I0459943

Book of 1st Enoch (Study Edition)

1 Enoch

First Century Version

Text, cross references and footnotes developed by
Jerry D. Franklin

Cassilis Publishing
jfranklin@frontiernet.net
21st-century-scribe.com
FACEBOOK: The Book of Enoch, second temple and early Christian era literature

All references and quotations of the Dead Scrolls are from, Wise, Michael, Abegg, Martin and Cook, Edward, 2005. *A New Translation, The Dead Sea Scrolls*, Harper One or Milik, J. T. 1976. *The Book of Enoch Aramaic Fragments Qumran Cave 4*, Oxford at the Clarendon Press.
Dead Sea Scroll reference numbers may be unfamiliar to readers who have not seen them before. This volume uses Aramaic rather than Roman numerals unless referencing Milik's work. For instance, 4Q204 5.2.17 would be the 204th scroll found in cave 4 at Qumran, fragment 5, column 2, line 17. Please note that some early scrolls were not assigned cave numbers. Common scrolls without numbers are CD Geniza A or B, 1QapGen, and 1QS.

Echoing Paul L. Maier—"I have not abandoned the traditional BC/AD year-by-year chronology, since BCE is irritating and lengthy. Non-Christians should not object, since they may interpret BC as simply 'before common (era)' and AD as 'after demarcation' With either definition, everyone knows the extraordinary human hinge involved here."[1]

Cover design created by Image Creator, from Microsoft Designer, Jan 31, 2024, under November 14, 2023, designer terms. "Two Essenes walking"

Paperback ISBN: 979-8-9923000-0-0
Hardcover ISBN: 979-8-9923000-1-7

[1] Maier, Paul L., 2021. *The Genuine Jesus, Fresh Evidence from History and Archaeology*, Kregel Publications, pg. 14.

Dedication

To all lovers of truth, who seek it wherever it may lead.
May this volume aid you in your search.

The influence of 1 Enoch on the New Testament has been greater than that of all the other apocryphal and pseudepigraphal books taken together.
R. H. Charles

What appears most likely is that the religious texts that informed Jesus and the early churches cannot be limited to the books that were finally received into the Hebrew Bible biblical canon.
Lee Martin McDonald

1 Enoch is "arguably the most important text in the corpus of Jewish literature from the Hellenistic and Roman periods."
George Nickelsburg

The book of 1 Enoch is also classified as (scripture at Qumran), since it is presented as revelation, is preserved in many copies, served as the model for the Qumran calendars, and may be quoted in the Pesher on the Apocalypse of Weeks (4Q247).
Peter Flint

Any general Bible reader who has not read 1 Enoch has yet to discover one of the most important sources of information about the thought world and cultural currents of Second Temple Israel at the turn of the eras. Any biblical scholar who does not regularly re-read 1 Enoch with her/his classes has no business teaching about Second Temple Israel or the Jesus movement and early church.
John H. Elliott

About the Editor

Jerry Franklin, is an objective evangelical Christian, independent researcher, and member of the international Enoch Seminar. He hails from a scientific background holding a BS and MS in the fields of natural science. He is in the midst of obtaining an MA degree in biblical exposition.

Contents

SOME PREVIOUS ENGLISH EDITIONS OF 1 ENOCH

Laurence, R., (1821) (1838) This edition is based only on one late Ethiopic manuscript of "middling quality" and is often unreliable.[2]

Baty, J., (1839) This edition is based on only a limited number of texts, and it of course dated; being before the important manuscript discoveries of the 20th century. It is surprisingly accurate in places such as 1En 7:2 where it agrees with modern scholarship; since he correctly, in that case, followed the early 9th century text of George Syncellus. His variant verse numbers from later translations make it difficult to use.

Dillmann, August, (1851) (1853) Despite being in German, his landmark edition deserves mention. His translation (1851) was based on 5 texts and he published a commentary 2 years later.

Schodde, G. H., (1882) Schodde relied on German scholarship by Dillmann and Schürer, producing a readable text based on five Ethiopic manuscripts.

Charles, R. H., (1912) This edition, while groundbreaking for its time and heavily used to the present, has become dated due to textual discoveries and critical research since it was written.

Knibb, M., (1978) This version is very valuable for its notes, sifting the textual evidence from a wide variety of manuscripts.

Isaac, E., (1983) This edition follows the oldest Ethiopic manuscript (Tana), with some consultation of a few others. He worked with 2080 (fifteenth century), 4437 (seventeenth century) and 4750 (seventeenth century).[2a] It is valuable also, since Isaac is a native speaker of Ge'ez, the Ethiopic language. However, his translation is particular to his individual style.

Black, M., (1985) Black's edition, though not in modern language, presents interesting though not always accepted ideas. It is the first English edition to incorporate textual evidence that came to light in the 20th century (Chester Beatty papyri and Dead Sea Scrolls).

Olson, D., (2004) Olson's edition is brilliant, readable, and based on recent textual evidence. But is unfortunately out of print.

Nickelsburg G. and VanderKam J., (2012) This edition is very scholarly and based on the full variety of manuscript evidence available at the time of writing. It is accompanied by a massive two volume commentary that is indispensable for serious students of the *Book of Enoch*. The text suffers somewhat in readability due to its scholarly nature and does not contain cross references or other important material unless one wades through the voluminous commentaries. However, their work is a landmark in the study of 1 Enoch.

LIST OF ABBREVIATIONS

---

[2] OL pg. 281.

[2a] P pg. 59, note 1.

ANCIENT DOCUMENTS
Bible and Apocrypha

Gen	Genesis
Ex	Exodus
Lev	Leviticus
Num	Numbers
Deut	Deuteronomy
Josh	Joshua
Judg	Judges
Ruth	Ruth
1Sam	1 Samuel
2Sam	2 Samuel
1Kgs	1 Kings
2Kgs	2 Kings
1Chr	1 Chronicles
2Chr	2 Chronicles
Ezra	Ezra
Neh	Nehemiah
Esth	Esther
Job	Job
Ps(s)	Psalms
Prov	Proverbs
Eccl	Ecclesiastes
Song	Song of Songs
Isa	Isaiah
Jer	Jeremiah
Lam	Lamentations
Ezek	Ezekiel
Dan	Daniel
Hos	Hosea
Joel	Joel
Amos	Amos
Obad	Obadiah
Jonah	Jonah
Mic	Micah
Nah	Nahum
Hab	Habakkuk
Zeph	Zephaniah
Hag	Haggai
Zech	Zechariah
Mal	Malachi
Tob	Tobit
Jdt	Judith
AddEsth	Additions to Esther
Wis	Wisdom of Solomon
Sir	Sirach (Ben Sira)
1Bar	1 Baruch (Baruch)
LetJer	Letter of Jeremiah
PrAzar	Prayer of Azariah
Sus	Susanna
Bel	Bel and the Dragon
1Mac	1 Maccabees
2Mac	2 Maccabees
Mt	Matthew
Mk	Mark
Lk	Luke
Jn	John
Acts	Acts
Rom	Romans
1Cor	1 Corinthians
2Cor	2 Corinthians
Gal	Galatians
Eph	Ephesians
Phil	Philippians
Col	Colossians
1Thes	1 Thessalonians
2Thes	2 Thessalonians
1Tim	1 Timothy
2Tim	2 Timothy
Tit	Titus
Phlm	Philemon
Heb	Hebrews
Jas	James
1Pet	1 Peter
2Pet	2 Peter
1Jn	1 John
2Jn	2 John
3Jn	3 John
Jude	Jude
Rev	Revelation

Pseudepigrapha

AddDan	Addition to Daniel
Ah	Ahiqar
AnonSam	An Anonymous Samaritan Text
ApAb	Apocalypse of Abraham
ApAdam	Apocalypse of Adam
ApDan	Apocalypse of Daniel
ApEl	Apocalypse of Elijah
ApEzek	Apocalypse of Ezekiel
ApMos	Apocalypse of Moses
ApocEzek	Apocryphon of Ezekiel
5ApocSyrPss	Five Apocryphal Syriac Psalms
AscenIs	Ascension of Isaiah
ApSedr	Apocalypse of Sedrach
ApZeph	Apocalypse of Zephaniah
ApZos	Apocalypse of Zosimus
ArisEx	Aristeas the Exegete
Aristob	Aristobulus
Art	Artapanus
AsMos	Assumption of Moses
Bar	Baruch
2Bar	2 (Syriac Apocalypse of) Baruch
3Bar	3 (Greek Apocalypse of) Baruch
4Bar	4 Baruch
BkNoah	Book of Noah
CavTr	Cave of Treasures
ClMal	Cleodemus Malchus
Dem	Demetrius
ElMod	Eldad and Modad
1En	1 (Ethiopic Apocalypse of) Enoch
2En	2 (Slavonic Apocalypse of) Enoch
3En	3 (Hebrew Apocalypse of) Enoch
1Esdr	1Esdras
Eup	Eupolemus
EzekTrag	Ezekiel the Tragedian
4Ezra	4 Ezra[3]
FrgsHistWrks	Fragments of Historical Works
FrgsPoetWrks	Fragments of Poetical Works
GbRev	Gabriel's Revelation
GkApEzra	Greek Apocalypse of Ezra
HebApEl	Hebrew Apocalypse of Elijah
HecAb	Hecataeus of Abdera

[3] 4 Ezra, as used here and in the OTP1, includes chapters 3-14 which are a Jewish apocalypse, known as 4 Ezra; chapters 1-2, (known as 2 Esdras) and chapters 15-16 known as 5 Esdras. Both chapters 1-2 and 15-16 are Christian additions. But for the purposes of this book Chapters 1-16 as a whole will be called 4 Ezra. The naming of books attributed to Ezra is confusing. The chart on OTP1 pg. 516 is helpful. This apocalypse is called 2 Esdras in English bibles and 4 Esdras in the Latin Vulgate.

HelSynPr	Hellenistic Synagogal Prayers
HistJos	History of Joseph
HistRech	History of the Rechabites
JanJam	Jannes and Jambres
JosAsen	Joseph and Asenath
Jub	Jubilees
LAB	*Liber Antiquitatum Biblicarum*
LadJac	Ladder of Jacob
LAE	Life of Adam and Eve (*Apocalypse*, OTP2 pg. 259 f.)
LetAris	Letter of Aristeas
LivPro	Lives of the Prophets
LosTr	The Lost Tribes
3Mac	3 Maccabees
4Mac	4 Maccabees
5Mac	5 Maccabees
MartIs	Martyrdom of Isaiah
OdesSol	Odes of Solomon
PhEPoet	Philo the Epic Poet
PJ	*Paraleipomena Jeremiou*
PrJos	Prayer of Joseph
PrMan	Prayer of Manasseh
PrMos	Prayer of Moses
PrJac	Prayer of Jacob
Ps-Eup	Pseudo-Eupolemus
Ps-Hec	Pseudo-Hecataeus
Ps-Orph	Pseudo-Orpheus
Ps-Philo	Pseudo-Philo
Ps-Phoc	Pseudo-Phocylides
PssSol	Psalms of Solomon
QuesEzra	Questions of Ezra
RevEzra	Revelation of Ezra
SibOr	Sibylline Oracles
SyrMen	Syriac Menander
TAb	Testament of Abraham
TAdam	Testament of Adam
Thal	Thallus
Theod	Theodotus
THez	Testament of Hezekiah
TIsaac	Testament of Isaac
TJac	Prayer of Jacob
TJob	Testament of Job
TMos	Testament of Moses
T12P	Testaments of the Twelve Patriarchs
TReu	Testament of Reuben
TSim	Testament of Simeon
TLev	Testament of Levi

TJud	Testament of Judah
TIss	Testament of Issachar
TZeb	Testament of Zebulun
TDan	Testament of Dan
TNaph	Testament of Naphtali
TGad	Testament of Gad
TAsh	Testament of Asher
TJos	Testament of Joseph
TBenj	Testament of Benjamin
TrShem	Treatise of Shem
TSol	Testament of Solomon
VisEzra	Vision of Ezra
VisIs	Vision of Isaiah
Vita	*Vita Adae et Evae* (Life of Adam and Eve, 0TP2 pg. 258 f.)

Josephus

Ant	*Jewish Antiquities*
Apion	*Against Apion*
Life	*Life of Josephus*
War	*Jewish Wars*

Philo

Abr.	*De Abrahamo*
Giants.	*On the Giants*
Good Person	*That Every Good Man Is Free*
Hypoth.	*Hypothetica*
QGen1	*Questions and Answers on Genesis 1*

New Testament Apocrypha and Pseudepigrapha

ActsJn	Acts of John
ActsPaul	Acts of Paul
ActsPer	Acts of Perpetua and Felicitas
ActsPhil	Acts of Philip
ADAM	Acts of the Disputation of Archelaus with Manes
AThm	Acts of Thomas
Aploan	*Apokalypsis tou hagiou lōannou*
ApMos	Apocalypse of Moses
ApPaul	Apocalypse of Paul
ApPet	Apocalypse of Peter
ApThom	Apocalypse of Thomas
ApVirg	Apocalypse of the Virgin
Barn.	Epistle of Barnabas
1Clem	1 Clement
2Clem	2 Clement
Did	Didache

GBart	Gospel of Bartholomew
GEbion	Gospel of the Ebionites
GEgyp	Gospel of the Egyptians
GHeb	Gospel of the Hebrews
GMatthias	Gospel of Matthias
GNic	Gospel of Nicodemus
GPet	Gospel of Peter
GPhil	Gospel of Philip
GThom	Gospel of Thomas
GTr	Gospel of Truth
NJoA	The Narrative of Joseph of Arimathea
ProtJames	Protoevangelium of James
PrPet	Preaching of Peter
PseudClemHom	Pseudo-Clementine Homilies
PseudClemRec	Pseudo-Clementine Recognitions
QuesBart	Questions of Bartholomew
RevSteph	Revelation of Stephen
ShepHerm	Shepherd of Hermes

Early Church Fathers

AdvHaer	Epiphanius, *Adversus haereses*
An.	*Tertullian, On the Soul/De anima*
Apol.	*Tertullian, Apology/Apologeticus*
Apol. A	*Apology of Aristides (Barlaam and Josaphat)*
1Apol.	Justin Martyr, *First Apology*
2Apol.	Justin Martyr, *Second Apology*
AposCon	Apostolic Constitutions
Cels.	Origen, *Contra Celsum*
CommGen	Procopius of Gaza, *Commentary on Genesis*, part I
CommIsa	Basil Caesar, *Commentary on Isaiah*
CommJn	Origen, *Commentary on the Gospel of St. John*
Defem	*Tertullian, De cultu feminarum*
De anima	*Tertullian, The Soul*
DeSpec	*Tertullian Of public shows*
DialTrypho	Justin Martyr, *Dialogue with Trypho*
DivInst	*Lactantius, Divine Institutes*
Ecl.	*Clement of Alexandria, Extracts from the prophets/Eclogae propheticae*
Epid.	*Irenæus, Demonstration of the Apostolic Preaching/Epideixis tou apostolikou kērygmatos*
ExcerPss	*Origen, Excerpta in Psalmos*
Haer.	*Irenæus, Against Heresies/Adversus haereses*
HE	*Eusebius, Historia ecclesiastica*
HebQuaestinLibGen	*Jerome, Hebrew Questions on the Book of Genesis*
Hom	*Macarius, Spiritual Homilies*
Idol.	Tertullian, *De Idolatra*

Inst.	Commodian, *Instructiones*
Leg.	*Athenagoras, A Plea for the Christians/Legatio pro Christianis*
Or. Graec.	*Tatian, Oratio ad Graecos (Pro Hellēnas)*
Paid	*Clement of Alexandria, the Tutor (Paidagōgos)*
Philoc	*Origen, Philocalia*
Prax.	Tertullian, *Against Praxeas*
PrEv	*Eusebius, Praeparatio evangelica*
Princ	*Origen, De principiis*
Ref	*Hippolytus, Refutation of All Heresies*
Res.	Tertulian, *De resurrection carnis*
Strom	Clement of Alexandria, *Stromata*

Gnostic Texts

PiSop	Pistis Sophia

Rabbinics

Ab	Abot

Words in **bold** correct errors in the text.
[ ] Words inside are interpolations, insertions into the text.
< > Restored words
( ) Words supplied to clarify the translation. Also they occasionally indicate a parenthetical comment within the text itself.
† † Indicates corruption in the text
… Indicates lost words

References and translations referred to in this study edition by abbreviation:

B	Baty, John 1839. *The Book of Enoch the Prophet.*
BAS	Porter, Josias L 1866. *The Giant Cities of Bashan and Syria's Holy Places.*
BL	Black, Matthew 1985. *The Book of Enoch, or 1 Enoch: A New English Edition*, Brill.
BO	Boccaccini, Gabrielle 1998. *Beyond the Essene Hypothesis*, Eerdmans.
C	Charles, R. H. 1912. *The Book of Enoch, or 1 Enoch*, Oxford: Clarendon.
DSS	Dead Sea Scrolls.
E	Boccaccini, Gabrielle. 2005. *Enoch and Qumran Origins*, Wm. B. Eerdmans Publishing.
ESV	ESV® Bible (The Holy Bible, English Standard Version®), copyright © 2001 by Crossway, a publishing ministry of Good News Publishers.
G	Golb, Norman 1995. *Who Wrote the Dead Sea Scrolls? The Search for the Secret of Qumran.*
H	Holmes, Michael W. 2006. *The Apostolic Fathers*, 3rd edition.
H1	Heiser, Michael S. 2019. *A Companion to the Book of Enoch* Vol. 1.
H2	Heiser, Michael S. 2020. *A Companion to the Book of Enoch* Vol. 2.
I	Isaac, E. 1983. *1 (Ethiopic Apocalypse of) Enoch A New Translation and Introduction* contained in *The Old Testament Pseudepigrapha Vol. 1,* edited by James H. Charlesworth. Doubleday.

K Knibb, M.A. 1984. "1 Enoch," trans, *The Apocryphal Old Testament. ed. H.F. D. Sparks; Oxford: Clarendon, 169-319.*

LXX Pietersma, Albert and Wright, Benjamin G., eds., 2007. *A New English Translation of the Septuagint*, Oxford University Press.

M Milik, J. T. 1976. *The Book of Enoch Aramaic Fragments Qumran Cave 4*, Oxford at the Clarendon Press.

N Nickelsburg, George W. E. and VanderKam, James C. 2012. *The Hermeneia Translation 1 Enoch,* Hermeneia. Fortress Press.

N1 Nickelsburg, George W. E. 2001. *1 Enoch 1: A Commentary on the Book of 1 Enoch, Chapters 1-36; 81-108.* Hermeneia. Fortress Press.

NV2 Nickelsburg George W. E. and Vanderkam, James C., 2012. *1 Enoch 2, A Commentary on the Book of Enoch Chapters 37-82*, Hermeneia. Fortress Press.

O Origen, *The Sacred Writings of Origen*, Translated by Frederick Crombie (1827-1889)

OL Olson, Daniel C. 2004. *Enoch A New Translation*, Bibal Press.

OLS Olson, Daniel C., 2022. *The wicked angels of 1 En. 69:4–15: Part 1: New evidence and proposals for the names; Part 2: The nature and purpose of the list.* Journal for the Study of the Pseudepigrapha (*JSP*) Volume 31, issue 3.

OTP1 Charlesworth, James H., ed. 1983. *The Old Testament Pseudepigrapha Vol 1*. Doubleday.

OTP2 Charlesworth, James H., ed. 2015. *The Old Testament Pseudepigrapha Vol 2*, fourth edition. Hendrickson Publishers.

P Charlesworth, J.H., ed. 2013. *Parables of Enoch A Paradigm Shift*, Bloomsbury T&T Clark

R Boccaccini, Gabriele, ed. 2007. *Enoch and the Messiah Son of Man, Revisiting the Book of Parables*, Grand Rapids, MI/Cambridge, UK: Eerdmans.

T Tiller, Patrick A. 1993. *A Commentary on the Animal Apocalypse of 1 Enoch.* Scholars Press.

VF Vanderkam, James and Flint, Peter. 2002. *The Meaning of the Dead Sea Scrolls* Harper Collins Publishers.

W Wise, Michael O., Abegg, Martin G. Jr. and Cook, Edward M. 2005. *A New Translation, The Dead Sea Scrolls.* HarperCollins Publishers.

LIST OF EXCURSUSES

INTRODUCTION

In this accurate readable edition of *The Book of Enoch*, enthusiasts have the best, most recent scholarship compiled at their fingertips. The goal is neither to promote nor "debunk" The Book of Enoch (1 Enoch) but simply let it speak for itself. This volume will correct both the inflated beliefs and unfair criticisms many make of The Book of Enoch. You will understand it as written, in all its insights, surprises and complexities. The goal of this edition is for readers to understand this important text that continues to shape our world through its widespread but mostly unrecognized influence.

Jesus and his disciples were very familiar with this text and it was foundational to their world view. With 1 Enoch you are not reading anything that Jews and Christians of the first century were not reading, and in most cases, regarded as scripture. Nickelsburg calls 1 Enoch "arguably the most important Jewish text of the Greco-Roman period."[4]

To understand what Jesus Christ taught, and who He claimed to be, you need to understand The Book of Enoch. "The Aramaic Book of Enoch, of which a fragment was included in the American exhibitions, very considerably influenced the idiom of the New Testament and patristic literature, more so in fact than any other writing of the Apocrypha and Pseudepigrapha."[5] "The presence of Enoch texts among the Dead Sea Scrolls, the literary and ideological connections with Old and New Testament documents, and the uncountable ramifications of Enoch ideas and concepts in the many Judaisms of the Second Temple period (including early Christianity) have made the study of Enoch literature a central issue for any specialist in ancient Judaism and Christian origins."[6]

Have you ever wondered why the New Testament has so much assumed theology and imagery that is so original from that found in the Old Testament? The Book of Enoch is the most influential book in that regard. "There is little doubt that 1 Enoch was influential in molding New Testament doctrines concerning the nature of the Messiah, the son of Man, the messianic kingdom, demonology, the future, resurrection, final judgement, the whole eschatological theatre, and symbolism. No wonder, therefore, that the book was highly regarded by many of the earliest apostolic and Church fathers."[7]

This volume is an attempt to bridge the divide between scholarship on the Book of Enoch and the modern-day Church, which in most cases has an inaccurate perception of the book. The cross references include both canonical writings, and literature that is non-canonical, or historical. Underlined cross references are those which appear to be especially linked to the text of 1 Enoch. Cross references include the Old Testament, New Testament, Apocrypha, Dead Sea Scrolls, Jubilees, second temple literature, first and second century AD Jewish writings, the writings of contemporary historians, and Christian Church fathers. It is recommended that readers digest this information dense book slowly and carefully; as much of the material is new and groundbreaking. The footnotes are critical to gaining a more complete understanding of 1

---

[4] N1 pg. xxiii.
[5] G pg. 366. See also P pgs. 338-339
[6] R, Boccaccini pg. 8.
[7] OTP1 pg. 10.

Enoch and should not be neglected. Consider also, the very complete subject and scripture indexes; as they will be of great benefit in the study of this book.

What can you expect to gain by studying this edition of the Book of Enoch?

This book more than any other, will help you think like a first century Christian or late 2nd temple Jew. This will help prevent you from imposing your world view, era and culture on scripture, and thus imagining false interpretations.

The Book of Enoch will help you more fully understand both the Old and New Testament.

You will better understand the Messianic expectations of the first century. When Jesus referred to himself as the "Son of Man" (85 times, all but four by Jesus) you will know what he meant after reading this book.

The Book of Enoch will help you understand the unseen spiritual realm of watchers, angels, and demons taken for granted by Jews and Christians in the first century.

The second temple period, and first century were full of literary activity. This edition will help you understand this world and where the Book of Enoch fits in that world.

Reading 1 Enoch will help you understand the roots of Enochian Judaism and Jewish Mysticism.[8] Scholars are now understanding that first century Judaism was much more complicated and diverse than previously believed. It is also apparent that Christians are more Jewish than previously realized.[9] Yet Christianity arose not from all of Judaism, but from a distinct subset of Judaism that valued the Enochic texts.

This edition provides alternative readings for difficult passages rather than giving a single reading. The text of the Book of Enoch, due to its history of poor preservation is "rougher," being not as well attested and preserved as the Bible. So alternative readings are very helpful. This edition seeks to bring the dedicated, and in some cases, lifelong, work of scholars into a form that is compact and understandable; with information a reader needs to know. This volume contains thousands of cross references to other literature of the period. These texts are presented to help the reader understand the world view of first century Jews and Christians. They are not by any means all regarded as scripture.

This is a serious reference book for 1 Enoch. The reader can do anything from just reading the text, to glancing at footnotes for understanding, to diving deep. The goal is to understand what the text really says, and how it fits in the world of its time. This reference edition is like an expansive wilderness for you to explore. You can go innumerable directions. The editor prays that it will be a rich blessing to you. Readers are encouraged to form their own conclusions. The editor's opinions and insights are occasionally included in excursuses and footnotes.

History of the Book of Enoch

---

[8] N1 pg. 1.

[9] W pg. 35.

> "The books or sections of Enoch were written by orthodox Jews, who belonged to the apocalyptic or prophetic side of Judaism, and by Judaism is here meant, not the one-sided legalistic Judaism that posed as the sole and orthodox Judaism after the fall of Jerusalem in AD 70, but the larger and more comprehensive Judaism that preceded it. This larger Judaism embraced both the prophetic and the legalistic elements."[10]

Scholars consider the Book of Enoch to be a specific genre of literature, valued by an Enochic sect of turn of the era Judaism. The Book of Enoch was highly regarded and read by Jews and Christians of the first century. It was often referenced or quoted by church fathers. It continued to be highly regarded by mainly Christians into the fourth century. Evidence of this is that scribes continued to copy it.

> "We have evidence that they copied the Greek text in the fourth century (Chester Beatty Papyrus [see Fas. 8]) and in the sixth Century. (Codex Panopolitanus; edited by Bouriant in 1892). Copying a work is laborious and reflects admiration for it and the need to preserve it, or part of it."[11]

After the disastrous Bar-Kokhba revolt in AD 132-135, the Jewish rabbinical attitude toward apocalyptic thought hardened. Their view after the failed Jewish revolts was stated as follows:

> "Whoever looks at four matters, it would have been better for him had he never entered the world: Anyone who reflects upon what is above the firmament and what is below the earth, what was before Creation, and what will be after the end of the world. And anyone who has no concern for the honor of his Maker, who inquires into and deals with matters not permitted to him, deserves to have never come to the world."[12]

Despite being highly regarded by many Christians previously, beginning in the fourth century church fathers such as Augustine, Jerome and Hilary looked upon the Book of Enoch (which as we will see is largely synonymous with 1 Enoch) with disfavor. A late reference to 1 Enoch outside Ethiopia was by George Syncellus around AD 800.[13] "The use of Enochic materials for chronographic[14] purposes appears again in the twelfth-century chronicles of George Cedrenus, who uses material from Syncellus, and of Michael of Syria, who cites Annianus as his source."[15] Excerpts of the Book of Watchers from Syncellus were printed in Scaliger's 1606 *Thesaurus temporum*. These excerpts (1En 6:1–9:5, 9:1–10:15, 15:8–16:2, 26:9–25, 26:26–27:7) were reprinted in the 17th and 18th centuries and discussed in multiple forms and settings, both in Greek as well as in Latin, French, German, English, and Italian translation. It was notably printed in Johann Albert Fabricius' 1713 *Codex pseudepigraphus VT.* Interest generated by these partial copies inspired a European quest to find the complete book of Enoch in Ethiopia.

---

[10] C pg. ciii.
[11] Charlesworth James H., 2008. *The Parables of Enoch and the Apocalypse of John*, In "Jewish and Christian texts in Contexts and Related Studies" pg. 198. **It has now been established that cave 7 at Qumran contained a Greek copy of portions of the Admonitions of Enoch** (E pg. 224-233). (7Q4.1; 7Q4.2; 7Q8; 7Q11; 7Q12; 7Q13; 7Q14).
[12] Mishnah Ch*agigah* 2:1 (ca. AD 190-230).
[13] N1 pg. 95.
[14] "Chronographic" recording time intervals.
[15] N1 pg. 95. See also N1 pg. 15.

Greek copies had been translated into Ethiopic (Ge' ez) "between about 340 and 525 C.E., more probably earlier (i.e., 340-400) than later (400-525)."[16] Nickelsburg cites reasons the *Book of Enoch* was readily accepted in Ethiopia.

> "In short, 1 Enoch took root in Ethiopia because: (a) it was brought there by missionaries who came from an environment that had long cherished the book; (b) its worldview spoke to the Ethiopians' worldview, and the environment it imaginatively portrayed resonated with their environment; and (c) Ethiopian Christianity lacked the theological and intellectual counterforces that lead to the book's rejection in Mediterranean Christianity."[17]

It existed in multiple Ethiopic texts, as it is to this day part of the Ethiopian Orthodox Tewahedo Church and Eritrean Orthodox Tewahedo Church canon.[18] In addition, the Ethiopian Jews known as the Falashas include it in their canon. Present-day protestants in Ethiopia generally do not favorably receive the Book of Enoch because they hold to the 66-book canon, and consider the Book of Enoch as heretical, even though they are unable to identify heresies contained in it. Bibles printed today in Ethiopia are mixed in their inclusion of the Book of Enoch.

Four copies[18a] of 1 Enoch (*Mäshafä Henok*) were brought back to Europe by Scottish traveler James Bruce (while searching for the source of the Nile) in 1773. In 1800, parts of the text were published in Latin.[19] In the 1800's these and other copies were translated into English and published. A widely circulating present day text is a translation by R. H. Charles which was based on 23 Ethiopic manuscripts.[20] Nickelsburg was aware of forty-nine pre-1900 Ethiopic manuscripts of 1 Enoch.[21] Olson was aware of "more than 60."[22] Loren Stuckenbruck has catalogued over 120 manuscripts of 1 Enoch. Of these more than 25 can be dated to the sixteenth century or earlier.[23] "There is no doubt that the Ethiopic archetype contained all of these 108 chapters."[24] In 1931 the Chester Beatty-Michigan Papyrus was purchased on the antiquities market. The Greek Text, copied by a careless scribe, which was marred by more than

---

[16] R pg. 364. Piovanelli, *"A Testimony for the Kings and the Mighty Who Possess the Earth" The Thirst for Justice and Peace in the Parables of Enoch.*

[17] N1 pg. 108.

[18] Wanger, Anke, 2011. *The Biblical Canon of the Ethiopian Orthodox Tewahedo Church.*

[18a] G. Boccaccini, "James Bruce's 'Fourth' Manuscript: Solving the Mystery of the Provenance of the Roman Enoch Manuscript," JSP 27 (2018) 237–63, esp. 237–41, introduces the story of Bruce's conveyance of the Enoch manuscripts to Europe, and argues for a previously unknown fourth manuscript (now Vat. et. 71) commissioned and transported by Bruce and then donated to the Antonelli Library after his meeting with Pope Clement XIV.

[19] N1 pg. 109.

[20] English translations include Laurence (1838), Baty (1839), Schode (1882), R.H. Charles (1893) (1912), Knibb (1978), Isaac (1983), Uhlig (1984), Black (1985), Olson (2004) and Nickelsburg/VanderKam (2012). Knibb and Isaac based their translations on a single manuscript with Isaac translating the oldest Ethiopic manuscript. Black's edition was largely a revision of Charles. Uhlig created his own German "eclectic text composed of what he considered to be the best readings from the whole corpus of Ethiopic, Greek, and Aramaic evidence" (N1 pg. 18). Nickelsburg and Vanderkam did the same. Olson's English translation also uses the whole corpus and stives to be "more natural-sounding" "without sacrificing accuracy" (OL pg. 20).

[21] N1 pg. 16.

[22] OL pg. 20.

[23] Stuckenbruck, Loren. T., 2013. *The Book of Enoch: Its Reception in Second Temple Judaism and in Christianity.* pg. 39.

[24] N1 pg. 21.

three dozen omissions, nevertheless proved to be extremely valuable.[25] It is believed to have originally included the entire text of the *Book of Enoch* but only chapters 91-107 were recovered. In the early 1950's, fragments of *1 Enoch* were identified in the Dead Sea Scrolls. Eventually it was determined that at least 12 copies of 1 Enoch were stored at Qumran. Eleven were from cave 4 and one from cave 7.[25a] This makes Enoch one of the most highly regarded (based on number of copies) texts to be found at Qumran. The Ethiopic texts are generally in agreement with the fragments found at Qumran. No fragments of the *Parables* (Chapters 37-71) or *The Eschatological Exhortation* (Chapter 108) were found at Qumran.

This edition of *1 Enoch* takes into consideration texts from all sources in pursuing the goal of an accurate engaging text. Alternative readings are quoted in the footnotes. The *Book of Enoch* is studied worldwide, and scholars meet biannually to present papers and discuss findings at the Enoch Seminar. Most Christians and Jews have still not heard of *1 Enoch* despite its mention in Jude and heavy use in 2 Peter. As we will discover, much of the New Testament was heavily influenced by the Book of Enoch. In fact, trying to understand Christian theology and thought without the Book of Enoch is like trying to assemble a puzzle with a third of its pieces missing. Recent, sensationally titled books have capitalized on the story of the watchers and giants; however, there is far more value to be found in 1 Enoch than just watchers and giants.

What texts make up the Book of Enoch (1 Enoch)?

"The division of 1 Enoch into five large 'books' with two appendices has been accepted by almost every scholar who has worked on this text for the past 150 years."[26] These books were written at different times by different authors; "all of which presumably once circulated separately"[27] Some scholars break out chapters 1-5 into a separate category, but this is the general division.

1. *The Book of Watchers* (1-36)
2. *The Book of the Parables/Similitudes* (37-71)
3. *The Book of Astronomical Writings* or *Book of the Heavenly Luminaries* (72-82)
4. *The Book of Dream Visions* (83-90)
5. *The Admonitions or Epistle or Apocalypse of Enoch* (91-105)
6. *Birth of Noah* (106-107)
7. *The Eschatological Exhortation* (108)

Tigchlaar summarizes the textual background of the books of 1 Enoch as follows: "If anything, the comparison of the codicological and the historical data suggest that there were different collections of the books of Enoch, and there are no grounds to rule out the possibility that in between the Qumran evidence of the second and first centuries B.C.E. and the Ethiopic evidence, there were different combinations of booklets."[28] The situation is even more complex. The books listed above are certainly made up of books from previous works. At least nineteen distinct

---

[25] N1 pg. 14.
25a VF pg. 195. Some scholars dispute the Greek copy from cave 7 since it is extremely fragmentary. E pg. 237-239
[26] N1 pg. 2.
[27] W pg. 295.
[28] R Tigchelaar, pg. 104.

literary traditions can be identified within 1 Enoch. "These distinguishable traditions may be listed as follows "(1) Ch. 1-5; (2) 6-11; itself a blend of two-three traditions (3) 12-16; (4) 17-19; (5) 21-36; (6) 37-71 into which (7) a number of Noah traditions are interspersed; (8) 72-80; (9) 81-82.4a; (10) 82.4b-20; (11) 83-84; (12) 85-90; (13) 90:1-10, 18-19; (14) 93:1-10 + 91:11-17; (15) 92:1-5 + 93:11-94:6 and 104:9-105:2; (16) 94:7-104:8; (17) 106:1-12 + 106:18-107:3; (18) 106:13-17; (19) 108."[29] Scholars differ, of course, in how these sections should break out, with the above as only an example. This editor would additionally break out 70:3-71:17 as an interpolation. Additional works attributed to Enoch may be lost, as indicated by (Jub 12:27; 21:10; TSim 5:4; TLev 10:5; TDan 5:6 and TBenj 9:1).

What about 2nd and 3rd Enoch?

The reader should be aware that the books of 2 Enoch and 3 Enoch also exist. 2 Enoch is clearly dependent on the Book of Watchers and the Book of Heavenly Luminaries.[30] It is interesting especially from a Christian apologetics perspective. In the editor's opinion, it is evidence for an early composition of portions of the New Testament. But first a little background is in order.

2 Enoch (late AD 1st century to early 2nd century) may have been one of the texts that Origen (AD 185-253) considered as the Books of Enoch which he distinguished from the *Book of Enoch* (probably what we consider 1 Enoch) and said they "do not circulate in the Churches as divine"[31] It is almost certain[32] that Origen is referencing 2 En 24:2-5; 25:3-5; or 33:4 in *De principiis* 1.3.3. This evidence would argue that 2 Enoch was circulating in the third century and Origen had a copy. 2 Enoch is clearly inferior to 1 Enoch and outside of mainstream Christian or Jewish thought; this would have been easily recognized by the early church. For this reason, it likely did not circulate among the churches as widely as 1 Enoch, just as Origen said. If the link with *De principiis* 1.3.3 is not accepted; the date of 2 Enoch is very much disputed. "There must be something very peculiar about a work when one scholar, Charles, concludes that it was written by a Hellenized Jew in Alexandra in the first century B.C., while another, J.T. Milik, argues that it was written by a Christian monk in Byzantium in the ninth century A.D."[33] Until 2009 the earliest known manuscript of 2 Enoch was from the 14th century. The full text is extant only

---

[29] Stuckenbruck, Loren T. 2013. The *Book of Enoch: Its Reception in Second Temple Jewish and in Christian Tradition*. pg. 8.

[30] Examples of 2 Enoch's dependency on 1 Enoch include: 200 fallen angels (2En J 4:1; 18:3 (OTP1 pg. 110; 130-131); 18:3 (OTP1 pg. 130)); storehouses for weather elements (2En 5-6 (OTP1 pgs. 112-113); Enoch interceding for angels (2En 7:4-5; (OTP1 pgs. 114-115); visit to paradise/ tree of life fragrance (2En 8:1-3 (OTP1 pgs. 114-115)); place of punishment/angels of punishment (2En 10:2-3 (OTP1 pgs. 118-119)); condemnation of the abuse of the poor (2En 10:5 (OTP1 pgs. 118-119)); celestial visits by Enoch (2En 11-12; 19; 36:2 (See OTP1)); gates of heaven (2En 13-16 (OTP1 pgs. 122-130); Satan as the prince of the fallen angels (2En J 18:3, (OTP1 pgs. 130-131) cf. 1En 54:6); Mt. Hermon, angels broke the promise (2En 18:4 (OTP1 pgs. 132-133)); beautiful daughters of men taken by angels (2En 18:4 (OTP1 pgs. 132-133)); earth defiled (2En 18:4 (OTP1 pg. 132)); lawlessness, giants/monsters, enmity (2En J 18:5 (OTP1 pg. 132); judgement of the angels under the earth by God (2En 18:7 (OTP1 pg. 132)); common names for archangels; Michael, Gabriel, Vrevoil=Uriel (2En 21-22 (OTP1 pgs. 136-140)) ; Enoch is a scribe, associate of angels and astronomer (2En 40:1-4 (OTP1 pgs. 164-165); Enoch instructs his children and gives them books (2En 47:1-2 (OTP1 pgs. 174-175)).

[31] *Cels.* 5.54.

[32] This link is not universally accepted among scholars, but the link seems compelling. 2 Enoch has an extensive creation section in chapters 24-33 that would not have escaped Origen's notice. Chapter 24 of 2 Enoch would apply directly to Origen's argument in *De principiis* 1.3.3.

[33] OTP1 pg. 95.

in Church Slavonic, but small Coptic fragments have been known since 2009.[34] These 2009 Coptic fragments date from before AD 1172 and possibly 969. They contain chapters 36-42 of the short recension of 2 Enoch. The Church Slavonic version itself represents a translation from an earlier Greek version.[35] It is quite possible that the Coptic fragments were also translated from Greek.

It exists in multiple recensions with J and A being used in the Old Testament Pseudepigrapha.[36] The text has been added to, modified and deleted from.

> In spite of its evident biblical style, there is no point at which it can be shown to depend on the text of the New Testament, barring obvious Christian glosses, whose extraneous character is betrayed by their presence in only one manuscript or at most in manuscripts of one family. There is not a distinctly Christian idea in the book.[37]
>
> This does not mean that the work is Jewish; it lacks some of the most distinctive and definitive tenets of main-line Judaism. In fact, it knows nothing of developments between the Flood and the end of the world, so there is no place for Abraham, Moses, and the rest; there is no reference to the Torah." "If the work is Jewish, it must have belonged to a fringe sect."[38]

Leonhard Rost, writes:

> The association with the West is all the more remarkable in that the Greek recension of the book (which represents at least an important stage in the formation of the tradition, if not the crucial initial stage) undoubtedly came into being in Egypt within the circle of Hellenistic Jews who were influenced but not overwhelmed by the intellectual milieu represented by Philo. Since the author had before him Sirach, the Ethiopic Enoch, and the Wisdom of Solomon, but states the Temple was still standing (51, 59, 61, 62, 68), the work should probably be dated in the first half of the first century C.E. Its final form is due to a Christian revision in the Eastern Church dating from the seventh century.[39]

Anderson writes that: "2 Enoch could derive from any region in which Jewish, Greek, Egyptian and other Near Eastern ideas mingled."[40] However given the apparent allusions to the New Testament, Christian influence must also be added to the mix. The text itself gives clues to having been written prior to AD 70[41] but that assumes the literary and philosophical unity of 2

---

[34] Hagen, Joost L. 2012. *No longer 'Slavonic' only, 2 Enoch attested in Coptic from Nubia.* In *New Perspectives on 2 Enoch* pgs. 5-34.
[35] OTP1 pg. 94.
[36] OTP1 pgs. 91-213
[37] OTP1 pg. 95.
[38] OTP1 pg. 96.
[39] Rost, Leonhard, 1976. *Judaism Outside the Hebrew Canon*, pg. 112.
[40] OTP1 pg. 96.
[41] Orlov, Andrei A., 2012 *The Sacerdotal Traditions of 2 Enoch and the Date of the Text, Marquette University e-Publications@Marquette*, pgs. 106-109.

Enoch.[42] The editor holds a working hypothesis that 2 Enoch was written between AD 62 and 70 (likely the middle of the range) by a well-educated yet conflicted "Enochic Jew" with exposure to Christianity.

2 Enoch is not a text with significant usefulness to the general student of the Bible, but because of its potential first century composition and dependence on portions 1 Enoch and the New Testament it warrants study by specialists in the field, and Christian apologists.

As far as 3 Enoch (AKA *Sefer Hehalot*) is concerned; P. Alexander summarizes:

"All things considered, then, though 3 Enoch contains some very old traditions and stands in direct line with developments which had already begun in the Maccabean era, a date for its final redaction in the fifth or sixth century A. D. cannot be far from the truth."[43] Nickelsburg writes "3 Enoch is a complex, layered text of Jewish Merkabah traditions that was composed probably in the fifth or sixth century C.E. and that indicates some loose knowledge of the Enochic tradition."[44] It is a text without significant usefulness to understanding of the New Testament.

Excursus: Does 2 Enoch help establish a pre-AD 70 date for the Gospel of Matthew and Epistles of Paul?

Scholars disagree on the date 2 Enoch was written, but many think it was composed in the late 1st century. If this date is accepted, then 2 Enoch's parallels with the New Testament may show a dependency on it. While it is not Christian in origin; numerous parallels with the New Testament are contained in 2 Enoch 49-53. It seems that a Christian interpolator would have been more overt in his efforts to Christianize the text.

2 Enoch may have expanded the reference by the apostle Paul in (2Cor 12:2) to the third heaven[45] into 10 levels (2En 3:1-22:1). Paul's comment about the angelic language in (1Cor 13:1) may be the basis for celestial speech in (2En 19:3 recission A).[46] (Col 1:16), regarding God creating things visible and invisible, may have been used in (2En 48:4). The powers and authorities of Eph 6:12 appear, to have been borrowed for (2En 20:1 recission J). The prohibition on taking vengeance, and letting God be the avenger in (Rom 12:19) is picked up in (2 En 50:4). A link may be conjectured between (Acts 17:23 and 2En 67:3) concerning the invisible/unknown God. In the general epistles a comparison can be made between (James 1:27 and 2 En 42:9) concerning orphans and widows in their affliction.

In the gospels, Matthew and especially the Sermon on the Mount are used; compare gates of hell (Mt 16:18 and 2 En 42:1); let your yes be yes (Mt 5:34, 37 or Jas 5:12 and 2En J 49:1-2); the concept of being persecuted for righteousness's sake (Mt 5:10 and 2En 50:4); abiding in

---

[42] Suter, David W., 2012 *Excavating 2 Enoch: The Question of Dating and the Sacerdotal Traditions*, Saint Martin's University, pg. 6n and 10.
[43] OTP1 pg. 229.
[44] N1 pg. 81.
[45] The third heaven in 2 Enoch 8 (OTP1 pgs. 114-116) is an Edenic paradise where God rests, surrounded by fire with a fragrant tree of life with every type of fruit. From it flows two streams that divide into four. The scene is reminiscent of (Rev 21:10; 22:1-2).
[46] OTP1 pg. 133. However, see The Songs of the Sabbath Sacrifice Mas1k 2.1 (W pg. 467).

meekness (Mt 5:5 and 2En 50:2); the Sower (Mt 13:1-8 and 2En 42:11). In the other gospels, similar themes include nothing kept secret (Mk 4:11; Lk 8:17; and 2En 50:1); and many rooms (Jn 14:2 and 2En 61:2-3)

2 Enoch shares some imagery with Revelation as well; which may have been written near the same time. These include a heavenly Jerusalem (Rev 21:10 and 2 En J 55:2); nothing incorruptible on the new earth (Rev 21:27 and 2En 65:10); and great light in paradise (Rev 22:5 and 2 En 65:10)The likelihood of Christ, Paul and James borrowing from 2 Enoch is extraordinarily unlikely given its unorthodox theology. Dating 2 Enoch before AD 70 is a valid minority position, due to the mentions of the temple, offerings, and/or sacrificial worship in (45; 51:4, 59: 61:4-5; 62:1-2; 68:5-7). If the Temple had been non-existent, it is very difficult to justify the inclusion of these references. Given the concentrated parallels with the Gospel of Matthew and the earlier Epistles of Paul it is hard to argue the author(s) was not influenced by them. Assuming we have something close to an original text; this research helps pin 2 Enoch to AD 62-70 and it also argues for an early date, as conservative scholars have long maintained; at least for Matthew, and some of the Pauline Epistles.

Dates of composition for the Book of Enoch

All the books in 1 Enoch are Jewish in origin (showing no trace of Christian influence), and were composed originally in Aramaic with words borrowed from Hebrew by different unknown authors. Olson, in a minority position, postulates a Hebrew original for the *Book of the Parables*. They were all written prior to the time of Christ. The Book of the Watchers and The Book of Heavenly Luminaries are the oldest known Jewish religious writings outside of the Old Testament itself.

The *Book of the Watchers* (chapters 1-36), "was completed by the middle of the third century B.C.E." "The earliest traditions in the book may predate the Hellenistic period" [47] "The first and third sections of the Book of Enoch are the oldest known Jewish religious writings outside the Old Testament itself."[48]

The Book of the Parables/Similitudes (chapters 37-71). The Parables were written in the late first century BC.[49] "The Parables can be dated sometime around the turn of the era,"[50] to as late as 20 C.E.[51] "no part of the Parables (chapters 37-71) has been preserved on any Qumran *MS*."[52]

Book of Heavenly Luminaries aka. The Book of Astronomical Writings (chapters 72-82) "…has its roots in the Persian period and is probably the oldest of the Enochic traditions.[53] *The Book of*

---

[47] N1 pg. 7.
[48] OL pg. 1.
[49] N1 pg. 7.
[50] N pg. 5.
[51] Charlesworth, James H., ex. ed. 2008. "Jewish and Christian tests in Contexts and Related Studies" in *The Pseudepigrapha and Christian Origins*, pg. 244.
[52] N1 pg. 21.
[53] N1 pg. 7-8.

the Heavenly Luminaries in the Dead Sea Scrolls is always found on separate scrolls that contain no other part of 1 Enoch.[54]

The *Book of Astronomical Writings* is found in an expanded form in the Dead Sea Scrolls. "Four Aramaic manuscripts among the Dead Sea Scrolls contain a substantially longer form of this part of *1 Enoch*, and these manuscripts are collectively called Astronomical Enoch to differentiate them from the '*Reader's Digest*' form that has come down in Ethiopic. None of the Qumran manuscripts of *Astronomical Enoch* preserve any of the other six divisions of 1 *Enoch*, so it appears that *Astronomical Enoch* did indeed circulate separately from the other Enochic literature"[55] Olson dates it to the third century BC or earlier.[56]

The Book of Dream Visions (chapters 83-90) "In its present form, the latter vision dates to (the) time of Judas Maccabeus (ca. 165 BC), although a prior form *may* date to the end of the third century or beginning of the second century."[57]

Admonitions of Enoch (chapters 91-105) Nickelsburg[58] and Olson[59] both place the date of composition in the second century BC.

Birth of Noah (chapters 106-107) The composition of this text is generally placed between 150-33 BC.

An Eschatological Exhortation (chapter 108) was the last section of 1 Enoch written— which would place its composition between the turn of the era and the first two decades of the common era. Therefore, it would be within the lifetime of Christ!

The traditions behind the oldest parts of 1 Enoch appear to be contemporary with, or older than the Old Testament, since the Old Testament assumes knowledge of the Enochian backstory. Olson summarizes:

> It is common to read in contemporary scholarly literature that the two oldest sections of Enoch, the 'Book of the Watchers' and the 'Astronomy Book,' were written in the third century BCE, but in fact the only thing we know is that they are *at least* that old. Then there is the fact that Old Testament passages crucial to the Enochians, like Gen 5:22-24, Gen 6:1-4, and Lev 16:8-10, are unusually allusive and cryptic. These scriptures know more than they are telling us.[60]

Olson continues:

---

[54] N1 pg. 21.
[55] W pgs. 295-296.
[56] OL pg. 8.
[57] N1 pg. 8.
[58] N1 pg. 8.
[59] OL pg. 8.
[60] OL pg. 6-7.

> Then too, investigations into the Mesopotamian background of the Enoch figure strongly suggest that both Genesis and the oldest parts of the Book of Enoch made independent use of the same ancient sources. More than one conclusion can be drawn from such findings, but the full range of possible implications has not yet been considered.[61]

Did Enoch write the Book of Enoch?

That the traditions in 1 Enoch are older than portions of the Old Testament, does not mean the book itself is older. In his commentary on 1 Enoch 1:2; Heiser points out: "Enoch is here referred to in third person, making it clear that the biblical Enoch of Genesis 5:21-24 is *not* cast as the author of 1 Enoch. Rather, an unknown writer purports to quote the biblical Enoch, so 1 Enoch is about Enoch, not authored by Enoch"[62]

No serious scholar thinks 1 Enoch was written by biblical Enoch; although a substantial amateur following exists that holds to Enochic authorship. Charlesworth writes, "while some today claim that the Books of Enoch were composed by Enoch, no scholar trained in the leading institutions of higher learning would agree with any of these conclusions."[63]

Some of the reasons Enochic authorship is rejected include:

To have been written by biblical Enoch, *The Book of Enoch* would have been written in Aramaic[64] at a minimum 1400 years before Aramaic,[65] or any other alphabetic writing was known to exist. Cuneiform, the first writing, was developed by the Uruk people at the start of the bronze age around 3300 BC.[66] Clay tokens with pictorial symbols preexisted Cuneiform.[67] Scholars maintain that neither the Aramaic nor Hebrew language existed during the time of a biblical Enoch. However, a recent examination of two unprovenanced cuneiform tablets inscribed with unusual text may extend the usage of "a kind of Hebrew" back to 1800 BC or earlier.[68] But still this is far short of the time of a Biblical Enoch which would have been well prior to 3000 BC.

---

[61] OL pg. 6-7.

[62] H1 pg. 27.

[63] Charlesworth, James H., 2008. *The Parables of Enoch and the Apocalypse of John,* In "Jewish and Christian texts in Contexts and Related Studies", pg. 241.

[64] **Scholars agree that the original language of most of 1 Enoch was Aramaic with words borrowed from Hebrew. "The discovery of the Qumran Aramaic Enoch MSS. makes it virtually certain that Aramaic was the language in which chaps. 1-36, the Book of Giants, and chaps. 72-107 were composed, although the authors may have drawn on some Hebrew sources. Whether the Book of Parables (chaps. 37-71) and chap. 108 were composed in Hebrew or Aramaic is less certain, since no Aramaic fragments of either section were found at Qumran"** (N1 pg. 9).

[65] Aramaic is thought to have first appeared among the Aramaeans about the late 11th century BCE. *Encyclopedia Britannica.*

[66] Walker, C. 1987. *Reading the Past Cuneiform.* British Museum. pg. 9.

[67] Overmann, Karenleigh A. 2019. *The Neolithic Clay Tokens,* in *The Material Origin of Numbers: Insights from the Archaeology of the Ancient Near East,* Piscataway, NJ, USA: Gorgias Press, pgs. 157-178.

[68] One of the authors of the paper announcing this find, "can hardly conceal his excitement over this text and from other parts of it that contain names of gods as well as expressions of love. 'It's pretty incredible. They were actually speaking a kind of Hebrew. It's not really Hebrew, but it's close to Hebrew," he says. Cohen describes their language as "the mother of Hebrew" and says that "most scholars agree that Hebrew developed from it and is related

The description of God descending on Mount Sinai in 1En 1:4 would have had no significance to a biblical Enoch.

The description of Petra (28:1) and a spice trade in the *Book of Watchers* (chapters 29-32) places that account at least as late as the first temple period.

The description of the topography of Jerusalem and its description as the center of the earth in chapter 26 would have had no meaning to anyone prior to the time of Abraham.

The massive dependence of 1 Enoch on the Old Testament proves that it was written after the bulk of the Old Testament. The *Book of Parables* is highly dependent on Old Testament texts that would have postdated a biblical Enoch. Even the older *Book of Watchers* shows dependence on Job, Psalms, Isaiah, and Ezekiel.

The mention of the "land of Dan" and "waters of Dan" southwest of Hermon in 1En 13:7 dates the text to well after the conquest of the promised land (Josh 19:47).

The reference to a "rejection of the timeless heritage of the fathers" in 1En 99:14, would have made no sense before there was a timeless heritage.

The reference to "maintain the covenant" in 1En 108:1 could not have been written before a covenant existed; either with Noah, Abraham or Moses.

The reference to festivals in 1En 82:7, 9 is obviously referring to Jewish festivals which would post-date a biblical Enoch by 2000 years!

The use of Greek terms like "Tartarus" in 20:2 and "sirens" in 96:2 plus the Greek cosmology reflected in (1En 17:4-18:4) shows the influence of Hellenization which would have only occurred long after the time of biblical Enoch.

Iron is mentioned numerous times in the *Book of Parables* (52:2, 6, 8; 54:3, 56:1 and 67:4) and in the Book of Watchers (8:1). It is well known that iron implements and weapons of war, did not exist prior to the beginning of the iron age in approximately the 12th century BC. This would have been thousands of years after the time of a biblical Enoch.

The Parthians and Medes are mentioned in 56:5 of the Book of Parables. Although people groups identified as the Medes existed from as early as the 11th century, the kingdom of the Parthians and Medes only existed from 247 BC to AD 224. Both would have been long after a biblical Enoch.

The use of the Septuagint in 106:18 establishes that the *Birth of Noah* was written after the development of the LXX in the early to mid-3rd century BC (See note 2198). Likewise, the use of

---

to it" (Krebenick, George. 2022. *Two Remarkable Vocabularies: Amorite-Akkadian Bilinguals!* Revue D'Assyriologie Et D'Archèologie Orientale 2022/1 (Vol, 116) pgs. 133-166).

the Septuagint in 71:12 dates the suspected interpolation into the *Parables of Enoch* to after the development of the LXX (see note 1426).

The Books of Enoch were known to have circulated separately. This would not be the case, if it was composed in antiquity by a single author.

The *Animal Apocalypse* (1En 85-90) is a retelling of Israel's history in minute detail. To consider it a prophecy would be very farfetched. After 90:13, the section becomes less accurate, indicating that it was originally written between 165 and 160 BC.

The imagery and theology of the *Book of Enoch* is quite different from the Old Testament and did not appear until well into the second temple period (516 BC to AD 70). If it had appeared in the time of biblical Enoch, it would have undoubtedly influenced the Old Testament beyond the influence from the *Book of the Watchers* seen in Daniel and Jeremiah. Another argument against authorship by a biblical Enoch is the revolutionary nature of the text itself. If it existed from antiquity, the astonishing doctrines it contains would have found their way into the books of the Old Testament, or other early second temple literature.[69]

Why was it written in Enoch's name?

From the second temple period, well into the common era, authors wrote under assumed names. The examples are extremely numerous. They include 4 Ezra, 2 and 3 Baruch, Testaments of the Twelve Patriarchs, Apocalypse of Adam, Apocalypse of Abraham, Testament of Abraham, Testament of Isaac, Testament of Jacob, Testament of Moses, Testament of Solomon, Testament of Adam, Apocalypse of Daniel, Apocalypse of Elijah, Vision of Ezra, Treatise of Shem etc. and etc. If the reader is concerned that the authorship is unknown, it should be remembered that the authorship of many biblical books are clearly unknown. At a minimum these include Joshua, Judges, Ruth, 1 Samuel, 2 Samuel, 1 and 2 Kings, 1 and 2 Chronicles, Esther, Job, much of Psalms, much of Proverbs, all of Lamentations, and in the New Testament 2 and 3 John, and Hebrews. In the apocryphal books, the authorship is unknown in Tobit, Judith, additions to Esther, Wisdom of Solomon, 1 Baruch, Susanna, Bel and the Dragon, and 1 and 2 Maccabees.

Daniel Olson has an excellent comment on pseudonymous authorship.

> "Were these pen names mere frauds? Did these writers wish to give their ideas unwarranted authority by faking 'long lost' books of Adam, Enoch, Moses, Ezra, and others? It is indeed probable that some pseudepigraphal works are nothing more than cheap tricks, but it is equally probable that many works in the Pseudepigrapha are products of good faith, written by Jews (and also Christians) who felt they were the true spiritual heirs to the name and authority of their adopted literary personae. The device may also have been a way of shielding the real author from persecution, since many of these books were critical of the political and religious status quo of their day." He continues on the same page: "What can certainly be said is that the device was common,

[69] The teachings of the earlier portions of 1 Enoch did find their way into later second temple writings such as Jubilees and the Testaments of the Twelve Patriarchs. These doctrines exploded into use in the pages of the New Testament, and formed the basis of Christianity.

> used not only by Jews but throughout the ancient world, and that it is unlikely that the ancients felt the same way we moderns do about such things. Perhaps it is wisest to view pseudonymous authorship as a literary device that can be used with equal ease to spout lies or to proclaim truth."[70]

Charles weighs in on the same subject.

> "The Book of Enoch is for the history of theological development the most important pseudepigraph of the first two centuries B.C. Some of its authors—and there were many—belonged to the true succession of the prophets, and it was simply owing to the evil character of the period, in which their lot was cast, that these enthusiasts and mystics, exhibiting on occasions the inspiration of the O.T. prophets, were obliged to issue their works under the aegis of some ancient name. The Law which claimed to be the highest and final word from God could tolerate no fresh message from God, and so, when men were moved by the Spirit of God to make known their visions relating to the past, the present, and the future, and to proclaim the higher ethical truths they had won, they could not do so openly, but were forced to resort to pseudonymous publication."[71]

David L. Dungan opines:

> "The idea of putting the actual name of the author on a writing does not seem peculiar to us, but it was a very peculiar, indeed offensive, idea back then." He notes that "Greek philosophy rebelled against this ancient custom of anonymity and pseudonymity on the grounds of a new, positive evaluation of the unique creativity of each individual person. It was the complete opposite of a centuries-old custom of anonymous or pseudonymous authorship found throughout the ancient world."[72]

It should not be overlooked that all the books of 1 Enoch are anti-establishment. *The Book of the Watchers*, while based on a genuine ancient tradition; can also be seen as a polemic against the corrupt Jewish priesthood of the third century BC. *The Book of Parables* openly introduces an "Anointed One;" who when he comes, "will destroy the kings and the mighty and give them over into the hands of the righteous and the holy" (37:5). The *Book of Heavenly Luminaries* advocates the use of a solar calendar rather than a lunar one used by the Temple authorities of the time—an act that would have been considered seditious. *The Book of Dream Visions* calls for open war against foreign oppressors (90:19). *The Admonitions of Enoch* look forward to a great purging of iniquity when the "Holy Lord" comes forth in wrath and with punishment to execute judgment upon the earth (91:5-9); especially on the decadent rich (98:2). (98:12) predicts that the righteous will cut off the necks of the sinners (rulers) and put them to death. *The Birth of Noah* looks forward to a time when "evil and wickedness will come to an end;" "when there arise generations of righteousness" (107:1). The *Eschatological Exhortation* in Chapter 108 anticipates days when "an end is made of those who work evil and the power of evildoers is finished" (108:2).

---

[70] OL pg. 19.

[71] C pg. X.

[72] Dungan, David L. 2007, *Constantine's Bible, Politics and the Making of the New Testament*, Fortress Press.

Composition, or possession, of any of these works could result in severe persecution or death (See 1Mac 1:56-57). By writing them as a vision in the name of Enoch, the author has a layer of protection, and the readers can claim that they are reading religious literature—which they indeed were. Writing the books as if they were from ancient writers was a way to make the communication of doctrine and world view more enjoyable and memorable for the reader.

Did the authors expect readers to believe that Enoch really wrote the books? Undoubtedly some did think that Enoch wrote the *Book of Enoch.* Tertullian was one of those defended the Enochian authorship of 1 Enoch and its status as scripture.

> I am aware that the Scripture of Enoch, which has assigned this order of action to angels, is not received by some, because it is not admitted into the Jewish canon either. I suppose they did not think that, having been published before the deluge, it could have safely survived that world-wide calamity, the abolisher of all things. If that is the reason for rejecting it, let them recall to their memory that Noah, the survivor of the deluge, was the great-grandson of Enoch himself; and he, of course, had heard and remembered, from domestic renown and hereditary tradition, concerning his own great-grandfather's 'grace in the sight of God,' (Genesis 6:8) and concerning all his preachings; since Enoch had given no other charge to Methuselah than that he should hand on the knowledge of them to his posterity. Noah therefore, no doubt, might have succeeded in the trusteeship of his preaching; or, had the case been otherwise, he would not have been silent alike concerning the disposition of things made by God, his Preserver, and concerning the particular glory of his own house.
>
> If Noah had not had this conservative power by so short a route, there would still be this consideration to warrant our assertion of the genuineness of this Scripture: he could equally have renewed it, under the Spirit's inspiration, after it had been destroyed by the violence of the deluge, as, after the destruction of Jerusalem by the Babylonian storming of it, every document of the Jewish literature is generally agreed to have been restored through Ezra.
>
> But since Enoch in the same Scripture has preached likewise concerning the Lord, nothing at all must be rejected by us which pertains to us; and we read that 'every Scripture suitable for edification is divinely inspired.' (2 Timothy 3:16) By the Jews it may now seem to have been rejected for that very reason, just like all the other portions nearly which tell of Christ. Nor, of course, is this fact wonderful, that they did not receive some Scriptures which spake of Him whom even in person, speaking in their presence, they were not to receive. To these considerations is added the fact that Enoch possesses a testimony in the Apostle Jude. (Jude 1:14-15) (*Tertullian, The Apparel of Women, Book 1,* Chapter 3:1-3) See also (*Apol.* 22) where he again calls the book of watchers scripture.

Jude, who was clearly in the tradition of an Enochic Jew (if it is fair to use that description), at first glance seems to have considered Enoch to be the author of the Book of Enoch.

> It was also about these that Enoch, the seventh from Adam, prophesied, saying, "Behold, the Lord comes with ten thousands of his holy ones, to execute judgment on all and to

> convict all the ungodly of all their deeds of ungodliness that they have committed in such an ungodly way, and of all the harsh things that ungodly sinners have spoken against him. (Jude 14-15)

No one doubts this is a reference to the Book of Enoch. But it is very possible that he was simply referring his readers to the text; not necessarily claiming authorship by a biblical Enoch. This is similar to James 5:11 where James refers to Job, an obvious literary creation, saying: "You have heard of the steadfastness of Job." Chapter 108 is thought to have been written in Jude's lifetime! He certainly would not have viewed it as having been written by a Biblical Enoch.

As you explore this text of the Book of Enoch, the reasons for the dating of each section of the Book of Enoch are given in the introduction to each book. Where evidence arises that the text could not have been written by Biblical Enoch; observations are often included in the footnotes of the text.

Excursus: Qumran and the Dead Sea Scrolls, scholars debate theories.

Scholars have been intensely debating the significance of the Khirbet Qumran ruins where the Dead Sea Scrolls were found. The predominant theory, after much debate and textual study, is that Qumran was a community of an Essene sect (the Yahad) founded circa 175-150 BC with the Qumran settlement established between 100-50 BC. This is known as the Groningen hypothesis. This sect was in opposition to the existing priesthood in Jerusalem and over time developed distinctive features from the larger Essene movement and was not limited to Qumran. During the Jewish revolt in AD 66-73 their settlement was destroyed in battle, but the precious scrolls were preserved in nearby caves.

Pliny is quoted in support of the site being Essene.

> On the west side of the Asphaltitis (Dead Sea), but out of range of the noxious exhalations of the coast, is the solitary tribe of the Essenes, which is remarkable beyond all the other tribes in the whole world, as it has no women and has renounced all sexual desire, has no money, and has only palm-trees for company. Pliny, *Natural History* 5.73

The scholarly community has sought to make sense of the evidence found at Qumran with various theories proposed. Inconsistencies remain. The "writing tables" were actually benches that had been fastened to the wall. Dr. Pauline Doncel-Voûte' concluded that the chances of the room designated as a scriptorium, actually being such, was nil.[73] The room did not contain "the slightest hint of most of the materials that bona fide scribes used constantly in their work."[74] "It has been identified as a "Roman-period triclinium, or dining room. The Romans did not sit to eat, but instead reclined on cushioned couches."[75] Now that the scrolls have been examined, it

---

[73] W pg. 23; G pg. 319.
[74] G pg.27-28.
[75] W pg. 23.

has been found that hundreds of different scribes are responsible for them. Of the 981 scrolls determined to have been on site, only about a dozen are scribal repeats.[76]

Wise et. al observes:

> The Standard Model's romantic image of sustained scribal activity at Qumran suffered yet another challenge with the release of all the scrolls in late 1991. Now that scholars could examine the totality of the manuscript evidence for themselves, a puzzling fact became evident: hundreds of different scribes appeared to have written the scrolls. Since each writer had a distinct handwriting, just as we do, it was possible to isolate individual scribes and determine which scrolls each had copied. Not only were hundreds of different scribes responsible for the texts, but very few seemed to have written more than one scroll. Only about a few dozen "repeats" have been identified.[77]

It is not possible that this number of scrolls were copied on site.[78] This fact, coupled with the knowledge that at most, only 10-20% of the deposited scrolls have survived even in fragments; gives an impossible number of scribes who would have had to be on site to produce the scrolls. The number of scrolls deposited at Qumran was truly staggering (perhaps 5000 scrolls originally existed). Estimates of the sites population during the time range from 50 to 150. It is difficult to imagine why so many scrolls would be needed for such a small population. Why would a community of at most 150 people need 24 manuscripts of Genesis, 21 of Isaiah, and up to 20[78a] of 1 Enoch?

Other scrolls were found in a jar near Jericho in the time of Origen (AD 185-254) during the reign of Antoninus Severus (AD 211-217). This find included a Greek translation of the Bible (which Origen used in his Hexapla) along with other Hebrew and Greek biblical texts.[79] A large find of Old Testament and Hebrew manuscripts including 200 psalms of David were found in a cave "near Jericho" in the late 8th century. This find included "various passages quoted in the New Testament as coming from the Hebrew Bible, but which had never been found there." This cache was referenced in a letter by the Nestorian Patriarch Timotheus I of Seleucia.[80] Jericho, being 8 miles or 12.9 kilometers from Qumran, would have been a very inconvenient repository for sectarians at Qumran; but would have been a convenient location for scrolls being spirited from Jerusalem, or other localities in the area, before the siege in AD 70. Or perhaps Jericho was home to another sectarian/Essene community as the cave complex at Arabel may have been.[80a]

---

[76] W pg. 23.
[77] W pg. 23.
[78] W pg. 23.
78a Abegg, Flint and Ulrich in *The Dead Sea Scrolls Bible,* (1999) pg. 481 state that 20 copies of 1 Enoch were found. Curiously Flint later (2002) maintains that only 12 copies of 1 Enoch were present at Qumran (VF pg. 195).
[79] G pg. 105, 108.
[80] G pg. 107-108. These finds were collaborated by the Jewish Karaite scholar Ja' qub al-Qirqisani (tenth century) and the Muslim authors Shahrastani (1076-1153) and al-Biruni (973-ca. 1050) (.BO pg. 158). (Cf. Driver, G. R. 1951. *The Hebrew scrolls, from the neighborhood of Jericho and the Dead Sea*. pg. 25-26).
80a Ben-Daniel, John & Gloria. 2019. *Saint John and the Book of Revelation: From Essenes to End-Times.* Ch 1

Josephus,[81] Pliny the Roman historian,[82] the Refutatio Omnium Haeres 9.XIII, and the Jewish philosopher Philo[83] describe the Essenes as predominately celibate[84] but the scrolls are replete with rules on marriage.[85] In support of celibacy, excavations have shown the main cemetery at Qumran predominantly contains the bodies of men aged 20 to 50+ lacking signs of violent death. These bodies belonged to men who were born elsewhere, and some bodies appear to have been transported in. However, burials outside the main cemetery site contain the bodies of women and children.[86] Moreover, Josephus[87] and Philo[88] record that the Essenes rejected slavery; but rules governing slavery are found in the scrolls.[89] The scrolls are strongly calendar focused, yet Josephus and Philo say nothing about this in their descriptions of the Essenes.[90]

The scrolls display a wide variety of recensions; Norman Golb comments:

> These scrolls, along with the many other biblical texts and text fragments discovered in the caves, show that at the time the scrolls were hidden, there was not yet a single authoritative text of scriptural writings but rather different versions of the same text that circulated widely among the Palestinian Jews. Some of these versions were closer to that of the (Greek) Septuagint version of the Bible, others to the Samaritan tradition, and still others to the traditional Masoretic text of the Hebrew scriptures that has survived among the rabbinic Jews until today. These various recensions indicate considerable diversity among the Palestinian Jews who used them. It is most difficult to imagine that any single sect would have refrained from making an important priority of definitely fixing its own version of holy writ.[91]

Khirbet Qumran was destroyed by a Roman siege after the capture of Jerusalem.[92] This fact makes the case that the occupants at that time, far from being pacifist Essenes,[93] were Sicarii, Zealots or others fighting in the Jewish resistance movement.[94] Philo says that the Essenes pursued only peaceful occupations[95]—and yet the War Scroll (1QM) gives detailed prescriptions for the conduct of a very real, though future, armed conflict against the powers of darkness.[96]

---

[81] *War* 2.8.2 §§ 120-121; *Ant* 18.2.5 §§21.

[82] Pliny, *Natural History* 5.73.

[83] Philo of Alexander, *Hypothetica* 11.14-15.

[84] W pg. 25. "ESSENES (etymology doubtful; probably two words are represented, "Essenes" and "Essæi": Essenes = Ἐσσηνοὶ = צנועים, "the modest," "humble," or "pious ones" [so Josephus in most passages; Pliny, in "Historia Naturalis," v. 17, used "Esseni"]; Essæi = Ἐσσαῖου = חשאים, the "silent" or "reticent" ones." Jewish Encyclopedia

[85] W pg. 25; CD 13.16-17 (W pg. 75); $1QS_a$ 1.8-11 (W pg. 138); 4Q416 3.20-4.13 (W pg. 488-489).

[86] G pg. 16-18. The graves containing women and children are on the periphery of the main graveyard and in two small, separated cemeteries. Boccaccini, G. 1998. *Beyond the Essene Hypothesis* pg. 45. The few bodies of women found in the main cemetery were determined to be secondary Bedouin burials. (VF pgs. 53, 250, E pg. 277).

[87] *Ant* 18.2.5 §§21.

[88] *Good Person* 7.79; *Hypoth.* 11.4.

[89] W pg. 25; 4Q159 2-4.1-3 (W pg. 232); CD 11:12 (W pg. 72); CD 12.10-11 (W pg. 73).

[90] W pg. 25.

[91] G pgs. 362-363.

[92] G pg. 12-14; W pg. 21-22.

[93] Philo, *Good Person* 7.78.

[94] G pg. 35.

[95] *Good Person* 7.78.

[96] W pg. 25.

The supposed dining room to feed 200 men would require an enormous amount of food and about 30 ovens. In fact, "only a small number of ovens" have been found."[97] Most of the Qumranites may have lived in small huts or tents away from the main structure but congregated there for common meals and fellowship. The majority of the stepped pools were unsuitable for ritual baths (mikva'ot) since they used "drawn" rather than free flowing water. "Besides, if the place were filled with Essenes who wanted to take a daily purifying bath, they could easily have gone down to the springs near the shore of the Dead Sea without resorting to the 'huge construction project" of building all these pools."[98]

Longtime excavator of Qumran, Yizhak Magen proposes a different use of the stepped pools:

> Floodwaters from these streams carried the clay to the site, which then sank in collecting tanks prepared for this purpose. Other sites in the area received floodwaters in this way but not from streams that contained fine potter's clay. Qumran was the only one. This, then, became the basis of the Qumran pottery industry. Indeed, the extremely elaborate and sophisticated water supply complex at Qumran, including some very large pools, was designed precisely to bring this precious clay-filled water into the site and make it available to the potters.[99]

Michael Wise et. al summarizes: "The logical inference is that most of the scrolls came from elsewhere. Indeed, once that much has been conceded, the burden shifts and it becomes necessary to prove that *any* of the scrolls were written at Qumran."[100]

However, the scrolls do have direct ties to the Qumran site, both from common pottery and the presence of a more permanent type of library with wooden shelves in cave 4. Based on the content of the scrolls most scholars believe the site was not a center for the main body of Essenes but housed a sectarian branch (the Yahad) of the larger Essene movement. At some point the site was a farming center for grains and date palms, but during the revolt and during the siege of Masada it was a military outpost.[101] That the site was used for pottery production is evidenced by "many pottery kilns, as well as scores of whole vessels, numerous production rejects, 'huge' quantities of industrial waste and tens of thousands of clay fragments found at the site."[102] In the same article, Yizhak Magen, who excavated at Qumran intermittently for ten years, states "Your vison of a couple hundred celibate Essenes paddling around praying whenever they were not copying scrolls in a special room designated 'the scrollery,' only to end up buried in a silent

---

[97] *Qumran—The Pottery Factory, Dead Sea Scrolls Not Related to Settlement, Says Excavator; Biblical Archelogy Review,* Sept/Oct 2006. pg. 29.
[98] *Qumran—The Pottery Factory, Dead Sea Scrolls Not Related to Settlement, Says Excavator; Biblical Archelogy Review,* Sept/Oct 2006. pg. 28.
[99] *Qumran—The Pottery Factory, Dead Sea Scrolls Not Related to Settlement, Says Excavator; Biblical Archelogy Review,* Sept/Oct 2006. pg. 28.
[100] W pg. 23. Davila also regards I "as a hastily assembled collection of libraries" E pg. 359
[101] Mizzi, Dennis, *Were Temple Offerings Buried at Qumran? Biblical Archeology Review* Fall 2023 pg. 58. Also see the work area marker onsite at Qumran.
[102] *Qumran—The Pottery Factory, Dead Sea Scrolls Not Related to Settlement, Says Excavator;* Biblical Archelogy Review, Sept/Oct 2006. pg. 28.

cemetery of more than a thousand single graves, is a work of the imagination, not history or archaeology," ... "This conclusion, he says is 'inescapable.'"[103]

It is probable that most scrolls were spirited out of Jerusalem before the Roman siege that resulted in the destruction of Jerusalem in AD 70. A few similar scrolls, in similar jars, have been found at Masada. Josephus says besieged Masada was occupied by the Sicarii.[104] This would provide an explanation for the famous copper scroll; as it could be a map to where temple treasure would have been hidden by the resistance. It is very likely that most of the scrolls were spirited away from Jerusalem with the temple treasure before the siege than that they were composed on site. All scholars concede that texts like 1 Enoch were not composed at Qumran.[104a] Some scrolls may have been transported in by those joining the sect.

Others transporting and hiding the scrolls may have been Zealots and Sicarii led by someone like Simon, son of Giora, who Josephus wrote of, as entering and gaining possession of Jerusalem prior to Roman siege.[105] Josephus even writes of Simon: "at the valley called Paran, he enlarged many of the caves, and many others he found ready for his purpose; these he made use of as repositories for his treasures, and receptacles for his spoils, and therein he laid up the fruits that he had got by plundering; and many of his partisans had their dwelling in them;..."[106] The valley of Paran included the area of Qumran and beyond. The copper scroll (3Q15) strongly bolsters the Jerusalem origin case with its mention of hidden texts, priestly garments, temple vessels and consecrated offerings which could only have come from a ransacked Jerusalem temple. Additionally, some of the scrolls (especially the sectarian ones) may have been composed and hidden by devout members of the "Yahad" as described in the *Community Rule* aka. *Charter of a Jewish Sectarian Association*, found with the Dead Sea Scrolls.[107] Charlesworth maintains that the scrolls were removed by the "leading Aaronic priests and Levites of the Temple."[108] It is known that writings were taken out of Jerusalem by Jews who fled to caves prior to the siege of AD 70 and the Bar Kokhba revolt (AD 132-136).[109] It could also explain why the very valuable scrolls were not retrieved, since those who hid them, were in all probability slaughtered by the Romans, sold into slavery, or committed suicide at Masada.

This does not mean most of the scrolls were not Essene in origin, since the Essenes certainly had a community in Jerusalem.[110] But it explains how the content of the scrolls differ from accounts

---

[103] Ibid.

[104] *War* 4.7.2 §§400; 4.9.5 §§516. Sicarii is translated as bandits.

[104a] McDaniel, P pg. 345-346

[105] *War* 4.9.3-12 §§ 503-584.

[106] War 4.9.4 §§ 512-513.

[107] 1QS, 4Q255-264a, and 5Q11. Yahad (Hebrew יַחַד) means together, unity, community. See Ezra 4:3 "We together" NASB. For texts behind the meaning see Isa 50:8 and Ps 133:1

[108] Charlesworth, James H. 2008. *The Parables of Enoch and the Apocalypse of John*, In *Jewish and Christian texts in Contexts and Related Studies*, pg. 213.

[109] G pg. 51.

[110] Concerning the Essenes: "And they dwell in many cities of Judea, and in many villages, and in great and populous communities" (Philo, *Hypothetica* 11.1)). "They have no one certain city; but many of them dwell in every city" (*War* 2.8.4 §§124) (cf. Refutatio Omnium Hareres 9.15). See Riesner, R. 1992. *Jesus, the Primitive Community, and the Essene Quarter of Jerusalem*, in Charlesworth, J. H. Ed. 1992. *Jesus and the Dead Sea Scrolls*. Davila rightly sees the DSS texts "as a hastily assembled collection of libraries belonging to utopian groups within a broadly cohesive but multifaceted and internally inconsistent Essene/sectarian movement." (E 359)

of the Essenes given to us by Josephus, Pliny and Philo.[111] Qumran is probably the Essene community complex described by the non-Jewish writer Pliny, but defining the Essenes by the documents found at Qumran is challenging. Qumran, at the time of its destruction, was taken by force; with a defensive wall (that had been breached), numerous arrow heads and tower. Josephus documented that early in the chaos preceding the first Jewish revolt, legal documents in Jerusalem were destroyed.[112] Much more likely than being copied in the desert, many of the scrolls were hurriedly collected, from multiple sources, certainly including Jerusalem, by those wise enough to realize that Jerusalem could not stand against Rome; or fearing their destruction before the Romans even arrived.[113]. They were then added to the existing sectarian library at Qumran, which for the time being was under firmer Jewish control.

Who did write 1 Enoch?

Nickelsburg comments:

> "Indirect evidence from the contents of 1 Enoch allows us to flesh out the profile of the Enochic authors. They were learned in the writings that were becoming Israel's scriptures. Even if they did not explicitly quote these texts, they interpreted them by rewriting narratives and conflating terminology from prophetic texts. …Their Israelite identity notwithstanding, they were familiar with non-Israelite mythic traditions and used them for their own purposes."[114]

It must be remembered that the Books of 1 Enoch were composed over a period of over 300-700 years by at least nineteen authors.[115] "The putative authors of 1 Enoch, 4 *Ezra, and 2 Baruch are* scribes. Wisdom vocabulary is omnipresent, with the Daniel authors being called *maśkîlîm*. The claim by all of these authors that they saw visions should not be dismissed on modern rationalistic grounds."[116] "They claimed divine authority for their words."[117] Scribes who were "trained for the kingdom of heaven," were viewed by Christ as prophets who found treasures in older writings and disclosed new revelation.[118] "These writings owe their present forms and their settings in 1 Enoch to the labors of a long series of authors, redactors, tradents, copyists, translators, and anthologists, such that the collection itself is an artifact of the continued cultivation of Enochic traditions in the second temple period and well beyond" (Reed E pg. 339).

What language was 1 Enoch written in?

Most scholars think I Enoch was written in all its parts in Aramaic with a few words borrowed from Hebrew. "The consensus of more recent scholarship, however, is opposed to positing a Hebrew original, judging it more coherent to have an Aramaic original that occasionally

---

[111] For more, see Glob, Norman, 1995. *Who Wrote the Dead Sea Scrolls*, and W pg. 14-35.
[112] *War* 2.17.6 §§426-428.
[113] *War* 2.16.
[114] N1 pg. 66.
[115] N1 pg. 67. Stuckenbruck, Loren T. 2013. *Early Christianity* Vol 4 pg. 8.
[116] N1 pg. 70.
[117] N1 pg. 66; 1En 104:10-13.
[118] Mt 13:51-52.

borrowed Hebrew words for specific reasons of wordplay."[119] Since there was not a Hebrew original, rabbinic Jews were reluctant to consider 1 Enoch as canonical. However, Daniel 2:4-7:28 and Ezra 4:7b-6:18 were also written in Aramaic, and the Jews who placed the scrolls at Qumran certainly valued 1 Enoch, despite its Aramaic text, judging by the sheer number of copies.

Was 1 Enoch used in the New Testament?

The Book of Enoch is quoted in Jude 14-15 and referenced in Jude 8 and 2 Peter 2:4. "It influenced Matthew, Luke, John, Acts, Romans, 1 and 2 Corinthians, Ephesians, Colossians, 1 and 2 Thessalonians, 1 Timothy, Hebrews, 1 John, Jude and Revelation…There is little doubt that 1 Enoch was influential in molding New Testament doctrines concerning the nature of the Messiah, the Son of Man, the messianic kingdom, demonology, the future, resurrection, final judgement, the whole eschatological theater, and symbolism" [120] R. H. Charles, a very influential scholar of 1 Enoch, stated that: "The influence of Enoch on the New Testament has been greater than all the other apocryphal and pseudepigraphal books taken together."[121] Nearly all the writers of the New Testament were familiar with 1 Enoch. That Jesus was familiar with and believed at least some of the books of 1 Enoch is a given.[122] The editor is of the opinion that the Book of Enoch is the single most influential text behind the New Testament, and one cannot adequately understand the New Testament without the study of the Book of Enoch.[123]

Why did the Book of Enoch disappear in the western church?

"Jesus and the early churches clearly welcomed and cited many sacred religious texts, but there is no evidence that they adopted a fixed collection of Scriptures" (McDonald, P pg. 355)." Rabbi Akiba/Akiva Ben Joseph (AD ca 50-132), known as the father of Rabbinic Judaism, was a central figure in deciding which books were accepted by rabbinic Jews.

> In the first place, Akiba was the one who definitely fixed the canon of the Old Testament books. He protested strongly against the canonicity of certain of the Apocrypha. . .
> To the same motive underlying his antagonism to the Apocrypha, namely, the desire to disarm Christians—especially Jewish Christians— who drew their "proofs" from the Apocrypha, must also be attributed his wish to emancipate the Jews of the Dispersion from the domination of the Septuagint, the errors and inaccuracies in which frequently distorted the true meaning of Scripture, and were even used as arguments against the Jews by the Christians. *JewishEncyclopedia.com*
>
> In making that determination, Akiba made the judgements that he thought were best, in light of the evidence and purpose that he had. The declaration of the completion of the canon was a doctrinal decision. It was a declaration that the contemporary revelations of

---

[119] H1 pgs. 57-58.
[120] E. Isaac, OTP1 pg. 10.
[121] Charles, R. H. 1893. *The Book of Enoch*, General Introduction, Pg. 41.
[122] The Editor has done significant unpublished research on the influence of The Book of Enoch on the New Testament. If the Lord wills, this will be published soon.
[123] Ibid.

> other groups of Jews (including those at Qumran (Essenes) and the Talmidei Yeshua (disciples of Jesus)) were not divinely inspired or sanctioned. Since the Rabbis held political power at that time, the decision strengthened their position. (Gruber, Daniel, 2013. *Rabbi Akiba's Messiah,* pg. 109)

Akiba went on to standardize a Masoretic text without key texts supportive of Christianity.

> The standardization of the text, to whatever extent that occurred, offered an opportunity for those doing the "standardizing" to choose those variations which were most in accord with their own beliefs. It then led to seeing that all other versions were eliminated. It is not likely that this was an impartial, disinterested exercise. The Rabbis and their followers were a minority sect seeking power. In their reasoning, and in their determination of binding law, they freely changed the text they kept. (*Rabbi Akiba's Messiah* pg. 110) (See also *DialTropho* 72-73)

Since Christians were using the Septuagint in their apologetic, Akiba's follower, Aquila, gave the Greek-speaking Jews a Greek rabbinical Bible altered to remove key passages supportive of Christianity from the LXX. (*Rabbi Akiba's Messiah* pg. 111, *DialTropho* 71)

Olson makes a good point concerning the declining acceptance of the Enoch tradition among the Jews.

> The Rabbinic Judaism which came to dominate Jewish religious life after the twin disasters of the first and second Jewish revolts (66-70 and 132-135 CE) had little sympathy for the apocalyptic brand of Judaism represented by Enoch and similar literature, and these books only survived because Christians continued to value them... Also, the Enochic tradition spoke of righteousness and acceptance before God, but it paid scant attention to Mosaic law or even to membership in the nation of Israel, and its mysticism was seen as a dangerous distraction from practical Torah observance. Although some of the legendary material in Enoch did live on in esoteric streams of Jewish mysticism, the Book itself ceased to have any influence as a serious religious text and eventually was no longer copied.[124]

A major factor in the rejection of The Book of Watchers by Christians, must have been legitimate doubt that it could have been written by Biblical Enoch. As we have seen, Tertullian revealed this was a concern voiced by critics in his defense of the Book of Enoch. (See quote on pg. 15) Augustine also cited uncertainty of the antiquity of the Book of Watchers as one of the reasons for his rejection of the text.

> But it is not without reason that these writings have no place in that canon of Scripture which was preserved in the temple of the Hebrew people by the diligence of successive priests; for their antiquity brought them under suspicion, and it was impossible to ascertain whether these were his genuine writings, and they were not brought forward as genuine by the persons who were found to have carefully preserved the canonical books by a successive transmission. (*The City of God,* Book 15, Chapter 23) (AD 420)

---

[124] OL pg. 2.

In Christian circles, the personage of Enoch, over time, became associated with the Gnostics, and Manicheans. The text of 2 Enoch, which seems to be from a separate Enochic tradition of a fringe sect,[125] may have been conflated with 1 Enoch in the minds of early Christians.[126] [127] Zosimos of Panopolis a Gnostic mystic and early alchemist attributed the corruption of alchemy to the fallen angels (See the Chronography of George Sykellos). The person of Enoch could have thus become associated with heresy and Gnosticism. [128] The "son of man" interpolation in 1 Enoch 71:14 may have served to cast doubt on the Parables if it was present in circulating copies. However, none of these issues were new to the early-4th century when Enoch fell out of favor. What changed was severe persecution under Diocletian (encouraged by Galerius) that began on March 31, 302 initially against the Manicheans. Here is a portion of that edict.

> We order that the authors and leaders of these sects be subjected to severe punishment, and, together with their abominable writings, burnt in the flames. We direct their followers, if they continue recalcitrant, shall suffer capital punishment, and their goods be forfeited to the imperial treasury. An official edict called the *De Maleficiis et Manichaeis* compiled in the *Collatio Legum Mosaicarum et Romanarum* and addressed to the proconsul of Africa

On February 23, 303, Diocletian also compelled Christians to turn over their sacred books to the authorities to be burned. The Christians tried to salvage as much of their sacred literature as possible by turning over to them less important texts that were not considered sacred. This edict remained in effect until 311. This severe widespread edict would have fallen especially hard on Enochic literature since it was used by both Manicheans and Christians. It would certainly have been more acceptable to hand over Enochic texts rather than New Testament texts when given the choice. The likely result was that Enochic texts became very rare.

Philastrus, bishop of Brescia (AD 330- before 397), who did not have access to a copy of The Book of Enoch, included the fallen Angel theory in his list of Heresies. Diversarum hereseon liber CVIII. Pseudo-Jerome followed his lead, calling Enoch heresy in *Breviarium in Psalmos* 133.3 (non-LXX) (AD 400). At the same time John Chrysostom (AD 347-407) in his homily on Gen 5:32–6:1 called the angel tradition "fanciful fictions." He gave a long explanation 'to refute the fanciful fictions. Pseudo-Jerome cited the use of the Book of Watchers by the Manichaeans as a major reason for the author's rejection of it.

> **Like the dew of Hermon that descends on Mount Zion. Dew Hermon.** We read in a certain apocryphal book, that at the time when the sons of God descended to the daughters of men, they descended to Mount Hermon, and there entered into an agreement, how they should come to the daughters of men, and marry them to themselves. It is a most manifest book, and is reckoned among the apocrypha, and the old

---

125 OTP1 pg. 94, 96.

126 Estimates of 2nd Enoch's date of composition vary from the first century BC to AD 9th century (OTP1 pg. 95).

127 Scholars are coalescing around a mid-1st century date for the composition of 2nd Enoch. Orlov, Andrei A. 2012. The Sacerdotal Traditions of 2 Enoch and the Date of the Text, in *New Perspectives on 2 Enoch No Longer Slavonic Only* eds Orlov, Andrei A. and Boccaccini, Gabriele pgs. 103-116.

128 For an example of potential heresy see 2En J 64:5 (OTP1 pg. 64) where Enoch "is the one who carried away the sin of mankind". Passages with apparent Gnostic influences include (2En 25:1-5 (OTP1 pgs. 144-145); and 2En J 30:16 (OTP1 pg. 152)).

> interpreters have spoken of it: but we have said some things: not for authority, but for commemoration. Like the dew of Hermon, which descends on Mount Zion. I read in a certain book about this apocryphal book confirming his heresy. What does he say? The sons of God, he says, who came down from heaven, came to Hermon and lusted after the daughters of men. Angels, he says, are those who descend from the heavens, and souls which have longed for bodies. For the bodies are the daughters of men. Have you seen how the Manichaean dogma arose? For as the Manichaeans say that souls longed for human bodies, and were associated with the pleasure of bodies: so also those who say that angels longed for bodies, that is, the daughters of men, do they not seem to you to be saying the same thing as the Manichaeans? It is now a long time to say against them: but I only wanted to judge, concerning which volume, as if by this occasion, they confirm their dogma. Hermon is interpreted in our language, ἀνάθημα, that is, condemnation. *Breviarium in Psalmos* 132.3 LXX (AD 400)

Like Augustine (see pg. 26 and 254-256), the author of the Pseudo-Jerome text above, appears to have never read, and indeed did not possess a copy of the Book of Enoch.[129] From the above quote, two things are clear. 1. The author did not have a copy of the Book of Watchers, let alone the rest of the Books of Enoch; choosing to reject it sight unseen. 2. He rejected it out of hand due to its use by the Manichaeans.

Jerome himself was to be a major decision maker on whether the Book of Enoch would be preserved. As one of the few church fathers at the time who could speak Hebrew, and presumably Aramaic, he held great influence. He did not translate it with the rest of the apocrypha into the Latin Vulgate. There is no evidence that it was ever translated into Latin, aside from a few quotes.[130] Even though it was translated into Greek; between 150-50 BC[131] the use of Aramaic and Greek began to fall into disuse. 1 Enoch gradually disappeared. That the post-Nicene fathers were almost uniform in embracing the "Sethite view" in opposition to the "angel view" is testament to 1 Enoch's scarcity in the western church by the 5th and 6th centuries. Existing copies, facing the disapproval of the church, were not translated, copied or preserved.

It seems strange that Jerome would let the rabbinic Jews of Bethlehem decide the Old Testament cannon. The Jews had long since, to the best of their ability, purged their scriptures of positive potential references to Christ. It is certain that under the Pharisees, and Rabbi Akiba's successor's leadership, powerful apologetic texts positive to Christianity such as The Parables, The Admonitions of Enoch and The Eschatological Exhortation would have been purged from Pharisee controlled libraries in the first and second centuries. Given that The Book of Enoch was popular with a competing sect of Judaism (Essenes-like groups) and Christians would have ensured it was not preserved by the Rabbinic Jews founded by Rabbi Akiba.

Irenæus (AD 130-202) is useful here; speaking of the virgin birth section of the Septuagint:

---

[129] *Breviarium in Psalmos* it no longer attributed to the Church Father Jerome although it does have antiquity.

[130] These quotes in Latin include Pseudo-Cyprian Ad Novatianum 16 (quotes 1:9); Tertullian, *Idol.* 4 (quotes 99:6-7) and a ninth century Latin *MS* (quotes 106:1-18). "While these quotations and allusions might attest a Latin version of the Book of Enoch, the evidence is slim and far from compelling" (N1 pg. 14; cf. P .pg. 360-361).

[131] E pg. 87 (Larson); N1 pg. 14.

> But it was interpreted into Greek by the Jews themselves, much before the period of our Lord's advent, that there might remain no suspicion that perchance the Jews, complying with our humor, did put this interpretation upon these words. They indeed, had they been cognizant of our future existence, and that we should use these proofs from the Scriptures, would themselves never have hesitated to burn their own Scriptures, which do declare that all other nations partake of [eternal] life,[132] and show that they who boast themselves as being the house of Jacob and the people of Israel, are disinherited from the grace of God."[133]

Tertullian (AD 155-220) made a similar observation:

> But since Enoch in the same Scripture has preached likewise concerning the Lord, nothing at all must be rejected by us which pertains to us; and we read that 'every Scripture suitable for edification is divinely inspired.' (2 Timothy 3:16) By the Jews it may now seem to have been rejected for that very reason, just like all the other portions nearly which tell of Christ. Nor, of course, is this fact wonderful, that they did not receive some Scriptures which spake of Him whom even in person, speaking in their presence, they were not to receive. To these considerations is added the fact that Enoch possesses a testimony in the Apostle Jude." (Jude 14-15) *Tertullian, The Apparel of Women, Book 1, Chapter 3:1-3*

Augustine (AD 354-430) seems to have rejected the writings of Enoch without reading them.

> Whether Augustine had firsthand knowledge of 1 Enoch, or any part of it, is doubtful, since he accepts the authenticity of the part of chap. 1 quoted in Jude but rejects the veracity of the story of the watchers, which follows right after the prologue. In any case, his rejection of the writings is tied to his rejection of material contained in them.[134]

Thus, the most influential decision makers of the 4th-5th century church (Philastrus Augustine, Jerome and Chrysostom) rejected the Enochian texts without personal examination. Lower ranking church authorities and the laity had little choice but to follow their lead. The Christian war on paganism and idolatry was undoubtedly also a factor in the suppression; as belief in other spiritual beings who could be considered "gods" was strongly discouraged.

A factor in the suppression of 1Enoch was that it became culturally unthinkable that angels would mingle sexually with humans. The change in view away from the watcher tradition was complete by the late 6th century. The 7th century text, *The Cave of Treasures,* blatantly attacks the watcher tradition and substitutes its absence with Sethite mythology.

> Methuselah and Noah spent their lives alone upon the mountain, because all the children of Seth had gone down from the fringes of paradise toward the plain to the children of

---

[132] The *Book of Enoch* is clearly implicated in this statement; as it predicts the inclusion of the gentiles in the kingdom of God (The Book of Watchers 10:21; Parables 48:4; Dream Visions 90:33, 38; Admonitions 91:14; 100:6).

[133] Irenæus, *Against Heresies* 3.21.1.

[134] N1 pg. 95. The Jews were the first to deny angels the ability to sin, calling the idea blasphemy (DialTrypho 79).

> Cain. The manly sons of Seth mingled with Cain's daughters, and there were conceived and borne by them valiant men, the sons of giants in the likeness of towers. The former authors erred concerning this when they wrote that angels came down from heaven and mingled with the daughters of humankind, and that from them were born those famous heroes. It is not true, for they are saying this without knowledge. Look, my fellow-readers, and understand that this does not lie within the nature of spiritual beings, nor in the nature of demons who are impure, evil-doers and lovers of adultery, because among them there is neither male nor female, and not a single one has been added to their number since they fell. If the devils could mingle with women, they would not leave a single virgin in the whole human race whom they would not violate. *Cave of Treasures*, 15:1-8 (AD 590-628)

Another example from the same time period is the *Conflict of Adam and Eve with Satan* AKA *The Book of Adam and Eve* or *1st and 2nd Adam and Eve.*

> And when they looked at the daughters of Cain, at their beautiful figures, and at their hands and feet dyed with colour, and tattooed in ornaments on their faces, the fire of sin was kindled in them. Then Satan made them look most beautiful before the sons of Seth, as he also made the sons of Seth appear of the fairest in the eyes of the daughters of Cain, so that the daughters of Cain lusted after the sons of Seth like ravenous beasts, and the sons of Seth after the daughters of Cain, until they committed abomination with them. 2nd Adam and Eve 20:31-32 (AD 6th century)

The Sethite tradition would have been utterly unknown to Jesus, His disciples, Jews of the time, and Christians in the 1st and 2nd centuries. It has no manuscript evidence until Julius Africanus (AD 160-240) proposed it as an idea in AD 221. See: (*Chronographia of Julius Africanus fragment 2, In Georgius Syncellus, Chron.*, p. 19, al. 15. (AD 221). Jews as early as AD 155-160 considered the idea that angels could revolt and sin as blasphemous (*DialTrypho* 79). The first recorded mention on the Jewish side of an alternative to the fallen angel tradition comes from the rabbinic writing *Bereshit Rabbah* 26:5. It is thought to have been written in the third century in Palestine. It identifies the fathers of the Nephilim as the *benei haelohim* "great men" or "judges." In addition, it says: "Rabbi Shimon ben Yoḥai used to curse anyone who would call them [translating the words literally, as] "children of god." (Rabbi Shimon ben Yohai lived in the second century and was a loyal student of Rabbi Akiba).

It appears that in both the Rabbinic Jewish and Christian camps a "conspiracy" against the Book of Enoch occurred. Rabbi Akiba, more than anyone else, is the reason the book of 1 Enoch did not find its way into the church cannon. He initiated the effort that eventually consolidated the majority of Jews under the control of the Rabbis and thus made Judaism conform to the dictates of their, at the beginning, minority sect. The books of other Jewish sects were banned from his cannon. A translation of the Masoretic text was shaped to the benefit of his rabbinic controlled sect, and a new Greek translation to replace the Septuagint was put into place. In this manner, a minority sect of Judaism was able to gain majority control of Judaism by the 6th century.

It then became imperative for Christians to make their own determination concerning 1 Enoch. The early church fathers, into the early 4th century, mostly embraced 1 Enoch. However, later church fathers largely turned to Rabbinic Judaism (opponents of Christianity) for guidance on the Old Testament canon; rather than to sects like the Essenes, who had by that time had virtually disappeared. The Jewish Encyclopedia admits the Essenes were the forerunners of Christianity. What little consideration of the text of 1 Enoch that occurred, was misinformed and reactionary after the mid-4th century.

McDonald (P pg. 330) notes:

> Despite the majority of the churches eventually rejecting the sacred status of 1 Enoch after the fourth century. It continued to be used after that by some Chrisitan communities for centuries, and continued to be a part of the Manichean and Ethiopian Christian Scriptures. The listing of 1 Enoch in apocryphal (thereby rejected) literature continued well into the sixth century, (Pseudo-Athanasis, *Synopsis*) and even in the mid-ninth century, the *Stichometry* of Nicephorus shows the continuing popularity of 1 Enoch long after its official rejection. This rejection appears to have begun with Origen or in his generation. Subsequently there are fewer references to 1 Enoch and it increasingly is found in rejected categories in various catalogues of the Church's sacred writings. This shows that Enochic literature continued to have an influence on subsequent generations of Christians. Why would it show up in categories if it had long been rejected and no one was using it.

It is unfortunate that 1 Enoch was suppressed to the point of being virtually lost to the west, since as we will see, it was obviously very important to Jesus, his disciples, and early Christians. Much misunderstanding of the New Testament and Christian theology has resulted from disuse of the Book of Enoch. It is time for it to reassume its proper prominent role in Christianity.

The Book of the Watchers

Background of *The Book of the Watchers*

Original language: Aramaic,[135] translated into Greek[136] then into Ethiopic (Ge' ez).[137]

Author and provenance: Multiple authors are undoubtedly involved. However, if one were to assume a single author, he was a pious, locally well-traveled Jew, who was very familiar with Jerusalem[138] and upper Galilee. He appears to have been involved in the spice trade[139] perhaps in procuring spices for the second temple. He was obviously an unabashed lover of trees who appreciated fragrances. It was written in Palestine, most likely upper Galilee.[140]
Date: Third century BC or earlier (pre 500 BC). "A scholarly consensus for the date of the Book of Watchers places the extant Aramaic form sometime in the third century BCE based on the paleography of the Qumran fragments; some suggest pushing the date farther back into an earlier Hellenistic period or perhaps the Persian period."[141] "The earliest traditions in the book may predate the Hellenistic period, and the book as a whole was completed by the middle of the third century B.C.E."[142] The Book of the Watchers belongs "to the earliest Enochic tradition and represents the oldest layer of the Qumran manuscript tradition… The earliest layer of the Enochic tradition thus reflects a strong Mesopotamian influence."[143] "The accurate references to locations in Upper Galilee in chapters 6-16… suggest that that section of the corpus may have been composed in this northern region."[144] This text is a composite writing that drew on older sources of unknown antiquity; parts of which may predate Gen 6:1-4. [145]
Important notes: Extensive parts of the Book of the Watchers were found in the Dead Sea Scrolls. 50% of the text is covered in the Dead Sea Scrolls.[146] In addition, it is thought that the opening columns of the Genesis Apocryphon (1QapGen or 1Q20) "probably told the story of the watchers and the women."[147] A complete Greek manuscript (*The Codex Panopolitanus*), of 1 Enoch 1:1-32:6a dating to AD 500-600 along with incomplete texts of the *Gospel of Peter* and the *Apocalypse of Peter*, was discovered in 1886/87 in a grave, in the Coptic cemetery at

---

[135] N1 pg. 1.

[136] The *Codex Panopolitanus* is a Greek manuscript containing 1En 1:1 -32:6a. It dates to the fifth or sixth century (AD) and was discovered in 1886/87 in a grave in a Coptic Cemetery at Akhmim (Panopolis) Egypt. This manuscript., however, has its own unique readings, both longer and shorter than the Ethiopic. In general, however, it corresponds quite closely to the Ethiopic (N1 pg. 12).

[137] The translation from Greek to Ge' ez is thought to have occurred in the fourth to the sixth centuries AD after Christianity was adopted as the official religion of Axum. In Ge' ez, Enoch is called Henok.

[138] See chapter 26 and (M pg. 25-26).

[139] See chapters 29-32 and (M pg. 25-26).

[140] *N1 pgs. 65 and 119.*

[141] Wright, Archie T., 2018. "*Introduction to the Book of Watchers*," in *Early Jewish Literature: An Anthology*. Eds. Embry, Brad, Wright, Archie T. Herms, Ronald. Olson in *An Enochic Reading of Gen 6:1-4 from the Beginning of the Persian Era?* 2018, *Wisdom Poured out Like Water: Studies on Jewish and Christian Antiquity in Honor of Gabrielle Boccaccini*, proposes a pre-500 BC date based on correlations between Gen 6, 19 and Judges 19-21.

[142] N1 pg. 7.

[143] R pg. 346-347, Fröhlich, *The Parables of Enoch and Qumran literature.*

[144] N1 pg. 65.

[145] OL pg. 10, Reeves E pgs. 376-377.

[146] N1 pg. 11.

[147] N1 pg. 76; W pg. 90.

Akhmim (Panopolis), Egypt. The Book of Watchers provides critical background for Gen 6:1-4. The giants (actually three types of progenies from the watcher/human women union) are well attested in ancient literature. The *Book of Watchers* serves as background for the *Parables* (1En 37-71) and the *Animal Apocalypse* (1En 85-90). It is also the background for *Jubilees* 5:1-19, and the *Damascus Document* (CD 2:2-3:12, 4Q180, and 4Q510-11). Many scholars now believe that the Book of Watchers antedates the Book of Daniel, making it the prototypical apocalypse.[148] "Chapters 6-11, usually considered an excerpt from the lost 'Book of Noah,' are the heart of the book, and probably the oldest piece in 1 Enoch."[149] "The influence of the 'Book of the Watchers' on later writers and thinkers is incalculable. Quotations of it, and allusions to it in early Jewish and Christian literature far outnumber references to all the rest of the Enochic writings combined."[150]

The Book of the Watchers (Chapters 1-36)

Written for a Remote Generation

1 1 The blessing[151] of Enoch: Deut 33:1; Gen 5:18-22
the words with which he blessed the righteous chosen,[152] 5:6-8; Mt 22:14
who will be present on the day of tribulation, 48:1; 58:1-2; 61:13; 62:12-15; Zeph 1:15-18
to remove all the enemies.[153] 62:2; 65:10; 69:27; 91:8; 94:1
2 He took up his discourse[154] and spoke,[155] [156]
"(Oracle of) Enoch,[157] a righteous man, whose eyes were opened Ps 78:2-4; Num 24:2-4, 15-17

---

[148] N1 pg. 119.

[149] OL pg. 10. Lost "Book of Noah" cf. Jub 10:13; 21:10.

[150] OL pg. 11.

[151] Portions of 1En 1:1-9 are found in the DSS (4Q201 Frag. 1 Col. 1.1-8 and 4Q204 1.1) or (4QEn^a 1 i (M 142-143)).

[152] **Who would not want to be one of the chosen/elect of God?** 1 Enoch also uses the term in (38:2, 3, 4; 39:6, 7; 48:1; 58:1, 2; 61:13, 62:12, 13, 15; and 70:3). Here and 5:6-8 are the only uses in 1 Enoch outside *The Book of Parables*. It is used in the Old Testament; (1Kgs.3:8; I Chr. 16:13; Ps. 89:3 (LXX 88.4); lsa 65:9, 15, 22; cf. Dt. 7:6; 14:2). It also appears in the Dead Sea Scrolls; (1QM 12.1, 4; 1QS 9:14; CD 4.3 "the chosen of Israel"). New Testament appearances include; (Mt. 22:14; 24:22, 31; Mk. 13:20, 22, 27; Lk. 18:7; Rom. 8:33; Col. 3:12; 2 Tim. 2:10; 1Pet 1:1 and 1Pet. 2:9 "the chosen race").

[153] The Greek text (Gk.^{a}) adds to this verse: "and the righteous will be delivered."

[154] "Discourse" is also translated "Parable" or "proverb." (4Q201 1.1.2 (W pg. 280) and N have "discourse".

[155] **"Enoch is here referred to in third person, making it clear that the biblical Enoch of Genesis 5:21-24 is *not* cast as the author of 1 Enoch. Rather, an unknown writer purports to quote the biblical Enoch, so 1 Enoch is about Enoch, not authored by Enoch" (H1 pg. 27).**

[156] "It was known at an early time that there were intriguing parallels between Enoch, the seventh man, and Enmeduranki, the seventh king in some versions of the Sumerian king list" (NV2 pg. 371). Enmeduranki of Zimbir (the city now known as Sippar) was an ancient Sumerian king, whose name appears in the *Sumerian King List* as the seventh pre-dynastic king of Sumer. He was said to have reigned for 21,000 years. A myth written in a Semitic language tells of Enmeduranki, subsequently being taken to heaven by the gods Shamash and Adad, and taught the secrets of heaven and of earth.

[157] "Oracle of" is not original to the text and is assumed to have been lost by omission, given the rest of the text's similarity with the Balaam oracle in Numbers 24:3-4" (BL pg. 103-104).

by God, a vision of the Holy One, who is in heaven,[158] was	15:1; 89:28; 1Q201 1.1.1-8
shown to me.	4Q534 2.15
I heard everything from the words of the watchers[159] and holy	Rev 1:1; Lam 4:14 LXX; Dan 4:13, 17, 23
ones; so, I fully understood what I saw.	
Not for this generation,	Dan 8:26; 12:4, 9; Jub 4:19; Gen 49:1
but for a distant generation do I speak.[160]	92:1; 1Pet 1:12

The Coming of God to Earth in Judgement

3 Concerning the chosen I speak, and concerning them I	
take up my parable.	
The Holy Great One will come forth from His dwelling,[161]	91:7; Ex 19:11; Ezra 5:8; Dan 2:45; Mic 1:3
4 and the everlasting God[162] shall come down upon the earth,	Deut 33:2; Judg 5:4-5; Hab 3:3
and tread on Mount Sinai.[163]	18:8; 25:3; 77:1; Mic 1:3-4; Neh 9:13 Amos 4:13
He will appear with his mighty army, and	Isa 26:21; Zech 2:13; Rev 19:11-16
he will shine in the strength of His might from the heaven of	Deut 10:14; 1Kgs 8:27; 2Chr 2:6; Eph 6:10
heavens![164]	TLev 3:1-8
5 All will be afraid. The watchers[165] will quake; and seek to	Ex 19:16; Jas 2:19; Jub 4:15

---

[158] A Greek manuscript (Gk[a]) reads: "a vision of the Holy One and of heaven."

[159] Nickelsburg has: "From the words of the watchers and holy ones I heard everything;" **The use of "watcher" here is thought by many scholars to predate its use in (Dan 4:13, 17, 23).** "And behold, a watcher, a holy one, came down from heaven" (Dan 4:13). Just like the author of Revelation (1:1), the author of this section receives his knowledge from heavenly beings.

[160] **The author states that this book was written for those who will be living in a remote time of tribulation. This is picked up by Peter "It was revealed to them that they were serving not themselves but you, in the things that have now been announced to you through those who preached the good news to you by the Holy Spirit sent from heaven, things into which angels long to look" (1Pet 1:12).**

[161] 1:3b to 1:9 is a classic theophany. "What is new and original in Enoch is that it is no longer—as in the classic theophanies at Deut 33:2; Num 24:1-4; and Judg 5:4-5 an account of a mighty act of God in the past, but a prediction of his future advent in a universal judgement but couched in the language of the Biblical theophanies. **The passage is of special importance, not only because Jude 14-15 cites v. 9 as a scriptural prediction of the advent of God or Christ in judgement, but also as the foundation, in the tradition-history of Hebrew theophanies, for the New Testament doctrine of the Second Advent"** (BL pg. 105).

[162] "The everlasting/eternal God" (cf. Gen 21:33; Isa 40:28; Dan 5:4 LXX; Rom 16:26; Jub 13:8; and Sib. Or. 3.698)

[163] God is here descending to his dwelling on Mt. Sinai. Compare Deut 33:2; Ps 68:7-8; Judg 5:4-5; and Hab 3:3-5, where God is seen coming from the south in judgement. **Prior to the time of Moses, Mount Sinai would have had no meaning to anyone; this is strong evidence that The Book of Watchers was written in the second temple period rather than in the time of a biblical Enoch.**

[164] The phrase "heaven of heavens" indicates the highest heaven. (Deut 10:14, 1En 60:1, 71:5, 1Kgs 8:27, and TLev 3:1-4) The highest level contains God's throne and palace surrounded by innumerable celestial beings. Isaac translates 1:4 as: "And from there he will march upon Mount Sinai and appear in his camp emerging from heaven with a mighty power."

[165] **"Watchers" originates from Hebrew/Aramaic and means "to be awake." It is a term for celestial beings of the unseen realm.** For watchers in the Bible see (Daniel 4:13, 17, 23). Watchers can be fallen, or loyal to God. Papias, relying on an unknown Daniel source, makes mention of loyal watchers "But Michael and his warriors who are the watchers of the universe helped humanity, as Daniel taught, by giving the Law and by making the prophets wise" (*A Danielic Pseudepigraphon Paraphrased by Papias,* Lourie, in *Old Testament Pseudepigrapha*, Bauckham et. al. pg. 441). In 1 Enoch, as used in this verse, "watchers" are most often fallen. Nickelsburg (N1 pg. 140) describes a watcher as "one that sits up or continues awake at night." Nickelsburg choses this definition in light of

hide themselves in all ends of the earth.
Even the ends of the earth shall be shaken, and great fear and
trembling shall seize them to the very limits of the earth.[166]
6 The lofty mountains will be shaken, fall, and crumble to dust,
and the high hills shall be made low,
and melt like wax before the flames.[167]

7 The earth will be torn open,
and everything on the earth will perish,
and there shall be a universal judgement.
8 But with the righteous he will make peace,[168]

and will keep safe the chosen,[169] [170]
and mercy will be upon them,
and they will all belong to God![171]
He will prosper and bless them and help them all.
The light ‹of God› will shine upon them,[172]
‹and He will make peace with them›.[173]

Hag 2:6-7; Isa 24:16; 26:20; GbRev 23-25
Jer 25:30-31; 1Sam 2:10; Job 9:6; Lk 21:26
10:13; 13:3; 69:1; 102:2-3; Ps 59:13
Rev 6:14-15; Judg 5:5; Ps 18:7; SibOr 3.680
Isa 40:4; 64:1-2 LXX; Mic 1:4; Hab 3:6
52:6; Ps 97:5; Jdt 16:15; 2Pet 3:7, 10
Bar 5:7; Mic 1:4
Nah 1:5; Isa 24:19-20; Zech 14:4; Ps 50:22
90:18; Zeph 1:2-3, 18; 3:8
80:8; Gen 6:17; Jude 15
45:6; Rom 5:1; Jn 14:27; Eph 2:14
OdesSol 9:6
Wis 3:1-9; Lk 17:34-37; Col 1:19; 1QS 9.14
Mal 3:17
Isa 9:2; 60:1
Ps 97:11; Jn 1:4, 9; 1Jn 1:7; 4Q440 3.16
Rom 5:1; Num 6:24-26; Jn 16:33

---

other places in 1 Enoch, (39:12, 13, 40:2; 61:12; and 71:7) where they are described as "those who sleep not." The Ancient Babylonians created apkallu figurines and buried them in the foundation of buildings to protect the buildings. These were called *matserey* which translates to watchers. The use of the term here is certainly borrowed from Babylonian sources. Outside the Book of the Watchers in 1 Enoch, the term is used only in 93:2 and some texts of 91:15. Watchers are also found in the *Book of Giants* (4Q532 2.7); (4Q534 2.15) and Jubilees (4:15, 22). Good watchers are found in (1En 1:2; 12:2, 3; 20:1 (the archangels are watchers); 33:3; 93:2); whereas evil ones are found in (1En 6:2; 10:9, 15; 12:4; 13:10; 14:1, 3, 4; 15:2, 9; 16:1,2; and possibly 91:15).

[166] Nickelsburg reconstructs verse 5 as: "All the watchers will fear and <quake>, and those who are hiding in all the ends of the earth will sing. All the ends of the earth will be shaken, and trembling and great fear will seize them (the watchers) unto the ends of the earth." The prison for angels, at the ends of the earth, is also mentioned in (10:13; 18:10-19:1 and 21:7-10). That God rules to the ends of the earth is also found in (Ps 59:13; 67:7; Isa 41:5). Since this verse is speaking of the final judgement, it **indicates that watchers will again be active on the earth, at the end of the age, as Christ prophesied (Lk 17:26-27) and Paul indicated (2Thes 2:3-9).** "The man of lawlessness" "the son of destruction" as used by Paul is quite certainly a reference to a yet future demigod descendent of the watchers (cf. Isa 13:3).

[167] For mountains melting like wax, see also (4Ezra 8:23), (cf. V*ita* 49:3). Isaac translates "wax" as "honeycomb."

[168] **This peace was accomplished through the work of Jesus Christ. "Therefore, since we have been justified by faith, we have peace with God through our Lord Jesus Christ" (Rom 5:1). This is therefore a prophecy of the work of Christ reconciling mankind to himself.**

[169] No longer is all of Israel blessed, but only the chosen and righteous remnant from among them (Isa 65:8-9).

[170] **This is a promise that the chosen will be kept safe in the time of tribulation.** This does not appear to be the flood judgement since the flood lacked the appearance of ten thousand holy ones (vs 9). Even preterists would have to agree; this account can only match the future "day of the Lord" judgement (Rev 19:11-16), since the mountains were not thrown down at the fall of Jerusalem in AD 70 (vs. 6).

[171] Some Ethiopian commentators have: "they will become God's property" (OTP1 pg. 13n t). Black postulates that this line may have originally read "And they shall all be/become sons of God" (BL pg. 108).

[172] OL, I and K, also have: "The light of God will shine upon them." "Of God" is omitted in (Gk.[a]). N omits: "of God." Jesus is the light (Jn 1; 3:19; 8:12; Eph 5:8; Rev 22:5). This verse can be taken as a prophecy of Christ with or without "of God." For light of God see (1En 5:7; 38:2,4; 45:4; 50:1; 58:3-6; 92:4; 96:3; 108:11-12).

[173] "And he will make peace with them" is found only in the Greek (Gk.[a]). This carries the idea of a cessation of God's anger. Jesus Christ is the one who makes peace with mankind through the cross (Rom 5:1; Eph 2:14; Col 1:20).

9 Behold! He comes[174] with ten thousand[175] holy ones[176]	14:22, 40:1; 60:1; 71:8; Mt 26:53; Zech 14:5
	Jude 14-15; 4Q531 24.1; Dan 7:10; Job 5:1
to execute judgement on all,	Deut 33:2; Ps 96:13; Rev 19:14; 1Thes 3:13
and to destroy all the ungodly,	Isa 63:1-4; 4Q530 2.2.16-19
and to convict all flesh	*Vita* 51:9; Isa 66:16; Jer 25:31
for the works of wickedness which they have godlessly committed,	Dan 8:13
and the proud and hard words that ungodly sinners have	5:4; 27:2; 91:7; 94:9; 96:7; Jude 15
spoken against Him."[177] [178]	100:9; 101:3; 108:6; Ps 139:20; Mal 3:13

Steadfastness of Creation in Contrast to Man

2 1 Consider all of creation and observe the works of heaven,	41:5; 69:20-21; Ps 8:3; 147:4; Gen 1:14-15
how the heavenly luminaires[179] do not change their paths or	82:7-20; 83:11; TNaph 3:2-4:1; 1QHa 9.14
the stations of their orbits.[180]	4QEnc 1i; OdesSol 16:13-17; Job 37:14
How each of them rises and sets in order, in its appointed time.[181]	80:7; PssSol 18:10-12; 1QS 10.3-5
At their fixed seasons they appear,	Sir 16:26-28; 43:1-29; Jer 31:35-36
and do not violate their proper order.[182]	Neh 9:6; 1Clem 20:1-12; Job 38:33
	2Bar 48:9, Jude 6, 13

---

[174] **It is thought that the very early Christian, Aramaic password, "maranatha!" "Our Lord come/our Lord has come" (1Cor 16:22; cf. Rev 22:20; *Didache* 10:6) arises from this passage.** That Paul uses an Aramaic word in an otherwise Greek letter indicates that it was a password among early Christians. Isaac notes that "Ethiopian commentators who follow this reading argue that the perfect tense is used to emphasize that "he will certainly come" (OTP1 pg.13n u). " *Ad Novatianum* 16 quotes (1:9) in Latin calling it scripture by using the phrase "as it is written."

[175] Isaac notes the Ethiopian word used here, *te'lft,* designates ten thousand times a thousand (OTP1 pg. 13n t). Nickelsburg with support from Black (BL pg. 108) translates it as "myriads of his holy ones."

[176] These "holy ones" are powerful, highly positioned spiritual beings (See Job 15:15; Dan 4:13, 17, 23; 8:13). This celestial army will include chosen humans (cf. Dan 7:22; Mt 19:28; 25:31; Lk 22:30; 1Cor 6:2; 1Thes 3:12; 2Thes 1:7; Rev 19:14; Jub 24:29; Wis 3:7-8; Sir 4:11, 15; 1En 38:5; 90:19; 95:3; 96:1; 98:12; 108:12; 1QpHab 5:4-5)

[177] **Verse 1:9 is quoted in (Jude 14-15). Jude also references 60:8 in Jude 14 indicating that he had both the *Book of Parables* and the *Book of Watchers* available to him or more likely memorized. Jude, by saying "Enoch prophesied," indicates he viewed the text as scripture. The common vocabulary in Jude, and the Greek texts, point to a single translator for the original Greek version of 1 Enoch.**

[178] An interpolator of the Life of Adam and Eve (100 BC to AD 200) roughly quoted this text and viewed it as referring to the second coming of Christ. "And on the stones themselves was found what Enoch, the seventh from Adam, prophesied before the Flood, speaking of the coming of Christ, 'Behold, the Lord will come in his holiness *to pronounce judgement on all* and to convict the impious of all their works which they spoke of him, sinners and impious, murmurers and irreligious, who walked according to their lust and whose mouth has spoken pride'" (*Vita* 51:9 (OTP2 pg. 294)).

[179] Orderly nature is contrasted with disobedient mankind. The author, as did most at the time, believed heavenly beings were responsible for the motions of the cosmos. The ideas in 1 Enoch 2-5 and 101 are amplified and have close parallels with one of the earliest Christian writings outside the New Testament (1 Clement (AD 100) 19:3-20:12). These either came from 1 Enoch or a common tradition (N1 pg. 87). Other period texts have the same popular Jewish theme. Charles (8 f.) cites parallels from (Sir 16:26-28; 43:1-29; TNaph 2:9; 3:2-3: PssSol. 18.12-14). The closest verbal parallel is (TNaph 3:2-3) although a dependance has not been shown.

[180] A substantial fragment of 1:9-5:1 was found in the DSS (4QEnc 1 i) (M pg. 184-185) or 4Q204 1.1 and 4Q201 1.2 (W pg. 281).

[181] This sentence is missing in DSS (4QEnc) due to homoeoteleuton (similar sound endings to words), but is present in (4Q201 1.2) (M pg. 147).

[182] For the last phrase Knibb has: "and they do not transgress their law."

2 Observe the earth and consider the works that take place on it.
That from the beginning until the consummation, nothing on earth changes, — 1QS 10.4
but all the works of God are on display before you.
3 Observe the signs of summer and winter, — Isa 18:6; Gen 8:22
examine the signs of winter,
how the whole earth is filled with water, — 41:3; 60:20; 39:5; 42:3
and clouds and dew and rain fall down upon it.[183] — 82:15-20; 1Q34bis

3 1 Observe that all trees become withered in appearance, and — 4Q201 1.2
all their leaves are shed, except fourteen trees,[184] which do not — 82:16, 20; Jub 21:12; TLev 9:13
shed their leaves, but whose foliage remains up to two or three
years until the new comes.[185]

4 1 Observe the signs of summer, how the heat of the sun burns
and scorches;[186] and you seek shelter and shade from before it, — Sir 43:2-4
because of the heat, and the earth burns with the scorching heat, — Ps 19:6
and you cannot tread on the dust or on the rocks because of its
heat.

5 1 Consider all the trees; their green leafage springs forth and
covers them; and all their fruit appears in glorious splendor.
Pay attention, and consider all these works and reflect
that the God who lives for ever and ever has created all these works. — Sir 18:1; Rev 4:10; 10:6; 15:7
2 All his works carry on year after year, accomplishing their — Gen 8:22; Ps 74:17
tasks for him without deviation, and all perform his commands.
3 Observe how, the seas and rivers in like manner, carry out and — 101:6-7
do not alter their works from his commands.[187] — 1Clem 20:1-12
4 But you have perverted your works! — TNaph 4:1
And have not stood firm nor done according to his commandments,
but you have transgressed against him, — 4QEn^a 1 ii; Is 1:4

---

[183] Black observes: "The pieces on spring and summer at 82:15-20 probably supply the missing portions of the text of Ch. 2:3 (in a fuller recension)" (BL pg. 111).

[184] The fourteen trees do not appear to be related to wood sources for Temple sacrifice, as are the 12-13 listed in Jubilees 21:12 though many, but not all appear to be evergreen. Fourteen evergreen trees are named in *Geoponica* book 11, chapter 1. "(The *Geoponica* is a medieval collection of ancient Greek and Roman agricultural writings. The section in question may have been originally written by Mago of Carthage and translated into Greek in the 1st. c. BCE)" (OL pg. 28). The *Geoponica* reads: "The evergreen trees that do not shed their leaves in the winter are fourteen; the palm, the citron, the strobilus, the bay, the olive, the cypress, the carob, the pine, the ilex, the box, the myrtle, the cedar, the willow, and the juniper" (Geoponica 11.1).

[185] A substantial fragment of the DSS closely parallel to this passage has been preserved in (4QEn^a 1 ii) (M pgs. 145-147).

[186] Isaac has: "how the heat of the sun is upon (the earth) and dominates her."

[187] 1En 5:3 is missing from one of the DSS (4Q201 1.2).

and spoken proud and hard words[188] 1:9; 27:2; 101:3; Jude 15-16; Deut 29:19
with your unclean mouths against his majesty! Isa 6:5
You hard of heart! You shall have no peace. 16:3-4; 94:6; 98:11,16; 100:8; Ezek 3:7
99:13; 101:3; 102:3; 103:8; Isa 48:22; 57:21

The Destiny of the Wicked

5 Therefore, you shall curse your days, 4Q201 1.2.10-17; Job 5:5
and the years of your life will come to nothing.
The years of your destruction will be multiplied under an Deut 28:15, 45
everlasting curse; you shall not have mercy or peace![189] [190] 12:6; 38:6; 39:2; 50:5; 62:9
6 Then you shall leave your names to be an everlasting curse Isa 65:15; Zech 8:13
for the righteous.
Those who curse will curse by you.[191] Jer 24:9; 25:18; 26:6; 29:22
Even the sinners and ungodly shall curse by you. Jer 42:18; 44:8, 12, 22; Ps 102:8

The Destiny of the Righteous

[But the chosen will rejoice, and they shall have remission of
sins,[192] and all mercy and peace and clemency; Ps 80:19; OdesSol 9:6
salvation they shall have, a good light, and they shall inherit 1:8; Isa 60:21; 65:9
the earth.
But for all you sinners there shall be no salvation,
but upon all of you a curse will abide.][193]
7 For the chosen, there will be light and joy[194] and peace, 58:2-4; Pss 37:9.11, 22, 29; Wis 4:15
and they will inherit the earth.[195] Mt 5:5; Num 6:25-26
But for you, the wicked, there will be a curse. 97:10
8 Then shall wisdom be given to the chosen, 48:1; 42:1-2; 84:3; 91:10; 93:10
and all of them shall live and shall sin no more, 91:17; Jer 31:33-34; Ezek 36:25-27

---

[188] **Jude 15 "all the harsh things that ungodly sinners have spoken against him." may be drawn from this verse.**

[189] The Greek text adds: "or peace" as here. That the wicked will have no peace is found in (1En 12:5-6; 13:1; 16:4; 94:6; 98:11, 16; 99:13; 101:3; 102:3; 103:8).

[190] The idea here is: "The wicked will 'curse their days' in this life, but in Gehenna, their years will he prolonged 'under an everlasting curse'" (BL pg. 113).

[191] The person or groups name would be inserted into the curse. For example, see "The LORD make you like Zedekiah and Ahab, whom the king of Babylon roasted in the fire," (Jer 29:22). **The dependence of this passage on (Isa 65:15) establishes that it was written after Isaiah.** "You shall leave your name to my chosen for a curse, and the Lord GOD will put you to death, but his servants he will call by another name" (Isa 65:15).

[192] This is the only positive mention of the forgiveness of sins in the Book of Enoch.

[193] This large part of 5:6 is not present in the Ethiopic texts and appears to have been omitted in the DSS but is present in the Greek. Olson (OL pg. 30) speculates that it may have been lost by homoioteleuton (the repetition of ending words where the copyists eye skipped from "curse" to "curse" in this case). Knibb excludes this passage from his translation.

[194] N has grace in place of joy. Black (BL pg. 115) notes that this word is associated with festive joy.

[195] **"Inherit the earth" (1En 5:7) and "humble=meek" in 5:8 make this a very likely source for one of the most famous sayings by Jesus Christ: "Blessed are the meek for they shall inherit the earth" (Mt 5:5).** Just as Israel inherited Canaan, so those made righteous, will inherit the entire earth.

either through sinning unwittingly[196] or from pride. 1Jn 3:9; Zeph 3:11-13
But those who have wisdom are humble.[197] Prov 11:2; 15:33; James 3:13
9 And they will transgress no more, 1QS 4:18-26
nor will they be judged all the days of their lives,
nor shall they die by the fury of God's wrath, Isa 42:25
but they shall complete the full number of the days of their lives, 10:17; 25:6; 96:8
and their lives shall be increased in peace. Jub 23:27-31; Isa 65:20-22
The years of their happiness will increase in gladness Isa 35:10; 51:11
and lasting peace throughout all the days of their lives.[198]

The Rebellious Angels Descend on Mount Hermon

6 1 And it came to pass when the children of men had multiplied, Jub 5:1
in those days were born to them beautiful and comely daughters. Jub 4:22
2 And the watchers, the sons of heaven,[199] saw them and desired 2Pet 1:4; 2:4; 1Cor 11:10; Job 1:6; 2:1 Deut 32:8; Ps 29:1; 89:6; Dan 3:25
after them,[200] and they said one to another: "Come, let us Tg Jon on Gen 6:1-2; TReu 5:6
choose for ourselves wives from the daughters of men,[201] 15:1-7; 69:4,5; Gen 6:1-4
and let us beget children for ourselves."[202] [203] [204] [205] Jude 6; 2Bar 56:12; Gen 3:15

---

[196] I has: "being wicked" in place of "sinning unwittingly." C translates: "ungodliness," OL has: "inadvertence," N has: "godlessness," K has: "forgetfulness;" this text follows Black with "unwittingly." It carries the idea of unintentional error.

[197] This text of 5:8 follows the Ethiopic which is considered more original in this case. The Greek Codex Panopolitanus (Gr^{Pan}) is thought to contain a scribal addition. It reads: "Then wisdom will be given to all the chosen and all these will live and they will not sin anymore either by truth or by pride. And there will be light in the enlightened man and knowledge in the man of understanding, and they will not err." (Litvinau, Fiodar, 2019, *A note on the Greek and Ethiopic text of 1 Enoch 5:8*, in *Journal for the Study of the Pseudepigrapha* Vol. 29(1) 28 – 35)

[198] Black translates this line as "and the times of their festivals will be filled with joy and lasting peace during all the days of their lives."

[199] Black references Lods: "Lods thinks that 'sons of heaven' replaces 'sons of God' of Gen. 6.2, since the Judaism of the Greek period found the latter objectionable" (BL pg. 116). Sons of God is the reading in most of the LXX manuscripts of Gen 6:2 and virtually all English translations. Cf. similar Masoretic text alterations in Deut 32:8, 43.

[200] Some texts add here "and lusted after them."

[201] Gk^s has: "daughters of earth." 1 En 6:1-6 exists in an ancient Christian Syriac text.

[202] **Part of the watcher's motivation for this sin was producing children. It is thought that by ruling through their children they might obtain dominion over the earth. These half human "demi-gods" could then legally participate in the dominion over earth granted by God in (Gen 1:26, 28).**

[203] **Genesis 6:1-4 assumes the readers know the backstory found here in 1En 6-9. The belief that watcher type beings mated with human women was well known and widely accepted among the ancients; as attested in ancient writings from the time. "Some scholars have even argued that Gen 6:1-4 is a pruned version of *Enoch 6*"** (OL pg. 7n14). **The consequences of this rebellion were catastrophic for all involved.**

[204] In (Jub 5:6), the angels are sent by God to earth before rebelling. The proper events may be that the watchers were sent to observe and aid man but were then tempted into sin. The idea that these angels were sent, appears in the writings of the church fathers (Irenæus, Tertullian, Cyprian, Clement of Alexandria, Lactantius, Commodianus, Epiphanius and Pseudo-Clementine).

[205] (1En 6:2) is viewed by scholars as the text, or at least the tradition, Paul had in mind when he wrote "That is why a wife ought to have a symbol of authority on her head, because of the angels" (1Cor 11:10). Angels were believed

3 And Shemihazah,[206] who was their leader, said to them:
"I fear you will not want to do this deed, and I alone shall pay
the penalty for committing a great sin."[207]
4 And all of them answered him and said: "Let us all swear an
oath, and bind one another with a curse that none of us turn back
from this plan until we carry it out and do this deed."[208]
5 Then they all swore together and bound one another with a Lev 27:29; Acts 23:14
curse.[209] *CommJn* 6.217
6 There were in all two hundred[210] who descended[211] in the 106:13; Jub 4:15; 4Q530 7.2.11
days of Jared[212] on the summit of Mount Hermon;[213] and they Lk 3:37; Josh 12:1-5; 2En 18:3-4

---

especially to be in the midst of congregations of believers (CD 15.17 (W pg. 68.); 4Q491 B 1-3.10 (W pg. 168); 4Q289 1.5 (W pg. 375); and 1QSa 2.8-9 (W pg. 140)). Glob comments: "The practice of women going without a hair covering veil was, according to Paul, unacceptable to the angels. The practice was perhaps regarded as daring; while humans may have tolerated it, the angels were apparently deemed to be more sensitive to such matters" (G pg. 376). "Paul's comments in 1 Corinthians 11:10 indicate that Paul feared angels could be tempted" (Heiser, Michael S., 2018, *Angels* pgs. 125, 127).

> "Paul's reference to the angels betrays a subtle warning that more than just social relationships between men and women are at stake; ultimately, wearing veils is a matter of maintaining the cosmic order. The head coverings are prophylactic in the sense that they protect this order by helping to draw boundaries between distinct, yet sometimes socially overlapping, spheres more clearly." "The head coverings also function to keep women distinct from the angels who, for the sake of this argument, are considered an essentially different order of creation." (Stuckenbruck, L. T., Spring 2001. *Why should women cover their heads because of the angels? (1 Corinthians 11:10)***.** *Stone-Campbell Journal.*, 4 (2). pgs. 231-232).

Tertullian agrees with this interpretation of Paul's view even mentioning the fallen angels in (*On the Veiling of Virgins* 7 and *Of Prayer* 22).Unlike the Romans, Essenes were even very modest in their bathroom habits, using either a roofed enclosed facility or by finding a secluded spot and wrapping a mantle around oneself, apparently so they would not offend spiritual entities that might be present (Refutatio Omnium Haeres 9.20) or drive away the Shekinah. (Cf. Jub 3:30-31; 7:20; 11QTemp 46.13-15 (W pg. 615)).

[206] Shemihazah, "My name has seen", "my" is God, so it reads "God has seen." Here, and in (6:7, 8:3, 9:7, and 10:11), he is portrayed as the leader of the watchers. He is also presented as the leader in (4Q203 8.5 (W pg. 294)).

[207] **Some scholars, such as Nickelsburg, theorize that the watcher story is a polemic against priests who intermarried with foreigners in violation of (Deut 7:3, cf. Ezra 9:2). However, it is apparent that the watcher tradition predates the second temple period. So, at most, it was appropriated and reshaped as a polemic against priests who married foreigners.**

[208] Portions of 6:4 through 7:5 are found in the Dead Sea Scrolls (4Q201 1.3 (W pg.281) and of 6:4-8:1 in (4QEn[a] 1 iii (M pg. 150-151)).

[209] Their mutual agreement did them no good, but instead shows premeditation in the rebellion.

[210] In *The Book of Giants* there are also references to 200 celestial beings: "two hundred [garden]ers that from heaven [came down…]" (4Q530 7.2.11 (W pg. 294)); (cf. 2En 18:3(OTP1 pgs. 130-131)).

[211] Origen refers to 1En 6:2, 6 in his *Commentary on John* 6:25 (ca. 226-229). "as it is written in the Book of Enoch—if any one cares to accept that book as sacred—in the days when the sons of God came down to the daughters of men." See (N1 pg. 91) and (M pg. 152).

[212] Jared was the son of Mahalalel and father of Enoch (Gen 5:15-18; 1En 37:1; Lk 3:37).

[213] It has long been believed by many scholars that **the transfiguration of Jesus occurred on the summit of Mount Hermon possibly near the spot where these rebellious angels descended** (Matt 17:1-2; Mark 9:2; Luke 9:28-29; BAS pg. 16). Small wonder that Jesus was speaking of the gates of hell in Caesarea Philippi, as he approached Mt. Hermon and the cave of Pan was a gateway to the realm of the dead/Hell. He was well aware that Mt. Hermon was the capital of the rebellious watchers. Mt. Hermon has a documented history of negative religious activity, including the worship of Pan, and other false deities of the era, dating back to at least 300 BC. Along the

called the mount "Hermon"[214] because they swore and bound Isa 14:13; Ps 68:15-16; Sir 24:13
one another with a curse upon it.
7 And these are the names[215] of their chiefs:
Shemihazah, their leader;[216] [217] 4Q203 8.5; 4Q201 1.3
Arteqoph, second to him;[218] 69:2-3; 90:21-23

---

road to Damascus, which passes along the southeast side of the mountain; Paul had his vision prior to his conversion experience. Nickelsburg notes **"In summary, a stunning mass of literary, epigraphic, and archeological evidence, stretching from the third millennium B.C.E. to the middle of the first millennium C.E. attests that Canaanites, Israelites, Greeks, Romans, and Christians treated the area around Hermon as sacred territory"** (N1 pg. 247). Mount Hermon is portrayed in opposition to Mount Zion in Ps 68:15-16. It is also seen as a mountain in opposition to God in Isa 14:13. The cedar forest (Hermon and Lebanon), was an important abode of the divine council in Mesopotamian thought (Lipinski, *El's Abode: Mythological Traditions Related to Mount Hermon and to the Mountains of Armenia*," Orientalia Lovaniensa Periodica II, (Leuven, 1971), pgs. 13-69). In the *Epic of Gilgamesh* tablets 2-5, Gilgamesh climbs the mountains of Hermon to receive a message from Shamash.

[214] **"Hermon" may mean "devoted to destruction" or "to swear an oath (H1 pg. 59-60). The watcher tradition is very old, predating the *Epic of Gilgamesh* (2100 BC) where the cedar mountain identified by name as Mount Hermon is the dwelling place of the gods (tablet 5).** (See also references by Hilary of Poitiers, Tractatus super Psalmos 132.6; and Pseudo-Jerome, *Breviarium in Psalmos* 132.3, (see rough translation on pg. 23)). Mount Hermon is mentioned in two Mesopotamian incantation bowls (*AIT* 2; 27) "will bring down upon you the curse and the proscription and the ban which fell upon Mount Hermon and upon the monster Leviathan and upon Sodom and upon Gomorrah" (*AIT* 2.6).

[215] These names are taken from Nickelsburg's translation. He notes: "Two overall patterns are noteworthy among the angelic names. First, according to the interpretation above, several names emphasize God's judicial activity. The conspiracy is carried out in spite of the awareness that God judges those who oppose him. It is an act of deliberate rebellion carried out with full knowledge of the consequences. Second, the names help to identify the conspirators and give some sense of the authority and the scope of the conspiracy. The names suggest that the chiefs are high angels in charge of the orderly functioning of the heavenly and earthly phenomena: in heaven, not Uriel to be sure, but the angels over sun, moon, stars, shooting stars, thunder, and lightning; on earth, the angels in charge of sea and mountains, as well as the critical rainy season and its clouds and rain. At the same time, the list lacks names associated with many other cosmic, meteorological, and geographic phenomena, and the total of two hundred angels is a small part of the thousands that a text such as 82:4-20 associates with the stars alone." Justin Martyr notes, relating to 1 Enoch, that the angels identified themselves with their names. "For whatever name each of the angels had given to himself and to his children, by that name they (mankind) called them" (*The Second Apology* 5).

[216] The fallen angels are organized in a hierarchy. Compare (Ephesians 6:12). "For we do not wrestle against flesh and blood, but against the rulers, against the authorities, against the cosmic powers over this present darkness, against the spiritual forces of evil in the heavenly places."

[217] Šemîhăzāh, Samîazâz, or Semyaz, ("my God has seen" "the Name sees" "the Name has seen" "heaven has seen" or "he who watches the heavens"). His very name indicates that God has seen his rebellion. "This name turns up in the Jewish and Manichaean Book of Giants, and in the Mishnaic medieval summary of it, as well" (M pg. 155). A derivative of his name ("Smhyz'") appears on a Manichaean incantation bowl (M pg. 299). He is named in the book of Giants from the DSS as the leader of his companions (4Q203 8.5). Milik quotes a Sogdian text, *The Coming of the Two Hundred Demons*, naming the two sons of Sahmizâd "two(?) sons were borne by . . . One of them he named 'Ohyà (['wy]y'); in Sogdian he is called "Sâhm, the giant" (s'ym kw'y). And again, a second son [was born] to him. He named him 'Ahyâ ('γ'); its Sogdian (equivalent) is "Pât-Sâhm" (p'ts'ym)" (M pg. 299). Ohya and his twin brother Hahya are prominent in fragments of the Book of Giants (6Q8 1; 4Q203 4,7_a; 4Q531 22.9; 4Q530 2.2.15). In the Babylonian Talmud (Niddah 61a (18)) Sihon and Og were sons of Ahijah, son of Shamhazai (cf. Deut 31:4; Josh 9:10; 1Kgs 4:19; Ps 135;11). He and the 200 are mentioned in the *Cronography* of Michael the Syrian, indicating the watcher story survived until the 12th century in Antolia.

[218] 'Ar 'tĕqop, Arâkîba, ´Ar 'tĕqoph or Arataqoph, ("earth is power" "earth is mighty" "land of the mighty one" "the strong one of the Earth" or "earth is a stronghold"). This name may indicate that earth is considered as a protection from Gods judgement. Nickelsburg notes: "This would offer an interesting foil to the previous name: Heaven may see what we do, but Earth will provide a defensible fortress against Heaven's wrath" (N1 pg. 179).

Remashel, third to him;[219]
Kokabel, fourth to him;[220] Isa 14:13; 3En 14:4; 17:7
Tamiel, fifth to him;[221]
Ramel, sixth to him;[222] 2Bar 55:3; SibOr 2:215
Daniel, seventh to him;[223]
Ziqel, eight to him;[224] 3En 14:4
Baraqel, ninth to him;[225]
Asael, tenth to him;[226] 4Q180.1.7,8; 4Q203 7a.6
Hermani, eleventh to him;[227]
Matarel, twelfth to him;[228]

---

[219] Remaš᾽ēl, Râmêêl, Ramt᾽el or Ramshiel ("burning ashes of God" is the preferred meaning but possibly ("evening of God"). Milik is confident the name refers to "the volcanic activities of the earth's crust" (M pg. 155). Black agrees (BL pg. 119). Other mentions include (2Bar 55:3 (OTP1 pg. 640) and SibOr 2.215 (OTP1 pg. 350 n p2).
[220]Kôkabîêl, or Kōkab ᾿ēl ("star of God"). Black and Olson note this name may be associated with Isa 14:13 which can be read "You said in your heart, 'I will ascend to heaven; I will raise my throne above Kokabiel…", (BL pg. 120; OL pg. 32). **This possibly makes Kokabel the proud subject of Isa 14. Note also that Isa 14:20d-21 could easily apply to the watcher tradition. The use of this name in Isaiah hints at the antiquity and prominence of this angel's name** (1En 8:3). In 3 En 14:4 and 17:7 Kokabi̇̈el oversees the stars
[221] ᾽Orām᾽ ēl, ("God is their light") or 'armûmāh ᾽ēl ("God is prudence" N1 pg. 180). The Ethiopic at this position in 69:2 which is used here has "Tamiel" Tâmîêl, ("Perfection of God?" "God is perfect" "God has completed"). This name is defective in the DSS and is uncertain.
[222] Râmîêl, ra ᾿m᾽ ēl, Rumyal, ("thunder of God").
[223] Dânêl or Daniel, ("God is my judge" "God is judge"). The Ugaritic text, *The Tale of Aqhat,* tells of a wise man named Dan᾽ el who lived in the Golan Heights region prior to the middle bronze age 1900-1550 BC. Since he is named in order between Noah and Job in Ezekiel 14:14, 20 (cf. 28:3), and the name there is spelled Danel, rather than Daniel, he may have been the Danel referred to in *The Tale of Aghat* (See Finegan, J., 1989. *Myth and Mystery: An Introduction to the Pagan Religions of the Biblical World* Pg. 147-151). That Ugaritic Danel, though fully human, is a close associate with the "gods" in the region of Mt. Hermon enhances the probability of an association of some type with this angel name. It is also interesting that Job is viewed in tradition to have lived in Bashan which is near Mt. Hermon. Heiser notes: "To muddle things even more, Jubilees 4:20 has Enoch marrying the daughter of *Dân᾽ êl*. Whether this figure from Ugaritic literature is the referent of these biblical verses (his character is nowhere as pristine as the biblical Daniel) or the Enoch tradition in Jubilees actually has Ugaritic Dan᾽ el in Enoch's family is far from clear or coherent" (H1 pg. 64-65). It is possible that Danel, the father of Enoch's wife, (whose name was Ednî in Jub 4:20) was the same person as that in the Ugaritic tradition. But he would not be related to the watcher Danel since the later was not human.
[224] Êzêqêêl or zîq ēl, ("shooting star of God") Black (pg. 120) translates ("fireball of God). See (1En 8:3). In 3En 14:4 Ziqi̇̈el oversees comets.
[225] Barâqîjal or Baraq᾽ ēl, ("lightning of God"). According to Dead Sea Scroll fragment (6Q8 1.2-5), from the Book of the Giants; Baraq᾽ el is the father of the giant Mahaway (W pg. 292). He is not to be confused with Barakiel, the father of Lamech's wife Betanosh, (Jub 4:28) as the Hebrew spelling is different. See (1En 8:3). In 3En 14:4 Baraqi̇̈ el oversees lightning.
[226] Asâêl or 'āśa ᾽ēl, ("God has made") Azazel is the most notorious of this group. As is apparent later in 1 Enoch, he is the first of the watchers to fall, and he then enticed the others. The name appears in (8:1; 9:6; 10:4, 8; 13:1; 54:5; 55:4; 69:2; 4Q180 1.7, 8; and 4Q203 7a.6). See also (88:1).
[227]Armârôs, Pharmaros, Arearos, but Hermoni is preferred ("The one of Hermon"). Armârôs is read by Black and Nickelsburg as Hermānî. **The name "Hermon" occurs as the proper name of a subordinate deity of the Egyptian Elephantine pantheon found in a text among the fifth century BC Elephantine papyri which predate The Book of the Watchers (H1 pg. 67-68). This shows that at least some of these names originate from antiquity and were not just made up by the author of the Book of Watchers**. Black observes: "Mount Hermon could have been named after the deity; perhaps as a place with a cultic sanctuary where oaths were taken; it may also have been associated with practices related to ban-execration such as 'spell binding' or the practice of the black arts generally." See (1En 8:3).
[228] Matr᾽ el, Mātār᾽ ēl is preferred, ("rain of God").

Ananel, thirteenth to him;[229]
Setawel, fourteenth to him;[230]
Shamshiel, fifteenth to him; [231]
Sahriel, sixteenth to him;[232]
<Tummiel>, seventeenth to him;[233]
Turiel, eighteenth to him;[234]
Yamiel, nineteenth to him;[235]
Yehadiel, twentieth to him;[236] [237] [238]
8 These are their chiefs of tens.[239]

Excursus: Qasr Antar, a Roman era temple on the summit of Hermon

Near the summit of Mount Hermon, and indeed over the entire mastiff, are a complex of more than thirty temple sites attesting to cultic activity stretching far back into antiquity. At the end of his section on Mount Hermon, Nickelsburg observes: **"In summary, a stunning mass of literary, epigraphic, and archeological evidence, stretching from the third millennium B.C. E. to the middle of the first millennium C.E., attests that Canaanites, Israelites, Greeks, Romans, and Christians treated the area around Hermon as sacred territory."**[240]

As an example: "There is a sacred building made of hewn blocks of stone on the summit of Mount Hermon. Known as Qasr Antar, it was the highest temple of the ancient world, sitting at 2,814 meters (9,232 ft) above sea level. It was documented by Sir Charles Warren in 1869. Warren described the temple as a rectangular building, sitting on an oval, stone plateau without

---

[229] Anânêl, ("cloud of God"), **"Both 'Anan' el and 'Ananî are deity names in the Elephantine papyri."** (H1 pg. 69) **That these names from independent older sources, match names in this list of watchers, establishes that they were not randomly created and appear to be the names of genuine "gods from antiquity."**

[230] Zaqîêl, sĕtāw' ēl, Sithwa' el ("winter of God").

[231] Samsâpêêl, Sasomaspe e' el, or Shamshiel ("sun of God").

[232] Śahrî' ēl, Satarêl, Sariêl ("moon of God") Worship of the moon god was widespread in the Canaanite area. Beth-yerah, the house of the moon god, Yerah, is a 50–75-acre site on the southwestern shore of the Sea of Galilee initially built ca. 3000 BC. It is located immediately north of where the Jordan river currently flows out of the Sea of Galilee and just south of where it used to flow out of the Sea of Galilee. Worship of the sun, moon, and stars is forbidden in (Deut 4:19-20). See (1En 8:3) for this angel's function.

[233] Tummî'ēl ("perfection of God") ("God has completed").

[234] Tûrî ' êl, ("mountain of God").

[235] Yamî'ēl or Yōmî' ēl or Jômjâêl ("sea of God" or "day of God") The name appears in (Gen 46:10; Ex 6:15; Num 26:12? and 1Chr 4:24?).

[236] Yĕhaddî'ēl ("God will guide") so Nickelsburg; Black and Knibb have Zehor'el (brightness of el).

[237] "As commentators note, the two lists – the one in 6:7 and the one in 69:2-3 – are identical (with spelling problems) apart from a scribal lapse or two" (R pg. 90, VanderKam, *The Book of Parables within the Enoch Tradition*).

[238] Nickelsburg observes that "The angelic names, which are often corrupted in the Gk and Eth, are largely attested in Aram" (N page 24). That the Aramaic numbered the watchers, as in this text, as attested in Dead Sea Scroll fragment (4Q201 1.3). For a detailed examination of the watcher names see (H1 pgs. 60-71, M pgs. 152-157, BL pgs. 119-124 or N1 pgs. 179-181).

[239] For 6:8, Black has: "These are the leaders and their dekadarchs." In the second temple period and earlier, military units were organized in tens, fifties and hundreds. In Alexander the Great's army, a dekadarch was originally a leader of ten and after reorganization, a leader of sixteen men.

[240] N1 pg. 247.

roof. He removed a limestone stele from the northwest of the oval, broke it into two pieces and carried it down the mountain and back to the British Museum, where it currently resides."[241]

The Greek language inscription on the stele, dated to the 3rd century AD, was translated by George Nickelsburg to read: "According to the command of the greatest a(nd) Holy God, those who take an oath (proceed) from here."[242] Douglas Hamp translates it as "According to the command of the great bull god Batios, those swearing an oath in this place go forth" which he amplifies to "According to the command of the great bull-god Satan, the great snake-dragon of Bashan that those swearing an oath in this place go forth."[243] That Jesus chose Mount Hermon as the location of His transfiguration,[244] with it's complex of temples, even in His time, was bold and revealing. This showed He was very aware of the spiritual warfare involved and the significance of Mount Hermon in the spiritual world. With Hermon being the center of angelic rebellion, it would follow that it also was the "very high mountain" where the devil showed Jesus "all the kingdoms of the world and their glory" during His temptation.[245]

The Watchers Take Wives, Giants Born

7 1 These (leaders) and all the rest (of the two hundred watchers),[246] took for themselves wives from all whom they chose; and they began to go into them and to defile themselves with them, and they taught them sorcery and incantations,[247]

4Q530 7.11
86:3; 106:14; Gen 6:2; *Haer.* 4.36.4
Ecl. 53; TReu 5:6; Jub 7:21; *1Apol.* 5
Tob 6:14; Wis 12:4; PiSop 20; *Apol.* 35

---

[241] Wikipedia, *Temples of Mount Hermon.*
[242] N1 pg. 247.
[243] (Hamp, Douglas, 2021. *At Satan's Command, a New Translation of Mt Hermon Batios Inscription*).
[244] Mt 17:1-2; Mk 9:2-3; BAS pg. 16.
[245] Mt 4:8-9.
[246] Olson (pg. 34) notes: "Interestingly, the prominent sins mentioned in this chapter, which precipitate the Flood, include forbidden forms of marriage, eating and drinking." This matches the actions Jesus describes before the flood (cf. Mt 24:36-39: Lk 17:26-27). "But concerning that day and hour no one knows, not even the angels of heaven, nor the Son, but the Father only. For as were the days of Noah, so will be the coming of the Son of Man. For as in those days before the flood they were eating and drinking, marrying and giving in marriage, until the day when Noah entered the ark, and they were unaware until the flood came and swept them all away, so will be the coming of the Son of Man (Mt 24:36-39). Perhaps in Mt 24:38 Jesus was not speaking of benign normal human activity; but depravity rarely practiced through subsequent human history. Marriage—watchers to humans, eating—the sustenance of humans or even humans themselves, drinking—blood. This would not have been lost on Christ's listeners as they well knew what activity preceded the flood. However no textual clues link 1 Enoch 7 to Christ's statements so He likely was only emphasizing the suddenness of His return in judgement and the obliviousness of people, not a return of Nephilim like activity. On the other hand it is quite possible Jesus is referencing the lost apocalypse of Noah or 1QapGen 6, which also speaks of the "days of Noah."
[247] In other words, they taught magic, incantations and potions. The *Apkallus,* of Babylonian religion, were seen as having been given the superior knowledge that founded their great civilization. These spiritual entities were seen as good by the Babylonians but evil by the Jews. "The Babylonian elite taught that the divine knowledge of the *apkallus* had survived the flood through a succeeding post flood generation of *apkallus*—giant, quasi-divine offspring fathered by the original preflood *apkallus*" (Heiser, Michael S., 2015. *The Unseen Realm* pg. 108).

and showed them the cutting of roots and herbs.[248 249 250] SibOr 1:93-103; Jub 10:12
2 And they became pregnant by them and bore gigantic 86:4; 1Q23:9-15; *Ant* 1.3.1; Leg 24
off-spring of three kinds. Giants[251] were born to them, Jub 5:1; 7:21-24; Jdt 16:7; CD 2.17-19
and the Nephilim were born to them on the earth, Gen 3:15; *QGen1* 92; Num 13:33
and the Elioud were their offspring.[252 253] 4Q203 8.6-8; 4Q181 2.1-2; Deut 2:10-11
3 These devoured the entire produce of the toil of the sons of men, 4Q531 Frags 1.1-8; 4Q201 1.3.17-21
and men were unable to sustain them.[254] Jub 5:2; 7:22; Jerm 3:24; 5:17; SibOr 1:100
4 Then the giants treated them violently and acted with conspiracy 1Q23 Frags. 1.6.22; Gen 3:15; 6:5, 11
to kill mankind and to devour them.[255 256] Sir 16:7; Num 13:32; 3Mac 2:4
5 They began to sin against the birds and beasts of the earth,[257] Gen 6:12; 9:4; Jub 7:24

---

[248] Some have found a basis for genetic engineering in "cutting of roots". In reality, it was for medicinal and magical purposes. This is speaking of botanomancy, which is a method of divination by means of the burning of leaves, herbs and tree branches and other magical uses of plants. It is an occult practice even to the present day. The Essenes used roots for healing (*War* 2.8.6 §§136). (Cf. Jub 10:12)

[249] This account that angels took wives of human women is echoed by early church fathers, Justin Martyr (AD 100-165), Irenæus (AD 130-202), Athengoras of Athens (AD 130-190), Clement of Alexandria (AD 150-215), Tertullian (AD 155-220), Clementine Homilies (2nd to 4th century) and historians of the period, both Josephus (AD 37-100) and Philo (20 BC-AD 50). Irenæus affirmed that angels, like humans, have free will (*Haer.* 4.37.1).

[250] Clement of Alexandria writes: "To which also we shall add, that the angels who had obtained the superior rank, having sunk into pleasures, told to the women the secrets which had come to their knowledge; while the rest of the angels concealed them, or rather, kept them against the coming of the Lord." (*Stromata* 5.1.10.2) **Clement is here saying that the watchers that fell, revealed secrets that were going to be revealed at the coming of the Lord. Since these were the worthless secrets (1En 16:3); imagine what technological secrets and wisdom will be revealed at his second coming!**

[251] Josephus, along with other period writers, associated these giants with the giants of Greek mythology (cf. *Ant* 1.3.1 §§73; *Leg.* 24). The Greek titans would roughly equate with the fallen watchers. It is generally acknowledged that the Greek myths were imported from the near east. The titans are substituted for watchers in Judith 16:7.

[252] **The watcher tradition brings a different twist to (Gen 3:15): "I will put enmity between you and the woman, and between your offspring and her offspring; he shall bruise your head, and you shall bruise his heel." Certainly, the second half of the verse is a prophecy of Christ. However, the offspring (seed) of the serpent are the giants and the offspring of Eve are humans. Thus, humans and the giants (including their unclean spirits) are to be continually at enmity with each other.** (cf. OdesSol 22:3)

[253] The wording of this verse follows Olson's reasoned approach (OL pg. 34, 263-265).

[254] Isaac has: "These (giants) consumed the produce of all the people until the people detested feeding them." Olson has: "These devoured the entire produce of the toil of men, but the men were still unable to sustain them." This event is also described in the account in the Book of Giants (4Q531 Frags 2-3 (W pg. 291)). Jeremiah borrows imagery from this passage (Jer 3:24; 5:17); equating the destruction wrought by the giants, to what will befall Judah.

[255] "To devour them" Black argues against inclusion of these words since they are not found in the Aramaic. Olson also excludes them. However, Nickelsburg, Knibb, Isaac, and Charles following the Greek, include them. That the giants were cannibals is implied in (Num 13:32-33) and overtly stated in (Jub 7:22).

[256] **The protoevangelium, "I will put enmity between you and the woman, and between your offspring and her offspring; he shall bruise your head, and you shall bruise his heel." (Gen 3:15) must be seen not as a loathing between mankind and snakes but as a massive spiritual war between the forces of God and those of the devil. This war between the offspring of the woman and the offspring of the devil is revealed here as the sons of the fallen watchers openly try to kill mankind! To have not chosen a side is to have chosen the wrong side.**

[257] **Up to this time, animals had not been given to man for food. See Genesis 2:16 compared to 9:2-3. The sin was compounded since they were eating flesh with the blood (Lev 17:14; Jub 6:7). However, another possibility may be that they made human animal chimeras. Ancient texts seem to indicate that Azazel may have had goat like characteristics since he is linked with the scapegoat (Lev 16:8-22) and goat demons are mentioned in Lev 17:7; and 4Q385a 1a-c.7 (W pg. 442). From the Book of Giants, it can be inferred that Mahaway, Ohyah, and Hahyah (hybrid beings from the Book of Giants) had bird-like characteristics (4Q530**

against reptiles that creep along the ground,	Hos 4:2-3
and the fish of the sea.[258]	
Then they began to devour one another's flesh,[259]	87:1; 98:11; 1Sam 14:32-34; Acts 15:20
and they were drinking the blood.[260]	Jub 5:2, 7-9; 6:7; 7:23, 25; 21:6; Lev 17:14 Lev 19:26; Rev 16:6; Deut 15:23; Gen 9:4 Ezek 33:25; Lk 17:26-27; Acts 21:25
6 Then the earth made accusation against the lawless ones [261]	2Thes. 2:7-9; 4Q203 8.9; Gen 4:10; 6:11
concerning everything which was done upon it.	Job 31:38

Excursus: Were the giants 3000 cubits (4500 ft.) tall?

The incredible height of the giants used in the translations by Charles, Knibb, Black and Isaac, but not by Baty, Olson or Nickelsburg is certainly a translation error, and does not describe the height of the giants at all. It is speculated by Olson (OL pgs. 264-265) that a Greek translator did not know what to make of the Greek transliteration of the rare word *naphēleim* which comes from the Hebrew *nĕpilîm*. Olson observes: "This would point to a Greek copyist who simply did not know what to make of the word. If that is true, he must have found Enoch 7:2 nearly unintelligible, and he ended up shortening and rewriting the verse, keeping the "three" for his "three thousand cubits" and perhaps drawing on other legends then current about the giants' great height" (OL pg. 265). Following the Greek text by George Syncellus, with consideration of (Jubilees 7:21-24 and the "elephants camels and donkeys" of 1 Enoch 86;4; 87:4; 88:2; 89:6, Nickelsburg has: "And the giants begot Nephilim, and to the Nephilim were born †Elioud†. And they were growing in accordance with their greatness." Baty (1839) has: "And there were born unto them three sorts, the first were great giants, and to the giants were born Nephilim, and to the Nephilim were born Elioud." Olson translates: "The women became pregnant by them and bore to them gigantic offspring (of three kinds): Giants were born to them, and the Nephilim were born to them on the earth, and the Elioud were their offspring." Knibb, following Gk[a], reads similarly to Charles. "And they became pregnant and bore large giants and their height was three thousand cubits." This would indicate giants at least 4500 ft. high! Some texts have 300 cubits which would still be a physically impossible 450 ft. If the giants were this tall, it would be difficult to envision them being disturbed by a flood!

7.2.4). "A giant and a sage in the account of Berossus, named Oannes, was part man, part fish; his six successors were also ichthyomorphic. As a matter of fact, the antediluvian sages (abgal — apkallu or adapu) of the Sumerian and Babylonian literature were half-men, half-fish, the kw/ullu-fish who in primeval times rose up from the sea in order to bring culture to men" (M pg. 313).

[258] The wording of (1En 7:5-6) appears to have been fuller in the Aramaic but has a long omission by homoeoteleuton (M pg. 168). Notably the word "heavens" found in (4Q201 1.3.21 (W pg. 282)) and in Milik's translation of "and (creatures) in the waters and in the heaven" in (En[b] I ii) cannot be satisfactorily placed (M pg. 167-168) (Cf. Gen 1:20-21).

[259] This could be read that they were eating the flesh of the animals. As such Black has: "They began to do violence to and to attack all the birds and the beasts of the earth and reptiles (that crawl upon the earth], and the fish of the sea; and they began to devour their flesh, and they were drinking the blood" (1En 7:5). Other translators are more like this text.

[260] **The giants may be the origin of prohibitions on the eating of blood** (Cf. Gen. 9:4, Lev 3:17; 7:26-27; 17:10-14; 19:26; Deut 12:16, 23-25; 15:23; 1Sam 14:32-34, Acts 15:20, 29; 21:25; and Jub 6:6-8; 7:28-33; 21:6) **Idols were seen by early Christians as controlled by bloodthirsty demons** (Jub 21:5-6; *Leg* 26; *Haer.* 3.12.6; 5.25.1; *Apol.* 22).

[261] Paul refers to the Antichrist as the "Lawless One" (Gk anomos) in (2Thes 2:3, 8-9). Lawless ones are mentioned here, and in (1En 22:13; 96:2).

Quoting this passage in the early 9th century, George Syncellus had "And they bore to them three kinds: first large giants, and the giants begot the Nephilim, and to the Nephilim were born Elioud. And they grew according to their greatness, and they taught themselves and their wives' charms and spells." There were three different types of offspring, or quite possibly three different successive generations of progeny. See note on 86:4. Also see (1En 10:9; 87:4; 88:2 and 89:6). In the Book of Giants, in multiple places, the wives of the Watchers "begot giants and monsters" who seem to be different types of beings (4Q531 Frag. 1; 4Q203 Frag. 7a; 4Q530 Frag. 2 Col 2.20; Frag. 7 Col 2.8; and 4Q531 Frag. 7:2-4 (W pgs. 291-295). 2 Enoch describes some of the progeny of the watchers as "great monsters" (2En J 18:5 (OTP1 pg. 132)). Jubilees 7:22 also references different types of progenies. "They fathered (as their) sons the Nephilim. All of them were dis-similar (from one another) and would devour one another: the giants killed the Naphil; the Naphil killed the Elyo; the Elyo humanity; and people their fellows" (VanderKam translation; Vanderkan James C. Jubilees, 2020. The Hermeneia Translation, Fortress Press). Olson (pg. 34) sees all three classes of giants in Genesis 6:4. "The Giants are the *gibbōrîm* ('mighty men,' or 'heros'), apparently a particular type as well as a general name for all three types. Nephilim probably means 'the fallen ones.' The word Nephilim appears also in Num 13:33, and the Nephilim are there equated with the 'sons of Anak' (=the Anakim) and these in turn with the 'Rephaim' in Deut 2:10-11. The mysterious Elioud appear again in Enoch only in 86:4. The word is most likely a Greek transliteration of Heb *yeled* ('child'). Their presence in Gen 6:4 is implied by the fact that the daughters of men 'gave birth' (*yāldû*) to the children of the sons of God." (4Q203 8.8, W pg. 294) states that the giants had children, "wives of their sons"; presumably from human wives or giant women. That being said, (CD Geniza A 2:17-19 (W pg. 53)) reads "When they went about in their willful heart, the Guardian Angels of Heaven fell and were ensnared by it, for they did not observe the commandments of God. Their sons, who were as tall as cedars, and whose bodies were as big as mountains, fell by it." However, Geniza texts A and B originate much later, being from the tenth and twelfth centuries C.E. (W pg. 49). (Amos 2:9) obviously using hyperbole, also describes the Amorites as having "height like the height of the cedars and who were as strong as the oaks." Nickelsburg observes: "This excessive height, vastly out of line with the height attributed to Og (9 cubits, Deut 3:11) and Goliath (6 cubits and a span, 1 Sam 17:4), may well be related to a tradition that ascribed immense height to angels (T. Reub. 5:7; 2 Enoch 1:4; Gos. Pet. 40)" (N1 pg. 185-186).

Milik notes that the three types are absent in important Aramaic texts from the DSS as the fragments frustratingly do not contain that crucial phrase. Milik filled in the gap with text from Charles indicating the enormous height. However, a reference to the three types is still found in the Aramaic texts as Milik observes "an unmistakable reference to it, which is based on a play on words and assonances" (M pg. 240). It should be noted that since demons were viewed as being the spirits of departed giants; it is significant that Jesus recognized different types of demons (Mk 9:29). These types, perhaps, correspond in some way to their pre-death natures or perhaps individual personalities. Other references to descendants of these beings tend to break them into groups that may or may not be descended from the Nephilim. The Rephaim occur in (Gen 14:5; 15:20; Deut 2:20; 3:11; Josh 12:4; 13:12) the Emim in (Gen 14:5; Deut 2:10-11) the Anak or Anikim in (Num 13:22-33; Deut 2:10-11; Josh 11:21-22; 15:13-14; 21:11; Jud 1:20) and giants in (Gen 10:8-9 LXX, 2Sam 21:15-22). The reason "giants" is used as a generic term in 2 Samuel is likely because those giants had fled from other territories such as Bashan and the hill country of Israel, and had lost tribal and familial identity.

Mankind is Taught Angelic Knowledge

8 1 Asael[262] [263] taught men to make swords of iron,[264] and 69:6; Lev 16:8-10; *Haer.* 1.15.6
breast-plates of bronze,[265] and every instrument of war. [266] 13:2; 86:1-2; 4Q180 1.7-9
He showed them the metals of the earth [267] 65:6-8; Gen 4:22; 4Q534 1.2.15
how to work gold to fashion it suitably, and concerning silver, *Defem* 1:2; 2:10; *Idol.* 2
to make bracelets and ornaments for women;[268] Isa 3:16-24; 1Pet 3:3
and he instructed them about antimony, and eye-shadow,[269] *Epid.* 18

---

[262] **The narrative now flashes back to focus on the specific sin of Asael that precipitated the rebellion of the watchers. He gave mankind the knowledge they then use to aid them in the seduction of the rest of the rebellious watchers. This is why all sin will be recorded against him (1En 10:8) and why the sins of all Israel are sent to him (Lev 16:7-10).** This text, following the DSS, reads Asael, matching (1 Enoch 6:7). The "Gk and Syn have respectively 'Azalzel' and 'Aseal' at 6:2 and then 'Azael' after that. Eth faithfully preserves 'Asael' at 6:2 but has 'Azazel' from then on" (OL pg. 34). For a parallel in the Dead Sea Scrolls, see (4Q180 1.7-10).
[263] The name Azazel is a corruption of Asael found in (1En 6:7).

> The name Asa'el appears to have been known by the Greek translator(s) of the Book of the Watchers, but the translators of the Eth. identified the demon with Azazel (עֲזָאזֵל, 'z'zl), mentioned in Lev 16:6-10. The identification is much earlier, however, and is attested in (4Q180 frg. 1.7-8), a MS. from the first century C.E. where עֲזָזָאל is twice mentioned in connection with the angels who spawned the giants. In the Parables, the name of this figure appears four times (54:5; 55:4; 69:2 twice), always spelled *'azāz'ēl* or some orthographic variant thereof. Given the early attestation of both עֲזָזָאל in 4Q180 and עֲסָאֵל /עֲשָׂאֵל in the Aramaic Enoch fragments, it is impossible to decide whether the name in the original form of the Parables was Asael or Azazel (NV2 pg. 202).

[264] **"Make swords of iron" places this text firmly in the iron age. The iron age did not begin in earnest until the twelfth century BC; long after the age of a biblical Enoch** (Collins, Steven, and Holden, Joseph M., 2001. *Harvest Handbook of Bible Lands,* pg. 129). The Essenes avoided the manufacture of weapons to avoid being involved in crafts that were taught by evil angels. (*Good Person* 78)
[265] Or copper. The text of Codex Panopolitanus adds a gloss in this location "teachings of angels." Olson makes a case that this gloss and the ones at 15:11 and 18:15 may have been inserted into the Codex Panopolitanus as headings by the gnostic alchemist Zosimos or his students. Olson, D. *From the Alchemist's Library? Zosimos of Panopolis and Codex Panopolitanus*
[266] Portions of 8:1-4 are found in the Dead Sea Scrolls (4Q202 1.2, 3; 4Q201 1.4 or 4QEn^b 1 ii; 4QEn^b 1 iii).
[267] Metal working was used for the making of molten images. The Parables relate metalworking to idolatry (65:6-8) and weapons of war (52:1-8). **Zosimos of Panopolis (ca. AD 300) attributed the corruption of the knowledge of alchemy to wicked fallen angels who perverted the authentic art of alchemy, originally revealed to Hermes and written in the book of Chemeu, which originated with Agathodaimon.** See The Chronography of George Sykellos. Bronze working was considered by ancient cultures to be an act of magic. (E pg. 143 n8)
[268] Peter may have had this passage in mind when writing (1 Peter 3:3), "Do not let your adorning be external—the braiding of hair and the putting on of gold jewelry, or the clothing you wear—".
[269] Eye paint (Arabic, kohl) was often associated with women of ill repute. Nickelsburg (N1 pg. 195) discusses substances that were likely used. The introduction of cosmetics was seen as an aid to sexual seduction (2 Kgs 9:30; Jer 4:30; Ezek 23:40). See also *Targum Yerushalmi Gen 6:2* where it reads, describing these daughters of men: "(they) were beautiful with their eyes painted and their hair combed and walking in nakedness of flesh."

and all manner of precious stones[270] and about dyes.[271] [272] [273] [274] [275] [276] Jub 4:15; PseudClemHom 8:14
And the sons of men fashioned them for themselves and for their 2Apol. 5
daughters and transgressed; and lead the holy ones astray.[277] [278] 86:2; Jub 5:2, 19; TReu 5
2 And there was much godlessness on the earth; and they were made SibOr 3:231-233
corrupt in all their ways.
3 Shemihazah taught incantation[279] and the cutting of roots.[280] 6:3,7; 7:1; 4Q201 1.4; *Epid.* 18
Hermani taught sorcery for the loosing of spells, magic, 10:7; 95:4; Ex 7:11 Tob 8:2
and sophistry.[281] Ezek 13:1; Dan 7:10-11;PiSop 20

---

[270] This indicates the women were well-to-do.

[271] Dying clothing was the chief industry of Phoenicia (Baumgarten. 1981. *The Phoenician history of Philo of Byblos: a commentary* pg. 157). Some translate "dyes" as "coloring tinctures."

[272] According to (Jub 4:15) the watchers were there to instruct humankind in judgement and righteousness. "... for in his days the angels of the Lord descended on the earth, those who are named the Watchers, that they should instruct the children of men, and that they should do judgement and uprightness on the earth." Knowledge that men would have discovered gradually under God's direction were given all at once and used for evil purposes. Azâzêl, by teaching war, may have gained an edge, making him dominant and especially destructive. See (1En 9:6 and 10:8).

[273] For 1En 8:1 Isaac has: "And Azaz' el taught the people (the art of) making swords and knives, and shields, and breastplates; and he showed to their chosen ones bracelets, decoration, (shadowing of the eye) with antimony, ornamentation, the beautifying of the eyelids, all kinds of precious stones, and all coloring tinctures and alchemy."

[274] Other references for the disclosure of forbidden knowledge include: (1En 7:1; 9:6; 10:7; 16:3; 65:6-11; and 69:8-11, 14-16).

[275] Tertullian discusses 1En 8:1 in *On the Apparel of Women* 1.2.

[276] Isaac adds after, "about dyes"; "and alchemy," he states it means literally, "transmutation of the world." He explains that "Ethiopian commentators explain this phrase as 'changing a man into a horse or mule or vice versa, or transferring an embryo from one womb to another" (OTP1 pg. 16 n 8d). The Aramaic is of no help here, as it is in a gap, and it is not found in Greek or Syncellus. Olson, finding support in Ethiopic manuscripts, translates it as "And the world was changed". Olson finds a parallel in 1En 86:2. Zosimos of Panopolis, an early (late 3rd to early 4th century) alchemist, understood this verse as referring to alchemy.

[277] This sentence is omitted in Ethiopic and Gk[a] (Akhmim) but it is found in Gk[s] (Syncellus).

[278] Some texts, such as the one before us, blame the fall on the women, implying that the women were active in seducing the watchers as in (TReu 5:6). Azazel, as in 86:1-4, enabled the rebellion by first teaching seductive arts.

> For it was thus that they charmed the watchers, who were before the flood. As they continued looking at the women, they were filled with the desire for them and perpetrated the act in their minds. Then they were transformed into human males, and while the women were cohabitating with their husbands they appeared to them. Since the women's minds were filled with lust for these apparitions, they gave birth to giants. For the Watchers were disclosed to them as being as high as the heavens. (*Testaments of the Twelve Patriarchs,* (Second Century BC) OTP1 pg. 784)

Targum Pseudo-Jonathan: Genesis 6:2, agrees: "The sons of the great ones saw that the daughters of men were beautiful, that they painted their eyes and put on rouge, and walked about with naked flesh. They conceived lustful thoughts, and they took wives to themselves from among all who pleased them." Others blame the Watchers, 1En 6:1-5; Jub 7:21; and Justin Martyr's Second Apology 5: "But the angels transgressed this order; and were captivated by love of women, and produced children who are called demons." **The illicit unions were likely initiated by both the women and/or the watchers depending on the attractions involved.**

[279] Milik has: "spell-binding" (M pg. 157).

[280] Shemihazah and his operatives are blamed for teaching humankind occultic practices here and in 7:1, and 9:8. The Quran has a story of Babylonian angels named Harut and Marut teaching magic to humans. Quran 2:102. Jaber, Hanan, 2018. *Harut and Marut in The Book of Watchers and Jubilees.* Cf. Idris/Enoch in Q 19:56 and 21:85.

[281] A Greek text (Gk.[s]) reads: "the eleventh, Pharmaros, taught charms, spells, magical skills and the release of spells." The Aramaic is incomplete but appears to have had a long text comparable to that of Gk[s]. (See footnote in

Baraqel taught the signs of the lightning flashes. Jub 8:3; 12:16-20
Kokabel taught the signs of the stars.[282][283] *Or. Graec.* 8.1; *Idol.* 9
Ziqel taught the signs of the comets.[284] *Ecl.* 53
Arteqoph taught the signs of earth.[285]
Shamshiel taught the signs of the sun. Rev 6:10
Sahriel taught the path of the moon.
And they all began to reveal secrets to their wives and to their children.
4 And as men perished,[286] they cried, and their cry went up before 9:2; Gen 4:10; Ex 2:23
heaven.[287][288] Neh 9:27; Sir 35:16-18

Excursus: A sampling of other accounts of the fall of the watchers.

> For a woman cannot force a man openly, but by a harlot's bearing she beguiles him. Flee, therefore, fornication, my children, and command your wives and your daughters, that they adorn not their heads and faces to deceive the mind: because every woman who useth these wiles hath been reserved for eternal punishment. For thus they allured the Watchers who were before the flood; for as these continually beheld them, they lusted after them, and they conceived the act in their mind; for they changed themselves into the shape of men, and appeared to them when they were with their husbands. And the women

---

Knibb's text). "The Elephantine deity associated with this name was known for spell binding and oath taking, who punishes oath breakers with his destroying curse" (H1 pg. 67-68). In 2010, Henryk Drawnel published an important study touching on the angel list in 1 En. 8:3, persuasively anchoring the text in a Babylonian environment.

> Drawnel conducts a detailed examination of the magic arts and sciences described in 7:1 and 8:3 and shows convincingly that the teachings of the watchers closely match the teachings and practices of the āšipus, a prestigious group of Babylonian incantation priests, characterized by Drawnel as medico-magical scholars and scribes who preserved the Babylonian cuneiform traditions well into the early centuries of the Common Era (OLS pg. 156 citing Henryk Drawnel, "*Between Akkadian ṭupšarrūtu and Aramaic ספר: Some Notes on the Social Context of the Early Enochic Literature*," RevQ 95 (2010), pgs. 373–403).

[282] Astrology was extremely widespread in the Mediterranean world from the fourth century BC on. (N1 pg. 199-200) Abraham turns from the practice in (Jub 12:16-20). It was a way for man to play God by attempting to gain knowledge rightly forbidden to man. (Jub 8:1-4) contains an account of how astrology was reintroduced after the flood. Psedo-Eupolmus (prior to 100 BC) attributes the discovery of astrology to Enoch (9.17.8-9; (OTP2 pg. 881)). Tertullian attributes the knowledge of astrology to the fallen angels (*Idol.* 9). ". . . presuming that we are led by the unchangeable will of the stars. One thing only I advance, that those angels who forsook God, who were lovers of women, were also the discoverers of this curious art, and on that account were condemned by God."
[283] Olson has: "Kaokabel taught how to read the signs of the stars." Knibb has: "portents." Gk.[S] has "the fourth taught astrology."
[284] Others suggest "shooting stars", or "fire balls".
[285] Black suggests this means: "meteorological or climatic predictions."
[286] Men perished due to the deprivations and cannibalism. Predominantly the guilty perish in the flood; since the innocent have already been killed!
[287] For other passages where the cry of man or prayers ascend to Heaven, see (1En 9:2-3, 10; 22:5; 47:1-2; 97:5; 104:1; and Rev 6:10).
[288] For 1En 8:4, Olson suggests a combination of the more elaborate Greek and Syncellus texts to arrive at: "After this the giants began to devour human flesh, and men began to decline upon the earth. Then men cried out to heaven, saying: 'Bring our suit before the Most High, and our devastation before the Great Glory, before the Lord of all lords in majesty.'" But for his translation he goes with what appears to be the reading in the Dead Sea Scrolls: "And they all began revealing secrets to their wives, and inasmuch as some of human kind was perishing from the earth, their cry went up before heaven."

lusting in their minds after their forms, gave birth to giants, for the Watchers appeared to them as reaching even unto heaven. *Testament of Reuben,* 5:4-6 (2nd century BC)

But for what degree of zeal they had formerly shown for virtue, they now showed by their actions a double degree of wickedness, whereby they made God to be their enemy. For many angels of God accompanied with women, and begat sons that proved unjust, and despisers of all that was good, on account of the confidence they had in their own strength; for the tradition is, that these men did what resembled the acts of those whom the Grecians call giants. But Noah was very uneasy at what they did; and being displeased at their conduct, persuaded them to change their dispositions and their acts for the better: but seeing they did not yield to him, but were slaves to their wicked pleasures, he was afraid they would kill him, together with his wife and children, and those they had married; so he departed out of that land. Josephus, *Antiquities of the Jews* 1.3.1 §§72-74 (AD 95)

And the daughters of Cain with whom the angels had companied conceived, but they were unable to bring forth their children, and they died. And of the children who were in their wombs some died, and some came forth; having split open the bellies of their mothers they came forth by their navels. And when they were grown up and reached man's estate they became giants, whose height reached unto the clouds; and for their sakes and the sakes of sinners the wrath of God became quiet, and He said, "My spirit shall only rest on them for one hundred and twenty years, and I will destroy them with the waters of the Flood. *Kebra Nagast*, Chapter 100 (AD 14th century)

And when the angels of God saw the daughters of men that they were beautiful, they took unto themselves wives of all of them whom they chose." Philo *On The Giants* Chapter 2 (time of Christ)

The prophetic interpretation concerning Azazel and the angels wh[o went in to the daughters of man,] [so that] they bore mighty men to them. And concerning Azazel [who taught them][to love] iniquity and to pass on wickedness as an inheritance, all […] […] judgements, and the judgment of the council of […] Dead Sea Scrolls 4Q180 1.7-10 (W pg. 269)

When they went about in their willful heart, the Guardian Angels of Heaven fell and were ensnared by it, for they did not observe the commandments of God. Their sons, who were as tall as cedars, and whose bodies were as big as mountains, fell by it. Geniza Document A, CD 1.17-19 *A New Translation The Dead Sea Scrolls* Wise, Abegg and Cook 2005 pg. 53.

This Ptolemy, however—a careful investigator of these matters—does not seem to me to be useless; but only this grieves (one), that being recently born, he could not be of service to the sons of the giants, who, being ignorant of these measures, and supposing that the heights of heaven were near, endeavored in vain to construct a tower. And so, if at that time he were present to explain to them these measures, they would not have made the daring attempt ineffectually. Hippolytus of Rome, *The Refutation of all Heresies* Book 4 Chapter 12 (ca. AD 210)

He made for people to see-and entrusted the care of men and women and of things under heaven to angels whom He appointed over them. But the angels transgressed this order, and were captivated by love of women, and produced children who are called demons. And besides later they enslaved the human race to themselves, partly by magical writings, and partly by fears and punishments which they occasioned, and partly by teaching them to offer sacrifices and incense and libations. St. Justin Martyr, *The Second Apology* 5. (AD 150-157)

When Almighty God, to beautify the nature of the world, willed that that earth should be visited by angels, when they were sent down they despised His laws. Such was the beauty of women, that it turned them aside; so that, being contaminated, they could not return to heaven. Rebels from God, they uttered words against Him. Then the Highest uttered His judgment against them; and from their seed giants are said to have been born. By them arts were made known in the earth, and they taught the dyeing of wool, and everything which is done; and to them, when they died, men erected images. But the Almighty, because they were of an evil seed, did not approve that, when dead, they should be brought back from death. Whence wandering they now subvert many bodies, and it is such as these especially that ye this day worship and pray to as gods. *The Instructions of Commodianus in Favour of Christian Discipline. Against the Gods of the Heathens. Chapter 3* (AD Mid-3rd century)

And for a very long while wickedness extended and spread, and reached and laid hold upon the whole race of mankind, until a very small seed of righteousness remained among them: and illicit unions took place upon the earth, since angels were united with the daughters of the race of mankind; and they bore to them sons who for their exceeding greatness were called giants. And the angels brought as presents to their wives teachings of wickedness, in that they brought them the virtues of roots and herbs, dyeing in colours and cosmetics, the discovery of rare substances, love-potions, aversions, amours, concupiscence, constraints of love, spells of bewitchment, and all sorcery and idolatry hateful to God; by the entry of which things into the world evil extended and spread, while righteousness was diminished and enfeebled. Irenæus, *The Proof of the Apostolic Preaching* 18 (AD late 2nd century)

For they possessed freedom in that time in which they were created. And some of them came down and mingled themselves with women. At that time they who acted like this were tormented in chains. But the rest of the multitude of angels, who have no number, restrained themselves. 2 Baruch 56:11-15 (AD 100-120)

Now the giants were on the earth in those days and afterward. When the sons of God used to go in to the daughters of humans, then they produced offspring for themselves. Those were the giants that were of old, the renowned humans. Gen 6:4 LXX[289]

---

[289] Pietersma, Albert and Wright, Benjamin G., 2007. *A New English Translation of the Septuagint.*

Excursus: Which came first: The Book of Watchers or Genesis 6:1-4?

The author of Genesis 6 is obviously assuming prior knowledge on the part of his readership. His readers already knew the identity of the sons of God, the Nephilim, and the mighty men who were of old. No long or even short explanation was needed. Modern readers who do not know the Book of Watchers backstory are not so fortunate.

> When man began to multiply on the face of the land and daughters were born to them, the sons of God saw that the daughters of man were attractive. And they took as their wives any they chose. Then the LORD said, "My spirit shall not abide in man forever, for he is flesh: his days shall be 120 years." The Nephilim were on the earth in those days and also afterward, when the sons of God came in to the daughters of man and they bore children to them. These were the mighty men who were of old, the men of renown. Genesis 6:1-4

A *Book of Watcher* type tradition certainly already existed when Genesis 6 was written. Genesis 6 is referencing a tradition from a known written or oral source of which his readership was well acquainted.

Black agrees and summarizes.

> On the whole the balance of evidence- and literary borrowing one way or the other is obvious—seems to favour the priority of the Enoch tradition, since it is, after all, the Enoch legend of the watchers to which Gen. 6 is so briefly alluding. A possible alternative explanation of the inter-relationship of the two narratives is that both, Gen. 6 and En. 6 are descended from a common literary ancestor, which need not have circulated only in an Aramaic form.[290]

Excursus: Is the Scapegoat identified with the watcher Azazel?

Olson is firm concerning the identification of Asael with the scapegoat: "A comparison of 10:4-8 with the day of Atonement ritual (cf. Lev 16:8-26), where we find a goat sent off "to Azazel," leaves little doubt that Asael is indeed Azazel." (OL pg. 34). Black is also convinced "There seems little doubt that 'Azaz' el at Lev. 16 is the same fallen archangel or watcher." "He appears in fact as the forerunner or prototype in Hebrew demonology of Satan or Belial of later traditions." (BL pg. 121) His association with the goat may be behind passages like (Lev 17:7) which mentions "goat demons" and follows soon after the day of atonement ceremony. Origen links Azazel and the goat with Satan (Cels. 6.43). "He was evidently not a simple he-goat but a giant who combined goat-like characteristics with those of man" (M pg. 313). Collins explores the association of Azazel and the goat, further speculating that Azazel had been the ruler of a monstrous race of demons named the *seirim* or he-goats (Collins, 1997, *From the Ashes of Angels*, pg. 252). This ancient association could well be behind the loathing of the goat in Jewish and Christian circles and the use of the goat head in the Sigil of Baphomet, the official insignia

[290] BL pg. 125.

of the Church of Satan. (2Chr 11:15) mentions goat idols, and elsewhere in ancient texts goats have negative connotations (Isa 13:21; 34:14; Philo, *The Posterity and Exile of Cain* 20 (72)). Heiser is one of the few who does not see a link between Leviticus 16 and the Asael of this passage (H1 pg. 79 and H2 pg. 137-138). But the Talmud clearly ties the two together. After discussing the temple ceremony, it reads: "The school of Rabbi Yishmael taught: Azazel is so called because it atones for the actions of Uzza and Azael. These are the names of "sons of God" who sinned with "daughters of men" and thereby caused the world to sin during the generation of the Flood" (Yoma 67b.7)(cf. Midrash of Shemhazai and Azazel). If, as seem certain, the Azazel goat in Leviticus 16:10 is based on the Asael from the *Book of the Watchers* then the fallen watcher tradition and the name Asael predates the Pentateuch! For other texts on Azazel see (The Temple Scroll 11Q19 26:3-13; The Book of Giants 4Q203 7_a; *Haer.* 1.15.6; and ApAb 13:6-14; 14:5; 20:5; 22:5; 23:11 and 31:5). The scapegoat ritual of Yom Kippur and the bird ritual of the *metzora* where sin/impurity is transferred onto an animal and it is sent away; have parallels in Eblaite, Hittite, Ugaritic, and Neo-Assyrian apotropaic (designed to avert evil) rituals.

The most ancient example of a sending away ritual was uncovered in the Ebla archives (Tell Mardikh in Modern Syria) from the twenty-fourth century B.C.E. A tablet describes a ritual in which an animal is sent away in order to purify the house of the dead prior to a royal wedding: 'We purify the mausoleum before the entrance of (the gods) Kura and Barama. A goat, a silver bracelet (hanging from) its neck, towards the steppe of Alini we let it go.' Here the goat is sent out, dressed up in a decorative silver bracelet, and carries with it the impurity, allowing the gods, and later the king and queen, to enter the mausoleum as part of the wedding ceremony" (Ayali-Darshan, *The Scapegoat Ritual and Its Ancient Near Eastern Parallels,* The Torah.com).

Men bring Suit before God Concerning Abuses by Fallen Angels and Giants

9 1 Then Michael, Sariel,[291] Raphael and Gabriel observed carefully[292] — 40:8-10; 87:2; 1QM 9.15-16
from the sanctuary of heaven, — Wis 9:10; Ps 14:2; 4Q201 1.4
and they saw much blood shed on the earth.[293] — Jub 7:23; *DeSpec* 27
The whole earth was full of wickedness and violence which men — 8:2; Gen 6:11

---

[291] The archangel Sariel is replaced in many other later sources and in rabbinic literature with the name Uriel. (Cf. SibOr 2:215). Black observes "It would seem that 1En 9:1 Aramaic preserves an old, probably the oldest, tradition of the names of the four archangels" (BL pg. 129). The names of Michael and Gabriel are picked up without introduction in the later book of Daniel (8:16; 9:21; 10:21; 12:1) and the New Testament (Lk 1:19, 26; Jude 1:9; Rev 12:7).

[292] "The names mean, respectively Michael ("Who is like God?") Sariel ("God is my prince"; i.e., leader, captain) Raphael ("Healer of God"; i.e., "God's healer"; or "God heals") Gabriel ("God is my Warrior")" (H1 pg. 88). These same four names are found in the War Scroll (1QM 9.14-16 (W pg. 156)). Three other archangels are named in chapter 20; Raguel, Saraqâêl, and Remiel, bringing the total to seven. This matches (Tobit 12:15): "I am Raphael, one of the seven holy angels, which present the prayers of the saints, and go in before the glory of the Holy One." **"A complement of four, and later seven, named archangels (here "holy ones" 9:3) appears first in 1 Enoch 9-10 and then becomes something of a staple in Jewish and Christian literature"** (N1 pg. 207). Four "living creatures" are also seen as throne guardians in (Ezek 1:5). (Cf. ApMos 40)

[293] **In 1 Enoch, 2nd Temple period literature, and in the thoughts of the anti-Nicene church fathers, the world's depravity did not originate solely from Adam and Eve, but also, and more importantly, from the fall of the watchers, and the rebellion of the "gods" placed in charge of the nations (Ps 82).**

were committing upon it.[294]
2 And entering in, they spoke to one another,
"The earth, made without (inhabitants), raises the voice of the cries 87:1; 84:5; Deut 24:15
of the children of earth to the gates of heaven.[295] Ex 3:7; Jas 5:4; Isa 26:21
3 Now to (us), the holy ones of heaven,[296] the souls of men are making Rev 8:3-4; OdesSol 23:1
their suit,[297] complaining with groans and saying:
"Bring our case before the Most High, and our destruction before the
Great Glory,[298] before the Lord of all lords in majesty." Job 33:23: 2Pet 1:17
4 Then Raphael, Michael, Sariel and Gabriel went in,
and said to the Lord of the Ages:[299] Our Great Lord, Lord of the Ages, 1Tim 6:15; Rev 17:14; 19:16
Lord of lords, God of gods[300] and King of kings; your glorious throne Deut 10:17; Dan 2:47; Jer 17:12
endures for all generations from eternity, and your Name is holy and Phil 2:9; Tob 3:11; 4Q202 1.3
great and blessed unto all ages! Ps 45:6
5 For you have created all things and have authority over all;[301]
and all things are open and uncovered before you. Mk 4:22; Sir 42:18; Heb 4:13
You see all things, and before you, there is nothing that can be hidden. Mt 10:26
6 You see what Asael[302] has done, that he has taught all iniquity 84:4; 86:1

---

[294] DSS fragments that bear on chapter 9 include (4QEn[a] 1 iv; 4QEn[b] 1 iii; 4Q201 1.4; and 4Q202 1.3). Additional fragments of 1 Enoch were alleged to be held by the Kando family but were determined to be modern forgeries. This includes XQpapEnoch MS 4612/8 (1En 7:1-5); MS 4612/12 (1En 8:4-9:3) and MS 4612/6 (1En 106:19-107:1), Elgvin, Torleif and Langlois, Michael, 2019. *Looking Back: (more) Dead Sea Scrolls forgeries in the Schoyn Collection, Revue de Qumran* 31 (1) [113}, 111-133.

[295] **Compare with 7:4, mankind is being devoured. The situation is so serious that the earth is being depopulated! If as the Lord said: "For as were the days of Noah, so will be the coming of the Son of Man." the conditions on earth will grow much worse from the present!** The angelic intercessors of heaven sit at heaven's gateway like human judges at a city gateway (Ruth 4:1-2).

[296] The suit is brought before the divine council of God. Compare Psalm 82:1. The council of God is composed of high-ranking spiritual beings, "gods, rulers, judges, divine ones" אֱלֹהִים (Elohim). God אֱלֹהִים (Elohim) presides over this council.

[297] That the complaints are being directed at the archangels is present in all English translations and is indicated in (4Q201 1.4.9-11). Other instances of angelic intercession on man's behalf may be found in (Tob 12:12-15; Job 5:1; 33:23; Zech 1:12-13; and Rev 8:3). An especially notable passage on angelic intercession is found in the *Testament of Levi* 3:3-9." Origen (AD 185-253) fully accepted the idea of not only angelic intercession, but angelic warfare on behalf of the saints (Cels 8.64). Irenæus mentions the possibility of invocations directed at presumably fallen angels (*Haer.* 2.32.5.)

[298] "Great Glory" is also used in (1En 14:20 and 102:3) (cf. 2Pet 1:17 "majestic glory").

[299] The title "Lord of the Ages" is attested in the DSS, *Tales of the Patriarchs,* ("Eternal Lord" 1QapGn 20.12-13; and 21.2 (W pgs. 100 & 102)).

[300] "God of gods," God is God of all the other heavenly beings (gods). For other uses, (Deut 10:17, Dan 2:47, and 1Cor 8:4-6). "King of kings," God is king over all earthly kings. For other uses see (1En 63:2, 4, 84:2, 2 Mac 13:4, 3 Mac 5:35, 1Tim 6:15 and Rev 15:3; 17:14; and 19:16). "God of the ages," God is eternal and exists through all the ages past and future. Other references occur in (1En 1:4, 5:2, and Sir 36:17).

[301] God's omnipotence is emphasized, along with His omniscience, eternality, and creative action. The approach to God by the four angels begins with praise and the greatest reverence.

[302] Asael is identified here as the first one to rebel. In the *Book of Giants*, Asael is also implicated in teaching iniquity (4Q203 7a.6). Shemihazah and Azazel are also both named in the Manichean Book of Giants texts. Nickelsburg believes "the material about Asael, moreover, has been imported from the Greek myth of Prometheus, or some Near Eastern version of it" (N1 pg. 29). Prometheus was punished by Zeus for defying the gods by stealing fire from them and giving it to humanity in the form of technology, knowledge, and civilization itself. The possibility exists that the dependence my flow in the opposite direction; given that the fallen watcher tradition predates Genesis 6.

upon the earth, and all deceitfulness in the land. 4Q180 1:7-10
He has revealed the eternal mysteries[303] which were preserved in heaven
and made them known to men; 2Cor 12:4
so that the most learned of the sons of men could put them into practice.
7 And Shemihazah has made known spells; he whom you gave authority 6:7
over those who are with him.[304]
8 And they have gone in to the daughters of men upon the earth, Gen 6:1-4
and have lain with women defiling themselves,[305] 7:1; 86:4; Rev 14:4
and have revealed to them all kinds of sins.[306] *Epid.* 18
9 And behold! The daughters of men have borne from them sons, *2 Apol* 5; 4Q203 7a; AThm 32
giants,[307] half breeds; and the whole earth has been filled with 4Q531 1; Jub 5:2; 7:21
wickedness.[308] Gen 6:5, 11
10 And now the spirits of the souls of those who have died are crying Rev 6:10; Gen 4:10
and making their suit to the gates of heaven. 8:4; Lk 18:7
Their groaning has ascended and they cannot escape the presence of Acts 10:4
the iniquities that are being done on the earth.[309] Sir 42:18-19
11 You know all things before they come to pass.[310] 39:11; Jdt 9:5-6; Isa 42:9; 44:7-8
You see these things, but you leave them alone,[311] and you do not tell 89:71, 77; Susannah 13:42

---

303 **"Mysteries" Is a loan-word from Persian meaning literally "secrets." Concerning celestial mysteries, Black notes "It came to be a key eschatological concept in apocalyptic literature, probably originally deriving from its use in Enoch,** where it occurs again at (10:7; 16:3; 104:10; 106:19), and in the Parables at (61:5; 65:11; 68:1; 69.16f)" (BL pg. 131).

304 **Nickelsburg sees two traditions. "According to the one, the rebellion, led by Shemihazah, consisted in the mating of watchers and women, while the other involved the revelation of heavenly secrets, and was led by Asael, whose name ("God has made") may have alluded to the metallurgical revelations that facilitated the fabrication of weapons, jewelry, cosmetics and dyes"** (NV2 pg. 202).

305 **Olson has insight here: "They have lain with women, defiling themselves. Compare Rev 14:3 -4a: '*And they sing a new song before the throne and before the four living creatures and the elders; and no one is able to learn the song except the 144,000, the ones who have been redeemed from the earth. These are they who have not defiled themselves with women, for they are virgins.*' These verses have long puzzled bible commentators, but most of the problems vanish if one recognizes that John is consciously alluding to Enoch: the redeemed who refuse to submit to the Beast's evil world system are likened to the holy angels who did not rebel against God when, on one famous occasion, others did. The fallen angels of Enoch leave a gap in the heavenly hierarchy to be filled, perhaps, by the 144,000 who have committed no such apostasy"** (OL pg. 36).

306 Gk^{s} adds: "and taught them to make charms for producing hatred." N adds here "and have taught them to make hate-inducing charms." Nickelsburg says these charms are "to win (back) one's beloved" (N1 pg. 213).

307 Gk^{a} "titans" Gk^{s} "giant sons" The etymology of the word "giant" from Greek *Gigas* (usually in plural, *Gigantes*), indicates a race of divine but savage and monstrous beings. The word is of unknown origin, probably from a pre-Greek language. "Derivation from *gegenes* "earth-born" is considered untenable." (See "giant" in the Online Etymology Dictionary)

308 In the Book of Giants, consisting of the Manichaean texts and Dead Sea Scroll fragments (4Q203, 4Q530-532, 6Q8, 1Q23 and 2Q26) "The stock figures of the giants come alive. They have names, they have dreams, they worry over them, discuss them, and seek to have them interpreted. In various of these respects, they recall narratives about their fathers, the watchers" (N1 pg. 173). **Gilgamesh is named in the Book of Giants.**

309 The last sentence of 9:10 could alternatively be interpreted with the idea that the souls groaning cannot cease because of the continuing iniquities occurring on earth.

310 This is a plain statement of God's foreknowledge and omniscience.

311 So Gk$^{a\ s}$.

us what we should do to them on account of these things."[312] Zech 1:12; 2Pet 2:11

Excursus: Mysteries of God

God has mysteries He keeps from mankind and even from his heavenly servants (1En 9:6 and notes). The revelation that God has mysteries came from the Book of Enoch. The concept of mysteries was picked up by the Apostle Paul in the New Testament. Mysteries include:

The greatest mystery; the advent, ministry and gospel of Christ. (Rom 16:25; 1Cor 2:7; Eph 1:9; 3:3; 3:9; 6:19; Col 1:26, 27; 2:2; 4:3; 1Tim 3:9; 3:16)

The intimate relationship between Christ and the Church. (Eph 5:32)

The Gentiles being fellow heirs with the Jews. (Eph 3:6)

The man of lawlessness. (2Thes 2:7)

The rapture. (1Cor 15:51)

For mysteries in the Book of Revelation see (Rev 1:20; 10:7; 17:5; 17:7).

Of course, Christ himself knew about the secrets of God; He himself being the greatest secret. "And he said to them, 'To you has been given the secret of the kingdom of God, but for those outside everything is in parables,'" (Mk 14:11)

All secrets will eventually be known. "For nothing is hidden that will not be made manifest, nor is anything secret that will not be known and come to light." (Lk 8:17)

Excursus: "I said you are gods"

> Jesus answered them (the Jews who were going to stone him), 'Is it not written in your Law, 'I said, you are gods'? If he called them gods to whom the word of God came—and Scripture cannot be broken—do you say of him whom the father consecrated and sent into the world, 'You are blaspheming,' because I said, 'I am the Son of God'? (John 10:34-36)

This verse is fundamentally and continually misunderstood because of a lack of understanding of the unseen realm of the Kingdom of God. 1 Enoch helps us understand, as it gives us a glimpse into the "unseen realm." The "gods" the Lord is referring to, are not human judges, as many interpret. They are אֱלֹהִים (Elo-him); the term Jesus uses here in Greek is θεός (*theós*). Although

---

[312] **The angels know God is going to act and are asking for specific instructions. This gives interesting insight into the operation of God's Kingdom. This appears to be the passage behind (2Pet 2:11). "Whereas angels, though greater in might and power, do not pronounce a blasphemous judgment against them before the Lord." These archangels though greater in power than the fallen watchers do not "pronounce a blasphemous judgment" before the Lord but politely asked God what they were to do.**

this term is often used of the Most High God it is also used of lesser spiritual beings. Yahweh יְהוָה (Yah-weh) always refers to the Most High God. This is not polytheism, these "gods" are created beings, subject to the Most High. Jesus distinguishes Himself from these Elohim and places himself above them by saying he is the one "whom the father consecrated and sent into the world…" The scripture Jesus seems to be referencing in (Jn 10:34-36), is (Ps. 82:1): "God has taken his place in the divine council; in the midst of the gods (Elohim) he holds judgement" Christ refers to this council in Mt 5:22 "whoever insults his brother will be liable to the council." We see this same type of Divine Council in (1En 9:3) where they are called the "holy ones of heaven". It is also seen in 1En 9:4 in the text, where God is "the God of gods." If there were not "gods" or they were imaginary beings, this appellation would be meaningless; a joke. An understanding of this concept is crucial to proper understanding of 1 Enoch, 2nd temple writings, early Christian writings and the Bible. It will also enhance your spiritual world view.[313]

Excursus: What about Adam and Eve?

Where does Adam and Eve fit into the account of the watchers? Second temple Jews and early Christians ascribed the origin of sin more to the fallen watchers than to Adam and Eve. The similarities of the accounts are apparent. A fallen watcher, (the serpent who is not named in Genesis, likely a seraph) temps Eve, (a human woman), with forbidden knowledge. Moreover, as with the watchers, both the serpent and the humans involved, receive divine punishment. The story of Adam and Eve serves as a subset, or example of the corruption sown by the watchers in passing forbidden knowledge to mankind. The serpent of Eden is in actuality a seraph identified by name in 1En 69:6 as Gadreēl. Without doubt, the fallen watcher tradition predates the story of Adam and Eve in Genesis.

Excursus: *Epic of Gilgamesh*, *Atrahasis Epic*, and other Mesopotamian stories; do they stand behind Genesis 1-10?

The *Epic of Gilgamesh*, while existing in different forms, is regarded as the oldest surviving notable literature in the world. Its sources date from 2100 BC. Found on clay tablets, it appears to have been written in independent stories that were then used as source material for a combined epic. It is thought that Genesis and the Epic draw from a common source. Three different Babylonian stories of the flood have survived: the *Sumerian Flood Story*, the eleventh tablet of the *Gilgamesh Epic*, and the *Atrahasis Epic*. The *Epic of Gilgamesh* describes a world similar to Homers Iliad and Odyssey which appear to have used elements of the earlier *Epic of Gilgamesh*. The world of the Epic is full of numerous "gods," and these "gods," as in 1 Enoch, interact and interbreed with humans. Gilgamesh himself, is described as two thirds "god" and one third human.[314] Gilgamesh is arrogant, moody, filled with lust, often angry and violent. Humans are despised and abused as lower beings.

"Gilgamesh sounds the tocsin for his amusement, his arrogance has no bounds by day or night. No son is left with his father, for Gilgamesh takes them all, even the children; yet the king should

---

[313] I would commend to you Michael S. Heiser's book *The Unseen Realm*, Lexham Press, 2015 for an introduction into this subject.
[314] Epic of Gilgamesh Prologue.

be a shepherd to his people. His lust leaves no virgin to her lover, neither the warrior's daughter nor the wife of the noble; yet this is the shepherd of the city, wise, comely, and resolute."[315]

This is a very similar and independent description of the sons of the watchers found in 1 Enoch and elsewhere. Enkidu, Gilgamesh's adopted brother and companion, is introduced as a star that fell from Heaven. Gilgamesh, who is also named in the *Book of Giants*, and Enkidu would be very good candidates for the referents in Genesis 6:4.

"The Nephilim were on the earth in those days, and also afterward, when the sons of God came in to the daughters of man and they bore children to them. These were the mighty men who were of old, the men of renown." Both Gilgamesh and Enkidu die in the Epic, thus showing that humans mixed with "gods" are mortal.

The *Epic of Gilgamesh* supports the Enochian interpretation of Genesis 6:1-4 over the Sethite interpretation championed later in church history. The Epic has a watcher of the forest, doors of Hell, seven years of famine, an ocean at the end of the world, a garden of the gods, and a bull of heaven. It has a flood story (from roughly 1200 BC) that is followed point by point in Genesis. In this story, the "god" Ea warns Ut-napishtim, the Noah figure, in a dream to build a huge boat and "then take up into the boat the seed of all living creatures." The boat in the Epic, being round, is distinctly un-seaworthy. The rain only lasts 6 days, in contrast to Genesis where it lasts forty days. A dove, a swallow and a raven are released. After exiting the boat, a sacrifice is made to the "gods."

Siduri's advice to Gilgamesh, "As for you, Gilgamesh, fill your belly with good things; day and night, night and day, dance and be merry, feast and rejoice. Let your clothes be fresh, bathe yourself in water, cherish the little child that holds your hand, and make your wife happy in your embrace; for this too is the lot of man" seems to find use in Ecclesiastes 8:9 "Enjoy life with the wife whom you love, all the days of your vain life that he has given you under the sun, because that is your portion in life and in your toil at which you toil under the sun."

> The parallels between the stories of Enkidu/Shamhat and Adam/Eve have been long recognized by scholars. In both, a man is created from the soil by a god, and lives in a natural setting amongst the animals. He is introduced to a woman who tempts him. In both stories the man accepts food from the woman, covers his nakedness, and must leave his former realm, unable to return. The presence of a snake that steals a plant of immortality from the hero later in the epic is another point of similarity. However, a major difference between the two stories is that while Enkidu experiences regret regarding his seduction away from nature, this is only temporary. After being confronted by the god Shamash for being ungrateful, Enkidu recants and decides to give the woman who seduced him his final blessing before he dies. This is in contrast to Adam, whose fall from grace is largely portrayed purely as a punishment for disobeying God."[316]

---

[315] Epic of Gilgamesh Book 1, THE COMING OF ENKIDU.

[316] Gmirkin, Russell, 2006. *Berossus and Genesis, Manetho and Exodus*. Continuum. p. 103. Mitchell, Stephen (2010) [2004]. Gilgamesh: *A New English Version*. Simon and Schuster.

The Atrahasis epic also includes a story with elements common to Genesis. It has man formed from a mixture of clay and a slain "god." Men are required to do hard work. Ellil, the main god, calls for a flood to destroy humans after they have multiplied on earth, because they are disturbing his sleep. A man, Atra-Hasis, and his family are preserved on a boat during a seven-night flood. Animals, including wild animals, are saved on a boat that was also loaded with food. The other gods are horrified by the flood and regret that it happened. The Atrahasis account is thought to be the common source for the *Epic of Gilgamesh* and the Biblical flood account. The reasons for this belief include 1. Both Genesis and the Atrahasis account are written in 3rd person. 2. The flood story, like in Genesis, is only a few generations after creation. 3. Like Genesis, in the Atrahasis epic, the god Enki announces to Atrahasis that the flood will come on the seventh night.[317] 4. In Gilgamesh, Utanapishti is called Atrahasis twice.[318] 5. In both Genesis and the Atrahasis epic, animals come in two by two.[319] 6. In both, the respective "god" declares there will be no more floods.[320] 7. In Genesis 9:1, man is commanded to be fruitful and multiply, which is likely a reactive counterbalance to the Atrahasis epic where mankind's procreation is instead limited by divine decree.[321] [322]

A separate tablet CBM 13532, actually CBS 13532, was translated fancifully by Hermann Hilprecht in a 1910 publication. It was popularized by the Institute of Creation Research (ICR) until "translation" issues were discovered. ICR has placed the following disclaimer on their webpage but amazingly left active (as of the time of this writing) the original article promoting the tablet. "Editor's note: Since this article was published, ICR has learned that Hilprecht's translation, by his own admission, included Bible-centric verbiage not found on the tablet. ICR thus no longer advocates this tablet as having any more apologetic value than other cuneiform-inscribed Flood stories such as the Epic of Gilgamesh.[323]

Another Mesopotamian flood text, known as the *Erra Epic* from the early first millennium BC, has been recovered in at least thirty-six specimens from multiple sites, including Assur, Babylon, Nineveh, Sultantepe and Ur. In it the Babylonian high god Marduk permanently banished the *apkallus* to the subterranean waters deep inside the earth. These *apkallus* were divine beings who possessed great knowledge in the period before the flood. Many were considered to be evil but some were good and fought against demonic powers. *Apkallus* mated with human women producing hybrid divine human offspring.

> Figures of *apkallus*, the Mesopotamian counterparts to the sons of God, are known through the work of Mesopotamian archaeologists. They were buried in rows of boxes as parts of foundation walls for Mesopotamian buildings to ward off evil powers. These

---

[317] Compare (Gen 7:4, 10) and the Atrahasis epic (3.1.37).

[318] Epic of Gilgamesh 11.49, 197.

[319] Finkel, Irving., 2014 *The Ark before Noah: Decoding the Story of the Flood* (London: Hodder & Stoughton) pg. 365.

[320] Compare Gen 8:21; and 9:11 with a statement toward the end of the Atrahasis epic, in a Neo-Babylonian fragment, when the god Ea declares: "Henceforth let no flood be brought about, but let people last forever!"

[321] Atrahasis 3.7.2–8.

[322] Day, John. 2020. *The Mesopotamian Origin of the Biblical Flood Story*, The Torah.com.

[323] For the standard (correct) translation of tablet CBM 13532, see (Lambert, W. G. and Millard, A. R., 1999. *Atra-Hasis: The Babylonian Story of the Flood.* Winona Lake, IN: Eisenbrauns, pg. 127).

> boxes were referred to by Mesopotamians as *mats-tsarey*, which means 'watchers.' The connection is explicit and direct.[324]

The Genesis account undoubtedly originated from sources in Mesopotamia. Josephus in fact equated the two flood accounts.[325] This similarity establishes the antiquity of the Genesis text but it also establishes a dependance of Genesis on these Mesopotamian accounts. Genesis 1-11 may have been a supplement to the Genesis text[326] or may have been original to the text.

Evidence that Moses had access to a written Hebrew language has recently come forth. The Khirbet Qeiyafa ostracon, dating from the time of King David, is thought by many scholars to have been written in an archaic, dialectal form of Hebrew, but scholars differ in decipherment of the text.[327] Additionally two Amorite/Canaanite cuneiform tablets dated to 1800 BC, found in Iraq, have been found to contain a Hebrew precursor language. One of the authors, "Cohen, adds that the text proves "beyond a shadow of a doubt" that already in the second millennium B.C.E there was a spoken language that was very close to Hebrew, which has been heretofore only known from the first millennium B.C.E."[328] This "mother of Hebrew" text significantly moves back the existence and use of Hebrew to the time of Abraham; well before Moses! So, it can no longer be argued that Moses did not have access to a written Hebrew like language.

God Sends the Archangels to Execute Judgement on the Fallen Angels and the Giants

10 1 Then the Most High declared and the Great Holy One spoke!
And he sent Sariel[329] to the son of Lamech, saying:[330]
2 "Go to Noah and say to him in my Name, 'Hide yourself!' Isa 26:20-21; 1Pet 2:20
and reveal to him the End that is approaching; 16:1
that the earth will be completely destroyed; 3Mac 2:4
and tell him that a Deluge is about to come on the whole earth;
to destroy all things from the face of the earth. Gen 6:7, 17; 7:17-24; Jub 7:25
3 Instruct the righteous one, the son of Lamech, Jub 5:5; Gen 6:8-9
what he should do to preserve his life and his offspring for all time."[331] Sir 44:17

---

324 Heiser, Michael S. 2015. *The Unseen Realm*, pgs. 104-105.
325 *Ant* 1.3.6 §§93-95; *Apion* 1.19 §§128-131; Josephus even mentioned flood survivors in *Ant* 1.3.5,6 §§89,95.
326 Possibly during the Babylonian exile.
327 Donnelly-Lewis, Brian 2022. *The Khirbet Qeiyafa Ostracon: A New Collation Based on the Multispectral Images, with Translation and Commentary.* Bulletin of the American Society of Overseas Research vol 388
328 *Revue d'Assyriologie et d'archéologie orientale Jan 2023.*
329 "Sariel" ("God is my prince" or "prince of God") as used in 20:6.
330 DSS containing portions of chapter 10 and 11 include (4Q202 1.4; 4Q204 1.5; 4QEn[a] iv; 4QEn[a] 1vi; 4QEn[b] iv; and 4QEn[c] iv).
331 This text follows Syncellus for 10:3, which more full than the Ethiopic/Greek, finding possible support in a small DSS fragment.

From him a plant shall be planted, — 4Q433a
and his seed will endure for all generations of eternity."[332] — Wis 14:6
4 To Raphael[333] he said, "Go, Raphael, and bind Asael by his hands — 13:1; 54:4-5; 2Pet 2:4; Tob 8:2-3
and feet and cast[334] him into the darkness — Mt 22:13; Jude 6; Ps 44:19
and split open the wilderness which is in the desert of Dudael[335] and — 88:1; 90:21-23; Ps 94:13
throw him into it. — 54:5-6; Jub 5:6 ; Isa 24:21-22
5 Throw on him[336] sharp and jagged stones, and cover him with darkness — 92:5; 2Sam 18:17; Josh 10:16-17
and let him abide there for an exceedingly long time. — Mt 8:12; 25:30; Isa 24:22
Cover his face, and let him not see the light.[337] — Jub 5:10; Job 40:13
6 And on the day of the great judgement he will be hurled into the — Rev 19:20; 20:10
blazing fire. — 1QS 4.13
7 Heal the earth[338] which the watchers have desolated, — 4Q534 2.15
and announce the restoration of the earth, that I shall heal its wounds — 4Q203 8.5-12; Rom 8:20, 21
that the sons of men shall not altogether perish[339] because of the — 2Chr 7:14
mysteries which the watchers have disclosed and taught their sons. — 7:1
8 The whole earth has been made desolate by the works of the teaching[340] — Gen 6:11-12
of Asael; record against him all sins."[341] — 6:3; Lev 16:10, 21; 17:7

---

[332] The "seed of Noah" includes all mankind; but specifically, the righteous and the Messiah will be the ones to endure for all generations of eternity. Noah's wife was named Emsârâ, the daughter of Râkê'êl according to (Jub 4:33). In 1QapGen 6.6 Noah's wife is also named Emzara (W pg. 93).

[333] Raphael (Rāpā'ēl, "God has healed"). His healing activity is demonstrated in (1En 10:7; 40:9; Tobit 3:17; and 12:14).

[334] "The Greek verb rendered 'cast into hell' is tartaroo, the verb found in the classical Greek story for the destination of the rebel Titan, a tale with clear relationships to the apkallu story that provides the original context for Genesis 6:1-4" (H1, pg. 98). Nickelsburg sees a link between the Prometheus myth and Azazel.

> "The Asael material has significant points of similarity to the Prometheus myth, especially to Aeschylus's version of it." Speaking of this version in *Prometheus Bound* he opines: "Of particular interest in the present context, he taught the mining of copper, iron, silver, and gold –an expansion on the idea of his theft of fire. For his rebellion against Zeus, he is taken into the wilderness where he is chained hand and foot to the side of a cliff. When he continues his insolence against the high god, Zeus opens up the rock and Prometheus is entombed until a later time when he will be subjected to terrible torment." (N1 pg. 193)

[335] **Dûdâêl, is in the wilderness east of Jerusalem, at the escarpment of the Yarden Valley below the Bet-Hudedon (Beth Hadudo) rock; given that is where the goat is sent to Azâzêl.** (Lev 16:10, 22; Yoma 6:8) (See The Jewish Virtual Library "Azazel"). (See note on 10:8).

[336] Gk[a s c] has "and place under him".

[337] Some associate 5000-year-old Rujm el-Hiri with its concentric rings of stones, as a prison for Azazel. See the excursis pg. 66, "Galgal Rafaim".

[338] Baty has: "reanimate the earth" Isaac has: "give life to the earth"

[339] **The situation was so dire that mankind faced annihilation.** The mysteries revealed were so dangerous they could destroy human life. Some mystical groups from antiquity, until present day, claim they possess forbidden anti-diluvian secrets. These include the Chaldeans, Magi, soothsayers, astrologers of Babylon, Druids, Egyptian priests, Brahmins, Gnostics, snake brotherhoods, Kabbalists, Freemasons and elements of the modern-day new age movement (Wayne, Gary., 2014. *The Genesis 6 Conspiracy*).

[340] Asael taught weaponry, metallurgy, cosmetics and female adornments (1En 8:1).

[341] Azazel is sent the scapegoat in (Lev. 16:8-10 and 11Q19-21 26). "But the goat on which the lot fell for Azazel shall be presented alive before the Lord to make atonement over it, that it may be sent away into the wilderness to Azazel" (Lev 16:10). The Temple Scroll, among the DSS, is more descriptive: "Then he shall wash the blood of the sin offering from his hands and feet and approach the living goat. He is to confess over its head all the iniquities of

9 To Gabriel[342] the Lord said: "Go, Gabriel, against the bastards,[343] Sir 16:7
the half breeds, and the children of fornication; and destroy Isa 14:20-21; Jub 5:7-10
the children of the watchers from among the sons of men. 3Mac 2:4; Wis 14:6
Muster them (for battle), and send them, one against the other, Jub 5:6-11; 7:22; 4Q531 7.4-6
in a war of annihilation;[344] for length of days they shall not have. 88:2; Bar 3:26-28
Ps 21:4; 55:23

10 Their fathers will present requests to you, 12:6; 13:4-6; 14:7
but no petition shall be granted on their behalf.
They hope to live an eternal life, Gen 6:3
and that each of them would live five hundred years."[345] Ps 21:4
11 The Lord said to Michael:[346] "Go, Michael, and declare to Rev 12:7; 14:4; TNaph 3:1
Shemihazah and the others with him, who united with the daughters 7:1
of men, so that they were defiled by them in their uncleanness. Jub 4:22
12 And when their sons perish, and they see the annihilation of their 12:6; Dan 9:24-27; Jub 5:10

---

the children of Israel, as well as all their guilt and sins, thus putting them upon the goat's head. Then he shall send him away to Azazel in the wilderness led by a man prepared for the moment. The goat shall carry away all the iniquities" (11Q19-21 26.10-13 (W pg. 605). **In the 2nd temple period, the sin of the watchers was viewed as the source of human depravity more so than the sin of Adam and Eve; and Asael, as the first to fall, is singled out for special punishment** (N1 pg. 195). By laying hands on the goat, the priest was ascribing all sin to Azazel. Sin is thus sent back to its source, i.e. since Azazel brought sin to the world, now sin is being given back to him. In Genesis 6:5, man's wickedness flows directly from the sins of the sons of God and Nephilim presented in 6:1-4. "The actual destination of the goat is not specified in Leviticus, but according to the Mishnah (*m. Yoma 6.8*), the goat is sent to 'Beth ha-Dudo' (meaning 'a jagged, pointed place'), about three miles from Jerusalem (but according to the Talmud, 12 miles, or perhaps 10—the Rabbis disagreed)" (OL pg. 38). Olson continues "Beth ha-Dudo is clearly the Dudael mentioned here. The meaning of 'Dudael' is uncertain, but in view of its identification with Berh ha-Dudo, it probably means 'jagged mountains of God'" (OL pg. 38 referencing BL pg. 134 and M. K pg. 87). Charles called the same place where the goat was taken "Beth Chaduda" (C pg. 189). Martin also agrees with this location and further opines: **"The place that the Azazel Goat (the Scapegoat) was taken in the ritual of the Day of Atonement is where Satan will be kept for the Millennium. Again, it is also the place in the wilderness where Christ defeated Satan during His forty days of temptation. Everything fits perfectly in this prophetic scenario."** (Martin, Ernest L., Edited by David Sielaff, February (2010) 1981. *The Lake of Fire: Where Is it Located?* Online edition).

342 Gabriel ("God is my warrior").

343 "Bastards" is used, because the conception of the giants is considered illegitimate, since it violated God's command. In the Dead Sea Scrolls, which display a literary dependency on this text, the spirits of the giants and demons, are referred to as "bastard spirits" (*rwhwt mmzrym*) (4Q510 1.5-7; 4Q511 35.7; 48+49, 51; and 4Q444 Frags. 1-5 Col. 1.4-8). N has: "to the bastards, to the half-breeds, to the sons of miscegenation." Again, three types are named, as in 7:2 and 86:4. Milik notes "In En. 10:9 the descendants of the Watchers and the daughters of men are likewise divided into three categories: mamzérayä—the bastards, the sons of courtesans, the children of the Watchers" (M pg. 240). See notes on (1En 7:2).

344 Most of the giants were to be immediately destroyed by internecine war (cf. Jub 5:7-11). They had physical bodies, so they could be killed; however, their spirts survived. In (Jub 10:5-9), a tenth part of the giant spirits, upon request, remained available to Mastêmâ, the chief of the evil spirits, and the rest were imprisoned. But they are not allowed to "have power over the sons of the righteous from now on and forevermore" (Jub 10:6). In *The Book of the Giants* (4Q531 22.3-8) the giants recognize the futility of fighting "angels who] reside in [Heav]en."

345 Nickelsburg has, "Length of days they will not have; and no petition will be (granted) to their fathers in their behalf, that they should expect to live an everlasting life, nor even that each of them should live five hundred years."

346 Michael ("Who is like God?"). Michael is the protector of Israel in later literature. Other uses are found in (Dan 10:13, 21 and 12:1). "Late Daniel" scholars (175-164 BC), which are the majority, would argue that The Book of the Watchers preceded The Book of Daniel. Even if Daniel was early (6th century BC) it appears to be dependent on the Book of Watchers with its inclusion of watchers and archangels.

beloved ones,[347] bind them for seventy generations[348] in the valleys — 14:5-7; 54:5; 69:28; 88:3; 90:23 Lk 3:23-37; 10:17-20; TLev 16:1
of the earth,[349] until the great day of their condemnation, — 67:4-7; Isa 24:21-22; Rev 20:1-3
the time of their final end, until the everlasting judgement becomes — 16:1; Mt 8:29; Jude 6; Jub 5:7-11
absolute. — DialTrypho 141
13 Then they shall be led away to the fiery abyss,[350] to torment, — 18:11; 21:7,10; 54:1-6; 90:24
and in a place of incarceration, they shall be imprisoned for all — 108:5; 1Pet 3:19; 2Pet 2:4
time.[351] [352] — ApPet 20-33; Rev 20:1-3, 10, 14
14 And everyone who is condemned and destroyed,[353] will be bound — 2Pet 2:4; Rev 19:20
together with them until the fixed time[354] of judgement which I will — 67:4-13; 103:7-8; Matt 25:41
administer.[355] Then they will perish for all ages.[356]
15 I will (then) destroy all the spirits of the bastard sons of the watchers, — 56:1-4; Jub 10:5-9; *Apol.* 22
because they have wronged mankind.
16 I will cut off all perversity from upon the face of the earth, — Isa 60:21; 61:3; Gen 6:7, 13
and every evil work shall come to an end. — 62:8; 84:6; 93:2, 5, 10
Then let the plant of righteousness[357] and truth appear. It shall be a — Jub 7:34; Gen 49:9 LXX
blessing, and deeds of righteousness and truth shall be planted — $4Q433_a$
with joy forever.[358]

---

347 "Beloved ones", the children of the watchers (cf. Jub 5:10). Killing of children in front of parents, was a means of torture in ancient times (2 Kgs 25:7; Jer 52:10; *Ant* 13.14.2 §§380; *War* 1.4.6 §§97). But in this case the "children/giants" murdered each other.

348 Seventy generations, i.e. "the rest of time", to the end of history. (H1 pg. 105) It should be noted that 70 generations occurred from Enoch to Christ (Lk 3:23-37). The 70 generations were preserved in the DSS text, so this prophecy predates the time of Jesus. In (Lk 10:17-20) where Christ says "I saw Satan fall like lightning from heaven." marks the fulfillment of this prophecy. Christ makes plain that the "ruler of this earth is judged." (Jn 16:11).

349 Isaac has: "underneath the rocks of the ground." Knibb has: "under the hills of the earth." Black does not accept a reading of hills (Bl pg. 137). See 67:4 where the imprisonment of the angels is in a valley.

350 I has: "bottom of the fire", B has "taken to the lowest depths of the fire" i.e. lowest depths of hell.

351 The pharisees believed in Hell (*Ant* 18.1.3 §§14).

352 Olson makes a good point, **"The Book of Enoch must be credited with playing a major role in forming the terrible picture of Hell as a fiery pit into which the wicked will be thrown to perish forever. Such a place is foreshadowed in Isa 66:24, but the specific idea that Gehenna is a bottomless pit of fire originally intended for the Devil and his angels, taken for granted in the New Testament, is first met in these pages"** (OL pg. 38).

353 Black has: "And everyone who is consumed by lust and is corrupted".

354 **Wicked, unredeemed, humans will be condemned to the same prison as the fallen watchers. This matches the teaching of Christ. "Then he will say to those on his left, 'Depart from me, you cursed, into the eternal fire prepared for the devil and his angels'" (Mt 25:41).**

355 **Archangels are assigned tasks, but God himself presides over the final judgement.**

356 For 1En 10:14 Isaac has: "And at that time when they will burn and die, those who collaborated with them will be bound together with them from henceforth unto the end of (all) generations."

357 "Plant of righteousness and truth" seems to be referring to the Messiah of Israel (cf. Isa 53:2); however other references seem to apply the plant to the righteous ones of Israel. "Other references in Enoch give us a clue: 'Israel springs from a seed that 'is sown' by God, 62:8: hence it is established as 'a plant of the seed forever,' 84:6; is called 'the plant of uprightness,' 93:10; and 'the plant of righteous judgement,' 93:5" (Charles, R. H., 1913. *Commentary on the Pseudepigrapha of the Old Testament*, vol. 2, pg. 194 n. 16). It is also an image used often in the DSS (1QS 8.5; 11.8; where it is applied to the party of the *Yahad).* The plant/vine also has ties to the concept of Messiah. (Mitchell, David C., 2021. *Messiah ben Joseph* pg. 33). Christ compares the kingdom of heaven to a plant (Lk 13:19). Paul applies plant imagery to Israel as the olive tree and the gentile Church as grafted in where Jewish branches were broken off (Rom 11:16-24).

358 **In 10:16-11:2 the author is wholly given to describing the messianic kingdom as a restored Eden.**

The Righteous on Earth are to be Blessed

17 And all the righteous will be saved,[359] — 5:9
and shall live till they beget thousands; — Gen 9:1; DivInst 7.24
and all the days of your youth and of your old age will be — Isa 65:20-22; Zech 8:4
completed in peace.[360] — Jer 3:16
18 Then shall the whole earth be tilled in righteousness, — Ezek 28:26
and it shall all be planted with trees,[361] laden with blessing. — Gen 2:9; Rev 22:2
19 And all luxuriant[362] trees will be planted in it; — 25:4-6
and they will plant vines, and the vine which they plant will — Gen 9:20
produce a thousand measures of wine,[363] [364] — cf. Isa 5:10
and of every seed which is sown upon it, each measure will produce — 2Bar 29:5; Amos 9:13
a thousand measures;[365] — Isa 5:10
and a single measure of olives will produce ten baths of oil.[366] — AdvHaer 5.33.3-4
20 And as for you. Cleanse the earth from all filth, — Rev 21:8
and from all injustice and from all lawlessness and from all godlessness. — Zech 13:1-2
All the unclean[367] things that have been brought about on the — Gen 7:4, 23
earth—these remove from the earth.
21 And all the sons[368] of men are to become righteous, and all — Isa 45:23; Jub 5:12; Rev 21:26
nations[369] shall serve and bless me, — Isa 2:1-4; 60:10-14; Phil. 2:9-11
and all shall worship me and prostrate themselves (before) me.[370] — 48:5; 50:2; 90:30; 33; 91:14
22 And the whole earth shall be freed from all defilement and
from all uncleanness, and wrath and torment;[371] and I will — Rev 21:4, 24-27

---

[359] Most translators have "will escape" rather than "will be saved." In support of this text, (W pg. 283) translates "will be saved" in (4Q204 1.5). This expresses an act of saving on the part of God, rather than a chance escape. However, Milik translates "will escape" from 4QEn[c] 1 v. (M pg. 190).

[360] For other references to a long/eternal life; (cf. 1En 25:6; 58:3, 6; 71:17; 96:8.).

[361] Trees were evidence of prosperity (BL pg. 139).

[362] Or "pleasant/delightful trees" N has "trees of joy".

[363] Some Greek texts have "wine in abundance".

[364] N has: "a thousand jugs of wine" (N1 pg. 227 notes), "excavated jugs range from 1.4-4.5 liters in volume." The amounts in this verse "are of miraculous proportions."

[365] The text reads a thousand seah. A seah of wheat was about 15 liters. One thousand seah, is 15,000 liters.

[366] **Irenæus, referencing Papias (bishop of Hierapolis, writing AD 130), who knew the Apostle John, claims Jesus taught images of future agricultural abundance similar to this passage from 1 Enoch. "The elders who saw John the disciple of the Lord used to teach in regard to these times, and say: The days will come, in which vines shall grow, each having ten thousand branches, and in each branch ten thousand twigs, and in each twig ten thousand shoots, and in each one of the shoots ten thousand clusters, and on every one of the clusters ten thousand grapes, and every grape when pressed will give five and twenty metretes of wine"** (Irenæus, *Against Heresies* 5.33.3); (cf. 2Bar 29:5). **This is evidence that Jesus knew The Book of the Watchers.**

[367] **The progeny of the watchers were unclean because they are mixed beings. When the gospels speak of unclean spirits, they are referring back to the children of the watchers who were killed and have now become the demons that infest the earth.** See (1En 15:8).

[368] The original text reads sons, but it is intended of course, that women are included in mankind, so some translate children.

[369] N has: "peoples" in place of "nations."

[370] "And prostrate themselves (before) me" is found only in Ethiopic. All nations will be in submission to God.

[371] N1 has: "wrath or scourge," for 10:22. I has: "And the earth shall be cleansed from all pollution, and from all sin, and from all plague, and from all suffering; and it shall not happen again that I shall send (these) upon the earth from generation to generation forever."

never again send a Deluge upon it unto generations of generations and forever. Gen 8:21; 9:11

11 1 In those days I will open the storehouses of blessing that are in Ps 85:10-13; 90:17
heaven so that I may send them down upon the earth, over the work Deut 28:12; Mal 3:10
and labor of the sons of men. Isa 65:21-22
2 Then peace and truth will be united for all the days of eternity, and Isa 32:17
for all generations of humanity.[372]

Excursus: Evil spiritual beings from the wrong side of the tracks.

The Book of Enoch provides great insight into the understanding of evil spiritual forces. The variety of names for the "chief evil one" and the ways in which they are used are not always consistent across second temple and New Testament literature.

Satan/devil (Hebrew: Satan שָׂטָן) (Greek: Satan Σατανᾶς, ᾶ, ὁ)/(Greek: devil, diabolos διάβολος, ον) (adversary[373]; accuser) is the head evil entity, and leader of the rebellion against the kingdom of God in the New Testament. In the Old Testament, he is the one who accuses people against God in a prosecutorial role. Satan is a prominent figure in the *Book of Job* (600-300 BC) (Job 1:6-2:7) where he has access to the throne of God and serves in a prosecutorial role. The name is used in (1Chr 21:1) (written after 400 BC)[374] where he is introduced with no explanation, as an already known entity, who incites David to number Israel. In (Zech 3:1-2) (640-609 BC) Satan is also in a prosecutorial role. Satan is mentioned in an appeal to God in a "new" Psalm found at Qumran "let not Satan rule over me" (11QPs[a] vs 14). Many hundreds of years after these OT uses, the name Satan is again used in the Parables of Enoch. It is used in the plural twice (40:7 and 65:6) where it seems to be speaking of adversaries against humans. A key verse in understanding the role of Satan is (1En 54:6) where he is firmly identified as the chief evil spiritual being (cf. *Apol.* 22).

Then Michael, and Raphael, and Gabriel, and Phanuel—will take hold of them on that great day, and hurl them on that day into the burning furnace, that the Lord of Spirits may exact vengeance on them for their unrighteousness in becoming servants of Satan and leading astray those who dwell on the earth." 1En 54:6

This verse blames the enticement of the 200 watchers on Satan.[375] In the New Testament, Satan is the chief evil entity and takes a more prominent role than in the Old Testament. He tempted Christ, and Jesus equates Satan with the term Devil (Mt 4:1-11; Lk 4:1-13). Satan is also equated with the devil in Revelation (Rev 12:9; 20:2) and (TJob 3; 26:6; 27:1). He has a kingdom (Mt 12:26; Lk 11:18; Rev 2:13). He is the God of this world, and it lies in his power (Jn 12:31; 14:30;

---

[372] Some translators, based on a postulated abbreviation in G[a] have, "all the generations of eternity" or "all generations of men." Isaac has: "generations of the world."
[373] *Cels.* 5.94
[374] ESV pg. 697. A date late in the 4th century BC seems most plausible (The New Oxford Annotated Bible pg. 583).
[375] See the footnote on 1En 54:6 for more information. (cf. 2 Enoch 18:3)

16:11; Eph 2:2; 2Cor 4:4; 1Jn 5:19). He is the "evil one" (Mt 5:37; 6:13;[376] 13:19, 38; Jn 17:15; 2 Thes 3:3; Eph 6:16; 1Jn 2:13-14; 3:12; 5:18-19). He has the power of death (Heb 2:14). He is involved in deceiving and harming humans (Mt 13:18; Mk 4:15; Lk 8:12; 22:31; Acts 10:38; 26:18; 2Cor 2:11; 11:14; 2Thes 2:9; 1Tim 5:15; 2Tim 2:26; 1Pet 5:8; Rev 12:9, 12; 20:10). He causes physical afflictions (Lk 13:16). He can enter into people (Lk 22:3; Jn 13:27). He has his own people (Mt 13:38-39; 1Jn 3:8). He can test and hinder Christians (1Cor 7:5; 2Cor 12:7; Rev 2:10). He can be resisted by humans (Acts 26:18; Eph 4:27; 6:11; James 4:7). Christ delivers His followers from his domain (Col 1:13). Christ gives His followers power over Satan and his followers (Lk 10:19). He is a liar and murderer, and had a beginning (Jn 8:44; 1Jn 3:8; cf. 1QS 3.24-25). He is engaged in cosmic warfare against God (Heb 2:14; Rev 12:7-9). He will be defeated and punished by Christ (Lk 10:18; Jn 12:31; 16:11; Rom 16:20; Rev 2:9; 20:2, 10).

Azâzêl/Asael (Hebrew עֲזָאזֵל) is the first angel to fall (1En 86:1; N1 pg. 195) and a leader of ten fallen angels (1En 6:7; 69:2). He taught humans warfare, metallurgy, jewelry making, eye shadow and colored dyes. He is especially singled out for teaching wickedness, deceit, and revealing mysteries (1En 9:6; 13:2 ApAb 13:9; 14:4; 20:7; 31:5; 4Q180 1.7-8). He is bound in the desert, in darkness, in Dûdâêl (1En 10:4). He is confined to earth (ApAb 13:7-8; 14:5-6; 20:6). To him is ascribed all sin (1En 10:8; ApAb 13:14). He is singled out as the leader of the watcher rebellion (1En 86:1; 88:1; 4Q181 2.1-2). He is a leader of hosts (1En 55:4; ApAb 14:6). He has his people (ApAb 22:5; 23:10-14). He is the recipient of the sin born by the scape goat (Lev 16:8-26; 11Q19 26.3-13; Yoma 39a.6; *Cels*. 5.93). The righteous are protected from him (ApAb 13:9-14). Those who follow idols will putrefy in his "worm" belly and be burned by his tongue (ApAb 31:5). He is mentioned in the Book of Giants (4Q203 7a.6) and he is also mentioned as having his face turned toward darkness on an incantation bowl (M163) that also names Jesus. See notes on (1En 8:1; 10:4 and 10:8). Azazel worships Christ in (ApAb 29:6-7). If he is the Satan of (1En 54:5-6) then Azazel and Satan are synonymous, since Azazel is viewed as the first one who fell and the other angels were subject to him. According to the 2005 translation of (ApAb 31:5) by Alexander Kulik; Azazel is the "evil one" and thus equated with the chief evil entity. "And those who followed after the idols and after their murders will rot in the womb of the Evil One—the belly of Azazel, and they will be burned by the fire of Azazel's tongue" (ApAb 31:5). Origen (*Cels*. 6.43) equates Azazel with the serpent and ApAb 23:10-11 seems to place Azazel in Eden.

Beliar/Belial (Hebrew: beliyyaal, בְּלִיַּעַל) (Greek: Βελίαρ, ὁ) (without worth; worthless) This word (not as a name) is used extensively in the Old Testament; frequently as a descriptor for worthless people. The expression "son" or "man of Belial" means simply a worthless, lawless person (Jud 19:22; 20:13; 1Sam 1:16; 2:12). It is also used extensively in the Testament of the Twelve Patriarchs (137-63 BC) and in Jubilees (1:20) (161-140 BC) as a proper name. In the New Testament it is found only in (2Cor 6:15), where Paul used Belial as a name for Satan, the personification of all that is evil. Belial rules over men (Jub 1:20; CD 12.2) and brings charges against them (Jub 1:20). He was created for the pit (1QM 13.11). He makes men stumble (Jub 1:20; TReu 4:7; CD 4.13-18), but he can be resisted (TReu 4:11). He has his people (Jub 15:33;

[376] The Lord's prayer is better translated as many translations have it "deliver us from the evil one". (Mt 6:13) seems not to be referring to abstract evil, but to a person, hence the *masculine/neuter singular* adjective with the article.

1QS 2.4-5; 3.20-21 1QM 11. 8; $1QH_a$ 12.14-15; $1QH_a$ 15.6; 4Q177 Frags 12-13.1.16; 4Q434 1.1.12; TIss 6:1) and has a time and place of dominion (QS 1.18; 2.19; 1QM 13.4; 1QM 13:11; 4Q286 2.8; 5Q13 5). He is in charge of the hordes of angels who will fight in the final battle (1QM 1:5, 13-15; 11.8; 13.2; TDan 5:10-11; Rev 12:7-8). He is behind terror and persecution (1QS 1.17) and plans to destroy the righteous (4Q177 Frags 12-13.1.9; 11Q11 5.3). He will be defeated, bound and punished in the eternal pit of fire (4Q88 10.8; 4Q286+4Q287 2.1-6; TLev 18:12; TDan 25:3; $4QPs^f$ 10.10). He is the angel of the pit and the spirit of Abaddon[377] (4Q286+4Q287 2.7). He will not be forgiven (4Q286 2.10). The War Scroll describes him. "You yourself made Belial for the pit, and angel of malevolence, his [dominio]n is in darkne[ss] and his counsel is to condemn and convict. All the spirits of his lot, the angels of destruction, walk in accord with the rule of darkness, for it is their only [des]ire" (1QM 13.11-12). Belial and Satan are synonymous. Belial is the dominant name for the chief evil one in the DSS where the name is used at least 20 times.

Mastema (Hebrew: *Mastēmā*; מַשְׂטֵמָה; *śtm*) (Ge' ez መስቴማ) ("hatred," "hostility," "enmity," or "persecution") (Cf. Hos 9:7,8, ESV "hatred" derived from *śtm*). "The prince of malevolence" (4Q225 2.1.9 and 2.2.7) is especially the one who brings testing and trials on people in general and especially believers such as; Abraham, (4Q225 2.2; Jub 17:16; 18:9) Sons of Noah, (Jub 10:8, 13) Terah, (Jub 11:11-13) Moses, (Jub 48:2-3) and the Egyptians, (Jub 49:2) (he is presented as the destroying angel cf. Ex 12:23). He is over the angels of malevolence (4Q225 2.2.7; Jub 19:28). He is separate from Belial, and Belial receives advice from Mastemah (4Q225 2.2.14; 4Q226 7.6), but he seems to be called Satan in (Jub 10:11) and is equated with Satan in (ActsPhil 13). His angels' rule over people (4Q390 1.11; 2.1.7). He rules over demons and spirits (Jub 10:1-13; 11:5; 11Q11 2.4). He is an accuser (Jub 48:15,18). He is bound and released by angels, as needed, to serve the purposes of God (Jub 48:15-18).

Shemihazah (Hebrew: Samyaza שמחזי) (Greek: Σεμιαζά) ("the (or my) name has seen," "he sees the name," or "I have seen"). He is the chosen leader of the 200 watchers who rebel against God and choose human wives (1En 6:3; 4Q203 8.5). He taught humans spell casting and the cutting of roots (1En 8:3). He is the father of two giants in the Book of Giants.[378]

Beelzebub, also spelled Beelzebul or Belzebuth (Hebrew: *Ba ʿal-zəḇūḇ* בַּעַל-זְבוּב) ("Lord of the Flyers", or the "Lord of the Flies"). His name is derived from a Philistine god, formerly worshipped in Ekron. He is first mentioned in (2Kgs 1:2-16). The scribes and Pharisees accuse Jesus of driving out demons by the power of Beelzebul. (Mk 3:22; Mt 12:24,27; Lk 11:14,19; cf. Mk 10:25) but Jesus immediately changes the name in the discussion to Satan, which along with the devil, is His preferred appellation for the chief evil entity. The DSS, the religious literature of time of Jesus, by far, predominately used Belial as the name for the chief evil one. In fact, the editor knows of no use of the singular name Satan as the chief agent of evil anywhere in the Dead Sea Scrolls. The Pharisees did not seem to use it either; at least not in the gospels. Mastema is the preferred name in Jubilees. Jubilees does sometimes refer to Satan in the plural (Jub 23:29; 40:9; 46:2; and 50:5). But Jubilees does not use Satan as a title or name. Other than its Old Testament uses (1Chr 21:1; Job 1;6-2:7 and Zech 3:1-2) a title or name of Satan is very rare in Jewish literature prior to its dominant use in the New Testament. Suddenly after hundreds of

---

377 Cf. Rev 9:11.

378 See note 217.

years of non-use; Satan was used as a name in the *Parables of Enoch* (53:3; 54:6), where he is identified as the chief of the forces of evil. That Jesus and the early Christians used Satan or the devil predominantly, indicates they were getting the name possibly from the Old Testament but more likely from the recently composed *Parables of Enoch.* This indicates their high view of the Book of Enoch, since they use Satan in preference to the name Belial which was much more common in their literary world. To this day, the *Book of Enoch* has shaped Christianity's vocabulary in this regard.

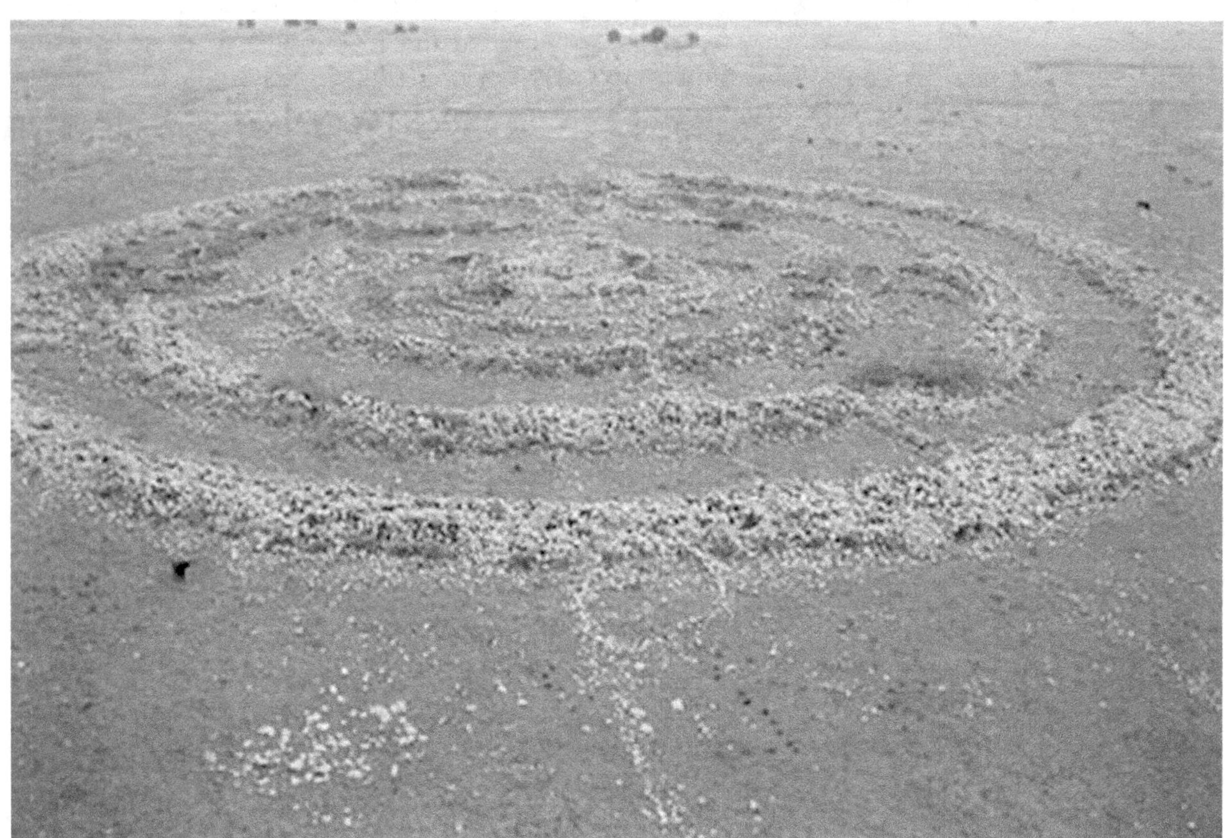

Gilgal Rafaim Author unknown licensed under CC BY-SA

Excursus: Galgal Rafaim

Some have drawn a connection between Galgal Rafaim (can be translated "circle of the giants") and the burial place for Azazel. "Throw on him sharp and jagged stones, and cover him with darkness and let him abide there for an exceedingly long time. Cover his face, and let him not see the light" (1En 10:5). Also "And he said to me: 'Those are being prepared for the hosts of Azazel, so that they may seize them and cast them into the lowest part of hell, and with jagged rocks they will cover their jaws, as the Lord of Spirits commanded'" (1En 54:5).

Ancient Galgal Rafaim, (modern name Rujm el-Hiri or Rujum Al-Hiri), dating from 3500 to 2700 BC is known as the "Stonehenge of the Levant." "Gilgal" roots back to "Galgal" meaning wheel; although the wheel shape is not apparent except from above. It is located in the area of ancient Bashan (Bathan "serpent" in ancient Canaanite)[379] not far from Mount Hermon which is in the present-day Golan Heights. This is the area of the kingdom of Og from the time of Moses.[380] Og was a remnant of the Rephaim; being of hybrid human/Nephilim ancestry. Ashtaroth and Edrei,[381] which are the closest cities in antiquity, mean "gateways to the underworld in Ugaritic texts."[382]

The massive stone circles are composed of 42,000 partially worked basalt stones which surround a central cairn. Some think an important burial lies beneath the cairn. Its shape is difficult to determine from ground level. The circles are surrounded by hundreds of mysterious stone Dolmens which are also found throughout the Levant. It was obviously a place of great importance in antiquity, given the immense effort expended in construction.[383]

Enoch is Sent to Pronounce Judgement on the Watchers

12 1 And before these things[384] Enoch was taken up, and none of the Sir 49:14; Gen 5:24 LXX
children of men[385] knew where he had been taken, or where he was Jub 4:21-23; Wis 4:10-15
or what had happened to him.[386] [387]
2 But his dealings were with the watchers, and his days were Heb 11:5; Sir 44:16
with the holy ones.[388] [389] Dan 4:13, 17, 23
3 I, Enoch, was standing, praising the Lord of majesty, the King of the

---

379 Heiser, Michael S., 2015. *The Unseen Realm*, pg. 200.
380 Deut 3:1-13.
381 These were Og's capital cities, (Joshua 12:4: 13:12).
382 Heiser, *Supernatural Seminar*, part 4, 20 min. mark.
383 It is estimated the construction of Galgal Rafaim required more than 25,000-man hours!
384 "Before these things" "These things can refer to the entire sequence of events beginning with the fall of the two hundred watchers (Ch 6-11), or, more specifically, to the divine commission to the archangels (Ch. 10), or even to the fulfilment of the prediction of the coming Deluge" (BL pg. 141). Charles takes this to mean Enoch was taken up before the angels interceded for mankind and God pronounced His judgement (C pg. 27).
385 Literally, "none of the sons of men." The LXX of Gen 5:24 has Enoch being "transferred" or "changed".
386 Jubilees explains that Enoch was with the angels of God for 6 jubilees of years, (294 years). "And he was moreover with the angels of God these six jubilees of years, and they showed him everything which is on earth and in the heavens, the rule of the sun, and he wrote everything down" (Jub 4:21).
387 Portions of the DSS containing very small portions of Chapter 12 include 4QEn[a] 1 vi; and 4QEn[c] 1 v.
388 (Gen 5:24) reads: Enoch walked with אֱלֹהִים Elohim, and he was not, for אֱלֹהִים Elohim took him. Hebrew would allow for the first "god" he walked with to be a group of watchers/angel(s). (Jubilees 4:23) would indicate that the second "god" could be a group of watcher/angels also. "And he was taken from among the children of men, and we conducted him into the Garden of Eden in majesty and honor and behold there he wrote down the condemnation and judgement of the world, and the wickedness of men." According to (Jubilees 4:23) it appears Enoch returned to "the children of men" before he was taken away for the last time. The pairing of "watchers" with "holy ones" is very similar to (Daniel 4:13, 17, 23) and the texts seem to be dependent on one another or a common tradition. Most likely Daniel is dependent on the Book of Watchers. Scholars are divided, but the theory that the Book of Daniel is dependent on the Book of Watchers is gaining ground (R pg. 207, Kvanvig).
389 These holy ones are the same celestial beings that 2Pet 2:10 and Jude 8 refer to as "glorious ones." Kvanvig writes: "As a whole, the relationship between Genesis and the Watcher story seems more complex than the idea that the Enochic scribes simply used Genesis as a source." (R pg. 203n, *The Son of Man in the Parables of Enoch*) **The evidence would indicate that The Book of the Watchers and Genesis 6:1-4 came from a common tradition.**

ages. And behold! Watchers of the Great Holy One called me and said:[390] [391] 15:1
TAb B 11:3-10
4 "Enoch! Scribe of righteousness! Go, declare to the watchers of *Haer.* 4.16.2
heaven who have abandoned the high heaven, and the holy eternal 4Q203 Frag. 8.1; 2Chr 6:20
sanctuary and have defiled themselves with women;[392] 7:1; 15:4; Rev 14:4; Jude 6
and have done as the sons of earth do, and have taken to themselves Gen 6:2
wives: (say) 'You have wrought great desolation on the earth; 9:2; Isa 26:21
5 and you shall have neither peace nor forgiveness![393] 5:4; 1QS 2.8; 2Pet 2:4
6 And inasmuch as they delight themselves in their sons,
the slaughter of their beloved ones they will see, 10:12; 14:6; 56:3-4
and they shall lament over the destruction of their sons Jub 5:10
and make perpetual supplication: but they shall have neither mercy
nor peace.'" 5:4-5

Excursus: Does the Book of the Watchers explain 1 Peter 3:18-4:6?

(1 Peter 3:18-22) has long been a subject of controversy. In the RSV it reads:

For Christ also suffered once for sins, the righteous for the unrighteous, that he might bring us to God, being put to death in the flesh but made alive in the spirit, in which he went and proclaimed to the spirits in prison, because they formerly did not obey, when God's patience waited in the days of Noah, while the ark was being prepared, in which a few, that is, eight persons, were brought safely through water. Baptism, which corresponds to this now saves you, not as a removal of dirt from the body but as an appeal to God for a good conscience, through the resurrection of Jesus Christ, who has gone to heaven and is at the right hand of God, with angels, authorities, and powers having been subjected to him (1Pet 3:18-22).

---

[390] Enoch also has scribal duties in 93:2. Enoch is described as a scribe, and a noted scribe, in the Book of Giants (4Q203 8:1 and 4Q530 2.2.14, 22). He is also a scribe of righteousness in (TAb B 11:3-10 (OTP1 pg. 900)). Other scribes, or references to presumed scribes of heaven, are found in (Ps 69:28; Isa 4:3; 65:6; Jer 17:13; Ezek 9:2; Dan 7:9-10, 10:21, 12:1 and Mal 3:16). "The idea of a celestial scribe is probably derived from Babylonian sources" (BL pg. 143). Heavenly records assume prominence in the Book of Revelation (17:8; 20:12, 15; 21:27). Other references to scribal activity in 1 Enoch are found in (14:1; 15:1; 39:1-2; 68:1; 72:1; 81:1-2; 83:2; 92:1; 93:1; 100:6; 103:1-4; 104:11-13; and 108: 1, 10).

[391] **"By 3300 BC, people were writing in both Egypt and Mesopotamia and made use of specific surfaces on which to express their ideas"** (Collins, Stephen, and Holden, Joseph M., 2001. *Harvest Handbook of Bible Lands*, Pg. 116). **Scholars are quite certain that the Book of Watchers was written in Aramaic; so, although it originated from prior traditions, it was not directly written in the time of biblical Enoch when Aramaic as a language did not exist.**

[392] This verse gives a clue to the identity of the 144,000 strong celestial army in Rev 14:1-4 who have not defiled themselves with women. The 144,000 would be those who are faithful to God, unlike the fallen angels who were unfaithful to God and did defile themselves with women. See n305.

[393] **Redemption and forgiveness are not available to the watchers but fortunately are richly available to humans.** "He is very patient and forgiving, covering the sin of those who repent of wrongdoing." (The Damascus Document Geniza A with 4Q267 Col. 2. 4-5 (W pg. 53). Repent and be baptized every one of you in the name of Jesus Christ for the forgiveness of your sins, and you will receive the gift of the Holy Spirit (Acts 2:38). And you, who were dead in your trespasses and the uncircumcision of your flesh, God made alive together with him, having forgiven us all our trespasses, by canceling the record of debt that stood against us with its legal demands (Col 2:13-14).

The traditional view is that Christ, either in a preincarnate state, or during his three days in the tomb, or soon after, preached to the humans in hell. It is even mentioned in the Apostles creed which places this decent during His time in the tomb.

> I believe in Jesus Christ, his only Son, our Lord,
> who was conceived by the Holy Spirit
> and born of the virgin Mary.
> He suffered under Pontius Pilate,
> was crucified, died, and was buried;
> he descended to hell.
> The third day he rose again from the dead.
> He ascended to heaven
> and is seated at the right hand of God the Father almighty.
> From there he will come to judge the living and the dead.

The Moffatt Bible[394] links Enoch's proclamations in the Book of Watchers (chapters 12-13) with I Peter 3:19. In that version of the bible it reads:

> Christ himself died for sins, once for all, a just man for unjust men, that he might bring us near to God; in the flesh he was put to death but he came to life in the spirit. (It was in the Spirit that Enoch also went and preached to the imprisoned spirits who had disobeyed at the time when God's patience held out during the construction of the ark in the days of Noah — the ark by which only a few souls, eight in all, were brought safely through the water.) 1 Peter 3:18-20.

Moffatt postulated[395] that the word Ἑνὼχ (Enoch) was dropped from the text due to a scribal blunder at an early point. Thus, 'in which also Enoch' (EN Ω KAI ENΩX) became simply 'in which also,' leaving a construction which makes *Christ* the one who went and made proclamation to the spirits in prison who had sinned before the Flood. In theory, such a blunder could have been either that of a copyist who skipped over the repeated letters or that of a scribe taking dictation who assumed the reader was hesitating and repeating part of what he had, uh, what he had just said. But even if the emendation is rejected—and it has no manuscript evidence—the passage still appears to be an allusion to the events of the *Book of Enoch*."[396]

---

394 The New Testament of the Moffatt Bible, the first English modern language bible, was translated by James Moffatt and first published in 1922. It was very popular in the 1930's.

395 Moffatt was not the first one to broach the possibility of a missing "Enoch" in the text. He cites work by Dr. Rendal Harris. In addition, Goodspeed's 1923 New Testament translation had a similar rendering. No other known translation has followed this lead, which is understandable, since no text of 1 Peter has been found with the name Enoch in the text. For the reasoning behind his translation concerning the dropping of the name Enoch from the text; (see *The Moffatt Commentary; the General Epistles Peter James and Judas* pg. 144-145). For those who also embraced this idea, (see B. Metzger, "Learned Printers and Biblical Scholarship," *Journal of Religion* 32 (1952) 256, 261-62).

396 OL pg. 44.

Moffatt's restoration thus has the text in 1 Peter referring to this account of Enoch proclaiming to the "spirits in prison."[397] While unidentified in any ancient text of 1 Peter, this assumption makes sense and greatly clarifies the passage. Given the abundant scribal slips know to be in New Testament texts;[398] this conjecture is entirely plausible. However, the textual alteration would have had to precede Irenæus (ca. AD 130-200) who references the text as we have it, combined with Eph 4:9 (*Haer.* 4.27.2).

That Peter knew Enoch is shown by his reference to 1En 1:2 in 1Pet 1:12. A key to the passage is the identities of the "spirits in prison"[399] and "those who are dead." The identities in 1 Peter 3-4 match the Book of Watchers tradition. The "spirits in prison" (1Pet 3:19) = fallen watchers (1En 10:4-8; 18:14-16) and "Those who are dead" (1 Peter 4:6) = children of the watchers (1 En. 15:8-16:1, Jub 10:1-11). Peter speaks of their present state in his time, rather than their state in the time of Enoch's preaching (1En 12:4-14:7). (1 Peter 4:6) is also linked to the watcher tradition, since it is theme-wise revisiting (1 Peter 3:19). But here Peter switches to the children of the watchers "those who are dead" who "were judged in the flesh the way people are" (see Ps 82:6-7 for a group of God's divine council judged like people). That they are not human is obvious when he says, "the way people are." If they were people, that statement would be unnecessary. The children of the watchers, especially the Rephaim, were all killed and are notorious for inhabiting the realm of the dead. (Ps 88:10; Prov 2:16-18; Isa 26:14). The progeny of the watchers hoped to be forgiven (they weren't) and hoped they "might live in the spirit the way God does." If this view is correct, then Peter is using Enoch's effort of preaching to the imprisoned fallen watchers, and their progeny by default, as a type of Christ appealing to those who are still living in sin that they might "live in the spirit." Enoch is thus held up by Peter as an example of preaching to the lost. If Enoch was willing to preach to the worst; the fallen watchers and their giant/demon offspring, then Christians should do no less.

Enoch Announces God's Judgement to the Watchers

13 1 So, Enoch, went to Asael and declared: "You shall have no 5:4; 10:4; Isa 57:21
peace:[400]a severe sentence has been issued against you, to bind you. Rev 6:4; Jub 4:22
2 You will have neither clemency or mercy, nor request granted to you, 2Pet 2:4
because of the wrongs you have revealed, and all the deeds of 8:1-2

---

[397] But consider the early creedal hymn in (1Tim 3:16); "He was manifested in the flesh, vindicated in the spirit, seen by angels, preached among the nations, believed on in the world, taken up in glory." "Seen by angels" could have other meanings and is far from proclaimed to fallen watchers in prison. This doctrine most likely sprang from a scripture removed from Jeremiah by the Jews in the early 2nd century which read: "The holy Lord remembered His dead Israel, who slept in the land of sepulture; and He descended to them to make known to them His salvation, that they might be saved." (See Haer. 3.20.4; 4.22.1; 4.33.12; 5.31.1; Epid. 78a and *DialTrypho* 72). This may also be the source for a similar passage in OdesSol 42:10-20.

[398] Bruce, F. F. 1943. revised 1997. *The New Testament Documents; Are They Reliable* pg. 19. This by no means indicates that the New Testament is unreliable. The thousands of copies available and abundant quotes by church fathers have allowed scholars to correct textual issues and produce a very accurate New Testament text for our use. See also Haer. 5.30.1.

[399] In the Old Testament, spirits were always non-human celestial beings. The use of the word "spirits" in (1Pet 3:19) is the only use in 1 or 2 Peter. In Mark, which was influenced by Peter (*HE* 6.14), every use of the word spirits in plural refers to non-human beings.

[400] "No peace," i.e. no rest for eternity.

godlessness, injustice, and sin which you have shown to the children of 9:6; 4Q180 1.7-8
men."[401]
3 Then I went and spoke to them all together, and they were afraid, 1:5
and fear and trembling gripped them.[402] Jas 2:19
4 And they asked me to write for them a memorandum of petition
that they might obtain forgiveness,[403] and that I should recite their DialTrypho 141
memorandum of petition before the Lord of heaven.[404] Acts 10:4
5 For they were unable any longer to speak or even lift up their eyes Isa 59:2; Ezra 9:6
to heaven out of shame for the sins for which they had been Lk 18:13; Leg. 25:1
condemned.[405]
6 Then I wrote out the memorandum of petition,[406] and their requests, *Haer.* 4.16.2
with reference to their spirits and their deeds individually,[407] and
regarding their requests that they might obtain forgiveness and
tolerance.[408] [409]
7 And I went off and sat down by the waters of Dan,[410] Josh 19:47
in the land of Dan,[411] which is south-west of Hermon; Gen 14:14; Mt 16:13-20

---

[401] "This is a clear reference to what the Watchers taught humankind and its subsequent result, the acceleration and proliferation of depravity." "This is the more enduring catastrophe in the Second Temple Jewish mindset with respect to pre-flood transgressions of the boundary between heaven and earth. The Nephilim giants are only the immediate threat" (H1 pg. 121).

[402] **These powerful spiritual beings are in extreme fear of judgement by Holy God. "Even the demons believe—and shudder!"** (James 2:19)

[403] Unlike humans, the Watchers know better than to try to hide their sin, make excuses, or deceive God.

[404] It is interesting that Enoch becomes an intercessor for the fallen watchers since he can appeal to God and they can't. We should not underestimate the power of the prayer of a righteous person. (Jas 5:16-18). Enoch is also an intercessor in (Jub 4:24-25).

[405] Sin separates from God. They were no longer able to approach God.

[406] That Enoch was a writer is prominent in (Jub 4:17-19, 23). "The repetition of the verb *sahafa* ("to write") and the noun *mashaf* ("book, writing") in vv 17-23 indicates that the traditions associated with Enoch are thought of as written traditions—the compositions of Enoch 'the scribe'" (N1 pg. 73). Enoch's role as a writer is also prominent in the later works of (2 Enoch A 36:2-3 and TAb Recension B 11:3-10).

[407] The watchers, like humans, are judged individually not collectively.

[408] Fragments of 13:6 to 14:8 have been found in the DSS, (4Q204 1.6 or 4QEn^c 1 v).

[409] For 13:6, Nickelsburg very plausibly has "Then I wrote out the memorandum of their petition, and the requests concerning themselves, with regard to their deeds individually, and concerning <their sons> for whom they were making request, that they might have forgiveness and longevity." Nickelsburg's construction introduces a concern on the part of the watchers of seeking forgiveness for their sons (cf. 1En 12:6; 14:6).

[410]This spot is well known. It is modern day Banias (Caesarea Philippi). "'The waters of Dan' are the stream that rises near and on Tel Dan and forms one of the headwaters of the Jordan River. The location of the stream given in the text is precise: Dan is just south of the western slope of Mount Hermon" (N1 pg. 247). "Caesarea Philippi had an ancient reputation for being a place where revelations took place, and both Peter's confession and the Enochic revelations are associated with Caesarea Philippi as well" (R pg. 318, Walck). Josephus mentions that Herod built a temple in this location (*Ant* 15.10.3 §§363-364); the remains of which can be seen today. The commissioning of Levi in the *Testament of Levi* occurs in this area also; Abel-Main is near Tel Dan (TLev 2:3) (N1 pg. 246). Other prophetic visions that occur near rivers may be found in (Ezek 1:1, and Dan 10:4). The waters of Dan locality is named as Baal-gad, "troop or city of Baal," in Joshua (11:17, 12:7; 13:5). It was a place where Baal was worshipped as the giver of "good luck" (cf. Isa 65:11). It was probably the same as Baal-hermon (Jud 3:3; 1Chr 5:23).

[411] **The mention of the region of Dan here, may indicate that the Book of the Watchers was written after the events of Judges 18 or was at least edited afterward.** Since Dan in the north did not exist prior to the period of the judges, the use of Dan similarly dates an interpolation in Genesis. "The town of Laish in northern Canaan was

and I was reading the memorandum of their requests until I fell asleep.
8 And behold! Dreams came to me, and visions fell upon me,
until I lifted up my eyes to the gates of heaven, and I saw visions of
wrath, and a voice came, saying: "Speak to the sons of heaven[412] to 6:2
rebuke them."
9 Then I woke up and went to them; and they were all seated,
assembled together, and mourning, in Abel-maim,[413] which is between TLev 2:3-5
Lebanon[414] and Senir,[415] with their faces covered. Deut 3:9; Song 4:8; 2Chr 16:4
10 And I recounted before them all the visions I had seen in my sleep;
and I began to speak words of truth, and the vision, and to reprimand the 1Cor 6:3
celestial watchers.[416]

Excursus: What is the *Book of Giants*? Another Enochic text.
The Book of Giants is known through both Manichean and Qumran fragments.

> Besides fragments of the previously known 1 Enoch, fragments of another Enoch story, the *Book of Giants* was known through "scattered allusions and fragmentary Asian manuscripts of a version known and used by the adherents of the Manichean heresy of the third and fourth centuries C.E.[417] The seven fragmentary Qumran scrolls of Giants show the composition is at least five hundred years older than previously thought.[418]

The very fragmented texts from Qumran have been pieced together, more or less.[419] While Enoch is mentioned twice in the work as a scribe; *The Book of Giants* focuses much more on the

---

renamed 'Dan' in the period of the Judges (Judg. 18:29). The use of the name 'Dan' here indicates that this account was edited sometime later" (Note on Genesis 14:13-16 in ESV). **However, since Dan means "judge" the possibility exists that the Gen 14:14 reference to Dan may be a place name memorializing the place where the fallen watchers were judged.**

412 Cf. Gen 6:2 "sons of God."

413 **Abel-Main is a known location in upper Galilee**, based on a parallel with TLev 2:3-5, Abel-Main (water meadow) is the name that Abel-Beth-Maacah was known by in the Persian period. It is mentioned in (2Sam 20:14; 1 Kings 15:20; 2Chr 16:4 and TLev 2:3). It is about "7 kilometers west-northwest of the "waters of Dan," at the mouth of the valley between the Lebanon range to the west and Mount Hermon" (N1 pg.250). It is currently known as Tel Abil. **This geographical region was known for the worship of Pan, a demigod, who like the watchers, was also infamous in his sexual desire for human women.**

414 **Neither Dan nor Lebanon would have been place names in the time of a preflood Enoch.**

415 Senir is the Amorite name for a peak near Mt. Hermon (Deut. 3:9; 1Chr 5:23; Ps 29:6; Ezek 27:5; Song 4:8). Senir was at least symbolically the home of Solomon's bride. "Come with me from Lebanon, my bride; come with me from Lebanon. Depart from the peak of Amana, from the peak of Senir and Hermon, from the dens of lions, from the mountains of leopards" (Song of Solomon 4:8). **Each of the three peaks of Mount Hermon had a name (Amana, Semir and Hermon). Solomon is calling his bride (a type of the Church) to leave the place of evil and come to Mount Zion, God's Mountain. (Cf. Ps 68:15-16). This shows that even in the time of Solomon, Hermon had a reputation as an abode of evil.** The symbolism is obvious, it is unlikely Solomon's bride worked at a ski resort on Mount Hermon. The area was thinly populated in his time.

416 **"Most scholars see this as a solemn assembly, not some casual follow-up encounter"** (H1 pg. 126). **This scene is a formal sentencing, similar to a courtroom. Paul may have had this verse in mind when writing (1Cor 6:3); "Do you not know that we are to judge angels."**

417 There is no doubt that the Book of Giants found among the DSS is the literary ancestor of the Manichean version. (Reeves, John C. 1992. *Jewish lore in Manichaean cosmogony: studies in the Book of Giants traditions*, pg. 31).

418 W pg. 290.

419 Qumran texts of the *Book of Giants* numbered ten and include (4Q203; 4Q530-532; 6Q8, 1Q23 and 2Q26).

giants themselves than does the Book of Watchers. They retell part of the Book of Watchers story and then elaborate on the exploits of Shemihaza's twin sons Ohya and Hahya. They name Enoch, Mahway, Azazel, and notably Gilgamesh, who is also known from the Epic of Gilgamesh.

Excursus: King David knew and believed in the fallen watcher tradition.

David and his soldiers killed lots of giants.

> There was war again between the Philistines and Israel, and David went down together with his servants, and they fought against the Philistines. And David grew weary. And Ishbi-benob, one of the descendants of the giants, whose spear weighed three hundred shekels[420] of bronze, and who was armed with a new sword, thought to kill David. But Abishai the son of Zeruiah came to his aid and attacked the Philistine and killed him. Then David's men swore to him, "You shall no longer go out with us to battle, lest you quench the lamp of Israel."
>
> After this there was again war with the Philistines at Gob. Then Sibbecai the Hushathite struck down Saph, who was one of the descendants of the giants. And there was again war with the Philistines at Gob, and Elhanan the son of Jaare-oregim, the Bethlehemite, struck down Goliath the Gittite, the shaft of whose spear was like a weaver's beam. And there was again war at Gath, where there was a man of great stature, who had six fingers on each hand, and six toes on each foot, twenty-four in number, and he also was descended from the giants. And when he taunted Israel, Jonathan the son of Shimei, David's brother, struck him down. These four were descended from the giants in Gath, and they fell by the hand of David and by the hand of his servants (2Sam 21:15-22).

Giants were not a myth to David, but a frightening real-life threat. David and his men were continuing the war on the giants begun by Moses (Deut 3:1-11). The Old Testament assumes knowledge of the existence of giants and of their origin.[421] Do we have evidence of where David thought these beings came from? Did he know the watcher tradition? The psalms from the time of David are full of supernatural imagery. We have the "strong bulls of Bashan" (Pss 22:12-13) who are viewed by Christians as demonic beings who would surround the cross of Christ. They are from Bashan; an area known as a center for Rephaim and evil spiritual activity. In (Pss 68:15-23) the many peaked mountain of Bashan (Hermon), the dwelling of the "gods" looks with hatred on the mountain of God. In (Psalm 82) God is dressing down members of his divine council of "gods" for judging unjustly and showing partiality to the wicked. This shows a belief in high spiritual beings, as does (Pss 89:5-7) where the divine council is mentioned again. The departed, Sheol dwelling, ex giants, the Rephaim (רְפָאִים, rə·pā·'îm) are mentioned in (Ps 88:10). These passages by themselves manifest a belief in high spiritual beings ("gods") and departed giants dwelling in Sheol. But overlooked (Pss 21:7-12) contains the key points of the watcher tradition.

---

[420] One shekel was 2/5 oz so the spear weighed 7 lbs., 4 oz or 3.3 kilos.

[421] Gen 6:4, for instance, presumes that the reader knows who the sons of God and the Nephilim are, since no explanation is provided.

> 7 For the king trusts in the LORD,
> and through the steadfast love of the Most High he shall not be moved.
> 8 Your hand will find out all your enemies;
> your right hand will find out those who hate you.
> 9 You will make them as a blazing oven
> when you appear.
> The LORD will swallow them up in his wrath,
> and fire will consume them.
> 10 You will destroy their descendants from the earth,
> and their offspring from among the children of man.
> 11 Though they plan evil against you,
> though they devise mischief, they will not succeed.
> 12 For you will put them to flight;
> you will aim at their faces with your bows.

(Ps 21:8) makes it plain that it is speaking of the enemies of God; who hate Him. This text parallels (Ps 68:16) where the mountain of Bashan looks with hatred on the mountain of God. God is not threatened by human enemies. These enemies of God (the rebellious angels/watchers) are from the spiritual realm. In (Ps 21:9) these spiritual enemies will be swallowed up in wrath, and fire will consume them.[422] Strangely, however, these spiritual enemies have descendants (the giants) on the earth among the children of men (vs. 10). These are the offspring, literally fruit (פִּרְיָמוֹ, pir-yā-mōw) of the spiritual enemies of God. This shows they are offspring through sexual relations. These crossbreed offspring must be destroyed from among the children of men. But until they are destroyed "they plan evil against God and devise mischief." Unfortunately, even after they are killed, The Book of the Watchers says the spirits of the giants continue with the same type of activity seen in (Ps 21:11).

> The spirits of the giants, the Nephilim, <lead astray>, do violence, and make desolate. They attack, they wrestle and dash to the ground, and cause illness. They eat nothing, but abstain from food but nevertheless hunger and thirst and cause illness. These spirits will rise up against the sons of men, and against the women, because they have proceeded from them" (1En 15:11-12).

In David's time, he and his soldiers were occupied with killing physical giants whose spirits then became demons.[423] (Ps 21:12) even describes their tactics for killing giants. Like David with his sling; rather than suffering in hand-to-hand conflict with a stronger foe; distance weapons were used. They evidently directed arrows at the face of the giants where armor did not protect them.

Those who disagree with this interpretation need to come up with an alternative. Who are these enemies? Are humans really a threat to God? Who are their offspring that must be destroyed from among the children of men? If they are human enemies, wouldn't it be obvious that their descendants are among the "children of men."

---

[422] This is one of the rare mentions of a fiery hell in the Old Testament. It is interesting that it seems to be applied to the rebellious enemies of God as in the Enochic tradition.
[423] Cf. 1En 15:8-9.

David, the presumed writer of Psalm 21, affirms, and in fact, assumes that his readers know, the main aspects of the watcher tradition. This pushes back the origin of the watcher tradition to long before the composition of the Book of the Watchers. Since the goat ritual in Leviticus 16:4-10 assumes a foreknowledge of an Azazel figure; and Genesis 6:1-4 assumes the reader knows the Book of the Watcher backstory of the rebellious angels; the tradition must predate these portions of the Pentateuch! The report of the spies in (Numbers 13:31-33) also assumes the participants and readers have knowledge of the watcher backstory. "The land, through which we have gone to spy it out, is a land that devours its inhabitants (cannibalism?) and all the people that we saw in it are of great height. And there we saw the Nephilim (the sons of Anak, who come from the Nephilim), and we seemed to ourselves like grasshoppers, and so we seemed to them" (Num 13:32-33). Undoubtedly, the watcher tradition substantially predates David, Joshua and Moses, going back to very ancient times! This would easily place the tradition before the Greek writings of the Iliad (8th-7th centuries BC) and the Theogony of Hesiod (750-650 BC) which give us the heroes of Greek mythology.

---

14 1 The Book of The Words of Truth; the reprimand of the eternal 13:8; 39:2
watchers who were from of old, in accordance with the command of
the Great Holy One in the dream which I saw.[424] [425]
2 I saw in my dream what I now speak with a tongue of flesh, 1Cor 13:1; Isa 50:4
and with the breath of my mouth, which the Great One has given to men; 84:1
that they might speak and understand with their hearts.
3 As he has created and destined the children of men to understand 4Ezra 4:22
words of insight; so, he has created and destined me to reprimand 1Cor 6:3; 12:8
the watchers, the sons of heaven.[426] 6:2; Jude 8
4 Watchers, I wrote down your petition, but in a vision, it was revealed
to me; thus, that your petition will not be granted to you for all the days
of eternity, and the sentence will be made final upon you, by decree. Dan 4:17, 24
5 From now on you shall no longer ascend to heaven throughout all the 45:2; *Leg.* 25; *Idol.* 9
ages,[427] and it has been ordered to bind you in bonds inside the earth 10:12; 18:16; 2Pet 2:4; Lam 3:34
for all the days of eternity.[428] Jude 6-7
6 And before these things, you shall see the destruction of your
beloved sons and all their sons, and the possessions of your beloved ones.
You will have no pleasure in them; and they will fall before you by 10:9; 12:6

---

[424] Here begins God's answer through Enoch to the petition from the watchers.

[425] Portions of chapter 14 are found in the DSS (4Q204 1.6.9-29; 4QEn^{b} 1 vi; 4QEn^{c} 1 vi; 4QEn^{c} 1 vii).

[426] **If God judges angels, then certainly man will be judged. This may be a source for Paul's teaching that "Do you not know that we are to judge angels?"** (1Cor 6:3). Note the cluster of other parallels with 1 Corinthians in (1En 14:2-3). Tongue of flesh-tongues of men and of angels (1Cor 13:1); understand words of insight-utterance of wisdom, utterance of knowledge (1Cor 12:8).

[427] The fallen watchers are banned from heaven for eternity.

[428] Suter and Nickelsburg think "the myths in chaps. 6-11 and the "commentary" on them in chaps. 12-16 are concerned primarily with the purity of priestly families, and the sin of the watchers is a paradigm of sinful priestly mixed marriages and sexual misconduct, which are also opposed in the Testament of Levi and the Damascus Document." (N1 pg. 119) If this is so, it is a repurposing of an existing tradition, since the watcher tradition clearly preexisted the second temple period.

the sword.[429]
7 Accordingly, you will not obtain your petition on their behalf,
nor for yourselves; for all your petitioning and pleading, not a single
word will be implemented from the document which I have written.[430]

Enoch Visits the Throne Room of God

8 The vision was shown to me as follows: Behold! Clouds were calling Matt 17:5; Dan 7:13; Ex 19:9 Ex 33:9-10; 34:5; Lev 16:2 Deut 4:11-12; 1Kgs 8:12
me in my vision, and thick clouds were crying out to me;[431] shooting Pss 18:7-13; 97:2-5; 104:1-4
stars[432] and lightning flashes were hastening me on and driving me, Ezek 10:4; Ex 24:16; Deut 5:22
and winds, in my vision, made me fly up, and lifted me upward and 39:3; 70:2; 2Cor 12:2; Acts 2:2
brought me to heaven.[433]
9 And entering, I drew near to a wall,[434] built of hailstones,[435] 71:5-6; Ezek 40:5
with tongues of fire[436] surrounding it on all sides; and it began to 60:3; Acts 2:3; Dan 7:9
terrify me.
10 I entered into the tongues of fire and drew near to a large house Ps 18:10-13; *ActsPer* 12
built of hailstones;[437] and the walls of the house were like stone slabs,[438] Isa 30:30; Ex 24:10
all of snow, and the floor was of snow.
11 Its ceiling was like shooting stars[439] and lightning flashes, Ezek 1:4-28; Rev 4:5-6

---

[429] The text of 14:6 is quite problematic. Black is most representative of an alternate translation "and that before these things you shall see the destruction of your beloved ones, and of all their sons and their flocks; and that you will have no heirs to them; and they will fall before you by the sword in total destruction." The mention of possessions is supported by Milik's translation of (4QEn^{c} 1 vi). Nickelsburg has "And that before these things, you will see the destruction of your sons, your beloved ones, and that you will have no pleasure in them, but they will fall before you by the sword."

[430] Nickelsburg contributes: "The text of this verse is problematic and perhaps missing a line" (N pg. 34).

[431] Kvanvig sees the clouds in this verse as inspiration for a later Daniel 7:13 (R pg. 207-208). Collins acknowledges the possibility but proposes that they draw on a common tradition (R pg. 218). Nickelsburg maintains that Daniel's heavenly throne room vision as based on 1 Enoch 14 (N1 pgs. 77 and 254). Nickelsburg includes a table of the many similarities in the throne room visits described in (Isa 6; Ezek 1-2; Enoch 14-16; and Daniel 7) (N1 pg. 255-256).

[432] "Shooting stars" is also variously translated as "thunders," "path of stars," "meteors," or "fire-balls."

[433] Other visions of the throne room or heavenly presence of God include: (Ex 19:16, Ps 18:6-15; 97:1-6; 104:1-4, Isa 6:1-6; Ezek 1:4-3:15; Dan 7:9-10; 1En 39:3-41:2; 71:1-17; Rev 4-6).

[434] This protective outer wall surrounds a structure viewed by some scholars as a heavenly temple with the watchers as priests and by other scholars as a royal court with courtiers similar to ancient near eastern and Hellenistic kingdoms. Esler sees similarities with the Persian palace precinct at Pasargadae. (Esler, Philip F. 2017. *God's Court and Courtiers in the Book of the Watchers: Re-Interpreting Heaven in 1 Enoch 1-36)*

[435] N has: "hailstones", I has: "white marble", B has "stones of crystal".

[436] The tongues of fire and rushing wind that carried Enoch to the throne of God, accompany the Holy Spirit to earth on the day of Pentecost (Acts 2:1-4).

[437] This forecourt protects the throne room of God, or more accurately protects those approaching the throne room of God. Sacchi speculates that the author reached ecstasy through opposite extreme physical sensations of heat and cold (E pg. 402).

[438] The word "stone slabs" is used only here. It's meaning is uncertain. Various translators have "like a tessellated (checkered) floor", "flagstones", "paving stones", "mosaics of marble", and "mosaic made of hailstones". It is interesting to note that the elders of Israel saw a pavement of sapphire under the feet of God on Mount Sinai (Ex 24:9-10).

[439] N and OL have: "shooting stars," C and K have "path of the stars," B has "stars violently agitated".

and amid them (were) fiery Cherubim,[440] 17:1; 20:7; 61:10; 71:7
and their heaven was like water.[441] [442] Ps 148:4; TLev 2:7; Ezek 10:5
12 A flaming fire encircled all its walls, and its doors blazed with fire. Zech 2:5; Rev 15:2
13 I went into that house. It was hot as fire and cold as snow;[443]
and there was no delight of life in it;[444] horror overwhelmed me,
and trembling took hold of me.
14 And shaking and trembling, I fell on my face. Ezek 1:28
And I saw in a vision,[445]
15 and behold! Another house,[446] greater than the first one, TLev 2:8
and its door was completely opened opposite me, Rev 4:1
and it was entirely constructed with tongues of fire.[447] Ezek 28:14, 16
16 In every respect it so excelled in glory and splendor and majesty that
I am unable to describe to you its glory and grandeur.
17 And its floor was of fire, and its upper chambers were lightning- Ex 24:10
flashes and the path of stars, and its ceiling was of blazing fire.[448]
18 I looked inside[449] and saw a lofty throne; and its appearance was TLev 5:1; Isa 6:1; *TMos* 4:2
like crystals of ice and the wheels[450] thereof were like the shining sun, 1Kgs 22:19; Dan 7:9
and the sound of cherubim.[451] Ezek 1:15-26; 3:13; 10:5
19 And from underneath the throne issued rivers of blazing fire, Ezek 47:1; Rev 22:1
and I was unable to look on it. Ezek 1:28

---

440 Cherubim are four-winged, four-faced angelic beings who guard the Garden of Eden (Gen 3:24; Ex 25:19). They are close attendants of God (Ezek 10:1-22).

441 "Like water" placid and blue. Charles has "clear as water." Compare (Ezek 1:22): "Over the heads of the living creatures there was the likeness of an expanse, shining like awe-inspiring crystal, spread out above their heads." See also (Ezek 10:1) (cf. Gen 1:7). Olson sees "Their heaven was like water" as a possible early anti-Aristotelian gloss.

442 "These waters are thematically important in Enoch since the flood results from unleashing them. The association of these waters with judgement may be one reason why in the time of the new heavens and new earth, there will be 'no longer any sea' (Rev 21:1)" (OL pg. 44) (cf. 1En 89:2).

443 A very unusual place, fire and ice don't normally mix. But "fire ice", or methane clathrate is a known icy substance which burns.

444 B has: "No trace of joy or of life was there;" I has simply: "there was nothing inside it."

445 This was a fearful experience, not a visit to paradise!

446 The heavenly Holy of Holies. The throne room of God. The earthly temple, in comparison, was only a poor imitation of the heavenly throne room (Ex 25:9). That God has a palace or temple in heaven is commonly found in the Old Testament (2Sam. 22:7, Ps. 11:4; 18.6; 29.9; Isa 6:1; 63:15; Mic. 1:2; Hab. 2:20).

447 The fallen being, described in Ezekiel's lament over the King of Tyre, was an "anointed guardian cherub" on the holy mountain of God, and walked in the "midst of the stones of fire" (Ezek 28:14-16).

448 This heavenly throne room may sound bizarre, but it has been reported in a great many near death experiences. Randy Kay's experience is representative. "Indeed, the 'city' I viewed in Heaven sparkled like a cut diamond with abodes of various heights and magnificently adorned designs unlike any architectural elements I have witnessed on earth. In the center I saw angels standing around a court surrounded by a floor made of deep blue stones that gave forth what appeared to be a blue flame through which the angels walked; and before the angels rested a glorious figure whom I knew was God the Father, whose white hair and robe flowed elegantly through the wind. I still recall the ethereal wonder of Heaven and the consuming love of Christ as if it is still happening" (Kay, Randy, 2021. *Revelations from Heaven*, Destiny Image Publishers, Inc. pg. 55).

449 Enoch did not enter this "house" which is symbolized by the earthly Holy of Holies.

450 "Wheels" (cf. Ezek 1:15-21; and 10:9). This scene of wheels and flames/crystals appears to be depicted on the rear panel of the Magdala stone found in the pre-70 synagogue excavation at Magdal (Tarichaeae), an important city in Galilee in the time of Christ. This may indicate use of the Book of Watchers in that location (P. pgs. 159-169).

451 N has: "voice (or sound)", I and B have: "voice", OL "has sound". OL adds "Cherubim are quite noisy in Ezekiel" (OL pg. 46).

20 The Great Glory sat upon it,[452] and his robe was brighter than — 102:3; 2Pet 1:17; TLev 3:4
the sun, and whiter than any snow.[453] — Dan 7:9-10; Matt 17:2
21 No angel was able to enter this house, or to look on his face, — Ps 104:1-4; Ex 33:20
because of its splendor and glory; and no human[454] was able to look — 1Tim 6:16; Jn 1:18; 1Jn 4:12
on him.[455]
22 Blazing fire[456] encircled him, and a great fire stood in front of him, — 40:1, 60:1; Ps 97:3-4
so that none who surrounded him could draw near to him; — 1:9; 71:8-13; Dan 7:10; Rev 5:11
ten thousand times ten thousand stood before him, — 2En 33:4; Sir 42:21; Rom 11:34 *Haer.* 2.7.4; 4Q530 2.2.16-19;

how

but he had no need of counsel; in his every word was a deed.[457] — Sir 42:15; Ps 33:11; Isa 40:13-14 1Cor 2:16

23 And the watchers and holy ones who approached him — 22:6; 93:2
did not turn away from him, by night or by day, — Rev 4:8; 7:15; Lk 2:37
nor do they depart from him.[458] [459] — 39:12
24 As for me, till then I had been prostrated on my face, trembling. — Dan 10:8-10
And the Lord called me with his own mouth and said to me:
"Come here, Enoch, and hear my word." — 91:1
25 Then one of the holy angels came to me and he raised me up and — Dan 8:17-18; 10:8-15
stood me (on my feet) and brought me to the door and I bowed
my face low. — 39:14

God Addresses the Fallen Watchers

15 1 He spoke and said to me: I heard his voice: "Fear not, Enoch, — *Abr.* 17; Rev 4:1
righteous man and scribe of truth![460] Come here and hearken to my voice. — Jub 10:17; Heb 11:5; Sir 44:16

---

[452] "Great Glory." This unusual name for God is also found in 102:3 and in 9:3. It is paralleled in (2 Peter 1:17) and it is also found in (TLev 3:4).

[453] Kvanvig, holding to a late date for Daniel, asserts that Daniel 7 was patterned on 1 Enoch 14. "This concerns above all the throne imagery in Dan 7:9-10." **"It appears that the scribe of Daniel 7 borrowed the language from 1 Enoch 14-15 to create a transcendent scene for the enthronement of his eschatological figure, the son of Man."** (R pg. 207-208) Black opines: **"How are these passages related? Are we to explain Enoch as an expanded Deut 5:22 description based on Daniel or is the account in Daniel an abridged adaptation, in a new composition, of the fuller descriptive imagery in Enoch? Their literary interrelationship cannot be denied"** (BL pg. 150).

[454] "Human" literally "creature of flesh."

[455] Even angels cannot behold Holy God. Nickelsburg observes: "**Thus through his imagery the author is describing a God who is totally transcendent, overpowering in his glory, unapproachable to humans and most angels,**" (N1 pg. 265).

[456] K has: "a sea of fire burnt around him"

[457] Gk omits: "but he had no need of council" but includes: "in his every word was a deed." Ethiopic, in contrast, includes: "but he had no need of council" but excludes: "in his every word was a deed."

[458] This may be the origin of the name watcher as "one who is awake". (N1 pg. 266) (See 39:12)

[459] Olson, speaking of (14:18-23), contributes: "**This passage is so similar to Daniel 7:9-10 that some kind of connection seems undeniable. Now that the 'Book of the Watchers' is known to be much older than previously thought, many scholars believe that Daniel borrowed from *Enoch* rather than vice versa. The whole argument obviously depends on one's dating of the two books, and conservative scholars continue to maintain a pre-Maccabean date for Daniel, but since no one really knows how old this portion of *Enoch* is, even an early date for Daniel does not necessarily prove its priority**" (OL pg. 46).

[460] Some translators have: "scribe of righteousness."

2 Go and declare to the watchers of heaven, who have sent you to *Haer.* 4.16.2
intercede on their behalf: it is you who should be petitioning on 13:4-5; 39:5; 40:6; 47:1-2
behalf of men,[461] and not men on behalf of you! Rev 8:3-4
3 Why have you left the high heaven, the eternal sanctuary; and Isa 33:5; Sir 24:4; Gen 6:2
lain with women? And defiled yourselves with the daughters of men, 10:11; Lev 15:16-18; Jude 6
and taken wives for yourselves, and acted like the sons of earth Rev 14:4; Jub 7:21-22
and begotten giants (as your) sons?[462] Gen 6:4; *Haer.* 1.10.1
4 You were holy ones, spirits,[463] that live forever,[464] 7:1; 12:4;OdesSol 23:1
yet you defiled yourselves upon the women,[465] and have 6:2; Lev 15:19-24; PssSol 8:13
begotten (children) by the blood of flesh. CD^a 5:6-7
Like the children of men, you have lusted after flesh and blood,[466] 9:2; 1Pet 3:20; 2Pet 2:4
just as they do who die and perish.[467] Pss 82:6-7
5 It was for this reason I gave them wives [468] that they might cast
seed into them and thus, beget children by them, that nothing should
ever fail them upon the earth.
6 But as for you, you formerly were spirits that live forever, immortal

---

[461] Intercession of angels on behalf of suffering humankind has ancient roots, even back to the "Sumerian texts where the divine council of Sumer deliberated justice between both humans and gods" (H1 pg. 142 referencing David J. A. Clines, Job 21-37, WBC 18A (Nashville: Thomas Nelson, 2006), pg. 735). This can also be seen in Job 5:1, "Call now; is there anyone who will answer you? To which of the holy ones will you turn?" The fallen watchers have sinned so deeply that not only can they not do one of their primary functions, but they must also have a man intercede for them! Christ himself now intercedes on behalf of humankind (Isa 53:12, Heb 7:25).

[462] Mixing of seed was forbidden in Leviticus 19:19, "You shall keep my statutes. You shall not let your cattle breed with a different kind. You shall not sow your field with two kinds of seed, nor shall you wear a garment of cloth made of two kinds of material." It may be that the prohibition in Lev 19:19 is a memorial reminder of the sin of the fallen watchers mixing their seed with that of humans in defiance of God's command. The prohibition in Leviticus may indicate knowledge of the sin of the watchers from the earliest times. It also was a reminder to avoid mixture with the surrounding nations.

[463] "Holy ones and spirits—the Hebrew bible uses the same terminology for members of the heavenly host" (H1 pg. 143). Many second temple Jews had a much richer view of the heavenly host, seeing heaven as populated by "glorious ones" (11QPs^a vs 16 The Apostrophe to Zion); "utterly holy ones" (4Q400 1.1.18) and "godlike beings" (4Q400 1.1.20) who form a council (4Q400 1.2.9). God the Father is "the holiest of the Holy Ones" (11QPs^a vs 1 The Hymn to the Creator); and "King of the divine beings" (4Q400 1.2.7).

[464] "Angels are not 'timeless' in the sense of being eternal beings. They had a beginning as created beings. They are immortal (Luke 20:36), but that immortality is ultimately contingent, based on God's authority and pleasure" (Heiser, Michael S., 2018. *Angels* pg. 170).

[465] This phrase carries the idea of being defiled through intercourse with women in their time of menstruation (Lev 15:19-24, CD^a 5:6-7 (W pg. 56)). It could also indicate virginal blood.

[466] Charles (C pg. 36) and Black (BL pg. 152) both note that bloodthirstiness could be involved here, but they discount it as foreign to this passage. Demons and ancient "gods" were known to have a thirst for blood (1En 15:4; *2Apol.* 12; *Cels.* 8.30, 60, 61, 62, 63; *Leg.* 26; 27; *Apol. 22, 23*).

[467] "Clearly, the sin of taking human wives and procreating with them is in view. But why does this sin have such disastrous consequences? The repetition of wording in the indictment elucidates the nature of the main sin 1) 'blood of women' 2) 'blood of flesh' 3) 'blood of men' 4) 'flesh and blood.' The primary significance of these four pairs involving blood and people is that in procreation and reproduction (involving blood) the Watchers have mixed the immortal with the line of *mortal* (or fleshly) humanity. This is reinforced by the last statement 'you have done as they do – flesh and blood, who die and perish' (4) The Watchers are not of flesh and blood but have entangled themselves with a race of flesh and blood. Not only have the Watchers procreated with women, but they have condescended to mix things of the heavenly realm with those of the earthly realm, which is a sin of cosmic grandeur" (Jasko, A., 2012. *Did Jesus Know 1 Enoch 15?* pg. 10).

[468] Nickelsburg more literally, has "women" in place of "wives."

for all generations of the world.[469]
7 For this reason, I did not appoint wives for you;[470] because for celestial spirits, heaven is their dwelling.[471] Mt 22:29-30; Mk 12:25 Lk 20:34-36

The Slain Giants are the Origin of Demons

8 And now the giants, born of both spirit and flesh shall be called 7:2; Jub 10:5; Zech 13:2

---

[469] **Being immortal, there was no reason for angels to perpetuate themselves though children; whereas humans because of death, would die off without procreation. Nickelsburg sums up the issue; "In short, the watchers have violated the created order, transgressing the boundary between the spheres of heaven and earth, spirit and flesh, and in so doing they have defiled their holy state. It is a combination that evidently makes their sin unforgivable (12:5; 16:4). No atonement can remove that uncleanness derived from an act that was not only forbidden but that violated the created order of the universe**" (N1 pg. 272). Olson notes; "'A rabbinic midrash on Hanna's prayer at Shiloh (1 Sam 1:11) reflects exactly this idea. According to Midrash Samuel 2:4, Hannah prayed: 'Lord of the Universe! The celestials never die, and they do not reproduce their kind. Terrestrial beings die, but they are fruitful and multiply. Therefore, I pray: either make me immortal, or give me a son!'" (trans. Bamberger, B. 1952. Fallen Angels [Philadelphia: Jewish Publication Society] 11) (OL pg. 69n15). Midrash Samuel was written after the 11th century.

[470] Nickelsburg has from vs 6 into 7: "But you originally existed as spirits, living forever, and not dying for all the generations of eternity; therefore I did not make women among you.' The spirits of heaven, in heaven is their dwelling:" Note Nickelsburg without telling us why, translated that he made no women (not just wives) among angels. OL translates 15:7 as: "The reason I did not provide wives for you is that the proper dwelling of heavenly spirits is—heaven!" Other than Nickelsburg all other translators have wives. This has bearing since the question always arises about the gender of angels. Heiser informed us that angels "cannot be gendered, since they are spirit beings and gender is a biological attribute. When angels assume visible form or flesh to interact with human beings, Scripture always has them male. The flesh they assume is gendered because it is flesh, not because that corporality is an intrinsic part of angelic nature." (Heiser, Michael, 2018, *Angels*, Lexham Press)

[471] **Jesus certainly had this verse, and or perhaps (1En 51:5 b-d, see note, 69:11), in mind when in (Mt 22:29-30) he responds to the Sadducees. "But Jesus answered them, 'You are wrong, because you know neither the Scriptures nor the power of God. For in the resurrection, they neither marry nor are given in marriage, but are like the angels in heaven.'" Jasko maintains that "1 Enoch 15 is the best fit out of the extant Early Jewish literature." as the text Jesus is referring to** (Jasko, A. 2012. *Did Jesus Know 1 Enoch 15?*). **Note in (Mt 22:29 and Mk 12:24-25) Jesus calls this passage from Enoch and presumably the entire Book of Watchers scripture!!!** The parallel passage is (Luke 20:34-36); "And Jesus said to them, 'The sons of this age marry and are given in marriage, but those who are considered worthy to attain to that age and to the resurrection from the dead neither marry nor are given in marriage, for they cannot die anymore, because they are equal to angels and are sons of God, being sons of the resurrection.'" See also (Mk 12:24-25) "Jesus said to them, "Is this not the reason you are wrong, because you know neither the Scriptures nor the power of God? For when they rise from the dead, they neither marry nor are given in marriage, but are like angels in heaven." Olson speaking of (Lk 20:34-36) as being dependent on 1En 15; concurs: **"This passage is surely the background against which Jesus's words should be understood."** (OL pg. 46). **That Jesus calls the *Book of the Watchers* scripture is immensely significant! Jesus even uses the same line of reasoning from (1En 15:5-7) in (Lk 20:36); "for they cannot die anymore" as to why humans will not be married in the next life. It should not be overlooked that Jesus, in these gospel passages, is strongly affirming that His saints will live forever! It should also not be overlooked that Jesus is calling a non-canonical book scripture!**

mighty spirits upon the earth,[472] [473] and on the earth[474] shall be their 106:17; Or. Graec 16; Mk 5:4
dwelling. Lk 11:24-26; Gen 6:4; AThn 32
9 Evil spirits[475] shall come forth from their (fleshly) bodies, 19:1; Leg. 24-25; *2Apol. 5*
for from humans they came into being, and from the holy watchers *Apol.* 22
was their beginning and the origin of their creation. They will be *Inst..* 3
called 'evil spirits' upon the earth, and such they shall be. Eph 6:12; 1Jn 4:1
10 As for celestial spirits, heaven shall be their dwelling: 2Chr 6:21, 39
but for terrestrial spirits, born upon the earth, on the earth
shall be their dwelling-place.[476] [477] Isa 26:14; Ezek 32:21-31
11 The spirits of the giants, the Nephilim,[478] <lead astray>,[479] Jub 10:1-11:5; *Leg* 26
do violence,[480] and make desolate. They attack, they wrestle Acts 19:12-13; Eph 6:12

---

472 Some translate "evil spirits on the earth." This text follows Olson, relying on Greek rather than Ethiopic, Syncellus has, "mighty spirits upon the earth" This of course brings to mind Gen 6:4 and the supernatural strength of the demon in Mk 5:4.

473 **You can see evidence in the Old Testament that the authors believed that the spirits of the giants are imprisoned.** "The mighty chiefs ('ê·lê) shall speak of them, with their helpers, out of the midst of Sheol" (Ezek 32:21) and in (Isa 14:20b-21) "May the offspring of evildoers nevermore be named! Prepare slaughter for his sons because of the guilt of their fathers, lest they rise and possess the earth, and fill the face of the world with cities." In (Jub 10:5-9), 90% of the demons are confined; but at the request of Mastêmâ, 10% were allowed to roam the earth. Imagine if they were all loosed upon humankind! **These remaining 90% of giant spirits appear to be the "locusts" released from the pit in Rev 9:1-3 (cf. Isa 13, esp. 13:3). The belief that demons came from the giants, and are spirits of the giants, is not generally recognized in modern western Christianity, but was accepted as fact in the time of Christ, and among the early Church fathers. Their physical deaths freed their spirits to torment humankind until the end of the age. This is the origin of the unclean spirits mentioned so often in the gospels. They are unclean because of their mixed parentage.** "Centuries before Jesus Christ, Enochic Jews specifically anticipated the destruction of the demons as an eschatological event. In light of this, it can hardly be accidental that the Gospel writers see Jesus's exorcisms as a sure sign of the advent of God's kingdom. '*But if I drive out demons by the finger of God, the kingdom of God has come to you*' (Luke 11:20 NIV)" (OL pg. 48). "Early Christian writings which reflect this explanation for the origin of demons (include): Justin Martyr, *Second Apology* 5 (ca. 150 CE); Athenagoras, *A Plea for the Christians* 24-25 (ca. 170); Tertullian, *Apology* 22 and *On Idolatry* 4 (ca. 200); Commodian, *Instructions* 3 (mid-3rd c.); Lactantius, *Divine Institutes* 2:25 (ca. 300-25); *Clementine Homilies* 8:18 (2nd-4th c.). **At least by the 2nd c. rabbinic Judaism began to reject these Enochic ideas, and the Talmudic and Mishrashic demonology is very different from Enochic**" (OL pg. 69 n16). For instance, b.Chagigah 16a holds that demons can multiply like humans. Olsen later adds to his list "Justin Martyr *First Apology* 5 (ca. 150 CE); Minucius Felix, *Octavius* 26-27 (late 2nd C.); and Cyprian, Treatise 6 (*On the Vanity of Idols*) 6-7 (247 CE). Note how Athenagoras (*Plea* 25) and Lactantius (*Divine Institutes* 2:15) carefully distinguish between the two kinds of wicked spirits loose in the world, as does Eusebius in his *Commentary on Isaiah* 13:3" (OL pg. 69 n21).

474 Isaac adds: "and inside the earth."

475 Heiser (H1 pg. 145), described these as *Pneumata ischura* "powerful spirits." "Because of their dual nature, the giants are both eradicable and immortal. On the one hand, the body of their flesh can die. On the other hand, their spirits have continued existence" (N1 pg. 267).

476 **Because of their hybrid and unclean nature, the giants cannot dwell in heaven. They are confined to earth.**

477 (1En 15:10) is viewed by many scholars as an ancient translator's expansion.

478 The use of "Nephilim" is uncertain here. Some Ethiopic texts read "clouds" which could be taken as a misreading of Nephilim. Black and Olson both support the use of Nephilim. That the Nephilim shed blood is backed up by (1QapGen 6.19 (W pg. 94)).

479 "Lead astray" is chosen to resolve a textual issue. It was chosen by Nickelsburg since it is a demonic activity in (1En 19:1) and is a central demonic activity in Jubilees which is dependent on this section of 1 Enoch (Jub 7:27; 10:2, 8; 11:5; and 12:20).

480 Verse 11 is a "snarl of textual problems" (N1 pg. 273). N has; "And the spirits of the giants <lead astray>, do violence, make desolate, and attack and wrestle and hurl upon the earth and <cause illnesses>." I has; "The spirits of

and dash to the ground,[481] and cause illness. They eat nothing, Mt 17:15; Lk 9:39, 42; Mk 9:18
but abstain from food[482] but nevertheless hunger and thirst and Mic 6:14
cause illness.[483] 4Q560
12 These spirits will rise up against the sons of men,[484] and Gen 3:15
against the women,[485] because they have proceeded from them.[486]

16 1 From the days of the slaughter, destruction and death of the giants, 10:12; Sir 16:7
the spirits which came forth from their bodies will go on destroying, 7:2-6; 22:3; Leg. 24-25; Jn 10:10
without incurring judgement.[487] In such ways they will destroy, Mt 13:29, 39

---

the giants oppress each other; they will corrupt, fall, be excited, and fall upon the earth and cause sorrow." B has; "The spirits of the giants shall be like clouds, which shall oppress, corrupt, fall, quarrel, and wound on earth." Olson postulating that "clouds" in the Ethiopic text is a misreading of "Nephilim" has; "The spirits of the giants, the Nephilim, oppress and destroy. They pounce and wrestle. They toss about upon the earth and cause crushing oppressions." The textual issues are unfortunate, since **this is the earliest Jewish text describing demonic influence**.

[481] That demons cause humans to be dashed to the ground is apparent in the gospels (Mt 17:15; Mk 9:18; Lk 9:42). The Codex Panopolitanus text contains a gloss "hard spirits of giants" at this position.

[482] **Being spiritual beings, they do not eat. This is the significance of the resurrected Jesus eating the piece of fish in front of his disciples (Lk 24:42-43).** This demonstrated that his body was resurrected and not just his spirit and that He was not a demon impersonating Jesus. **These spirits of the giants are punished by having an insatiable appetite and thirst but being unable to eat or drink.** Intense thirst is a staple of eternal punishment (Mt 12:43; Lk 11:24; 16:24).

[483] "Cause illness" This can also be read as "strike and smite", or "stumble." "Cause illness" is another possible reading; it was chosen for this text since it is a demonic activity cited in (Jub 10:12-13; Lk 7:21; 8:2; and Acts 19:12-16). Black has "and they collapse" "The idea seems to be that those who are possessed by such evil spirits collapse through their abstention from food and drink i.e. through their fasting." (BL pg. 153) Matthew Goff sees the idea of movement with the spirits roaming and wandering (Goff, Matthew., 2010. *Monstrous Appetites: Giants, Cannibalism and Insatiable Eating in Enochic Literature*; *Journal of Ancient Judaism*. pg. 41).

[484] Olson observes: **"Literal children may be intended. From earliest cuneiform tablets down to modern day folklore, it has been commonly believed that certain types of demons harbor an especially lethal hostility towards small children"** (OL pg. 48).

[485] **The incidence of rape and sexual assault on women (as well as on men) seems particularly high among those involved in overtly occult encounters and occult worship practices** (Hawkins, 1996. *Witch Craft: Exploring the World of Wicca,* Grand Rapids: Baker, pgs. 60, 79-81).

[486] **The spirits of the giants are hybrids of humans and watchers. As such, they neither belong in the world of man nor in eternal heaven. After their death, either in internecine battle, or in the flood, or killed afterward they became the demons the world is beset with to this day. No place was found for them in heaven, so they remain on earth until the great final judgement.** Eusebius of Caesarea also confirms that the spirits of the giants are demons, (*Preparation for the Gospel* book 5). Athenagoras is very clear. "These angels, then, who have fallen from heaven, and haunt the air and the earth, and are no longer able to rise to heavenly things, and the souls of the giants, which are the demons who wander about the world, perform actions similar, the one (that is the demons) to the natures they have received, the other (that is the angels) to the appetites they have indulged." (*A Plea for the Christians* 25). Other second and third century Christian writings that describe the giants as malevolent demons include (TSol 5:1-5; 17:1; Tertullian's *Apol.* 22; Lactantius, *The Divine Institutes* 2:15 and Commodianus, *Instructions* 3). "The giants would be furious that God rescued Noah's righteous descendants from the Flood and had not rescued them, and so their spirits would conceivably delight in afflicting humans out of jealousy and malice." "Their goal is thus to reproduce in humanity their own godlessness, war, and chaos, and eventually to make them taste death, that is, the separation of soul and body that they experienced under God's wrath" (Micallef, Jesmond, *eXORCISMS*. pg. 87).

[487] **No immediate earthly judgement will be taken on the demons** (see 10:12). This is reflected in the gospels, "And behold, they (the demons) cried out, what have you to do with us, O Son of God? Have you come here to

until the day of the end, until the great judgement, Mt 8:29; Mk 5:7; Jub 10:5-11
when the great age will be completed.[488] 55:4; Rev 10:5-7; TLev 18:12
It will be consummated all at once.[489] 94:1; 95:6; 96:1,6; 1Thes 5:2-3 Mt 24:36-44; 2Pet 3:10; Rev 3:3

2 And now say to the watchers, who were once in heaven,
who sent you to petition on their behalf.
3 'You were in heaven, but all (it's) secrets had not yet been revealed to Mt 24:36-37; Ezek 28:3
to you,[490] and worthless mysteries you knew,[491] [492] and these Job 15:15; 1Pet 1:12; 11QPs[a] 5[a]
you made known to women in your hardness of heart;[493] 98:11
and by these secrets women and men multiplied evils upon 100:8; *Strom* 5.1.10.2
the earth.' 7:1; 8:3
4 Say to them, therefore. 'You shall have no peace.'" 5:4; Isa 48:22

---

torment us before the time" (Mt 8:29). That Matthew made no explanation of these words, indicates his readership knew the backstory. **See also (Jub 10:5-11), which states that in order for the evil spirits of the giants to stop oppressing humans they must be bound in the place of condemnation, i.e. with the watchers.** As Hippolytus (AD 170-235) says, "This person, (Christ) exercising the righteous judgement of the Father towards all men, hath prepared a just sentence for everyone, according to his works; at whose judgement-seat when all men, and angels, and demons shall stand, they shall send out one voice, and say, just is thy judgement" (*An Excerpt From Josephus' Discourse to the Greeks Concerning Hades* (6) found in *The Complete Works of Josephus*, Flavius Josephus, Translated by William Whiston). (Note this passage is more correctly attributed to Hippolytus of Rome (d. ca. AD 236), than Josephus). The demons have no power over the righteous (Jub 10:6; Acts 19:15; *Cels.* 8.27; 8.34; 8:36) Origen proclaims: **"But the Christian—the true Christian, I mean—who has submitted to God alone and His word, will suffer nothing from demons, for He is mightier than demons"** (Cels 8:36).

[488] Isaac, while admitting a difficult reading of Ethiopic, adds here: "until everything is concluded (upon) the Watchers and the wicked ones." For 16:1, Olson has: "From the days of the slaughter, destruction, and death of the Giants, the spirits which emerged from the souls of their flesh will continue to destroy without incurring judgement. In such a state they will destroy until the Day of the End: the great judgement (in which the great age will be consummated), and everything concerning the Watchers and the wicked will be finished."

[489] The watchers, giants, and godless had reign on the earth; but their unrestricted dominion was crushed by Christ. **The Gospels point to Jesus's power over the demons as a sign of the arrival of the kingdom of God.** "But if it is by the Spirit of God that I cast out demons, then the kingdom of God has come upon you" (Mt 12:28) (See also Lk 11:20). But the final judgement awaits the end of the age. The suddenness of the return of God in judgement is emphasized here, as it is in Mt 24:36-44; 1Thes 5:2-3; 2Pet 3:10; and Rev 3:3 (cf. 1En 94:1; 95:6; 96:1, 6; 98:16).

[490] **Unrevealed mysteries in heaven remain. The mysteries the watchers revealed, are not as valuable as the others unrevealed. That angels do not have full knowledge, is evident from the New Testament.** "But concerning that day and hour no one knows, not even the angels of heaven nor the Son, but the father only" (Mt 24:36). The Yahad, a Jewish sect mentioned the Dead Sea Scrolls, were very careful who they revealed secrets to; requiring a two-year blameless apprenticeship prior to acceptance into the Yahad (*Charter of a Jewish Sectarian Association, Community Rule*, 1QS 8.10-12).

[491] In place of "worthless mysteries," B has: "a reprobated secret," I has: "rejected mysteries," N has: "and no mystery was revealed to you; but a stolen mystery you learned;" OL has: "rejected ones."

[492] **That God does not fully trust angels, is a biblical concept** (See Job 4:17-18; 5:1; 15:15; 1Pet 1:12).

[493] "Hardness of your hearts" is a common saying of Christ (Mt 19:8; Mk 3:5; 10:5; 16:14).

Enoch's First Journey Through the Cosmos

The Unseen Realm

17 1 And they took me[494] and led me away to a certain place,
inhabited by beings who were like blazing fire,[495] and when they wished, 64:1; Ezek 1:13-14; Heb 1:7 Ps 104:4
they took on the appearance of men.[496] 14:11; 19:1; 2Cor 11:14
2 Then they lead me away to a place of stormy darkness,[497] and to a Job 38:17, 19; Ps 23:4
Mountain[497a] whose summit reached to heaven. 1:4; 18:8; 25:3; 77:1; Gen 28:12
3 I saw the place of the luminaries,[498] and the treasuries of the stars, 77:2; Job 38:22-23; Isa 14:13
and of thunderpeals, to the outermost reaches,[499] where (I saw) Deut 32:41; Hab 3:9; Lam 3 13
a bow of fire, arrows and their quiver, and a fiery sword and all the Gen 3:24; Ps 7:12-13; 18:14
lightning-flashes.[500] 41:3; 43:1-2; 44; 59; 60:13-15
4 Then they led me away to the waters of life[501] and to the fire of the 23:2-4; 48:1; Zech 9:14; Jn 4:10

---

[494] The angels here take Enoch on his first journey, chapters 17-19. Other texts with an "interpreting angel motif," as the scholars call it, are (Ezek 7-11; 40-48; Zech 1-6; Dan 7-8; 4 Ezra; and 3 Baruch). The journey finds similarities with the Epic of Gilgamesh and the Babylonian world map (N1 pg. 279). Nickelsburg dates chapters 17-19 to "a date early in the second half of the third century B.C.E. for the present form of this section." He sees them as "later than chaps. 12-16 and (they) are presupposed by chaps. 20-36" (N1 pg. 279). The dependence on Job (see cross references) unsurprisingly indicates that Job was written earlier. The idea that 1 Enoch 17-19 is a separable subsidiary work is maintained by Charles, Nickelsburg, VanderKam, Himmelfarb, Bautch, Knibb, and Reed.

[495] These fiery beings which can take human form, are not otherwise identified.

[496] **This remarkable statement indicates that celestial beings can change shape to appear as men.** This is a biblical concept. "And no wonder, for even Satan disguises himself as an angel of light" (2Cor 11:14). "Do not neglect to show hospitality to strangers, for thereby some have entertained angels unawares." (Heb 13:2) In the 2Cor 11:14 passage, Paul may have texts from *The Life of Adam and Eve* in mind. "Then Satan was angry and transformed himself into the brightness of angels" (*Vita* 9:1 (OTP2 pg. 260)) and "Then Satan came in the form of an angel and sang hymns to God as the angels." (LAE apocalypse 17:1 (OTP2 pg. 277)) In the pseudepigraphal work *Testament of Job*, Satan disguises himself as a beggar (TJob 6.4-7.6 (OTP1 pg. 841-842)), the king of the Persians (TJob 17.2; OTP1 Pg. 846), and later as a bread seller (TJob 23.1 (OTP1 pg. 848)). In the Jewish book 2 Baruch (AD 100-120) "those who proved to be righteous on account of my law" are contrasted with the those who despised my law. Both change form. The righteous "will be changed into any shape which they wished, from beauty to loveliness and from light to the splendor of glory." The unrighteous are changed into "startling visions and horrible shapes; and they will waste away even more" (2Bar 51:1-11 (OTP1 pg. 638)). (1Enoch 19:1) teaches us that the spirits of the angels can assume many different forms; not limited to just human. In support of this belief; demons were able to enter pigs when Jesus cast them out (Mt 8:32; Mk 5:13; Lk 8:33).

[497] I has: "into a place of whirlwind."

[497a] This mountain has been postulated as Mt. Zaphon, AKA Jebel Aqra, on the Syrian Turkish border or Mt. Hermon.

[498] i.e., the sun and moon (H1 pg. 159).

[499] N has: "depths of the ether." Since Enoch is viewing the heavens from a high mountain, he is likely viewing deep into the ether, the upper regions of space, or heavens. I has: "the ultimate end of depth".

[500] The lightning flashes are the arrows of the almighty (cf. 2Sam 22:14-15; Ps 144:6).

[501] "Waters of life" is replaced by Black with "subterranean waters." B has: "splashing stream". I, K and OL have "waters of life." Living Waters, *mayim chayyim*, is a term used in the Old Testament for moving/flowing water (Song 4:15, Zech 14:8) (H1 pg. 160). It is referenced of God in (Jer 2:13) "fountain of living water."

west which receives every setting of the sun.[502] [503] 77:2
5 And we came to a river of fire[504] whose fire flowed like water 23:2-4; Rev 19:20; 20:14-15
and was pouring into the great ocean[505] toward the west. 14:19; 77:5; Dan 7:10
6 I saw the great rivers, and I reached the great river[506] and the Job 26:10; Phaedo 111D; 113A
great darkness, and I went to the place where no flesh walks.[507] 1QS 4.13; Job 38:17
7 And I saw wintry winds of darkness,[508] and the place where the Job 37:9
waters of the deep gush forth.[509] Ps 24:2; Job 38:16
8 I saw the mouth of all the rivers of the earth and the mouth of the abyss.

18 1 I saw the store chambers[510] of all the winds, and I saw how he 41:4; 60:12, 19-21; Ps 135:7
used the winds to set in order all created things, and I saw the Prov 8:29; Isa 24:18; 40:21
firm foundations of the earth. Ps 18:15; Jer 31:37; 2Sam 22:16
2 I saw the corner-stone of the earth;[511] and I saw the four winds[512] Job 38:4-7; Isa 11:12; Mk 13:27
that support the earth and the firmament of heaven. Rev 7:1; Mt 24:31; Ezek1:22
3 I saw that the winds spread out the expanse of heaven.[513] They 34; Job 26:7; 36:29; 37:16; 38:18
are stationed between heaven and earth; they are the pillars of heaven. Job 9:6-8; 26:11; Ps 75:3
4 I also saw the winds which rotate the sky and bring to (their) setting 72:5; 73:2; 76:4-12

---

[502] **"Closely paralleling the present passage, is the idea in Babylonian, Canaanite, and Israelite religious writings that God dwells on a mountain, from the foot of which issue great rivers of water"** (N1 pg. 284).

[503] "This is scarcely Gehenna, although the Talmud says that the sun is red in the evening because it passes the gate of Gehenna, and red in the morning when it passes the garden of Eden (Baba Bathra 84a)" (BL pg. 156). "It seems these verses (17:4-8) are describing the underworld. The "waters of life" are there, according to Mesopotamian mythology, and the "river of fire," according to Greek. Still, the fire which receives the setting sun and the river of fire flowing in to the western sea (the Mediterranean) suggest nothing so much as a sunset on the ocean and the blazing stream of its reflection—seen with the eyes of a mystic or poet" (OL pg. 50).

[504] For a description of a river of fire see (1QH$_a$ Col 11.30-33 Hymn 14 (W pg. 183)). The river of fire may be identified as Pyriphegethon, from Greek literature. However, here it is not in the underworld, but discharges itself into the sea. (Cf. Plato's Phaedo 111D; 113A-C)

[505] Scholars identify this as the great sea, the Mediterranean.

[506] Oceanus (Greek) or "bitter river" (Babylonian), was thought to circle the inhabited world. In ancient Greek cosmogony the RIVER OKEANOS (Oceanus) was a great, fresh-water stream which encircled the flat disc of the earth. "Cf. the encircling waterbody on the Imago Mundi. As to the geography presumed in these chapters, it is best to suggest that our author knew a popular geography that was a composite of Mesopotamian and Greek ideas" (Gasson, *Greek Influence*, 11: Hengel, *Judaism and Hellenism*, 1:197-98). (Cf. Greek: Plato's Phaedo 112E; Homer Iliad 18.607-8; 21.194-96; Odyssey 10.510-12; 11.13; 24.11-12; Hesiod Theogony 789-791; Works and Days; Strabo Geographica 1.1.8-9; Herodotus finds the idea laughable History 4.36)

[507] This text follows Gk[a]. Isaac from Ethiopic, reads: "where all flesh must walk cautiously." Knibb reads: "where all flesh walks." N has: "where no human walks." OL has: "where no flesh walks." Hieser, (H1 pg. 162), refers to it as "the realm of the dead i.e., Hades." Nickelsburg speculates that since it is in the far northwest, no humans live there due to the cold (see 76:11-12) (N1 pg. 283-284). This reflects a Greek cosmology (Homer Odyssey 24.12ff).

[508] This text follows Gk[a]. Following Ethiopic; K has "mountains of the darkness of winter;" OL has "mountains of the storm clouds of winter" This reading would match (Jer 13:16) (C pg. 39).

[509] Water gushing/fountains of the deep (cf. Gen 7:11, 8:2; Prov 8:28; and 1En 89:3, 7).

[510] "Store chambers of all the winds" (cf. Ps 135:7; Jer 10:13; 11Q6 26.15).

[511] N has here "I saw the foundation of the earth and the cornerstone of the earth." B has "I beheld the stone corners of the earth." Ancient cosmology viewed the earth as a building or temple. The cornerstone of the earth is mentioned in the Bible only in (Job 38:6). "Foundations of the earth" is a common idea in the Bible (cf. 2Sam 22:16; Job 38:4; Pss 18:15; 82:5; 102:25; 104:5; Prov 8:29; Isa 24:18; 40:21; 48:13; 51:13,16; Jer 31:37; Mic 6:2; Zech 12:1; Heb 1:10; Sir 16:19).

[512] "Four winds" (cf. Jer 49:36; Ezek 37:9; Dan 7:2; 8:8; 11:4; Zech 2:6; 6:5; Mt 24:31; Mk 13:27; Rev 7:1).

[513] N has: "height" instead of "expanse" others have: "vault."

the orb of the sun, and all the stars.[514] Job 38:24, 33
5 I saw the winds on the earth bearing the clouds.[515] I saw the paths Ps 104:4; Gen 28:12
of the angels;[516] and I saw at the ultimate extremities of the earth, 33:2; Job 28:24
the firmament of the heavens above.
6 I proceeded southward[517] and saw a place which burns night and Jub 8:22
day where there were seven mountains of precious stones, three 21:3; 24:1-3; 52:2-6; 67:4; 77:4
towards the east, and three lying towards the south.[518] Rev 17:9; 4Ezra 2:19
7 And of those toward the east one was of stones of varied hues, Ezek 28:17-20
another of pearl[519] and one was of <jasper>;[520] those towards the Rev 21:18-20
south were of flame-colored stone.[521] Phaedo 110 D-E
8 The one in the middle was pressing up to the heavens, like the 1:4; 17:2; 25:3; 77:1
throne of God, and it was of antimony,[522] [523] and the summit of the Isa 14:13; Jub 4:26; Ex 24:9-11
throne was of sapphire.[524] Ezek 1:26; 10:1
9 I saw a flaming fire, and beyond those mountains[525] 24:1; 71:2; Ezek 28:13

The Abyss and Prison for the Stars

10 I saw the edge of the great earth, and there the heavens come to 33:2; Prov 8:27-28
an end.[526]
11 I saw a deep chasm,[527] with pillars of heavenly fire, Rev 20:1

---

514 "This language reflects a non-scientific cosmology in that it has the winds propelling the motion of the sun and stars." (H1 pg. 185)

515 I has: "I saw the souls carried by the clouds."

516 The paths the angels use in their travels between the realms.

517 Some texts omit "southward."

518 These mountains are visited again in the vision of 24:1-3.

519 Pearl is ambiguous; other suggestions are emerald, carbuncle and rubies.

520 N states, "the identity of the stone is unknown"; he has jasper in his translation. I, OL and K following Ethiopic have "healing stone", B has "variegated stone." K notes the text is very doubtful. For other references to precious stones see (Isa 54:11; Tob 13:16). Olson notes that "healing stone" is possibly corrupt for Jasper. Josephus, describing the Essenes, notes "They also take great pains in studying the writings of the ancients, and choose out of them what is most for the advantage of their soul and body; and they inquire after such roots and medicinal stones as may cure their sickness" (*War* 2.8.6 §§ 136).

521 Black suggests carnelian, a fiery red stone. Compare the stones of fire in (Ezek 28:14, 16).

522 Charles and Isaac have "alabaster" in place of "antimony."

523 N has "antimony" which is bright and silvery white. OL notes "'stibium,' a crystalline metal usually found in a lead-gray ore" is also a possibility (OL pg. 52). In the ancient near east, God is often seen as dwelling on mountain tops. It is argued credibly that this mountain of God's throne is Sinai. For a discussion see (OL pg. 267-268). Others locate it in the north as a sort of Mount Olympus.

524 N has: "lapis lazuli." Sapphire is associated with God's throne in the Old Testament (Ex 24:9-10; Ezek 1:2 6-28; 10:1). The foundation of the walls of New Jerusalem also contain precious stones (Rev 21:18-20). The image of mountains made of precious stones is very ancient. Consider *The Curse of Agade* (written before 2200 BC) line 110 "To splinter it, like the lapis lazuli mountain" (Cooper, Jerrold., 1983. *The Curse of Agade*, John Hopkins University Press. pg. 11). This mountain is identified as Mt. Sinai (cf. 1 En 77:1).

525 I has: "inside those mountains." These mountains are protected and surrounded by flaming mountain ridges (cf. 1En 24:1).

526 Knibb has: "there waters are gathered together" in place of "and there the heavens came to an end".

527 (1En 18:10-11) has parallels to Hesiod's description of Tartarus in the Theogony (713-736). "Tartarus, the prison of the Titans, is located at 'the ends of the huge earth'. It is 'a great gulf', so deep that a falling bronze anvil would

and I saw in it pillars of fire descending, which were 21:7-10; ADAM 32
immeasurably high and deep.[528] [529] 2Bar 59:5

{Many scholars insert 19:1-2 here}

12 And beyond that chasm[530] I saw a place which had no firmament 21:1-3
of heaven above, nor foundation of earth beneath it; 108:3; Jer 4:23-26 LXX
there was no water in it, and no birds, but it was a desolate Gen 1:2
and horrible place.[531]
13 There I saw seven stars,[532] like great burning mountains, 21:3; Rev 1:16, 20; 8:8; Isa 14:13
and concerning these; when I enquired,[533] Jer 51:25; Deut 32:22
14 the angel said to me: "This place is the end of the heavens and 108:3-6; Mt 8:12; 25:41; Jude 6

---

take ten days to hit bottom, the same distance as from heaven to earth, and a man would take a year to reach its floor" (N1 pg. 286-287). Other parallels from the Theogony include the Titans buried under rocks, (1En 10:4-5) and bound in chains in Tartarus (1En 54:3). Hesiod was a well-known early Greek poet living between 750-650 BC. These passages indicate Greek influence on the text.

[528] "Immeasurably high and deep" can be thought of as a bottomless pit (Cf. Rev 9:1-2, 11, 11:7, 17:8, and 20:1). This prison for the angels is also described in (1En 21:7-10).

[529] I am not accepting Nickelsburg's translocation of 19:1-2 to this position. He notes the reason for his translocation: "As it is preserved, the text narrates Enoch's progress to two places, followed by two angelic interpretations. Additionally, in Enoch's next journey, from west to east (chaps. 21-32), the order of stations suggests the transposition here of 19:1-2 between 18:11 and 18:12" (N pg. 39). He also writes "These verses read most naturally as an interpretation of 18:11. Otherwise we would have 18:9b-11 with no explanation and 18:12-13 with two explanations." (N1 pg. 287) While Nickelsburg's repositioning has merit, he admits that in the DSS (4QEn[c] 1 viii); 18:12 almost certainly follows 18:11.

[530] Isaac has: "on top of that pit"

[531] "The next place to which Enoch is led is 'a place that lies outside not only the inhabited world, but also the bounds of the cosmos. Enoch is beyond the terrestrial disk, the atmosphere and the heavens. Enoch has eclipsed even the waters that surround the earth disk or make up the firmament.'" (Bautch, *A Study of the Geography of 1 Enoch 17-19: "No One Has Seen What I Have Seen" (Supplements to the Journal for the Study of Judaism) pg. 141* s) Heiser calls this Hades like prison, an "anti-Eden," as it is truly as opposite from the beauty and abundant life of Eden as imaginable. (H1 pg. 174) The lack of water in places of punishment is a consistent theme.

[532] Olson suggests: "The author is probably condemning the widespread worship of the seven planets (i.e., Sun, Moon, Mercury, Venus, Mars, Jupiter, Saturn)." (OL pg. 52) (Cf. 80:7) He continues: "It is possible, however, that the author is thinking of the seven stars of the Pleiades, located in the constellation Tauris." That the Pleiades were bound, was a Greek myth that is also found in (Job 9:9; 38:31 and Amos 5:8). In Greek mythology the seven daughters of the titan Atlas and the nymph Pleione became these stars. For stars as symbols of celestial beings or humans, see also, (1En 86:1-3; 104:2, Job 38:7; Isa 14:12; Dan 8:10; 12:3 and Rev 9:1, 12:4).

[533] Olson observes "These verses (12-13) bear a striking resemblance to (Jer 4:23-26), a poem about primordial chaos which forms part of Jeremiah's lengthy oracle about the doom of Judah (Jer 4:5-31). The resemblance is still closer if we read Jer 4:26 with the LXX, which has "burnt with fire" instead of "laid in ruins.' The entire oracle of Jer 4:5-31, in fact, appears to presuppose a cosmological background similar to what is described here in Enoch 18 and 21." (OL pg. 52). **The question arises whether Jeremiah precedes, or does 1 Enoch, or did they originate from a common tradition. In another article Olson opines "The oracle of Jer. 4.5-31 is chiastic in structure, featuring within it a short, 'apocalyptic' poem (vv. 23-28). Comparison with the 'Book of the Watchers' (chs. 1-36 of 1 Enoch), suggests that the Enochic mythology of the fallen angels lies behind this poem. Seen within the full context of the 'Book of the Watchers', obscure elements of the larger Jer. 4:5-31 chiasm become clear, particularly if a double meaning of cities as 'city/watcher' is recognized. Since the relevant Enochic materials do not appear to be dependent on Jeremiah, Jer. 4:5-31 probably presupposes the Enochic mythology, which echoes elsewhere in Jeremiah.**" (Olson, Daniel C., 1997. *Jeremiah 4.5-31 and Apocalyptic Myth, "Journal for the Study of the Old Testament*" Vol. 22 73 (1997) pgs. 81-107). **That the Book of Watchers tradition predates the Book of Jeremiah (before 550 BC) is a monumental observation!**

Prov 30:4; Job 28:24; 38:21
the earth: this has become a prison for the stars and the hosts of heaven. 10:13; 1Pet 3:18-20; 2Pet 2:4
15 The stars which are rolling over[534] in the fire—these are 108:4; Isa 24:21-22; Jude 13
they which transgressed the commandment of the Lord in the TNaph 3:3
beginning of their rising[535] [536] [537] because they did not come forth at Rev 9:1
their proper times.[538] [539] 80:6; Gen 1:16
16 And he was angry[540] with them, and he incarcerated them[541] Jude 6; Rev 20:3, 10
for ten thousand years, until the time of the completion of the 21:6; Isa 14:15
punishment for their sins." [542]

19 1 The angel Uriel said to me: "There shall stand the angels who Rev 9:20
have mingled[543] with women, but their spirits,[544] assuming *Idol.* 4; 15; *Inst.*.3
many different forms[545] —bring destruction on men and lead them astray, 17:1; Deut. 32:17; *QGen1* 92

---

[534] "'Rolling over' could be a textual corruption for 'burning'" (N1 pg. 289). Olson translates "The stars which turn in these flames—"

[535] "These are the "wandering stars" Jude mentions in (Jude 13). They are wandering because they did not come forth at their proper time in accordance with God's order of the universe. They are therefore in disobedience. Some think comets are the wandering stars. This is an astral rebellion taking place in prehistoric times (Olson, Eerdmans's Commentary.on the Bible: First Enoch).

[536] Isaac has: "because they did not arrive punctually."

[537] The Greek text includes a gloss here: "So that there is an empty place outside of heaven"

[538] This may mean some angels transgressed from the beginning of their creation.

[539] I has: 'did not arrive punctually" The Essenes were fixated on numbers and especially the calendar. They held to a 364 day rather than a 360-, or 365-day year. "[A] striking characteristic of the Essene calendar is it's concern for numerical symmetry, precision and regularity" "where each of the four seasons is of precisely equal length". (Beckwith, Roger T. 2001. *Calendar and Chronology, Jewish and Christian: Biblical, Intertestamental and Patristic Studies* (Leiden: e. J. Brill, 2001), pgs. 101, 106). This Essene solar calendar was at odds with the lunar calendar that was followed by the Sadducees and Pharisees. This resulted in a major source of disagreement as temple activities were supposed to be in sync with the calendar. The lunar calendar required continuous adjustment whereas the Qumran sect calendar did not. "The Qumran sect believed this misalignment occurred because there had been disruption in the heavens-when the Watchers sinned. The cosmic malfunction was their fault." (H1 pg. 178) In Mesopotamia, the proper time of the rising of the seven stars of the Pleiades was a good omen, whereas if the Pleiades did not rise at the expected time, it was an evil omen.

[540] Olson reads "furious."

[541] These stars are symbols of celestial beings.

[542] For 18:16 Isaac has: "And he was wroth with them and bound them until the time of the completion of their sin in the year of mystery." Baty has "in a secret year." Nickelsburg has "ten thousand years" which is meant as an uncountable number of years.

[543] The Greek verb is *migentes* ("mixing with") (N1 pg. 181).

[544] Here, and in 13:6 **a distinction seems to be made between the physical presence of the watchers and their spirits.** Olson notes: "Apparently such radical bifurcation is still possible for them since their assumption of flesh was not natural. **This means that there are two types of evil spirits operating in the world: the spirits of the original 200 fallen Watchers and the spirits of the slain Giants—the demons**." (OL pg. 54) This may be behind Christ's statement responding to his disciple's inability to cast out an unclean spirit: "And he said to them, 'This kind cannot be driven out by anything but prayer'" (Mk 9:29). Some Church fathers were careful to distinguish between these two kinds of wicked spirits active in the world (Lactantius, *Divine Institutes* 2:15, Athenagoras *Plea* 25, Eusebius *Commentary on Isaiah* 13:3).

[545] Once again, (see 17:1) we are told that the **spirits of angels/demons can assume different forms**. See (TReu 5:6); "Then they were transformed into human males". Paul in (2Cor 11:14) states: "And no wonder, for even Satan disguises himself as an angel of light." Enoch is at the place where the fallen Watchers are imprisoned. The spirits are the spirits of the fallen angels, who have now been loosed upon the world to deceive. In Origen's time (AD 184-

so that they sacrifice to demons as gods,[546] until the great judgement, 15:8; 99:7; Jub 10:5-9; 11:4-5 1Cor 10:20; Jub 22:17; Mt 8:29
in which they will be finally judged. 45:2; 56:4; TLev 14:1; Ps 106:37
2 And the wives of the angels who transgressed shall become sirens."[547]
3 And I, Enoch, alone saw the vision: There is not one man who has Dan 10:7-8
seen as I have seen; the extremities of all things that exist.[548] 37:4; *Princ* 4.1.35; *Ecl.* 2

The Seven Archangels

20 1 And these are the names of the holy angels who keep watch.[549] 12:2; Rev 8:2; Zech 4:2, 10
2 Uriel,[550] one of the holy angels, namely, the one in charge of the 4Ezra 4:1; ApMos 40

---

253), worshiping idols was equated with worshiping demons. "For that which is offered to idols is sacrificed to demons, and a man of God must not join the table of demons. As to things strangled, we are forbidden by scriptures to partake of them, because the blood is still in them; and blood, especially the odour arising from blood, is said to be the food of demons" (Origen, *Against Celsus*, Book 8.30).

[546] The belief that sacrificing to idols is the same as sacrificing to demons has a long history. "So they shall no more sacrifice their sacrifices to goat demons, after whom they whore" (Lev 17:7). Origen (AD 184-253) makes numerous references to demons being the "gods" to which ancient people sacrificed (*Origen, Against Celsus*, Book 7.35-8.62). See also: (Pss 96:5 LXX; 106:36-38, Deut 32:17, 1Cor 10:20-21; Rev 9:20; Jub 1:11; 11:4-5; 1En 19:1 and Bar 4:7). **That demons impersonate the pagan gods was the overwhelming view of the early church fathers.** Examples include Justin Martyr, (*First Apology* 5; *Second Apology* 5); Commodianus, (*Against the Gods of the Heathens* 3); Tertullian, (*Of Idolatry* 4); Minucius Felix, (*Octavius* 26-27); and Cyprian, (*Treatise 6, On the Vanity of Idols* 6-7).

[547] I has: "peaceful ones" rather than "sirens." K has: "will become peaceful." OL has: "will have peace." B has: "and their wives also shall be judged," N, BL and C have: "sirens." Sirens are prominent in ancient Greek mythology. Sirens (seirēn) seems to be the correct reading as peaceful appears to be a mistranslation by the Ethiopic translator. In Greek mythology the term refers to deceitful, charming women, sometimes depicted as "half-women, half-birds," who lure and then slay men." (Bautch, Coblentz., 2003. *A Study of the Geography of 1 Enoch 17-19: "No One Has Seen What I Have Seen" (Supplements to the Journal for the Study of Judaism)* pg. 132). Belief in literal sirens was discouraged in the 4th century western church as paganism was strongly denounced. It may be that a siren can be understood as a "female" demon possibly a succubus. In the LXX [Septuagint] the term was sometimes rendered "desert owl" (Mic 1:8, Isa 13:21; Isa 34:13). "Sirens" are chosen here, since the women are everywhere otherwise condemned and usually blamed for enticing the watchers. All that being said, the "shall have peace" in the Ethiopic text is not without merit. With the judgement of their "fallen celestial husbands" the women are freed from a possibly abusive relationship (cf. 7:1). If they were innocent, and were taken against their will by the watchers, there is no reason for them to be punished.

[548] Olson translates: "The extremities of the cosmos, the totality of creation." Origen (AD 185-253) refers to 19:3 and 21:1 in (*De Principiis* 4.1.35) saying: "I have walked on even to imperfection." "I beheld the whole of matter." Also, Clement of Alexandria (ca. AD 150-215) roughly paraphrases 19:3 in (*Eclogae prophetica*e 2).

[549] Chapter 20 begins an account of Enoch's second journey. It introduces the angels who will serve as Enoch's guides in this journey. In Greek, they are "angels of the powers". Nickelsburg states: "The expression 'holy angels' here and in each of the subsequent verses is suspicious. We should probably read 'watchers and holy ones,' the term being slightly paraphrased here" (N1 pg. 295). The angels/watchers here, are not fallen, and have oversight over different realms and tasks. Seven angels are also found in (81:5; 87:2; Rev 1:20; 8:2, 6; 15:1; 21:9; Tob 12:15; ApMos 40:7; and TLev 8:2). Enoch was well acquainted with angelic beings; given the extensive time he spent with them (1En 12:2). **That the archangels are introduced here, with such a lengthy description, indicates, as is believed by most scholars, that the Book of Watchers is the first introduction of them in literature. From then on, the names of the archangels are used with the assumption that the reader is familiar with them, both in the Bible and other period literature.**

[550] Uriel in 1 Enoch, is over both the cosmos (33:3-4; 72-82), and Tartarus (19:1; 20:2; 21:5-9; 27:2). Uriel appears in the apocryphal book 4 Ezra (4:1; 5:20; 10:28) as the helper of Esdras. Isaac has: Suru' el in place of Uriel. Uriel

cosmos and Tartarus.[551] 2Pet 2:4; Jude 6; Job 40:15 LXX
3 Raphael,[552] one of the holy angels, who is over the spirits of men.[553] 9:1; 10:4; 40:9; Tob 12:15
4 Raguel,[554] one of the holy angels who tends the hosts of the
luminaries as a shepherd.[555] 23:4
5 Michael,[556] one of the holy angels, who has been put in charge of 10:11; Dan 10:13, 21; 12:1
the good ones of the people,[557] being also entrusted with rulership of 9:1; 40:9; Rev 12:7
the people themselves.[558]
6 Sariel[559] one of the holy angels, who is in charge of the spirits 10:1-3; 27:2; LadJac 3:1-3
who sin against the spirit.[560] 1QM 9.15
7 Gabriel,[561] one of the holy angels, who is in charge of Paradise, 9:1; 10:9-10; 32:3-6; Lk 1:19
the serpents (seraphim? [562]) and the cherubim.[563] 14:11; 40:9; Gen 3:1-4, 24
8 Remiel,[564] one of the holy angels,[565] whom God set over those 2Bar 63:6

---

means "light/light—bearer of God" (H1 pg. 234). In 1 Enoch he is mentioned in (19:1; 21:5, 9; 27:2; 33:3; 72:1; 74:2; 75:3-4; 78:10; 79:6; 80:1; and 82:7).

551 "Tartarus is the deepest level of Hell in Greek mythology, the abode of the Titans" (OL pg. 54). **Tartarus occurs in the New Testament only one time (2Pet 2:4) where it is clearly referencing the Book of the Watchers.** B has: "over alarm and terror" Isaac has: "of eternity and of trembling." Knibb has: "of thunder and of tremors" Nickelsburg has: "of the world and Tartarus" Olson has: "of the cosmos and of Tartarus."

552 Raphael is the healer (40:9). He is the angel who accompanies Tobit (Tobit 3:17; 5:4; 7:8; 8:2; 9:1, 5; 11:2, 7; 12:15). Mentions in 1 Enoch include: (9:1; 10:4; 22:3, 6; 32:6; 40:9; 54:6; 68:2-4; 71:8, 9, 13).

553 Examples of angels guiding spirits who have passed away are found in: (Luke 16:22, TJob 47:10-11, 52:1-12, TAbA 20:10-12).

554 Raguel, or Reul (friend of God) is also named in (1En 23:4).

555 The translation of this passage by many translators (N, C, I, and K) as "who takes vengeance on the world of the luminaries" is likely a "misunderstanding of an underlying Aramaic verb meaning 'follow (like a shepherd)'" (OL pg. 54). The idea is that he is "the shepherd of the luminaries" (N1 pg. 188, BL pg. 36, 162-163)).

556 Other appearances of Michael include: (Dan 10:13, 21; 12:1; Jude 9; Rev 12:7; 1QM 17.6-7; 4Q470). In 1 Enoch he is named in (9:1; 10:11; 24:6; 40:9; 54:6; 60:4-5; 67:12; 68:2-4; 69:14,15; 71:3, 8, 9, 13).

557 "The good ones of the people." Michael is the protector of the righteous and holy, the elect, see 25:4-5. OL has: "who has been entrusted with the benefits of the people, being also entrusted with rulership of the people themselves;" N has: "who has been put in charge of the good ones of the people." BL has: "who has been put in charge of the blessings to come to the people (of Israel)."

558 B has: "rules the nation" rather than "being also entrusted with rulership of
the people themselves." I has: "for (he is) obedient in his benevolence over the people and the nations" N omits "being…themselves", as not original. K has "in charge of the nation."

559 Sariel cf. Ladder of Jacob 3:1-3; 4QEn[a] 1 iv 9.1; 1QM 9.15. C and K have Saraqâêl 'he who has mastery over all'

560 Instead of "who is in charge of the spirits who sin against the spirit" in agreement with N; OL has: "who is over the spirits of men who commit spiritual sin;" K has: "who is in charge of the spirits of men who cause the spirits to sin." Ethiopic could read: "Sariel, one of the holy angels, who is in charge of the spirits of the sons of men who sin against the spirit." Is this a clue to the unpardonable sin (Mt 12:30-31; Mk 3:28-30; Lk 12:8-10)?

561 Gabriel is also mentioned in: (Dan 8:16; 9:21). He is the angel of the enunciation both for John the Baptist and Christ in (Lk 1:19, 26). In 1 Enoch, mentions of Gabriel occur at (9:1; 10:9; 40:9; 54:6; 71:8, 9, 13). In 1En 40:9 he is "set over all the powers." He is the "king of the angels, the prince of princes" in *Gabriel's Revelation* 80-81.

562 The serpents should most likely be Seraphim. In Gen 3:24 the flaming sword many be related to a seraph. In Genesis 3:1-5 the serpent was not a talking snake but a seraph. Seraphim are a six-winged angelic order of lightning like, fiery attendants of God (Isa 6:2–7).

563 Cherubim are four-winged, four-faced angelic beings who guard paradise (Gen 3:24; Ex 25:19). They are close attendants of God (Ezek 10:1-22).

564 "Remiel may mean ("El/God lifts up"). The name suggests "God raises" (as in resurrection)" (N1 pg. 190). Other texts that mention him are (4 Ezra 4:36 (Jeremiel = Remiel)), (2Bar 55:3 ("the angel who is set over visions")), and (2Bar 63:6 "his angel who speaks with you").

565 Baty adds here: "who presides over repentance, and the hope of those who will inherit eternal life."

who rise (from the dead).
The names of the seven archangels.[566 567 568] 81:5; Rev 1:4, 16, 20; 3En 17:1-3 OdesSol 4:8

The Second Journey

The Angelic Prison

21 1 I traveled[569] to a formless void.[570 571] *Princ* 4.1.35; 1QS 4.13
2 and there I saw a terrible thing; neither heaven above, 18:12; Gen 1:2; Ps-Philo 28:7
nor a firmly founded earth below, but a place with no Mt 8:12; 22:13; 25:30

---

[566] **Olson comments on this verse as "one of the very earliest clear references to the resurrection in Jewish literature."** (OL pg. 54) **It predates the passages about resurrection in (2 Maccabees 7:9, 14 and 12:43-44) by over a century.** References to human resurrection in 1 Enoch occur in (22:13; 51:1; 61:5; 62:15-16; 90:33; 91:10; 103:4). For another early reference see (TBenj 10:5-9). However, Olson may be overlooking Old Testament passages about the resurrection of the dead (Ps 16:10; 133:3; Isa 66:22; Dan 12:2-3; Hos 6:2); some of which are clearly speaking of a bodily resurrection (Isa 26:19; Ezek 37:12).

[567] Nickelsburg, and this text, add a sentence in this location found in Greek but not Ethiopic, "The names of the seven archangels." For the seven angels see: (Rev 1:4, 16, 20; 8:2; and possibly Zech 4:2,10).

[568] Enoch's familiarity with watchers/angels reminds readers of Gen 5:22: "Enoch walked with God after he fathered Methuselah 300 years and had other sons and daughters," and Gen 5:24 "Enoch walked with God, and he was not, for God took him." The word for God in both passages is Elohim, which is the same term used for the members of the Council of God in Psalm 82:1. Enoch walked so intimately with the watchers/angels/Elohim that they took him prior to death. No other human has had such intimate communion with the Council of God than Enoch. See 1En 19:3. Due to Enoch's inside knowledge, his name was a popular pseudonym for the body of outside the Jewish mainstream (i.e., antiestablishment) literature. This literature arose in the third century BC or earlier and continued until AD second century.

[569] "Traveled," "(ephodeuō; "to make rounds")" The material here is very similar to (parallel to) chapters 18 and 19. Enoch now begins to revisit the places in chapters 18-19 in reverse order as Enoch moves eastward. Olson opines: "The repetition of motifs and ever shifting landscape are very like a dream. This whole portion of *Enoch* (chs 17-36) has an authentically surreal atmosphere matched by few other apocalypses" (OL pg. 56).

[570] "Void," literally: "where nothing is done." This is the outer darkness spoken of by Christ: "I tell you, many will come from east and west and recline at table with Abraham, Isaac, and Jacob in the kingdom of heaven, while the sons of the kingdom will be thrown into the outer darkness. In that place there will be weeping and gnashing of teeth" (Mt 8:11-12. Cf. also Mt 22:13; 25:30;1QS 4.13)

[571] Verse 21:1 was quoted by Origen (AD 184-253) "I have walked on even to imperfection." (*De Principiis* 4.1.35) **Origen considered the texts to be authentic and Enoch to be a prophet, whose writings were "scripture"** (N1 pg. 92). **However, Origen also states "the books which bear the name Enoch do not at all circulate in the Churches as divine"** (*Against Celsius* 5.54). **But it must be kept in mind, that in his time, the bizarre text of 2 Enoch was most likely also "circulating in the name of Enoch." That he had access to 2 Enoch is implied in (*De Principiis* 1.3.3, AD 220-230) where Origen seems to be referencing 2En 24:2-5; 25:3-5; or 33:4.**

order[572] and terrible.[573] [574] Jude 13; Jer 4:23-26
3 And there I saw seven stars of heaven bound together, 10:4; Rev 8:8; Job 38:31
like great mountains, and burning in fire. 18:6; 12-16; 24:2
4 Then I said: "For what sin have they been bound?
Why have they been cast down here?" Rev 9:1; Isa 14:15
5 Then Uriel, one of the holy angels who was with me and a leader
among them,[575] spoke to me, saying: "Enoch, why do you ask 25:1
and why are you eager for the truth? Dan 7:16
6 These are (some) of the stars of heaven who have transgressed 80:6; Jude 13
the commandment of the Lord, and were bound here till the completion Isa 24:21
of ten thousand years,[576] the time demanded for their sins."
7 And from there I traveled to another place, even more terrible than Rev 20:1-3, 14
the former; and I saw dreadful things—a great fire there burning and
blazing. And that place had a narrow cleft (extending down) to the
abyss, filled with columns of great fires descending; 18:11; 2Bar 59:5

---

[572] "No order" is translated by others as "chaotic."

[573] **This type of void has been reported in numerous near-death experiences.**

> "The second type of experience involved 'a paradoxical sensation of ceasing to exist entirely, or of being condemned to a featureless void for eternity ... Sometimes ... a sense of despair that life as we know it, not only no longer exists, but in fact never did, that it was all a cruel joke'" (Greyson, Bruce, and Bush, Nancy Evans, *Distressing Near Death Experiences*, Psychiatry 55:95-110 1992, pg. 101).
>
> An example experience is: "A man who was attacked by a hitchhiker felt himself rise out of his body: "I suddenly was surrounded by total blackness, floating in nothing but black space, with no up, no down, left, or right ... What seemed like an eternity went by. I fully lived it in this misery. I was only allowed to think and reflect." Another example: "It was no longer a peaceful feeling; it had become pure hell. I had become a light out in the heavens, and I was screaming, but no sound was going forth. It was worse than any nightmare. I was spinning around, and I realized that this was eternity; this was what forever was going to be.... I felt the aloneness, the emptiness of space, the vastness of the universe, except for me, a mere ball of light, screaming" (Bush, Nancy Evans, and Greyson, Bruce, 2014. *Distressing Near-Death Experiences: The Basics,* The Journal of the Missouri State Medical Association. 111(6): 486–491).

[574] "This place-and so the Watchers' prison- is separate from god's ordered world" (H1 pg. 191).

[575] Nickelsburg has: "he was their leader". In 24:6, Michael is presented as the leader. This likely means he was a leader among them or "a leading angel among them"; the equivalent of an archangel. (BL pg. 37, 164)

[576] B has: "infinite number of days," I has: "10 million years," N has: "ten thousand years" It is an infinite period. The infinite time period matches the infinite magnitude of their sin. Charles notes that among the Greeks; ten thousand years was the sentence imposed on "sinful souls" (C pg. 45). (Cf. Plato Phaedrus 248E).

neither their extent nor their size was I able to see nor to discern.[577] [578]
8 Then I said: "How fearful is this place and terrible to look on!"
9 Then Uriel, one of the holy angels who was with me,
spoke up and said to me: "Enoch, why are you so afraid and terrified?" 108:3-6
And I replied: "(I am terrified] on account of this fearful place and
before this painful spectacle."
10 And he said to me: "This place is the prison for the angels. 18:14; 19:1; 1Cor. 6:3; Jude 6
Here they will be imprisoned for an eternity."[579] [580] 10:13; Mt 25:41; 2Pet 2:4
Ps 36:12; DialTrypho 141

Sheol

22 1 From there I was transported to another place; and he (Uriel)
showed me towards the west, a large and lofty mountain of
flint-hard rock,[581]
2 and there were four caverns in it,[582] deep and wide and very smooth: *Ant* 18.1.3 §§14
three of them were dark, and one illuminated, with a fountain of water Lk 16:25; 1QH$_a$ 14.20
in its midst. And I said: "How bare these caverns are, and how
deep and dark they appear."[583]
3 Then Raphael, one of the holy angels who was with me, answered

---

[577] **Falling into a fiery abyss has been reported in near-death experiences; these are most certainly underreported due to the intense mental anguish involved.**

> "The third type, represented by the smallest number of accounts, features graphic hellish symbolism such as threatening demons or falling into a dark pit" (Greyson and Bush, *Distressing Near Death Experiences*, Psychiatry 55:95-110 1992, pg. 105).
>
> An example experience is: "A woman who attempted suicide felt her body sliding downward in a cold, dark, watery environment: 'When I reached the bottom, it resembled the entrance to a cave, with what looked like webs hanging.... I heard cries, wails, moans, and the gnashing of teeth. I saw these beings that resembled humans, with the shape of a head and body, but they were ugly and grotesque.... They were frightening and sounded like they were tormented, in agony'" (Bush and Greyson, *Distressing Near-Death Experiences: The Basics,* The Journal of the Missouri State Medical Association. 111(6): 486–491).

[578] Milik identified DSS fragment (En^c xxi) with 21:2-4 but Black places it in 21:7 (M pg. 228-229 and BL pg. 164).
[579] **The thought of hell as a place for "the devil and his angels" is somewhat new to the Jewish world in Enoch. While not inconsistent with the Old Testament, passages such as this are what Jesus is referring to in Mt 25:41. "Then he will say to those on his left, 'Depart from me, you cursed, into the eternal fire prepared for the devil and his angels."**
[580] Job 4:18 reveals that God charges the angels with error. **This is evidence that the belief in fallen angels goes back to the ancients since Job is usually dated to the 6th century BC or earlier.** Origen considered the Book of Job to predate Moses (*Cels.* 6.43).
[581] Olson notes: "The west was the land of the dead in Egyptian, Greek, and Mesopotamian thought. Some Babylonian myths feature an underworld located inside a mountain" (OL pg. 56).
[582] These hollow places are inside the mountain, think of a mountain with caves on the sides. Since they are smooth; climbing out is not an option. "Here the righteous dead are put into a separate category from the three divisions of the unrighteous dead. The bright spring of water is an image apparently drawn from classical Greek material about Hades" (H1 pg. 200). **Josephus applied this passage to the beliefs of the Pharisees** (*Ant* 18.1.3 §§14; *War* 2.8.14).
[583] **These four caves seem to be meant for people who died before the flood.** This is apparent in 1En 22:12 "murdered in the days of the sinners" and in 22:13 "who were partners with the lawless ones." These could be the "spirits in prison" mentioned in (1 Peter 3:19) and those who are dead in (1 Peter 4:6).

me saying: “These caverns exist as gathering places for the spirits Isa 24:22; Ezek 26:20
of the souls of the dead,[584] for this very purpose they were fashioned 90:18; 100:4-5; 102:5, 11; 103:7
that here all the souls of the children of men should be assembled.[585] [586]
4 And see, these pits are fashioned in this way for their incarceration, 63:10
until the day they will be judged, until the time of the last day Jn 5:28-29; Isa 26:19
of the great judgement which will be executed upon them.”[587] 16:1; 51:1; Dan 12:2; *War* 2.8.14
5 There I saw the spirit of a dead man crying out unceasingly and
making accusation; and his lamenting reached up to heaven as he 9:2-3; Rev 6:9-11
cried and made suit.[588] 4Ezra 4:35-37
6 Then I asked Raphael, the watcher and holy one who was with me,[589]
and I said to him: “Whose spirit is this whose voice is thus going forth
and complaining to heaven?”
7 And he answered me, saying: “This is the spirit that came forth from LAE 22:4-5
Abel;[590] killed by his brother Cain. Gen 4:10; Jub 4:3; Lk 11:51
He will bring accusations against him until his seed perishes from Heb 11:4; 12:24; Mt 23:35 1Jn 3:12
the face of the earth, and from the offspring of men his seed is 39:1; Ps 21:10; Jub 5:6-7
obliterated.”[591] [592] Rev 6:10

---

[584] This is the abode of the Rephaim, the shades, the place of the dead. The Rephaim are quasi-divine dead warrior kings who inhabit the underworld (Heiser, Michael S., 2015. *The Unseen Realm*, pg. 200). (See Isa 14:9-11; 26:14)

[585] Portions of 22:3-6 are found in DSS (4Q206 1.22); and portions of 22:3-7 are found in DSS (4QEn[e] 1xxii).

[586] **This passage displays a belief in the afterlife at a very early point in Judaism. This is the first time a Jewish writer describes the Greek tradition of an afterlife where people are separated due to their deeds on earth. This would argue for a composition during the Hellenistic period. Olson observes: “The entire chapter in fact, fairly swarms with concepts also found in Greek, Egyptian, Babylonian, and Ugaritic literature, to say nothing of later Judaism and Christianity”** (OL pg. 56). Charles observes: “This is the most ancient account of the doctrine of Sheol from the Pharisaic or Chasid standpoint, but clearly this doctrine cannot have leaped into life full-grown as it appears here, but must already have passed through several stages of development (C pg. 46).

[587] The human dead are kept separate until the great judgement when they are told to “Depart from me, you cursed, into the eternal fire prepared for the devil and his angels” (Mt 25:41). “Come, you who are blessed by my Father, inherit the kingdom prepared for you from the foundation of the world” (Mt 25:34). “Do not marvel at this, for an hour is coming when all who are in the tombs will hear his voice and come out, those who have done good to the resurrection of life, and those who have done evil to the resurrection of judgment” (Jn 5:28-29). Even in Christ’s time, the resurrection was far from universally accepted (Mt 22:23-33).

[588] The Ethiopic is plural and the Greek is singular for those making suit. The Greek is correct since it is obviously only Abel. Verse 7 tells us this is the voice of Abel making suit against Cain and those like him and their posterity. The idea is similar to that found in (Gen 4:10-11, Mt 23:34-36, Lk 11:50-51, and Heb 12:24).

[589] 1En 22:6 is illuminating in the Aramaic of the DSS. The Ethiopic and Greek of this verse have “angel” but the Aramaic has “watcher and holy one”. **This “suggests that elsewhere in this section, where there are no Aram counterparts, *holy angel* may also have translated Aram *watcher(s) and holy one(s)*”** (N pg. 42 note *a*).

[590] **Abel and Cain serve as types for martyrs and their murderers who will certainly face judgment** (cf. Rev 6:10). **This was especially poignant in the second temple period when this was written, given the brutal persecution of observant Jews.**

[591] “Seed of Cain” Cain’s seed would have been destroyed in a universal flood assuming none survived.

[592] **This verse indicates that the line of Cain was especially involved in mixing with the watchers since they are singled out for annihilation. (cf. Jub 5:6-7) The writer of Hebrews seems to be alluding to this verse in 11:4 where Abel “though he died, he still speaks.”**

The Four Caverns

8 Then I asked about all the caverns, why are they separated, 41:8
one from the other?[593]
9 And he answered me, saying: "These three[594] have been made to keep
the spirits of the dead separated. 56:8; Lk 16:19-31, esp. 26
And this one has been kept separate for the spirits of the righteous,[595] 39:4-5; Heb 12:23; *Ref* 9.22
where there is a bright fountain of water.[596] 17:4; 48:1; 96:5-6; *ActsPer* 7, 8
10 And that one was fashioned for the spirits of the sinners who die
and are buried in the earth; but judgement has not been carried out
upon them in their lives.[597] [598]
11 Here their spirits shall be set apart, in this great pain, 99:11
till the great day of judgement; (the day) of scourgings and torment 103:6-7
of those forever accursed, (that there will be) retribution on their Mt 22:13

---

[593] This text follows Gk[a]. Knibb following the Ethiopic, translates 22:8 as: "Then I asked about him and about the judgement on all and I said, 'Why is one separated from another?'"

[594] N1 sees three as "secondary" or not in the original.

[595] See 39:4-5 and 104:6 where the righteous are already in heaven with the righteous celestial beings rather than in Sheol. This argues that this passage is speaking of the pre-flood dead.

[596] **This description of Sheol matches Christ's parable in (Luke 16:19-31); with the division and the extreme thirst exhibited by the rich man but with Lazarus having access to water.** Olson notes the tradition of extreme thirst in Sheol "was common throughout the ancient world, attested, for example, in Greek cults and in Assyrian religion" (OL pg. 58). It is also found in Jewish and Christian sources (4Ezra 8:59 and Lk 16:24). A similar description of a bright well-watered eternal state, likely drawn from this passage, is found in (*The Passion of the Holy Martyrs, Perpetua and Felicity* 2.4, AD 203). A bright well-ventilated place of rest for souls, was also a doctrine of the Essenes (*Ref* 9.XXII). A similar, but expanded, description of Sheol/Hades can be found in *An Extract Out of Josephus's Discourse to the Greeks Concerning Hades* which is also attributed to Hippolytus (ca. AD 170-236). The Apocalypse of Zephaniah states that the saints always exist in light (ApZeph 2:7).

[597] 1En 22:9 describes the place for the righteous. Verses 10 and 11 seem to describe the place for sinners who were not punished in life and now undergo scourgings and torments in this pit. Verse 12 describes the place for those who were murdered on earth and now make suit for vengeance. This place ties back to verses 5-7. These souls are not in the righteous category. Verse 13 describes a place for those who were lawless, godless, and impious. The argument can be made that verses 12 and 13 refer to the generation of the flood. This line of thought is strengthened by *The Apocalypse of Zephaniah* 6:15 (100 BC to AD 175) which reads in part: "I am the great angel, Eremiel, who is over the abyss and Hades, the one in which all the souls are imprisoned from the end of the Flood, which came upon the earth, until this day." So there seems to be a separation between pre-flood and post-flood souls. In Enoch 20:8, Remiel=Eremiel is set over those who rise, but these souls who partnered with the giants in 22:13 do not rise. Olson weighs in on this subject: "If we put *Enoch* 20:8: 22:13 and Apoc. Zeph. 6:15 together, we get a consistent picture. It seems the author of the apocalypse of Zephaniah interpreted the inhabitants of cavern four in Enoch 22:13 as wicked humans from before the flood, a unique class who will not rise again." See also Mishnah Sanhedrin 10:3: "The generation of the Flood have no share in the world to come, nor shall they stand in the judgement. Was this idea originally inspired by Ps 88:10 and Isa 26:14, which can be interpreted as teaching that there is no resurrection for the Rephaim (RSV: shades)?" (OL pg. 70)

[598] This category would include the rich man in (Lk 16:25-26): "But Abraham said, 'Child, remember that you in your lifetime received your good things, and Lazarus in like manner bad things; but now he is comforted here, and you are in anguish. And besides all this, between us and you a great chasm has been fixed, in order that those who would pass from here to you may not be able, and none may cross from there to us.'" Note also that the rich man was buried, but Lazarus was carried away by angels (Lk 16:22). Lazarus would be in the illuminated place with the bright fountain of water (22:9). That is why he had access to water and the rich man did not (Lk 16:24).

spirits. There they shall be bound for ever.[599]
12 And that (third) cavern has been separated off for the spirits
of those who have accusations to bring and disclosures to make 103:14-15; Rev 6:10
with regard to their destruction, when they were murdered in the
days of the sinners.[600]
13 And that (fourth cavern) has been fashioned for the spirits of men
who are not righteous but rather sinners—wholly godless,[601] who were
complete in transgression, and of the transgressors Dan 12:2
who were partners with the lawless ones.[602] Mt 7:23; 10:28; ApZeph 6:15
Their spirits will not be punished on the day of judgement,
but neither will they be raised, from there?" [603] [604] 20:8
14 Then I blessed the Lord of glory[605] and said: "Blessed be the Judge
of righteousness,[606] and blessed are you, O Lord of majesty and 1Cor 2:8; Jas 2:1
righteousness, who rules over the world!"

The River of Fire

23 1 From there I was carried off [607] to another place, toward the west,
right to the ends of the earth.
2 And I was shown a blazing fire which ran without resting or pause 14:19-23; 17:4-5
in its course, (holding to it equally) by day and by night. Phaedo 111D; 113A

---

[599] At the end of (1En 22:11), Ethiopic adds: "even if from the beginning of the world" which may be an addition (gloss) by a scribe.

[600] These are spirits who were "murdered in the days of the sinners." They don't fall into the category of the righteous ones in the illuminated cavern; but they have information relevant to form cases against their murders in the fourth cavern. The days of sinners would apply to the preflood days, and their murderers would include the giants (OL pg. 58).

[601] Isaac has: "but sinners and perfect criminals,"

[602] "Lawless ones" these are the fallen watchers and their progeny (1En 7:6). Paul describes the Antichrist using the term "lawless one" (2Thes 2:8-9). This indicates the Antichrist will be a fallen watcher or more likely a hybrid demigod. **This parallel, and Christ's statements in Mt 24:37-39 and Lk 17:26-27 concerning conditions before His return, would argue for an appearance of fallen watchers at the end of the age! Many humans will find themselves judged for being partners with the fallen angels and demons.**

[603] (1En 22:13-24:1) is found in the DSS (4QEn[d] 1 xi).

[604] This group seems like it should be the one most subject to judgement, but it is not. Nickelsburg opines: "The simplest explanation is that different from those described in vv 10-11, these sinners were judged during their lifetime, and for that reason they need not be recompensed either immediately after death or at the great day of judgement" (N1 pg. 308). A more likely explanation is that just as the righteous in the illuminated well-watered space have already been found to be righteous (22:9); the "wholly ungodly" have no need for judgement and have already been judged and are suffering eternal torment in this place. Their sins are so obvious that they need no further legal proceeding. It is also apparent that since this group is specifically named as partners with the lawless ones, (preflood evil spiritual entities), this group is limited to people from before the flood. Note: Dan 12:2 "many" not "all."

[605] "Lord of Glory" is used often in *1 Enoch* (25:3; 27:3, 5; 36:4; 40:3; 63:2; 75:3; 83:8) but nowhere else in pre-Christian texts. The Book of Enoch is the likely source Paul draws this term from in (1Cor 2:8) and James draws from in (Jas 2:1).

[606] This text follows the Aramaic. Ethiopic reads: "Blessed by (be?) my Lord, the Lord of Righteousness." Gk.[a] reads: "Blessed are you, Lord of Righteousness" (K pg. 212).

[607] "Aramaic reads *wblt* (4QEn[d] 1 11:3), which means 'I was transported.' Other language of Enoch being 'transported' is found in 1 Enoch 14:8; 32:2; 36:1" (H1 pg. 202).

3 And I asked: "What is this (fire) that has no rest?"
4 Then Raguel,[608] one of the holy angels who was with me, answered
and said to me: "This flaming current is the fire in the west which
tends[609] all the luminaries of heaven." 20:4

Mountain Paradise and the Tree of Life

24 1 And, from there I was transported to another place on the earth,[610]
he showed me mountains with fiery ground between them,
glowing in the night.[611]
2 I went beyond them and saw seven magnificent mountains, of precious 18:6-9; Rev 7:9
and beautiful stones, each differing from the other, Phaedo 110 D-E; Ps-Philo 12:9
but all (the mountains) were precious, glorious and beautiful in Ezek 28:11-14
appearance.
Three of them (laying) towards the east, were firmly set one on the other,
and three to the south, one on the other, with deep, rugged ravines,
not one of which approached any other.[612]
3 The seventh mountain (was) in the middle of these, and it rose Ps 48:1-2
above them in height resembling the seat of a throne; and fragrant 18:8; 25:3; OdesSol 11:15
trees surrounded it. ApPet 15-16
4 Among them was a tree with a fragrance such as I have never at any Ezek 31:7-9; 15-18
time smelt, and no tree among them, nor any other, flourished like it; Pss 1:3; 92:12, 14
it had a fragrance beyond all fragrances, and its leaves and flowers Prov 11:24; 13:12; 15:4
and wood never wither;[613] its fruit is beautiful, resembling the clusters Gen 3:22; Ezek 47:12
of the date-palm. 32:3-6; Rev 22:2 OdesSol 11:16
5 Then I said: "How beautiful is this tree and fragrant! Sir 24:12-17
(How) pleasant are its leaves,
and (how) very lovely to the eye are its blossoms!"[614] [615] Prov 3:17-18
6 Then Michael, one of the holy and revered[616] angels who was with me, 20:5

[608] Nickelsburg uses: "Reuel" meaning "shepherd of God". C, BL, OL, I and K all have "Raguel." In 20:4 he is the one "who tends the host of the luminaries as a shepherd."
[609] K and C have: "persecutes" in place of "tends". N has "pursues"; OL has "tends." The idea may be, that the fire in the west keeps the luminaries in order and burning. Thus, the combination of a shepherd tending, and the fire igniting (persecuting) the stars.
[610] Ethiopic but not Greek, adds this phrase placed at the beginning of 24:1 indicating a change in location; "from there I was transported to another place on the earth." Nickelsburg does not include it, viewing it as secondary. Black, Knibb, and Isaac include it. Aramaic is no help.
[611] This phrase is from Aramaic, attested in (1QEn^d 1 xi); "the ground between them was of burning fire" (M pg. 218).
[612] **This dwelling place of God with the tree of life, is a paradise virtually inaccessible to threats; given the remoteness, flames, terrain and height. Not to mention, it would be guarded by multitudes of powerful celestial beings.** Enoch, like Isaiah, is seeing a future abode of God and his elect (cf. Isa 2:2-3).
[613] **That the tree does not wither forever, indicates that this is the tree of life (cf. 25:4-6).**
[614] Some Ethiopic texts have "fruit" in place of "blossoms" which is found in G^a.
[615] (1En 24:1-5) describes an earthly Eden.
[616] Greek omits "revered" or as some translate "honored", but it is included in the Ethiopic.

and was their leader, responded[617]

25 1 and said to me: "Enoch, why are you so inquisitive concerning
the fragrance of this tree, and why do you desire to learn the truth?" 21:5
2 I answered him: "I desire to learn about everything, but most of all,
about this tree!" GbRev 31
3 He answered: "This high mountain which you see, whose summit
is like a throne of God, is (indeed) the throne on which the great 18:8; Isa 2:2-3
Lord, the Holy One of glory,[618] the everlasting King, will sit when he 1:3-4; 17:2; 22:14; Deut 10:17
descends to visit the earth with goodness. 1:8; 5:6-9; 77:1; 1Cor 2:8
4 And as for this fragrant tree, no mortal shall be allowed to touch it 24:3-4; Gen 2:9; 3:3, 22; 2En 8:3
until the great judgement,[619] when he requites vengeance on all, Rev 2:7; 22:14; ApPet 15-16
and brings everything to eternal consummation. Isa 34:8; 61:2; 63:4
Then it will be given to the righteous and holy.[620] TLev 18:10-11; Prov 3:18
5 Its fruit shall be given to the chosen for food;[621] and it shall be Rev 2:7; Ps 92:12-14
transplanted to the sacred place beside the house of God,[622] Rev 22:2,14; 4Ezra 8:52
the everlasting King.
6 Then they will rejoice with great joy, and enter into the holy place;
and its fragrance will permeate to their very bones; Isa 66:14; Sir 49:10; 4Ezra 2:12
they shall live a long life upon earth such as your fathers lived;[623] 2Bar 73:2-7; 74; Gen 3:22-24
and in those days no sorrow, or plague or torment,[624] 10:17; Wis 3:1-4; Rev 21:4; 22:2
nor calamity will touch them." 4Ezra 7:123; Isa 65:17-25
7 Then I blessed the God of glory, the King of the ages, 14:20

---

[617] **Michael is the archangel or chief angel. This likely means he is an archangel over other angels who are not archangels.** Michael is mentioned several times in Daniel, "The prince of the kingdom of Persia withstood me twenty-one days, but Michael one of the chief princes, came to help me" (Dan 10:13). "But now I will return to fight against the prince of Persia; and when I go out, behold, the prince of Greece will come. But I will tell you what is inscribed in the book of truth; there is none who contends by my side against these except Michael, your prince" (Dan 10:21). "At that time shall arise Michael, the great prince who has charge of your people" (Dan 12:1). Michael is also named in (Jude 9) "But when the archangel Michael, contending with the devil, was disputing about the body of Moses, he did not presume to pronounce a blasphemous judgement, but said, 'The Lord rebuke you.'" Jude 9 shows, that even a fearsome being like Michael, does not take judgement into his own hands but leaves judgement to God. The Jude 9 reference is thought to be from the lost final portion of the *Assumption of Moses,* Aka. *Testament of Moses* written AD 6-33.

[618] G^a reads (literally), "the great Lord, the Holy One of Glory" (H1 pg. 209) (cf. 1Cor 2:8; Jas 2:1).

[619] **No one is allowed access to the tree of life until after the Day of the Lord. The tree of life in (Revelation 2:7 and 22:1-2, 14) is based on (Ezek 47:12) but modified to match this passage of 1 Enoch. Unlike Ezek 47:12, but like 1 Enoch, in Revelation, it is single tree, it is the tree of life, it is in the paradise of God. Its fruit is only for the elect, and the elect are allowed access to it. Common to all three texts; the trees are for food and healing. Clearly John in Revelation is drawing on 1 Enoch as a source.**

[620] Ethiopic has righteous and humble in place of righteous and holy.

[621] Isaac, from Ethiopic, has "for life" in place of "for food."

[622] "House of God" = Jerusalem.

[623] Note, this is a long but not eternal life. Charles opines: "The writer of 1-36 has not risen to the conception of an eternal life of blessedness for the righteous, and so has not advanced a single step beyond the conceptions found in Isa 65; 66" (C pg. 53). But alternately the writer could be describing a millennial period rather than an eternal state.

[624] **John is clearly pulling from 1 Enoch 25:6 for Rev 21:4. "He will wipe away every tear from their eyes, and death shall be no more, neither shall there be mourning, nor crying, nor pain anymore, for the former things have passed away." This demonstrates John's high regard for The Book of the Watchers.**

who has prepared such things for the righteous! Ps-Philo 26:6, 14
And has created such things and promised to give (them) to them.

Excursus: What about the Book of Jasher?

The Book of Jasher/Jashar (Sefer ha-Yashar) is mentioned in the Masoretic text of Josh 10:13 "And the sun stood still, and the moon stopped, until the nation took vengeance on their enemies. Is this not written in the Book of Jashar?" The Book of Jasher is however, not mentioned in the LXX text of Josh 10:13. 2Sam 1:18 reads: "and he said it should be taught to the people of Judah; behold, it is written in the Book of Jashar." The LXX reads "behold it is written in a book of the upright." Sefer ha-Yahar means book of the upright. A possible 3rd mention is in 1Kings 8:53 LXX "a book of the song."

A Book of Jasher, named after the one in the bible, first appeared printed in Rabbinical Hebrew in Venice in 1625 published by Joseph Ben Samuel. There may have been a previous edition of this same text printed in Naples in 1552. Joseph Ben Samuel presented two dramatic scenarios for the transmission of the text to his time, for which no evidence has been found. Leon Modena (1571-1648) recognized it as a forgery, soon after its publication. (Leon Modena's *Ari Nohem*, MS A ed Libowitz 1929 pp73-74). However, this book of Jasher was widely printed in Europe over the next 200 years, becoming very popular. "In the compiling of the work the following sources were made use of, namely: the Babylonian Talmud; Bereshit Rabbah; Pirḳe R. Eliezer; the Yalḳut; the Chronicle of Moses; Yosippon; Midrash Abkir; and various Arabic legends. That Italy, however, was the land of its origin seems evident from the author's knowledge of Italian names, as Tuscany, Lombardy, and the Tiber (x. 7-36), and also from the description of the rape of the Sabines (xvii. 1-14). The appearance of Arabic names, such as Sa'id, Allah, Abdallah, and Khalif, only tends to show that the book was written in southern Italy, where Arabic influence was strongly felt even in the eleventh century" (Jewish Encyclopedia "Yashar"). Its authenticity was challenged in early November of 1828 when debate about another "Book of Jasher" AKA "Pseudo-Jasher" appeared. This totally separate 37-chapter work had been published in English by Jacob Ilive, a Christian Deist, in 1751. This forgery led to an investigation of Joseph Ben Samuel's 1625 text. Moses Samuel, a Hebrew scholar of Liverpool, translated the Hebrew text of Joseph Ben Samuel's book into English in 1839. In 1840, Mordecai Manuel Noah and A. S. Gould published Moses Samuel's translation. This is the text most commonly circulating today in English. (Chiel, Arthur A., *The Mysterious book of Jasher,* Judaism, A Quarterly Journal, Issue 103, Vol 26, Number 3, Summer 1977, pgs. 367-374.)

The date and provenance of the text are nowhere near that of the Biblical book of Jasher, having a 2500-year gap! No trace of the text has been found in any collection of ancient manuscripts. It was not referenced in any of the later books of the Old Testament. No fragment of it was found among the Dead Sea Scrolls. It was not referenced by the writers of the New Testament, nor by the Church fathers, nor has it been accepted by rabbinic Judaism. By all appearances it is a product of the medieval period. Unbelievably, in spite of all this, the Book of Jasher has a large and loyal following among amateurs who accept it as the Book of Jasher mentioned in the Bible. It is even promoted as such by some leaders in the Christian community, who thus instantly lose credibility! Specialist scholars in the field universally and rightfully shun the Book of Jasher as a medieval forgery.

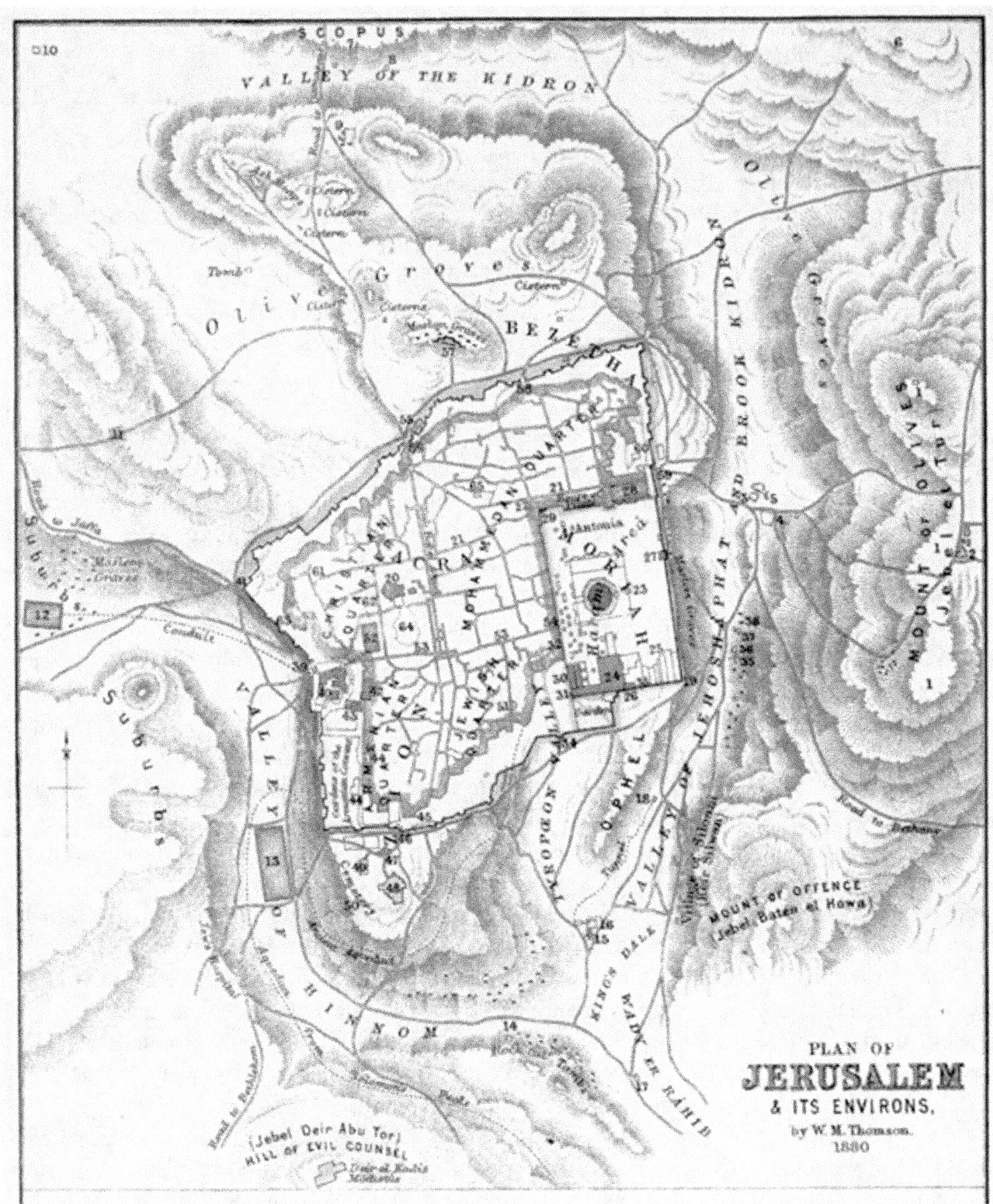
SCOPUS
VALLEY OF THE KIDRON
Olive Groves
BEZETHA
Suburbs
VALLEY OF HINNOM
KIDRON BROOK
Olive Groves
MOUNT OF OLIVES
MOHAMMEDAN QUARTER
CHRISTIAN QUARTER
ARMENIAN QUARTER
JEWISH QUARTER
MORIAH
OPHEL
VALLEY OF JEHOSHAPHAT
TYROPŒON
KING'S DALE
WADY ER RÂHIB
MOUNT of OFFENCE
(Jebel Baten el Howa)
(Jebel Deir Abu Tor)
HILL OF EVIL COUNSEL
Road to Bethany
Road to Jaffa
Road to Bethlehem
Moslem Graves
Conduit
Cistern
Tomb
Antonia
Village of Siloam
PLAN OF
JERUSALEM
& ITS ENVIRONS,
by W. M. Thomson.
1880

Jerusalem, the Center of the Earth

26 1 And from there I was transported to the center of the earth,[625] and 90:26; Ezek 5:5; 38:12; Jub 8:12
I saw a blessed place,[626] where there were trees, with branches alive and 10:18-19; Rom 11:17-24
sprouting [from a tree that had been cut down].[627] [628] [629] Job 14:7-9; Num 17:8; Heb 9:4
2 And there I saw a holy mountain,[630] and coming forth from beneath
the mount, from the east side, a stream: and its descent was Ezek 47:1-12
towards the south.[631]
3 I saw towards the east another mountain higher than the first;[632]
and between them a ravine deep and narrow,[633] and through it, a
stream ran alongside this (higher) mount.
4 And to the west was another mount,[634] lower than it and of no
great height, and a ravine at its foot between them, deep and dry,[635]
and another valley[636] at the apex of the three mountains.
5 All the ravines were deep and narrow, of hard rock,
and no tree was growing in them.
6 I marveled at the mountains and I marveled at the ravines;
indeed, I marveled exceedingly.[637]

---

[625] N and OL have "center." **In (Jub 8:12, 19 and Ezek 5:5; 38:12); Jerusalem/Mount Zion is called the center, middle, or navel of the earth just as Delphi was regarded amongst the Greeks** (C pg. 54). Gehenna is also located in the middle of the earth (1En 90:26). Jerusalem is certainly at a crossroads, and is the center of God's interest and plans, both past and future. This passage is "an unmistakable geographical outline of Jerusalem and its immediate environs" (BL pg. 172).

[626] Gk[a] reads "a blessed, *well*-watered, place." The word for "Blessed", is "fertile" in Ethiopic (cf. 89:40; 90:20).

[627] Portions of 25:7-27:1 are found in DSS (4QEn[d] xii).

[628] N has: "and I saw a blessed place where there were trees that had branches that abide and sprout." The image of a felled tree resprouting is an allusion to Jerusalem rising again after the Babylonian exile. **If original to the text, this indicates that *The Book of Watchers* was written after the Babylonian exile, when the nation of Israel would be rising again like a felled tree. This description of the terrain of Jerusalem indicates great familiarity on the part of the author. This depiction of the terrain of Jerusalem would have had no meaning to a person in biblical Enoch's time.**

[629] For 26:1, Baty has: "I went from thence to the middle of the earth, and saw a happy and fruitful land, in which branches continually germinated from the trees which were planted thereon:" I has: "And from there I went into the center of the earth and saw a blessed place, shaded with branches which live and bloom from a tree that was cut." N omits: "from a tree that had been cut down" seeing it as a later gloss (i.e. a margin comment that made itself into the text). Charles, Milik and Knibb also see it as a gloss.

[630] Mount Moriah; the Temple mount.

[631] This is the Gihon Spring, a source for the brook of Kidron flowing in a southerly direction.

[632] The Mount of Olives.

[633] The Kidron Valley (In tradition this is synonymous with the Valley of Jehoshaphat; see Joel 3:2, 12).

[634] This is the Hill of Evil Counsel across the Hinnom valley from Jerusalem.

[635] The Hinnom Valley.

[636] The Valley of Gehenna

[637] **This is obviously a description of the topography near Jerusalem. The author describes the location as if the city did not yet exist, making it appear as an antediluvian description. This will be the future site of Gods capital. The significance of Jerusalem only increased after this composition, when it became the site of the crucifixion and resurrection of the Chosen One.**

The Accursed Valley of Judgement (Gehenna)

27 1 Then I said: "Why is this land blessed, and all of it full of trees,
but that valley is accursed?"[638] [639] 53:1; 56:1-4
2 Then Uriel,[640] one of the watchers and holy ones who was with me,
answered me and said to me: "This accursed valley is for those who. 54:1-6; Jer 7:31-34; 19:1-6
are cursed forever.[641] Here shall all the accursed be gathered together 90:26-27; Mt 5:22,29,30; 10:28
who utter with their mouth blasphemies against the Lord,[642] 1:9; 5:4; 101:3; Isa 66:24
and speak hard words against his glory. Here they shall be gathered. Jude 15; ApPet 21, 27; Mal 3:13
This shall be their place of judgement.[643] Rev 16:16
3 The spectacle of righteous judgement will come upon them Ps 91:8
in the last days, for all time;[644] in the presence of the righteous. Isa 66:24; Mic 4:1-7; Dan 12:2
Here the godly will bless the Lord of glory, the everlasting King. 48:9; 62:12; 4Ezra 7:36-38
4 In the days of judgement (of the accursed), they will bless him for Zech 12:9-11; Mal 4:1-3
the mercy he has bestowed upon them." Dan 12:13; Eph 2:8-9
5 Then I blessed the Lord of glory. His glory I made known, 1Cor 2:8
and I praised (him) in a manner worthy of his majesty.[645]

---

[638] The fertile blessed place of the righteous on Mount Zion is contrasted with the accursed valley Gehenna.

[639] Olson explains: "**Here the 'accursed valley' (i.e., Gehenna) is identified with the place of punishment for the wicked (i.e., Hell) for the first time in Jewish literature, an identification only vaguely hinted at in (Isa 66:24). By New Testament times the identification was so taken for granted that the Greek word translated "hell" throughout the New Testament is simply *geenna.*"** (OL pg. 62).

[640] N rightly has "Sariel", "God is my prince" in place of Uriel (cf. 20:6).

[641] **This is the Valley of Hinnom (gēy 'hinnôm) in Hebrew, or Gehenna (gēhinnām) in Aramaic. It is located south of Jerusalem and was noted for pagan worship, burning incense to Molech, and throwing children into the fire during the time before the exile** (Jer 7:31-34, 19:1-6, 32:35; 2Kgs 16:3; 23:10-14; 2Chr 28:3, 33:6). Gehenna became interchangeable with the place of Hell in the New Testament (Mt 5:22, 29, 30; 10:28; 18:9; 23:15; 23:33; Mk 9:43, 45, 47; Lk 12:5 Jas 3:6).

[642] This verse may give insight to the unforgivable sin passages (Mt 12:31, Mk 3:29, and Lk 12:10). (Cf. 1Sam 2:25)

[643] **The Book of Enoch here places the final battle of good vs evil in Jerusalem, as does a properly understood (Rev 16:16) "And they assembled them at the place that in Hebrew is called Armageddon." Armageddon in Greek, (Ἀρ¦μαγεδών (Har¦magedōn)), is properly translated as Mount of Assembly i.e. Jerusalem, not the Plain of Megiddo which has no mountain.** That the final battle will be in Jerusalem, is also evident in (Zech 12:9-11, 14:2-5; 4Ezra 13:32-38; Joel 3:2; Ezek 39:2; SibOr 3:660-674; Rev 20:9).

> And on that day I will seek to destroy all the nations that come against Jerusalem. And I will pour out on the house of David and the inhabitants of Jerusalem a spirit of grace and pleas for mercy, so that, when they look on me, on him whom they have pierced, they shall mourn for him, as one mourns for an only child, and weep bitterly over him, as one weeps over a firstborn. On that day the mourning in Jerusalem will be as great as the mourning for Hadad-rimmon in the plain of Megiddo (Zech 12:9-11).

This will be a spiritual battle, more than a human based one (Heiser, Michael S. 2015. *The Unseen Realm, Recovering the supernatural worldview of the Bible.* Chapter 41). See also (4 Ezra 13:32-38: where the Son fights from Mount Zion; also note the battle of divine beings in the (Songs of the Sabbath Sacrifice 4Q402 Frags 1-4).

[644] The spectacle of the judgement of the cursed wicked will be a reminder for the righteous throughout all time (cf. Isa 66:24).

[645] Enoch blesses God because the righteous will be shown mercy and the evil judged. Note the righteous are saved because of mercy (grace); not works (cf. 1En 27:4; Eph 2:8-9).

Journey to the East: The Spice Route

28 1 And from there I went on into the midst of a mountainous
part of the desert,[646] and I saw an isolated wilderness,[647] in a place
full of trees and plants,[648]
2 with water gushing over it from above. Joel 3:18; Ps 107:33-38
3 It rushed in a copious torrent[649] towards the northwest,
causing mist and dew to ascend on every side. Jer 10:13; 51:16

29 1 From there I went into yet another place in the desert,
approaching to the east of this mountainous region.
2 And there I saw <trees of the field>[650] exhaling the fragrance Ex 30:23
of frankincense and myrrh.[651] These trees were similar to nut[652] trees. Mt 2:11; Song 4:6, 13

---

[646] Milik found clues about the author in these chapters:

> The most original part of his literary composition, that which describes the surroundings of Jerusalem and the lands of spices (1En 26-32), reveals some details about the actual person of the author and the approximate date of his work. He was certainly a Judaean, since he looks upon Jerusalem as the center of the earth, and the hill of the temple of Jerusalem as 'the sacred mountain' par excellence (26:1-2). He was perhaps himself a Jerusalemite, for he has an excellent knowledge of the environs of the Holy City (26:2-27:1); at the very least he must have travelled there frequently. His information about the aromatics and their botanical habitats—obviously gained from hearsay—suggests fairly clearly, in my opinion, that he was engaged, in his role as a modest official, in the perfume and spice trade. This hypothesis is confirmed by his reference to a second town which he must have known *de visu*, namely Petra, the capital of the Nabataeans. He admires above all the aqueduct of the city, impressive remains of which can still be seen today in the es-Siq gorge of the Wâdi Mûsa. (M pg. 25-26)

These chapters read like a travel account for places the author has personally traveled.

[647] "Wilderness," Black and Dillmann, identify this wilderness as the Arabah, an area south of the Dead Sea.

[648] "The textual situation in these chapters is especially complex due to the plethora of sometimes obscure proper names, the technical nature of the subject matter, and the disagreements among Gk, Eth, and two Aram mss." (N pg. 47). For a general guide to location; chapter 28=Petra; 29=Arabia; 30=the lake and marshlands of 'Ain el-Garr in Lebanon.

[649] Isaac has "waterfall." If this is indeed describing Petra, the water gushing from above would be from Petra's well known water collection system.

[650] This word is very unclear. Olson has "uncultivated trees" in place of Nickelsburg's "<trees of the field>." Milik has "wild trees." Black has "*juniper trees*," Knibb, and Isaac have "trees of judgement."

[651] Both frankincense and myrrh are grown in Arabia as well as Africa. Frankincense was a component of the incense used in temple worship (Ex 30:34-38). Myrrh was used in sacred anointing oil (Ex 30:23) in perfumes, in medicines, and for embalming (N1 pg. 324). They were of course gifts presented to the infant Jesus (Mt 2:11). That spices from Arabia traded as far as Jerusalem is confirmed by a 10th BC century inscription engraved on a clay jar rim, "aromatic labdanum" (galbanum Ex 30:34). The pottery fragment was found at Ophal just south of the Temple Mount and was determined to be written in language stemming from the Kingdom of Sheba (todays Yemen) — over 2,000 kilometers (1,240 miles) away! The clay for the jar originated in the Jerusalem area, thus confirming the presence of a native Sabaean language speaker from Sheba in Jerusalem, indicating extensive trade contact between the two localities (Vainstub, Daniel, 2023. *Incense from Sheba for the Jerusalem Temple*, Jerusalem Journal of Archaeology 4:42–68).

[652] Some translate "almond trees."

30 1 And beyond these things, I went far to the east, and I saw
another vast region, valleys full of water that does not fail;[653] [654] Isa 58:11
2 and I saw aromatic cane[655] with a fragrance like mastic.[656] Jer 6:20; Sus 13:54
3 On the flanks of those valleys I saw fragrant cinnamon;[657]
and beyond the valleys I was carried on towards the east.

31 1 I was shown other mountains, and I also saw trees on them,
from which flowed the resins known as storax[658] and galbanum.[659] Ex 30:34-38; Sir 24:15
2 Beyond those mountains I was shown another mountain,
to the east of the ends of the earth,[660] and on it were aloe trees; [661] Prov 7:17; Num 24:6
and all the trees in it were full of fruit and it was like the husk
of the almond nut.
3 When an incision is made in those trees, a pleasant odor is
released from them; and when that bark is ground,
it is sweeter than any perfume.[662]

32 1 Beyond these mountains, roughly north and to the east of them,

---

[653] Milik associates this valley "with the lake and marshlands of 'Ain el-Garr in Lebanon, where the sweet reed and cala-mus grew" (M pg. 28). K and OL, following an Ethiopic text, have "valleys full of water, the kind that never fails." OL notes: "This phrase is not in the Gk, but it helps create an allusion to Isa 58:11 in this verse and is probably original."
[654] Fragments of 28:3 to 32:3 were found in the DSS (4Q204 1.12; 4QEn^c 1 xii; 4QEn^e 1xxvi)
[655] Nickelsburg identifies this aromatic grass with the genus *Cymbopogon*; which grows in Lebanon but was also "imported from India and its environs" (N1 pg. 325) (cf. Ex 30:23).
[656] Mastic is excreted by the resin glands of certain trees, notably, the mastic tree (Pistacia lentiscus), and dries into pieces of brittle, translucent resin. When chewed, the resin softens and becomes a bright white and opaque gum. The flavor is bitter at first, but after some chewing, it releases a refreshing flavor similar to pine and cedar (Wikipedia). Black translates: "camel-hay" for mastic, arguing that since reeds are involved, camel hay is a better translation than the tree-based mastic (BL pg. 177).
[657] Cinnamon was native to Ceylon and the coast of India. It was used as a food spice and as a perfume. It is mentioned in (Ex 30:23).
[658] "Storax" is usually translated in the Bible as "balm" (N1 pg. 325). This resin comes from *Liquidambar Orientalis*, commonly known as oriental sweetgum or Turkish sweetgum. Used as a "love potion" and perfume by the Egyptian Queen Cleopatra, the oil has also been used as a medicine since the Hippocratic period. The ancient Egyptians also used the oil during embalming. Amphora filled with the oil unearthed from sunken Phoenician ships show that sweetgum oil occupied an important place in Mediterranean trade in the past (cf. Gen 37:25).
[659] "Galbanum was a resin exuded from the lower stem and rootstock of the species *Ferula gummosa* Boiss. (fennel), a tall herbaceous plant of the carrot family. It was native to Persia and was a component of the sacred incense (Ex 30:34, Sir 24:14-15)" (N1 pg. 325).
[660] "East of the ends of the earth" Black speculates that this is India or China which would be home to aloe.
[661] This "type of *Aloe*, the so-called lignaloes, was the dark, fragrant heartwood taken from the decaying eaglewood tree (*Aquillaria agallocha* Roxb.) which was native to India and Ceylon" (N1 pg. 325) (cf. Num 24:6).
[662] Most of the spices mentioned in chapters 28-32 were used in worship on the Temple Mount, and would have been familiar to the readers.

I was shown other mountains, filled with choice nard,[663] *tspr*,[664] Song 4:13-14
cardamon[665] and pepper.[666]
2 From there I was carried to the east of all these mountains, Gen 2:8
far from them to the east of the earth;[667] and I was conveyed 77:3, 6-7
above the Erythraean Sea[668] but I went further still and was carried above 1QapGen 21:17
the darkness, far away from it.[669] 4Q206 1.26.18-21

The Paradise of Righteousness

3 I passed by the Paradise of Righteousness,[670] and I saw from afar its trees, 60:23; 61:12
growing there in tremendous numbers: large, sweet-smelling, tall, 77:3; Gen 2:9; 3:24
exceedingly beautiful and glorious. (I saw) the Tree of Knowledge,[671] 25:3-6
whose fruit the holy ones eat[672] and learn great wisdom. 82:3
4 That tree is in height like the fir,[673] and its leaves are like (the leaves of) 24:4

---

663 "The first spice mentioned is nard..., often called spikenard, an oil derived from the roots of *Nardostachys joatmansi* (Wall.) D.C., a plant native to the Himalayas and used for perfumes and medicinal ointments (Zohary, Plants, 205; Lőw, Flora, 3:482-488; Miller, *Spice Trade*, pgs. 88-92) (cf. Song 1:12; 4:13). **This is the costly spice Jesus was anointed with before his crucifixion (Mk 14:3).**

664 This word is linked by Nickelsburg to a component of the sacred incense called *onycha* in (Ex 30:34). The substance is thought to have been derived from a marine animal (N1 pg. 326).

665 "Cardamon is probably identical with the cardamom of modern commerce, . . . and was native to Malabar in southwest India" (N1 pg. 326).

666 Substantial portions of 32:1-32:6 were found in the DSS (4Q204 1.26-27; 4QEn[c] 1xii; 4QEn[e] 1xxvi; 4QEne 1xxvii).

667 In the *Epic of Gilgamesh, The Search for Everlasting Life*, thought to have been written in 2100 BC, Gilgamesh makes a long journey to the East "So Urshanabi the ferryman brought Gilgamesh to Utnapishtim, whom they call the Faraway, who lives in Dihnun at the place of the sun's transit, eastward of the mountain."

668 "Erythraean Sea", literally "Red Sea" was a name used in antiquity for the Red Sea. "The 'Red Sea' referred in antiquity, variously (depending on the authors), not only to the Arabian Gulf but also to the Persian Gulf and the Indian Ocean" (N1 pg. 326). The Greeks derived the name from an eponymous King Erythras. The modern country of Eritrea was named after the ancient Greek name.

669 This passage from the DSS is translated: "And from there I was carried [east]ward of all these mountains, far away from them, to the east of the earth, and [I] was made to pass [hig]h above [the] Red [Sea], but I went farther still and was carried abo[ve] the darkness, far away from it. And I was made to come to the Garden of Truth" (4Q206 1.26.18-21 (W pg. 285)). The darkness is likely referring to the darkness separating the world of the living from the netherworld (cf. 1En 17:6). Crossing through an area of darkness is a staple of near-death experiences.

670 "Paradise of righteousness" (cf. 20:7; 60:8; 23; 61:12; 70:3; 77:3). In 70:3 "the place of the chosen and the righteous ones" is located in the northwest, in agreement with Greek tradition that places Elysium in the west. Here paradise is in the east, which agrees with oriental tradition. (Cf. TJob 40:3; 52:10)

671 Nickelsburg has tree of wisdom; Gk[a] has tree of knowledge.

672 That angels eat, is possibly indicated in (Pss 78:23-25), where manna is described as the bread of angels. Black speculates: "Perhaps the tenses are wrong and we should render "of which the saints shall partake and understand great wisdom."

673 Or possibly cypress.

the carob,[674] and its fruit is like the clusters of the vine,[675] shining brightly; Gen 3:6
and its fragrance penetrates far beyond the tree.
5 Then I exclaimed: "How beautiful this tree is, 24:5; Ab 3:10
and how pleasing is its appearance!"[676]
6 Then the watcher and holy one who was with me, Raphael,[677] answered:
"This is the Tree of Knowledge from which your father of old and your mother Gen 2:17; PiSop 134
of old[678] before you ate; and they learned wisdom, and their eyes were opened, 4Q206 1.27.9-10
and they knew that they were naked, and they were driven out of Gen 3:7, 22-24
the garden."[679]

Excursus: Does a complete Aramaic copy of the Book of Enoch, (including The Book of the Parables), from the caves of Qumran exist?

Avi Katzman, quoting the late John Strugnell, reports a complete copy of Enoch in Aramaic has been found and is in private hands.

> Regarding the scrolls, [John] Strugnell claims at least four other scrolls have been found that have not yet come to light: "I've seen, with my own eyes, two." One of the two is a complete copy of the Book of Enoch.[680] According to Strugnell, Israeli archaeologist Yigael Yadin is the reason these scrolls have still not come into scholarly hands. After the Six-Day War, Yadin confiscated the famous Temple Scroll from a Bethlehem antiquities dealer known as Kando. Yadin paid Kando $250,000, (according to Yadin, the sum was $105,000), to encourage anyone else with scroll materials to come forward. But this was not enough, says Strugnell: 'Yadin gave Kando two hundred fifty thousand dollars where we'd offered Kando one million five weeks earlier. When the owners of the manuscripts heard that, they just crossed the Jordan River.'

---

674 The carob tree is an evergreen legume native to the Mediterranean area; whose pods are a food for animals and humans. Carob pods were often used as animal feed, and in times of famine, as the last source of human food. They are commonly identified as the pods the prodigal son wished to eat (Luke 15:16). Its leaves are 10 to 20 centimeters (4 to 8 inches) long, oval, alternate, pinnate, and may or may not have a terminal leaflet.

675 Genesis does not name the fruit from the tree of knowledge. This is the first known attempt to describe the fruit produced by the tree of knowledge (apples are a recent tradition) (OL pg. 64). Grapelike fruit are also identified in the *Apocalypse of Abraham* 23:6 (OTP1 pg. 700) (AD 1st to 2nd century); and 3 *Apocalypse of Baruch* 4:8-17 (OTP1 pg. 667-668) (AD 1st-3rd century).

676 This is the only line of Enochic literature quoted anywhere in the Mishnah or the two Talmuds: "Rabbi Jacob said: if one is studying while walking on the road and interrupts his study and says, 'how fine is this tree!' [or] 'how fine is this newly ploughed field!' scripture accounts it to him as if he was mortally guilty" (Mishnah 'Abot 3:10, Aka Pirkei Avot, in English it translates "chapters of the fathers/categories" written AD 4th century). Apocalyptic literature like 1 Enoch, was seen as a distraction from study of the Torah by rabbis in AD 2nd century and later.

677 Nickelsburg emends Raphael to Gabriel here, following the sequence in 20:7. Since this scene is in paradise, Gabriel is expected (cf. 20:7).

678 This is referring to Adam and Eve and the tree of the knowledge of good and evil (Gen 2:16-17; 3:1-7). .

679 "Although Ben Sira may contain the earliest datable allusion to the story of Adam and Eve, the earliest reflections of Gen 2-3 occur most likely in the Book of the Watchers." (Collins, 2004. *Before the Fall: The earliest Interpretations of Adam and Eve, in The Idea of Biblical Interpretation: Essays in Honor of James L. Kugel*. pg. 296). **The watcher tradition predates and was more attested in ancient literature than the tradition of Adam and Eve.**

680 It is not clear if this "complete copy of the Book of Enoch" includes the *Parables* and *The Eschatological Exhortation*.

> These scrolls, like the Temple Scroll, came from Cave 11 at Qumran, according to Strugnell. The manuscripts are now 'somewhere in Jordan. Various people own them. Several of them have been sold to big bankers. They're investments for these people. There's no point in forcing a sale. If they really need cash — as one seems to now — I have the money.' As for the other two scrolls — the ones Strugnell has not seen — '[Lankester] Harding [the director of Jordan's Department of Antiquities] on his death bed told me he'd seen three, only one of which I've seen — so that makes four.' "Strugnell is not concerned that the scrolls may deteriorate before scholars can look at them: 'They're all being kept very carefully; no one need worry about them. They're a better investment than anything on the Israeli or the New York stock exchanges,' he added.[681]

Strugnell has passed from this life; but indications that additional scroll fragments exist have popped up from time to time. In 2008, Charlesworth affirmed that "Obviously, some Qumran scrolls were destroyed by Bedouin and some are still in the possession of Arabs – and two of them are of 1 Enoch but not portions of chs. 37-71."[682] Who knows what tomorrow will bring? But anecdotal evidence exists that a full scroll of Enoch, sadly excluding the Parables and most likely The Eschatological Exhortation, is being held by private parties.

Journey to the Ends of the Earth

33 1 From there I went to the ends of the earth[683] and saw huge beasts. 18:12
Each differed from the other; and birds with a variety of appearances, Dan 7:3
beauty and call, each different from the other.[684]
2 To the east of these animals I saw the ends of the earth on which the 10:14; 18:5
heavens rest, and the gates of the heavens open.
3 I observed how the stars of heaven come forth, and I counted the gates 36:2-3; 75:7
through which they proceed, and I wrote down all their places of exit,
each one individually, according to their number and their names, 93:14; Gen 15:5
according to their conjunctions and positions, their seasons and their months, 72:1; 82:7-8; Jub 4:21
as Uriel, one of the holy watchers who was with me, showed me. Wis 7:17-19
4 He showed all things to me and wrote it down; additionally, he wrote down Job 38:33

---

[681] Shanks, H. 1993, *Understanding the Dead Sea Scrolls: a reader from the Biblical archaeology review* , pg. 262.
[682] Charlesworth, James H., 2008. *The Parables of Enoch and the Apocalypse of John*, In "Jewish and Christian texts in Contexts and Related Studies", pg. 222. Charlesworth, after 40 years of searching, almost found the scroll in Damascus. It is an Aramaic version of 1 Enoch which has been broken into two parts. P pg. 345 n49.
[683] Ancient world cosmology viewed the world as a disk like an upside-down bowl on a plate of the same diameter with waters above and beneath. Enoch now travels to where the bowl and plate meet.
[684] B has: "and birds different in their appearances and forms, as well as with notes of different sounds." Strange beasts were thought to inhabit the far reaches of the earth. Envision ancient maps with sea monsters and beasts at the end of the world. That the author does not name them, indicates this may be what he had in mind. Another interpretation is that these are beasts associated with the constellations. Or it could be Leviathan and Behemoth mentioned in (1En 60:7-8). "Dillmann suggests that Enoch may be here drawing on a legend based on Gen 2:19-20 that beyond Eden, at the ends of the earth, lay a land with all kinds of wild creatures, beasts and birds" (BL pg. 180).

for me their names, their appointed times[685] and their groupings.[686] Ps 147:4; Isa 40:26

North

34 1 And from there I was transferred northwards to the ends of the earth,
and I was shown a wonderous creation situated at the ends of the whole earth.
2 There I saw three open gates of heaven; through each of them north winds 18:2-3
go forth; when they blow, there is cold, hail, hoarfrost, snow, dew and rain.
3 Through one gate they blow beneficially: but when they blow through 76:6, 8, 10
the other two gates, it comes forcefully and causes affliction upon the earth.
And violently do they blow.[687] [688]

West

35 1 From there I proceeded towards the west to the ends of the earth, and I
saw there three gates of heaven opened, just as I had seen in the east—the
same number of gates and the same number of outlets.[689]

South

36 1 From there I was taken to the south, to the ends of the earth,[690] 76:1-14
and there I saw three gates of the heavens open;
and there come forth from them the south winds: for dew and rain.

East

2 Then from there I was taken towards the east, at the ends of the earth,
and I was shown three gates of the heavens open_towards the east,
and above them were smaller gates. 33:3; 75:7
3 Through each of these smaller gates pass the stars of heaven 75:4-7
proceeding to the west along the paths which have been shown them. 83:11; 1QH^{a} 9:14
4 And with every observation I offered continuous praise,
and I shall always praise the Lord of glory, who has created great 1Cor 2:8
and glorious wonders, that he might show the grandeur of his work Eph 3:10

---

[685] "Appointed times" C, I, and K have: "laws," OL and BL have: "ordinances," N has: "appointed times".

[686] "Groupings" C, I, and BL have: "companies," OL from Ethiopic has: "groupings," N and K have: "functions." The verse has a military connotation (BL pg. 180).

[687] A Sirocco is a Mediterranean area wind that comes from the Sahara and can reach hurricane speeds, especially during the spring season. ". . . and behold a great wind came across the wilderness and struck the four corners of the house, and it fell upon the young people, and they are dead, and I alone have escaped to tell you" (Job 1:19).

[688] Some translators such as Nickelsburg omit "And violently do they blow."

[689] Portions of chapters 35-36 were found in the DSS (4QEn^{c} 1 xiii).

[690] Enoch now completes his travels to the ends of the earth at each of the four directional quadrants.

to his angels, and to the spirits[691] of human beings,[692] 61:13
so that they might see the effect of his might and glorify 2Bar 54:18
the great work of his hands, and bless him forever.[693]

Excursus: When were the Parables (Chapters 37 to 71) written? And why it matters.

Why it matters.

The time of composition for the Parables of Enoch is critical for two reasons. The Parables contain substantial information about the identity of the Son of Man; the term Jesus used most often in referring to himself through all four gospels. The Book of Parables interchangeably uses the titles Anointed One, Righteous One, Son of Man and Chosen (Elect) One. All these titles were used of Jesus Christ in the New Testament. A pre-Christian era date would make it an amazing and important prophetic text that the Lord was pointing his listeners toward. By calling himself the Son of Man, Christ is identifying himself as the one from the Parables who sat from before creation on the throne of God. A later first century date, though still important, would be written by an author looking back at the time of Christ—and the Lord would not be referring his listeners to the Son of Man passages in 1 Enoch but exclusively to references found in the Old Testament.

While the name "son of man" is used often in the Old Testament; in only three places is it speaking of a heavenly personage. The Son is identified as the divine Messiah in the amazing Ps 2 prophecy about the Lord's anointed, which is best read in context. (Ps 2:7) reads: "I will tell of the decree: The LORD said to me, 'You are my son; today I have begotten you.'" Then in (Prov 30:4) a divine Son of God is also mentioned. "Who has ascended to heaven and come down? Who has gathered the wind in his fists? Who has wrapped up the waters in a garment? Who has established all the ends of the earth? What is his name, and what is his son's name? Surely you know!"

Daniels famous prophecy in chapter seven describes a scene where the son of man is presented before the Ancient of Days.

> I saw in the night visions, and behold, with the clouds of heaven there came one like a son of man, and he came to the Ancient of Days and was presented before him. And to him was given dominion and glory and a kingdom, that all peoples, nations, and languages should serve him; his dominion is an everlasting dominion, which shall not pass away, and his kingdom one that shall not be destroyed (Dan 7:13-14).

Jesus was obviously pointing listeners back to these passages by calling himself the Son of Man.

---

[691] Knibb has: "souls" in place of "spirits". Isaac simply reads: "winds".
[692] Some manuscripts read "spirits of human beings" and others "spirits and human beings".
[693] Milik and Nickelsburg (N1 pg. 335), believe *The Book of Heavenly Luminaries* (1En 72-82) was originally juxtaposed at the end of Chapter 36 and that it was later interrupted with the subsequent interpolation of *The Book of Parables.*

THE BOOK OF PARABLES

The Book of Parables, which equates the Son of Man with the Chosen/Elect One, adds additional important electrifying details, found nowhere else at the time, about this "Son of Man" personage. "On that day My Chosen One shall sit on the throne of glory: and he shall test their works." (45:3) On that day, I will cause my Chosen One to dwell among them," (45:4) "And there I saw One who had a head of days, and His head was white like wool, and with him was another, whose face had the appearance of a man; and his face was full of grace, like one of the holy angels" (46:1) "This is the Son of Man to whom belongs righteousness, and righteousness dwells with him; and he will reveal all the treasures of that which is hidden. For the Lord of Spirits has chosen him, and his destiny is to triumph before the Lord of Spirits in truth forever." (46:3) "This Son of Man whom you have seen, shall rouse up the kings and the mighty from their soft beds and the strong from their thrones! He shall loosen the reins of the powerful and crush the teeth of sinners." (46:4) "He will hurl down the kings from their thrones and kingdoms, because they do not extol or praise him; nor humbly acknowledge who bestowed their kingdoms upon them." (46:5)

Then we have the incredible chapter 48:

2 At that time, the Son of Man was named in the presence of the Lord of Spirits,
and his name before the Antecedent of Time.
3 Before the sun or the constellations were created,
before the stars of the heaven were made,
his name was named before the Lord of Spirits.
4 He shall be a staff for the righteous that they may lean
on him and not fall, and he shall be the light of the Gentiles,
and the hope of those who grieve in their hearts.
5 All who dwell on earth shall fall down and worship before him,
and will glorify and bless and celebrate with song the Name of the Lord of Spirits.
6 For this (reason) he was chosen and hidden in his presence
before the world was created and forever.
7 The wisdom of the Lord of Spirits will reveal him to the holy and righteous.
For he will preserve the portion of the righteous,
because they loath and despise this world of unrighteousness;
and hate all its works and ways in the Name of the Lord of Spirits.
For in his name, they will be saved,
and he will become the avenger of their lives.

This clearly matches the Messiah of Christianity, predicted in a Jewish text from just before the time of Christ! It was to be the last in a long line of prophecies of the Messiah, preparing the way of the advent of the divine Lord Jesus Christ. It was critical that they accept him. Instead, he was rejected, and the Jewish temple which had stood in one form or another for over 900 years was destroyed, never more to be rebuilt. A pre-Christ date for the Parables would forever end the charge that Jesus never claimed to be God. If Jesus claimed to be God in His Jewish culture; (He did) skeptics then face the trilemma of deciding if He was a liar, lunatic, or God incarnate.

Secondly, a pre-Christ date for the parables would mean Jesus was very familiar with The Book of Parables as he was quoting from it and referencing it extensively. 1 Enoch as a whole, is easily the foundational book of the New Testament and thus Christianity. The Parables of Enoch influenced the development of the doctrine of Christ since it was widely read among early Christians. It has a large number of touch points with the New Testament, yet it does not appear to be Christian in origin. The opportunities for better understanding the New Testament through the study of the Parables of Enoch are immense.

External evidence for the composition date of the Parables

Literature from Qumran

Charlesworth addressed the fact that no fragments of The Book of The Parables have been published from Qumran. "Cumulatively, perhaps we possess only about 10 to 20 percent of the manuscripts that were in the Qumran caves before, or in, June 68 C.E. Thus, the absence of identifiable fragments of the Parables of Enoch from Qumran is neither remarkable nor a viable reason for dating the composition."[694] Speaking of the two caves that were numbered together as cave four Charlesworth elsewhere states "There may have been four hundred documents in those two caves, but it is conceivable that we have only about 2 percent of what had been placed there."[695] Many compositions are not found there, including 1 Maccabees, and the Psalms of Solomon.[696] It should be noted that no part of the Book of Esther is found among the Qumran literature and only 1 fragment of 2 Chronicles has been found. In addition, no part of Nehemiah has been found unless one counts "Ezra-Nehemiah as one book-as, indeed, it is so regarded in Jewish tradition—since only a fragment of Ezra, but not Nehemiah, has been identified."[697] Thousands of unidentified fragments still exist and many works have not been identified. "In general, then, the rule should be that absence from Qumran proves nothing."[698] There is some evidence that the Book of Giants took the position of the Parables in the Dead Sea Scrolls. However, it has been reported: "Obviously, some Qumran scrolls were destroyed by Bedouin (and some are still in the possession of Arabs-and two of them are of Enoch, but not portions of chapters 37-71)"[699] The Parables were likely added to the other books of 1 Enoch in the late 1st or early 2nd centuries (P pg. 352). Boccaccini very plausibly postulated that the Parables were composed by the more moderate main Essene branch[699a] "after the schism between Qumran and Enochic Judaism" and therefore the Parables did not appear at Qumran (BO pg. 144).

Due to the obvious theological underpinnings *The Book of Parables* provided for the claims of Jesus Christ; copies were quite likely purged from Jewish libraries (cf. P pg. 68). After all, Jewish animosity toward Christians was in full swing by AD 68. Jewish scribes and librarians

---

694 R pg. 456, Charlesworth; P pg. 44

695 R pg. 456, Charlesworth.

696 R pg. 455, Charlesworth.

697 Crawford, Sidnie White, 1996. *Has Every Book of the Bible Been Found Among the Dead Sea Scrolls? Bible Review,* October 1996. An unprovenanced fragment of Nehemiah, ostensibly from the Dead Seas Scrolls, that was displayed in the Museum of the Bible, was determined in 2018 to be a modern forgery. (The Times of Israel, *US museum says 5 fragments in Dead Sea Scroll collection are fake,* 23 October 2018).

698 R pg. 446; Stone, *Enoch's Date in Limbo; or, Some Considerations on David Suter's Analysis of the Book of Parables*.

699 James H. Charlesworth, Ex. ed., 2008. "*Jewish and Christian texts in Contexts and Related Studies*" in *The Pseudepigrapha and Christian Origins*, pg. 240.

699a Other Essene communities have been tentatively identified at En el-Ghuweir, Beit Safafa and the Arbel Cave village. Ben-Daniel, John. 2022. *The Arbel Cave Village: Remains of an Essene Commune*, pg. 10.

likely purged scrolls containing *The Book of Parables* from their repositories before their contents were transported to Qumran. Christians were obviously using *The Book of Parables* heavily in their apologetic and writings as evidenced by its use in the gospels. Rejection of Christ would have meant rejection of the writings most supporting His claims to messiahship. Stephen (AD 36),[700] the apostle James (AD 44), members of the Jerusalem church (AD 44)[701] and James the brother of Christ with others (AD 62)[702] were brutally martyred soon after the life of Christ. So it would be no surprise that writings favorable to the Christian apologetic would have been purged from Jewish libraries, especially when Jewish conversions to Christianity were taking place. In fact, it would have been very unlikely that they would not have been removed! Irenæus (AD 130-202) speaks to the Jews willingness to destroy scrolls unfavorable to their views. Referencing the virgin birth section of Septuagint, he states:

> "But it was interpreted into Greek by the Jews themselves, much before the period of our Lord's advent, that there might remain no suspicion that perchance the Jews, complying with our humor, did put this interpretation upon these words. They indeed, had they been cognizant of our future existence, and that we should use these proofs from the Scriptures, would themselves never have hesitated to burn their own Scriptures, which do declare that all other nations partake of [eternal] life, and show that they who boast themselves as being the house of Jacob and the people of Israel, are disinherited from the grace of God."[703]

Justin Martyr (AD 100-165) makes a similar charge concerning Jewish changes from the LXX.

> "And I wish you to observe, that they have altogether taken away many scriptures from the translations effected by those seventy elders who were with Ptolemy, and by which this very man who was crucified is proved to have been set forth expressly as God, and man, and as being crucified, and as dying; but since I am aware that this is denied by all of your nation, I do not address myself to these points."[704]

Dating from quotes by the Church Fathers.

Since the Parables of 1 Enoch were referenced by early church fathers, they must have been in circulation in the early church by the 2nd century.

Origen (184 –253 CE)

"We are not to suppose that a special office has been assigned by mere accident to a particular angel: as to Raphael, the work of curing and healing; to Gabriel, the direction of wars; to Michael, the duty of hearing the prayers and supplications of men" (De Principiis, chapter 8.1).

---

700 Acts 7:54-60.
701 Acts 12:1-3.
702 Martyrdom of James (*Ant* 20.9.1 §§200; *HE* 2.23). Persecution of Christians by Jews was still active at the time of the Second Jewish revolt in AD 132-136 (*1Apol.* 31) (Gruber, Daniel, 2013. Rabbi Akiba's Messiah. 250-284)
703 Irenæus, *Against Heresies* 3.21.1.
704 Justin Martyr, Dialogue with Trypho 71

1 Enoch 40:9-10 And he answered: "This first is Michael, the merciful and long-suffering, and the second who is in charge over all the diseases and every wound of the children of men, is Raphael; and the third, who is in charge of all the powers, is Gabriel: and the fourth, who is set over the repentance (leading) to hope of those who will inherit eternal life, is named Phanuel." These, then, are the four angels of the Lord of Spirits and the four voices I heard in those days.

"The name Jared is etymologically akin to it, if I may say so; it also yields the meaning going down; for Jared was born to Maleleel, as it is written in the Book of Enoch— if anyone cares to accept that book as sacred—in the days when the sons of God came down to the daughters of men" (*Commentary on John* 6.25).

1 Enoch 37:1 THE VISION OF WISDOM THAT ENOCH SAW—The son of Jared, son of Mahalalel, son of Kenan, son of Enosh, the son of Seth, the son of Adam.

Tertullian (155-220 CE)

Tertullian seems to be loosely referencing the Parables in this text; note he calls it scripture. It is certainly applicable to the theological point he is trying to make on bodily resurrection.

> But that you may not suppose that it is merely those bodies which are consigned to tombs whose resurrection is foretold, you have it declared in Scripture: And I will command the fishes of the sea, and they shall cast up the bones which they have devoured; and I will bring joint to joint, and bone to bone. You will ask, will then the fishes and other animals and carnivorous birds be raised again, in order that they may vomit up what they have consumed, on the ground of your reading in the law of Moses, that blood is required of even all the beasts? Certainly not. But the beasts and the fishes are mentioned in relation to the restoration of flesh and blood, in order the more emphatically to express the resurrection of such bodies as have even been devoured, when redress is said to be demanded of their very devourers. Now I apprehend that in the case of Jonah we have a fair proof of this divine power, when he comes forth from the fish's belly uninjured in both his natures — his flesh and his soul (*On the Resurrection of the Flesh* chapter 32).
>
> *1 Enoch 61:5 Those measurements will reveal all that is hidden in the depths of the earth, those who have been destroyed by the desert, those who have been devoured by the fish of the sea and by wild beasts, so that they may return and rely on the day of the Chosen One; for no one shall be destroyed before the Lord of Spirits, and no one can be destroyed.*

It also appears that Tertullian was speaking specifically of *The Book of the Parables* in the following quote. However, other passages in 1 Enoch can be seen as speaking of Christ such as 1:9 or 90:37-38.

> But since Enoch in the same scripture has preached likewise concerning the Lord nothing at all must be rejected by us which pertains to us; and we read that 'every scripture suitable for edification is divinely inspired' [2 Timothy 3:16] By the Jews it may seem to

> have been rejected for that very reason, just like all the other portions nearly which tell of Christ. Nor of course, is this fact wonderful, that they did not receive some scriptures which spoke of Him whom even in person, speaking in their presence, they were not to receive. To these considerations is added the fact that Enoch possesses a testimony in the apostle Jude. [Jude 14-15] (*The Apparel of Women,* Book 1 Chapter 3:3)

In one place (*Adversus Marcionem* 5.1.8) "Tertullian uses the phrase 'Lord of Spirits' (domino spirituum) instead of 'the Lord who is the Spirit' while quoting 2 Cor 3:18 from memory, and it has been suggested that familiarity with this title from the Parables could have influenced Tertullian's recollection.[705]

Irenæus (130-202)

The earliest Church father use of the Parables, may be in a poem quoted in *Against Heresies.* "The mere mention of "Azazel" raises suspicion of an Enochic allusion, since this name is almost unknown in Greek and Latin patristics"[706] The exception being Origen's *Against Celsus* 6.43.[707] "The author of the poem in (*Adversus haerese* 1.15.6) the "divinely inspired elder," is generally identified as Irenæus' predecessor, Pothinus, the first bishop of Lyons and probably, like Irenæus, a native of Asia Minor."[708] Pothinus died in the persecution of AD 177 (Eusebius, *Historia ecclesiastica* 5.1.29-31; 5.5.8), so his poem cannot be dated later than the mid-170s, making it one of our earliest and most direct patristic allusions to the *Parables.*"[709]

> Both rightly and fittingly, therefore, in view of your boldness, has the divinely inspired elder and preacher of the Truth burst forth against you in the following poetic lines:
> Marcus, maker of idols, observer of portents,
> Skilled in astrology and in all arts of magic,
> Whereby you confirm your erroneous doctrines.
> Showing wonders to whomever you lead into error.
> Showing the works of the apostate Power,
> Marvels which Satan, your father, teaches you always
> To perform through the power angelic of Azazel,
> Using you as the precursor of Godless evil.
> Such are the words of the God-loving elder.
> *Against Heresies 1.15.6, Unger/Dillow translation*
>
> *1 Enoch 54:4-6 I asked the angel of peace who went with me, saying: "These chains—for whom are these being prepared?" And he said to me: "Those are being prepared for the hosts of Azazel, so that they may seize them and cast them into the lowest part of hell, and with jagged rocks they will cover their jaws, as the Lord of Spirits commanded. Then*

---

[705] R pg. 493, Olson, referencing FF Bruce, *The Canon of Scripture* pg. 86.
[706] R pg. 495, Olson, *An overlooked Patristic Allusion to the Parables of Enoch?*
[707] R pg. 495, Olson, *An overlooked Patristic Allusion to the Parables of Enoch?*
[708] R pg. 496, Olson, *An overlooked Patristic Allusion to the Parables of Enoch? Citing Unger and Dillow, St. Irenæus of Lyons against the Heresies* pg. 55 and *"Pothinus" in Oxford Dictionary of the Christian Church.*
[709] R pg. 496, Olson, *An overlooked Patristic Allusion to the Parables of Enoch?* The line about Azazel in the Roberts /Rambaut translation is more explicit for our purposes; it reads "by means of Azazel, that fallen and yet mighty angel."

Michael, and Raphael, and Gabriel, and Phanuel—will take hold of them on that great day, and hurl them on that day into the burning furnace, that the Lord of Spirits may exact vengeance on them for their unrighteousness in becoming servants of Satan and leading astray those who dwell on the earth."

The Irenæus (Asia Minor/Gaul), Tertullian (Carthage), and Origen (Alexandria/Caesarea) quotations and parallels are evidence that Enoch's Parables were in wide circulation among the Church as early as the 2nd century.

Evidence from early Jewish and Christian texts

One of the earliest references to the Parables of Enoch is found in the Odes of Solomon, a very early collection of Christian, almost Jewish, hymns, likely composed in Syriac. The best date and provenance for the Odes is AD 100 (certainly before AD 125), near Edessa or Antioch (an area known to be frequented by the Apostle John). Some have speculated that it may have been composed in Pella; a place early Christians fled to avoid the destruction of Jerusalem in AD 70. Check the index for more examples, esp. OdesSol 18:6 vs. 1En 58:6. It is obvious the Odist had a copy of the Parables of Enoch. The Ode (30:1-2) is fairly obviously drawn from 1 Enoch 48:1.

Ode 30:1-2 Fill for yourselves water from the living spring of the Lord, because it has been opened for you. And come all you thirsty and take a drink, and rest beside the spring of the Lord.

1 Enoch 48:1 And in that place I saw the fountain of righteousness, which was inexhaustible, and around it were many fountains of wisdom. All the thirsty drank from them, and were filled with wisdom, (then) their dwellings were with the righteous, the holy and chosen.

Another example from the Odes of Solomon

Ode 36:3 (the Spirit) brought me forth before the Lord's face, and because I was the Son of Man, I was named the Light, the Son of God.

1 Enoch 48:2-4 At that time, the Son of Man was named in the presence of the Lord of Spirits, and his name before the Antecedent of Time. Before the sun or the constellations were created, before the stars of the heaven were made, his name was named before the Lord of Spirits.
He shall be a staff for the righteous that they may lean on him and not fall, and he shall be the light of the Gentiles, and the hope of those who grieve in their hearts.

Another very early text, with striking parallels to the Parables, is 4 Ezra,[710] thought to have been written around AD 100, with content dated prior to AD 70.[711] "In other words it seems that the content of the Parables has influenced 4 Ezra, which has content that can be dated to before AD

[710] 4 Ezra, as used here and in the OTP1, includes chapters 3-14 which are a Jewish apocalypse, known as 4 Ezra; chapters 1-2, (known as 2 Esdras) and chapters 15-16 known as 5 Esdras. Both 1-2 and 15-16 are Christian additions. But for the purposes of this book Chapters 1-16 as a whole will be called 4 Ezra. The naming of books attributed to Ezra is confusing. The chart on OTP1 pg. 516 is helpful. This apocalypse is called 2 Esdras in English bibles and 4 Esdras in the Latin Vulgate.
[711] H2 pgs. 246-247.

70."[712] Parallels are numerous, but include (4 Ezra 6:49-52) and (1 Enoch 60:7-9, 24); (4 Ezra 7:32f) and (1 Enoch 51:1, 3); and (4 Ezra 7:37) and (1 Enoch 62:1).[713]

> 4 Ezra 6:49-52 Then you kept in existence two living creatures; the name of the one you called Behemoth and the name of the other Leviathan. And you separated one from the other, for the seventh part where the water had been gathered together could not hold them both. And you gave Behemoth one of the parts which had been dried up on the third day, to live in it, where there are a thousand mountains; but to Leviathan you have the seventh part,[714] the watery part; and you have kept them to be eaten by whom you wish, and when you wish.
>
> *1 Enoch 60:7-9 And on that day two monsters were separated from one another, a female monster called Leviathan to dwell in the abyss of the ocean over the fountains of the waters. But the male is named Behemoth, who covers with his breast an empty desert named Dundayn, east of the Garden where the elect and righteous ones dwell, where my great-grandfather was taken up, the seventh from Adam, the first man whom the Lord of Spirits created. I asked another angel to show me the might of these monsters, how they were separated in one day the one into the abysses of the sea, and the other into the dry land of the desert.*
>
> *1 Enoch 60:24 And the angel of peace who was with me said to me: "These two monsters, are prepared for the great day of the Lord to provide food for <the chosen and righteous>, so that the punishment of the Lord of Spirits may fall upon them and not come forth in vain. Children shall be slain with their mothers, and children with their fathers.*
>
> 4 Ezra 7:32-37 And the earth shall give up those who are asleep in it; and the chambers shall give up the souls which have been committed to them. And the Most High shall be revealed upon the seat of judgement, and compassion shall pass away, and patience shall be withdrawn; but judgement alone shall remain, truth shall stand, and faithfulness shall grow strong. And recompense shall follow, and the reward shall be manifested; righteous deeds shall awake, and unrighteous deeds shall not sleep. Then the pit of torment shall appear, and opposite it the Paradise of delight.[715] Then the Most High will say to the nations that have been raised from the dead, "Look now, and understand whom you have denied, whom you have not served, whose commandments you have despised!"[716]
>
> *1 Enoch 48:10 On the day of their distress there shall be rest on the earth, and they will fall down before them and not rise again. There shall be no one to grasp them with his*

---

[712] H2 pg. 247.

[713] OTP1 pg. 522.

[714] "Seventh part" refers to one seventh of the earth being covered with water, which is just the opposite of reality.

[715] **Interestingly this line appears to be referencing the Book of Watchers chapters 26-27, strengthening the link with the Book of Enoch in general and indicating that the author of 4 Ezra had familiarity with both the Book of Watchers and the Book of Parables. It thus appears that by this time in the first century, the two texts (and conceivably the others) had been combined into one corpus; or less likely, the author had separate copies of the two books.**

[716] All quotes from 4 Ezra are from the translation of 4 Ezra by (Metzger, B.M., 1983. OTP1 pgs. 517-559).

hand and raise them up, for they have denied the Lord of Spirits and His Anointed One. Blessed be the Name of the Lord of Spirits!

1 Enoch 51:1-3 1 In those days the earth will give back that which has been entrusted to it. Sheol will give back that which has been deposited there, and Abaddon shall repay that which it owes. For in those days, my Chosen One shall arise, and choose the righteous and holy from among them; for the day on which they will be saved has drawn near. My Chosen One shall in those days sit on my throne, and from his mouth will pour forth all the secrets of wisdom and council. For the Lord of Spirits has appointed him and glorified him.

1 Enoch 62:1 Then the Lord of Spirits commanded the kings and the mighty and the exalted, and those who possess the land, and said: "Open your eyes and lift up your eyebrows; see if you are able to recognize the Chosen One!"

(2 Enoch J 18:3), thought by most to have been written prior to AD 70; names Satanail as the leader of the 200. This would seem to be dependent on 1 Enoch 54:6 where the 200 are identified as servants of Satan. However, the name Satanail may be a later Bogomil[717] interpolation as it is not found in the shorter recension (A).

The earliest text (outside the New Testament) dependent on the Book of the Parables is *The Wisdom of Solomon* which is dated by Winston to the evil reign of "Caligula" 37-41 AD.[718] This Book is thought to have been written in Alexandria Egypt and was considered canonical by some church fathers. It is very interesting that the Wisdom of Solomon dates to immediately after the ministry of Jesus Christ. Winston, who wrote the definitive book on The Wisdom of Solomon, stated that the phrase "being well-pleasing to God" in Wis 4:10-11 is clearly a reference to Enoch.[719] This phrase follows the reading of the LXX in Gen 5:22 and 24 where Enoch is mentioned.

Nickelsburg opines: "In addition to demonstrating an interest in the figure of Enoch, the Wisdom of Solomon draws on traditions found in the Enochic corpus. Most striking are the parallels between the story of the scene of the righteous one's exaltation in Wis 4:20-5:8 and the description of enthronement of the Chosen One in 1 Enoch 62-63."[720]

The dependence of the Wisdom of Solomon on the Parables and other parts of 1 Enoch is generally accepted by scholars. Nickelsburg sums up his discussion of this dependency of the Wisdom of Solomon on the Parables by using it to date the Parables, "Evidence from the NT and

---

[717] Bogomilism, was a Gnostic dualistic sect that flourished in Europe in the 10th through 15th centuries. It was founded in the First Bulgarian Empire by the priest Bogomil during the reign of Tsar Peter 1 in the 10th century. Satanail, in their heresy, was the older of two sons of God with the younger being Christ.

[718] Winston, David, 1979. *The Wisdom of Solomon, A New Translation with Introduction and Commentary*, pg. 23.

[719] Ibid. pg. 139.

[720] N1 pg. 78.

the Wisdom of Solomon suggest the early decades of the common era as a terminus ante quem."[721] [722]

The Wis 4:20-5:8 passage includes elements from the heavily messianic Isaiah 52-53 combined with the messianic 1 Enoch 62-63.[723] It is difficult not to think of Jesus when studying Wisdom chapters 2-5. This indicates that within 4-8 years of the resurrection, as far away as Alexandria, the Parables may have been used to substantiate the Messianic claims of Jesus Christ.

Samaritan traditions

The Samaritan's have preserved traditions concerning the angel Phanuel that appear to have come from the Book of Parables.[724] Olson writes:

> Phanuel is also found in esoteric Samaritan traditions, where he is named as one of the four chief ruling angels (the others are Kabbala, Anusa, and either Zilpa or Nasi). The Samaritans also name three devils: Azazel, Belial, and Jasara. Thus, the Samaritans agree with the Parables in naming Phanuel as one of the four archangels and Azazel as the chief demon. This is further evidence that the "Parables" is not of Christian origin, since it is unlikely that the Samaritans would take this information from Christian sources, and these Samaritan traditions predate the rediscovery of the Book of Enoch."[725]

This indicates that either the Parables share a common tradition with the Samaritan texts, or the Parables were preserved for some time among the Samaritans; and the text was at one point considered authoritative enough to influence their beliefs.

Evidence from the New Testament

Nickelsburg writes "The earliest evidence for the Christian use of the Parables and/or the traditions contained in them is to be found in the New Testament itself."[726] Speaking of The Revelation to John of Patmos he also writes "As a revelation set in heaven depicting events related to the coming judgement, this work may well reflect knowledge of the Parables. In any case, its portrayal of a savior who is son of Man, Servant (Lamb that is slain), and Messiah draws on the tradition that dominates the soteriology[727] of the Parables, if not on that work itself."[728]

Ample evidence of dependence and parallels between The Book of the Parables and the New Testament will, God willing, be presented in a future book by the editor. The parallels can be chased down, by pursuing the cross references in this volume. Olson, speaking of the caution by

---

[721] This quote is from (NV2 pg. 62). Please see (NV2 pgs. 61-62, 258; 318-19; N1 pg. 78-79) for a fuller presentation of these parallels between The Wisdom of Solomon and the Parables of Enoch.

[722] "Terminus ante quem" is the date before which a document must have been written.

[723] See (NV2 pg. 258) for a comparison. He links Wis 5:1 with 1En 62:2a and 62:3ab; Wis 5:2 with 1En 62:3c and 62:4-5; Wis 5:4 with 1En 62:1b, 3c; Wis 5:4-8 with 1En 63:1-11 and Wis 5:5 with 1En 62:6, and 63:2-3.

[724] 1 Enoch 40:9; 54:6; 71:8-13.

[725] (OL pg. 137 n6) referencing Montgomery, J. A. 1907. *The Samaritans: The Earliest Jewish Sect*, pgs. 218-219.

[726] NV2 pg. 70. (See also P pg. 45, 53)

[727] The doctrine of salvation.

[728] NV2 pg. 70.

modern scholars in embracing the use of The Book of the Parables by the New Testament, is useful here:

> This forward shift in dating, however, means that modern specialists have been timid about positing any influence from the "Parables" to the New Testament, even though it is widely conceded that at a minimum, Matt 19:28 and 25:31, with their descriptions of the Son of Man seated on his throne of glory and presiding at the Last Judgement, are probably dependent on *Enoch* 62-63; 69:26-27."
> This caution is excessive. There have been a number of close, detailed studies of the "Parables" in recent decades, with particular attention to the "Son of Man" figure, and it may be that we are losing the forest for the trees. Perhaps it is time to step back a little, take a broader look, and make some common-sense observations. First, if Matthew had a copy, so could any number of others, and if we allow that the 'Parables' influenced the Gospels in even one place, there is no point in denying influence in other places that give that appearance. Second, while a number of parallels between the "Parables" and the New Testament can be replicated from other literature, such as *4 Ezra* or various Qumran texts, no other writing of that era even comes close to the "Parables" in providing such a remarkable *set* of similarities to the New Testament: the "Parables" unambiguously combines the heavenly "son of man" from Daniel 7, the Davidic king, and the Isaianic "Servant of the Lord" into a single figure, and then gives him no less than four names used of Jesus Christ in the gospels. The occurrence of exactly this cluster of significant motifs in two different works, especially when combined with sometimes striking verbal parallels, strongly suggests direct acquaintance.[729]

Chapter 108, which was written after the rest of the corpus of 1 Enoch, has dependance on the rest of 1 Enoch. Nickelsburg defends the reliance of 1 Enoch 108 on the Book of Parables:

> The concluding announcement of the judgement of the righteous and sinners (vv 11-13, 14-15) employs important motifs and imagery found in chapters 102-104 and 62-63. Since none of these parallels to the earlier chapters indicate the use of independent, more primitive tradition…, it seems likely that chap. 108 was composed as the conclusion to a form of the corpus that included at least chaps. 1-71, 81:1-82:4, and 85-105."[730]

If, as appears proven beyond reasonable doubt, material was pulled from chapter 108 for Matthew, and 1 Peter, this indicates that all of 1 Enoch was completed prior to the composition of these books. Since Matthew is thought to have been written in AD 55-65,[731] this is further evidence that the entire corpus of the Parables predates the ministry of Christ.

The Epistle of Jude is almost certainly quoting 1En 60:8 in Jude 14 "the seventh from Adam' and 54:6 in Jude 6 "great day." 60:8 is in a section of the Parables that is viewed as a Noahic interpolation. This indicates that the interpolation and the Parables proper were written early in

---

[729] OL pg. 12
[730] N1 pg. 553.
[731] ESV pg. 1815. However, the presence of thirteen direct parallels between Mt 24:8-44 and 1Thes 4:14-5:8 is very strong evidence that the gospel of Matthew was in circulation at the time 1 Thessalonians was composed in AD 49-51.

the first century at the latest; since Jude is typically dated to the mid 60's.[732] The references to the Book of Watchers in the book of Jude indicate that the Parables and the Book of Watchers were circulating together when Jude composed his epistle.

Evidence of the New Testament's dependence on the Parables abounds. Nowhere is this more evident, than in the Gospel of Matthew. In this regard Chiala comments:

> Another factor that makes us tend toward Matthew's dependence on the Book of Parables, and not vice vera, is that the essential characteristics that the Book of Parables attributes to the Son of Man can be found in Matthew, but he reverse is not true. The first element in Matthew that is totally foreign to the Enochic tradition is the series of sayings about how the Son of Man must die. If the Book of Parables is a Christian text, it is hard to imagine why the author would have left out this central part of the Christian kerygma.[733] And if it is a Jewish text that was written in the Christian era, it is hard to see why the author would have taken material from a Christian text such as the Gospel of Matthew. Furthermore, unlike the author of the Parables, the Gospels never seem to explain the nature, origin, and functions of the Son of Man, but they make a point of emphasizing those traits that are never attested in the earlier tradition, such as his power to forgive sins 'even' on earth, and his passion and death." He continues "By the time the Evangelists were writing the Gospels, and probably by the time of Jesus' ministry, the Son of Man was a familiar figure, but what was truly familiar about him was his role as eschatological judge."[734]

It is quite possible that the Book of Parables was so well known among early Christians that no need existed to identify the "nature, origin and functions of the Son of Man" since it was already laid out in the Parables.

Even the term Son of Man serves to date the Parables.

> By the end of the first century C.E., it seems that all 'Son of man' language is attentively avoided, and this should weigh as a critical factor in dating the Book of Parables. Once the Christian era had begun, there was no longer any mention of the Son of Man in Judaism, not even among the specific group of Jews who wrote the Second Book of Enoch, and later the third Book of Enoch. Christian literature also abandoned the title, and Christology developed around the titles of Messiah and Son of God.[735]

The text of the Parables in this edition contains 615 cross references between the Book of Parables and the New Testament. Of these, 182 are direct links (underlined). This is firm evidence that the Parables are directly related to the New Testament and the nature of the references establish the Parables were written before the New Testament. Regarding the similarities of (1En 51, 61;2-5; 62;14-150 with Mk 13:26-27 McDaniel (P pg. 346) states "If

---

[732] ESV pg. 2447.

[733] "Kerygma" is a Greek word used in the New Testament for "proclamation."

[734] R pg. 168 Chiala. Jesus is never asked to explain the term "son of man," it seems to be readily understood.

[735] R pg. 178 Chiala. But see *Haer.* 3.19.1; 3.19.2; 3.20.2; 4.33.11; 5.21.1, 2, 3; *Prax.* 2; 27; and Irenæus fragment LII.

Mark accurately reflects Jesus' understanding of this messianic Son of Man role, then it is likely that Jesus was familiar with the *Parables of Enoch* or that their tradition (oral) was circulating in Galilee or the land of Israel in the time of Jesus." He further comments that Jesus' self-designation as the Son of Man must be original to Him since it does not occur elsewhere (with very few exceptions).

Internal dating of the Book of Parables.

Parthians and Medes

The Parthians and Medes (this kingdom existed from 248 BC to AD 224, the Medes were included after 174 BC) are held up for special abuse in 1 Enoch 56:5. This is viewed as a reaction to the invasion of Judea by the Parthians in 40 BC as described by Josephus. (*War*, 1.13.1-8 §§248-265) John Ben-Daniel sees the Parthian invasion as useful not just for dating but in locating the author. He writes

> It should be evident that the residents of Arbel, Magdala, and the surrounding region of Eastern Galilee, witnessed precisely the same three pivotal aspects of the Civil War that are alluded to in the Parables of Enoch. The author may indeed have been resident in this area." "Since these scenes from the eschatological war in the Parables (*1En* 56-57) read like a personal recollection of the most dramatic and pivotal moments of the Civil War from 40-37 BCE, the text can provide geographical as well as historical details about the author. Most significantly, it reads as if it is being recalled by an observer who was stationed high-up in the Arbel cliffs, overlooking the Plain of Ginnosar, and seeing with his own eyes the most momentous events take place from his lofty vantage-point.[736]

Although the Parthians remained a threat, the invasion would have become yesterday's news after years and decades so it was likely interpolated into the Parables not long (certainly within a generation) after 40 BC. Archeologists have confirmed this invasion. "The Parthian invasion of 40 is now documented by recent excavations along the western littoral of the Dead Sea."[737] "The hoard of twenty bronze coins of Mattathis Antigonus (40-37 B.C.E.) discovered near the bathhouse and on the paved patio surrounding the swimming pools of the Hasmonean winter palace in Jericho are also, most likely, evidence of the Parthian invasion of 40 B.C.E."[738] Luca Arcari compares the chronological phases of the invasion as described by Josephus, with 1 Enoch 56:5-7 and finds that the Parthian invasion of 40 BC could well stand behind the Enochian text.[739] However some scholars see the Enochic text as problematic.

The problem is, the wording of the passage suggests that that Jerusalem was not taken and that the invaders fought among themselves and were destroyed (56:7-8). In addition, a second invasion from the east seems to be envisaged (57:1-2). Needless to say, none of this happened.

---

[736] Ben-Daniel, John, The Parables of Enoch (1Enoch 37-71): Provenance and Social Setting, pg. 13-14.

[737] R pg. 458. Charlesworth, *Can we discern the Composition Date of the Parables of Enoch?*

[738] Netzer, E. 1993. *Jericho – Exploration Since 1973*, in *The New Encyclopedia of Archaeological Excavations in the Holy Land*, 1993.

[739] R pg. 478-486, Luca Arcari, *A Symbolic Transfiguration of a Historical Event: The Parthian Invasion in Josephus and the Parables of Enoch.*

Whatever the historical reality, this passage seems to be a metaphor for an eschatological defeat of Jerusalem's enemies.[740]

It should be taken into consideration that Josephus was writing from a later time (AD 75-79) while the account in the Parables is much earlier. It is possible that Josephus was the inaccurate one. Nevertheless, the invasion serves as a time marker for the Parables.

Theft of land

"Through taxation and intrigue, Herod and his hierarchy controlled virtually two-thirds of the fertile land by the time he died."[741] Not only did Herod steal the land of small landowners but also large estates.[742] "Most of these new landowners were not Jews and lived away from the land they owned; they even lived outside the Land, as is evident in Jesus' parable of the wicked tenant farmers. The demotion of Jews from landowners to tenant farmers was exceptional during Herod's reign."[743] This land theft is reflected in the Book of Parables and the new owners are singled out as future subjects for judgement. (38:4-5; 45:5; 46:4; 48:8; 54:1-2; 62:2; 62:3-6; 62:9; and 63:12). The "dry ground" referred to so often in these passages is the fertile ground, as opposed to the swampy ground, that was not drained and farmed until the 19th and early 20th centuries AD. The swampy areas were near the coasts, west of the Kinneret and especially in the land of the Hulah Valley.[744] "This conclusion seems to follow the probability that the provenience and origin of the books of Enoch is most likely in Galilee. For example, the Watchers do not descend on a spot in Judea. They descend on Mount Hermon in Upper Galilee. Moreover, the best location for those who live near swamps – non-dry ground—and lament the loss of dry ground to the Herodians and their henchmen is the Hulah Valley, the large swampy area from Dan or Banias to Bethsaida or Capernaum."[745] "Archaeological excavations reveal "The appearance of large, sumptuous manor houses and palatial abodes"[746] in the Herodian period. "Almost all the new landlords were Romans and others who were considered pagans by Jews. When the Jewish author called them "the powerful" (1En 46:4; 54-55) "the strong" (48:8), and "the mighty" (62:2), he revealed his feelings of impotence in a land that had been promised to him as a descendent of Abraham."[747] By AD 66 an estimated 70% of the arable land shifted from small and ordinary farms to large and wealthy farms owned by Herodians or Romans.[747a] Funds from this confiscation were used by Herod for massive building projects including the Herodium, Caesarea Maritima, Sebaste, Masada, the Temple and the Antonia Fortress. The use of the words "the kings of the earth" in 48:8 clearly denote Roman emperors, "but some Jews may have included King Herod in that group since he was judged to be non-Jewish and perceived to be pro-Roman, even a Roman."[748] "Most scholars will have little difficulty

---

[740] R pg. 391. Grabbe, *The Parables of Enoch in Second Temple Jewish Society.*

[741] R pg. 463, Charlesworth, *Can We Discern the Composition Date of the Parables of Enoch.* (See also P. pg. 51)

[742] This matches the account in Josephus (*Ant* 17.11.2 §§304-314) of the delegation of the Jews sent to Caesar in Rome to complain of conditions (see esp. *Ant* 17.11.2 §§307).

[743] R pg. 463, Charlesworth.

[744] R pgs. 460-461, Charlesworth. (See also P pg. 49)

[745] R pg. 465, Charlesworth.

[746] R pg. 464, Charlesworth.

[747] R pg. 464, Charlesworth. (See also P pg. 48)

[747a] P pg. 181 and 183. (Cf. Ant 17.11.1-2 §§303-308

[748] R pg. 465 Charlesworth.

perceiving that the Book of Parables is an anti-Herodian polemic."[749] This is very strong evidence dating the Parables to the later reign of king Herod or shortly thereafter (30-4 BC).[750]

Bloodshed

1 Enoch 47 mentions the blood of the righteous three times. The reign of king Herod (37-4 BC) was certainly a time when the blood of the righteous was shed. The slaughter of the innocents by Herod as related in Matthew 2:16-18 doesn't even merit a mention by Josephus amid the other Herodian atrocities. A prime example of his cruelty, directed toward the righteous, is his treatment of the young men who pulled down the golden eagle Herod had placed above the great gate of the temple. They were burnt alive and otherwise put to death (*War* 1.33.4 §§655).

Baths of Callirrhoe

1 Enoch 67:8 closely matches the account of king Herod's sickness, just before his death, and his attempted treatment by luxuriating in the warm baths of Callirrhoe, which is mentioned by Josephus.[751]

Now those waters will perform a service for the kings, the mighty, the exalted, and those who occupy the dry ground, for the healing of their flesh, but for the judgement of their spirits. Their spirits are full of lust, so that their flesh is punished, for they have denied the Lord of Spirits. Every day their punishment is plainly visible to them, and yet they still do not believe in his Name. 1 Enoch 67:8

Herod's death is dated to late March of 4 BC. "Since, according to Josephus, Herod died before Passover, which in 4 B.C.E. fell on April 11, and Herod's journey to Callirrhoe took place after the lunar eclipse, which occurred on the night of March 12/13, we know that the journey must be dated to the second half of March."[752]

The question arises, as to whether these are the springs of Callirrhoe or another set of warm springs. "Pliny, who clearly was interested in such matters, mentions only two sets of hot springs in his literary tour of Palestine, those at Callirrhoe and at Tiberias (Natural History 70-72), but only with regard to the former does he speak of "the celebrity of its waters" (*aquarium gloriam*)."[753] Rabbinic writings referred to Lasha (Gen 10:19) as Callirrhoe. Callirrhoe is mentioned by Ptolemy in *Geography* 5.15. Gaius Julius Solinus (AD 3rd century) in *De mirabilibus mundi* 35.4 refers to Callirrhoe as a "well proved medicinal source of heat." "At a later date, the sixth century Mababa map eloquently attests the thermal bath's continuing importance. Finally, archaeological evidence confirms that they were in use during Herod's reign, as the most significant of the remains of building structures, coins, and pottery found there are all clearly Herodian."[754] The springs are still used in the present day.

---

[749] R pg. 465, Charlesworth.
[750] NV2 pg. 63-64.
[751] Josephus *War* 1.33.5 §§657; Josephus *Antiquities* 17.6.5 §§168-172 esp. 171.
[752] R pg. 475, Hannah, see footnote 27. Callirrhoe is a 3.5 hour chariot ride from Jerusalem.
[753] R pg. 470, Hannah.
[754] R pg. 471, Hannah.

1 Enoch 67:8 is a known interpolation inserted into the text of the *Book of the Parables.*[755] "The interpolator could have added this passage only after the fateful events of 4 B.C.E., but his allusion would have the most force if Herod's demise was a recent occurrence and still fresh in the memory."[756] This establishes that the text itself dates from before Herod's death. Please see the footnotes for 67:6-13 for a closer examination of this subject.

1 Enoch 46:5-6 as well, could be read as a reference to Herod's rise to kingship and death which were both attributed to God. "Nor humbly acknowledge who bestowed their kingdoms upon them"[757] "And worms shall be their bed, and they shall have no hope of rising from their beds, because they do not exalt the name of the Lord of Spirits."[758]

Convergence of paradigms

Speaking of the Parables, Boccaccini writes:

> The document as a whole therefore testifies to a stage in which the encounter and merging of the Sapiential, Messianic, and Apocalyptic Paradigms were still at their inception – a stage that parallels the earliest origins of the Jesus movement and is the logical premise for the theological developments in Paul and the later Christian tradition....It is difficult to imagine that someone, either Christian or Jew, could "forge" so well after the year 50 a text like the Parables of Enoch that so well fits in this quite distinctive (and chronologically well confined) stage in the development of Second Temple Jewish thought.[759]

Argument from silence

Major events after the time of king Herod are not alluded to in the Parables. On this subject Piovanelli opines:

> On the other hand, the text is apparently silent about the circumstances of the king's death; the troubles that disrupted his succession; the Roman occupation of Judea, Samaria and Galilee; the military resistance that ensued; Caligula's attempt to have his own statue introduced in the temple, and more significantly, the destruction of Jerusalem in 70 C.E., not to mention the hope to rebuild the Holy City before the tragic epilogue of the Second Jewish War, in 135 C.E.[760]

It should be pointed out that the text does speak obliquely of the circumstances of Herod's death in 67:8-13.

---

[755] R pg. 472, 473-474 Hannah.
[756] R pg. 476, Hannah.
[757] Cf. *Ant* 15.10.5 §§ 373-376
[758] Cf. *Ant* 17.6.5 §§169
[759] R pg. 288. Boccaccini.
[760] R pg. 376. Piovanelli.

What scholars think

The dating of the Parables/Similitudes has been intensely debated by scholars. Baynes[761] concludes "Although a minority view argues for a post-Christian date, a growing scholarly consensus places the composition of the Similitudes around the turn of the millennium or somewhat later in the first century AD." R. H Charles dated the Parables between 94 and 79 BC.[762] Bock[763] writes in his conclusion, "The starting point for such discussion is the strong likelihood that the Parables of Enoch are Jewish and most likely were composed prior to the work of Jesus of Nazareth or contemporaneous with his Galilean ministry." Charlesworth[764] dates the Parables (Similitudes) to the Herodian period 34-4 BCE. Nickelsburg, agreeing with Stone, concludes: "With these considerations in place, I date the Parables between the latter part of Herod's reign and the early decades of the first century C.E., with some preference for the earlier part of this time span."[765]

Charlesworth sums up the findings of the 2007 Enoch seminar which dealt specifically with the dating of the Parables.

> In the first section we observed that the Parables of Enoch is now reevaluated by a world-class team of experts working in the Enoch seminar. They have concluded, unanimously, that the Parables of Enoch are Jewish. They have agreed, almost unanimously, that the Parables of Enoch were composed in the late first century B.C.E. or in the early decades of the first century C.E. The provenance of the Parables of Enoch, according to many Enoch experts, is most likely Galilee.[766]

Elsewhere Charlesworth notes:

> Third, Enoch specialists working in the Enoch Seminar have concluded, almost unanimously, that the Parables of Enoch is not only Jewish but was composed during the Herodian period, or more precisely sometime between 40 B.C.E. and 20 C.E., most likely somewhere in Galilee.[767] Charlesworth has since established scholarly consensus around a narrowed date range of 20-4 BC.[768]

---

[761] Baynes, Leslie, 2018. *Introduction to the Similitudes of Enoch*, in Early Jewish Literature: An anthology vol. 2. pg. 259-260.
[762] R. H. Charles, *The Book of Enoch*, section II, page 108.
[763] Bock, *Dating the Parables of Enoch: A Forschungsbericht*, pg. 112.
[764] Charlesworth, James H. 2013. *The Date and Provenience of the Parables of Enoch*, in *Parables of Enoch: A Paradigm Shift* eds. James H. Charlesworth and Darrell L. Bock; *Jewish and Christian Texts in Contexts and Related Studies*, pgs. 37-57.
[765] NV2 pg. 62-62.
[766] Charlesworth, James H., Executive editor, 2008. "Jewish and Christian tests in Contexts and Related Studies" in *The Pseudepigrapha and Christian Origins*, pg. 259. The holdout among scholars at the time, was the late M. Knibb who argued for a date in the second half of the first century. R pg. 467, Charlesworth, *Can We discern the Composition Date of the Parables of Enoch?*
[767] Charlesworth James H. Executive editor, 2008. *Jewish and Christian tests in Contexts and Related Studies* in *The Pseudepigrapha and Christian Origins*, pg. 244.
[768] R pg. 465, 467, Charlesworth, *Can we Discern the Composition Date of the Parables of Enoch?*
[768a] P pg. 369. Charlesworth summarizing Grant Macaskill P. pgs. 218-230

Charlesworth elsewhere concludes:

> In his detailed survey, (Grant) Macaskill shows that it is unlikely that the author of the Parables of Enoch knew and depended on Matthew. The overlap in themes shows that the Parables of Enoch preceded Mathew. Thus we have a literary confirmation of what philology, historiography, and archeology have illustrated: the early existence of the Parables of Enoch.[768a]

Sacchi concludes:

> I think that after the Camaldoli meeting (2007) the adjective "tentative" should be dropped, given the impressive amount of evidence gathered in support of a pre-Christian origin of the document. The burden of proof has shifted to those who disagree with the Herodian date. It is now their responsibility to provide evidence that would reopen the discussion."[769]

Conclusion

Dating the Parables to the reign of king Herod is quite remarkable. Scholars have not come to this conclusion lightly. Christ and the writers of the New Testament knew all the Books of 1 Enoch because it was written before their ministry/compositions. They used thoughts and language from 1 Enoch extensively, including the Parables. The Book of Parables prepared the way for the Lord. That makes it one of the most, if not the most, influential writings in history, as it was written mere decades prior to the start of Christ's ministry!
The highly regarded James H. Charlesworth, summarises:

> The Book of the Parables (1 Enoch 37-71) appears to be a Jewish work that antedates Jesus, and the author seems to imagine a connection among the Messiah, the Righteous one, and the Son of Man. The work most likely took shape in Galilee, not far from where Jesus centered his ministry. He, thus, could have been influenced by this writing or the traditions preserved in the Parables of Enoch. In this case, his own self-understanding may have been shaped by the relationship between the Son of Man and the Messiah that is found only in the Parables of Enoch. If those in the Enoch group were known as the great scholars who had special and secret knowledge, and if they lived in Galilee, then Jesus would most likely have had an opportunity to learn firsthand about their teachings through discussions and debates.[770]

Are these the scribes Jesus referred to in Mt 13:52? "Therefore every scribe who has been trained for the kingdom of heaven is like a master of a house, who brings out of his treasure what is new and what is old."

The fact that the portrayal of the Messiah in the Parables of Enoch, especially chapters 45; 47; 48; and 61:8-63:12, matches exactly the messianic claims of Christ and the apostles is remarkable! In fact, given His extensive knowledge of the Parables and His frequent reference to

---

[769] R pg. 511, Sacchi.
[770] R pg. 467, Charlesworth.

the "Son of Man" it is not improbable that Christ himself knew, or knew of, the author! The timing and place of its composition could not have been more fortuitous in supporting the ministry of Jesus Christ. 1 Enoch and the Parables must be studied and taken seriously. How is it possible to understand Christianity without it? As you read The Book of Parables, and indeed all of 1 Enoch, note the New Testament quotes, parallels, theology, and images throughout; confident that the entire document, less the possibility of some interpolations, precedes the Christian era. This text is from the very dawn of Christianity! "How could Jesus not have known the Parables of Enoch, if it was composed about Jesus' time and in areas of Galilee that he frequented." (Charlesworth P pg. 372

The Book of Parables or Similitudes

Background of The Book of Parables

Original language: Hebrew or Aramaic[771], translated into Greek and then Ethiopic (Ge' ez).[772] No significant text of the Parables currently exists other than in Ethiopic.

Author and provenance: Jewish, Galilee, perhaps in Migdal=Taricheae? Caves of Arabel?[772a]

> Study of the text of *The Book of Parables* finds that although it draws from a variety of literary sources, these have been shaped by a firm compositional hand, to produce a text that has been artfully constructed on a literary and oral level. It is therefore justified to consider it as the product of a single author, with the interpolation of some additional material from other hands."[773]
>
> The Book of the Parables (1En 37-71) appears to be a Jewish work that antedates Jesus, and the author seems to imagine a connection among the Messiah, the Righteous One, and the Son of Man. The work most likely took shape in Galilee, not far from where Jesus centered his ministry. He, thus, could have been influenced by this writing or the traditions preserved in the Parables of Enoch. In this case, his own self-understanding may have been shaped by the relationship between the Son of Man and the Messiah that is found only in the Parables of Enoch. If those in the Enoch group were known as the great scholars who had special and secret knowledge, and if they lived in Galilee, then Jesus would most likely have had an opportunity to learn firsthand about their teachings through discussions and debates."[774]

Date: The Book of Parables was most assuredly written during the reign of king Herod (37-4 BC) or soon after. This date is supported by; 1. The reference to the Parthian invasion of Israel in 40 BC. (56:5). 2. The wicked immoral kings luxuriating in the hot water spas referring to king Herod's visit to Callirrhoe days before his death in 4 BC. (67:8-13), 3. The parables show no Christian interpolation and are Jewish in composition. 4. The Parables have been shown to have influenced the authors of the New Testament. 5. The portrayal of Jews as having been pushed off their land or made tenant farmers matches the time of king Herod. 6. The text mirrors the world view of 4 Ezra and 2 Baruch, both AD first century compositions which appear to contain parallels to The Book of the Parables. 7. Unlike 4 Ezra and 2 Baruch it does not mention the fall of Jerusalem in AD 70. 8. Parallels from the Book of Parables appear in 1st century Jewish and Christian texts. "Cumulatively, then, dating the Parables of Enoch to the time of Herod the Great

---

[771] Nickelsburg argues for Aramaic, (NV2 pg. 32, 251). Olson and Black Hebrew (OLS pg. 21; P pg. 75-76).
[772] N1 pg. 15-16, NV2 pg. 33.
[772a] Magdala Stone and Synagogue: P pgs. 159-169; 186-191. Caves of Arabel: Ben-Daniel, John & Gloria 2019. *Saint John and the Book of Revelation: From Essenes to End-Times*, pg. 6.
[773] Daniel, John Ben, *The Parables of Enoch (1Enoch 37-71): Provenance and Social Setting* pg. 2.
[774] R pg. 467, Charlesworth.

and the Herodians has become conclusive."[775] Charlesworth is on target with his proposed date between 20 and 4 BC (he later proposed 37 BC to the time of Jesus ministry). [776]

<u>Important notes</u>: That no literary bridge exists between the Book of Parables and The Book of Heavenly Luminaries is evidence that the Book of Parables circulated separately and was not composed in its present position in 1 Enoch.[777] No part of the Book of the Parables have been published from the literature found at Qumran. The Parables form the basis of the doctrine concerning the expected person of the Messiah/Christ. Christ and the New Testament writers show broad knowledge of the text in their discourses and writings. The titles Son of Man, Chosen One, and Righteous One are used extensively in the text and in the New Testament. "Although the Parables were not composed as a Christian text, the parallels between the Parables' and the Gospels' teaching on the Son of Man suggest a common milieu for the branch of the early Jesus movement and the community that generated the Book of Parables."[778] It may be argued that the Book of the Parables along with The Admonitions of Enoch and Chapter 108 are among the most important books ever written, since they form the foundation of so many New Testament passages. In fact, "the content of the Parables may have influenced not only early Christian theologies, but also Jesus' formative culture and teaching."[779] "We cannot simply assume, however, that all its ideas originated with this book. Even if the specific theology of the author is essentially sui generis,[780] it is very likely that the general outlines of his thought predate the Parables."[781] "Jesus certainly shared the same type of Judaism with the Enoch groups and at the same time and place." The *Book of Parables* was an important precursor to the ministry of Jesus Christ, introducing the Son of Man to the Jewish world of His day (cf. Jn 9:35-39).

"In creating his book, the author of the Parables drew, first of all, on traditional Enochic material from the Book of the Watchers and a source like the Astronomical Book, following to some extent the order of the Book of the Watchers."[782] Evidence for this is readily found in the near identical angel lists in 6:7 and 69:2-3. It is also thought that the Book of Giants was used as a source (P pg. 72). "The author also drew heavily on biblical sources, both for the form of his book, using Ezekiel and Zech 1-8, for example, and for specific thematic concerns. He reworked and incorporated biblical material, especially the Danielic Son of Man, the Anointed One of Ps. 2 and Isa 11, the Servant of Deutero-Isaiah, and possibly traditions about preexistent wisdom."[783] The polemics in the Book of Parables would have marked it as anti-establishment and are undoubtedly one reason it was written pseudonymously. The wicked oppressors of the region certainly would not have appreciated predictions that they would be given over into the hands of the righteous and holy, (1En 38:5) or be hurled from their thrones and kingdoms (1En 45:5). However, the Parables, though they come close; do not reach the level of righteous furor found

---

[775] R pg. 467, Charlesworth.
[776] R pg. 465, Charlesworth, *Can we Discern the Composition Date of the Parables of Enoch?* (P pg. 52).
[777] R pg. 91 VanderKam.
[778] NV2 pg. 66.
[779] R pg. 507 Sacchi.
[780] Sui generis: means "of its/their own kind", "in a class by itself."
[781] R pg. 499 Sacchi.
[782] R pg. 44 Nickelsburg, *Discerning the Structure(s) of the Enochic Book of Parables*.
[783] R pg. 76-77, Wright, *The Structure of the Parables of Enoch: A Response to George Nickelsburg and Michael Knibb*.

in the Psalms of Solomon (70-45 BC).[784] The Parables present the Messiah in a unique way, and in accordance with Christian Christology. "The Messianic doctrine in 37-71 is unique, not only as regards the other sections of Enoch, but also in Jewish literature as a whole. The Messiah pre-exists from the beginning (48:2), he sits on the throne of God, (51:3), possesses universal dominion, (62:6); all judgement is committed unto him, (69:27), and he slays the wicked by the word of his mouth, (62:2)."[785] Walck concluded "This study of the features of "the Chosen One" and "the Son of Man" in the *Parables of Enoch* and the Synoptic Gospels reveals that many similarities can be noted, some of which strongly suggest that the *Parables of Enoch* was known to the Evangelists and its theology incorporated into the Synoptics. Now that most specialists on the Book of Enoch date the Parables of Enoch near the end of Herod the Great's reign, it becomes obvious that the masterpiece (was) available in the period when the Gospels were written." (P pg. 266).

Interpolations: According to Darrell Hannah, most scholars today would agree that the Parables contain interpolations from a Noah apocryphon, although the precise delineation of these interpolations is still debated. Hannah has proposed 1En 54:7 –55:2; 60:1-10, 24-25; and 65:1 - 69:25 as certain, and chapter 64 as a likely interpolation.[786] The Noah apocryphon is viewed by scholars as an otherwise lost text that at some point in antiquity was interpolated into the text of the Parables.[787] "The Noachic materials form a coherent whole and seem to be additions or interpolations drawn from a separate text. Although it seems clear that the Noachic passages are copied from another text, the question of who inserted the Noachic narrative still remains. Was it the author of the entire text or a later scribe?"[788] The source of the interpolations may be the book of Noah mentioned in Jub 10:13 and 21:10. No evidence exists of an earlier text of the Parables without the Noachic additions. "Since the Noachic passages fit contextually in the ensemble of the book, I think it better to attribute the insertion of the passages to the author himself, who found in ancient texts passages useful for his intellectual construction."[789] If this is the case, the Noachic passages are not interpolations at all. That the son of man sayings in Matthew (24:37) and Luke (17:26) draw parallels between the days of the son of man and the days of Noah may indicate that the Noahic interpolations were present in the text by the early first century.[790] However, another interpolation exists. "For example, 56:5-57:3a has peculiarities that make it so out of character with the view of the rest of the Book of Parables that the passage would appear at the very least to have been taken over from elsewhere and may well have been added at a secondary stage."[791] However the interpolations could be original and important to the text, juxtaposing imagery of the first judgment of the flood with that of the final judgement.

Nickelsburg postulates the original text and arrangement as follows:
Introduction chap. 37

[784] See esp. PssSol 17:21-35 (OTP2 pg. 667-668).
[785] C pg. 66.
[786] R pg. 473. Hannah, *The Book of Noah, the Death of Herod the Great and the Date of the Parables of Enoch, in Enoch and the Messiah Son of Man.*
[787] R pg. 472, Hannah.
[788] R pg. 501 Sacchi, *The 2005 Camaldoli Seminar on the Parables of Enoch: Summary and Prospects for Future Research.*
[789] R pg. 502, Sacchi.
[790] R. pg. 47, Nickelsburg. But see also 1QapGen 6 esp. 6.9.
[791] R pg. 502, Sacchi and Knibb, *The Structure and Composition of the Parables of Enoch.*

Parable 1	chaps. 38-44
Parable 2	45:1-54:6; 56:1-4
Parable 3	58:1-59:3; 60:11-22; 61:1-63:12; 64:1-2; 69:2-12, 26-29
Conclusion	70:1-2[792]

The most controversial section of the Book of Parables are chapters 70:3-71:17. This is due to 71:14 where Enoch himself is identified as the Son of Man. One would expect the Book of the Parables to end at 70:2 since Enoch is at that point taken by a "chariot of the wind". Sacchi comments on this discrepancy and references Knibb.

> Nevertheless, he (Knibb) can affirm with sufficient certainty that (1) chaps. 70-71 belong to a late stage in the formation of the Parables, and (2) these chapters contain the narration of the ascent of Enoch to heaven and his identification with the preexistent Son of Man. This means that the last two chapters, though belonging to the text that tradition has handed down to us, are not the work of the same author of 1En 37-69, and so the identification of Enoch with the Son of Man.[793]

Throughout the rest of the Parables, the Son of Man and Enoch are clearly distinct figures. (1 Enoch 70:3-71:17) for this reason, and others, is viewed by some scholars as an early interpolation that contradicts the rest of the text.

The Book of Parables (Chapters 37-71)

For Those Who Come After

37 1 THE VISION [794] OF WISDOM[795] THAT ENOCH Isa 1:1

---

[792] NV2 pg. 19.

[793] R pg. 503, Sacchi referencing Knibb.

[794] The use of the term "vision" with its obvious similarity to Isa 1:1, introduces the Book of Parables as a prophetic text. In Num 12:6, God says he speaks to prophets through dreams and visions. Other places where "vision", (in Hebrew, <u>hă·zō·wn</u>, חָזוֹן) is mentioned or used to introduce a prophetic text include (Ezek 12:23-24; Joel 2:28; Obad 1:1; Nah 1:1; and Hab 2:2-3). **The scribe is clearly calling on the reader to consider the Parables as a prophecy divinely revealed.** This would not have been done lightly, especially at the time of Herod. Scribes viewed using their own name as sinful. This is one reason why texts were written under pseudonyms, as in the present case. "And now I know this mystery, that sinners will alter and copy the words of truth, and pervert many and lie and invent great fabrications, and <u>write books in their own names</u>" (Translation of 1En 104:10 by N). Speaking of (1En 104:10), Nickelsburg opines "Thus the text appears to have spoken about people who wrote writings in their own names. This could mean people who attached their own names to their literary compositions. But the idiom can also mean "with their own authority" (N1 pg. 633-534). **In (Mt 23:34) Jesus says that "prophets, and wise men and scribes" were sent from God. He is thus giving authority to each of the three categories. Hence scribes and wise men functioned as revelers of God's visions, the same as prophets.**

[795] The original title of what we call the Book of Parables, was Enoch's "Vision of Wisdom;" which derives from this verse. The name Book of Parables derives from 1En 68:1. "The use of a superscription parallels the beginning of the Book of the Watchers (1:1), the Book of the Luminaries (72:1), the Epistle (92:1), and the concluding 'book' (108:1), but not the Dream Visions (chaps. 83-90) and the narrative about Noah's birth (chaps. 106-7). **The full genealogy included here suggests that the Book was written to be read independently of these other units, even if it reflects knowledge, for example, of the Book of the Watchers"** (NV2 pg. 85).

SAW[796]—The son of Jared, son of Mahalalel,[797] son of Kenan, *CommJn* 6.25; Gen 5:3-19
son of Enosh, the son of Seth, the son of Adam.[798]
2 This is the beginning of the words of wisdom[799] 1:2-3; Ps 111:10; Sir 1:4, 14; Wis 6:17
which I lifted my voice to speak, declaring to those who dwell Prov 1:7; 4:7; 9:10
on the earth:[800] "Listen, you men of old; [801] and consider,
you men of latter days, the words of the Holy One which I 1:2; 92:1; 82:1
shall speak in the presence of the Lord of Spirits![802] [803] Num 16:22; 27:16; 2Cor 3:18; Heb 12:9
3 It is proper to declare such things to those of former times, 2Mac 3:24
but from those who come after, let us not withhold Ps 78:1-4
the beginning of wisdom.
4 Until the present day, the Lord of Spirits has never given Jub 4:17
such wisdom as I have now received, as my insight allows,[804] 19:3; 1Cor 2:7
and in accordance with the good pleasure of the Lord of Spirits, Lk 12:32
who has given to me the inheritance of eternal life. Jn 3:16; 1Jn 5:11
5 Three parables were entrusted to me, 60:1; 68:1

---

[796] This text reflects the original beginning postulated by Nickelsburg. "All Ethiopic manuscripts begin with *the second vision that he saw*, almost certainly a gloss that postdates the section's incorporation into the corpus and relates the Parables to Enoch's vision recounted in the Book of the Watchers" (N pg. 50). Other translations begin with "The second vision which he saw" (NV2 pg. 85). Note that Enoch is in the third person; the writer is speaking about what Enoch saw. **The author makes it plain up front that this is a vision, not actual events.**

[797] "In his commentary on John, (6.25) Origen observes that: 'Jared was born to Maleleel, as it is written in the Book of Enoch'" (R pg. 492 Olson, *An overlooked Patristic Allusion to the Parables of Enoch?*) Origen's Commentary on John dates to ca. AD 226-229.

[798] No part of Chapters 37-71 has been published from the Dead Sea Scrolls. No Greek or Latin texts exist other than quotes from the church fathers. The text is therefore almost solely dependent on the Ethiopic writings.

[799] The phrase "beginning of the words of wisdom" may mean the most important, or best part of wisdom, (NV2 pg. 88). "In the Parables, wisdom is an entity that belongs to the divine realm, where it is a property of God, the Son of Man, and the angels (42:1-2; 48:1, 7; 49:1, 3; 51:3; 61:7, 11; 63;2; 69:8)" (NV2 pg. 88).

[800] "On earth" literally "on dry land."

[801] N has: "O ancients" in place of "you men of old."

[802] **"Lord of Spirits" is the most frequent title for God in the Parables, occurring 102 times** (NV2 pg. 91). In the Bible a similar usage is found in (Num 16:22; 27:16), "the God of the spirits of all flesh." (1 Clem 64:1) reads: "Finally, may the all-seeing God and Master of spirits and Lord of all flesh." (Hebrews 12:9) uses "Father of spirits." (2Cor 3:18) reads: "Lord who is the Spirit." (Rev 22:6) comes close with "God of the spirits of the prophets." (2Mac 3:22-29); has a frightful appearance of the "Sovereign of spirits and of all authority" which prevents Heliodorus, an official of the Seleucid king, Seleucus, from removing money from the temple. ($1QH^{a}$ 18:10; W pg.195) translates: "Behold, you are Chief of the gods and King of the glorious, Lord of every spirit and Ruler over every creature." ($1QH_{a}$ 9:10-11; W pg. 178) states: "You (God) have formed every spirit." "Lord of spirits" was thus a term in use prior to the composition of the Parables where it is used extensively.

[803] 1En 37:2 has parallels with 1En 1:2. **This indicates that the Parables were written after the Book of the Watchers and the writer of the Parables had the Book of Watchers in hand. But the lengthy introduction of Enoch in 37:1 establishes that the Parables were written to stand alone.**

[804] **This is a remarkable, electrifying claim from the scribe who wrote the Parables. The revelation the scribe has been given, exceeds all previous wisdom! Given the amazing contents of the Parables, and the time they were written, this claim is amply justified. He is fully aware of the implications of what he is claiming. An observant Jew, at this time just before Christ, would sit up and take notice at this claim. Given that the penalty for false prophecy is death (Deut 13:1-5; 18:20-22), this statement is remarkable. He is revealing to the holy, chosen people of the end times, the mystery that the Messiah is near, and their salvation is at hand! If he is writing from Galilee during the life of Christ, did he actually know Christ? Given that these passages, and the Son of Man title were so heavily used by Jesus, it is impossible to argue that Jesus and this text are not linked.**

and I recounted them to those who dwell upon the earth. Rev 3:10

The First Parable

The Coming Judgement of the Wicked

38 1 The First Parable.[805] When the congregation of the 46:8; 53:6; 62:8; Ps 111:1
righteous appears,[806] the sinners shall be judged for their sins, 2 Thes 1:7-10; Ps 1:5; 74:2; 149:1
and be driven from the face of the earth;[807] 52:9; 53:2; Mt 25:41
2 And when the Righteous One[808] appears before the eyes of the 53:6; OdesSol 42:2; Isa 53:11
righteous, whose works[809] depend on[810] the Lord of Spirits; 40:5; 43:4; 46:8; PssSol 17:26-29
and when the light[811] appears for the righteous and elect 1:1, 8; Jn 1:4-5; Isa 9:2; 60:1; 1QS 3.20
who dwell on the earth, where then will be a dwelling place
for sinners?
And where (will be) a resting-place for those who have denied Lk 12:8-10; Mt 12:32; Rev 3:8

---

805 A parable is: "merely an elaborate discourse, whether in the form of a vision, prophecy, or poem" (C pg. 70).

806 "Congregation of the righteous" means "the exclusive people of God," "the eschatological community of God's people" "the people of God, the true Israel" (NV2 pg. 96-97). Other similar usages are (Ps 1:5; 74:2; 111:1; 149:1; and PssSol 17:16). (4Q171 1-2.2.5) reads "This refers to the company of his chosen, those who do his will." (W 249). These are the resurrected elect, see (51:1-2; 61:1-5; and Rev 19:14). At the end of days, when they are revealed, creation will be set free from its bondage (Rom 8:18-23). The term is also used in (4Q164 1.3 (W pg. 241)). Other uses of "congregation of the righteous" in 1 Enoch are unique to the Parables in (46:8; 53:6 and 62:8).

807 "Driven from the face of the earth" (cf. 53:2; 62:10; 63:6; 11; 69:28; Job 18:18; TAb A 11:5; 12:1-2; and ApZeph 4:1-7). **Chapter 38 is a description of the great final judgement.**

808 **The "Righteous One" is a highly elevated celestial being, the Messiah God, who is to be revealed and appear on earth. The Book of Parables, written just before the ministry of Christ is a major part of His unveiling.** The name "the Righteous One" may be from (Isa 53:11) where he will "make many to be accounted righteous, and he shall bear their iniquities." **Jesus is the only wholly righteous one who ever lived.** In 1En 92:3 the "righteous one arises from sleep" which predicts his resurrection and thus the dual nature with his humanness since spiritual beings are immortal. In the remarkable (47:1, 4), the blood of the righteous one ascends from the earth into the presence of the Lord of Spirits and is found fully acceptable. **1 Enoch therefore predicts the Lord's death, atonement and resurrection.** 1 John 2:1 has: "Jesus Christ the righteous." The name "righteous one" is used of Jesus Christ in (Acts 3:14; 7:52; and 22:14). For other uses of "Righteous One," see (1En 53:6; Isa 24:16; DialTrypho 136; the amazing Wis 2:12-22 and "messiah of righteousness 4Q252 5.3).

809 "The 'elect works' are those of the righteous. **It is interesting that the Book of the Parables appears to define 'righteousness' not as works or having to do with human meritorious performance"** (H2 pg. 37).

810 "Depend on," hang on, believe on. After a discussion of passages related to the "concept of 'faith' or 'faithfulness'' (39:6; 58:5 and 61:4). Nickelsburg opines: **"These passages suggest that the righteousness of the righteous is the fruit of faith, and this is begotten of the revelation that is promulgated in the parables" (NV2 Pg. 97, 101). This is the same concept of faith leading to righteousness found in (Rom 10:17; Eph 2:8-9; and Gal 3:2).**

811 "Light" (cf. Isa 9:2; 60:1; Jn 1:4-5).

the Name of the Lord of Spirits? [812] [813]   45:1, 2; 48:10
It had been better for them if they had not been born.[814]   Mt 26:24; Mk 14:21
3 When the secrets of the Righteous One are revealed,   49:4; 61:9; Mt 13:35; Lk 10:21
the sinners will be judged.[815] And the wicked will be driven from   Ps 1:5; Rev 20:14
the presence of the righteous and chosen.   4QPs^{f} 6-7; Mt 22:11-14
4 From then on, it will not be the mighty and exalted[816] who   62:6, 9; 63:1,12; Ps 37:11; Mt 5:5
possess the earth.[817] [818] They will not be able to look at the faces   Ex 34:29-35; 1Cor 2:6; Jas 5:1-6
of the holy, for the light of the Lord of Spirits shall shine on the   Jn 8:12; 12:46; 2Cor 4:6; Bar 2:35
faces of the holy and righteous and elect.[819]   92:4; 104:2; 108:12
5 At that time shall the kings and the mighty perish,[820]   Rev 6:15; Ps 149:6-9

---

[812] The answer is: they will find no rest or dwelling place (cf. 63:6). In contrast, the "Righteous One" goes to prepare a place for the righteous chosen (1En 39:4-5; 41:2; Jn 14:2-3).

[813] "Denied the Lord of Spirits" (see also 41:2; 45:1-2; 46:7; 48:10; 60:6; 67:8-10). The end of 46:7 reads: "All their deeds manifest iniquity, and their power rests upon their riches. Their devotion is to the gods which they have fashioned with their own hands. But they deny the name of the Lord of Spirits." In Rev 3:8 it is said that the Church in Philadelphia has "not denied my name."

[814] **"It had been better for them if they had not been born" Christ applies this verse to Judas, who is an excellent example of a denier of the Lord of Spirits.** (Mt 26:24; Mk 14:21) **This verse can be taken as a prophecy of Judas.** Christ may be citing it to draw attention to this passage; as He often did elsewhere. However, it was a common idiom especially in later sources (cf. Jerm 20:14; 4Ezra 4:12; 2Bar 10:6; ApSedr 4:2; 2En 41:2; Mishna Hagigah 2:1; and Babylonian Talmud Berakhot 17a).

[815] For this line Nickelsburg has: "When his hidden things are revealed to the righteous, the sinners will be judged," OL and I, relying on key Ethiopic texts as here, have: "When the secrets of the Righteous One are disclosed, sinners will be judged" Christ was hidden for ages and generations until the time He was revealed (Col 1:26).

[816] These mighty and exalted are prominent oppressors of the righteous and enemies of the Lord of Spirits in the Parables. From the fifteen mentions of them in the Parables (38:4-5; 46:4-6; 48:8; 53:5; 54:2; 55:4; 62:1, 3, 6, 9; 63:1; 63:12; 67:8, 12) clues to their identity can be gleaned. Using the terms from the translation by Nickelsburg; as "kings" they have political status, and "mighty" indicates political and military power. They are "strong" and "exalted" and through their possession of the land and by other means they oppress the righteous chosen. They shed the "blood of the righteous" (47:2) and they are idolaters (45:1-2; 46:5-7) (NV2 103-106). Nickelsburg prefers the later part of Herod's reign (37-4 BC) for the date of the composition of the Parables (NV2 pg. 62-63). If this is the correct date, these oppressors would be "the Roman rulers of Palestine and/or their clients in the Herodian house" (NV2 pg. 63). For a description of conditions at the time of Herod see (*Ant* 17.11.2) and if a slightly later date is preferred see (*War* 2.2-3). For a date after Christ, just before the Romans march on Jerusalem see (*War* 3.1-3). The editor agrees with Nickelsburg and Charlesworth that "**when the parables criticize the kings and the mighty who possess the earth (land), they are referring to the seizure of Hasmonean estates and other tracts of land and the granting of them to the king's friends, who are often non-Jews**" (NV2 pg. 63). This would argue for conditions late in Herod's reign.

[817] "Those who possess the earth" may also be read as "those who possess the land." In the time of the parables, Jews were being pushed off their land and replaced with rich and powerful friends of Herod (cf. 48:8; 55:4; 62:1-2; 63:1; 67:8).

[818] This reminds one of the statement by Christ, "Blessed are the meek, for they shall inherit the earth" (Mt 5:5). But Christ's source is more likely (Ps 37:11).

[819] This brings to mind the glory of God, reflected in the face of Moses, after coming down from Sinai (Ex 34:29-30). All of the chosen will have faces that shine (cf. Dan 12:3 and 2Cor 3:13-18).

[820] The sinners in the Parables are often identified as the kings and/or the mighty. This image of judgement is carried over into Rev 6:15-17 and broadened to sinners at all stations of life; "Then the kings of the earth and the great ones and the generals and the rich and the powerful, and everyone, slave and free, hid themselves in the caves and among the rocks of the mountains calling to the mountains and rocks, 'Fall on us and hide us from the face of him who is seated on the throne, and from the wrath of the Lamb, for the great day of their wrath has come, and who can stand?'"

given over into the hands of the righteous and holy.[821] 91:12; 95:3; 98:12
6 From then on, no one will be able to induce the Lord of Spirits 5:5; 48:8-9; 63:1-11; 4Q405 23.1.12
to show them mercy, for their life will be at an end.[822] 4Ezra 7:115; 2Thes 1:9

The yet Future Descent of the Angels

39 1 And it shall come to pass in those days, that the chosen 1Tim 5:21; SibOr 1:307-310
and holy children[823] will descend from high heaven,[824] 1:5; 1En 6-7; Ps 21:8-12; Gen 6:2; Jude 6
and their seed shall become mingled with that of Dan 2:43
the children of men.[825] 4Ezra 5:8
2 In those days, Enoch received books of indignation and wrath, 1:5; 13:3; 14:1
and writings of trepidation and tumult.[826] [827] [828] Ezek 2:10; Rom 2:7-9

---

[821] Here, and in (1En 48:9; 50:2; 63:11; 90:19; 91:12; 95:3, 7; 96:1; 98:12; and 99:6, 16); the sinners are given into the hands of the righteous. In Jewish apocalyptic literature, this is known as the "time of the sword" where Jews are given a limited time to take vengeance on their enemies (example, Ps 149:6-9). This mirrors the time of Jewish vengeance in Esther 9:1-15. This is one aspect of Jewish apocalypticism that was not picked up by Christianity. The closest parallels in scripture include (Ps 37:34-36; 58:10; 91:8; 92:11 and Prov 29:16). A more active role for the righteous may be assumed in (Rev 17:14; 19:11-16); compare (1Thes 3:13; 2Thes 1:5-10; cf. Zech 14:5). Christianity has generally been content to leave vengeance to God (Rom 12:19, and Heb 10:30; cf. Deut 32:35).

[822] In place of "at an end," B has: "terminated" and I has: "annihilated." N remains with: "at an end."

[823] These are fallen angels. Since it parallels 1 Enoch 6:2, and the context indicates it, the elect and holy children should be understood as angelic beings. All scholars acknowledge that these are celestial beings.

[824] **This problematic verse may forecast a future appearance of fallen Watchers** (OL pg. 76, 269-270, BL pg. 196). It can be translated in future tense as here and by OL, BL, K, C and I. However, Nickelsburg (NV2 pgs. 107-108) translates this verse in past imperfect as summarizing the first watcher appearance. "In those days, sons of the chosen and holy were descending from the highest heaven, and their seed was becoming one with the sons of men."

[825] "Their seed shall become mingled with the children of men." This phrase links this passage with (Ps 21:8-12). It speaks of the enemies of God (watchers) and their descendants (giants) whose seed is among the children of man. The giants "who plan evil" against God and "devise mischief" are defeated by aiming "at their faces with your bows." This would be the best way to defeat a stronger armored foe from a distance and is exactly what David did with a sling rather than a bow. **If this interpretation of (Ps 21:8-12) is correct, it is a very early witness to belief in the watcher story by David, from the time of David, as Psalm 21 has been dated to his time!**

[826] For the first line of verse 39:2; Nickelsburg has: "In those days Enoch received books of jealous wrath and rage and books of trepidation and consternation." Isaac has: "And in those days Enoch received the books of zeal and wrath as well as the books of haste and whirlwind." Olson has: "books of indignation and wrath, books of agitation and disturbance." These books caused great fear among the fallen angels.

[827] "Knibb accepts the conclusion that (1En 39:1-2a) is an interpolation into the text, perhaps originating as a marginal comment. Charles is firm that it is an interpolation (C pg. 74). Nickelsburg, when he characterizes these verses as an allusion to the Book of the Watchers that summarizes 1En 6-11, seems to assume that they belong to the original text." (R pg. 73, Wright, *The structure of the Parables of Enoch: A Response to George Nickelsburg and Michael Knibb*). He acknowledges that they may be an interpolation. (NV2 pg. 107).

[828] **The parallels between 1En 39:2a (Ethiopic) and Rom 2:7-9 (Greek) are profound. Paul states in Romans "but for those who are self-seeking and do not obey the truth, but obey unrighteousness, there will be wrath and fury (Enoch uses indignation and wrath). There will be tribulation and distress (Enoch uses trepidation and tumult) for every human being who does evil." In both passages, there are four words in two pairs. Close comparison of the words—Ethiopic to Greek—gives meanings as close as two languages can. For the righteous rewards, Paul's use of "glory and honor and immortality" (Rom 2:7) is matched by Enoch's "blessedness and splendor" (1En 39:9), "radiant like the brightness of fire" (39:7), and "for ever and ever" (39:6). Paul's passage is clearly applied to humans whereas the Enoch passage is fallen celestial beings. Since they are in league, and in rebellion, this is not a substantial point of difference. Paul's clarification that he is**

There shall be no mercy for them,[829] says the Lord of Spirits.[830]

Excursus: Will there be a return of the giants in the end times?

All translators but Nickelsburg place (1En 39:1-2) in a future tense, as it is in this text. He places this verse in past and past continuous tense, rather than future tense. He acknowledges that it can be translated in future or past imperfect (NV2 pg. 107) but makes a good case for the past perfect. He translates: "In those days, sons of the chosen and holy were descending from the highest heaven, and their seed was becoming one with the sons of men." Thus, he views it as speaking of the fall which already occurred, not a future event. That being said, **a growing number of amateur, and some professional, Enochic scholars (including Olson pgs. 76, 269-270) see a future return of the watchers/giants prior to the Day of the Lord in this verse. This image could not have been far from both Christ's and his listener's minds when He said, "Just as it was in the days of Noah, so will it be in the days of the Son of Man"** (Lk 17:26; cf. Mt 24:37). The return of the watchers at the time of the end is implied in 1En 1:5 where the watchers are seeking to hide themselves on judgement day. 1En 1.5 likely influenced 1En 39:2. Heiser, who was not a translator, also sees this as a reference to the past watcher rebellion: "The reference is the Watchers under judgement (1 Enoch 12-16). Consequently, 1 Enoch 39:1-2 does not support the notion that 1 Enoch 39:1-2 forecasts a return of the Watchers and repetition of Genesis 6:1-4 at the end of days" (H2 pg. 47). Olson, speaking of 1En 39:1-2a, disagrees: "Most *Enoch* scholars have paid little attention to this passage, presuming it to be a misplaced fragment describing the fall of the Watchers, perhaps from the lost "Book of Noah" or some other Enochic work, and probably corrupt, since it inexplicably describes the angelic escapades in the days of Enoch's father as a *future* event. But Enoch 39:1 makes satisfactory sense when we realize that (it) is not alluding to the events of Enoch's day but rather to things yet to come" (OL pg. 269). (1En 1:5) does forecast a future return of the fallen watchers/angels and (1En 19:1) indicates continual activity of the spirits of the fallen angels. Christ's prophecy in (Lk 17:26-27) and Paul's statements in (2Thes 2:3-9) seem to indicate a return to fallen angelic activity in league with humans at the end of the age. That fallen spiritual beings will return at the end of the age, may also be present in Daniel. According to this interpretation, just as ancient Atlantis had 10 hybrid kings, the ten toes of the great statue are seen to represent ten end time kings of mixed parentage, clay=mankind, iron=fallen spiritual beings. But something goes wrong; "As you saw the iron mixed with soft clay, so they will mix with one another in marriage, but they will not hold together, just as iron does not mix with clay" (Dan 2:43). (Isa 13:3) may be predicting a return of the giants, with God actually using the giants as an instrument of judgement on mankind. "I myself have commanded my consecrated ones, and have summoned

---

speaking of human beings (Rom 2:9) would be odd if he was not referencing a text about fallen celestial beings. This establishes four facts. 1. The *Parables* were written before Romans. 2. Paul internalized by study, and/or memorization, this passage from the *Parables*, since he casually incorporated the words into his most famous epistle. 3. His study, and use of the text demonstrates that Paul highly regarded the *Parables*. 4. That he applies this passage to the end times, in Romans, demonstrates that he regarded this text in the Parables as applying also to the end times. All four facts have far-reaching implications.

[829] The past fallen watchers did not receive mercy as is described in 1 Enoch chapter 10. Future rebellious celestial beings will not receive mercy either.

[830] N omits the last line of 39:2. He notes; this sentence "appears to be a misplaced variant of 38:6a" (N pg. 51, NV2 pg. 107). However, it appears in all Ethiopic manuscripts. Olson omits it from 38:6 and places it here. Black sees it as deliberately parallel (BL pg. 196).

my mighty men (gibbor) to execute my anger, my proudly exulting ones." 4 Ezra 5:8 is quite clear in predicting strange end time events, including; "and menstruous women shall bring forth monsters." *Irenæus* predicted the Antichrist will be a hybrid "since he sums up in his own person all the commixture of wickedness which took place previous to the deluge, due to the apostacy of the angels" (*Haer.* 5.29.2) See also Hippolytus of Rome, *On Christ and Antichrist* 6

Dwelling Places of the Elect with the Chosen One

3 And in those days, a whirlwind snatched me up from the face — 14:8; 52:1; 70:2
of the earth and set me down within the confines of heaven.[831] — Rev 4:2; 2 Kgs 2:11
4 And there I saw another vision[832]—the dwellings of the holy, — 41:2; 71:16; Jn 14:2
and the resting-places of the righteous.[833] — TDan 5:12
5 There my eyes saw their dwellings among his righteous — 104:6
angels,[834] and their resting-places with the holy ones;[835]
and they were petitioning and supplicating and interceding on — TDan 6:2
behalf of the children of men.[836] — Cels. 8.64
Righteousness flowed like water before them,[837] — 48:1; 49:1; Amos 5:24; Jn 7:38

---

[831] Isaac has: "into the ultimate ends of the heavens." "The reference point is the dwelling of God, beyond the point where 'the heavens were completed' (1 Enoch 18:10; cf. 1 Enoch 24-26)" (H2 Pg. 47).

[832] "Another vision," Nickelsburg views these two words as interpolated (NV2 pg. 111).

[833] Jesus references this idea in (Jn 14:2), where He says "In my father's house are many rooms. If it were not so, would I have told you that I go to prepare a place for you." (Cf. 1En. 39:7) Jewish homes were overseen by the patriarch, while sons with their families typically lived in the same family complex.

[834] **This is the dwelling of holy humans with the righteous angels and the Elect One (1En 39:6)! "The passage reveals that the holy, the righteous, and the chosen who have died are not in the mountain of the dead (see chap. 22) or in Sheol (see 102:5) but already in heaven"** (NV2 pg. 112). This is also proclaimed in 1En 104:6.

[835] Verse 39:4 and the first two lines of 39:5 are a good example of a-b-b-a parallelism. Holy-righteous-righteous-holy. Many ancient texts including the Gospel of Matthew were written with parallelism.

[836] These are most likely angels interceding for humans (NV2 pg. 112) but the translation could allow for it to be the spirits of heavenly humans interceding for earthly humans. "Angelic intercession is an idea known in the Old Testament, but not in the New Testament. Old Testament intercession of the heavenly (non-human) holy ones for people is an idea that is related to the keeping of heavenly books. **After the advent and accomplished mission of Jesus the Messiah, He becomes the lone mediator between God and humankind** (1 Timothy 2:5)" (H2 pg. 50). However, Origen correctly observes that angels join their own prayers and intercessions with pious humans and that tens of thousands of sacred powers are on the side of those who are friends of God; even taking up arms against demons (Cels. 8.64). Heiser goes on to note that: "**The notion that heavenly beings were presumed to function as mediators between the leadership of the divine council and mortal humans, in effect functioning as witnesses for humans to plead their case in the context of unjust suffering, is a very ancient one, perhaps going back to divine assemblies as Sumer**" (Heiser, Michael S., 2018. *Angels: What the Bible Really says about God's Heavenly Host* (Bellingham, Wa:Lexham Press) pg. 49). Other mentions of angelic intercession on behalf of humans occur in (Job 5:1, 33:23; Tobit 12:12; 1 En. 40:6; 47:1-4; 99:3; 104:1; TDan 6:1-2 (messianic) and TLev 3:5-10; 5:5-7 and possibly Rev 8:3-4). Fortunately, Christ, the perfect one, is interceding for the Christian (Rom 8:34; Heb 7:25; 9:24-25).

[837] "Righteousness flowed like water before them" This is a candidate for the scripture Jesus quoted as he cried out before the crowd on the last day at the Feast of Booths. "On the last day of the feast, the great day, Jesus stood up and cried out, 'If anyone thirsts, let him come to me and drink. Whoever believes in me, as the **scripture** has said, 'Out of his heart will flow rivers of living water.' Now he said this about the Spirit, whom those who believed in him were about to receive" (John 7:37-39). Other, better, but still inadequate, candidates exist for this unknown scripture Jesus is quoting in front of a massive crowd. Other candidates are: (1En 17:4; 48:1; Jer 17:13; Isa 44:3;

and mercy like dew upon the earth; 2:3; 42:3
thus, it will be among them for ever and ever.
6 And in that place, with my own eyes, I saw the Chosen One[838] 49:4; Lk 9:35; 23:35; Isa 41:8, 9; 42:1
of righteousness and faithfulness, and in his day righteousness Isa 11:5
will prevail. The righteous and elect will be innumerable before Rev 5:11; 7:9-10; 19:1, 6
him for ever and ever.[839] 37:4; Deut 32:10-11; Ruth 2:12
7 And I saw their dwelling place beneath the wings[840] of the 71:16; Ps 17:8; 36:7; 57:1; 61:4; 63:7; 91:4 Lk 13:34; Isa 31:5
Lord of Spirits, and all the righteous and elect were radiant Mt 5:15; 13:43; 1QH$_a$ 15.27; Phil 2:15
like the brightness of fire[841] before him; and their mouths were 104:2; 108:13-14; 2Bar 51:10; Dan 12:3
full of blessing. Their lips were praising the Name[842] of the Lord
of Spirits. Before him righteousness and truth will never cease.
8 There I desired to dwell! My spirit longed for that abode. Jn 14:2-3; Ps 84:1-2; Wis 5:5; Heb 11:16
Indeed, my inheritance had already been assigned there, for thus 48:7; 1QH$_a$ 11:21-23; Mt 25:34
it had been reserved for me in the presence of the Lord of Spirits. Dan 12:13; Mt 6:20
9 At that time, I praised and exalted the Name of the Lord of
Spirits with blessings and praises; for he has established me for Ps 7:9
blessedness and splendor, according to the good pleasure of 71:14; Lk 12:32
the Lord of Spirits.
10 For a long time, my eyes gazed on that place, and I blessed
him and praised him, saying: "Blessed is he and may he be Dan 4:34; Tob 13:1
praised from the beginning and forever!" 61:11
11 In his presence, nothing ceases to be.[843] He knew before the 61:5; Eph 1:3-5; 1Pet 1:20

55:3; 58:11; Zech 13:1; 14:8). Some passages in the DSS are better candidates: (1QSb 1.6-7; 4Q418 81&81a 1; CD 3.16-17; 19.33; 4Q525 24.2). The closest candidate appears to be (4Q418 103.6 (W pg. 491)) but a critical portion is missing. **It is apparent that Jesus considered texts "scripture" that are not in the western canon. These scriptures probably include all the books of 1 Enoch and the Book of Jubilees (compare Jn 8:56 with Jub 16:20-27, esp. 26). The anti-Nicene church fathers who antedated the accepted OT canon, also considered some texts that are not in the Old Testament as scripture.**

[838] "Elect One" and "Chosen One" are interchangeable in translations, the term is used of the Messiah/Christ. The name "Chosen One" is applied to Jesus by God at the transfiguration (Lk 9:35) and derisively by the rulers at the crucifixion (Lk 23:35). Some manuscripts use "Chosen One" in (John 1:34). The Chosen One is the "dominant character" in the Parables (NV2 pg. 113). The title "Elect One" comes unmistakably from Isa 41:8, 9 (BL pg. 197). Charles more plausibly sees "Chosen One" deriving from (Isa 42:1) (C pg. 78). The Righteous One, the Anointed One, Chosen One, Elect One and the Son of Man are all titles for the same personage, since their functions are virtually identical. Compare (40:5; 45:3, 4; 49:2, 4; 51:3, 5a; 52:6, 9; 53:6; 55:4; 61:5, 8, 10; and 62:1). **That Jesus claimed to be this personage is beyond dispute.**

[839] **This is a strong statement of resurrection and eternal life for the elect.**

[840] Other cross references to the "wings" of God include: (Deut 32:10-11; Ruth 2:12; Ps 17:8; 36:7; 57:1; 61:4; 63:7; 91:4; Isa 31:5; Mt 23:37; and Lk 13:34). N has "And I saw his dwelling beneath the wings of the Lord of Spirits"

[841] Isaac has: "intense as the light of fire." Several translators have "fiery lights." The intensity of the light is indicated both in number and appearance (NV2 Pg. 124).

[842] "This 'Name' of the Lord of the Spirits is self-evident for any Jewish reader; it is יְהוָה, the revered Divine Name" (R pg. 239. Gieschen). This is the personal name of God. "A close reading of scriptural references to God's name shows that 'the name' (Hebrew, ha-shem) is another way of referring to God himself" (Heiser, Michael S. 2018. *Angels*, pg. 59).

[843] For the first sentence in 39:11; I has: "There is no such thing as non-existence before him." N has: "in his presence there is no limit.;" OL has: "In his presence nothing ceases to be." "In light of what follows, the point seems to be that there is no end to God's knowledge and foresight" (H2 pg. 53). It may be speaking of the eternality of the saints in paradise.

world was created what would be, forever, and for generation after generation that which is to come.[844] 9:11; 81:2; Isa 42:9; 46:10; Sir 42:19 CD 2.9-10; Jub 1:26
12 Those who sleep not,[845] bless you: they stand in the presence of your glory[846] and bless, praise, and exalt, saying: 61:12; 71:7 Rev 4:8
"Holy, holy, holy,[847] is the Lord of Spirits; he fills the earth with spirits."[848] 45:1; Isa 6:3; Wis 1:7
13 And in this place my eyes saw all those who sleep not.[849] 14:23; 40:2
They stand in his presence and bless saying: "Blessed are you, and blessed be the Name[850] of the Lord of Spirits forever and ever!" Lk 19:38 Ps 113:2
14 My face was transformed for I was unable to continue watching.[851] 14:19, 25; 106:2; Ex 34:29

---

[844] **This is a powerful statement of the foreknowledge of God.** See also the Thanksgiving Hymn (1QH$_a$ 9.7-29 (W pgs. 178-179)).

[845] "Those who sleep not." "The Ethiopic has *teguhān*, the equivalent to Aramaic *'îrîn*, 'Watchers'" (H2 pg. 53). These "watchers" are not fallen but watch over the Kingdom of God for good. The concept of watchers is likely "related to the Akkadian by virtue of the *apkallu* of Mesopotamian Lore" (H2 pg. 54) (cf. the interpolation at 1En 71:7-8 where God's throne attendants are described in more detail). "Sleep not" (cf. 40:2; 61:12; 71:7; 72:37).

[846] Glory "refers to the divine glory (kābôd), the splendid effulgence that radiates from the enthroned deity" (NV2 pg. 127). For other descriptions/mentions of God's glory in 1 Enoch see: (14:16, 20; 21; 47:3; 60:2; 71:7; 103:1; and 104:1). His glory is described in many Biblical texts.

[847] The Trisagion, "Holy, holy, holy," is found only here, and in Isa 6:3 and Rev 4:8. Numerous similarities exist between 1 Enoch 39-40 and Revelation 5-6, including the thousands of thousands attending the throne of God and multiple spirits. Olson observes: "The substitution of 'Lord of Spirits' for Isaiah's 'Lord of Hosts' supports the idea that the former is an interpretative paraphrase of the latter." In other words, 1En 39:12 is interpreting Isa 6:3. It is evident that the Lord's hosts are spiritual beings. **However, the use of the Trisagion in Rev 4:8 is dependent on this verse (39:12) rather than Isa 6:3. Isa 6:3 says nothing about "those who sleep not" as is found here (also 39:13), whereas Rev 4:8 reads "and day and night they never cease to say."**

[848] **"The world of the author of the Parables was one full of angelic beings and disembodied spirits of whom God was supremely Lord"** (BL pg. 198). Are these human spirits as in (Num 16:22; 27:16), or other spirits such as the seven spirits as in (Rev 1:4; 3:1; 4:5; and 5:6) or both? It is not supported by the manuscripts; but this verse may have originally read: "the earth is full of his spirit" as in (Wis 1:7), which reads: "Because the spirit of the Lord has filled the world." This would also be in sympathy with (Isa 6:3): "the whole earth is full of his glory."

[849] "Those who sleep not" are the attendants of God, the watchers. Always watchful. Seeing them establishes that Enoch is in the very throne room of God. Some Ethiopic manuscripts read "others who sleep not" or "all the watchers who sleep not" or "all from among those who sleep not" indicating they may not be the same beings as in (1En 39:12).

[850]"Blessed is He" or "blessed be you" is a widespread way to begin prayers in the texts found at Qumran. (See The War Scroll 1QM 13.1-2; 14:3-4; 8; 18.6; 1Q434 Frag. 1 Col. 1:1; Frag 2.10; 4Q511 Frag. 63-64 2.2, 4.1-3; and 4Q285 8+11Q14 Frag. 1 Col. 2.2 (W pg.370). (See also Tob 13:1 and Dan 4:34). It likely reflects a contemporary liturgy.

[851] For 39:14b I has: "And my face was changed on account of the fact that I could not withstand the sight." N has: "And my face was changed, for I was unable to see." This may mean that his face was changed so he would be able to see the vision that begins in 40:1. This is language similar to Luke's account of Jesus' transfiguration in (Lk 9:29), "the appearance of his face was different" (NV2 pg. 129). Or it may be his countenance changed due to fear and awe. In 2 Enoch 22, Enoch is transformed in appearance to "one of the glorious one, and there was no observable difference" (2 Enoch 22:10, F. I. Andersen translation OTP1 pg. 138-139).

The Four Archangels in God's Presence

40 1 And after that I saw thousands upon thousands and ten	1:9; 14:22-23; 4Q530 2.2.17; Dan 7:10
thousand times ten thousand,[852] beyond number and reckoning,	60:1; 71:8; Rev 5:11; 7:9; 19:1,6; *Haer.*2.7.4
standing before the glory of the Lord of Spirits.[853]	Jer 33:22; Heb 12:22; ApZeph 4:2
2 And I saw standing on the four sides[854] of the Lord of Spirits,	Ezek 1:5-11; 10:14, 21; Ex 33:14-15
four presences,[855] different from those that sleep not,[856]	TLev 3:5; TJud 25:2; Rev 4:6-8
and I learned their names, because the angel that went with me	Isa 63:9
and showed me all secret things made their names known to me.	Dan 2:29; 1QpHab 7.5
3 And I heard the voices of those four presences[857]	*Haer.* 3.11.8
as they uttered praises before the Lord of Glory.	22:14; 1Cor 2:8; Jas 2:1; 1QapGen 2.4
4 The first voice was blessing the Name of the Lord of Spirits	
for ever and ever.	
5 The second voice I heard blessing the Chosen One,	Isa 42:1; Lk 9:35; 13:35; 23:35
and the chosen ones,[858] who depend[859] upon the Lord of Spirits.	Mt 22:14; OdesSol 8:18
6 The third voice I heard petitioning and praying	Job 33:23; TDan 6:2
on behalf of those who dwell upon earth,	TLev 3:5
and interceding in the Name of the Lord of Spirits.[860]	Rev 8:3-4

---

[852] Isaac has: "I saw a hundred thousand times a hundred thousand, ten million times ten million, an innumerable and uncountable (multitude) who stand before the glory of the Lord of the Spirits" This image likely came from (1 Enoch 14:22 or Dan 7:10) since the multitude is standing (cf. Heb 12:22; 1En 1:9; 14:22; 60:1; 71:8; Rev 5:11; 7:9-10). Interestingly this image of a multitude standing and serving God also appears in the Book of Giants (4Q530 2.2.17-18 (W pg. 294) and may be one of the sources used in *Haer.* 2.7.4 since it is the closest known text.

[853] **The number of watchers/angels who rebelled is a small fraction of the total number of beings before the throne** (cf. 2Bar 55:14). Someone my respond that in Rev 12:4 the dragon sweeps "down a third of the stars of heaven and cast them down to earth." This Revelation passage undoubtedly points back to Dan 8:10 where the little horn: "grew great, even to the host of heaven. And some of the host and some of the stars it threw down to the ground and trampled on them." This is certainly referring to the saints who were killed during the reign of Antiochus IV. Therefore, the Rev 12:4 passage is most likely referring also to martyred or apostatized saints rather than fallen angels. (Cf. Plato *Timaeus* 41D-42A; Gen 15:5; and 2Bar 51:10 for stars representing humans).

[854] Both B and I have "four wings." "The word translated 'sides' denotes literally 'wings,' but it is also used figuratively to refer to a corner (of a garment or the earth). "The author may imagine that the divine throne is set on a square platform with one of the archangels at each corner" (NV2 pg. 132).

[855] Presences, literally "faces" Hebrew פָּנִים, Greek πρόσωπον, and Ethiopic gaṣṣ (NV2 pg. 132). "Angels of the presence" are also mentioned in (Isa 63:9; Lk 1:19; Jub 1:27-2:18; TLev 3:4-5; TJud 25:2; and 1QSb 4.25,26). **These angels of the presence are found in the very throne room of God (cf. Mt 18:10; Heb 9:24). Jesus tells us that these angels are protectors of little children (Mt. 18:10). "Here in Enoch, they are distinguished from the watchers (Cherubim, Seraphim and Ophanim) and identified (v. 9) with Michael, Raphael, Gabriel and Phanuel.**" (BL pg. 199)

[856] I has: "and saw four other faces among those who do not slumber," N has: "I saw four figures different from those who sleep not." (Cf. 39:12-13; 61:12; 71:7).

[857] In place of "presences" N uses "figures" I uses "faces."

[858] Chosen and elect are interchangeable. "Elect One" and "elect ones" could just as easily have been used.

[859] Depend upon or "hang upon." I has "who are clinging onto the Lord of the Spirits." N has "depend on."

[860] **Angels are seen as mediators in prayer for humans in (1En 99:3; Job 5:1; 33:23; Zech 1:12-13; and Rev 8:3-4). They are also mediators in (TDan 6:2) "Draw near to God and to the angel who intercedes for you, because he is the mediator between God and men for the peace of Israel. He shall stand in opposition to the kingdom of the enemy." In (TLev 3:5-6) Angels even offer sacrifices for men's "sins of ignorance." After the work of Christ, for a Christian, Christ is their mediator (1Tim 2:5). "For there is one God, and there is one**

7 I heard the fourth voice fending off the satans[861] — Job 1:8, 2:1-5; TDan 6:2
and forbidding them to come before the Lord of Spirits. — Zech 3:1-2; Rev 12:10; Num 22:22,32
to accuse those who dwell on the earth.
8 After that, I asked the angel of peace[862] who went with me, — TDan 6:5; TAsh 6:6; TBenj 6:1; Isa 33:7
who showed me everything that is hidden,
"Who are these four presences that I have seen,[863] — Ezek 1:5; Rev 4:6
and whose words I have heard and written down?" — 33:3
9 And he answered: "This first is Michael,[864] — 9:1; 10:11; 71:8
the merciful and long-suffering, and the second who is in charge — *Princ* 1:8:1; Ex 34:6
over all the diseases and every wound of the children of men,
is Raphael;[865] and the third, who is in charge of all the powers,[866] — 10:4; 4Q285 1.3; Rom 8:38; Eph 6:12

---

mediator between God and men, the man Christ Jesus." (See also Heb 9:15). Jesus is a much higher mediator than any other celestial being. Hebrews 1 may have been written to correct those in the authors time who were looking to angels as intercessors rather than to the much superior intercessor, Christ.

[861] These "Satans" are accusers, adversaries, or prosecutors seen in the singular with a definitive ("the satan") in (Job 1:8-2:5 and Zech 3:1-2 (the slanderer in LXX)). "Just as there are many devils but one devil, so there are many satans but one Satan" (OL pg. 80). Satan is also seen in a legal accusatory role in Rev 12:10; and as a proper name in 1Chr 21:1. In Hebrew it is שָׂטָן, in Greek κατήγορος here in Ethiopic it is haśśātān. Satan is found in the Parables in 53:3; 54:6 and "satans" in 65:6. Charles astutely observes: **"The Satans appear here for the first time in Enoch, 40:7. They seem to belong to a counter kingdom of evil, ruled by a chief called Satan, 53:3. They existed as evil agencies before the fall of the Watchers; for the guilt of the latter consisted in becoming subject to Satan, 54:6. This view harmonizes exactly with that of Gen 3:1 combined with 6:1-4. These Satans had the right of access into heaven, 40:7 (cf. Job 1:6; Zech 3)—a privilege denied to the Watchers, 13:5; 14:5. Their functions were threefold: they temped to evil, 69:4, 6; they accused the dwellers upon earth, 40:7; they punished the condemned. In this last character they are technically called 'angels of punishment,' 53:3; 56:1; 62:11; 63:1."** (C pg. 78) Speaking of Satan Fröhlich expounds: "The title is not found in any of the other sections of the Book of Enoch other than the Parables. The "fourth voice," Phanuel, is contending in a court scene against multiple accusers. **"The Book of Parables seems to know of a larger tradition on the Watchers than what we find in *The Book of the Watchers*. In the Parables, the Watchers are identified with Satan, a figure originating outside of Enoch literature"** (R pg. 350. Fröhlich).

[862] The angel of peace seems to be the only angel accompanying Enoch in the Parables. The guiding angel in *The Book of Watchers* is Uriel (21:5). This angel is mentioned again in (43:3; 46:2; 52:5; 53:4; 54:4; 56:2; 60:24 (an interpolation); he is unnamed in 61:2, 3; and 64:2). The angel of peace is mentioned also in the Testaments of the Twelve Patriarchs; TDan 6:5; TBenj 6:1; and TAsh 6:6 where he strengthens Israel, is a guide, and knowing him leads to entering eternal life. The origin of the term may involve Isa 33:7 "envoys of peace" since Jerome understood that passage as applying to the angels. (C pg. 77)

[863] These four angels are the same as those found in chapters 9-10 except Sariel is here replaced with Phanuel (1En 40:9).

[864] Michael, meaning "who is like God," "Is the great prince who has care of your people" (Dan 12:1). In the War Scroll (1QM 17:6-9 (W pg. 163)) he is also seen as the protector of Israel and his name, along with those of Gabriel, Sariel and Raphael are to be written on the shields of the tower soldiers (1QM 9.13-16 (W pg. 156)). His role in spiritual warfare is also apparent in (Dan 10:13). The four are mentioned again in (4Q285 1.3 (W pg. 369)). Some Ethiopic texts read "the holy Michael." He is mentioned also in (4Q529 (W pg. 539); and 1QM 17.7 (W pg. 163).

[865] Raphael, "god's healer" true to his name, in this passage he is the healer. This is also seen in (Tobit 12:14) "And now God sent me to heal you and Sarah your daughter-in-law. I am Raphael, one of the seven holy angels, which present the prayers of the saints, and go in before the glory of the Holy One." In (Tobit 3:17) Raphael also was sent to heal. "In rabbinic literature he was the power that presided over medicine." (C pg. 78).

[866] "The powers" has a military connotation (cf. TLev 3:3). "For the Hebrew mind these are the 'forces' of heaven in this quasi-military sense: blended, however, with Greek usage, 'powers' convey the idea of miracle-working agencies or agents" (BL pg. 200).

is Gabriel:[867] [868] and the fourth, who is set over the repentance 10:9; Acts 11:18; 2Cor 7:10; Lk 1:19, 26
(leading) to hope[869] of those who will inherit eternal life,[870] Heb 1:14; Gen 32:29-30; Mt 19:29
is named Phanuel."[871] Mk 10:17
10 These, then, are the four angels of the Lord of Spirits 87:2
and the four voices I heard in those days.[872]

41 1 After that I saw all the secrets[873] of heaven: how the 46:5; 2Cor 12:1-4
kingdom is divided,[874] and how human deeds are weighed in the 61:8; Dan 5:26-28; 1QS 3.17-4.18; Job 31:6

---

[867] Gabriel means: "God is my warrior." He destroys the giants in (1En 10:9); and in other texts serves as a messenger; (Dan 8:16; 9:21; and Lk 1:19, 26). Some Ethiopic texts read "the holy Gabriel" (cf. 1En 20:7). That he is the angel of the annunciation, shows the extraordinary importance of Christ's birth. He is mentioned in the DSS (4Q529 4 (W pg. 539))

[868] (1En 40:9) is paraphrased and commented on, by Origen in (*De Principiis* 1.8.1). "A similar method must be followed in treating of the angels; nor are we to suppose that it is the result of accident that a particular office is assigned to a particular angel: as to Raphael, e.g., the work of curing and healing; to Gabriel, the conduct of wars: to Michael, the duty of attending to the prayers and supplications of mortals. For we are not to imagine that they obtained these offices otherwise than by their own merits, and by the zeal and excellent qualities which they severally displayed before the world was formed" (O pg. 52). Note, he interestingly places the creation of these angels before the creation of the world.

[869] "Repentance (leading) to hope," (cf. Acts 11:18; 2Cor 7:10; 1Pet 1:3; Titus 3:7). This is a very important phrase showing the importance of repentance (getting on God's side) in salvation. Although salvation is a gift by grace, and not works, (Eph 2:8-9) God will not save those still in rebellion against Him, i.e. in the opposing kingdom.

[870] Inherit eternal life (cf. Mt 19:29; Mk 10:17).

[871] Phanuel means "turn" or "turn aside" as in turn to God. For other mentions of Phanuel in 1 Enoch see (54:6; 71:8, 13). Other uses of the name as a placename occur in (Gen 32:30; Judg 8:8, 17) and in (Lk 2:36) as the personal name of the father of the prophetess, Anna. It is similar to Sariel "turn aside." "The name Phanuel (*pnw'l*) is a play on Peniel (*pny'l*) from Genesis 32:30, the place where Jacob wrestled with the "man" who was actually an angel (Hos 12:3-4)" (H2 pg. 61 see also NV2 pg. 134 and DialTrypho 58, 126). He here replaces Sariel (1En 9:1, 4) in the list of four. He is named in (3 Baruch 2:5). **A more extensive body of angelic literature undoubtedly existed at one point.** Hints of this, exist in (4Q529; 4Q400-405; and 11Q17).

[872] (1En 40:1-10) is the first example of a vision-query-explanation literary form in the Parables that is frequent in The Book of Watchers and in The Book of Parables (NV2 Pg. 131). It occurs in (40:1-10; 43:1-4; 46:1-8; 52:1-9; 53:1-7; 54:1-6; 56:1-4; 61:1-5; and 64:1-2). It is also found in the apocalyptic literature of the Bible.

[873] "Secrets" "The Ethiopic term is *hebu' āt* ('hidden things')" (H2 pg. 65).

[874] It is unclear if this is the earthly realm, which the *Charter of a Jewish Sectarian Association* (1QS 3.17-4.18 (W pg. 120-121) divides between the rule of the prince of light which is over the righteous and the angel of darkness who is over the wicked. Or is it the celestial realm, which the ancients going back to Mesopotamia, divided into 7 levels. Irenæus is an example of this thought: "Now this world is encompassed by seven heavens, in which dwell powers and angels and archangels, doing service to God, the Almighty and Maker of all things: not as though He was in need, but that they may not be idle and unprofitable and ineffectual" (*Epid.* 9). Or is it simply referring to the coming and going of earthly kingdoms as Isaac translates: "how a kingdom breaks up."

balance.[875] [876] [877] Ps 62:9; Prov 16:2; 24:12; 4Ezra 3:34
2 There I saw the dwelling-places of the chosen, and the Jn 14:1-2; Mt 22:14
resting places of the holy, and I saw with my own eyes
the sinners—all who deny the Name of the Lord of Spirits, 38:1-2
being driven away from there, and being 48:8-9; Jer 49:20; 50:45; Mt 7:23
dragged off; and they could not stand because of the scourge[878] TAb A 11:5; 12:1-2; ApZeph 4:1-7
which went forth from the Lord of Spirits.[879]
41(9) For no angel or satan[880] has power to hinder:[881] because 40:7; Rom 8:38-39
the Judge[882] sees them all and passes judgement on them all 1:7; Jn 5:22; 5:27; Acts 17:31
in his presence.

Excursus: Wisdom found no place in Jerusalem.

"Verses 42:1-2 describe Wisdom's futile attempt (as in Prov 1:24-25) to dwell in the world of humans (at the temple), while v. 3 recounts how Iniquity fills the vacuum left by Wisdom's departure" (NV2 pg. 138). Iniquity finds a welcome home on earth, being soaked up like rain in a desert. Nickelsburg notes concerning chapter 42, "**the poem can be understood as an outright attack on the notion that the Mosaic Torah embodies heavenly Wisdom and, thus as a denigration of the Torah as an effective catalyst of the righteous life. Wisdom descended but found no home in the Torah or among the Jewish people, and after she**

---

[875] (1En 41:1) brings to mind (Dan 5:26-28). "MENE, God has numbered the days of your *kingdom* and brought it to an end; TEKEL, you have been *weighed in the balances* and found wanting; PERES, your *kingdom is divided* and given to the Medes and Persians" (NV2 pg. 137). Like the kingdom of Belshazzar, the kingdom of the kings and mighty in the Parables, who oppress the righteous and chosen, will be ripped from their hands. This allusion to Daniel indicates that the Parables, unsurprisingly, were written after Daniel. "An allusion to Dan 5 would support the view that the historical situation of the writer and his readers was that of the Seleucid or Roman period" (BL pg. 202).

[876] Nickelsburg sees a literary problem with 41:1-44:1. To resolve this problem he advocates the following sequence. "41:1-2 + 41:9; + 42:1-3 + 41:3-8 + 43:1-44:1 (a + cd + b + e)." He goes on to say "It seems better to ascribe these continuities to the hand of an author bringing together traditions than to an interpolator who found a piece (chap. 42) that just happened to have suitable points of connection at both ends" (NV2 pg. 135). His sequence has been adopted in this text.

[877] That mankind's deeds are weighted in the balance is a common theme (cf. 43:2; 60:12; 61:8; Job 31:6; Ps 62:9; Prov 16:2; 21:2; 24:12; 4Ezra 3:34; 4:36; TAb 12:8). Charles observes: "In Enoch, as in the O. T., this idea is not incompatible with the doctrine of divine grace; but in the Talmud it is absolutely materialized, and man's salvation depends on a literal preponderance of his good deeds over his bad ones" (C pg. 79).

[878] **The image of God punishing the wicked offends modern sensibilities. But those who had suffered from murdered loved ones, torture, and intense persecution, found hope in the certainty of God's retributive justice.** The Jewish, *Testament of Abraham*, Recension A, (AD 75-125) is especially graphic. "While he was yet saying these things to me, behold (there were) two angels, with fiery aspect and merciless intention and relentless look, and they drove myriads of souls, mercilessly beating them with fiery lashes. And the angel seized one soul. And they drove all the souls into the broad gate toward destruction" (TAb A 12:1-2). Given what Jews of that time suffered, at both the hands of the Romans and their own people; retribution upon the wicked was demanded.

[879] This thought picks up again in 41:9, which most translators agree should be shifted to the position it has in this text.

[880] "Satan" is found in the reliable Tana manuscript but is absent in others.

[881] N reads: "For no angel hinders and no power is able to hinder." Some manuscripts have "no authority or power has the power to hinder." **Nothing can interfere with the judgment and vengeance of God!**

[882] Christ is the judge: "For the Father judges no one, but has given all judgment to the Son," (Jn 5:22). And he has given him authority to execute judgment, because he is the Son of Man. (Jn 5:27).

returned to heaven, the Torah could promote nothing but iniquity" (NV2 pg. 139). Heiser agrees: "For some Second Temple Jews, particularly those who produced "Enochian" material, the Torah was *not* the apex of divine revelation" (H2 pg. 77). With the Messiah personified as Wisdom in 1En 48:1-3 and 49:1-2, **chapter 42 can be seen as a prediction of the rejection of the Messiah, who came to earth, but found no place (rejected in Jerusalem) and thus returned to heaven.** For the corruption in Judaism, see Mt 23. It is also a statement that the law cannot produce righteousness, but only increase sin, as the apostle Paul observed. "But now the righteousness of God has been manifested apart from the law, although the law and the Prophets bear witness to it" (Rom 3:21). **The New Testament link between Jesus and Wisdom was strategic. The Torah was not the agent of creation, enthroned with God; that was Jesus.** "Olson observes: "**In the messianic future, Wisdom will return, poured out like water for the thirsty (48:1; 49:1) and given to the chosen (5:8; 91:10). This poem is a direct slap at (Sir 24:1-12 and Baruch 3-4), which declare that Wisdom took up a permanent abode among the people of Israel in Law and Temple**" (OL pg. 84).

The Descent of Wisdom and Iniquity

42 1 Wisdom found no place[883] where she[884] might dwell; 48:1; Prov 1:20-33; Mt 8:20; Lk 9:22, 58
so, her dwelling-place came to be in heaven. 84:3; Prov 8-9; Mk 8:31
2 Wisdom set out to make her dwelling among the Sir 24:1-11; 51:13-14; Lk 11:31
children of men, Wis 6:12; 9:10; Jn 1:1-11
but found no dwelling-place. 94:5; Mt 8:20; 21:42; Lk 9:58; 11:49
(So) Wisdom returned to her place, 5:8; 49:1; Job 28:12-14, 20-24; 4Ezra 5:9
and took her seat[885] among the angels. Bar 3:9-4:4; Phil 2:9

---

[883] "Place" "In the OT the Heb. מָקוֹם (māqôm; LXX τόπος) is often employed with reference to Jerusalem and its temple" (NV2 pg. 140). **Charlesworth links this verse with the saying of Jesus that "the Son of Man has nowhere to lay his head.** (Mt 8:20; Lk 9:58; and the Gospel of Thomas Log. 86) (R pg. 466, see also P pg. 248). **Like Wisdom, Christ came to earth and was rejected before returning to be seated in His place among the angels. If this verse is meant to be about the Messiah, which it certainly appears to be, then this nicely crafted poem is an amazing prophecy of the Messiah's rejection in Jerusalem and resurrection to the heavenly throne!** The biblical passage on Wisdom personified in (Prov 8) does not include this earthly rejection and return to heaven. However, (Prov 1:20-33), while not including the return to heaven, does contain a rejection leading to the destruction of Jerusalem which would apply equally well to both the Babylonian and Roman sieges. Unlike (Sir 24:7-11), where wisdom finds a home in Jerusalem; the text before us has Jerusalem rejecting wisdom. This text was proven by history to be correct. Jesus sees the rejection of wisdom as not just when he, the ultimate messenger of wisdom (Lk 11:31), was rejected; but when all God's messengers were rejected. "Therefore also the Wisdom of God said, 'I will send them prophets and apostles, some of whom they will kill and persecute,'" (Lk 11:49). Consider also (Mt 11:19 and Lk 1:17; 7:35) where John the Baptist is included as a messenger of the Wisdom of God. (Cf. Eph 3:10)

[884] "The reason for the feminine pronoun references in this and other biblical passages (as well as Second Temple Jewish literature) is that the word translated "wisdom" (chokmah) is grammatically feminine" (H2 pg. 72). Heiser's comment would assume an original composition of the Parables in Hebrew or Aramaic with the gender carried through Greek and into Ethiopic.

[885] In place of "took her seat," OL has: "found refuge" while I has: "settled permanently."

3 Iniquity[886] went forth from her chambers; 4Q184; Prov 1:24-33; 7:27; 9:13-18
those she did not seek, she found,[887] Zech 5:6-8
and dwelt among them. Ps 55:15
(Welcome) as rain in a desert
And dew on a thirsty land. 41:3

Secrets of the Weather

(41) 3 And there, I saw with my own eyes the secrets of the 2Bar 59:11
flashes of lightning and of the thunder, and the mysteries of the 17:3; 18:1-5; 43:1-2; 44; 59; 60:13-15
winds, how they are divided to blow over the earth, and the secrets 60:11-22; Job 38:24
of the clouds and dew. I saw the place where they come forth, Sir 43:14
and from which they saturate the dust of the earth. 2:3
(41) 4 There I saw closed storehouses. From them the winds 76; Jer 10:13; 51:16; 1Kgs 8:35; 11QPs[a] 8
are distributed, the store chamber of hail and winds, Job 38:22; Ps 33:7; 135:7
and the store chamber of mist and of the clouds: Deut 28:12; 2Bar 41:4
and its cloud hovers over the earth from the Gen 1:2; 2:6
beginning of the age.[888] [889]

Courses of the Sun and Moon

(41) 5 And I saw the storehouses of the sun and moon, from which 72-73
they go forth and to which they return—and their glorious return!
The splendor of the one is greater than the other; and their Ps 19:1-6
magnificent[890] orbit! And how they do not leave their orbit, 2:1
and they neither extend nor diminish their course, but they keep 69:13-25; 72-74
faith with one another according to the oath[891] by which they 83:11; Jer 33:20, 25-26
are bound together.

---

[886] Chapter 42 can be seen as a very brief summary of Prov 8-9 with lady Wisdom (8:1-9:12) contrasted against the woman of folly (9:13-18). Iniquity is personified as a woman here, as folly is personified as a woman in (4Q184). Is this a prophecy of the rejection of Christ (wisdom) but the embrace of Antichrist (iniquity)?

[887] It is easy for Iniquity to attract followers; she doesn't even have to look for them. Their ready acceptance of Iniquity intensifies their guilt in rejecting Wisdom.

[888] "Age" or "world." These are the clouds at creation (Gen 1:2) so the present age began at creation and will end with Christ's return and the judgement! (1En 16:1; Mt 13:39, 40, 49; 24:3; 28:20) Another "eternal age" will then begin (Mt 12:32; Mk 10:30; Lk 18:30). The present age includes marriage since mankind is physical and mortal; the age to come will not include marriage since mankind will be spiritual (Lk 20:34-36). The rulers and wisdom of this age will pass away (1 Cor 2:6, 8; 3:18). The present age is evil and Christ delivers us from it (Gal 1:4). Christ will reign in this age and the next one (Eph 1:21). Saints are to live righteously in the present age (1 Tim 6:17; Titus 2:12). Saints can taste of the powers that are to come in the present age (Heb 6:5). Christ will be with the saints until the end of the present age (Mt 28:20).

[889] For chambers of weather elements in the Old Testament; see (Deut 28:12; Job 38:22; Ps 33:7; 135:7; Jer 10:13 and 51:16).

[890] Black argues for "fixed or appointed orbit" (BL pg. 202). But N and OL have "splendid" and "magnificent" orbit. C has "stately."

[891] For more on this oath see (1En 69:16-25). Olson observes that the oath; "is connected to the Name of God which binds and orders the forces of the cosmos. It is this oath which the fallen angels violated, disrupting the divine order and unleashing chaos" (OL pg. 82).

(41) 6 First the sun goes forth and traverses its path according Sir 43:2
to the commandment of the Lord of Spirits, —his Name
will endure forever and ever.
(41) 7 Following this is the invisible and visible path,[892]
of the moon.[893] It completes[894] the course of its path 4Q209 7.2-3; 15-16
in that place by day and by night—the one holding a position Sir 42:19, 24
opposite to the other before the glory of the[895] Lord of Spirits.
They give thanks and praise, and do not rest; [896] Ps 148:3; PrAzar 3:63
because for them, giving thanks is rest in itself. 69:24
(41) 8 The many changes of the sun[897] produce both a blessing Sir 43:2-3; Ps 91:6
and a curse. And the course of the path of the moon
is light to the righteous, but darkness to sinners,[898]
in the Name of the Lord of Spirits, who created 22:8-13; Gen 1:4, 18
a separation between light and darkness, and divided the 1QS 3.13-4.18; 4,15-20; 11Q5 26.11
spirits of men,[899] strengthening the spirits of the righteous Heb 12:22-23
in the name of his righteousness.

The Lightning and the Stars

43 1 I also saw other flashes of lightning and stars of heaven;[900] 17:3; 104:2; Isa 14:12; 40:26; Lk 10:18
and I saw how he called them all by their names 69:21; Ps 147:4
and they hearkened unto him. Bar 3:33-34
2 I saw how they are weighed in a righteous[901] balance according 41:1; 60:12; 61:8; Job 31:6
to their amount of light, according to the width of their spaces Dan 12:3
and the time of their (first) appearing,[902] I saw how their 18:15
movement produces lightning,[903] and their revolution is

---

[892] This likely refers to the phases of the moon and the invisibility of a new moon.
[893] "The order of vv.6 and 7ab indicates again, the superiority of the sun over the moon" (NV2 pg. 144-145). In the translation by Charles, the sun is assigned a male pronoun and the moon a female pronoun.
[894] Lit. "works, executes."
[895] Some manuscripts omit "glory of the."
[896] Like the heavenly beings that "sleep not" the sun and moon are always faithful.
[897] Some texts read "the shining sun". K and N have "For the shining sun makes many revolutions."
[898] This may be a reference to the dispute over lunar and solar calendars (cf. 82:4-5; 80:1-5).
[899] **"Scholars have noticed that the language here is similar to that of the "two spirits" doctrine from Qumran, a doctrine that held that God created two spirits within humanity (spirits of truth and falsehood).** The belief is laid out (in) (1QS iii.13:17-25; iv. 15-20)" (H2 pg. 68).
[900] **The faithful stars of heaven symbolize the righteous while the falling stars/lightning symbolize the apostates (the kings and mighty) who have rejected the faith. When Jesus makes the remark "I saw Satan fall like lightning from heaven" (Lk 10:18). He may have had this passage in mind as Satan is the ultimate apostate.**
[901] "Righteous," Isaac has "impartial".
[902] **This appears to be a judgment of works among stars (the righteous), that remain without falling. This would be the judgement of the righteous saints spoken of by Paul in (Romans 14:10-12 and 2 Corinthians 5:10).** Black sees the stars as heavenly beings: "The stars and heavenly bodies are hypostatized; they are heavenly beings, with consciousness and conscience, to be assessed or weighted in a balance, like mankind, and to be so judged" (BL pg. 203-4). But 43:4 makes plain that they are "holy ones who dwell on the earth" (See note on 43:4).
[903] "Lightning" may refer to shooting stars" (NV2 Pg. 146).

according to the calculation of the angels, and (how) Sir 43:9-10
they keep faith with each other.[904]
3 I asked the angel who went with me who showed me what was
hidden: "What are these?"
4 And he replied: "The Lord of Spirits has shown you a parable 104:1-2
concerning them; these are the names of the holy ones who dwell Dan 8:10; 12:3; Mt 13:43
on the earth and believe on the Name of the Lord of Spirits
for ever and ever."[905]

44 1 I also saw another phenomenon regarding the lightning: Lk 10:18
how some stars arise and become lightning;
and these cannot remain with the others.[906] 14:5; 45:2

---

[904] For (1En 43:2) N has "I saw a righteous balance, how they are weighed according to their light, according to the breath of their spaces and the day of their appearing. (I saw how) their revolution produces lightning, and their revolution is according to the number of the angels, and they keep their faith with one another." Isaac has: "Their revolutions produce lightning; and in number they are (as many as) the angels; they keep their faith each one according to their names." This passage reflects Babylonian astrology. Galilee was known for having ties to the East. (P pg. 185)

[905] **This passage (43:1-chapter 44) depicts the stars as a representation in heaven of the exalted status of the saints presently living on earth. These stars of the earthly righteous are already shining in heaven.** The righteous elect are accorded honor, based on the amount of light they produce, how influential their light is, and how long their light has been shining or having appeared at the proper time (43:2). Since they dwell on earth (43:4), these are the human righteous on earth. That stars can represent humans, rather than angels, is known in apocalyptic literature. In (Daniel 12:2-3), from which this text obviously derives, it is clear that the star imagery in that passage reflects humans. Likewise, the stars "thrown down to the ground and trampled" in (Daniel 8:9-10) are righteous Jews, martyred during the reign of Antiochus IV. **This passage is important, because it affects the interpretation of (Rev 12:4): "And another sign appeared in heaven: behold, a great red dragon, with seven heads and ten horns, and on his heads seven diadems. His tail swept down a third of the stars of heaven and cast them to the earth." It is commonly taught, in some circles, that a third of the stars represent rebellious angels in league with Satan. Instead, these appear to be humans, who facing persecution, deny Christ, becoming apostates, thus losing their exalted status and therefore can no longer retain their shining status; "cannot remain with the others (1En 44)."** Many of those who do not deny Christ, become the martyrs, who are mentioned immediately following in (Rev 12:11). "And they have conquered him by the blood of the Lamb and by the word of their testimony, for they loved not their lives even unto death." **Thus, both (1En 43-44) and (Rev 12:4) (which assumes the reader has knowledge of the symbolism in 1En 43-44), have the same imagery of denying the faith and therefore falling out of heavenly position**. This idea is carried into (1 Enoch 45) thereby illuminating an otherwise difficult passage. This thought gives added depth to passages like (Mt 5:14-16; 10:33; 13:43; 16:24; 26:35; 2Tim 2:12 and Rev 2:13). This is an image that should be in the minds of Christians as they face persecution, as it will help them persevere.

[906] The stars that become lightning in this verse, are those who apostatize, and therefore cannot remain with the faithful. "The faithful luminaries are an image of the righteous, just as the wicked are symbolized by falling stars/lightning flashes." (OL pg. 84) Once the stars become a streak of lightning (or shooting star) they must stay that way and can no longer remain with the other stars. This imagery relies on (1 Enoch 18:14-15) where the fallen watchers are also referred to as stars. Like shooting stars, they can never return to their previous position. The sin of the watchers cannot be forgiven (1En 14:7). **The message of the text before us (43, 44 and 45:1-2) is that, like the watcher's transgression; the sin of denying the "Name of the Lord of Spirits" cannot be forgiven (45:1-2) (cf. Heb 6:4-6).** The restoration of those who denied the faith, in the face of persecution, was an important issue in the early church (*HE* 6:41, 42, 44) and undoubtedly also was in the Jewish community of the second temple period.

The Second Parable

The Eternal State of the Sinners and Elect Ones

45 1 This is the Second Parable concerning those who deny 38:2; Rev 3:8
the Name of the Lord of Spirits and the congregation of 38:1; Rev 13:6
the holy ones.[907] [908] 1QM 12.7
2 Into heaven they shall not ascend,[909] 14:5; 44
and on the earth, they shall not come:
such shall be the lot of sinners[910]
who have denied[911] the Name of the Lord of Spirits, Mt 10:33; 12:31-32; 2Tim 2:12; Lk 12:8-12
who are thus kept for the day of suffering[912] and distress. 2Pet 2:17; Jude 13
3 On that day, My Chosen One shall sit on the throne of glory[913] 61:8; 62:5; Lk 9:35; 23:35; Mt 19:28; 25:31
and he shall test their works. 47:3; 51:3; 55:4; 61:8; 62:2; 69:27, 29
Jn 5:22, 27; Mk 14:62; Isa 22:23; Sir 47:11
Jer 14:21; 17:12; Wis 9:10

And their dwelling places shall be innumerable.[914] 38:2; 2Thes 1:9; Jn 14:2
Their souls will be distressed within them when they Isa 8:21-22; Lk 13:35

---

[907] Some Ethiopic texts omit: "and the congregation of the holy ones" at the end of (1En 45:1). It is included here with support seen in (Rev 13:6) where the dragon is: "blaspheming his name and his dwelling, that is those who dwell in heaven." Support is also found in the DSS *War Scroll*: "For you have a multitude of holy ones in the heavens and hosts of angels in your holy abode to pr[aise] Your [truth.]" (1QM 12.7). It is included by OL, N, I, C, but excluded by K. Black has: "And this is the Second Parable concerning those who deny the Name of the Lord of Spirits and the *testimony* of the holy ones."

[908] "Black proposes that the original may have read "who deny the testimony of the holy ones" because the presumed Aramaic spelling of the respective "congregation" (*'dt*) and "testimony" (*'dwt*) are very similar. Consequently, Black suspects that the Aramaic text was misread by the Ethiopic translator" (H2 Pg. 85 citing BL pg. 204).

[909] This could be speaking of the kings and the mighty, who we will discover are the earthly villains of the Parables. They, like all unredeemed sinners, will not ascend to heaven or inhabit the restored earth (see 45:5) but be consigned to Gehenna. "Alternately, it could be speaking of the "angelic host of Azazel, who have lead humanity astray (54:5-6; 56:4), and who will not be able to return to heaven but will be consigned to hellfire (54:6; 56:4)" (NV2 pg. 149).

[910] These sinners are identified as the kings and the mighty elsewhere in the parables (cf. 38:5; 46:4-5; 48:8; 53:5; 54:2; 55:4, 62:1, 3, 6, 9; and 63:1).

[911] The Ethiopic verb used here for denied, *kehda* carries a variety of connotations: "deny, denounce, repudiate, reject, rebel" (NV2 pg. 149, Leslau, *Dictionary*, pg. 279).

[912] "Suffering" "The noun *serāh*, here translated 'affliction,' is a synonym derived from the Eth. root meaning 'to labor' and implies weariness, fatigue, or exhaustion (perhaps = Gk. κόπος)" (NV2 pg. 149).

[913] **Jesus Christ appropriates this image of the Chosen One/Son of Man sitting on the throne of glory to himself in (Mt 19:28 and 25:31). Jesus, by His claimed attributes in the gospels, clearly identifies himself with the Chosen One from the Book of Parables.** The image of the deity sitting on the throne is found in other Jewish literature; (cf. Isa 6:1-3; 22:23; Jer 14:21; 17:12; Ezek 1:26; Sir 47:11 LXX; PrAzar 3:56; Wis 9:10; 4Q405 23.1.3 (W pg. 474); and 11Q17.2+1+9.6 (W pg. 475)). (ApMos 39:3), while not deifying Adam, has him "sitting on his glorious (some translations have honorable) throne."

[914] "Innumerable" likely speaks to an immeasurable amount of time, an eternity of punishment (cf. 2Thes 1:9). As another opinion, Black proposes a misreading of the Aramaic into Greek; the original text may have read: "'oblations were without number' the idea being that of innumerable offerings to placate the wrath of God?" (BL pg. 205).

see my Chosen One,[915] | 38:2; 39:6-7; 4Ezra 7:36
and those who appeal to my glorious Name.[916] [917]
4 On that day, I will cause my Chosen One to dwell | 62:14; 105:2; Isa 42:1; Jn 14:23; Rev 21:1-3
among them,[918] and I will transform the heaven[919] and make it | 72:1; 91:16; Isa 65:17; 66:22; Jn 1:14
a blessing and light forever; | 1:8; 2Bar 32:6; 57:2
5 I will transform the earth[920] and make it a blessing: | 2Pet 3:13; Rev 21:1; 4Ezra 7:75
I will cause my elect ones to dwell upon it;[921] | Mt 5:5; OdesSol 8:18
but sinners and evil-doers[922] shall not set foot[923] on it. | Rev 21:27; 22:14-15
6 For I have provided[924] for and satisfied my righteous ones | 1:8; Ps 34:15; 2Bar 52:5-7
with peace and have caused them to dwell before me.[925] | OdesSol 9:6
But the judgement of the sinners is impending before me, | 69:27
that I might destroy them from the face of the earth. | Gen 6:7; 7:4, 23

Excursus: The Son of Man!

The introduction of the Son of Man (1En 46:2) in this text could not be more significant! This is the first of 19 uses of the title "Son of Man" in 1 Enoch. It is also used in Daniel. "I saw in the night visions, and behold, with the clouds of heaven there came one like a son of man, and he came to the Ancient of Days and was presented before him. And to him was given dominion and glory and a kingdom, that all peoples, nations, and languages should serve him; his dominion is an everlasting dominion, which shall not pass away, and his kingdom one that shall not be destroyed." (Dan 7:13-14). It is the term Jesus Christ uses most to refer to himself, occurring 82 times in the Gospels and a total of 86 times in the New Testament. Jesus had a way of referring to a text to draw attention to it. It is very unlikely that he only had Dan 7:13 in mind. The Parables of Enoch were obviously a text he was commending to his listeners in order to establish

---

[915] Here and in 45:5, N has "my chosen ones." K and OL, as in this text, have the singular "chosen one." The Ethiopic manuscripts are inconsistent here.
[916] Translators are divided on this corrupt textual line. Representative of an alternative translation is Charles: "And their souls shall grow strong within them when they see Mine Elect Ones, and those who have called upon My glorious name:" This text largely follows that proposed by Nickelsburg, which seems to be the best fix for multiple thorny translation issues (NV2 pg. 150 and Sjöberg, Erik, 1946. Der *Menschensohn im āthiopischen Henochbuch*, Acta Regiae Societatis Humaniorum Litterarum Lundensis 53; LUND: Gleerup, pg. 75).
[917] As in (Isa 66:23-24) and (Lk 16:22-23), those in paradise and hell can see each other. What is envisioned is the proximity of Jerusalem (paradise) with the valley of Hinnom (Gehenna). This is explicit in 4Ezra 7:36; "Then the pit of torment shall appear, and opposite it shall be the place of rest; and the furnace of Hell (Gehenna) shall be disclosed, and opposite it the paradise of delight."
[918] For dwelling among them, see also (Jn 14:23 and Rev 21:3).
[919] Why would Heaven need to be transformed? As the Book of Enoch makes abundantly clear, spiritual beings and angels transgress also. In addition, (Rev 12:7) speaks of war in heaven. So even heaven is marred by the rebellion!
[920] "Earth" would translate literally as "dry ground."
[921] Many Christians wonder if their ultimate dwelling place will be in Heaven or Earth. This verse settles the debate in favor of a renewed Earth. This passage agrees with and serves as background for Rev 21-22.
[922] "Evil-doers" here carries the connotation of the error of idolatry.
[923] "The latter verb, while it can denote simply "walk," may here have the stronger connotation of "tread" or "trample," as it has in 1:4; 46:7; 56;6: and 89:74" (NV2 pg. 151).
[924] Instead of "provided" both K and N have "seen."
[925] Commenting on the first two lines of 1En 45:6 Nickelsburg opines: "Thus for this author the judgement will bring to the righteous—the deprived and persecuted victims of the sinners—a time of wholeness, satisfaction, and wellbeing on the renewed earth; it is a vision that characterizes most of the strata of 1 Enoch" (NV2 pg. 152).

His identity. This passage in Enoch closely resembles (Dan 7:9-13), and the image of the Son of Man is most likely drawn from Daniel or (Ps 2:7; 8:4 (cf. Heb 2:6-8)); but amplified in the Parables of Enoch. The possibility that both Daniel and the author of the Parables were drawing from a common source has no evidence but remains a possibility. McDonald agrees: "I would agree that they (the Gospels) do reflect Jesus' perspective and his awareness and use of the *Parables of Enoch* in presenting his own identity as the apocalyptic Son of Man (P pg. 355)." Some of the other uses of Son of Man in 1 Enoch include (46:4; 48:2; 62:5, 7, 9, 14; 63:11; 69:26-29; 70:1; 71:14, 17 (possible interpolation)).

Introduction of the Son of Man

46 1 And there I saw One who had a head of days,[926] [927]
and His head was white like wool, — 71:10; 106:2; Dan 7:9; Rev 1:13-14
and with him was another, whose face had the appearance — Judg 13:6; Dan 7:13; Ezek 1:26
of a man; and his face was full of grace,[928] — 2Cor 4:4-6; Jn 1:14; Rev 1:16; 14:14
like one of the holy angels. — Acts 6:15
2 So I asked the angel of peace,[929] who went with me, — 4Ezra 2:44-47
and showed me all the hidden things,[930] concerning that — Dan 7:16
Son of Man, [931] who he was, and whence he was, — Ps 2:7; Dan 7:9

---

926 Instead of "who had a head of days" Isaac has: "to whom belongs the time before time". B "There I saw the Creator of days." The others remain with "head of days."

927 "Head of days" is based upon "Ancient of Days" in Dan 7:9, 13. Isaac, a native speaker of Ge' ez offers equivalents of "Chief of Days," "he who precedes time," "the beginning of days," "the First of days," "he who is of primordial days," "the Antecedent of time," (OTP1 pg. 34n46$_{a}$). It is used elsewhere in: (47:3; 48:2; 55:1; 60:2; 71:10-14). This text will follow Isaac and hereafter use "Antecedent of Time" as the best representation of this name for God.

928 Defining a proposed Semitic root word for "grace" Nickelsburg opines, "The noun is first a term of beauty. It denotes an aesthetically pleasing presentation or aspect of someone or something, and is properly the quality that someone or something possesses." "Thus, the figure here described is characterized by a humanlike face, which, however is surpassingly beautiful and graceful like the countenance of the angels" (NV2 pg. 157). For other instances of beautiful, transfigured faces see (TAb 12:5; Ex 34:29-30; Mt. 17:2; Jn. 1:14; Acts 6:15; Rev 1:16; and Rev 10:1).

929 One manuscript reads "angel of peace" in accordance with other uses in the Parables (40:8; 52:5; 53:4; 54:4; 56:2; 60:24 (an interpolation)). Nickelsburg places "angel of peace" in place of "angel" with the thought that "one of the holy angels" in the other manuscripts was inadvertently copied from the previous line.

930 "Hidden things" In the highly messianic passage of Isaiah 48:6-49:7, the Messiah is described as hidden (Isa 48:6; 49:2) but will now be revealed (Isa 48:6). This progressive revelation of the Messiah continues dramatically as He is further revealed here in the Parables. The Parables certainly affected the thinking of early Christians as they recognized the now reveled Messiah. Those who were enlightened in the time of Christ were preparing the way for the LORD (Lk 3:4; and 1QS 8.11-16). The fact that the lord Jesus was the mystery spoken of by the prophets, hidden not just from men, but also to beings in heaven, was not lost on the Apostle Paul. "To me, though I am the very least of all the saints, this grace was given, to preach to the Gentiles the unsearchable riches of Christ, and to bring to light for everyone what is the plan of the mystery hidden for ages in God who created all things, so that through the church the manifold wisdom of God might now be made known to the rulers and authorities in the heavenly places," (Eph 3:8-10). See also: (1Cor 2:7-8; Eph 1:9-10; 3:1-11; Col 1:26-27; 2:2; and 1Tim 3:16).

931 One critical Ethiopic text, Kebran/Tanasee, aka Tana, has: "the one who was born of men" in place of "that Son of Man."

(and) why he went with the Antecedent of Time?[932] Dan 7:13
3 He replied to me: "This is the Son of Man to whom Isa 9:6-7; 11:4; 32:16
belongs righteousness, and righteousness dwells with him; 71:14-16; Jer 23:5; Zech 9:9; PssSol 17:36
and he will reveal all the treasures of that which is hidden.[933] Mt 13:11-12; Col 2:3; Isa 45:3; Mt 6:19-20
For the Lord of Spirits has chosen him, Isa 42:1; 43:10; Lk 9:35; OdesSol 36:3
and his destiny is to triumph before the Lord of Spirits Col 1:15-17
in truth forever.[934] 1QS 4.23
4 This Son of Man whom you have seen, Dan 7:13
shall rouse up the kings and the mighty from their soft beds[935] 38:5; 56:5; Dan 4:34-35
and the strong from their thrones! Isa 49:7; Lk 1:52
He shall loosen the reins of the powerful Isa 45:1; Job 12:18, 21
and crush the teeth of sinners.[936] Ps 3:7; 58:6; Mt 13:42; 16:27

Judgement of the Earthly Kings

5 He will hurl down the kings from their thrones[937] and kingdoms, Col 1:16; PssSol 17:22-24; Dan 5:20

---

[932] Isaac translates Enoch's question as: "Who is this, and from whence is he who is going as the prototype of the Before-Time?" Olson translates: "Head of Days" as "Antecedent of Days." Referring to the Head of Days title, Olson opines: "No one English phrase can capture the title's sweep; the expression simultaneously carries ideas of supremacy, primacy, origination, and timelessness; 'He who precedes time,' 'chief of days,' 'The beginning of days,' 'The Before -time,' 'The Summation of days,' are all possible renderings" (OL pg. 88).

[933] The primary secret that was hidden was the Son of Man himself (1En 48:6; 62:6-7). The Yahad sect of Dead Sea Scrolls fame had hidden things that were not revealed to new initiates until they had proven themselves for two years, (1QS 6.14-23; 8:10-12). The Essenes, likewise, had a three year initiation period, see (*War* 2.8.7 §§137-138). These hidden things may be similar to the spiritual/heavenly things Christ is speaking of in (Jn 3:12). "If I have told you earthly things and you do not believe, how can you believe if I tell you heavenly things?" It may also be the reason he spoke in parables and did not cast His pearls before swine. However, He did come to reveal hidden things. This was to fulfill what was spoken by the prophet: "I will open my mouth in parables; I will utter what has been hidden since the foundation of the world" (Mt. 13:35). But He did not reveal the hidden things to everyone. "In that same hour he rejoiced in the Holy Spirit and said, 'I thank you, Father, Lord of heaven and earth, that you have hidden these things from the wise and understanding and revealed them to little children; yes, Father, for such was your gracious will'" (Lk 10:21). The Gnostics alleged that Christ's disciples withheld secrets from later Christians, but this idea is amply refuted by Irenæus (*Haer*. 3.3.1) and Tertullian (*Against Heretics*).

[934] For the last line of (1En 46:3), Knibb has: "for the Lord of Spirits has chosen him, and through uprightness his lot has surpassed all before the Lord of Spirits forever." I has: "and he is destined to be victorious before the Lord of the Spirits in eternal uprightness." N has, "and his lot has prevailed through truth in the presence of the Lord of Spirits forever." OL has, "His destiny is to triumph before the Lord of Spirits in eternal justice."

[935] "Soft beds," some royal thrones were more like couches than hard chairs.

[936] Loosen the reins that the rulers use to control their subjects. However, Black translates "loosen the loins of the powerful" and writes that "the expression means to demoralize, probably to disarm the powerful (Isa 45:1)" (H2 pg. 96 citing BL pg. 208). This is a word play. The reins the powerful use to control the righteous (like bits between their teeth) will be loosened, while the teeth of the wicked will be crushed.

[937] **Mary may reference a portion of this verse in the *Magnificat*, or at least a similar thought. "He has brought down the mighty from their thrones" (Lk 1:52).** A similar passage in Isaiah 14:9 is a taunt to Babylon, but instead the leaders of the earth are raised from their thrones. **Chapter 108 also contains similarities to the *Magnificat*. This indicates that young Mary had an Enochic world view, and that from an early age, Jesus was reared in an Enochic Jewish environment. In addition, James, the Lord's brother, was raised in a very devout manner; likely in the same sect of Enochic Judaism.** As quoted by Eusebius, Hegesippus speaking of James, says:

because they do not extol or praise him; Lk 1:52
nor humbly acknowledge who bestowed their kingdoms 63:7; Jn 19:10-11; Wis 6:1-3; Rom 13:1
upon them.[938] Dan 4:17, 25
6 He shall cast down the faces of the powerful Job 40:13; 2Bar 40:1-3
and they will be covered with shame;[939] 62:10; 63:11; 97:6; Jer 30:6; Job 17:13-15
darkness shall be their dwelling,[940] 63:6; Isa 14:9-14; 66:24; 1QS 4.13; Lam 3:6
and worms shall be their bed, Job 21:26; Mk 9:47-48; Jdt 16:17; Sir 7:17
and they shall have no hope of rising from their beds, 2 Mac 7:34; 9:5-12; *War* 1.23.5; Job 17:15
because they do not exalt the Name of the Lord of Spirits. Acts 12:23; Jude 8; Ps 36:12
7 There they are: judges of the stars of heaven! [941] [942] Dan 8:10; 1Cor 6:3
Raising their fists against the Most High! Isa 14:4-20; Job 15:25
But they tread upon the dry ground and occupy it. Dan 7:19, 23
All their deeds manifest iniquity,[943] 93:9
and their power rests upon their riches. 63:10; Job 17:13-17; Jas 5:1-6; Ps 52:7
Their devotion is to the gods which they have fashioned Jer 1:16; Isa 2:8; 45:20

> [Administration of] the church passed to James, the brother of the Lord, along with the apostles. He was called 'the Just' by everyone from the Lord's time to ours, since there were many James, **but this one was consecrated from his mother's womb.** He drank no wine or liquor and ate no meat. No razor came near his head, he did not anoint himself with oil, and took no baths. He alone was permitted to enter the sanctum, for he wore not wool but linen. (*HE* 2.23)

In addition, the Simeon of (Lk 2:25-35) who blessed and prophesied about the infant Jesus, is quite likely the "Simon, a man of the sect of the Essenes" mentioned by Josephus (Ant 17.13.3 §§346). It serves as a validation of the beliefs of this Jewish Enochic sect; that God chose those affiliated with them to rear the Chosen One.

[938] **Verses 5 -6 could well be read as a reference to Herod's rise to kingship and death.** "Nor humbly acknowledge who bestowed the kingdom upon them" (cf. *Ant* 15.10.5 §§ 373-379) "and worms shall be their bed, and they shall have no hope of rising from their beds, because they do not exalt the name of the Lord of Spirits" (cf. *Ant* 17.6.5 §§169). Jesus applies the idea that God places rulers in places of authority to Pilate. "Jesus answered him, 'You would have no authority over me at all unless it had been given you from above. Therefore, he who delivered me over to you has the greater sin'" (Jn 19:11). Paul likewise applied the idea to all rulers. "Let every person be subject to the governing authorities. For there is no authority except from God, and those that exist have been instituted by God. Therefore, whoever resists the authorities resists what God has appointed, and those who resist will incur judgment" (Rom 13:1-2). This again shows the Essene-like foundation of their belief system, as Josephus reports regarding the Essenes and the tremendous oath they take, "That he will ever show faithfulness to all men, and especially to those in authority, because no one obtains the government without God's assistance" (*War* 2.8.7 §§140).

[939] Black notes that the Ethiopic verb has the idea of making the face pale, and he cites Jeremiah 30:6 for a direct parallel: "why has every face turned pale?" The idea is to "turn white (as a ghost in our expression) with fear" (H2 pg. 96. citing BL pg. 208).

[940] Darkness shall be their dwelling (cf. Ps 88:6; 143:3; Lam 3:6).

[941] For this line Charles reads: "And these are they who judge the stars of heaven!" "The verb 'judge' is almost certainly a corruption" (NV2 pg. 154). He goes on to conjecture "cause to fall." And then posits "they judge." Black writes that the idea of 'judging' here "would make very poor sense" and opts for 'ruling'" (BL pg. 208). Olson rightly recognizes the sarcasm which is reflected in this text and our text follows his lead.

[942] Stars of heaven can be taken as celestial beings (1En 18:14), or wise and righteous humans, (Dan 8:10; 12:3; 1En 43; Rev 12:4). Either meaning can apply here. This is sarcasm directed at earthly human rulers who do not realize they are ruled from above; but instead think they rule heaven; or they do not realize that by oppressing the righteous, they are oppressing future celestial beings who are represented by the stars of heaven.

[943] In place of "iniquity," Isaac has: "oppression."

with their own hands.[944]
But they deny the name of the Lord of Spirits. Mt 10:33
8 They persecute[945] the houses of his congregation,[946] [947] 53:6; Mt 24:9; Acts 8:1; 2Tim 3:12 and
the faithful who depend upon the Name of the Ps 33:21
Lord of Spirits.

Excursus: Were the Essenes a target audience of the Parables of 1 Enoch?

I have the greatest respect for George W. E. Nickelsburg and have used his research extensively. However, is this statement of his true? "In similar fashion, the Parables indicate no parallels to Josephus and Philo's descriptions of the Essenes"[948] Charles also concludes that the Essenes were not an audience for the entirety of 1 Enoch.[949] The following are their reasons, with my response.

---

[944] "The accusation of idolatry seems to indicate that these rulers are gentiles (i.e., Roman), although one cannot exclude a reference to Herod the Great and his construction of temples dedicated to pagan gods" (NV2 pg. 160).

[945] "The precise nature of this persecution is unclear but would have been known to the author's audience" (NV2 pg. 161); but 47:1-2, 4; makes plain that it involved the death of the righteous.

[946] Some manuscripts read: "they will be driven from the houses of his congregation." Isaac translates a less likely reading: "Yet they congregate in his houses and (with) the faithful ones who cling to the Lord of the Spirits."

[947] This likely refers to synagogues (P pg.164). "The plural expression 'houses of his congregation' indicates a plurality of religious communities, who construe themselves as members of one community. This could refer to local assemblies, which were seen as subgroups of the Jewish people. Alternatively, an analogy might be in CD xiv.3, where a plurality of camps were governed by a single set of laws and therefore belong to some single religious group. There is, however, no evidence that the present author was an Essene" (NV2 pg. 161). **Given the similarities of the Parables of Enoch to the gospels of Christ; if it can be discovered who this proto-Christian community was; one will discover the very roots of Christianity.** That Jesus was associated with a non-majority religious community, with common beliefs, is evident from an honest reading of the plurals in (Jn 3:11). "Truly, truly, I tell you, we speak of what we know, and we testify to what we have seen, and yet you people do not accept our testimony" (Jn 3:11) (BSB). This expression gives us a clue as to the audience of the Parables. It was not a single isolated group, and it was experiencing persecution prior to the ministry of Christ. For other mentions of this congregation, see (1En 38:1; 53:6; and 62:8). According to Josephus, the Essenes escaped persecution under king Herod, due to the prophecy by Manahem (*Ant* 15.10.4-5 §§371-379). Philo, with family ties to Herod Agrippa 1, writing in the AD 40's agrees (Philo, "Apology for the Jews," 11.18; Taylor, 2012. pgs. 45-46). However, Josephus elsewhere speaks of Essene persecution during the first Jewish revolt (*War* 2.8.10 §§152-153). This may indicate that the Essenes were not the group spoken of here, and thus not the target audience of the Parables of 1 Enoch. However, that would be a generalization that overly simplifies the complex religious and political context of Judea at the time. This is a time period scholars still know relatively little about. It would also assume that the Essene movement was homogenous. Josephus documents different beliefs among the Essenes (*War* 2.8.13 §§ 160). The assumption that the Essenes were homogenous is dubious, knowing the tendency of religious groups to splinter; and given that the Essenes existed in separate semi-independent dispersed communities (*War* 2.8.4 §§124). The author of Refutatio Omnium Haeres (9.21) (third century) says as much **"The Essenes have, however, in the lapse of time, undergone divisions, and they do not preserve their system of training after a similar manner, inasmuch as they have been split up into four parties."** A multiplicity of at least minor differences is a certainty, especially since Josephus was writing decades after the incarnation of Christ and may have not been accurate in all details. Splintering of the movement is evident in (CD Geniza B 19:33-20:27), if that is indeed an Essene text. It may be best to view the DSS as an Essene/sectarian library supplemented with scrolls collected or gathered to a secure location, rather than an Essene defining collection. However, a great deal can be learned about the Essene movement when these texts are combined with the descriptions of the Essenes by Josephus, Philo, Pliny and the Refutatio Omnium Haeres.

[948] NV2 pg. 66.

[949] C ciii-civ.

Charles: The Essenes "entirely condemned marriage," but marriage is glorified and fruitful wedlock in 1 Enoch 6-36, has its place in the Messianic kingdom.[950]

Response: The Essenes did not entirely condemn marriage. Since most members of the Essenes were older, the majority were certainly married with children before joining and remained so; although abandoning marital life and sexuality while being part of the sect. The children they raised, born from others, were not themselves forbidden from matrimony.[951] In fact some Essene subsects allowed and valued marriage.[952] Josephus recounts "They do not absolutely deny the fitness of marriage, and the succession of mankind thereby continued; but they guard against the lascivious behavior of women, and are persuaded that none of them preserve their faithfulness to one man."[953] The Essenes were the spiritual elite of the time. They did not impose their celibacy on everyone. Celibacy was something they chose, in order to concentrate on their devotion to God. Paul reflects this thought: "I want you to be free from anxieties. The unmarried man is anxious about the things of the Lord, how to please the Lord. But the married man is anxious about worldly things, how to please his wife, and his interests are divided. And the unmarried or betrothed woman is anxious about the things of the Lord, how to be holy in body and spirit. But the married woman is anxious about worldly things, how to please her husband" (1Cor 7:32-34). Jesus expressed a similar opinion. "The disciples said to him, "If such is the case of a man with his wife, it is better not to marry." But he said to them, "Not everyone can receive this saying, but only those to whom it is given. For there are eunuchs who have been so from birth, and there are eunuchs who have been made eunuchs by men, and there are eunuchs who have made themselves eunuchs for the sake of the kingdom of heaven. Let the one who is able to receive this receive it" (Mt 19:10-12).

Charles: "The Essenes objected to animal sacrifice" and "no such objection is found in 1 or 2 Enoch." "In the former passage at 89:50 the temple sacrifices are referred to with complete approval in the words 'and they offered a full table before Him'".[954]

Response: The Essenes objected to the impure temple worship of the 2nd temple period (see 1En 89:73). In contrast, the full table before the Lord mentioned in (1En 89:50) which indicates an endorsement of the temple cult, refers to the early 1st temple period when the sacrifices were considered pure. The Essenes most likely rejected temple sacrifice due to the corruption in the temple so aptly brought to light by Christ (Mt 21:12). In addition, the contention by Charles that the Essenes did not offer sacrifices may not be entirely accurate. Josephus recounts: "and when they send what they have dedicated to God into the temple, they do not offer sacrifices because they have more pure offerings of their own; on which account they are excluded from the common court of the temple, but offer their sacrifices themselves."[955]

Charles continues: "Furthermore, not a word is said on behalf of certain characteristic beliefs of Essenism—such as the necessity of bathing before meals and at other times, the duty of having

---

[950] C pg. ciii.
[951] *Refutatio omnium Haeres* 9.13.
[952] *Refutatio omnium Haeres* 9.23.
[953] *War* 2.8.2 §§121.
[954] C pg. civ.
[955] *Ant* 18.1.5 §§19. (Cf. 1QS 9.4-5; Good Person 75)

all things in common and of having common meals, the rejection of anointing the body, the claim that all were free and that none should be slaves."[956]

Response: This is an argument from silence, which is always dangerous. There was no reason to include these practices in an apocalyptic text attributed to biblical Enoch. While not in the Parables; slavery is condemned in the *Admonitions of Enoch* (1En 98:4).

Nickelsburg states "In addition, the Parables indicate no interest in issues of vital concern to the Qumranites or their satellites: the Mosaic Torah, halakic exposition, matters of purity, the temple cult and the priesthood, the calendar as such, and pesher interpretation of the Prophets. Additionally, the Parables double reference to the resurrection of the dead (51:1; 61:5) has no counterpart in the Qumran sectarian scrolls."[957]

Response: If the Qumran sect had parted ways with the main Essene movement, then the sectarian scrolls at Qumran may not reflect beliefs and practices in the larger Essene community. The Essenes would have had little interest in the temple cult since they did not offer sacrifices at that location.[958] Pliny's mention of an Essene community in the general vicinity of Qumran certainly does not limit the Essenes to that location.[959] His statement that the DSS contain no reference to the resurrection is puzzling considering the sectarian text (1QH$_a$ 19.15 (W pg. 196)) clearly speaks of resurrection. Resurrection is also prominent in other DSS texts that are not strictly considered sectarian (4Q521 Frags 7+5 Col 2.7-15 (W pg. 531); 4Q525 14.2.13-14 (W pg. 536); 4Q385 2.8 (W pg. 448); CD-A 7.4-6 (W pg.58).

Below are historical observations concerning the Essenes (in regular print) from Josephus, Philo, Pliny and *The Refutation of All Heresies*, (*Refutatio omnium Haeres*).[960] These known facts about the Essenes from historic sources are in bold and the response from the Book of Parables is in italics.

Jews by birth.[961]
The Parables were written to a Jewish audience by a Jew.

They despised riches.[962]
The rich are seen as the enemies of the righteous (1En 46:7; 63:10).

They lived in many cities and were numerous.
They have no certain city, but many of them dwell in every city; and if any of their sect come from other places, what they have lies open for them, just as if it were their own; and they go in to such as they never knew before, as if they had been ever so long acquainted with them. For

[956] C pg. civ.
[957] NV2 pg. 66.
[958] *Ant* 18.1.5 §§19
[959] Pliny, *Natural History* 5.73.
[960] *The Refutation of All Heresies* was once attributed to Hippolytus; but is now thought to have been written in the third century.
[961] *War* 2.8.1 §§119.
[962] *War* 2.8.3 §§122.

which reason they carry nothing at all with them when they travel into remote parts, though still they take their weapons with them, for fear of thieves. [963]

"And they dwell in many cities of Judea, and in many villages, and in great and populous communities."[964] "There is a portion of those people called Essenes, in number something more than four thousand in my opinion, who derive their name from their piety"[965] "But there is not one city of them, but many of them settle in every city."[966]

Note: The Essenes were in no way reported by the sources as being confined to a location in the desert at Qumran, as is the prevailing opinion. Instead, they were scattered to such an extent that they could travel to remote cities and expect to find colonies of Essene brothers who would provide for their needs. Even the most ardent Essene Qumran supporters only postulate at most 200 Essenes living at the site!

...houses of His congregation... (1En 46:8).

They were exceedingly holy, haters of wickedness, and assistants of the righteous.
"But our lawgiver trained an innumerable body of his pupils to partake in these things, who are called Essenes, being, as I imagine, honored with this appellation because of their exceeding holiness."[967]

"And as for their piety towards God, it is very extraordinary;[968]

"…that he will always hate the wicked, and be assistant to the righteous"[969]

The wisdom of the Lord of Spirits will reveal him to the holy and righteous. For he will preserve the portion of the righteous, because they loath and despise this world of unrighteousness; and hate all its works and ways in the Name of the Lord of Spirits. And the wisdom of the Lord of Spirits hath revealed him to the holy and righteous; For he hath preserved the lot of the righteous, (1En 48:7).

Blessed are you, righteous and elect ones, for your inheritance is glorious.
The righteous shall be in the light of the sun, and the chosen in the light of everlasting life:
the days of their life will have no end, and the days of the holy will be innumerable (1En 58:2-3).

They believed souls are immortal.
They believe "that the souls are immortal, and continue forever;" and when released "rejoice and mount upward."[970]

[963] *War* 2.8.4 §§124-125.
[964] Philo, *Hypothetica*, or *Apology for the Jews 11.1.*
[965] Philo of Alexander, *Good Person 12.75.*
[966] *The Refutation of All Heresies*, *Refutatio omnium Haeres 9.15.*
[967] Philo, *Hypothetica*, or *Apology for the Jews 11.1.*
[968] *War* 2.8.5 §§128
[969] *War* 2.8.7 §§139
[970] *War* 2.8.11 §§154

"They teach the immortality of souls…[971]

"Now the doctrine of the resurrection has also derived support among these; for they acknowledge both that the flesh will rise again, and that it will be immortal, in the same manner as the soul is already imperishable. And they maintain that the soul, when separated in the present life, (departs) into one place, which is well ventilated and lightsome, where, they say, it rests until judgment."[972]

In those days the earth will give back that which has been entrusted to it.
Sheol will give back that which has been deposited there, and Abaddon shall repay that which it owes. For in those days, my Chosen One shall arise, and choose the righteous and holy from among them; for the day on which they will be saved has drawn near. (1En 51:1-2)

Those measurements will reveal all that is hidden in the depths of the earth, those who have been destroyed by the desert, those who have been devoured by the fish of the sea and by wild beasts, so that they may return and rely on the day of the Chosen One; for no one shall be destroyed before the Lord of Spirits, and no one can be destroyed. (1En 61:5)

The Lord of Spirits shall abide over them, and with that Son of Man they shall eat, and lie down and rise up for ever and ever. The righteous and chosen shall be raised up from the earth and cease to have downcast faces. They shall be clothed with garments of glory. This shall be your garment, a garment of life from the Lord Spirits: and your garments shall not wear out, nor your glory fade away in the presence of the Lord of Spirits. And the Lord of Spirits will abide over them, (1En 62:14-16)

They did not participate in temple sacrifices.
…because they are above all men devoted to the service {therapeutai] of God, not sacrificing living animals, but studying rather to preserve their own minds in a state of holiness and purity.[973]

No mention of temple sacrifice is found in the Parables.

They believed the righteous will be rewarded.
"…and esteem that the rewards of righteousness are to be earnestly striven for:"[974]

They will seek the light and find righteousness with the Lord of Spirits.
There shall be peace for the righteous in the Name of the Eternal Lord!
After this it shall be said to the holy ones, that they should seek the mysteries of righteousness the inheritance of faith, for it has become bright as the sun upon the earth, and darkness has passed away. (1En 58:4-5)

They did not seek treasure or make weapons of war.

---

[971] *Ant* 8.1.5 §§18
[972] *The Refutation of All Heresies*, *Refutatio omnium Haeres 9.22* (cf. also 1En 22:9)
[973] Philo of Alexander, *Good Peerson* 12.75.
[974] *Ant* 8.1.5 §§18

"not storing up treasures of silver and of gold, nor acquiring vast sections of the earth out of a desire for ample revenues,"[975]

Among those men you will find no makers of arrows, or javelins, or swords, or helmets, or breastplates, or shields; no makers of arms or of military engines; no one, in short, attending to any employment whatever connected with war, or even to any of those occupations even in peace which are easily perverted to wicked purposes; for they are utterly ignorant of all traffic, and of all commercial dealings, and of all navigation, but they repudiate and keep aloof from everything which can possibly afford any inducement to covetousness;[976]

And they despise wealth, and do not turn away from sharing their goods with those that are destitute. No one amongst them, however, enjoys a greater amount of riches than another. For a regulation with them is, that an individual coming forward to join the sect must sell his possessions, and present the price of them to the community. And on receiving the money, the head of the order distributes it to all according to their necessities.[977]

And it shall come to pass in those days that no one will be saved either by gold or by silver, and no one will be able to escape. There will be no iron for war, nor will anyone wear a breastplate. Bronze will be of no service, and tin will be useless and of no value, and lead shall not be desired. (1En 52:7-8)

They believed in a dark place of punishment for bad souls.
"While they allot to bad souls a dark and tempestuous den, full of never-ceasing punishments."[978]

He shall cast down the faces of the powerful and they will be covered with shame; darkness shall be their dwelling, and worms shall be their bed, and they shall have no hope of rising from their beds, because they do not exalt the Name of the Lord of Spirits. (1En 46:6)

They preserved the books of their sect and the names of the angels.
And will equally preserve the books belonging to their sect, and the names of the angels [or messengers.] [979]

See the extensive list of angels in 69:2-15. That a list was preserved from the Book of the Watchers in the Parables, would argue for an intended Essene audience.

The target audience for the Parables was a numerous Jewish sect with different congregations that despised riches. They did not seem to participate in temple worship. They believed in immortal souls, a place of punishment for bad souls, a bodily resurrection, extreme holiness, and they hated the wicked. They preserved the names of angels. Of all the known Jewish groups of

---

975 Philo of Alexander, *Good Person* 12.76.
976 Philo of Alexander, *Good Person* 12.78.
977 *The Refutation of All Heresies, Refutatio omnium Haeres 9.14.*
978 *War* 2.8.11 §§155.
979 *War* 2.8.7 §§142.

the time, the target audience best matches the Essenes, as described by Josephus, Philo, Pliny and the *Refutatio omnium Haeres*. There is no other known choice.

The Prayers of the Righteous and Blood of the Righteous One

47 1 At that time, the prayers of the righteous and the blood	7:6; 8:4; 9:3; Rev 8:3-4; Mt 27:24; Jas 5:16
of the Righteous One[980] [981] shall ascend from the earth	38:2; Isa 53:11; Wis 2:12-18; Lk 2:20
into the presence of the Lord of Spirits.[982]	Isa 57:1-2; OdesSol 42:2
2 In those days all the holy ones who dwell in the heights of	
heaven shall join together and supplicate and pray with one	
voice—glorifying, giving thanks, and praising the Name	Deut 32:43; Rom 12:1; Ps 72:14
of the Lord of Spirits; on account of the blood of the	Lk 11:49-51; Mt 23:32-36; Isa 26:21
righteous which has been poured out.[983]	Rev 19:2; Lam 4:13; Ps 79:10

---

[980] The "Righteous One" can also be taken as an impersonal "righteous one" meaning "every righteous person" (OL pg. 90). However, Olson, in his translation, uses "Righteous One" which is already familiar from 1 En 83:2. Scholars are divided on this issue. Nickelsburg argues that it should be taken as righteous ones based on the context in 1En 46:8 and 47:2. However, the context can easily favor "Righteous One", with the presentation of the synonymous "Son of Man" in 1En 48:2.

[981] **The title "Righteous One" originates from (Isa 53:11) but would have been well known to early Christians from the Parables and the Admonitions of Enoch (see Chapters 91-105), which was found among the DSS; assuming they circulated widely. The titles use by Peter in (Acts 3:14) "But you denied the Holy and Righteous One, and asked for a murderer to be granted to you," and Stephen; "Which of the prophets did your fathers not persecute? And they killed those who announced beforehand the coming of the Righteous One, whom you have now betrayed and murdered," (Acts 7:52); and Ananias; "And he said, 'The God of our fathers appointed you to know his will, to see the Righteous One and to hear a voice from his mouth" (Acts 22:14); would have cut like a knife and immediately identified Jesus as the suffering atoning Messiah who they put to death! (OdesSol 42:2) identifies Jesus with the Righteous One.**

[982] **Chapter 47 is a vision of a most remarkable divine council meeting (cf. Ps 82). Revelation 5-6 is dependent on this text, which is in turn, partially dependent on Dan 7:9-10. In this most important meeting, the blood of the "Righteous One" (47:1, 4) the prayers of the holy ones (47:2) and the blood of the righteous ones (47:2) are presented before the Antecedent of Time (God the Father). "Righteous One" in 47:1 and 47:4 is a collective singular, as if the blood of the "Righteous One" is mystically joined with that of the righteous, making them acceptable to the Antecedent of Time (47:4). The sacrament of Communion is a perfect image of this concept (1Cor 10:16). This is the same way it was expressed by Jesus: "And he took a cup, and when he had given thanks he gave it to them, saying, 'Drink of it, all of you, for this is my blood of the covenant, which is poured out (47:2) for many for the forgiveness of sins'" (Mt. 26:27-28; cf. Mk 14:24; Lk 22:20; Acts 5:28). It appears that this passage is the basis for the sacrament of communion!** That the righteous can also be a sacrifice acceptable to God, is expressed by Paul: "I appeal to you therefore, brothers, by the mercies of God, to present your bodies as a living sacrifice, holy and acceptable to God, which is your spiritual worship" (Rom 12:1). For I am already being poured out like a drink offering, and the time for my departure is near (2Tim 4:6). This blood of the Righteous One has purchased acceptance with the Lord of the Spirits (47:4). This is expressed by Paul, "For all have sinned and fall short of the glory of God, and are justified by his grace as a gift, through the redemption that is in Christ Jesus, whom God put forward as a propitiation by his blood, to be received by faith" (Rom 3:23-25) (cf. Acts 20:28; Rom 5:9; Eph 1:7; 2:13; Col 1:20; Heb 12:24; 1Pet 1:19; 1Jn 1:7; Rev 5:9; 7:14; 12:11).

[983] "Since chap. 47 is placed at a key and catalytic point in this authors narrative of the events that lead to the judgement of the kings and the mighty, this passage indicates an actual slaughter of 'the righteous' such as occurred in conjunction with the tearing down of the golden eagle that Herod installed in the temple (*War* 1.33.2-4 §§637-55), and/or, if one dates the Parables a little later, to the revolts that followed Herod's death in 4 B.C E. (*War* 2.2-3

And that the prayer of the righteous may not be in vain
before the Lord of Spirits,[984]
that judgement may be executed on their behalf,
and that their long-suffering may not be endless. [985] [986] [987]
3 In those days, I saw the Antecedent of Time when he seated
himself upon the throne of his glory, and the books of the living[988]
were opened before him. And all His host[989] which is in heaven[990]
above and his council stood before him.[991]
4 The hearts of the holy ones were filled with joy,
because the number of the righteous had been reached,[992] [993]

Rev 6:9-11; 8:3-4; Joel 3:21
Dan 7:21-22; Rev 6:10; 16:6; 17:6; 18:24
Rev 1:9; 2:3; 3:5,10; 4Ezra 4:33-37; Lk 18:7
60:2; 62:5; Dan 7:9-10; Ps 69:28
4Q530 2.2.16-19
45:3; 71:7; 4Q504 6.14; Phil 4:3; Mt. 25:31
104:1; 108:3; Jub 4:23; Rev 13:8; 20:12, 15
Lk 10:20; Mt 5:22
Lk 15:7, 10; TLev 18:5; Rom 11:25; OdesSol 23:1
Rev 6:10-11; 7:4; 2Bar 23:4-5; 4Ezra 4:36

§§4-13; 3.1-3 §§39-79)" (NV2 pg. 63). This being said, plenty of other instances of barbarity by Herod could easily explain this mention of persecution (See *Ant* 15:10.4 §§366-370).

[984] Instead of: "may not be in vain" K has: "that it may not cease." N remains with: "that it might not be in vain."

[985] (1En 47:2-4) is a substantially expanded form of (Deut 32:43 esp. LXX).

[986] For the last three lines in 47:2 Isaac has: "Their prayers shall not stop from exhaustion before the Lord of the Spirits-neither will they relax forever-(until) judgement is executed for them." **Let no one think that the suffering of the elect goes unnoticed by God. The blood of the martyrs is very special and precious to Him.**

[987] For this line N has: "and endurance might not be their (lot) forever." "For endurance … as an apocalyptic virtue, see (Rev 1:9; 2:2, 3, 19; 13:10 and 14:12)" (NV2 pg. 164).

[988] Other passages that mention or imply a Book of Life include: (Ex 32:32; Ps 69:28; Dan 12:1; Lk 10:20; Phil 4:3; Heb 12:23; Rev 3:5; 13:8; 17:8; 20:12, 15; 21:27). In 1 Enoch see also (103:2 and 108:3).

[989] Olson has: "all of his powers".

[990] In place of "And all His host which is in heaven above and His counselors stood before Him" Isaac, has: "And all his power in heaven above and his escorts stood before him."

[991] **What an incredible scene of the end time judgement! In a courtroom style proceeding, God with all the high heavenly beings around Him, sees the open "books of the living" which contain the names of those who have been petitioning and are now awaiting justification. The last name has just been written in this book! The holy ones are ecstatic that the one-time blood sacrifice of Christ is found acceptable; thus, allowing the elect named in the book to be accepted before God. Revelation 5-6:11 is clearly drawn from this passage and amplified. (Cf. OdesSol 23:1 where the holy ones have joy that grace is given to the elect)**

[992] In place of "had been reached," N translates: "for the number of <the righteous> was at hand;" OL has "for the sum total of righteousness had approached completion" "The remarkable parallel to the motifs in this passage in Rev 6:10-11 may indicate knowledge of the Parables" (NV2 Pg. 165). This is the first reference in Jewish literature of a number of the righteous needing to be filled; although (2 Baruch 23:4-5) is a close second. Please compare the phrases in Rev 6:10-11 of "they cried out," to (1En 47:1, 4) "avenge our blood" to (1En 47:2) "until the number" to (1En 47:4) and "should be complete" to (1En 47:4). Also see "The number of the children whom you long for, is fulfilled" (4Ezra 2:41)

[993] **This image is of the time when the last person on earth is redeemed by the blood of Christ. At that point, judgement can begin. This is the reason Christ delays His return.**

and the prayer of the righteous had been heard. Mt 18:14; Rev 8:3; Heb 12:23
And the blood of the Righteous One[994] had been found[995] [996] Isa 53:11; Jn 6:54-56; Heb 1:3; 9:11-14
fully acceptable before the Lord of Spirits.[997] Rev 5:9; Mt 26:28; 27:24; Col 1:20

The Son of Man!

48 1 And in that place[998] I saw the fountain[999] Isa 55:1; Ps 36:8-9; 46:4; 4Ezra 14:47
of righteousness[1000] which was inexhaustible, 96:6; OdesSol 11:6; 30:1-2; Ezek 47:1

---

[994] **When considering the life of Christ, and the certainty that He knew passages such as 1En 47 and Isa 53:11; even humanly speaking, He knew exactly what His mission of atonement was to be. His followers can be forgiven for being more focused on a Messiah to deliver them in the earthly political realm; since those predictions are very abundant in the Parables and other scripture; and still await future fulfillment. It appears that even the spiritual forces of evil were also deceived into expecting a political deliverer. Jesus dealt with the spiritual root of the problem, which was the only way to solve the rebellion problem once and for all.**

[995] **This is the first and only mention in Jewish literature, prior to the ministry of Christ, where the propitiation of Christ's blood is mentioned! That God legally requires a reckoning for the spilled blood of mankind is found in (Gen 9:5-6; 42:22; 2Sam 4:11; Ps 9:12; and Lk 11:50-51). Only the "Righteous One," Jesus Christ, was able to pay. In some manuscripts Pilate is quoted in (Mt 27:24) as saying "I am innocent of this righteous man's blood."**

[996] In opposition to the following quote, the Parables do here portray a suffering, and indeed, a dying "Righteous One." "Whereas the book of Parables does not portray a suffering Son of Man, the figure does identify with the oppressed righteous and elect. In a similar way, the suffering Son of Man in the gospels identifies with the oppressed by joining them in their suffering and by dying on their behalf. Thus, the suffering sayings reflect three similarities between the Gospels and the Parables: identification with the oppressed; the ruling being the oppressors; and the divine intention to act on behalf of the oppressed" (R pg. 321. Walck, *The Son of Man in the Parables of Enoch and the Gospels*).

"[997] **Unlike the earthly Temple, where the blood of animals was presented time after time; here the Righteous One presents his own blood in the Heavenly Temple one time, where it is accepted fully for all time** (cf. Heb 9:11-14)! Nickelsburg translates 47:4 as: "And the hearts of the holy ones were filled with joy, for the number of <the righteous> was at hand; and the prayer of the righteous had been heard, and (a reckoning of) the blood of the righteous one had been required in the presence of the Lord of Spirits." "The idiom (require a reckoning) suggests a process of inquiry or investigation appropriate to a legal proceeding, in which one would 'look for in the expectation of fixing blame,' or it may refer here to the careful searching of the heavenly books mentioned in v. 3" (NV2 pg. 165 citing Wagner 297 and BDAG, 302). Olson translates the line as "and the blood of the Righteous One had been found fully acceptable before the Lord of Spirits." **If this translation is correct, it appears to be the earliest revelation of the Messiah shedding his blood for the forgiveness of sin!**

[998] "In that place" the heavenly throne room.

[999] K and N have: "spring" in place of "fountain" in both occurrences in 48:1.

[1000] **The fountain here is God, the Son of Man, providing wisdom to all who will drink. The spring/fountain symbolize the abundant wisdom and righteousness freely given by God to those who thirst. For fountains, see also (1En 96:6; Ps 46:4-5; Jer 2:13; 17:13 Amos 5:24; and EBar 1:3). Jesus claimed to be this fountain: "On the last day of the feast, the great day, Jesus stood up and cried out, 'If anyone thirsts, let him come to me and drink. Whoever believes in me, as the scripture has said, out of his heart will flow rivers of living water.'" (Jn 7:37-38) Scholars are still looking for this exact passage that Jesus called scripture. He may have been paraphrasing any number of passages including this one. Whatever the origin; this statement of His was a very public and explicit claim to deity as the Anointed One!** The imagery of a fount of water is also found in the Qumran literature ($1QS_b$, ($1Q28_b$)) 1.6, it reads: "[...May He open for you] an eternal [fou]nt; may He never wi[thhold living water from] the thirsty." (4Q418 Frag. 81+81a 1) reads: "Open your lips as a spring to bless the holy ones and give praise like an eternal spring." The sectarian text (4Q418 Frag. 103.6) which may be the closest match, reads: "like a spring of living water that contains go[odn]ess." (4Q504 5.1) has: "[... They abandoned] the fount of living water [...] and served a foreign god in their land." See also (1QS 11.5).

	OdesSol 4:10
and around it were many fountains of wisdom.	17:4; Sir 24; Rev 7:17; 21:6; 22:1, 17 Bar 3:12; Mt 5:6; 2Bar 39:7; Jer 2:13; 17:13
All the thirsty drank from them,	22:9; 39:5; Jn 4:10, 14; 7:37-39; Prov 16:22
and were filled with wisdom,[1001]	49:1; Prov 8:22-31; OdesSol 6:11
(then) their dwellings were with the righteous, the holy and chosen.	1:1; 42:1-2; 1QS 11.7, 8, 16
2 At that time,[1002] the Son of Man[1003] was named[1004] [1005] [1006] [1007]	69:26; Rev 5:1-5; 19:12; Jn 17:5; Dan 7:13 OdesSol 8:19
in the presence of the Lord of Spirits, and his name before the	52:4; Phil 2:9; Isa 9:6; 49:1
Antecedent of Time.[1008]	Jn 1:3; Heb 1:2-3; Dan 7:13
3 Before the sun or the constellations[1009] were created,	Wis 9:2, 4, 9; Mic 5:2; Gen 1:14-19

[1001] **Jesus Christ claimed to be wiser than Solomon** (Mt 12:42 and Lk 11:31). See also (Mt 13:54 and Mk 6:2).

[1002] "At that time," means before creation; see (1En 48:3).

[1003] **Chapter 48 is the jaw dropping heart of the Book of Parables with its incredible introduction/prophecy of the identity of the Son of Man. "Far from being a scene of eschatological triumph inspired by Dan 7, this scene depicts the Son of Man as a preexistent being who was given a special name by the Lord of the Spirits in the primal 'hour' *before* creation began**" (R. pg. 240, Gieschen). John the Apostle identifies Jesus as the Son of Man (Jn 1:51; 3:13-14; 5:27; 6:27, 53, 62; 8:28; 9:35; 12:34; and 13:31). Jesus possesses the Divine Name in (Rev 19:12).

[1004] Chapter 48 is a commissioning scene for the Son of Man/Anointed One/Messiah/Christ/Righteous One. He is named, which gives Him the full authority and power of God.

[1005] "In 1 Enoch 'the name' by which the Son of Man 'was named' appears to be the Divine Name of the Lord of the Spirits because there are numerous references to 'the name of the Lord of the Spirits' throughout the Parables" (R pg. 240, Gieschen). "Second Temple Jewish literature evinces considerable interest in the Divine Name and the theophanic figure who possesses it. **A significant aspect of the understanding of the Divine Name in this literature is an emphasis on its power. This name is not another word among the myriad of words in the human language, but is the most powerful word of the world, even the very word that God spoke to bring the world into existence** (Ps 124:8)" (R pg. 244, Gieschen). See also (Jn 12:28; 3Jn 7; Rev 19:12).

[1006] "Several Jewish texts speak of the Divine Name as the hidden or secret name. For example, see (Gen 32:29; Judg 13:17; 1En 69:14; Jos Asen 15:12; Prayer of Joseph; Gos Thom 13; Gos Truth 38:7-40:29; and Gos Phil 54:5)" (R pg. 247, Gieschen). **Giving someone a name is part of calling that person for a special task** (BL pg. 210).

[1007] A son of man/messiah figure is also revealed in (4 Ezra 13:25-38). Some scholars, such as Heiser, (H2 pg. 165), date 4 Ezra prior to the Book of the Parables but most date it later, to about AD 100 (NV2 pg. 61, 121; OTP1 pg. 520).

[1008] **This verse establishes that some Jews in the late 2nd temple period knew about a duality in the God head that would later manifest itself in the Son of Man coming to earth in the incarnation. This in no way negates the Shema, *"Hear O Israel the Lord our God, the Lord is One"* (Exodus 6:4), as God is still one, but shows that God would manifest himself in human form. Divine Messianic expectations are abundant in the Dead Sea Scrolls, prime examples are the (Thanksgiving scroll Col 26.1-9 (W pg. 203-204) and 4Q491C 11.1.11-18 (W pg. 169)). An earthly king Messiah is predicted in the Psalms of Solomon (70-45 BC) (17:21-18:9) (OTP2 pgs. 667-669). However, outside the Old Testament, the description that best matches the person of Jesus Christ at His first coming and in Christian theology is found in the Parables of Enoch.**

[1009] "Charles and other older commentators thought "heavenly signs" meant the Zodiac, and this view was still maintained by Milik and Knibb. But Black and Neugebauer rightly point out that the Zodiac plays no role in Enochic astronomy (see Black pgs. 111, 210, 395)" (OL pg. 137 n10) (cf. Job 38:31-33). Other scholars (Laurence, Martin, Dillman and Hoffman) disagree, seeing two zodiac signs per gate.

before the stars of the heaven were made,
his name was named before the Lord of Spirits.[1010] [1011]
4 He shall be a staff for the righteous[1012] [1013] that they may lean
on him and not fall, and he shall be the light of the Gentiles,[1014]
and the hope of those who grieve in their hearts.[1015]
5 All who dwell on earth shall fall down and worship before
him,[1016]and will glorify and bless and celebrate with song the
Name of the Lord of Spirits.[1017]
6 For this (reason) he was chosen and hidden in his presence
before the world was created and forever.[1018]
7 The wisdom of the Lord of Spirits will reveal him to the holy

Ps 147:4; Prov 8:27; Heb 1:2-3
OdesSol 36:1-6; 41:15; Jn 1:1; 8:26, 58
Mt 12:15-21; Ps 23:4; Lk 2:32
61:3, 5; Isa 42:6; 49:6-7; 61:1; Acts 13:47
Jn 1:4-9; 8:12; Mt 5:4; Eph 3:6; Isa 61:1-2
10:21; 62:9; 63; 90:37; Isa 45:23; Ps 72:11
Phil 2:9-11; 4Q215a 1.2.8; Dan 7:14, 27
62:6-7; Isa 42:1; 49:2; 1Pet 1:20; Jn 1:1
4Ezra 12:32; 13:26, 52; 1QS 11.5.6,7
Rev 13:8; Tit 1:2; DialTrypho 61
1QS 4.24; Col 2:2-3; Eph 3:8-11; Lk 17:30

[1010] (1En 48:3) **is a clear statement of the preexistence of the Son of Man, Messiah/Christ. Jesus claimed preexistence (Jn 8:56-58). The apostle John unambiguously presents Jesus Christ as preexisting creation and as the possessor of the divine name (Jn 1:1-5; 17:6, 11-12). The possession of the divine name is like having the kings signet ring. All power and authority is given to the bearer.**

[1011] The Odes of Solomon are a very early (ca. AD 100) collection of Christian hymns. They appear to reference (1En 48:1-10), making it a very early extra-Biblical reference to the Parables. "In these verses (1En 48:1-10) we find a memorable description of a *fountain* of righteousness which was inexhaustible so that *all* the *thirsty drank* and were filled. This description may have influenced the Odist when he wrote (Ode 30:1f.), in which there is a similar picture of a living *spring* and the exhortation to *all* the *thirsty* to come and *drink*; moreover, the water that comes from the spring is described as boundless. Increasing the possibility of influence is the description in (1 Enoch 48:2-10) of the *Son of Man* who *was named* in the presence of the Lord of Spirits (cf. 48:3). It would be unwise to dismiss the possibility that this image influenced (Ode 36:1-3), in which the Odist claims that he was lifted up to heaven by the *Spirit* of the *Lord*; and then that Christ himself spoke and stated that he had been brought before the Lord's face and because he was the *Son of Man* he '*was named* the Light, the Son of God.' Increasing the possibility of dependence here on 1 Enoch by the Odist is the recognition that the *naming* of the Son of Man in apocalyptic and other intertestamental writings is apparently found in only these two documents" (Charlesworth, OTP2 pgs. 732-733). A parallel may also be found in (OdesSol 6:11); "Then all the thirsty upon the earth drank, and thirst was relieved and quenched" (OTP2 pg. 739).

[1012] One manuscript reads "staff to the righteous and holy."

[1013] (1En 48:4-7) has parallels with the language of (Isa 49:2-8).

[1014] N and K have "nations" in place of "gentiles." That the light of salvation will be available to the nations/gentiles is also found in (10:21; 90:38; and 91:14). The ministry of the Son of Man is to both Israel and the nations. The early Apostles were taken aback at the eagerly positive reception of the gospel among Gentiles. **Considering the events of the New Testament, and subsequent world history since the first century; Jesus Christ is the light of the Gentiles and can be the only one who fulfilled this prediction.** See also (Isa 42:6; and 49:6-7) where the Messiah will be a light to the gentiles.

[1015] **"By giving the Son of Man certain prerogatives, the text stresses his 'messianic' nature, an element absent from the book of Daniel. This Son of Man is the support for the righteous ones, the light of the Gentiles, the hope of those who suffer, the Chosen One. The language is clearly that of Isaiah and is borrowed from those passages of Isaiah that have strongly messianic overtones"** (R pg. 161. Chiala).

[1016] **Paul may have had (1En 48) in mind, given the parallels with (Phil 2:5-11); "Christ Jesus, who, though he was in the form of God, did not count equality with God a thing to be grasped, but made himself nothing, taking the form of a servant, being born in the likeness of men. And being found in human form, he humbled himself by becoming obedient to the point of death, even death on a cross. Therefore God has highly exalted him and bestowed on him the name that is above every name, so that at the name of Jesus every knee should bow, in heaven and on earth and under the earth, and every tongue confess that Jesus Christ is Lord, to the glory of God the Father." At the very least, Philippians reflects the Christology of chapter 48 and the balance of the Parables.**

[1017] Knibb has: "with psalms the name of the Lord of Spirits." N has: "and sing hymns to the name of the Lord of Spirits." "The wording of v. 5b may reflect Ps 18:49" (NV2 pg. 172).

[1018] **The Son of Man/Messiah existed before the world was created.** See also (1En 62:7).

and righteous. For he will preserve the portion of the righteous,   58:2; Ezek 9:4-6; 1Cor 1:30; Eph 1:8-9 Jn 8:28; 2 Bar 29:3, Jn 1:31
because they loath and despise this world of unrighteousness;[1019]   108:8-10; Ps 45:7; Gal 1:4; Jn 12:25
and hate all its works and ways in the Name of the Lord of Spirits.   1Jn 2:15-16; Lk 14:26
For in his name, they are saved,[1020]   50:3; Acts 2:21; 4:12; Rom 10:13; Jn 1:12
and he will become the avenger of their lives.[1021]   1Cor 6:11; Rom 12:19; Deut 32:35
8 In those days, downcast will be the faces of the kings
of the earth,[1022] and the strong who possess the land   38:4-5
because of the deeds of their hands. For on the day of their   4Ezra 13:37; Hos 10:8
anguish and distress they will not be able to save themselves.[1023]   45:2; 52:7; Rev 20:13-15; 1Cor 6:2-3
9 I will give them over into the hands of my chosen ones;[1024]   27:3; 38:5; 91:12; 95:3,7; 98:12; 2Bar 72:6
as straw in the fire[1025] so they will burn before   Isa 5:24; 47:14; Wis Sol 3:7; Mal 4:1 Div Inst 7.26
the face of the holy,[1026] as lead in the water they shall   Ex 15:7, 10; Rev 14:10; Obad 18
sink before the face of the righteous,
and no trace of them shall be found.[1027]   4Q418 69.2.8; Wis 5:9-12
10 On the day of their distress, there shall be rest[1028] on the earth,   52:8; 53:7; 91:17; Isa 14:7
and they will fall[1029] down before them and not rise again.   Ps 36:12; Jer 50:32; 4Ezra 7:36
There shall be no one to grasp them with his hand and raise   Isa 41:10; 51:18; Rev 6:15-16

[1019] Isaac has: "oppression" in place of "unrighteousness." Hating unrighteousness is a common theme in the Qumran Community Rule, (1QS 1.4, 10; 4.24). It appears that Jesus may be referring to this text or at least this idea when he says, "Whoever loves his life loses it, and whoever hates his life in this world will keep it for eternal life" (Jn 12:25).

[1020] **The concept of being "saved in His name" is found originally in (Joel 2:32). But this concept was expanded in the Parables of Enoch. It was picked up by the authors of the New Testament. We are saved only by His Name (48:7; 50:3; Acts 2:21; 4:12; Rom 10:13; Jn 1:12). The power of the Name of Jesus Christ is well demonstrated in modern day accounts of near-death experiences, and demonic/ "alien" encounters. It is also demonstrated in scripture (Mt 7:22; Mk 9:38; Lk 9:49; 10:17; Acts 16:18; 19:13-16). The power of the Name is prominent in the New Testament; but underestimated by modern day Christians.**

[1021] For this line K has: "and he is the one who will require their lives." I has: "and it is his good pleasure that they have life." N has: "and he is the vindicator of their lives." OL has: "and he will be the avenger of their lives."

[1022] "Kings of the Earth" These are Roman emperors." "But some Jews may have included King Herod in that group since he was judged to be non-Jewish and perceived to be pro-Roman, even a Roman" (R 465, Charlesworth).

[1023] For 48:8, Isaac has: "In those days, the kings of the earth and the mighty landowners shall be humiliated on account of the deeds of their hands. Therefore, on the day of their misery and weariness, they will not be able to save themselves." The kings and the mighty will be made helpless and be delivered to their victims for vengeance.

[1024] Being handed over into the hands of the chosen "is evidently derived from the biblical ideology of holy warfare" (N1 pg. 464). This image may be behind the scene of Christ's return in (Rev 19:11-16) indicating that the saints will be part of the armies of Heaven.

[1025] **This fire is certainly Gehenna which was envisioned as being in the valley just to the south of Jerusalem.**

[1026] Nickelsburg sees evidence for a connection between (1En 48:9; 49:2) and (Wis 3:7) (stubble/straw) (Wis 5:9-12) (no trace/no trace to be found) (NV2 pg. 176).

[1027] In (27:2-3; and 90:26-27) the righteous view the punishment of the wicked. In the Parables (48:9 and in 62:12-13) the judged are seen temporarily and then are not seen any more. In the story of Lazarus and the rich man, they are able to see each other for a seemingly long period of time (Lk 16:19-31). This indicates Lazarus and the rich man were in a Sheol type holding place awaiting the time of judgement. Likewise, in (4Ezra 7:32-36), souls are held until the time of judgement and at the judgement the place of torment and rest are opposite each other.

[1028] **This is a term for rest associated with "the peace or calm that follows the end of war or hostilities"** (NV2 pg. 176). See (Isa 14:7) for example.

[1029] **Both the elect and the wicked fall. One in worship (48:5); the other in judgement (48:10).**

them up, for they have denied the Lord of Spirits and His	38:2; Ps 2:2; Lk 12:9; Jude 4; Mt 10:33
Anointed One.[1030]	52:4; Acts 3:14; Rev 3:8; Mk 8:29
Blessed be the Name of the Lord of Spirits!	

The Chosen One!

49 1 For wisdom[1031] is poured[1032] out like water,[1033]	39:5; 48:1; 51:3; 1Cor 1:22-24, 30; Sir 24
and glory will not fail[1034] before him for ever and ever.	
2 For he is powerful in all the mysteries[1035] of righteousness,	4Q440 3.16
and iniquity will vanish like a shadow, with no place to remain.[1036]	Wis 5:9-12; Job 14:2
For the Chosen One has taken his stand[1037] before the	39:6
the Lord of Spirits. His glory is forever and ever,	Eph 3:21
and his might to generations of generations.	Dan 7:13-14; Ps 89:4; TLev 18:8
3 In him dwells the spirit of wisdom,	Isa 11:2
the spirit which gives insight,	61:11
the spirit of understanding[1038] and of might,	
and the spirit of those who have fallen asleep in righteousness.[1039]	81:4; 116:15; Col 3:3-4
4 He shall judge the things which are in secret,	38:3; Lk 8:17; 12:2-3; Eccl 12:14; Ps 90:8

[1030] Anointed One=Messiah. In place of "Anointed;" I, OL and K have "Messiah." N translates "Anointed One." **Anointed one (מְשִׁיחוֹ (mə·šî·ḥōw) is the language of kingly status in the Old Testament indicating this is referring to Messiah** (See Ps 2:2, 20:6, 45:7, and 89:20). Near the same time or slightly before the composition of the Parables, the term Messiah/Anointed One was also used in a technical sense in the highly messianic passage of (PssSol 17:32; 18:5, 7). Later it was used in (4Ezra 7:29; 12:32; 2Bar 29:3; 30:1; 39:7; 40:1; 70:9; 72:2). It was of course also used in the New Testament scores of times, as the equivalent term "Christ".

[1031] The personification of wisdom is identified as Christ in the New Testament. Compare (Wis 7:24-26 with Heb 1:1-3) with the common use of ἀπαύγασμα (apaugasma) "radiance" linking the two passages. Speaking of this passage; Nickelsburg opines, "Taken together, it is a complex and tightly packed presentation of the identity and function of the Son of Man" (NV2 pg. 177). Jesus identifies himself as the Wisdom of God (Mt 11:19; Lk 7:35; 11:49); as does Paul (1Cor 1:24, 30; 2:6-8; Eph 1:17; and Col 2:3).

[1032] Compare 47:2, "blood poured" and 49:1, "wisdom poured."

[1033] **In the writings of John, Jesus often used water as an image, with him being the source of water. See: (Jn 3:5; 4:10-14; 7:37-38; Rev 7:17; 21:6; and 22:1, 17). That water is lacking in Gehenna, serves to reinforce that Gehenna is away from the presence of Christ, the water bearer.** It is interesting that the progression of the equinox, in our time, is next entering Aquarius, the water bearer, which would forecast a return of Christ as the age of Pisces wanes.

[1034] In place of "not fail" Isaac has: "is measureless." Measureless unfailing glory is an attribute only of God and firmly places wisdom personified in the throne room of God. This is a powerful statement of the deity of the Messiah.

[1035] In place of "mysteries" an alternate reading could be "ways of."

[1036] In place of "remain" in agreement with Olson; I has: "foundation." K has: "existence." N has: "and will have no place to stand." C has: "continuance."

[1037] "To stand up (Heb. עָמַד, Aram… [qûm] is technical language for assuming a stance to execute judgement" (NV2 pg. 178).

[1038] Olson has "knowledge" in place of "understanding."

[1039] **The Elect One has a special relationship with the righteous dead, "those who have fallen asleep in righteousness." He will gather them together, be their vindicator, mediator, protector, and the judge of their oppressors. Paul says "For you have died and your life is hidden with Christ in God. When Christ who is your life appears, then you also will appear with him in glory" (Col 3:3-4). The spirits of the righteous dead dwell in Christ.**

and no one will be able to utter a lying word[1040] in his presence; 62:3; 67:9; Rom 2:16; Mt 12:36; Isa 11:3
for he is the Chosen One before the Lord of Spirits according Isa 42:1; Lk 9:35; 13:35; 23:35
to His will. Lk 12:32; Eph 1:9

The Righteous Saved

50 1 In those days a change will take place for the holy and 1Cor 15:51-54; TBenj 10:6-8
elect;[1041] the light of days[1042] shall remain upon them,
and glory and honor will again come to the holy.
2 On the day of distress, evil will be stored up against the Rom 2:5; Hos 13:12; Job 21:19; 1Thes 5:3
sinners![1043] [1044] But the righteous will be victorious in the Name TJob 4:6; Rev 2:7,11,17, 26; 3:5, 12, 21
of the Lord of Spirits: and he will cause others[1045] to witness this:
that they may repent[1046] 100:6; Rev 9:20
and abandon the works of their hands.[1047] 91:9, 14; TMos 10:7
3 Although they will have no honorable standing before the
presence of the Lord of Spirits, Rom 10:13; Acts 2:21; 4:12; Mt 20:1-16
yet through his Name they shall be saved,[1048] 1Cor 6:11; Jn 1:12; 20:31; Joel 2:32
and the Lord of Spirits will have compassion on them, Isa 54:7
for His mercy is great. 1Pet 2:10
4 And in his judgement, he is righteous. 61:9; 2Thes 1:5

1040 Isaac translates "vain words," N has "lying word," OL has "empty word." Black observes: "The expression means a great deal more than 'idle chatter' or 'careless talk:' it includes deceptive speech, including unfulfilled promises or covenants, false witness, all the evil that the tongue can create" (Bl Pg. 213). Since Christ the judge is all knowing, lies are useless.

1041 **The fortunes of the holy and elect will be reversed. The elect will have light and glory and honor, while the sinners will have distress and calamity.**

1042 Nickelsburg suggests a possible reading of "light of (many) days." "The difficult expression "light of days" seems to refer to the endless multiplication of days, the everlasting life, anticipated in 58:3, 6 in the description of the light-filled glorious future of the righteous" (NV2 pg. 182).

1043 Some manuscripts read "Evil shall have been treasured up" or "on which evil will have been stored up." Nickelsburg notes that the "exact wording of this clause varies in the mss" (NV2 pg. 180 n 2b and N pg. 64).

1044 For 50:1c-50:2a Isaac has: "and glory and honor shall be given back to the holy ones, on the day of weariness. He heaped evil upon the sinners"

1045 "Given the references to the righteous and their oppressors in vv. 1-2b, the "others" mentioned in this section must be either the gentiles not included among the oppressors of the righteous or other Israelites not included among the righteous, the holy, and the chosen" (NV2 pg. 182).

1046 This verse anticipates and predicts the conversion of the Gentiles. Others include (1En 10:21, 90:30, 38; 91:9; 91:14 and 100:6). Conversion of the gentiles is a major and surprisingly miraculous occurrence in the New Testament. See: (Mt 12:18, 21; Lk 2:32; Acts 9:15; 10:45; 11:1, 18; 13:46-48; 14:27; 15:3, 7, 12, 14, 17, 19, 23; 18:6; 21:19-25; 26:20, 23; 28:28; Rom 1:13; 3:29; 9:24; 11:11-13, 25; 15:8-16; 16:4 etc. and 1Pet 2:10).

1047 This is speaking of abandoning the worship of idols, who are the works of their hands.

1048 This text follows the majority manuscript reading "not have honor." Nickelsburg finds the reading in this text "easier and more suspicious" (N pg. 64). He translates "And they will have honor in the presence of the Lord of Spirits, and in his name, they will be saved;" **Whichever reading is chosen; this text establishes that idolatrous gentiles and jews can be saved after repentance through the power of the name and then receive mercy. This is a very Christian concept. Mercy through repentance is freely offered to all, through the blood payment for sin that was to be made by the Righteous One (1En 47:4). Those who persist in sin will perish before Him in judgement. In (1En 62:5-9 and 63:1-8 the kings and mighty do repent, but since it is after death, while before the throne (62:5 and 63:1), it is too late to receive mercy. Repentance is turning from idolatry or other sin and seeking allegiance with God. A switching of sides, so to speak.**

In the presence of his glory, iniquity shall assuredly not stand.
At his judgement, whoever does not repent
will perish before him.[1049] [1050]
5 The Lord of Spirits has spoken: "From then on, I will have
no mercy on them."

49:2; Deut 32:35
Lk 13:3, 5
4Ezra 7:33-34; 2Bar 85:10-15
5:5-6; 12:6; 60:5, 25; 61:13

The Resurrection of the Dead

51 1 In those days the earth will give back that which has been
entrusted to it.
Sheol will give back that which has been deposited there,[1051]
and Abaddon[1052] shall repay that which it owes.[1053]

Ps-Philo 3:10; 2Mac 7:9; 11; 29
4Ezra 4:40-42; 7:32-33; Dan 12:2
61:5; 103:4; Rev 9:11; 20:13-14
20:8; 22; Job 26:6; Jn 5:28-29

[1049] **It is easy to gloss over the message of judgement in the Parables, but it is central throughout. The Parables of Enoch were written not long before the ministry of Christ as a stark final warning to Israel, and as a presentation of the "Son of Man" giving them one last chance at national repentance. The judgment of Israel was sealed with the rejection and crucifixion of Christ. (*Cels.* 8.69; *HE* 3:5) The sentence was carried out by the Romans with unspeakable horror, in the total destruction of Jerusalem, the Jewish nation, and the Temple in 68-70 AD. (*War* books 4-7). The Parables, composed immediately before the time of Christ, were an amazing written warning to accompany His ministry. Throughout His ministry, He continued to point to the Parables. His use of the term "Son of Man," is only one way He sought to point those of His time to these passages, that so plainly testify of Him. Christ was obviously claiming to be the Son of Man/Chosen One/Righteous One from the Parables.**

[1050] **This passage makes plain that there are no second chances after death. If repentance does not occur before the judgement, it is too late.** This is also expressed in (4 Ezra 7:33-36) and in a beautiful passage in (2Bar 85:10-15).

[1051] **This is the first of two passages in the Parables that announce a resurrection of the dead; and like (1En 61:5), it precedes a description of the judgement. This appears to be a bodily resurrection since the earth gives "back that which has been entrusted to it."** The resurrection in (2Mac 7:11) also appears to be a bodily resurrection "receive these (hands) back again."

[1052] In place of "Abaddon" K and N have "destruction." C has: Hell; OL has Perdition. "But the Ethiopic term (*hagwal*) is thought by Black, Nickelsburg, and VanderKam to be a rendering of the Aramaic *'abdwn* (+Abaddon)" (cf. H2 pg. 120). The Hebrew term Abaddon (אֲבַדּוֹן *'Ăḇaddōn*, meaning "destruction", "doom"), and its Greek equivalent Apollyon (Ἀπολλύων, *Apollúōn* meaning "destroyer") often appear in conjunction with the place Sheol. It is the place of the dead. Both terms are used as names for the angel-king of the bottomless pit in (Rev 9:11).

[1053] Earth, Sheol, Abaddon/Hell/destruction, may complement each other or be synonymous. "Earth is where the body is buried. Sheol is the place to which the spirit or soul descends (see 1 Enoch 102:5)" (NV2 pg. 184). "The common term for 'earth' or 'land' *'erets*, is also used for the underworld (Jonah 2:6 [cp. 2:2, Isaiah 44:23), as the realm of the dead was conceived as being inside the earth" (H2 pg. 120). Destruction is a term that in the Hebrew Bible is synonymous with Sheol (NV2 pg. 184). Sheol and Abaddon are especially a place for the wicked (1QH$_a$ Col. 11.16-19 (W pg. 182)). The three expressions "entrusted," "deposited," and "owes" have financial connotations referring to money or a precious person or thing. "**Thus, the realm of the dead has only temporary custody of what belongs to God**" (NV2 pg. 184). Verse 51:1 "is paralleled by two texts from the end of the first century C.E., Pseudo-Philo's Liber *antiquitatum biblicarum* (*Biblical Antiquities*), and 4 Ezra" (NV2 pg. 184). Both these texts are Jewish, and from the first century, but scholars are divided on whether they depend on (1En 51:1). However, given the dating of the texts involved, the *Parables* would be the oldest. It is of course also paralleled in (Rev 20:13), especially in the Ethiopic version of Revelation (NV2 pg. 183). In any event, (1En 51:1) is a clear acknowledgment and anticipation of the post death existence of the unrighteous and their appearance for judgement before the throne of the Chosen One.

5a For in those days, my Chosen One shall arise,[1054]	39:6; Dan 12:1-3
2 and choose the righteous and holy from among them;[1055]	Mt 13:30; 25:31-33; Mk 13:27
for the day on which they will be saved has drawn near.	2Cor. 6:2; Lk 21:28; Isa 49:8
3 My Chosen One[1056] shall in those days sit on my[1057] throne,	45:3; 2Chr 9:8, 1Chr 29:20, 23; Rev 22:1
and from his mouth will pour forth all the secrets of wisdom	49:1, 3; 91:1; Isa 11:1-4; 1Cor 2:7-8
and council. For the Lord of Spirits has appointed him and	Mt 13:54
glorified him.	Jn 17:5
4 In those days, the mountains will leap like rams,	Ps 29:6; 114:4
and the hills will skip like lambs satisfied with milk.	Rom 8:19-23
The faces of all the angels in heaven will be radiant with joy.[1058]	47:4; Lk 15:7, 10; Mt 13:43
5b-d The earth will rejoice,[1059]	
and the righteous will dwell upon it and the elect	Ps 37:9; 29; Mt 5:5
will walk freely thereon.[1060]	

Mountains of Metal

52 1 Afterwards, in that place where I had seen all the visions of	23:1-24:1
of what is hidden (for I had been carried off in a whirlwind[1061]	14:8; 39:3; 70:2; 2Kgs 2:11; Job 38:1

[1054] Nickelsburg, Charles and Olson agree with the placement of this line here. "Arise" may be similar to the usage in (Dan 12:1) where Michael arises. "In Dan 12:1, the verb עֲמֹד ("to stand up") means to assume a posture for judgement" (NV2 pg. 185) and (Nickelsburg, George, W.E., 2007. *Resurrection, Immortality, and Eternal Life in Intertestamental Judaism and Early Christianity: Expanded Edition (Harvard Theological Studies) pg. 24)*. The Chosen One, is here arising in judgement, whereas Michael arose as a defender of Israel. In (1En 51:3) the Chosen One sits on the throne in judgement. See (chapters 62-63) for a description of this judgement.

[1055] **(Mt 25:31-33) is gleaned from the same images and eschatology as in (1En 51:2-3).** "When the Son of Man comes in his glory, and all the angels with him, then he will sit on his glorious throne. Before him will be gathered all the nations, and he will separate people one from another as a shepherd separates the sheep from the goats. And he will place the sheep on his right, but the goats on the left. Then the King will say to those on his right, Come, you who are blessed by my Father, inherit the kingdom prepared for you from the foundation of the world'" (Mt 25:31-33).

[1056] "Chosen one" Since it is in the first person, singular, it is best read as "my chosen one" in both instances (NV2 pg. 183).

[1057] Some manuscripts say "his throne." The Lord of Spirits and the Chosen One sit on the same throne (cf. Rev 22:1, 3). **The idea is that although the kings of Judah sat on the throne of the kingdom, it was ultimately God's throne (cf. 1Chr 29:20, 23; 2Chr 9:8).**

[1058] **Creation is joyful that judgement has finally been rendered** (cf. Rom 8:19-23, TLev 18:5).

[1059] Like so many Biblical and other texts contemporary with the *Parables*, this text looks forward to a renewed earth.

[1060] This text follows Issac, Nickelsburg and Olson. Knibb is quite different in the closing lines of this chapter, starting in 3c: "for the Lord of Spirits has appointed him and glorified him. And in those days the mountains will leap like rams, and the hills will skip like lambs satisfied with milk, and all will become angels in heaven. Their faces will shine with joy, for in those days the Chosen One will have risen; and the earth will rejoice, and the righteous will dwell upon it, and the chosen will go and walk upon it." It is also translated this way by Black and Chiala (NV2 pg. 183). That translation is based on the later manuscript group m,β which Nickelsburg translates "And all of them will become angels in heaven; their faces will be radiant with joy" (NV2 pg. 181). This idea of humans becoming like angels recurs in 69:11. Also compare (Mt 22:29-30 and Lk 20:34-36) where in Matthew, Jesus says that humans after the resurrection, "are like the angels in heaven" or in Luke, "equal to angels".

[1061] Olson has: "chariot of wind" in place of "whirlwind." Isaac has: "wind vehicle" and suggests "wind balls." For other descriptions of people caught up into another realm or whirlwinds in general compare (2 Kgs 2:11; Job 381; Isa 66:15; Jer 4:13; Ezek 1:4; Acts 1:9-11; 2Cor 12:2-4).

and they[1062] had taken me towards the west). Isa 66:15; Jer 4:13
2 There my eyes saw all the secrets of heaven which are destined
to happen upon earth: a mountain of iron, and a mountain of Dan 2:31-45
copper, and a mountain of silver, and a mountain of gold, 18:6-8; 24:2-25:3
and a mountain of soft[1063] metal, and a mountain of lead.[1064] Zech 6:1
3 I asked the angel who went with me, saying, "What are those
things which I have seen in secret?"
4 And he said to me: "All these things which you have seen
shall be under the dominion of his Messiah,[1065] 48:10; Dan 7:14
that he may be in command and hold power on the earth."[1066] 2Thes 1:7
5 And that angel of peace[1067] answered, saying unto me: 40:8
Wait a little, and all the secrets which surround the
Lord of Spirits shall be revealed to you.[1068]
6 And these mountains which your eyes have seen;
The mountain of iron, the mountain of copper, the mountain 67:4
of silver, the mountain of gold, the mountain of soft metal, Dan 2:35
and the mountain of lead,[1069]
all these shall be, in the presence of the Chosen One, 39:6; SibOr 2:197; 7:121
as wax in front of the fire,[1070] 1:6; 53:7; Ps 97:5; Isa 64:1-3 LXX

[1062] "The use of 'they' without any antecedent in the context 'may indicate that this sentence and perhaps the whole chapter or large parts of it have been taken out of context, or that something has dropped out. It is impossible to tell whether the original context of this passage, if there was such, still exists in the Book of Parables'" (NV2 pg. 188).

[1063] In place of "soft" Isaac has "colored."

[1064] Some scholars such as (Black, BL pg. 215; Heiser, H2 pg. 128), see these mountains as a succession of kingdoms as in (Daniel 2:31-45); especially in light of 1En 52:6. The kingdoms seem to degrade in quality, as does the value of the metal, until they are put in subjection to Messiah. Nickelsburg argues against a direct link with Daniel 2 since no succession of kingdoms is referred to and the list of metals only partially correspond (NV2 pg. 189). In Origen's (*Contra Celsum* 6.22), there is a description of a ladder with seven gates from the *Mysteries of Mithras.* That text associates these same metals (assuming tin is the soft metal) with the planets (C pg. 102). **A simpler explanation may be that these metals are simply the ones used to maintain warfare, and kingdoms in opposition to Messiah, but He will cut off the supply and need (see 52:6-8).**

[1065] Some scholars use "Anointed One" here, others have "Messiah."

[1066] Isaac translates the angel's reply as: "All these things which you have seen happen by the authority of his Messiah so that he may give orders and be praised upon the earth." Nickelsburg has "All these things that you have seen will be for the authority of his Anointed One, so that he may be powerful and mighty on the earth." "The point here is that "the world empires shall become subservient to the rule of the Elect One" (BL pg. 215).

[1067] This is the "angel of peace" named previously in 40:8 and 46:2. This angel will be named again in 53:4; 54:4; and 56:2. The appearance of this angel is appropriate in a text about the cessation of warfare.

[1068] Knibb, using different manuscripts translates: "Wait a little, and you will see, and everything which is secret, which the Lord of Spirits has established, will be revealed to you."

[1069] All six of these mountains will be destroyed, but a seventh one may be envisioned as God's Mountain, as in Nebuchadnezzar's dream. "Then the iron, the clay, the bronze, the silver, and the gold, all together were broken in pieces, and became like the chaff of the summer threshing floors; and the wind carried them away, so that not a trace of them could be found. But the stone that struck the image became a great mountain and filled the whole earth" (Daniel 2:35).

[1070] Isaac has: "like a honeycomb (that melts) before the fire." In (1 Enoch 1:6) the mountain melts at the advent of God but here at the advent of the Chosen One.

and like water which streams down from above.[1071] Mic 1:4; Nah 1:5
These mountains shall become helpless[1072] under his feet. Isa 13:7, 17
7 And it shall come to pass in those days that no one 53:1; 97:8-9
will be saved either by gold or by silver, 63:10; Dan 5:4, 23; Ezek 7:19; Zeph 1:18
and no one will be able to escape.[1073] 94:7; Isa 49:7-10
8 There will be no iron for war,[1074] Mic 4:3; Isa 2:4; Hos 2:18; Zech 9:10
nor will anyone wear a breastplate.[1075] 8:1; Ps 46:9, Gen 4:22; *Good Person* 78
Bronze[1076] will be of no service, 4Q242 Frag 1-3.7-8
and tin will be useless and of no value,
and lead shall not be desired.
9 All these substances will be rejected and destroyed from the 90:34
surface of the earth,[1077] when the Chosen One appears before 39:6
the face of the Lord of Spirits."

The Deep Valley—The Kings and the Powerful

53 1 There before my eyes, I saw an underworld with a gaping 54:1; 56:4; Isa 60:3, 5, 16
mouth,[1078] and all who dwell upon the land[1079] and sea and the
islands will bring to him gifts and presents and tribute,[1080] 52:7; 100:12; Pss 72:8-11; Rev 21:26

[1071] The similarity with (Mic 1:4) is apparent. "And the mountains will melt under him, and the valleys will split open, like wax before the fire, like waters poured down a steep place." (Mic 4:3, and Isa 2:4) are also shadowed in 52:8. ""The motifs of the fiery presence of the deity and the judgement function of the flood are near at hand" (NV2 pg. 191).

[1072] "Helpless," literally "tired," "weak," "powerless."

[1073] The image may be of trying to bribe or pay tribute to God on the day of judgement (See 100:12).

[1074] **The mention of widespread use of iron in warfare places this text firmly after the beginning of the iron age; which is generally agreed as starting around 1200 BC in the middle east** (Collins, Steven and Holden, Joseph M. 2001. *The Harvest Handbook of Bible Lands*, pg. 34). Iron works dating to earlier periods have been documented; possibly as early as 2200 BC in Anatolia. (*Hideo, Akanuma, 2008. "The Significance of Early Bronze Age Iron Objects from Kaman-Kalehöyük, Turkey" Anatolian Archaeological Studies. Tokyo: Japanese Institute of Anatolian Archaeology.* **17**: 313–320). Iron smelting also occurred in the Indian subcontinent as early as 1800 BC (Tewari, Rakesh, 2003. *"The origins of Iron Working in India: New Evidence from the Central Ganga Plain and the Eastern Vindhyas" Antiquity*. **77** (297): 536–545). **This reference to the widespread use of iron in warfare is another nail in the coffin for those who imagine authorship of the *Parables* by a biblical Enoch; as he would have lived prior to 3000 BC.** Iron is also mentioned in Gen 4:22.

[1075] The breastplate was made of leather and covered with metal (NV2 pg. 192).

[1076] Nickelsburg has "copper" in place of "bronze." The paring of this metal with tin in the next line would indicate the use of bronze, since copper and tin (12-12.5%) are combined to produce bronze. Bronze statues and idols were ubiquitous in this period. (Cf. Zech 6:1)

[1077] Mountains of metal would have been very attractive for exploitation by the kings and the mighty in order to increase their power. In the day of judgment, they will not protect from the wrath of God. When Messiah rules, there will no longer be a need for riches or instruments of war that were used for oppression. In addition, these metals, except for lead were used for the fashioning of idols (99:7; Dan 5:4, 23; Wis 13:10; and 4Q242 Frag 1-3.7-8).

[1078] K and N have: "deep valley, and its mouth was open" I has: "deep valley with a wide mouth." It may be the Kidron Valley (Isa 30:33; Rev 16:16). The location of the final battle is not Megiddo, but Jerusalem. (H2 pg. 131, Heiser, Michael S., 2015. *The Unseen Realm*, 368-375). "*Open mouths*—Most commentators take this to be another expression for the "hollow places" of 1 Enoch 22, which described the underworld realm of the dead" (H2 pg. 131).

[1079] Knibb has "dry ground" in place of "land".

[1080] The idea is that the gentile nations will bring gifts, presents and tribute to the Chosen One in Jerusalem.

yet that deep valley will not become full.[1081] [1082] 67:4; Joel 3:2, 12
2 The hands of sinners commit criminal deeds,
and everything that (the righteous) toil over, the sinners lawlessly 7:3; 103:11; Hos 4:8
devour.[1083] Sinners will be destroyed before the face of the Lord
of Spirits, and they shall be banished from the face of his earth. 38:1-4; 45:6; 63:11; 69:28; Jub 30:22
They will be punished for ever and ever.[1084] 1QS 4.12-14
3 For I saw all the angels of punishment[1085] continually preparing 41:2; 62:11; 63:1; 66:1; Mt 25:46; ApPet 20
all the shackles[1086] of Satan.[1087] 40:7; 54:3; 65:6; Ps 78:49
4 And I asked the angel of peace who went with me: 40:8
"For whom are they preparing these chains?" Ezek 7:23
5 And he answered and said to me: "They are preparing these for Nah 3:10; Dan 4:23
the kings and powerful of this earth, that they Ps 2:2; 149:7-8; Isa 14:9
may thereby be destroyed.
6 And after this, the Righteous and Chosen One[1088] will cause 39:6; 1Jn 2:1; Acts 3:14; OdesSol 42:2
the house of his congregation to appear; from then on, 38:1; 46:8; 62:8; Rev 19:11-15

1081 "Will not become full" "If the language of verse 1 points to the realm of the dead, the point is that the underworld can never be filled" (H2 pg. 132). Black has a superior interpretation, "The idea would seem to be that no amount of tribute or offerings would be sufficient to 'buy off' the Elect One" (BL pg. 217).

1082 "A number of commentators identify this valley with the Valley of Jehoshaphat" (NV2 pg. 195). See (Joel 3:2, 12) where the nations are gathered to the Valley of Jehosaphat, which is the Kidron Valley next to Jerusalem.

1083 For 52ab Knibb has: "And their hands commit evil, and everything at which the righteous toil, the sinners evilly devour." Olson offers: "Apparently, the overall meaning is that the wicked offer no tribute to God as others do (v1), but selfishly consume everything they produce—all of which is evil anyway" (OL pg. 98).

1084 Isaac has a quite different rendering of the difficult text of 53:2: "They shall fulfill the criminal deeds of their hands and eat all the produce of crime which the sinners toil for. Sinners shall be destroyed from before the face of the Lord of the Spirits—they shall perish eternally, standing before the face of his earth." Nickelsburg has: "Their hands commit lawless deeds, and everything that (the righteous) labor over, the sinners lawlessly devour. And from the presence of the Lord of Spirits the sinners will perish, and from the face of this earth they will be taken, and they will perish forever and ever." "Depending on whether one reads the verb 'perish,' with its one letter negative adverbial prefix (*'i*) or without it as two MSS. do, the last line of the verse refers either to the sinners' being eternally punished (and thus not perishing) or to their annihilation" (NV2 pg. 196). Compare the *Charter of a Jewish Sectarian Association*: "The judgement of all who walk in such ways will be multiple afflictions at the hand of all the angels of perdition, everlasting damnation in the wrath of God's furious vengeance, never-ending terror and reproach for all eternity, with a shameful extinction in the fire of hell's outer darkness. For all their eras, generation by generation, they will know doleful sorrow, bitter evil, and dark happenstance, until their utter destruction with neither remnant nor rescue" (1QS 4.12-14 (W pg. 121)).

1085 "Angels of punishment" are found in the Parables (41:2; 56:1; 62:11; 63:1; 66:1); in the Bible (Ps 78:49 LXX); in the Dead Sea Scrolls (1QS 4.12 (W pg. 121); CD 2.6 (W pg. 53)); and horrifyingly in the *Pseudepigrapha* (TAb A 12:1-2 (OTP1 pg. 889); ApZeph 4:1-7 (OTP1 pg. 511) and (ApPet 20). These appear to be a special class of sadistic angels in league with Satan who dwell in places of punishment and gather sinners to those places (cf. DialTrypho 105). Then they mercilessly delight in the punishment of those entrusted to them. At times they serve outside the place of the dead. These angels of punishment are the "locusts" of (Rev 9:1-11), who are released from the bottomless pit to torment mankind on the face of the earth. Please compare the description in (Rev 9:7) with (ApZeph 4:1-7). You, at all costs, want to avoid an encounter with these beings!

1086 "The reference is doubtless to the 'instruments, iron chains' referred to in 54:3. The kings and the mighty are to be shackled—appropriate punishment for those who in their lifetime put many into chains. Ironically, albeit appropriately, the material from which they fashioned their weaponry (52:8) will be the material of the chains in which they will be punished" (NV2 pg. 196).

1087 Satan is here seen as an agent of punishment. For a similar thought see (1Cor 5:5; 2Cor 12:7 and 1QapGen 20.16 (W pg. 101)).

1088 "Righteous One" here equated with the "Chosen One" is also used in (38:2; 92:3; Isa 53:11; Acts 3:14; 7:52; 22:14 and OdesSol 42:2).

they will not be hindered in the 62:8
Name of the Lord of Spirits.[1089] [1090]
7 And these mountains in the presence of his righteousness,[1091] 52:6; Ps 97:5
shall become level ground and the hills shall become like a Rev 16:20; Zech 4:7; Isa 30 25
fountain of water,[1092] 48:1; 49:1; Rev 21:6; Ezek 47:1-6
and the righteous shall have rest from the oppression of sinners." Dan 7:22

54 1 Turning and looking at another part of the earth, I saw
there a deep valley[1093] burning with fire. 10:12-13; 18:11; 21:7; 56:3-4
2 And they brought the kings and the powerful, 38:5; Isa 14:9; 24:21-22; 30:33
and hurled them into that deep valley.[1094]

The Deep Valley—The Hosts of Azazel

3 I saw there with my own eyes, how their shackles were being 56:1; Rev 20:1-3
fashioned; iron chains[1095] of immeasurable weight. 53:3; Jude 1:6; 2Pet 2:4; 1Chr 22:3, 14
4 I asked the angel of peace who went with me, saying: 40:8
"These chains—for whom are these being prepared?" 2Bar 56:13
5 And he said to me: "Those are being prepared for the hosts TLev 18:12; Mt 25:41
of Azazel,[1096] so that they may seize them and cast them into 8:1-10:8; 10:12; Isa 24:21
the lowest part of hell,[1097] and with jagged rocks they will 10:5; 2Pet 2:4
cover their jaws, as the Lord of Spirits commanded. DialTrypho 141
6 Then Michael, and Raphael, and Gabriel, and Phanuel—will 9:1; 20; 40:9
take hold of them on that great day, and hurl them on that day 10:4, 11-13; Rev 19:20; Jude 6
into the burning furnace, that the Lord of Spirits may exact Rev 20:1-3, 10; Mt 13:42; Isa 31:9
vengeance on them for their unrighteousness in becoming 65:6; *Haer.* 1.15.6; 2En 18:3; *Apol.* 22

[1089] The congregation of the righteous, will no longer face persecution, when they appear with the Chosen One.
[1090] 53:7 picks up where 52:9 left off.
[1091] For this line Isaac has: "And these mountains shall become (flat) like earth in the presence of his righteousness." Nickelsburg has: "And these mountains will be in the presence of his righteousness as <wax>" This passage strengthens the case that these mountains symbolize earthly kingdoms as in 52:2. Charles states "These mountains and the hills are symbols of the world powers as personated in the kings and the mighty" (C pg. 105).
[1092] The earthly kingdoms (mountains) will be replaced, and the fountain of God's wisdom (48:1; Rev 21:6) will reign supreme. An actual earthquake in Antioch (AD 115) involving Emperor Trajan, caused faces of mountains to collapse and new springs to form (*Cassius Dio* 68.25.6).
[1093] This is the Hinnom valley (Gehenna) lying to the south of Jerusalem (C pg. 105).
[1094] Nickelsburg has a note under 54:2, "(This) line has been displaced. 'The kings and mighty belong in the previous valley (53:5), not in this one, which is designated for the fallen angels (54:5)" (N pg. 68). However, (Mt 25:41) indicates that sinners and fallen angels will inhabit the same fire "Then he will say to those on his left, 'Depart from me, you cursed, into the eternal fire prepared for the devil and his angels.'"
[1095] **Due to the great power of angels, extraordinary restraints are required. The chains mentioned here find a place in the New Testament (Jude 6; and 2Pet 2:4). Only in the *Parables*, are chains mentioned in restraining rebellious angels. This establishes that Jude and Peter both knew and accepted the Parables as authoritative! That Christ knew the Parables of Enoch is therefore a certainty.** Chains binding angels are also mentioned in 2Bar 56:13 (AD 110-120).
[1096] Isaac has: "armies," and Olson has: "legions," in place of "hosts." Other scholars go with "hosts".
[1097] In place of "lowest part of hell," Nickelsburg has: "the abyss of complete judgement" Isaac has: "abyss of complete condemnation." (Cf. 1En 10:5, 12).

servants of Satan[1098] [1099] and leading astray those who dwell 40:7; 67:7; 69:3-12; Rev 12:9; 13:14
on the earth." TDan 5:6; Jub 10:11; AThm 32

The Flood

7 In those days, the punishment of the Lord of Spirits,
shall go forth, and all the chambers of waters which are above
the heavens, and all the fountains of waters which are beneath 2Pet 3:5-7
the earth will be opened.[1100] Gen 1:6-7; 7:11; 8:2
8 All the waters shall be joined with waters: that which is above 60:21-22
the heavens is the masculine, and the water which is beneath

[1098] **This verse is critical in understanding the nature of the evil powers. It indicates that Satan and his league of evil ones preexisted the fall of the watchers and recruited the watchers for evil purposes. He will be cast from heaven down to earth (Rev 12:7-12). Then he will be imprisoned and released before his final judgement (Rev 20:1-10). "This line is important, for it associates the sin of the Watchers with 'becoming subject to Satan,' something the earlier chapters of 1 Enoch that describe the Watchers rebellion do not do" (H2 pg. 138). Interestingly, this same line of thought is picked up by Irenaeus as he quotes a poem thought to be written by his predecessor, Saint Pothinus (AD 87-177). "Which Satan, thy true father, enables thee still to accomplish, by means of Azazel, that fallen and yet mighty angel" (*Against Heresies* 1.15.6) (cf. Jub 10:8-11). Lactantius (ca. AD 240-320) has the same view.**

> **When, therefore, the number of men had begun to increase, God in His forethought, lest the devil, to whom from the beginning He had given power over the earth, should by his subtlety either corrupt or destroy men, as he had done at first, sent angels for the protection and improvement of the human race; and inasmuch as He had given these a free will, He enjoined them above all things not to defile themselves with contamination from the earth, and thus lose the dignity of their heavenly nature. He plainly prohibited them from doing that which He knew that they would do, that they might entertain no hope of pardon. Therefore, while they abode among men, that most deceitful ruler of the earth, by his very association, gradually enticed them to vices, and polluted them by intercourse with women. Then, not being admitted into heaven on account of the sins into which they had plunged themselves, they fell to the earth. Thus, from angels the devil makes them to become his satellites and attendants. (*Divine Institutes* 2.15 (AD 305))**

The rebellion of Satan and his followers thus preexists and is separate from that of the Watchers (1En 6). Five satans are named in (1En 69:3-12). All that being said, this line could also be taken as equating Asael/Azazel with Satan (H2 pg. 139; N2 pg. 203). Given the association of Azazel with the goat, and the use of the goat head in the half human, half goat, half male, half female, Sigil of Baphomet (the official insignia of the Church of Satan (since 1966)); it would appear that Satanists are equating the two. The goat head is also used in the 1856 *Baphomet* "Sabbatic Goat" image and in the ancient pagan Krampus figure.

[1099] The link between (1En 54:6 and TDan 5:6) is somewhat baffling and deserves further exploration. The most likely explanations are that the TDan passage is an early second century AD interpolation from this text in the Parables, or possibly (2 Enoch J 18:3) into the Testament of Dan. There could also be a common tradition from a lost book of Enoch, which would be very interesting! (TDan 5:6) reads: "For I read in the Book of Enoch the Righteous that your prince is Satan and that all the spirits of sexual promiscuity and of arrogance devote attention to the sons of Levi in the attempt to observe them closely and cause them to commit sin before the Lord."

[1100] **"Although various elements and phrases in 54:7-55:2 have counterparts in Genesis 6-9, the common terminology that runs through 54:7-55:2 sets it apart as a piece of tradition in its own right"** (NV2 pg. 203).

the earth is the feminine.[1101] [1102]
9 All who dwell on earth, and those who dwell under the Gen 6:17; 7:21-23; Jub 7:25
ends of heaven shall be obliterated. 4Q370 1.6
10 For this reason, they will be destroyed: because they have
not acknowledged the iniquity which they have done
upon the earth.[1103]

55 1 After that the Antecedent of Time repented and said: 46:1-2; Dan 7:9, 13
"In vain have I destroyed all those who dwell on the earth."[1104] 10:22; Gen 8:21-22; Jer 2:30
2 He swore by his great Name: "From now on I shall not act
in this way toward all who dwell on the earth. I will place a sign
in the heavens; and it will be a pledge of faithfulness between Gen 9:8-17
me and them forever, so long as the heavens are above the earth. Deut 11:21
This is in accordance with my command."[1105]
3 "When I wish to take hold of them by the agency of the Rev 20:2
angels,[1106] on the day of tribulation and pain, in the face of my Mt 13:39-43; 16:27
anger and wrath, I will make my anger and wrath dwell upon 60:25; 62:12; 84:4; Jn 3:36
them," says the Lord of Spirits.[1107]
4 You mighty kings who occupy the earth! You are destined 62:1; 38:4-5
to behold my Chosen One, as he sits on the throne of glory 61:8; 69:29; Mt:19:28; 25:31

[1101] The male waters above and female below may be referencing the union of the watchers and women. Male waters above and female beneath was a common idea in rabbinic writings starting in the 4th century AD (OL pg. 100) (Cf. *Jerusalem Talmud Berakoth* 9:2:24; *Genesis Rabbah* 13:13; *Pirqe Rabbi Eliezer* 23:7).

[1102] Many commentators, but not all, view (1En 54:7-55:2) as an intrusive interpolation as it seems out of context. Charles listed seven reasons he believed it to be an interpolation. He went on to state: "The object of the interpolator is clear. Although the final world judgement is treated at length, there are only the briefest references to the first. It was to supply this defect in the Parables that an existing Apocalypse of Noah was laid under contribution" (C 106-107). Nickelsburg opines: "With the verses removed, the two parts of the remaining text (54:1-6; 55:3—56:4) present a continuous narrative with common elements, as well as a pair of parallel vision accounts" (NV2 pg. 200). In contrast Black notes "The view that 54:7-55:2 (Charles, Martin) is an 'interpolated' Noah apocalypse overlooks the evident dependence, here as elsewhere, of the parables, the 'Second Vision', on the older 'first vision,' in this passage the destruction of the watchers corresponds to the account at (1En 8:1-9:11) of the condemnation of the watchers, followed at 10:2 by an account of the deluge. The *Parables* follow the same pattern" (BL pg. 219).

[1103] For 54:10 Isaac has: "On account of the fact that they did not recognize their oppressive deeds which they carried out on the earth, they shall be destroyed by (the flood)." Nickelsburg has: "And when they have recognized their iniquities that they have done on the earth, then by these they will be destroyed."

[1104] Unlike Genesis 6:6-7 where God regrets creating man, here He regrets destroying man. Perhaps this is because the destruction has gone further than desired. This reminds one of the *Epic of Gilgamesh* (Book 5) where Ea rebukes Enlil for the destruction caused by the flood. "The expression 'in vain' may reflect the motif in Gen 8:21; human beings are evil from their youth, and this would inevitably lead to an endless series of floods" (NV2 pg. 204-205).

[1105] 55:2 ends the interpolation begun in 54:7. 55:3 picks up the theme of judgement from 54:5-6.

[1106] The first five words of 55:3 are confused and corrupt (BL pg. 220). Black proposes: "And this is my command [with regard to the host of Azazel] when I am pleased to seize them by the hand of the angels."

[1107] For 55:3 Isaac has: "'When I would give consent so that they should be seized by the hands of the angels on the day of tribulation and pain, already I would have caused my punishment and my wrath to abide upon them—my punishment and my wrath,' says the Lord of the Spirits." Nickelsburg has: "When I have desired to take hold of them by the hand of the angels, on the day of tribulation and distress in the face of my punishment and wrath, I will make my punishment and wrath dwell upon them,'" The idea is that the four angels named in 54:6 will take hold of the associates and army of Azazel, chain them and bring them to justice.

and judges Azazel,[1108] and all his associates, and all his hosts — 1Pet 3:22; Rev 20:12; Lev 16:8-10, 26
in the Name of the Lord of Spirits!

The Deep Valley—Punishment of the Children of the Host of Azazel

56 1 And I saw there, legions[1109] of angels of punishment, [1110] — 53:3; 54:1-6; ApPet 20
on the move, carrying scourges and chains[1111] — 8:1; 69:28; TAb A 12:1
of iron and bronze.[1112] — Dan 4:15
2 I asked the angel of peace who was walking with me: "To — 40:8
whom are these going, who carry the scourges?"
3 And he answered: "To their elect and beloved ones,[1113] — 14:6; Mt 13:38-42
that they may be cast into the chasm of the abyss of the valley. — Lk 8:28-31; Mt 25:41; Isa 24:22
4 That valley will be filled with their elect and beloved ones, — 10:12, 15; 53:1; 54:1
the epoch of their lives and the era of their glory[1114] will be at — 16:1; Mt 8:29
an end, and the days of their leading astray, will be counted no — 19:1; 69:27; Ps 82:6-7
more."[1115] — 58:3

Invasion by Parthians and Medes/Kings of the East

5 In those days, the angels will assemble,[1116 1117] — Dan 10:20-21
and they will rush eastward upon the Parthians and the Medes.[1118] — Isa 13:17; Acts 2:9; Rev 16:12

[1108] Azazel here is the leader of the 200 fallen spiritual beings if not the supreme evil one. The human kings will watch the enthronement of the Chosen One and His judgment of the fallen watchers. The mighty kings will watch the judgement of Azazel, realizing that they share the same fate. This is the same order of judgement as in (Rev 20:10-12). This mirrors the Azazel goat ritual (Lev 16:8-26), the focal point of the day of atonement, Yom Kippur.

[1109] Isaac has: "army" in place of "legion," others translate: "host."

[1110] "Angels of punishment" See note on 1En 53:3.

[1111] Isaac translates "chains" as "nets." Olson uses "scourges and shackles"; Charles "scourges and chains" and Knibb uses only "chains" since some manuscripts omit the word translated here as "scourges." Nickelsburg notes "'Chains' seems more appropriate for the metals mentioned here" (NV2 pg. 199).

[1112] Later Jewish magical and exorcism texts used iron and bronze chains to bind demons. In a 4th century magical text (the) "angels of disquiet" are bound using "chains of iron" and a "bronze yoke" (Morgan, M. 1983. *Sepher Ha-Razim: The Book of the Mysteries* {Chico: scholars Press, 1983} pg. 49). Chains did not prove effective with the Gerasene demoniac (Mk 5:4; Lk 8:29).

[1113] These are the demon offspring of the watchers and human women from I Enoch 7:2. Other references to them in the Parables are in 39:1 and 69:4-5.

[1114] Some manuscripts omit "and the era of their glory."

[1115] The demons in (Mt 8:29 and Lk 8:28-31) fear the fate described here.

[1116] Some manuscripts have "will return," in place of "will assemble". Heiser advocates that: "will assemble themselves" is better than "shall return" (H2 pg. 145). The angels of God are a celestial army operating behind human events.

[1117] **56:5-57:3a is rightly considered an interpolation into the text** (R pg. 58 Knibb and 502 Sacchi). It concerns an invasion by the Parthians and Medes (i.e. the kings of the east).

[1118] The Parthian kingdom (modern day Iran) existed from 247 BC to AD 224. The Parthians and the Romans were enemies for centuries from 66 BC to AD 217. That the Parthians are mentioned first, as in (Acts 2:9), but unlike (Dan 6:8), indicates this passage was written after the Parthians began to dominate the kingdom. This reference to the Parthian invasion may indicate a date for this interpolation into the Parables as soon after their invasion of Judea in 40-37 BC (*Ant* 14.13.3-10). Some see in 1En 56:5-7 a prediction of a future invasion from the east, or others a

They will stir up the kings so that a spirit of unrest,[1119] 99:4; Jer 51:1, 11; SibOr 5:93-110
shall come upon them. They will shake them off their thrones. 46:4-5; Isa 14:9; Rev 20:8
They will break forth as lions from their lairs,
and as famished wolves[1120] in the midst of their flocks.[1121]
6 Up they will arise, and trample underfoot the land of my Rev 11:2; Ezek 38:16
chosen ones. And the land of my chosen ones shall be before Mt 22:14
them a threshing floor, and a thoroughfare. Mic 4:12; Jer 51:33; Isa 21:10
7 But the city of my righteous ones will prove an obstacle Zech 12:2-4; 1Sam 14:20
to their horses[1122] and they will begin to fight among themselves. 10:9; Ezek 38:21; Hag 2:22; Judg 7:22
Their own right hand will prevail against themselves.[1123] Zech 14:13; Isa 19:2; Jer 13:14

---

recollection from Israel's past. Nickelsburg sums up as follows "All this having been said, one should exercise caution in employing these verses in the construction of an argument for the dating of the Parables. They may be consonant with a date after 40 BC and may even provide support for such a date, but they are not a firm foundation on which to *base* such an argument" (NV2 pg. 210). Others make a case that this verse, and other textual evidence, argue for a composition of *The Book of Parables* in its original form no later than 50 BC (Bampfylde, G., *The Similitudes of Enoch, Historical Allusions*, JSJ 15 {1984] pgs. 9-31). In this scenario, the threat of the formidable Parthian calvary would be checked by walled cities like Jerusalem (1En 56:7) Parthian calvary, bows, and superior armor were all factors in the disastrous defeat of the ambitious Roman procurator Crassus at Carrhae in 54-53 BC. **These Parthians and Medes, the ravagers of Judea from the east, and longtime enemies of Rome, are reused as end time enemies (kings from the east) of the region in (Rev 16:12). "The sixth angel poured out his bowl on the great river Euphrates, and its water was dried up, to prepare the way for the kings from the east." The Euphrates was generally seen as the limit of Roman control, with the Parthians and Medes controlling the area to the east of it. The constant tensions and often war between Rome and the Parthians from 54 BC until AD 217 undoubtedly serve as the backdrop of (Rev 16:12).**

[1119] **The idea is that of the angels violently shaking the kings and driving them to the battlefield. The belief is that spiritual forces lie behind human events; even with celestial beings accompanying military armies** (cf. Josh 5:13-15; Dan 10:20-21; TLev 3:3-5).

[1120] Isaac, of course, has: "hyenas."

[1121] Olson's translation, postulating a simple translation error, reads: "famished wolves from their dens."

[1122] This invasion by the Parthians and Medes is spoken of in future tense as if it were prophesying the Parthian invasion of 40 BCE where the Parthians sacked a portion of Jerusalem and all of Judea. "The elect are the Jews/Judeans, or occupants of Jerusalem" (H2 pg. 147). The account by Josephus of the Parthian invasion of 40 BC is somewhat different from how it is described here, but not fatally so. The city of Jerusalem was a hinderance to the Parthian calvary, but it was at least partially taken by them through treachery (*War* 1.13.2-9 §§250-270; *Ant* 14.13.3-4 §§335-39). Black notes: "Even though Parthian troops did penetrate to Herod's Palace and the Temple area; it is unlikely that they did so with a body of calvary. Jerusalem probably did prove a very real obstacle to their horses" (BL pg. 222). Josephus leaves no account of internecine war among the troops. However, with the greed of the notoriously treacherous Parthian troops seizing spoils, internecine war among them would not have been out of the question, especially with a blended army (*War* 1.13.9 §§ 268). In addition, the Jews were at civil war among themselves, some siding with the party of Antigonus, others with Hyrcanus II and some with Herod. If 56:7 is taken as applying to Jewish forces; then it is unquestionably included in the account by Josephus. All things considered, this text lines up well with that of Josephus. The account of the *Parables* was written much closer to the event; easily within the living memory of those involved. Whereas Josephus wrote over 110 years later; and only tangentially recounts the Parthian military actions and pillaging in Jerusalem. That the walls of Jerusalem are still standing, establishes a date of writing for the *Parables* prior to AD 70 when they were demolished. The author may see a parallel of the Parthian invasion with the invasion by Gog of the land of Magog and his armies as in Ezekiel 38.

[1123] Black postulates that this difficult line may have read literally "their faithfulness is not firm among themselves" or "they fail to keep faith with one another" which would match the meaning of the next line (BL pg. 222-223). No subsequent translator has picked up his rendering.

A man will not recognize his brother, nor a son, 100:1-3; SibOr 8:84
his father[1124] or mother,[1125] [1126] till there is
a (significant) number of corpses from among them,[1127] Nah 3:3
Their punishment will not be in vain!
8 In those days Sheol shall open its jaws,[1128] Num 16:32-33; Ex 15:12
and they will be engulfed therein; 22; 90:18; Isa 5:14; 14:9; Hab 2:5
and their destruction will be at an end.[1129]
Sheol will devour the sinners in the presence of the chosen ones. Prov 1:12; Jude 11

Legions from the Northwest

57 1 After that I saw another legion; chariots,[1130] loaded with Isa 60:3-4; 66:20-21
people,[1131] and they came upon the winds[1132] from the east, GbRev 67

[1124] Isaac omits "father." The other translations keep it.

[1125] For this line K has "and a man will not admit to knowing his neighbor or his brother," N has "a man will not acknowledge his brother." Eshel sees in 56:7: "an allusion to Matthias Antigonus, who bit off the ear(s) of his uncle Hyrcanus to prevent him from serving as high priest" (R pg. 509 referencing Eshel, *An allusion in the Parables of Enoch to the Acts of Matthias Antigonus in 40 B.C.E.?*).

[1126] It is unlikely that mothers would be on the battlefield. Heiser opines: "**It seems more coherent to go in a different direction, that the author has the angels tasked with judging the Parthians and the Medes adopt the tactic of having their armies turn against each other. The 'familial' language would then be metaphorical and speak of blended people groups now undermining themselves**" (H2 pg. 147). However, if this passage is speaking of the civil war and division among the Jews themselves, this language would be appropriate (See note on 56:7).

[1127] Nickelsburg has: "Until the number of corpses will be enough due to their slaughter."

[1128] N, K and I have "mouth" in place of "jaws."

[1129] For these lines Isaac has: "and they shall be swallowed up into it and perish."

[1130] Some translate "wagons" in place of "chariots" here and in 57:2. Assuming the Greek word behind the Ethiopian word (šaragallā) translated chariot is ἅμαξα, it can also mean cart or wagon.

[1131] Nickelsburg, who favors the third option, lists three possible interpretations of chapter 57 "(1) a majority of commentators see here a description of the return of the Israelite dispersion. (2) A few others understand it to refer to the arrival of another hostile army. (3) This may reflect prophetic predictions that the gentiles will flow to Jerusalem to pay tribute to the God of Israel" (NV2 pg. 213). A parallel text to the third option is found in (Isa 66:20). Another option may be derived from the recently discovered unprovenanced stone tablet "Gabriel's Revelation." This tablet is dated to the late 1st century BC to early 1st century AD, so the same time as the Parables of Enoch. Line 67 of the tablet reads "This is their chariot, that of the great ones[○of heaven.]." Adding to this are lines 26-29: "The God of the chariots will listen to the cry of Jerusalem and the cities of Judah and bring consolation for the sake of the hos[t]s of [the] angel Michael, and for the sake of those who have loved and asked him." This would indicate that the chariots represent a celestial army of "great ones" coming to the relief of Jerusalem (Rev 19:14) or glorified Chosen ones coming to inhabit a restored Jerusalem (see line 58). That they are coming from the East, where God's paradise, is located, and the chosen dwell, adds to this probability. John Ben Daniel postulates an alternative explanation based on three phases of the Jewish Civil War. "The author appears to have modelled his prophecy of the eschatological war between good and evil on these developments in the Civil War (40-37 BCE), in a way that suggests that he had personally witnessed them and they were still fresh in his memory. This establishes the date of the Book of Parables to the generation immediately following the Civil War, i.e., from 35 to 20 BCE. If another period of dire suffering and social inequality was the impetus for writing, one would have to look no further than the regional drought and famine of 25/24 BCE (Josephus, Antiquities 15.299-326). So far as the dating of the Parables is concerned, then, we arrive at a period from 35 to 4 BCE, which is to say, sometime during the reign of King Herod the Great" (Daniel, John Ben, 2021. *The Parables of Enoch (1Enoch 37-71): Provenance and Social Setting*).

[1132] This could potentially translate "like the winds" indicating speed.

and from the west toward the south.[1133] Ps 107:3; Isa 43:5-6
2 The noise of the rumbling of their chariots was heard, Jer 47:3; GbRev 26-28
and when this commotion took place, the holy ones
from heaven observed it, and the pillars of the earth were shaken Hag 2:6-7; Isa 13:13; 24:19-20
from their bases. It was heard from one end of the heaven to the Deut 30:4; Neh 1:9; Ps 75:3
other in one moment.[1134]
3 All will fall down and worship the Lord of Spirits.[1135] 62:9; 63:1; 90:30, 37; Isa 27:13
This is the end of the second parable.

The Third Parable

Blessing of the Righteous

58 1 I began to speak the third parable concerning the righteous
and the elect.
2 Blessed are you, righteous and elect ones, 2Tim 2:10; OdesSol 8:18; 23:2-3
for your inheritance is glorious. 48:7; Col 3:4
3 The righteous shall be in the light of the sun, 45:4-5; 50:1; Jn 1:4
and the chosen in the light of everlasting life: PssSol 3:11-12; Jn 8:12; Job 33:30; Ps 56:13
the days of their life will have no end, Dan 12:3: Jn 3:15-16
and the days of the holy will be innumerable.
4 They will seek the light and find righteousness with the 38:2, 4; Mt 5:6; 6:33; Jn 3:20-21; 12:35
Lord of Spirits.
There shall be peace for the righteous in the Name of the Mt 5:9; 4Q440 3.16; OdesSol 9:6
Eternal Lord![1136]
5 After this it shall be said to the holy ones,[1137] Eph 3:3-5; 9-10
that they should seek the mysteries of righteousness 39:6; 61:4; 11; Col 3:1-4; Mt 6:33
the inheritance of faith,[1138]
for it has become bright as the sun upon the earth, 102:7-8; Isa 60:1-3; Mal 4:2
and darkness has passed away. 4Q541 9.1.3-5; Jn 1:5; 1Jn 2:8

[1133] I, BL and OL have: "and from the west until noonday." K, C and N are the same as this text. From the east and the west may be "polar" expressions intended to convey the meaning "from the whole inhabited world" (BL Pgs. 223-224).

[1134] The manuscripts read differently. Knibb is typical of another reading having: "from the ends of the earth to the ends of heaven throughout one day."

[1135] Nickelsburg has "and they all fell down and worshiped the Lord of Spirits." The prostration and worship in v. 2f must refer to those who come riding on their chariots, but it could also include the holy ones who have been witnessing these events" (NV2 pg. 216).

[1136] For this line K has "Peace be to the righteous with the Lord of the world!"

[1137] Isaac translates "holy ones in heaven." Nickelsburg omits: "in heaven" positing that it has been misplaced into the text. This removes the ambiguity, making the subjects of the text the holy ones on earth. This would refer to humans who are to seek out the secrets of righteousness. These secrets, as Paul said, are ultimately found in Christ (cf. Col 3:1-4).

[1138] Isaac has: "the gift of faith." Nickelsburg has: "the lot of faith." This is a rare mention of faith in the *Parables*, for others see: (39:6; 43:2; 46:8; 58:5; and 61:4, 11). The wisdom of knowing that God will deliver the righteous from those who oppress them leads to faith as the righteous patiently await deliverance.

6 There shall be light inexhaustible,[1139] Rev 21:23-25; 22:5
and they will find that their days are without number.
For the former darkness shall have been destroyed, Rom 13:12; 1Jn 2:8; OdesSol 11:19
and light will endure before the Lord of Spirits.[1140] OdesSol 18:6; 21:3
The light of truth will endure forever before the Lord of Spirits.[1141] 5:6-7; 4Ezra 2:35

Secrets of Lightning and Thunder

59 1 In those days, I saw with my own eyes the secrets [1142] 41:3; 43:1-44:1
of the lightning flashes, and the luminaries,[1143] and their laws.[1144] 17:3; Job 36:30-33
They flash for blessing or a curse as the Lord of Spirits wills.[1145] 41:8
2 There I saw the secrets of the thunder. When it crashes in the 60:13-15
heights of heaven, the sound of it is heard among the dwelling Job 36:29-37:5, 13
places of earth. I was shown the sound of the thunder, Jn 12:29
for peace and blessing or for a curse, according
to the command of the Lord of Spirits.[1146] [1147] Sir 43:13,17
3 After that, all the secrets of the luminaries and lightnings
were shown to me, and they gleam for blessing and Job 38:24-27
contentment.[1148]

Mysteries of the Wind and Weather

60 11 And the other angel who went with me and revealed to
me what is hidden, showed me what is first and last, in heaven Mt 19:30; Mk 10:31; Lk 13:30

[1139] Knibb has: "ceaseless light" Isaac has: "light that has no end." OL translates: "And there will be boundless light."

[1140] For these two lines Isaac has: "For already darkness has been destroyed, light shall be permanent before the Lord of the Spirits," This imagery is widespread 2En 30:15; TAb 7; 1QS 3:13-4:26; 3Bar 6:13; Did 1:1; Barn. 18:1-20:2.

[1141] Nickelsburg views the last line of 58:6 to be a later addition to the text (NV2 pg. 220).

[1142] "Chapters 59-60 contain several literary disjunctions that indicate a displacement or an interpolation in the texts, or both" (NV2 pg. 221). This textual problem has been recognized since the earliest English translators. Nickelsburg attempts to resolve it by moving 60:11-23 to after 59:1-3 and then placing 60:1-10 and 60:24-25 together. This text follows this arrangement. He recognizes 60:7-10 and 24a as an interpolation.

[1143] "Luminaries" = sun, moon and stars.

[1144] "Their laws" or judgements; Knibb has: "and the regulations governing them."

[1145] Nickelsburg observes that: **"Common to all these texts is the notion that the cosmos operates according to a divinely established and regulated order**—thus, 'as the word of Spirits wills' (59:1b) and 'according to the word of the Lord of Spirits' (59:2e)" (NV2 pg. 226).

[1146] Nickelsburg notes: "These three lines are corrupt and commentators dispute how to resolve the problem." For these three lines he has "And there I saw the secrets of the thunder, †and (how) when it crashes in the heights of heaven, its sound is heard <in> the dwelling places of the earth, he showed me the sound of the thunder for peace and blessing, or for a curse†"

[1147] Black suggests that 1 Enoch 59 draws on (Job 36:30-37:5, 13; and 38:24-27) (BL pg. 224).

[1148] Nickelsburg inserts verses 60:11-23 here after 59:3 which seems to be a better fit, so it has been adopted in this text. He suspects the originality of 59:3. Regarding this juxtaposition of verses he comments: "Two factors support moving 60:11-23 to a position before 60:1-10. (1) The reference to the *two monsters* in v 24 presumes vv 7-10 immediately before vv 24-25. (2) Moving vv 11-23 forward before 60:1 juxtaposes material about the lightnings and thunders with the other cosmological material." (N pg. 72).

and in the heights, and beneath the earth in the depths,[1149] and
at the ends of heaven and in the foundations[1150] of the heavens, 2Sam 22:8; Ps 18:7
and in the storehouses of the winds; Jer 10:13; 11QPs^{a} 8
12 and how the winds[1151] are distributed, and weighed and 41:3-4; 61:8; Job 28:25
how the gates[1152] of the winds are numbered,[1153] according Jer 51:16; Ps 135:7; 11Q6 26.14-15
to the strength of its wind; and the intensity of the phases
of the moon, according to the power that is fitting;[1154]
and the division of the stars according to their names, 43:1-2
and how all the divisions are made.
13 And thunders according to where the sound falls, 17:3; 59:2
and all the divisions that are made in the lightning that it
may flash, and its legions may obey at once.
14 For the thunder has fixed pauses[1155] assigned to it while Job 28:26; 36:30-37:1-5
its peal awaits. The thunder and lightning are inseparable. Ps 81:7
Although they are not one, by the wind the two of them go
and are not separated.
15 For when the lightning flashes, the thunder utters its voice, Rev 10:3-4
the wind immediately enforces an appropriate pause,
dividing evenly between them. For the storehouse controlling 1QH$_{a}$ 9.14-15
their moments of occurrence is like the shore;[1156] each of them
at its proper time is held in with a bridle and turned back by
the power of the wind and driven forward according to the
many regions of the earth.
16 The wind of the sea is masculine and strong, and by virtue Sir 39:28-29
of its strength this wind draws back the sea with a rein; PrMan 3; Ps 104:7-10; Rev 16:5
and thus, it is driven and scattered into all the
boundaries of the land.[1157]
17 The wind of the hoarfrost is an angel unto itself, 76:6-13; Jub 2:2; Job 37:10

[1149] Nickelsburg has: "abyss" in place of "depths."

[1150] Isaac has: "extent" in place of "foundations."

[1151] K has: "spirits" in place of "winds" in all occurrences in chapter 60. Black suggests that "wind-spirit" be used in order to obtain the correct meaning (BL pg. 228).

[1152] N and K have: "springs" in place of "gates." OL has: "gates." In Ethiopic it is literally "fountains" but the word for "gates" is similar looking and fits the context, so it has been adopted by some translators.

[1153] I has: "weighed" in place of "numbered." N has: "{divided} and numbered."

[1154] K has: "power of *their* spirit;" in place of "power that is fitting;" N has: "according to the power of righteousness."

[1155] The thunder and lightning are under the command and control of God.

[1156] The use of "shore" here which is usually translated "sand" is based on Olson's reading, which assumes that the Greek word behind the text is *ammos* (ἄμμος), which in the New Testament, is almost always referring to sand at the seashore (cf. Heb 11:12; Rev 20:8). In ancient writing, the sandy shore was seen as a boundary which God fixed for the sea to restrain it. "The sand on the shore checks the movement of a body of water…, as the use of a rein checks the movement of a horse and allows it to move on" (NV2 pg. 230).

[1157] Charles has "all the mountains of the earth" in place of "all the boundaries of the land" In explanation he offers: "The flow of the sea is connected (with) its subterranean advance into the mountains to nourish the springs" (C pg. 117-118).

but the wind of the hail is a good angel.[1158] Ex 9:18-25
18 The wind of the snow, because of its power, never fails; Job 38:22; Jer 18:14
so that there is within the snow a unique wind that ascends
from it like smoke, known as frost.
19 The wind of the mist does not share lodgings with these
others in their storehouses, but it has a special storehouse;
because its path has the Glory in it, both in light and in darkness, Ex 19:9, 16, 19; 20:21; 1Kgs 8:10-11
in winter and in summer;[1159] and in its storehouse is an angel.[1160] 1QH^a 9.13-14
20 The wind of the dew has its dwelling at the ends of the 34:1-2; 36:1; 75:5; 100:11-13
heaven, and is connected with the storehouses of the rain, 54:8
and its course is in winter and summer. Dew clouds and storm
clouds are associated, and one supplies the other.
21 When the wind of the rain is to move out from its store Job 37:11-13
chamber, the angels come and open the chamber and lead it out.
When it is scattered over all the dry land,
it unites with all the waters on the land. 2:3
(If these waters always united with those of earth, 54:8
there would be ample water for the inhabitants of the earth.)[1161]
22 For these waters are nourishment for the ground 42:3; Job 38:25-27, 33-38
from the Most High who is in heaven. 41:3
Therefore, on this account, there is a measure for the rain Job 28:25-26; 37:11-13; Deut 28:12
and the angels are given charge of it.[1162] 61:1-5; 66:2
23 And all these things I saw toward the
garden of the righteous.[1163] 32:3; 61:12; 77:3

Shaking of the Heavens

60 1 In the year five hundred,[1164] in the seventh month, on the Gen 5:32; Lev 23:34; 4Q252 1.1.1-2.4

[1158] For 60:17 Isaac has: "The frost-wind is its own guardian and the hail-wind is a kind messenger." Hail which is so destructive to agriculture; was often an instrument of judgement against the enemies of God's people. (Cf. Ex 9:18-25; Josh 10:11; Wis 16:16, 22; Sir 39:29; 46:6; 4Ezra 15:13, 41).

[1159] I has: "both in the rainy season and the dry season;"

[1160] Manuscripts differ in the wording of this unusual line. It seems to be saying that since God hides His Glory in the cloud, it is holy, set apart and guarded by an angel. Examples include: (Ex 16:10; 19:9; 19:16; 24:15-16).

[1161] Nickelsburg believes a line is missing at the end of 60:21. Olson, relying on two Ethiopic texts (EMML 1768 and 6281 supported by G) attempts to recover the last two lines of (60:21) which are included in this text. If…earth.

[1162] K has: "and the angels comprehend it." OL has: "and the angels have custody of it."

[1163] 60:23 is problematic. "More likely it is associated with 60:7-10 +24, where we heard of 'the garden where the chosen and righteous dwell (v 8)'" (NV2 pg. 232). Nickelsburg speculates that it may be a scribal gloss that found its way into the text.

[1164] The flood occurred in the 600th year of Noah's life (Gen 7:6, 11; 4Q252 1.1.3). According to the Qumran pesher on Genesis (4Q252 1.1.8(W pg. 353) (cf. Gen 7:24) the "waters prevailed upon the earth one hundred and fifty days until the fourteenth day of the seventh month, on Tuesday" this was in the six hundredth year of Noah's life. This would be exactly 100 years after the time named here in 60:1; and also, on the eve of the Feast of Tabernacles/Booths. The timeline appears to be that God swore that mankind only had 120 years left before the flood (4Q252 1.1.2 (W pg. 353); Gen 6:3). Then with 100 years before the flood, the events of (1En 60:1-6) occur. It is an ironic twist that in the eschatological future, God in (Zechariah 14:16-19) will withhold rain (rather than send a deluge) upon nations that do not go up to the feast of tabernacles.

fourteenth of the month in the life of <Noah>,[1165] [1166] in that — Zech 14:16-19
parable[1167] I saw how the heaven of heavens was shaken violently, — 37:5; 68:1; 2Sam 22:7-16; Lk 21:26
and the host of the Most High, and the angels, thousands — 1:9; 14:22; 40:1; 71:8; Dan 7:9-10, 25
upon thousands and ten thousand times ten thousand,[1168] [1169] — Rev 5:11; *Haer.* 2.7.4; 4Q530 2.2.16-19
were greatly disturbed with a tremendous agitation.[1170]
2 And the Antecedent of Time was sitting on the throne of his — 46:1-2; 47:3
glory, and the holy and righteous angels were standing — 70:4
around him.[1171]
3 Great trembling seized me, and fear took hold of me, — 14:13-14; Isa 45:1
my loins collapsed and gave way,[1172] my kidneys[1173] lost control, — 71:11; Nah 2:10; Ps 69:23; ApZeph 6:9
and I fell upon my face. — Dan 8:16-18; 10:9-10
4 Then Michael[1174] sent another angel from among the holy ones — 14:24-25
and he lifted me up, and when he raised me up my spirit returned;
for I had not been able to endure the appearance of this host,
and the commotion and the quaking of the heavens.
5 Then Michael spoke to me: "What have you seen that has you
so shaken? Until today has the day of his mercy been in effect; — 50:3-5; 61:13

[1165] **Although "Enoch" is found here in all Ethiopic manuscripts, the scholarly consensus is that this should read "Noah."** The 500 years is drawn from Genesis 5:32 and Enoch's last age on earth was 365 as stated in Genesis 5:23. In addition, 1En 60:8, reveals that the text is speaking of Noah rather than Enoch (great grandfather, 7th from Adam; taken up). Nickelsburg also inserts <Noah> here. This passage appears to be an interpolation about Noah with the name changed to Enoch. (1QapGen 6.11-20) contains a vision where Noah interacts with a mighty watcher regarding the activity of those who dwell on the earth, the Nephilim, and the holy ones who mated with human women. "The obvious Noah context for the opening of this chapter is why scholars consider 1 Enoch 60 to have originally been an ancient 'Noah apocalypse' that has been added to the first fifty-nine chapters of 1 Enoch and then adapted to read "Enoch" in this first verse" (H2 pg. 159).

[1166] The seventh month, 14th day of the month is the day before the Feast of Tabernacles (Lev 23:34). In rabbinic literature the Feast of Tabernacles is associated with a banquet on the flesh of leviathan (60:24) (*Babylonian Talmud Baba Batra* 75a and *Pesiqta deRab Kahana* 187b).

[1167] "In that Parable. This phrase marks a clumsy attempt to connect this chapter with the main context but betrays the hand of the interpolator" (C pg. 113).

[1168] Isaac has: "ten thousand times a million and ten million times ten million." 60:1 clearly relies on Daniel 7.

[1169] Scholars consider 60:1-10, 24, 25 to be a Noahic interpolation into the text.

[1170] Commotion in heaven is not found in the Genesis account of events in heaven prior to the flood; but is found in *Atrahasis* II (18th century BC) where the commotion/noise caused by man is the cause of the flood.
The country was as noisy as a bellowing bull
The God grew restless at their racket,
Enlil had to listen to their noise.
He addressed the great gods,
The noise of mankind has become too much,
I am losing sleep over their racket.

[1171] OL and K have: "and the angels and the righteous stood around him," I is similar; thus having the righteous as humans. (cf. 70:4) This text follows Nickelsburg, having the holy and righteous as angels. This is supported by the use of "holy ones" in 60:4 and that "the righteous" are not expected to be standing among "the holy ones" (NV2 pg. 236).

[1172] For this line K has: "and my whole being melted."

[1173] "In biblical usage, the kidneys כִּלְיָה (kilyôt) are 'the seat of emotions from joy to deepest agony,' and thus the image is appropriate in a scene of sheer terror" (NV2 pg. 237). But yes, it was likely known then, that the kidneys were part of the urinary system; leading to a "vivid and colorful image." (NV2 pg. 237).

[1174] "Michael means 'Who is like God?'" (H2 pg. 162) For Michael in the Old Testament see (Dan 10:13, 21; and 12:1).

and he has been merciful and long-suffering towards those who 93:3
dwell on the earth.[1175]
6 But when the day, and the power, and the punishment,
and the judgement come, which the Lord of Spirits has prepared
for those who do not bow before the righteous <judge>,[1176]
and for those who deny the righteous judgement, 4Ezra 7:37; Mt 23:23
and for those who take his Name in vain[1177]—that day has been 38:2; 46:7; Ex 20:7; Deut 5:11
prepared, for the elect a covenant,[1178] but for sinners an Ps 89:3
inquisition."[1179]

Leviathan and Behemoth

7 And on that day[1180] two monsters were separated from 2Bar 29:4; Job 40:19; Ps 104:26
one another, a female monster called Leviathan,[1181] 4Ezra 6:49-52; Isa 27:1; Job 41

[1175] **"The author of the present section may well be asserting that God's patience allowed one hundred years to pass between the fall of the angels and the inception of violence in the world and the time of the flood in the 600th year of Noah's life** (Gen 5:32 | Gen 6:1-7:5 | 7:6). **A number of early Christian writers assert precisely such a one-hundred-year period, during which Noah built the ark and preached repentance.** A similar idea occurs in the Qumran pesher on Genesis (4Q252 i.1-3)" (NV2 pg. 237). "Michael is most likely speaking with a view toward the end of the one-hundred-year period" (NV2 pg. 238). This long time period demonstrates God's long suffering and being slow to wrath before bringing on the destruction of the flood.

[1176] In its original form, this is the judgement of the flood. As in this text, Nickelsburg uses "<judge>" postulating a mistranslation of Aram *dyn*. He translates 60:6 as follows: "And when the day and the power and the punishment and the judgement come, which the Lord of Spirits has prepared for those who do not worship the righteous <judge>, and for those who take his name in vain . . . And that day has been prepared for the elect, a covenant, for the sinners, a visitation." OL and others have: "do not bow before righteous judgement."

[1177] "Take His name in vain" "The idea here is representing God in an unworthy manner—bearing the name as His people in a way that denigrates God's own character and reputation" (H2 pg. 163). In other words, the people of God are misrepresenting Him by not keeping His commandments, thus bringing disgrace to Him. Heiser maintained that this is in accordance with its meaning in Ex 20:7.

[1178] The Noahic covenant (Gen 9:8-17).

[1179] N and K have "visitation" in place of "inquisition." C, OL and I remain with "inquisition." This is the judgement of those who perished in the flood both "giants" and humans.

[1180] Leviathan and Behemoth were created on the fifth day of creation (Gen 1:21; 4 Ezra 6:47-52 and 2 Baruch 29:4). The passages in 4 Ezra (late 1st century AD) and 2 Baruch (AD 100-120) are drawing from these verses in the Parables (BL pg. 227; 230). This is evidence for, at the latest, a first century or earlier date for the Parables.

[1181] Leviathan sometimes called "Rahab" in the bible (Job 9:13; 26:12-13; Ps 89:10; Isa 51:9); is an ancient symbol of evil in all its monstrous horror. It is attested by the name Lotan in Canaanite (Ugaritic) tales that describe a powerful, chaotic, violent, seven headed (cf. Ps 74:12-14; Rev 13:1;OdesSol 22:5) dragon-like deity who was defeated by Hadad-Baal. A similar type monster is found in numerous traditions. It inhabits the sea, it is pulled out of the sea and cast upon the land for the wild animals and birds to eat. Created on the fifth day of creation, it was defeated by God who showed His superior power when He divided the Red Sea, the domain of Leviathan (Job 9:13; 26:12-13; Ps 74:13-14; 89:10; Isa 27:1; 51:9; Ezek 29:3-5; 32:1-10;). Other references to Leviathan include (Ps 104:26; Job 3:8; 41:1-34 (detailed description); ApAb 21:4 and LadJac 6:13). Here in (1En 60:24); and in (4Ezra 6:49-52; and in 2 Baruch 29:4) both Leviathan and Behemoth are associated with food, to be eaten at a future date by those chosen of God. This idea of leviathan being the main course at an eschatological banquet is taken up in the *Babylonian Talmud Baba Batra* 75a. The idea of it being found at the end times can also be found in *Targum Pseudo-Jonathan* Gen 1:21: "And God created great beasts: Leviathan and his wife, which were prepared for the Day of Consolation" (OL pg. 139). The location of Behemoth in 60:8, near Eden, the place where the chosen and righteous dwell, "makes it a convenient pantry for those participating in the eschatological banquet" (NV2 pg. 241).

to dwell in the abyss of the ocean over the fountains of the waters. 89:7; Gen. 1:21; Gen 7:11
8 But the male is named Behemoth,[1182] who possesses for (his) Job 40:15-41:34; 4Ezra 6:51
pastureland [1183] a trackless desert named Dundayn,[1184] east of the 10:4; 33:2; 108:3; Gen 4:16
garden[1185] where the elect and righteous ones dwell, 32:3-6; 61:12; 70:4; *Haer.* 4.16.2
where my great-grandfather[1186] was taken up,[1187] the seventh 93:3; Sir 44:16; Jub 4:23; Gen 5:24
from Adam,[1188] [1189] the first man whom the Lord of Spirits Jub 7:39; *Vita* 51:9; Jude 14

As far as the female and male, this may relate to 1En 54:8 where the waters above are masculine and the waters below are feminine. Leviathan brings to mind the beast rising out of the sea in (Rev. 13:1-10) who most take as the Antichrist. (Daniel 7:1-8) describes nefarious spiritual beings who came out of the sea, at least one of whom, is transformed into a man; (Daniel 7:4). The last of these kings (Dan 7:17), is described in (Dan 7:19-28) in terms befitting the Antichrist. **This passage on Leviathan, who was defeated at the crossing of the Red Sea by God's control of his domain, (Isa 51:9) fits with the other imagery from Exodus in the text before us. This includes the drawing back of the sea (60:16); hail (60:17); and the cloud obscuring the divine glory (60:19). When Christ walked on the Sea of Galilee it showed His superiority over Leviathan. When the sea is no more (Rev 21:1), it shows God's final triumph over Leviathan (chaos).**

[1182] Behemoth (great beast, in Hebrew and Aramaic "beast" and "behemoth" are the same word), described in Job 40:15-24, is a mythological chaos monster. He is described as land dwelling, but near water, as here. Created on the fifth day of creation (4Ezra 6:47), he is a creature so powerful that only God can overcome him, so he may be spiritual in nature. "**The two chaos beasts are thus 'participants' in the judgement of the Flood in the Noah apocalypse. After the destruction, one (Leviathan) returns to the oceans and thereafter serves as the chaos beast of the sea; the other (Behemoth) becomes the chaos beast of the dried-up land after the Flood**" (H2 pg. 166). Since he dwells in Duidain/Dudael with Azaz' el he may be a representation of Azaz'el or at least a being that dwells with him under the jagged rocks. (See 10:4-5). This brings to mind the beast of (Revelation 13:11-18) who rises out of the earth. This is taken by many as the false prophet. (Cf. also Ezek 32:1-8). Behemoth was given a seventh part of the dry land with a thousand mountains and Leviathan was given the sea for a dwelling (4Ezra 6:51-52). They are both defeated by the messiah in (2Bar 29:4) and become food for those who survive to His coming.

[1183] Olson is followed here. He speculates: "assuming a Hebrew original for at least this Noah apocalypse, we suggest that the translator confused "field, land" and "his breast," which are spelled the same in Hebrew" (OL pg. 108). He states: "It seems to me more likely that the translator mistakenly read בְּשָׂדֵיהוּ (or בְּשָׂדֵהָ) rather than בַּשָּׂדֵיהוּ (or בַּשָּׂדָה)." (Journal for the Study of the Pseudipigrapha 31 (2022) 133). Black following the majority has: "But the male is named Behemoth, who covers with his belly an empty wilderness named Duidain(?), on the east of the Garden where the elect and righteous dwell,"

[1184] This name takes several forms. OL and I have: "Dundayin", C has: "Duidain" K has: "Dendayn." One manuscript has "yendayn." See 1 Enoch 10:4-5 for a possible clue, Duidain=Duda' el, which is a possible match for "Duidain" in this text. By being confined or located in the same lifeless, threatening place, Azazel and Behemoth may be linked. The possibility arises that Behemoth/Azazel is the beast of Revelation 13:11-18 where the beast is "rising out of the earth" as if he were imprisoned below it. Olson postulates that Dundayin may be the "Dedan" mentioned in (Isa 21:13; Jer 25:23; 49:8; and Ezek 25:13) (OL pg. 108).

[1185] I has: "garden of Eden" OL has: "paradise."

[1186] This would be Noah's grandfather Enoch. This confirms chapter 60 is, as Olson states: "a clumsily altered Noah apocalypse."

[1187] Knibb has: "received" in place of "taken up." Interestingly, Sir 44:16 is reserved as a blank in MasSir.

[1188] It seems that this is the source of the use in Jude 14 "the seventh from Adam" since the same language is used. The wording in (1En 93:3) is different "I was born the seventh". In the (Jubilees 7:39) text it is translated: "the seventh in his generation" or "its seventh generation." **The significance of this, is that it would establish that the author of Jude was quoting from a Greek translation of the *Parables of Enoch* and that this interpolation occurred prior to the time of Jude. This is evidence that *The Parables of Enoch* preexisted the composition of Jude.** However, it is remotely possible the phrase could be derived from a previous text common to both. This language is also picked up in a later Christian interpolation into the text of the Life of Adam and Eve, (*Vita* 51:9 (OTP2 pg. 294)).

[1189] "It was known at an early time that there were intriguing parallels between Enoch, the seventh man, and Enmeduranki, the seventh king in some versions of the Sumerian king list" (NV2 pg. 371). Enmeduranki of Zimbir

created.
9 I asked another angel[1190] to show me the might of these
monsters, how they were separated in one day[1191] the one
thrown into the abysses of the sea, and the other into the dry 2Bar 29:4
land of the desert.
10 And he said to me: "Son of man, you here wish to know
what is hidden."[1192] [1193] 65:11
24 And the angel of peace who was with me said to me: 40:8
"These two monsters, are prepared for the great day of the Lord 4Ezra 6:49-52; 2Bar 29:4
to provide food for <the chosen and righteous>, so that the Ps 74:14
punishment of the Lord of Spirits may fall upon them and 55:3; 62:12; Ezek 32:4-7
not come forth in vain. Children shall be slain with their mothers, Ex 20:5; Deut 5:9
and children with their fathers.
25 When the punishment of the Lord of Spirits rests upon them, 84:4
afterwards will be the judgement according to his mercy and 5:5-6; 50:3-5; 61:13
patience."[1194]

Angels Measure the Portions of the Righteous

61 1 I saw in those days how long cords[1195] were given to those Ezek 40:2-3
angels,[1196] and they acquired wings[1197] for themselves and Ezek 10:6-19

(the city now known as Sippar) was an ancient Sumerian king, whose name appears in the Sumerian King List as the seventh pre-dynastic king of Sumer. He was said to have reigned for 21,000 years. A myth written in a Semitic language tells of Enmeduranki, subsequently being taken to heaven by the gods Shamash and Adad and taught the secrets of heaven and of earth.

[1190] Some manuscripts read "the other angel" and others "this angel" and "that angel" (N pg. 76).

[1191] "This verse may suggest that the monsters were created and then thrown, respectively, into the sea and the dry land, or that, having their origin in the sea, the one is thrown into its depths, and the other onto the dry land" (NV2 pg. 242). (Cf. 4Ezra 6:47-52).

[1192] Isaac has the angel saying: "You, son of man, according (to the degree) to which it will be permitted, you will know the hidden things."

[1193] This is the only use of "son of man" being applied to a human in 1 Enoch except for potentially the controversial verse (71:14). "Son of man" is very commonly used when God addresses Ezekiel in the book of Ezekiel.

[1194] Nickelsburg inserts both verses 24 and 25 after verse 10. He then moves 60:11-23 to follow 59:3, as in this text.

[1195] Isaac is quite different for 61:1 having: "I saw in those days that long ropes were given to those angels; and hoisting up their own (respective) portions (of the ropes), they soared going in the direction of the northeast." In addition to being used for measuring, "These cords or ropes also function as staying devices for the righteous and chosen and are related to the coming resurrection of the righteous" (NV2 pg. 243). The measuring line was commonly used for measuring land like survey chains. They are measuring the place of the elect and righteous, see 70:3.

[1196] A variant of Eth[q] says: "two angels" in place of "those angels" (BL pg. 231).

[1197]The Ethiopian text "Tana" has "took their sections and flew off". Other texts have "took to themselves wings and flew off." Olson notes that either reading could be original to the text (OL pg. 112). "Contrary to popular opinion, there is no evidence from the Greco-Roman period and earlier that "angels" were outfitted with wings. In the Bible these appendages were attributed only to the Seraphim in (Isa 6:2) and the creatures that surround the chariot in (Ezek 1:6. 8-11). In neither of these passages are these beings said to be "angels" (מַלְאָכִים), and in both instances the wings function mainly to cover the body" (NV2 pg. 244). "The present passage follows this wingless tradition, but states that in the present case, the angels "take for them(selves)' wings…in order to bring them to the place of their

soared, going in the direction of the north.[1198]
2 I asked of an angel: "Why have they taken those cords and TJob 46:9-47:5
gone off?" He answered me saying: "They have gone to take 60:22; 70:3; Zech 2:1-2
measurements." Rev 11:1; 21:15; 5Q15; 4Q554
3 The angel who went with me said to me:
"These are the ones who will bring the measured portions Isa 65:17-25; Rev21:10-21
of the righteous,[1199] and the binding-ropes[1200] of the righteous Mt 16:19; Ps 16:6
to the righteous, so that they may rely[1201] on the Name of the 48:4; Mic 3:11; Isa 10:20
Lord of Spirits forever and ever.
4 The elect shall begin to dwell[1202] with the elect,
and these are the measures which shall be given for faith,[1203] 39:6; Rom 12:3
and for the strengthening of righteousness.[1204]
5 Those measurements will reveal all that is hidden 58:5
in the depths of the earth,[1205]
those who have been destroyed by the desert, 51:1-2; 90:33
those who have been devoured by the fish of the sea and Rev 20:13
by wild beasts,[1206] *Res.* 32.1; SibOr 2:221-235

---

mission" (NV2 pg. 244). Heiser weighed in on the subject: "As I have written elsewhere, the idea that angels in the Bible had wings is untrue. The misguided idea has its roots in the conflation of angels (*melakîm*) with *cherûbîm* and *śeraphîm*. All three of these terms describe roles or functions, essentially job descriptions, not the ontological nature of the heavenly beings that bear these labels" (H2 pg. 173). See also: (Heiser, Michael S., 2018. *Angels*, pgs. 164-167). Milik, an early translator and researcher of the Dead Sea Scrolls, cited this verse to support a late date for the Parables, translating, 'take wing," but the passage indicates that they do not have wings and must acquire them" (Greenfield and Stone, *Pentateuch*, pg. 65). Cherubim are also said to have wings in (4Q405 20.2.8 (W pg. 473)).

1198 "Paradise is the destination of the angels" (cf. 1En 60:8; C pg. 119). Isaac has: "northeast" in place of north while Nickelsburg has "northwest" in his notes (NV2 pg. 243). This matches 1En 70:3, but see also 1En 32:1-3.

1199 These appear to be surveyor angels who are laying out the New Jerusalem (Isa 65:17-25; Rev 21:10-21). These angels are laying out the portion of New Jerusalem/Paradise each saint will have; like the land of Canaan was portioned out to the tribes (Josh 13:6; 19; Num 33:54). Olson observes, speaking of (1En 61:3-5): "These verses speak of ropes, allotted portions, measured lengths, destinies, and unification (i.e., of separated things—in this case the saints living and dead). All these ideas are related to the Hebrew root, *hbl*. The original writing probably contained much wordplay" (OL pg. 112).

1200 Olson notes concerning the binding-ropes: "Apparently cords by which the righteous may bind someone or something." He sees a connection with Christ's words in (Mt 16:19): "I will give you the keys of the kingdom of heaven, and whatever you bind on earth shall be bound in heaven, and whatever you loose on earth shall be loosed in heaven" (OL pg. 112).

1201 "The image is that 'the Lord of Spirits is a rope that one can hang onto'" (NV2 pg. 245).

1202 Some manuscripts have "walk" in place of "dwell".

1203 The word "Faith" is rarely used in the parables. It is only used here, and in (39:6; 46:8; and 58:5). "Black notes that the word translated 'faith' more precisely means 'fidelity, faithfulness'" (BL pg. 232). But N, OL, I and BL translate "faith".

1204 Black postulates this may have originally read: "and to those who hold fast to righteousness."

1205 "Depths of the earth" Sheol, the land of the dead. The present abode of the dead is contrasted with their future dwelling in paradise.

1206 **Verse 61:5 was probably the text called scripture and paraphrased by Tertullian (AD 160-220) in *On the Resurrection of the Flesh* Chapter 32.1 "But, that you may not suppose that it is merely those bodies which are consigned to tombs whose resurrection is foretold, you have it declared in Scripture: 'And I will command the fishes of the sea, and they shall cast up the bones which they have devoured; and I will bring joint to joint, and bone to bone.'" This passage teaches a bodily resurrection, as does 1En 51:1. The point is that God will restore the righteous dead no matter what happened to their earthly bodies. That some Jews**

so that they may return and rely on the day of the Mk 13:27; Acts 2:20; 2Pet 3:10
Chosen One;[1207] [1208]
for no one shall be destroyed before the Lord of Spirits, 2Cor 5:1; Phil 3:20-21; Rom 8:23
and no one can be destroyed.[1209] 2 Mac 7:9, 11, 14, 29; Jn 5:28-29

The Chosen One is Praised in Heaven

6 All who are in the heights of heaven above received a
command and power and one voice[1210] and a single light like fire
was given to them.[1211] [1212] [1213]
7 And that one, the First Word, they praised, they exalted and Heb 4:12; Jn 1:1
glorified in wisdom, and they were wise in speech and in Acts 1:8; 2:2-4, 11, 14-41
the Spirit of Life.[1214] Isa 41:8; 42:1; 43:10; 49:7
8 The Lord of Spirits seated the Chosen One on the 45:3; 51:3; Heb 12:2; Mt 19:28; 25:31
throne of Glory.[1215] Ps 110:1; Heb 1:3, 13; 8:1; 10:12-13; 12:2
Eph 1:20; 2Bar 73:1

---

prior to this time believed in the resurrection, is displayed by statements made by the Jews brutally tortured by Antiochus (2 Mac 7:9, 11, 14, 20, 23, and 29).

[1207] **Judgement will be given to the Chosen One, i.e. Christ. The day of the Lord (Chosen One) is a day of judgement for sinners and hope for the righteous.**

[1208] For these lines Isaac has: "So that they all return and find hope in the day of the Elect One."

[1209] **This is one of the earliest statements that God will resurrect even bodies which have been destroyed. This is a strong statement in favor of the doctrine of bodily resurrection.** How bodies would be physically resurrected was a major controversy in the second century. It was extensively addressed by Athenagoras (Athenagoras, *On the Resurrection of the Dead* (AD 176-177)). A bodily resurrection is clearly taught in the New Testament (Jn 5:28-29; Rom 8:23; 2Cor 5:1; Phil 3:20-21).

[1210] "Perhaps the author here depicts the heavenly chorus singing in unison or perhaps in a unified harmony. In any event the expression denoted musical perfection, and the aural ("one voice") is complemented by the visual ("one light like fire"). Since angels are otherwise depicted as glorious creatures (Ps 104:4; Ezek 1:13-14; Dan 10:5-60), it is striking, and indicative of the extraordinary character of this event, that here they are given "one light like fire" (NV2 pg. 249).

[1211] Only a few manuscripts have "was given to them." But since it fills out the parallelism it appears to be original.

[1212] **In this throne room vision, a command goes forth from an unnamed leader to each group of the heavenly entourage who then erupts in powerful praise directed at the Chosen One. This is one of the most impressive throne room scenes in literature.** See also Rev 4-5.

[1213] **The similarities between (1En 61:6-7) and the events of Pentecost are notable and seem hardly coincidental. Is this a prophecy of Pentecost; the earthly enthronement of the Chosen one at the birth of the Church? Power (cf. Acts 1:8), one voice (cf. Acts 2:4-11), light like fire=tongues of fire (Acts 2:3); praised First Word i.e. Christ; wise in speech (cf. Peters speech Acts 2:14-40); Spirit of life (cf. Acts 2:4).**

[1214] For these lines I has "And him the First Word, they shall bless, extol, and glorify with wisdom." N has "And that one, before anything, they blessed with (their) voice," OL has: "And him, the First Word, they blessed, they exalted, they glorified in wisdom, showing themselves wise in speech and in the spirit of life." Olson admits that his translation may be over literal. He suggests other alternatives: "'And before uttering any (other) word, they blessed him.' or simply, 'before anything else, they blessed him.'" (OL pg. 112) This passage may stand behind the first verse in the Gospel of John. "In the beginning was the Word, and the Word was with God, and the Word was God" (Jn 1:1).

[1215] **1En 61:8-13 is a dramatic throne room scene where the entire heavenly kingdom of God is assembled to see the Chosen One enthroned in preparation for rendering judgment; both on those in heaven and on earth. The power and majesty of God's united assembled kingdom makes the watcher rebellion seem puny in comparison.** This scene may derive from knowledge of a text like the *Songs of the Sabbath Sacrifice* (4Q400-407; 11Q17 (W pg. 462-475)) which might also be behind some of the issues Paul addresses in Colossians 2:18 (W pg. 464).

He shall judge all the works of the holy ones in heaven above, 55:4; 62:2; 69:26-29; 91:15
and in the balance shall their deeds be weighed.[1216] [1217] 41:1; 43:2; 1Cor 6:3; 1Sam 2:3 4Ezra 3:34; 4:36

9 When he shall lift up his face to judge their secret ways 38:3; Ps 90:8; Rom 2:16; OdesSol 33:11
according to the word of the Name[1218] of the Lord of Spirits,
and their paths[1219] according to the righteous judgement
of the Lord of Spirits, then will they all with one voice celebrate
and praise and glorify and extol and sanctify the Name of the
Lord of Spirits.
10 All the hosts of the heavens will cry out;[1220] all the holy ones 4Q402 Frags 3-4.6-10
in the heights and the forces of the Lord, the Cherubim,[1221] 14:11,18; 20:7; 71:7; Ps 80:1; Ezek 11:22
Seraphin[1222] and Ophannin,[1223] and all the angels of power Mk 13:25; Isa 6:1-3; 2Thes 1:7; Ezek 1:20

[1216] **The Chosen One, Christ, will judge not only humans but also celestial beings.** In 61:9, the image that He lifts up his face shows a favorable judgement. This phrase is similar to (Isa 24:21) in that it includes the judgement of heavenly beings; however, Black sees this as a judgement of the elect ones (BL pg. 233). "'Chosen One' most likely derives from the Servant Songs in Isaiah where it is a common description of the Servant of the Lord in Isaiah (42:1; cf. 41:8, 9, 43:10, 20; 44:1, 2; 45:4; 49:7)" (P pg. 297).

[1217] **"The fact that the Beginning of Days yields the throne, symbol of judgement, to the Son of Man is a critical clue for dating the text. In the entire Hebrew bible, including the book of Daniel, it is God in person who judges. In the New Testament, on the other hand, judgement is entrusted to the Son"** (R pg. 161, Chiala). (Ps 110:1) may be an exception to Chiala's statement.

[1218] "God's name (YHWH), translated as 'Lord God' in most Bibles and roughly equivalent to the term 'Yahweh,' has long been considered so holy that it is unspeakable. During the days of the Jerusalem Temple, only the High Priest said the word out loud, and then only once a year, on the Day of Atonement. In Jewish theology and practice, there is still mystery and majesty attached to God's special name. The Tetragrammaton is considered "the name that comprises all" (Gaines, Janet Howe, 2023. *Lilith, Seductress, heroine or murderer?* Bible History Daily, Biblical Archeology Society Aug 6, 2023).

[1219] Isaac uses "conduct" in place of path.

[1220] In place of: "All the hosts of heaven will cry out" Olson has: "And he will summon on that day all the hosts of heaven." Isaac is similar with: "And he will summon all the forces of the heavens." Charles allows for both readings (C pg. 121).

[1221] "The Hebrew term translated "cherub" (kerûb) derives from Akkadian and refers instead to a guardian of sacred space" (H2 pg. 178).

[1222] *Seraphim* are heavenly beings who are guardians of sacred space (Isaiah 6:1-6). The term seraphim "is drawn from Egyptian throne terminology and conceptions." ...The relevant cobra species spit "burning" venom, can expand wide flanges of skin on either side of their bodies—considered "wings" in antiquity—when threatened, and are (obviously) serpentine. As Joines notes, the protective nature of the uraeus cobra is evident: 'a function of the uraeus is to protect the pharaoh and sacred objects by breathing out fire on his enemies'" (H2 pg. 179, partially quoting Karen R. Joines, *Winged Serpents in Isaiah's Inaugural Vision, Journal of Biblical Literature* 86.4 (1967):410-15).

[1223] Ophannin are a special type of winged spiritual beings linked to the Hebrew word ophan which is used in Ezekiel's vision of the glory of God in (Ezek 1:15 to 1:21). The "wheels", "ophan" in Hebrew, are described as living and having eyes in (Ezek 1:18-19). Wheels are associated with them again in (Ezek 3:13; 10:6-19; and 11:22). In *The Songs of the Sabbath Sacrifice*, wheel beings are mentioned. "The chariots of His innermost sanctum shall offer praise as one, and their Cherubim and wheel-beings shall marvelously bless [. . .] the chiefs of the divine building. They shall praise Him in His holy innermost sanctum" (4Q403 1.2.15-16 (W pgs. 470-471)). Holy Cherubim luminous wheel-beings are described in detail later in *The Songs of the Sabbath Sacrifice*, (4Q405 20.2 (W pg. 473).

and all the angels of dominions,[1224] and the Chosen One,[1225] 39:6; Col 1:16; 2Bar 59:11
and the other powers on the earth and over the water.[1226] Eph 1:21; 6:10-12; Rom 8:38-39
11 On that day they will lift up one voice, praising and glorifying Rev 1:4; ApPet 18
and exalting in the spirit of faithfulness, in the spirit of wisdom, 49:3; Isa 11:2
in the spirit of patience, in the spirit of mercy, in the spirit of Gal 5:22
justice and of peace, and in the spirit of goodness,[1227] Rev 5:11-14; 7:9-12
and shall all say with one voice: "Blessed is he, and may the
Name of the Lord of Spirits be blessed for ever and ever!" 39:10; Dan 2:20
12 All who sleep not[1228] in heaven above shall bless him,[1229] 39:12-13; 40:2; 71:7
and all the holy ones who are in heaven will praise him!
All the chosen ones who dwell in the garden of life, 32:3; 60:8; 70:3-4; OdesSol 8:18
and every spirit of light[1230] and every spirit of light capable of 1QS 3.25; Jas 1:17; 1Thes 5:5
glorifying, exalting and hallowing your blessed Name,[1231] Mt 6:9
and all flesh will glorify exceedingly and bless your Name for Ps 148
ever and ever.
13 For the mercy of the Lord of Spirits is great in quantity! 50:3-5; 60:5
He is long-suffering,[1232] and all of his deeds and all the 60:5, 25; 36:4; Num 14:18
dimensions of his creation, he has revealed to the righteous 1:1
and chosen in the Name of the Lord of Spirits.

The Chosen One on the Throne Judges the Kings and Powerful

62 1 Then the Lord of Spirits commanded the kings and the 4Ezra 7:37
mighty and the exalted,[1233] and those who possess the land,[1234] 55:4
and said: "Open your eyes and lift up your eyebrows;[1235] Rom 11:25; Ps 75:4-5

[1224] I has: "angels of governance" N has: "angels of the dominions." **"The two terms here are the Ethiopic equivalents of Greek *dynameis* ("powers") and *kuriotētes* ("lords" or "dominions"). That these two Greek terms are paired in the New Testament (Ephesians 1:21, Colossians 1:16) indicates that (1 Enoch 62) is a contextual background for Paul's material"** (H2 pg. 180). See also (Rom 8:38-39) where *archai* ("principalities") is paired with *dynameis.*

[1225] It is interesting that the "Chosen One" is included in this list. Since He is placed so far down the list, Olson postulates a scribal error (OL pg. 114).

[1226] "Over earth and over water" is a polar expression meaning over the entire earth.

[1227] Note that there are seven virtues named. Isaac has "generosity" in place of "goodness".

[1228] "Those who sleep not" are the constant attendants of God (1En 14:23; 39:12-13). "The Watchers. The Aramaic term ('îr) derives from either Ugaritic ġyr ('to protect') or Akkadian êru ('be wakeful')" (H2 pg. 180).

[1229] Isaac has for this line: "All the vigilant ones in heaven above shall bless him;"

[1230] "Every spirit of light," glorified humans and celestial beings. See also (1QS 3.25) "It is actually He who created the spirits of light and darkness, making them the cornerstone of every deed."

[1231] "Holy" is used instead of "blessed." In some manuscripts.

[1232] N has: "slow to anger" in place of "long-suffering."

[1233] **"These chapters depict the event toward which the whole of the Book of Parables has been pointing—the enthronement of the Chosen One and his judgement of the kings and the mighty"** (NV2 pg. 257).

[1234] Some manuscripts read "those who inhabit (or dwell on) the earth" others read as here. Land is used in this text since the kings and mighty in Galilee had come to possess the best land, displacing the righteous. Isaac translates "landlords".

[1235] I and OL have "eyebrows" in place of most translators "horns." "Lifting up one's horn denotes arrogance (Ps 75:4-5, which forbids the action) or, more neutrally, courage" (NV2 pg. 260). This appears to be a taunt, as in where

see if you are able to recognize[1236] the Chosen One!"	39:6; Isa 42:1; Jn 8:28
2 The Lord of Spirits seated him on the throne of his glory,[1237]	45:3; 69:27,29; Jer 17:12; Mt 19:28; 25:31; Rev 3:21; Phil 2:9-11; Ezek 1:26
and the spirit of righteousness was poured out upon him.	Isa 6:1-3; 11:2-4; 52:13-53:6
The word of his mouth will slay all the sinners,[1238]	Ps 110; Rev 19:15; 2Thes 2:8; Wis 18:15
and all the oppressors[1239] will perish from before his face.	Ps 2:1-12; 2Bar 40:1-3
3 There shall stand up on that day[1240] all the kings and the	Isa 49:7
governors, and the high officials and those who occupy the	38:4; 48:8; Isa 52:15; Wis 5:2
land,[1241] and they shall see him and recognize him,	Mk 13:26; Heb 1:3, 13; 8:1; 10:12-13; 12:2
because he sits on the throne of his glory.[1242]	45:3; Mt 25:31-34, 41-46
Righteousness is judged before him,	Isa 11:3-4; 24:21-22; 1Pet 4:18; Mt 16:27
and no lying word[1243] is spoken before him.[1244]	49:4; 67:9; Acts 10:42; 17:31; Jn 5:25-28
4 Then agony shall come upon them as upon a woman in labor,[1245]	Mt 24:8; Mk 13:8; Ps 48:6; Jer 4:31
for whom birth is difficult;[1246]	Isa 13:6-9; 21:3; 26:17; 37:3; 42:14
at the moment her child enters the mouth of the womb,	1Thes 5:3; Hos 13:10-14
and she has pain in giving birth.	Gen 35:17; Jer 22:23
5 One group of them will glance on the other,	

is your arrogance now? However, Heiser thinks "eyelids" makes much better contextual sense (H2 pg. 185). In that sense it would be more akin to "open your eyes".

[1236] Rather than "recognize", Collins proposes that "acknowledge" is a better translation. "Since the Chosen One is sitting on the throne of his glory, they quickly realize that he is their judge and acknowledge him as such" (R pg. 339 Collins, *The secret Son of Man in the parables of Enoch and the Gospel of Mark: a response to Leslie Walck*).

[1237] The throne of glory is mentioned in the Bible, see (1Kgs 22:19; Isa 6:1-3; Jer 14:21; 17:12; and Ezek 1:26). It is also mentioned in second temple literature, (1En 9:4; Wis 9:10; 4Q405 23.1.2 (W pg. 474); 11Q17 Frags 2+1+9.6 (W pg. 475) and concerning an earthly throne (Sir 47:11; 4Q161 Frags 8-10.3.19 (W pg. 238)). It is mentioned extensively in the Book of Parables; see (45:3; 47:3; 55:4; 60:2; 61:8; 62:2, 3, 5; 69:27, 29; and 71:7). The throne is the throne of God who shares it with the Son of Man/Chosen One. **Statements by Christ such as: "Jesus said to them, 'Truly, I say to you, in the new world, when the Son of Man will sit on his glorious throne, you who have followed me will also sit on twelve thrones, judging the twelve tribes of Israel'" (Mt 19:28). Also "When the Son of Man comes in his glory, and all the angels with him, then he will sit on his glorious throne" (Mt 25:31). These statements are obviously claims of messiahship/divinity and both are universally accepted by scholars as being reliant on the Parables.** In the Old Testament, only three passages allude to an enthroned Son of Man (Ezek 1:26; Dan 7:13-14 and Ps 110:1). Other New Testament references to the Christ on the throne include (Heb 12:2; Rev 20:11 and 22:3).

[1238] "The word of his mouth will slay all the sinners" See also (Isa 11:4; 49:2; 4Q161 8-10 3.15 (W pg. 238); 4Ezra 13:1-11; PssSol 17:24, 36; 2Thes 2:8; Rev 1:16; 19:15, 21). The references from Isaiah 11:1-4 in particular, are very specific to the Messiah and "are of great importance in considering the messianism of the Parables" (BL pg. 235).

[1239] Many translators have "unrighteous" in place of "oppressors".

[1240] On the day of judgement.

[1241] Isaac again has landlords in place of "those who occupy the land."

[1242] Previously the kings and mighty refused to acknowledge the Son of Man/Chosen One (1En 46:5-7). Now, before the judgement seat, they are forced to acknowledge Him; but it is too late to save themselves by pretending worship. They must recognize they have been persecuting the elect of the Chosen One.

[1243] Some translate "lying word" as "empty talk" or "nonsensical talk". The idea is the Chosen One cannot be fooled. His judgement will be based on truth.

[1244] **The great judgement scene described by Christ in (Mt 25:31-46) makes direct use of (1En 62-63) with some imagery from (1En 90:20-27).**

[1245] Woman in labor was a common idiom (Ps 48:6; Isa 21:3; 26:17; 42:14; Jer 4:31; 6:24; 13:21; 22:23; 30:6; 49:24; 50:43; Mic 4:9-10; Mt 24:8; Sir 48:19). This passage relies on (Isa 13:6-9).

[1246] "For whom birth is difficult" is present in all manuscripts but Nickelsburg omits it as: "almost certainly a doublet reading for verse 4c."

and they will be terror stricken,[1247] and their faces downcast.[1248]	Wis 4:20-5:3; Rev 6:15-16; 22:12
Pain shall seize them when they see that Son of Man[1249]	Isa 13:8; 52:15; 4Q416 1:11
sitting on the throne of his glory.[1250]	Mk 14:62; Mt 19:28; 24:30; 25:31 Lk 22:69
6 The kings and the powerful and all who possess	46:5
the land will (try to) glorify[1251] and bless and extol him	1Cor 2:6-9
who reigns over all—the One who was hidden.	Dan 7:14; Mt 28:18; Isa 45:15; Rev 1:5
7 For from the beginning the Son of Man was hidden,[1252]	48:6-7; Rom 16:25-26; Isa 49:2
and the Most High preserved him in the presence of his power,	4Ezra 12:32; Mt 11:25;Jn 1:1-3; Mk 8:27-30
and revealed him (only) to the chosen.	48:7; 2Tim 1:9-10; Lk 17:30; 1Pet 1:20
8 The congregation of the chosen and holy will be sown,[1253]	10:16; 38:1; 1Cor 15:42-44
and all the elect shall stand before him on that day.	Lk 12:8-9; 21:36; Wis 5:1
9 All the kings, the powerful, the exalted and those who rule the	
land will fall down before him on their faces, and worship	Phil 2:9-11; Isa 45:23; 52:15
and set their hope on that Son of Man[1254] and petition him and	46:3; Ps 2:10-12
plead for mercy from him.[1255]	63
10 But the Lord of Spirits himself will inspire such panic in	Ps 110:5-6
them[1256] that they will rush to escape from his presence.	2Thes 1:5-10

[1247] The suddenness of judgment is reminiscent of Jesus coming as a thief in the night (Mt. 24:44 and Lk 12:40).

[1248] For this line N has: "and will cast down their faces,"

[1249] **Jesus' favorite self-title "Son of Man" was evidently widely known prior to His ministry**. It was not a term to emphasize His humanity but a recognized title of a being. Jesus is never asked to explain the expression "Son of Man." It was recognized as a claim to deity (see 62:9) by the man born blind (Jn 9:35-38), and Caiphas (Mt 26:64). The title was familiar to the Sanhedrin (Lk 22:69), and a Jerusalem crowd (Jn 12:34). Black prefers manuscripts that here read "child of a woman" rather than others that read "Son of Man." (BL pg. 235-236).

[1250] **Christ alludes to this passage or a similar one (45:3; 47:3; 69:27) while threatening Caiaphas. "And Jesus said, 'I am, and you will see the Son of Man seated at the right hand of Power, and coming with the clouds of heaven.'" (Mk 14:62). Since the Son of Man is not seated in (Dan 7:13) but clouds are mentioned in (Dan 7:13) Christ's reference seems to be a blend of the two. This places Caiaphas in the category of the kings and mighty who will face judgement from the Chosen One. That Caiaphas is condemning Christ is beyond ironic, since their roles will be reversed at the great judgement, where Christ will be the judge.**

[1251] Isaac inserts, and this version follows: "shall (try to) bless" The attempt by the kings, powerful and landlords to now worship the Chosen One is futile. This is the worship they refused to give in (1En 46:5).

[1252] **That Christ was hidden from the beginning, and then revealed to the elect, is a theme in the writings of Paul** (cf. Rom 16:25-26; 1Cor 2:6-9; Col 1:26-27; 2Tim 1:9-10; and Tit 1:2-3. (Cf. 48:6-7; 69:26; Isa 45:15; and 4Ezra 13:26, 52). **Many commentators on (Rom 16:25-26) see the hidden mystery being the gospel, but it is obvious here, and in (1 En 48:6-7, and 2Tim 1:9-10), that the hidden mystery is Christ himself.**

[1253] Isaac has: "planted" in place of "sown" **The pairing of "sown" and "stand" may be speaking of the resurrection. This is the most likely reading in light of (1En 62:15-16). If so, this is the source of the imagery Paul is using in (1Cor 15:42-44). "So is it with the resurrection of the dead. What is sown is perishable; what is raised is imperishable. It is sown in dishonor; it is raised in glory. It is sown in weakness; it is raised in power. It is sown a natural body; it is raised a spiritual body. If there is a natural body, there is also a spiritual body."** Alternately, Paul may be referring to (1En 10:16) where a plant of righteousness and truth is established.

[1254] Nickelsburg has a note that Son of Man here and in 62:7 literally means: "'the son of the progeny of the mother of the living,' that is, Eve" (NV2 pg. 256).

[1255] For this line Isaac has: "they shall beg and plead for mercy at his feet." **The once proud and powerful kings are reduced to pleading for mercy from the one they persecuted unto death. But it is too late. Their petitions are rejected by the Lord of Spirits. In contrast, Christ did not plead for his life (Mk 15:3-4). That the Son of man is God, is established by His accepting worship.**

[1256] For this line Isaac has: "But the Lord of the Spirits himself will cause them to be frantic."

Their faces will be filled with shame,[1257]
97:6; Isa 13:8; 41:11-13; 44:9-11; Jer 51:51
and the darkness in their faces will grow deeper.
46:6; 62:5; 63:11; 4Ezra 7:125; Nah 2:10
11 He will deliver them to the angels of punishment,[1258]
53:3-5; ApPet 20; TAb A 12:1; Mt 16:27
to execute vengeance on them because they have
46:5-8; 48:9; Mt 13:41-43; Rev 14:19-20
oppressed his children and his chosen ones.
12 They will provide a spectacle for the righteous and for his
27:3
chosen ones, who will rejoice over them,
60:25; 84:4
because the wrath of the Lord of Spirits rests upon them,
55:3; Jn 3:36; Sir 5:6; Rev 19:15
and his sword is drunk from them.
63:11; Deut 32:42; Jer 46:10; Isa 34:5-7

The Salvation of the Righteous and Chosen

13 The righteous and chosen shall be saved on that day;
48:7; Dan 12:1; Lk 21:28; OdesSol 33:11
and never again will they see the faces of the sinners and
Ex 14:13; Wis 5:9-14; 4Q418 69.2.8
the lawless.
Isa 52:1
14 The Lord of Spirits shall abide over them,
38:2; 45:4; Zeph 3:17; Isa 55:1-2; 60:17-22
and with that Son of Man they shall eat,
Rev 3:20; 19:9; Isa 25:6-9; 55:1; Mk 14:25 Lk 13:29; 14:15-24; 22:16, 30; Mt 26:29
and lie down and rise up[1259] for ever and ever.
Wis 5:15; Zeph 3:13; Jn 14:23; Ps 23:5-6 Ps 26:4-5; Mt 8:11; Rev 21:3
15 The righteous and chosen shall be raised up from the earth[1260]
20:8; TBenj 10:6, 9; Dan 12:2; 2Mac 7:9
and cease to have downcast faces.
Mt 13:43; 1Thes 4:17; 2Bar 30:1-2
They shall be clothed with garments of glory.[1261]
Isa 52:1-2; 61:10; Dan 12:3; ApPet 17 Rev 6:11
16 This shall be your garment, a garment of life from the Lord
Mt 22:11-13; 4Ezra 2:39, 45; 2Cor 5:3-5
of Spirits: and your garments shall not wear out,
Rev 3:4, 5, 18; 4:4; 6:11; 7:9, 13, 14 Deut 8:4; 29:5
nor your glory fade away in the presence of the Lord of Spirits.
108:12; 2Bar 51:1-10

[1257] "'Shame' is a way of describing the loss of one's case in court, see (Isa 41:11-13; 44:9-11; 50:7-9)" (NV2 pg. 266).

[1258] Or "angels for punishment". However, we have already been introduced to angels of punishment (1En 53:3; 56:1; 63:1; 66:1). For a description and functions of angels of punishment see (TAb A 11:5; 12:1-2; ApZeph 4:1-7).

[1259] **"The verb pair 'lie down-rise up' denotes daily existence from start to finish, and this will include table-time at what will be, by definition, the messianic banquet"** (NV2 pg. 267). See also Rev 21:3. This verse also relates to the daily practical trials of the community the Parables were addressed to. "We can imagine that many Jews in this Enochic community are obviously exhausted, hungry, and so oppressed that they can find no rest" (R pg. 462 Charlesworth).

[1260] **The righteous and chosen are resurrected and raptured!**

[1261] For other mentions and descriptions of heavenly garments see (1Bar 5:1-2; PssSol 11:7; AscenIs 4:16-17; 8:14-15; 9:9-10; Isa 61:10; 2Cor 5:2-4; Rev 3:4-5, 18; 4:4; 6:11; 7:9; 13-14; 16:15; 19:7-8 and 1QS 4.7-8 (W pg. 121). These garments are associated with the heavenly feast in a parable of Christ (Mt 22:11-13).

The Mighty and the Kings Beg for Mercy

63 1 In those days the governors and the kings who possess	Isa 52:15
the earth will plead with the angels of punishment[1262] to whom	53:3; ApPet 20; TAb A 12:1; ApZeph 4:1-7
they were delivered up, to grant them a brief respite that they	62:11; Mt 13:40-43
might fall down and worship before the Lord of Spirits and	
confess their sins before him.[1263]	
2 And they will praise and glorify the Lord of Spirits saying:	62:6; Ps 138:4-5
"Blessed is the Lord of Spirits and the Lord of kings,	22:14
and the Lord of the mighty and the master of the rich,	
and the Lord of glory and the Lord of wisdom!	1Cor 2:8; Jas 2:1
3 Every secret thing will be brought to light; your power is	9:4-5; 38:3; 49:2; Job 12:22; Lk 8:17
from generation to generation,[1264] and your glory for ever	Mk 4:22
and ever. Deep are all your secrets, and innumerable,	84:3; Deut 29:29
and your righteousness is beyond all calculation.	
4 We have learned our lesson now: that we should glorify	Rom 14:11; Phil 2:10
and bless the Lord of kings and him who rules over all kings."	1Tim 6:14-16; Rev 17:14; 19:16
5 And they shall say: "Would that we might be given respite[1265]	
to glorify, praise and make confession[1266] before his glory!	
6 Now we are begging for a little rest but do not find it:	4Ezra 7:82
we pursue it, but obtain it not. Light has vanished from before us,	10:4-5; Lam 3:6
and darkness shall be our dwelling-place for ever and ever.	46:6; 2Thes 1:9; 1QS 4.13; Ps 143:3
7 For before him we have not made confession.	38:2
Nor glorified the Name of the Lord of Spirits and of kings,	46:5
but our trust has been in the scepter of our kingdom	Wis 5:5-8; Jer 17:5
and in our glory.[1267]	
8 But now on the day of our suffering and distress he does not	
save us, and we find no respite to make confession,	
that our Lord is true in all his deeds, and in his judgements	Col 3:25; Jub 5:15

[1262] The mighty and the kings will seek permission from the angels of punishment to plead for mercy from God. Nickelsburg speaks of: "Angels of punishment" "For these angels as a staple in Jewish eschatology, see 1 QS iv.12 and T Abr A 11:5, as well as CD ii.6 and less obviously, 1QS ii.5-7" (NV2 pg. 266). See also (4Q473 2.7; 1QM 13.12; 1QS 4:12; TAb A 12:1-2; and ApZeph 4:1-7). Angels of destruction may be different. In (4Q510 1:4-5) destroying angels are included in a list of malignant spirits "all the spirits of the destroying angels, spirits of the bastards, demons, Lilith, howlers, and [desert dwellers…]"

[1263] Nickelsburg notes: **"Having failed to receive mercy from the Son of Man and the Lord of Spirits, in anguish and self-pity they address their petition to their brutal angelic guards, only to be rejected again and dragged off to hell"** (NV2 pg. 268).

[1264] For this line Knibb has: "And everything secret is clear before you, and your power is for all generations" OL admits the line is obscure and translates "And in every hidden thing your power shines, from generation to generation" (OL pg. 118). This line agrees with Black "Every secret thing will be brought to light."

[1265] The language in this request for a respite "could then imply not only a request for a respite from their punishment but for a cessation of it" (BL pg. 237).

[1266] "Make confession"; "*Confess our faith*—The basis of salvation has been inconsistent (1 Enoch 60:6, 61:8), but here the appeal for mercy includes the content of faith, something that must be believed (and has heretofore not been believed) for the circumstances to change. See verse 7" (H2 pg. 194). "Make confession" has also been translated as "give thanks" (BL pg. 238).

[1267] For this line Nickelsburg has: "scepter of our kingdom and <throne of> our glory."

and his justice, and his judgements show no respect of persons.[1268] Acts 10:34-35; Rom 2:11; Eph 6:9
9 We vanish from before his face on account of our works,
and all our sins are justly reckoned up."[1269] 89:61-62
10 Then will they say to themselves: "Our souls are full of Mt 16:26; Ps 49:16-17; Jas 5:4
ill-gotten gains,[1270] but they will not keep us from going down 46:7; 52:7; 94:7-8; Lk 16:9, 19-31; Sir 5:8
into the flames of the torment of Sheol."[1271] 22; Isa 14:9-15; Ps 49:7-14
11 After that their faces shall be filled with darkness and shame 46:6; 97:6
in the presence of that Son of Man; Mt 7:23; 25:41; Lk 12:8-9
and they shall be banished from his presence, 32:6; 62:10; Gen 3:23-24; 2Thes 1:9
and the sword shall remain before his face in their midst.[1272] 62:12; 90:19, 34; Rev 19:15, 21
12 Thus spoke the Lord of Spirits: "This is the decree and the 14:4; 69:27
judgement, with respect to the powerful and the kings and the 38:5
high officials and those who possess the land,
before the Lord of Spirits."

Enoch sees the Fallen Angels

64 1 Then I saw other presences[1273] hidden in that place. 10:5-14; 17:1; 18:16; 40:2
2 I heard the voice of the angel saying: "These are the angels Mt 25:41
who descended to the earth, and revealed what was hidden Jude 6
to the children of men and they led the children of men astray 6-8
into committing sin."[1274]

[1268] **It is too late to repent after death, and wealth or social standing has no consideration. This is the same message as in the parable of the rich man and Lazarus (Lk 16:19-31).**

[1269] For this line Knibb has: "and all our sins have been counted exactly."

[1270] Other references to ill-gotten gains can be found in the Damascus Document (CD 6.15 (W pg. 57); 8.5-7 (W pg. 59)). **Leaders of the Christian Church were counseled by Paul and Peter to avoid the love of money** (1Tim 3:3; 3:8; Tit 1:7; and 1Pet 5:2).

[1271] For 63:9 Knibb has: "Then they will say to them, 'Our souls are sated with possessions gained through iniquity, but they do not prevent our going down into the flames of the torment of Sheol.'" Charles postulates that this may have read "into the stronghold of Sheol." "This theology echoes Matthew 16:26, 'For what will it profit a man if he gains the whole world and forfeits his soul?'" (H2 pg. 194-195).

[1272] "The reference to a "sword" and God's presence ("his face") takes the readers mind back to Genesis 3:24, where the cherubim 'and a flaming sword' guard the way to the tree of life after Adam and Eve were driven out of the Garden. The point is that those under judgment will be granted no access to God's presence" (H2 pg. 195).

[1273] Isaac has: "mysterious faces" in place of presences. K and N have "figures." Olson has: "presences." In Ethiopic it is literally "faces." These are the fallen angels in their place of condemnation along with the mighty and kings. Compare: "Then he will say to those on his left, 'Depart from me, you cursed, into the eternal fire prepared for the devil and his angels'" (Mt 25:41).

[1274] "In the Book of the Parables, the focus of the crime of the Watchers is not their sexual transgressions, but the revelation of forbidden knowledge to humans. See Enoch 54:3-6" (H2 pg. 195).

Excursus: The development of the concept of Sheol/Gehenna.

The following is an excellent summary of the development of the concept of Sheol by R. H. Charles.

> **Sheol.** This word has borne different meanings at different periods and also different meanings during the same period, owing to the coexistence of different stages in the development of thought. As these different meanings are to be found in Enoch, a short history of the conception will be the best means of explanation. (**1**) Sheol in the O.T. is the place appointed for all living, (Job 30:23) from its grasp there is never any possibility of escape, (Job 7:9). It is situated beneath the earth, (Num 16:30) it is the land of darkness and confusion, (Job 10:21, 22) of destruction, forgetfulness, and silence, (Pss. 88:11, 12; 94:17; 115:17). Nevertheless, the identity of the individual is in some measure preserved, (Isa 14:10; Ezek. 32:21; 1 Sam, 28:15 sqq.); but the existence is joyless and has no point of contact with God or human interests, (Pss. 6:5 30:9; Isa 38:11, 18). In the conception of Sheol there is no moral or religious element involved; no moral distinctions are observed in it; good and bad fare alike. But the family, national, and social distinctions of the world above are still reproduced, and men are gathered to their fathers or people, (Gen 25:8, 9; 35:29; Ezek 32:17-32); kings are seated on their thrones even there, (Isa 14:9, 10; Ezek. 32:21, 24). Thus the O.T. Sheol does not differ essentially from the Homeric Hades, Odyssey (xi, 488, 489). This view of Sheol was the orthodox and prevailing one till the second century B.C.; cf. (Sir. 14:16; 17:22, 23; 30:17; 1 Bar. 3:11; Tob. 3:10; 13:2:1) 1 Enoch 102:11 (i.e., where Sadducees are introduced as speaking). Individual voices indeed had been raised against it in favour of a religious conception of Sheol, and finally through their advocacy this higher conception gradually won its way into acceptance. (**2**) This second and higher conception of Sheol was the product of the same religious thought that gave birth to the doctrine of the Resurrection—the thought that found the answer to its difficulties by carrying the idea of retribution into the life beyond the grave. The old conception thus underwent a double change. Firstly, it became essentially a place where men were treated according to their deserts, with a division for the righteous, and a division for the wicked. And, secondly, from being the unending abode of the departed, it came to be only an intermediate state; (cf. 1En. 22; 51:1; 102:5 (?) Luke 16:22 (?)). (**3**) The conception underwent a further change, and no longer signified the intermediate state of the righteous and of the wicked but came to be used of the abode of the wicked only, either as their preliminary abode, (cf. Rev. 1:18; 6:8; 20:13, 14) or as their final one, (1En. 63:10; 99:11; 103:7). This was probably due to the fact that the Resurrection was limited to the righteous, and thus the souls of the wicked simply remained in Sheol, which thus practically became hell or Gehenna; (cf. Pss. Sol. 14:6; 15:11).[1275]

Charles does not here express the role of Christ in changing the concept. Sheol/Hades, the realm of the dead, including the righteous dead, was controlled by the Devil and the Rephaim. Christ, after His payment, descended into this realm and rescued His own, the righteous dead, from Satan's domain. From that point, the souls of the dead in Christ, no longer endure Hades but ascend directly into Paradise. The unrighteous dead, still in Hades, await the final judgement.

[1275] C pg. 127.

Excursus: Did the Noahic passages and interpolations from the Book of Parables exist *prior* to the time of Christ?

Nickelsburg promotes the idea that the Noahic interpolations predate the gospels.

> Our earliest evidence for the Noah material in the Parables appears to be the middle of the first century C.E. The parallel between "the days of Noah" and "the days of the Son of Man" in the "Q" tradition in Matt 24:37-39 || Luke 17:26-27 points to the Parables in a form that included the Noachic interpolations. This allows a terminus ante quem around the turn of the era also for 1 Enoch 65-66.[1276]

The New Testament associates the flood event with the second coming of Christ.

> For as were the days of Noah, so will be the coming of the Son of Man. For as in those days before the flood they were eating and drinking, marrying and giving in marriage, until the day when Noah entered the ark, and they were unaware until the flood came and swept them all away, so will be the coming of the Son of Man (Mt 24:37-39).

> Just as it was in the days of Noah, so also will it be in the days of the Son of Man. People were eating, drinking, marrying and being given in marriage up to the day Noah entered the ark. Then the flood came and destroyed them all (Lk 17:26-27).

In addition, the proximity of the flood reference, in concert with Enochic material in 2 Peter, suggests that the Noahic interpolations were present at the time 2 Peter was written.

> For if God did not spare angels when they sinned, but cast them into hell and committed them to chains of gloomy darkness to be kept until the judgement; if he did not spare the ancient world, but preserved Noah, a herald of righteousness, with seven others, when he brought a flood upon the world of the ungodly; (2Pet 2:4-5).

Jude 6-7 may indicate knowledge of (1En 67:8-13). It could be associating the location where the angels are imprisoned and Herod sought relief, at the waters of Callirrhoe, with the nearby sites of Sodom and Gomorrah (Sodom lies just 13 miles north of the springs[1277] and the main road passed nearby Sodom). The angels with their unnatural sexual sin, king Herod's known perverse sexual sins, and that of the Sodomites are thus all rolled into one geographic region. However, this evidence is far from conclusive, as the flood would naturally be associated with the watcher story; given that the whole point of the flood was to judge the Nephilim and those who learned unrighteousness from the watchers. It should also be kept in mind that the judgements of the flood, Sodom and the giants are also associated in other texts dated before Jude such as (3Mac 2:4-5; Jub 20:5 Sirach 16:7-8; TNap 3:4b-5). The sin of watchers practicing forbidden sex with women and men attempting homosexual sex with angels were associated together, in that both were forbidden.

[1276] NV2 pg. 279.

[1277] Collins, Steven, Scott, Latayne C. 2013. *Discovering the City of Sodom*, Howard Books.

Noahic Interpolations

Why the Flood Judgment is Coming

65 1 In those days, I, Noah, saw that the earth had warped Isa 24:18-20
downward[1278] and that its destruction was near.[1279] 83:3-4
2 And I picked up my feet and dashed to the ends of the earth,[1280] 106:8; Ps 61:2; 1QapGen 2.21-22
and shouted to my great-grandfather Enoch. 1Sam 28:5-15
Three times I cried bitterly, "Hear me! hear me! hear me!"
4 Thereupon at once there was a great quaking on the earth,
and a voice was heard from heaven, and I fell on my face.
5 Then my great-grandfather Enoch came and stood by me, and
said to me: "Why have you called me with a bitter cry and tears? 83:6; 1Sam 28:5-15
3 So, I said to him: "Tell me what is taking place on the earth 60:1-3; 102:1-2
that the earth staggers so, and violently shakes, lest I shall
perish with it."[1281] [1282]
9 After that my great-grandfather Enoch took hold of me by
my hand and raised me up, and told me: "Go, for I have asked
the Lord of Spirits about the quaking on the earth.[1283]
6 A command has gone forth from the presence of the Lord Mt 4:5
concerning[1284] those who dwell on the earth that this must be
their end.[1285] Because they have acquired all the secrets of the 7:1; Gen 6:5; Dan 2:10-11
angels, and all the violence[1286] of the satans,[1287] and all their 40:7
arcane powers,[1288] and all the powers of those who practice
sorcery, and the power of spells,[1289] and the powers of those Ex 32:24; Deut 18:10-14; Isa 49:9; 12

[1278] N and K have "tilted" In place of "warped downward." I has: "deformed" "According to the author's world view, the earth was a flat disc, which was now tilted precariously and (is) in danger of toppling" (NV2 pg. 281).

[1279] **Scholarly consensus since Lawrence's 1821 translation has identified 65:1-66:3; 67:1-68:1; and 69:2-25 as major interpolations into an earlier form of the Book of Parables** (NV2 pg. 277).

[1280] The end of the earth is the entrance to heaven where Noah could find his great-grandfather Enoch. (BL pg. 239) (C pg. 129) (1En 106:8).

[1281] Isaac has "perish with her in the impact."

[1282] N and OL move 65:3 to after 65:5 as in this text; as it plainly belongs there.

[1283] 65:9 is moved into this position as Enoch's discourse starts here and continues into 65:6.

[1284] Nickelsburg has: "against" in place of "concerning."

[1285] **"As the Book of the Watchers makes clear, the point here is not merely that humanity had learned secret knowledge, but that the result of doing so was humanity's corruption: 'And the whole earth has been corrupted through the works that were taught by Azâzêl. To him ascribe all sin'"** (1 Enoch 10:8) (H2 pg. 198).

[1286] K has "wrongdoing" in place of "violence."

[1287] **"Satan's followers, the watchers, are named in the plural only here and in 40:7. 'Satan' is used in the singular in 53:3 in association with the punishing angels, and in 54:6, evidently as an alternative title for Azazel, the archdemon of the Parables"** (NV2 pg. 283).

[1288] Isaac has: "occult powers."

[1289] In place of "and the power of spells" Isaac has: "all the powers of (those who mix) many colors. Nickelsburg has: "the powers of (brightly) color(ed garments)," Others are as in this text.

who make molten images for the entire world.[1290] 8:1-3; Ex 34:17; 2Kgs 17:16-17; 23:24
7 And furthermore, how silver is extracted from the dust Job 28:1-2
of the earth, and how mixed metals[1291] originate there.[1292]
8 For lead and tin are produced[1293] from the earth just as silver is. Num 31:22; Ex 22:17-21
They are produced in a flow, and an angel stands in the flow and
distributes them."[1294]
10 And he said to me: "Because of their iniquities, their Eccl 7:29
judgement shall be fully carried out and shall not be withheld
before me; because of the sorceries which they have searched Gal 5:20; Rev 18:23
out and mastered, the earth and those who dwell upon it shall
be destroyed.
11 These (watchers) will never have a place of refuge for ever,
because they have revealed to humanity what was secret, 60:10; Rev 2:24
and they have been condemned. But as for you, my son, the
Lord of Spirits knows that you are innocent and guiltless[1295] <u>Gen 6:9</u>
of this reproach concerning these mysteries.
12 He has established your name to be among the holy ones,
and will preserve you from among those who dwell on the earth, 83:8; Gen 9:1-11; 17:6-7; Sir 44:17
and he has established your righteous seed both for sovereignty[1296] 10:16; 67:3; 84:6
and for great honors. From your offspring will flow a 106:16,18; Deut 33:28
fountain[1297] of the righteous and holy without number forever." 48:1-2; Jn 4:13-14; 7:38; Ps 68:26

[1290] For 65:6 Isaac has: "An order has been issued from the court of the Lord against those who dwell upon the earth, that their doom has arrived because they have acquired the knowledge of all the secrets of the angels, all the oppressive deeds of the Satans, as well as all their most occult powers, all the powers of those who practice sorcery, all the powers of (those who mix) many colors, all the powers of those who make molten images;" Note his mention of the "court of the Lord" AKA the "Council of God" as in (Ps 29:1; 82:1; 89:5, 7; 4Q400 1.1.4-5; 4Q400 1.2.7-9; 4Q402 1.3; 4Q181 1.3-4; Job 1:6; 2:1: 38:7; 1Kgs 22:19-23; Dan 4:17). This is a ruling council of "god-like beings," who under God's oversight, control creation and all that is in it.

[1291] Most manuscripts say: "soft metal." Isaac has: "bronze."

[1292] Nickelsburg has: "and how soft metal <is poured out> on the earth."

[1293] This reading follows the Ethiopic Tana manuscript or D'. All the others say, "are <u>not</u> produced."

[1294] This text follows Knibb's common sense reading of this controversial phrase which literally means "and this angel runs." Since these metals are seldom found in pure form, they must be separated. Asael was preeminent as the watcher who introduced metallurgy and colored dyes (1En 8:1). The author may be viewing an angel underling of Asael as separating the metal. The melting point of silver is much higher than lead and tin. Nickelsburg translates the line as "an angel stands in it and the angel is preeminent." Olson has: "Within this flow stands an angel—an angel that runs ahead." Olson associates this angel with the smelting process that separates silver and lead and tin. Isaac has: "and he is a running angel." Running angels, those who do not remain at their post, are found in other early and later Jewish and Christian texts (*ApZeph* 9:4; *Ps-Philo* 11:5; *3En* 25:5; *Apocalypse of Paul* 35; *Questions of Bartholomew* IV, 47; *Sepher Ha-Razim* 1:200; 2:158; 3:39-40; 4:3; 5:6).

[1295] Isaac has: "pure and kindhearted." "Noah was untainted by the forbidden knowledge and its corruption" (H2 pg. 199).

[1296] Sovereignty i.e. kingship.

[1297] **The holy and righteous fountain coming from the seed of Noah is Israel. The righteous fountain is ultimately the Messiah. (See 48:1-2). The fountain that brings righteousness given by Christ is contrasted with the metallic fountain that brings corruption controlled by Azazel (65:8).**

The Floodwaters Prepared

66 1 After that, he showed me the angels of punishment,[1298] 53:3; Rev 9:14-15; ApZeph 4:1-7
who were prepared to go forth and let loose all the power of Rev 7:1-3; ApPet 20; TAb A 12:1
the waters which are beneath the earth in order to bring Gen 7:11
judgement and destruction on all who reside and dwell
on the earth.
2 But the Lord of Spirits gave orders to the angels who were 65:6
going forth, that they should not raise their hands[1299] 60:16, 21-22; Ps 10:12
but keep watch (over the water enclosures),[1300] for those angels Rev 7:2-3; 16:5; 1Pet 3:20
were entrusted with the powers of the waters.[1301]
3 Then I went away from the presence of Enoch.

Noah is Promised Salvation from the Flood

67 1 In those days[1302] the word of the Lord[1303] came to me, and MT 24:37-39; Lk 17:26
he said: "Noah, your lot has come up before me, a lot without Sir 44:17
blame, one of love[1304] and uprightness. Gen 6:9-16; 1QapGen 6.1-4
2 At this moment the angels are building a wooden (vessel),[1305] 10:1-3; 89:1; Gen 6:14-16; 1Pet 3:20
and when the angels have completed this work, Gen 7:16; Wis 10:4; 4Q422 2.5
I will place my hand upon it and preserve it, and there
shall come forth from it the seed of life and a transformation Gen 7:3; 8:15-17
shall take place so that the earth will not be empty (of inhabitants). 84:5

[1298] Like the angels in (Rev 7:1), these angels of punishment hold back judgement until the righteous are safe.

[1299] In place of "raise their hands" BL translates: "show their power." These angels of punishment are under God's control, who commands them to wait until the ark is built, before releasing the water.

[1300] **At the commandment of God, judgement is delayed, presumably until the angels complete the ark. "The idea of withholding or delaying an eschatological act until certain conditions are fulfilled occurs also in roughly contemporary literature."** (NV2 pg. 285) (For similar instances see Rev 7:1-3; 2Thes 2:1-8; 4Ezra 4:36-37; 2Bar 51:11 and 1Cor 15:23-28). **In a similar way, Christ's second coming is being delayed until the last soul is redeemed** (2Pet 3:9).

[1301] For 66:2 Knibb has: "And the Lord of Spirits commanded the angels who were *then* coming out not to raise *their* hands, but to keep watch; for those angels were in charge of the forces of the waters." Isaac has: "But the Lord of the Spirits gave an order to the angels who were on duty that they should not raise the (water) enclosures but guard (them)–for they were the angels who were in charge of the waters." The expression "*power* of the water(s) … conveys the same violent image as the verb … in Gen 7:11 ("all the fountains of the great deep burst forth") (NV2 pg. 285).

[1302] The days just before the flood.

[1303] "The word of the Lord came to me" is a standard prophetic formula.

[1304] "'Love' (Ethiopic *feqr*) is not ascribed to Noah in parallel passages. Here it might mean his love of others, but perhaps, more likely, it denotes his love of God. In this sense, if the love of God corresponds to piety, it could reflect the word pair 'righteous and pious'…" (NV2 pg. 287). Black postulates that it may have originally read "the lot of a lover of righteousness" (BL pg. 241).

[1305] That there was a supernatural hand in the construction of the ark is evident from Gen 7:16. "And those that entered, male and female of all flesh, went in as God had commanded him. And the LORD shut him in." **"Black observes that this is the only place in Second Temple Jewish literature that has angels building the ark"** (BL pg. 241). "The construction of the ark by the angels may be unique to this verse, although there is a possible exception in 89:1" (NV2 pg. 288). **1Pet 3:20 seems to have a passive role for Noah in preparing the ark as here.**

3 I will establish your offspring before me for ever and ever, Gen 9:1, 9, 11; 13:15
and I will scatter abroad those who dwell with you so that your Gen 10:32; 11:8; 15:5; Jub 8:8-9:15
seed, will not prove unfruitful on the face of the earth.
I will not (again) put (them) to the test on the face of the earth, Gen 8:21; 4Q422 2.11
rather they shall be blessed and multiply upon the earth in 65:12
the Name of the Lord."

The Fiery Underworld Prison for the Fallen Angels (Callirrhoe)

4 He[1306] will imprison those angels who have revealed iniquity 18:5-16; 54:1-6
(to mankind) in that burning underworld which my Mt 25:41
great-grandfather Enoch had formerly shown to me in the west 23:1-24:1
among the mountains of gold, silver, iron, soft metal,[1307] and tin. 52
5 I also saw that underworld, and in it was a tremendous Jn 5:2-14
turbulence and a churning of the waters.[1308]
6 And when all this was happening, fiery molten metal together 52:6
with the turbulence which convulsed those (waters) in that place
generated a smell of sulfur and it mixed with those waters.[1309] *Cels* 5.52-55; Rev 20:10
And that underworld of those deceiving angels who [1310] Jude 6
had led astray (mankind) burned beneath that land;[1311]
7 and through its caverns[1312] flow rivers of fire, where these

---

[1306] K and I have "they" in place of "He."

[1307] Jerusalem was to the west of a place of biblical Enoch. But directions are confused in this portion of the Parables. Isaac has: "bronze" in place of "soft metal."

[1308] **Surprising similarities exist between the pool of Bethesda account in (John 5:2-7) and the account of the waters (presumably near Callirrhoe) in 1 Enoch 67:5-8. Convulsion of water, angels, and healing are common to both.** N and K have: "disturbance" in place of "turbulence." For 67:5 Isaac has: "I also saw that valley in which there took place a great turbulence and the stirring of the waters."

[1309] The author appears to have had firsthand experience with volcanic activity.

[1310] **"The author associates this place of punishment with the whole region from the fiery Valley of Hinnom in Jerusalem ... down the Kidron Valley, and over to the east shore of the Dead Sea, where the author believes that the hot springs of Kallirrhoë (67:8-13) spew out sulfurous fumes emanating from the subterranean waters that boil from the molten metal that flows out from the seven mountains"** (NV2 pg. 289). **This location likely matches the hot springs resort of Hamrnarnat Ma'in, situated in Wadi Zarqa near Machaerus in modern day Jordan, or a place nearby. Sulfur mines in antiquity were also located in this area.**

[1311] **This text is mentioned in (Origen's *Against Celsus*, Book 5, Chap. 54-55). This text by Origen, when read very closely, and with understanding of the issues involved, appears to place the Parables into a legitimate Book of Enoch and *The Book of Dream Visions* section of 1 Enoch into the category of the Books of Enoch "which do not at all circulate in the Churches as divine."** The point is that "the 60-70 who descended" is from 1 Enoch 89:59 which is in the *Book of Dream Visions* which he seems to consider being of questionable divine origin. It introduces the 70 beings who misruled the nations. But then, when he immediately afterward discusses the "warm springs" (1En 67:8-11), Origen places that passage in the Book of Enoch. **Origen's (AD 185-253) discussion displays intimate familiarity with the Book of Enoch.**

[1312] "Caverns" From the context, these are subterranean rivers of burning lava. Most translate this word as "valley" "ravine" "deep valley" or "depths of the valley." The Ge' ez word used here, q^w allā, (ቈላ) (pl. q^w allāt) means valley, lowland, low place. However, it is connected in meaning to qalāy (pl. qalāyāt) 'depth (of river, sea), ocean, gulf, abyss, pit, ravine, gully, underworld, lower regions, (Lt) pool, pond' (Leslau - Comparative Dictionary of Geʿez (1987) pgs. 426 and 431). I have thus used: "underworld" or "caverns" in place of valleys in its occurrences where it is clearly referring to a subterranean setting. Uses of the word in the Book of Watchers are referring to

angels[1313] will be punished, who had led astray the inhabitants of the earth. 54:6; Mt 25:41
8 Now those waters will perform a service for the kings, the War 1.33.5; Ant 17.6.5
mighty, the exalted, and those who occupy the dry ground, 38:4
for the healing of their flesh, but for the judgement of their 1Cor 5:5
spirits.[1314] Their spirits are full of lust,[1315] so that their flesh
is punished,[1316] for they have denied the Lord of Spirits. 38:2
Every day their punishment is plainly visible to them,
and yet they still do not believe in his Name.[1317] [1318]
9 And the greater their carnal burning becomes, the greater
the price they will pay in their spirits forever and ever
for before the Lord of Spirits no one speaks a lying word.[1319] 49:4; 62:3; Rev 21:8; Mt 12:36-37
10 Judgement shall come upon them, because they believe

---

valleys such as (1En 24:2; 26:3; 26:4; 26:5; 26:6; 27:1; 27:2; 30:2; and 30:3). However in the Parables this word is referring to a flaming underworld (1En 53:1; 54:1?; 54:2?; 56:3; 56:4; 67:4; 67:5; 67:6; and 67:7).

[1313] Hot springs were viewed by some Rabbis, (*Babylonian Talmud: Tractate Shabbath Folio 39a),* and Christians (*The Martyrdom of Pionius the Presbyter and his Companions 4*) as evidence of a fiery place of judgement below the earth. The vanquished giants of Greek mythology were said to be buried under volcanoes, and to be the cause of volcanic eruptions and earthquakes.

[1314] **"A substantial majority of scholars see this passage (67:8-13) as an allusion to the last days of Herod the Great, when the ailing king unsuccessfully sought relief from a terminal illness in the hot springs of Kallirrhoë. The allusion provides a terminus post quem around 4 B.C.E. for the Noachic interpolation within which it stands"** (NV2 pg. 61). **"This still leaves open the earlier dating of the Parables text into which it was interpolated."** (NV2 pg. 61). Herod's visit to Callirrhoe was in March of 4 BC (R pg. 475 Hannah).

[1315] King Herod and his family were infamously sexually immoral (*Ant* 15.9.3 §§319-322; *War* 1.24.2 §§477). He had ten wives, one who was his cousin and another a niece (*Ant* 17.1.3 §§19-22; *War* 1.28.4 §§563) plus at least one concubine and likely more (*War* 1.25.6 §§511). Herod's son Alexander was known for pederastic relations with eunuchs (*War* 1.24.7 §§488-89; 1.25.6 §§511; *Ant* 16.8.1 §§229-231; 17.2.4 §§44). Darrell Hannah opines on the subject: "Is there another witness to this estimation of Herod in As Mos 6:2 where Herod is described as 'a man bold and shameless' (*homo temerarius et improbus*)? The latter term, *improbus* can have the connotation of 'lewd' and 'lascivious.' If this is the intended meaning, then we have here an earlier witness than Josephus. A late witness to Herod's reputation for licentiousness appears in (the Babylonian Talmud Bava Batra 3b 16), where it is asserted that he committed necrophilia with Mariamme's corpse" (R pg. 475 Hannah). The word for lust may also indicate the "pleasure and enjoyment that typifies a royal court" (NV2 pg. 291). The bones from his tomb, on the northern side of the Herodium, appear to have been scattered by revolting Jews at the beginning of the first Jewish revolt (AD 66-70).

[1316] According to Josephus, the 69 year old Herod's suffering, consisted of "a gentle fever upon him, and an intolerable itching over all the surface of his body, and continual pains in his colon, and dropsical tumors about his feet and an inflammation of the abdomen, and a putrefaction of his genitals, that produced worms" and "his genitals were rotting and produced worms" (*War* 1.33.5 §§656; *Ant* 17.6.5 §§169). This was seen as a just punishment for his cruelty and gross immorality.

[1317] "The issue of 'believing' on God's name is again present. See 1 Enoch 48:7, 60:6" (H2 pg. 207).

[1318] For 67:8, Isaac has, "Those waters shall become in those days a poisonous drug of the body and a punishment of the spirit unto the kings, rulers, and exalted ones, and those who dwell on the earth; lust shall fill their souls so that their bodies shall be punished, for they have denied the Lord of the Spirits; they shall see their own punishment every day but cannot believe in his name."

[1319] For the first line of 67:9, Nickelsburg has: "And the more their flesh is burnt, the more a change takes place in their spirits, forever and ever." "The point seems to be that the unrighteous will forever admit within their hearts that they were wrong not to believe in the Lord of Spirits. There is nothing in this verse or those that ensue that suggest a post mortem conversion and deliverance from the torturous judgement. In fact, that notion is specifically contradicted in verse 10" (H2 pg. 207).

in the lust of their flesh but the spirit of the Lord[1320] they deny.[1321] Mt 12:31-32
11 These same waters will undergo a change in those days; *Cels* 5.52
for when those angels are punished in them the heat of these
water-springs will change, and when they come up, *War* 7.6.3
the water of the springs will change and become cold.[1322] [1323]
12 I heard Michael speak up and say: "This judgement wherewith
the angels are punished serves as a warning for the kings and 55:4; 2Pet 2:4-5
the mighty who possess the land.[1324]
13 These waters of punishment minister to the healing of the
bodies of the kings and the lust of their flesh;[1325] [1326]
but they do not perceive and do not believe that these same Rev 21:8

1320 "Spirit of the Lord." Black theorizes that a theologically minded scribe may have altered this line from the more usual "deny the Lord of Spirits" (BL pg. 243).

1321 **It should be kept in mind how dangerous criticizing king Herod was. At the very time of the event of Herod bathing in the waters of Callirrhoe, he had gathered together in bonds "the most illustrious men of the whole Jewish nation, out of every village, into a place called the Hippodrome," intending to have them killed when he died, so people would be morning when he died! (War 1.33.6 §§ 659-660). John the Baptist was beheaded by king Herod's son for accusations like those stated in this text (Mt 14:1-12; Mk 6:14-20). This is certainly one reason for writing the Parables under a pseudonym!**

1322 "According to v. 11, the waters are heated when the angels are placed there for temporary punishment, but they cool when the angels are taken out to the place of their final punishment. This contrasting of hot and cold waters may have been inspired by second-hand knowledge of the hot and cold springs of Baaras (*War* 7.6.3 §§ 178-89)" (NV2 pg. 291-292). Josephus speaks of the different temperatures of the water at Callirrhoë and associates the area with the Baaras root which is used to drive away demons from those who are sick (*War* 7.6.3 §§ 180-187). The punished angels will at some time leave the prison they are confined in; at which point the waters will become cool. So, at some point they will be released as in (Rev 20:3).

1323 "The continuity between vv.4-6 and 7-11 suggests that both sets of verses were composed by the same author/interpolator, and the focus on the Enochic themes of the arrogance and punishment of "the kings and the mighty" indicates that these verses were composed with knowledge of the *Parables*" (NV2 pg. 292).

1324 **The kings and mighty who are using the springs to bring healing, do not understand that they are bathing in waters heated by the fiery punishment of the fallen watchers! Upon judgement they will be joining them in torment!**

1325 For the first line in 67:13, Isaac has: "For these waters of judgment are poison to the bodies of the angels as well as sensational to their flesh"

1326 "Josephus Flavius relates that, shortly before his death from complications of diabetes (Fournier gangrene and end-stage renal failure), Herod visited his villa at Callirrhoë, on the northeastern shores of the Dead Sea, where there were thermal baths, well known throughout the Empire for their healing properties. In his case, however, the waters did not help, and Herod died a few days later in severe pain, interpreted by some as divine punishment for his sexual immorality (*War* 1.656-58 (1.33.5); *Ant* 17.168-72 (17.6.5). Due to Herod's international fame, the circumstances of his death became widely known, so it should cause no surprise to find echoes and allusions in contemporary literature. In the Book of Parables, the fiery valley in which the rebellious angels were incarcerated to await judgment is identified with the valley that generates the thermal springs to which 'the kings and the mighty and the exalted' resort for healing. But because they have believed in satisfying their own pleasure and have denied the name of the Lord of Spirits, the place where they seek healing will also become the place of their judgment (1En 67:4-12). The allusion to Herod's judgment and death becomes even more evident when we discover that it was written as an update by the author of the Parables, and that this same author describes the punishment as a judgment for seeking (sexual) pleasure, a known fault of Herod, but a slight deviation from the reason stated in the rest of the text, namely, for persecuting and oppressing the righteous. This can therefore be understood as a specific allusion to Herod's terminal illness, in the light of his recent death in 4 BCE" (Daniel, John Ben 2021. *The Parables of Enoch (1Enoch 37-71): Provenance and Social Setting* pg. 13). **This interpolation therefore provides a terminus date for the Parables of soon after Herod's death. This dates the composition of the *Parables* to about the time of the birth of Christ** (OL pg. 122).

waters will change to become a fire which burns forever."[1327] [1328] 2Thes 1:9

68 1 [After this my great-grandfather Enoch gave me[1329] the
instruction[1330] of all the secrets in the parables that were given 37:5; 60:1
to him; and he gathered them for me in the words of
the Book of Parables.][1331]

Michael and Raphael Tremble at the Severity of the Judgement

2 On that day[1332] Michael answered Raphael[1333] and said: "The
power of the spirit seizes me[1334]and makes me tremble[1335] 2Pet 2:10-11; Jas 2:19
because of the severity of the judgement of the secrets[1336]—the
punishment of the angels.[1337] Who can endure the severity
of the sentence which is to be executed? They melt before it."
3 Michael spoke further and said to Raphael: "Who is there
whose heart[1338] has not felt softened over it?[1339] Who is not
shaken deep within himself by this word of judgement which

[1327] **(1En 67:4-13), taken together with the references to angels in chains (1En 54:3,4; 56:1; 69:28) and the angels weeping in (1En 13:9-10) appear to be the sources Celsus (ca. AD 178) in ignorance, conflates with (1En 89:59) in (Origen's *Against Celsus* 5.52-55 ca. AD 250). Origen's response to Celsus betrays his intimate knowledge of the *Parables*, *Book of Watchers*, and *Book of Dream Visions*. He would not have studied these books so closely if he did not regard them as important.**

[1328] **These hot springs are still a resort area in the present day. They are found on the northeast shore of the Dead Sea west of Machaerus (where John the Baptist was imprisoned and beheaded). "The site of an anchorage and a village that included a large villa and thermal bath complex constructed by king Herod, Kallirrhoë was visited by Herod in his last days as he and his physicians futilely sought to assuage the severe pains of his terminal illness (*War* 1.33.5 §§656-58; *Ant* 17.6.5 §§168-72). Although Josephus says that the waters of Kallirrhoë are sweet (*J.W.* 1.33.5 §657), he describes the hot springs of Baaras, some four kilometers to the east, as the source of hot springs that poured forth both bitter and sweet water, and he locates sulfur and alum mines in the area (J.W. 7.6.3 §§178-89). Evidently the author of the present section had a less-than-precise picture of the local geography" (NV2 pg. 290-291).**

[1329] Me=Noah

[1330] Charles observes: this "verse (68.1) comes from the redactor who combined the Parables and the Noah fragments." Heiser notes: "This line creates the impression that 1 Enoch 68 (and perhaps 67) was added after the *Book of Parables* had been written" (H2 pg. 209). Nickelsburg views the section as not original (N pg. 87). Black, Dillman, and Charles also agree that this passage is not original to the text. According to Nickelsburg's reconstruction the original *Book of Parables* does not pick up again until 69:2.

[1331] The Book of Parables gets its name from 68:1.

[1332] This is the day when God calls for the angels to execute judgement against the fallen watchers.

[1333] One manuscript reads: "And on that day the holy Michael answered Raphael," here and in 68:3 and 68:4.

[1334] Charles postulates that this text may have originally read "the power of my spirit seizes me" (C pg. 135).

[1335] Isaac has: "causes me to go up" in place of "makes me to tremble" but suggests other possibilities of "rouses me," "provokes me" and "angers me." For the whole phrase Nickelsburg has: "The power of the spirit seizes me and aggravates me," The image of lesser celestial beings trembling before a great deity is also found in ancient Akkadian texts (Kienast, *Igigu and Anunnakku according to the Akkadian sources*, found in Heiser, Michael S. and Clapper, Dorothea., tr. 2018., *The Anunnaki Gods According to Ancient Mesopotamian Sources*, pg. 56).

[1336] These are the secrets that the watchers revealed to humans.

[1337] In 68:2 and again in 68:3 Michael expresses sympathy for the fallen watchers. Intercession is not a possibility since the decree of God has already gone forth.

[1338] K has "mind" in place of "heart." N has "kidneys."

[1339] Some manuscripts read: "Whose heart would not feel convicted over it."

has gone out against them?" There were others who responded
to them in the same manner.[1340] [1341]
4 But as it happened, when they stood before the Lord of
Spirits,[1342] Michael said thus to Raphael, "In the sight of the
Lord, I will not support them, for the Lord of Spirits is angry
with them because they act as if they were like the Lord![1343] Isa 14:13-14; Ex 20:4
5 Therefore, everything that has been concealed[1344] will
come upon them forever and ever; for no angel or human[1345]
may receive that which properly belongs to God. But they by
themselves will receive their condemnation for ever and ever.

69 1 After this, the judgment will terrify them and make them 1:5
tremble [1346] because they have revealed this to those who dwell
on the earth."

Another List of the Fallen Angels

2 Behold, I name the names of those angels! These are their
names:[1347] [1348]the first of them is Semyaza, the second Artaqifa, 6:7; 8:1-3
the third Armen, the fourth Kokabiel,[1349] the fifth Turuel, the
sixth Rumel, the seventh Danyal, the eighth Niqael, the ninth

---

[1340] This text follows the Tana manuscript here.

[1341] Nickelsburg states that the last phrase of 68:3 can be translated as "'against those whom they have led out thus,' that is the fallen angels who are being led from temporary confinement, to permanent punishment" (NV2 pg. 293-94).

[1342] The location of the discussion now shifts to the throne room of God.

[1343] The point seems to be, that the fallen watchers have sought to take unto themselves the authority of God, by revealing secrets to humankind. For the first sentence of Michael's response Isaac quite differently has: "They shall not prosper before the eye of the Lord; for they have quarreled with the Lord of the Spirits because they make the image of the Lord."

[1344] The point may be that since they revealed hidden knowledge, now hidden judgements will come upon them. Knibb has: "Because of this the hidden judgement" in place of "Therefore, everything that has been concealed."

[1345] Black postulates this may have read "neither idol nor angel nor man" (BL pg. 245).

[1346] This verse belongs with 68:5. Scholars are divided as to whether this is speaking of the angels or the kings and mighty, but the weight of opinion is that it is the angels, since they have revealed the following secrets to those who dwell on the earth. Isaac has: "scream" in place of "tremble."

[1347] **Josephus recounts that preserving the names of the angels was important to the Essenes (*War* 2.8.7 §§ 142). "The unique collection of the names of the rebel angels, in a traditional form, within a work attributed to Enoch, almost certainly reflects this particular aspect of Essene piety. The somewhat awkward inclusion of the list of the names of the rebel angels in the *Book of Parables*, with an updated description of their transgressions (*1En* 69:2-15) and modelled on the original list in the Book of the Watchers (*1En* 6:3-8; 8:1-4), suggests that the author of the Parables was indeed fulfilling an obligation to 'preserve the names of the angels', which in turn would ensure the preservation of his book. This is significant as it would identify him, and the group which edited his work, as full members of the Essene community"** (John Ben Daniel, The Parables of Enoch (37-71): Provenance and Social Setting).

[1348] These names are taken from Olson and differ from the names in this text of 1En 6:7, which are taken from Nickelsburg; in order for the reader to appreciate the translation differences. Olson notes "The spellings here are taken from a variety of MSS, trying in each case to use the angel name least corrupted from the original preserved in the DSS of Enoch 6:7."

[1349] Kôkabêl means "star of God" (H2 pg. 215).

Baraqel,[1350] the tenth Azazel, the eleventh Armanos, the twelfth
Bataryal, the thirteenth Basasael,[1351] the fourteenth
Ananel, the fifteenth Turyal, and the sixteenth Sampisiel, the
seventeenth Yesrael, the eighteenth Tumael, the nineteenth Turel,
the twentieth Rumael, the twenty-first Ezezeel.[1352] [1353]
3 The following are the chiefs of their angels and their names, 40:7; 54:6
their leaders of hundreds, the leaders of fifties, and the
leaders of tens.
4 The name of the first is Yeqōn: [1354] [1355] This is the one who led
astray all the sons of God,[1356] and brought them down to the Job 1:6; 2:1; 38:7; Gen 6:1-4
earth, and led them astray through the daughters of men. 6:2

[1350] Barâqêl means "lightning of God" (H2 pg. 215). Baraq᾽el's Persianized name is Virôgdâd, meaning 'Given by the lightning,'. He is the father of Mahway in the Book of Giants (6Q8 1.4 (W pg. 292))

[1351] "Basasael" This name is not found in the list of watchers in 6:7 and Olson thinks it "should probably be deleted" (OL pg. 126). It's addition results in a list of 21 rather than twenty watchers as in 6:7. This is an inexplicable corruption in the text. Nickelsburg notes, "A scholarly consensus has identified the first of these lists (vv. 2b-3), as an interpolation of the list in 6:7-8" (NV 2 pg. 298). "It was introduced at a very late-stage m the transmission of the text of Enoch" (BL pg. 245, citing K).

[1352] The restating of names of the watchers of 6:7 here, indicates that the author was familiar with the *Book of Watchers*. Different translators use different forms of the names. For instance, in order, Nickelsburg has, Shemihazah, Arteqoph, <Remashel>, Kokabel, †Turel†, Ramel, Daniel, Ziqel, Baraqel, Asael, Hermani, Matarel, †Basasel†, Ananel, †Turel†, Shamsiel, <Sahriel>, <Tummiel>, <Turiel>, <Yamiel> and †Azazel†. The two lists have spelling differences and are subject to a scribal lapse or two (R pg. 90. VanderKam). Olson finds the names in this passage to be well preserved from the original text which he maintains is Hebrew (OLS pg. 134).

[1353] Loren Stuckenbruck informs us that, apart from the Book of Giants and the name 'Azazel', and "despite the influence of the Enochic accounts, the names of the chief angelic perpetrators of evil are conspicuously absent outside the earliest Enoch tradition". "This means that the convergence of the lists of angelic names in the Parables of Enoch (*1En* 69:2-15) is a singularity—a unique occurrence —and that the author, or authors, felt uniquely responsible for recording the names of the rebel angels." (Stuckenbruck, Loren T., 2017. *The Myth of the Rebellious Angels: Studies in Second Temple Judaism and New Testament Texts*, Grand Rapids MI/Cambridge UK: Eerdmans, pg. 82).

[1354] **These following five chief angels are the ones identified as "satans" in (1 Enoch 40:7 and 65:6) where the original 200 are condemned for being subject to Satan. Black refers to them as "a higher angelic echelon."** (BL pg. 245). **This would be the top level of evil rebellious beings who are ranked above the 200 from 1 Enoch 6. This gives added insight into the kingdom of evil. In the gospels, Christ prefers to use Satan or Devil in the singular for the head of the evil legions. This verse indicates that the evil forces are numerous and organized into an army. These names are unrelated to the 20 fallen watchers.**

[1355] "Yeqōn" means "he stands up" "to rise up" or "to rebel" in Hebrew or "idol" in Greek. As Knibb notes, יקים is a biblical name (Jakim) in (1Chr 8:19; 24:12). (Knibb, Michael A., *The Ethiopic Book of Enoch: A New Edition in the Light of the Aramaic Dead Sea Fragments* (2 vols; Oxford: Clarendon, 1978), 2:160). The name also appears on a Christian onomasticon (Heidelberg G 1359) dating from the third or fourth century, preserved on a scrap of papyrus and probably used as an amulet (OLS pg. 134).

[1356] I have chosen to remain with "sons of God" as did Charles. This would match the context of the rest of 1 Enoch. Knibb has: "the children of the holy angels" in place of "sons of God" in both 69:4 and 69:5. However, Knibb notes that "it is possible that the text derives from a false translation of 'all the (holy) children of God.'" Black discounts a mistranslation, postulating that the scribe was simply reluctant to use the term "sons of God" and thus substituted "sons of the angels." Black is firm on their identification as the watchers, the 'sons of God' of Gen 6.2" (BL pg. 246). Nickelsburg and Isaac have: "children of the angels" here. Olson translates: "angelic sons." Olson notes: "'Sons of the angels' (also v. 5; 71:1) is evidently another name for the watchers of *1 En.* 6–16, combining the idiom of MT Gen 6:2 (בני האלוהים) with that of the LXX (αγγελοι του θεου)" (OLS pg. 134). **These verses establish that the sons of God in Gen 6:2 (angels of God in the LXX) are fallen spiritual beings, not sons of Seth.**

5 The second was named Asbeēl:[1357] This one gave evil
counsel to the children of the holy angels and led them astray 4Q174 3.7-9
so that they defiled[1358] their bodies[1359] with the 7:1; Rev 14:4
daughters of men.[1360]
6 The third was named Gādriēl:[1361] This is the one who
showed the sons of men all lethal blows, and he led Eve astray,[1362] Gen 3:1-5, 13; 2Cor 11:3
and showed the weapons of death to the sons of men, the shield
and the breastplate, and the battle sword; every weapon of death 8:1; *Good Person* 78
to the sons of men.
7 From his hand they (the weapons of war) have gone forth upon
those who dwell on earth from that day through all ages.[1363]
8 The fourth was named Pēnēmuʾe:[1364] This one taught the Ps 11:7
children of men the bitter and the sweet[1365] and he showed Isa 5:20
them all the secrets of their wisdom. Rev 2:24

[1357] Asbeēl may mean "exorcist of God" "one who forsakes God" "thought of God" or "deserter from God." The name in Hebrew may mean "conjurer" or "sorcerer," which derive from ancient Alkadian. In this passage he seems to have taken the role of Semjaza (6:2) in leading the Sons of God astray, although Olson assigns that role to Yeqōn (OLS pg. 136).

[1358] Nickelsburg has: "ruined" in place of "defiled."

[1359] That angels can have physical bodies, is not without precedent. (See Gen 19:1-11; Tobit 5:4-5; TAb A 1:6-2:5 (OTP1 pg. 882), TAb B 2:1-3 (OTP1 pg. 896)).

[1360] **Does this verse help with understanding the identity of the 144,000 in Rev 14:1-4, who "have not defiled themselves with women"? The 144,000 however, are human; "virgins, redeemed from mankind." It may mean that these redeemed humans, now glorified, have become like the loyal unfallen spiritual beings who chose to not rebel.**

[1361] "Gādreēl has taken the role of Azâzêl in 8:1. The name may mean 'God is my helper' or 'God has helped Me'" (NV2 pg. 301). Dillmann proposed the meaning as: "to be lacking, to fail." Olson has the meaning as "fence (or wall) of God" with a meaning that he broke through the fence around Eden (OLS pg. 138-139). See also Vayikra Rabbah 26.2 and Eccl 10:8b. Ethiopic "Gādreēl" accurately represents the Hebrew גדריאל. (OLS pg. 137). A similar name is found on a military banner in (1QM 4.13). "The name has also been observed on an Aramaic incantation bowl from *Nippus*, the *Sefer HaRazim* (1:214), and the *Zohar* (*VaYaqhel* 202a). In this last source, which Daniel Olson suggests may have been influenced by the Parables, Gadre' el is responsible for wars that occur among nations, reminiscent of his role in 1En 69:6 as the one who introduces weapons to humanity" (R pg. 356-357). "Azazel *is* linked with the deception of Eve in Apoc Ab 22:5-23:12, just as we observe with Gadre' el in 1En 69:6" (R pg. 357 Bautch). "It may be possible to see faint traces of this tradition also in the Sefer Ha-Razim, although the argument here is admittedly more conjectural. Gadriel is one of forty-four angels in the seventh encampment of the first firmament, serving under an overseer named Bo'el (בואל)." "Also reviewing our four texts, we find Gadriel in service to an angelic shield-bearer in Sefer Ha-Razim and a divine charioteer in Isbell #9. He is a satanic arms-dealer in 1 Enoch and the angel in charge of warfare in the Zohar" (OLS pg. 138-139).

[1362] **This gives a name to the spiritual being behind the serpent in Gen 3:1. This is the only mention of Eve in 1 Enoch. This does not contradict the Bible, as the serpent is not named there. Seraphim are serpent like, so Gadriel was likely a seraph, who would have had serpent like features.**

[1363] Olson renders 69:7 as: "Through their agency death proceeds against those who dwell on the earth, from that day and through all ages." **War among humans is an extension of the war between the offspring of the woman and that of the serpent revealed in Gen 3:15. War, famine, and disease are all methods used to slay mankind while they are deceived as to the true spiritual forces behind the events.**

[1364] Pēnēmuʾe "the face(s) of death" (N2 pg. 303). Another possibility is "the face of terror" (OLS pg. 141). The name is obscure. Olson sees a possible parallel with "his (God's) face" :פָּנֵימוֹ, p̄ā-nê-mōw in Ps 11:7 (OLS pg. 126).

[1365] The idea of bitter and the sweet is likely from (Isa 5:20). "Woe to those who call evil good and good evil, who put darkness for light and light for darkness, who put bitter for sweet and sweet for bitter!" It has the idea of the devil's deception in calling evil good and good evil; such as is so common in the world.

9 He instructed mankind in writing with ink and papyrus,[1366] Jub 4:17
and thereby there are many who have gone astray from of old 98:15; 104:10; Prov 10:19; Eccl 10:14
and forever and until this day.
10 For men were not born for this purpose, to give confirmation
to their trustworthiness with pen and ink.[1367] Mt 5:33-37; Jas 5:12
11 For humans were not created to be different than the angels,[1368] 104:6; 2Bar 51:3-13; Gen 1:27, 31 DivInst 7.26
so that they should remain righteous and pure, and death, TAb A 18:1; Wis 1:12-15; 2:23,24
which destroys everything,[1369] would not have touched them.
But through this knowledge of theirs they are perishing, 4Q174 3.7-9; Gen 2:17
and through this power death is consuming us.[1370] 1Cor 15:25-26
12 The fifth was named Kāsdeyāe:[1371] This is the one who showed
the sons of men all the evil afflictions[1372] from spirits and Dan 2:2

[1366] The author here condemns the occultic writings of the Chaldean *āšipu*s who promulgate the teachings of the Babylonian gods who stand behind the evil angels reflected in this text. This is not a commendation of all writing, given that Enoch "was the first among men that are born on earth who learnt writing and knowledge and who wrote down the signs of heaven according to the order of their months in a book" (Jub 4:17)(See also 1En 15:1).

[1367] **It seems odd that writing in general would be seen in a negative context since it is otherwise lauded in 1 Enoch. It may be referring to contracts. Similar to (Mt 5:33-37 and Jas 5:12), a person's word should be sufficient with no need to solemnify a contract in writing. Alternatively, it may be that writing was used to preserve the knowledge that the rebel watchers imparted to man.** The Kish tablet is widely regarded as the oldest writing in the world that has been confirmed. This clay pictographic tablet was found in Iraq at the site of the ancient Sumerian city of Kish and has been dated to 3500-3200 BC. The oldest known writing on papyrus is the Egyptian *Diary of Merer* (also known as *Papyrus Jarf*). It consists of papyrus logbooks written over 4,500 years ago by "Merer," a middle ranking official with the title *inspector*. They are the oldest known papyri with text, dating to the 27th year of the reign of pharaoh Khufu during the 4th dynasty. The text, discovered in 2013, is written with (hieratic) hieroglyphs, and mostly consists of lists of the daily activities of Merer and his crew. The best-preserved sections (*Papyrus Jarf A and B*) document the transportation of white limestone blocks from the Tura quarries to Giza by boat (Stile, Alexander Oct. 2015. *The World's Oldest Papyrus and What It Can Tell Us About the Great Pyramids*, Smithsonian Magazine).

[1368] **Jesus many have had this verse or 51:5b-d (see note) and certainly 15:7 in mind in (Matt. 22:29-30; Mk 12:24; and Lk 20:34-36), where he tells the Sadducees "You are wrong, because you know neither the Scriptures nor the power of God. For in the resurrection they neither marry nor are given in marriage, but are like the angels in heaven" (Mt 22:29-30). No other ancient writing has been found other than 1En 15:7 that can be the source of this quote about marriage although the idea that saints will be equal with angels is commonly taught in second temple literature (Jasko, Andrew, 2012. *Did Jesus Know 1 Enoch 15?*). Note that in (Matt. 22:29 and Mk 12:24) Jesus thus calls *The Book of the Watchers* (15:5-7) and possibly the *Parables* (69:11) scripture. (2 Baruch 51:10), "For they will live in the heights of that world, and they will be like angels and be equal to the stars" would be a potential source of the statement by Jesus in Mark 12:25 but it "clearly postdates the gospels." (Jasko, Andrew. *Did Jesus Know 1 Enoch 15?* 2012. Pgs. 8-9) These passages are profound statements that man was created to be righteous and pure and immortal.**

[1369] Nickelsburg has: "ruins" in place of "destroys."

[1370] N has: "and through this power it devours us." OL has "Through this force, Death is devouring us." C has "and through this power it is consuming me." It may be an addition to the text.

[1371] Kāsdeyāe, possibly Aramic, "Chaldaean" in the sense of "astrologer," belonging to a group construed as magicians more generally (N2 pg. 303). "A certain, 'Kasdiel, the mighty angel, the prince of the Chaldeans' appears in Jewish incantation texts dating from the 3rd-8th c. CE." (OL pg. 128 citing Isbell *Corpus* 114-17). "Kāsdeyāe" looks like a straightforward transliteration of כשדיא") The Chaldean"). "As is well known, the gentilic became a technical term for a class of Babylonian wise men. That 'Kāsdeyāe' = 'The Chaldean' is also supported by the presence of one 'Kasdiel, the mighty angel, prince of the Chaldeans' in the incantation bowls" (OLS pg. 137).

[1372] OL has: "scourgings." K has: "blows" N and K have: "evil blows" in place of "evil afflictions"

demons, and the diseases of the embryo[1373] in the womb, 4Q510 1.5
so that it miscarries,[1374] [1375] and the afflictions of the soul, 99:5
the bites of the serpent,[1376] and the afflictions which come Ps 91:5-6, 13; 4Q525 15.4, 9; Deut 32:24
through the midday heat,[1377] and the son of the serpent is Lk 3:7; Mt 23:33; 2Kgs 4:18-19, 35
named Tabā'et.[1378]

The Oath of Creation

13 Here is the account of Kāsbeēl,[1379] the chief of the
oath[1380] which he showed to the holy ones when he was PrMan 3

[1373] Nickelsburg has: "foetus" in place of "embryo." Demons were commonly implicated in causing abortions, miscarriages, stillbirths and the death of infants. "Demons who attack child-bearing women, killing infants and producing miscarriages, were particularly well known in Mesopotamia, going back to the Sumerian Lamaštu, known in Babylon as Pāšittu and eventually manifested in Judaism as Lilith" (OLS pg. 144).

[1374] Miscarriages were widely thought of as being caused by evil spiritual entities. This facilitated a market for charms and incantation bowls thought to prevent them. As far as abortion and infanticide, numerous, later, first and second century AD condemnations of abortion exist, both Jewish and Christian (*Apion* 2:25 §§202; 1 Clement 57:7; Didache 2:2; *Athenagoras, A Plea for the Christians 35;* Apocalypse of Peter 25; *Apol.* 9; *An.* 26; (Minucius Felix) *Octavius* 30; *Ref* 9.7; Cyprian (*Epistles*) 48.2; SibOr 2:281 and Barnabas 19:5).

[1375] Isaac has: "the smashing of the embryo in the womb so that it may be crushed," N has "so that it aborts." "Nickelsburg and VanderKam draw attention to research on Jewish magical texts indicating 'that abortions were functions of demons that could be controlled by magic,' and that Qumran texts like 1QHxi.iii. 12-18 contain the notion of women being impregnated by serpents (who are thus the cause of ill-fated birth)" (H2 pg. 222).

[1376] "Bites of the serpent," (cf. Num 21:6-9; Deut 32:24; Isa 14:29; Amos 9:3).

[1377] This line is based on (Ps 91:5-6) which from ancient to modern times has been used as a text for exorcism. Olson informs: "In Jewish exorcism texts written on incantation bowls, Psalm 91 is quoted often. The rite of Exorcism still used by the Roman Catholic Church makes use of the Psalm" (OL pg. 140). "The closest parallel, however, comes from the Utukkū Lemnūtu exorcism texts, which make passing reference at one point to a dangerous demon known as "the 'watcher' of midday" (OLS pg. 145).

[1378] Tabā'et may be the name of a sixth satan, and the seventh; Charles, citing Schmidt proposes as "Hakael" (C pg. 138). It is also possible there were only five satans. Unfortunately, the text has been corrupted. For the last phrase of this awkward text, Knibb has: "the son of the serpent who is … strong" or Olson "the son of the serpent whose name is the Strong One" (OLS 141). Tabāet may be a form of the name of Tiamat who was a primordial goddess of the sea in ancient Mesopotamian religion and who plays a major role in the Enuma Elish creation epic. Olson opines: "Would a reference to Tiamat be out of place in the Parables? Enoch has already alluded to her indirectly in an image derived from Babylonian creation imagery, when he speaks of masculine upper and feminine lower waters (54:8). The latter are of course Tiamat in the Enuma Elish. Enoch has also confessed to a fascination with the primeval monsters Behemoth and Leviathan (60:7–10, 24). There is also a line from our verse, 'the bite of the serpent,' which might call to mind for some readers Amos 9:3: 'Though they hide from me at the bottom of the sea, there I will command the serpent to bite them.' Unlike the allusion in 54:8, the latter two examples are not specific to Babylonian mythology, but they do show an interest in serpentine monsters of the deep. According to the Enuma Elish, Tiamat is the mother of all the Chaldean gods, and if our author held views similar to what we see in LXX Ps 96:5 ('The gods of the nations are demons'), there is nothing incongruous about finding in his text a wicked angel named 'The Chaldean' described as the offspring of the serpent Tiamat, especially since Tiamat in the Enuma Elish goes to war against her patricidal offspring and produces a second brood, horrors such as giant snakes, dragons, scorpion-men, and 'fierce demons.'" (OLS pg. 142-143)

[1379] These verses may mean "Kāsbeēl tricked Michael into revealing the secret of the divine name. Kāsbeēl, in turn, revealed the name to his angelic colleagues, who used it in the oath that they swore as they conspired to rebel against God" (NV2 pg. 307). Kāsbeēl means "sorcerer of God" "sorcerer divinity" or "lying divinity." This wording accepts Olson's suggestion (OLS pg. 146).

[1380] Black has: "sum of the oath." He states, "It seems more likely to mean the numerical sum of the letters in the 'hidden name' contained in the oath" (BL pg. 247).

dwelling on high in glory. Its name is Bēqā.[1381]
14 This one tried to talk Michael into revealing to him the Judg 13:18; Phil 2:9; Heb 1:4
hidden Name,[1382] that they might pronounce it in the oath, 69:26; Isa 9:6; Rev 19:12-13; Isa 26:13
so that those who revealed all that was secret to the sons of men
might tremble before that Name and oath.[1383] 61:9; 1Pet 1:12; Jas 2:19
15 This is the power of this oath,[1384] for it is powerful and strong, Jub 36:7
and the responsibility for this inscribed oath was given to
Michael,[1385]
16 and they are his secrets.[1386] [1387] In regard to the oath and its
strength—through his oath the firmament and the heavens 2:1; Gen 1:1-2; 3En 13:1-2
were suspended before the age was created and forever![1388] 39:11; 48:6; 3En 13:1; Col 1:15-17

[1381] Isaac has: “his name was then Beqa;” Eth *Bēqā* = Gk βεκα = Heb בך and is found in the Hebrew of (Isa 26:13) which has been used as the source of mystical names and oaths. In Zohar *Shemoth* 9a–9b Beka=22 and symbolizes the Holy name comprising 22 letters (there are 22 letters in the Hebrew alphabet). These letters were thought by Jewish mystics to be used in the act of creation. See also Jub 2:15, 23: 3En 13:1-2.

[1382] “This description of the cosmogenic power of the Divine Name reflects similar understandings of the Divine Name as power in contemporary Jewish and Christian literature, even as the word used in creation.” (R pg. 242, Gieschen). Kāsbeēl, like human occultists, attempts to manipulate the elemental forces that create and sustain the world in order to tap into their power. They seek powers they cannot comprehend that are potentially catastrophic.

[1383] For (69:14-16), most scholars, and this text, follow manuscript Q which supplies “a clear and coherent text throughout.” (OL pg. 128)

[1384] “Oath” Eth *ʾAkāʾe* = Gk αχα = Heb אכא is spelled *alef-kap-alef* in the best Ethiopic manuscripts. “*Alef-kap-alef* in Hebrew (אכא) is the seventh of the seventy-two names that together make up what came to be regarded as the most powerful divine name in Jewish magic and mysticism. The names are derived from Exod 14:19–21, three verses of exactly seventy-two letters each. When combined, they yield the 72 three-letter names known collectively as the *Shem Ha-Mephorash*, that is, the “ineffable” or “explicit” name of God.”(Olson, Daniel, 2022. *The wicked angels of 1 En. 69:4–15: Part 1: New evidence and proposals for the names; Part 2: The nature and purpose of the list.* Journal for the study of the Pseudepigrapha 31.3) “Tremendous Oaths” were taken during initiation into the Essenes (*War* 2.8.7 §§139); “but swearing is avoided by them, and they esteem it worse than perjury, for they say that he who cannot be believed without [swearing by] God is already condemned” (*War* 2.8.6 §§135 (cf. *Ant* 15.10.4 §§371; *Good Person* 84). As with the Essenes, the avoidance of swearing is commended by Christ (Mt 5:34-37; 23:16-22) and His brother James (Jas 5:12). For the Essenes, “any oath of allegiance with any authority other than God would weaken the solidity and stability of the universe by challenging the ‘oath’ by which the world is sustained.” (Boccaccini, G. 1998, *Beyond the Essene Hypothesis* pg. 173)

[1385] For 69:15 Isaac has: “He (then) revealed these to the children of the people, (and) all the hidden things and this power of this oath, for it is power and strength itself. The Evil One placed this oath in Michael’s hand.” Heiser postulates: “Kasbe’el tricked Michael into revealing the secret of the divine name. Kasbe’ el, in turn, revealed the name to his angelic colleagues, who used it in the oath they swore as they conspired to rebel against God” (H2 pg. 224). However, the text as it is here and translated by the majority does not give certainty that Kasbe’ el was successful in gaining possession of the oath; but that Michael served as a protector of the Name until it was revealed (69:26).

[1386] “In view of what follows, the point seems to be that the revelation of the divine name and “oath names” results in the knowledge of how the heavens and earth came into existence (cf. verses 18-25)” (H2 pg. 225). **This oath appears to be related to the divine name, this name is the creative power behind creation and the maintenance of the cosmos. It is associated with the logos. See (1En 61:9) and note.**

[1387] “Vs 16-21, 26-29 are composed in poetic form with parallelism and 16-21 has a concluding recurring refrain of “from the creation of the age and forever” (BL pg. 248) (cf. 1En 48:6).

[1388] **This is a clear statement that the cosmos was in existence prior to the first day of creation.** N translates: “And <through that oath> the heaven was suspended. . . before the age was created and forever.” **This corresponds to Gen 1:1-2 where the heavens and the earth, according to the gap theory, are in existence before the first day of creation.** This may also be implied in (2Pet 3:5).

17 Through it[1389] the earth was founded upon the waters,[1390] — 2Pet 3:5; Ps 24:2; 136:6; 4Ezra 16:58-59
and from the secret recesses of the mountains sparkling water[1391] — Job 26:7; Ps 104:10, 13
comes forth, from the creation of the age and forever. — 71:15
18 Through that oath the sea was created and its foundations; — Ps 104:5-9
for the time of its wrath, he placed for it a barrier of sand, — 101:6; Prov 8:27-29; 2En 28:4
and it does not pass beyond its boundary — Job 26:10; 38:8-11; Jer 5:22; PrMan 2-3
from the creation of the age and forever.
19 Through that oath the depths are made firm, — Prov 8:28
and they have stood and are not shaken from their place
from the creation of the age and forever.
20 Through that oath the sun and moon complete their course,
and deviate not from their command — 2:1; 41:5-8; 83:11
from the creation of the age and forever. — OdesSol 16:13-17
21 Through that oath the stars complete their course,
and he calls them by their names, — 43:1; Isa 40:26; Sir 43:9-10; Ps 147:4
and they answer him from the creation of the age and forever. — Bar 3:34
22 Likewise with regard to the waters, to their winds, and to — Jub 2:2
all the breezes and their paths according to the different — 60:12; 77:1-3; Rev 7:1
varieties of the winds.[1392] [1393]
23 There are preserved the voice of the thunder and the flashes — 41:3
of the lightning. There are preserved the storehouses of the hail — 60:19-21; Job 38:22
and of the hoar-frost, the storehouses of the storm cloud[1394] — Haer. 2.28.2
and the storehouses of the rain and of the dew.
24 These all make confession[1395] and give thanks before the — Job 38:7; Neh 9:6; Ps 148:1-6
Lord of Spirits. With all their power they glorify, and their — 41:7; 82:3
every act of thanksgiving gives them nourishment. They will — PrAzar 35-56; Jn 4:34
praise and glorify and extol the Name of the Lord of Spirits — Add Dan 3:52-90
forever and ever![1396]
25 This oath is binding upon them, and by it they shall be
kept, and they shall keep to their paths, and their courses
are not disturbed.

[1389] "'It' refers to heaven. In this instance, "heaven" is likely an instance of metonymy, the use of one name or word for another in light of the close association between the two. Thus 'heaven' really refers to God, the Creator. As in the Bible, the earth was created and placed upon the waters (Psalm 136:6; cp. Genesis 1:9-10)" (H2 pg. 225).

[1390] **The traditional cosmology of the time is that the earth was founded on water** (Ps 24:2 and 136:6).

[1391] Black speculates that the original may have been "living waters" rather than "sparkling water."

[1392] For 69:22, Knibb has: "and likewise the spirits of the water, of the winds, and of all the breezes, and their paths, according to all the groups of the spirits."

[1393] 1En 69:22-24 is an interpolation into the text. These verses do not follow the poetic form of verses 17-21. (NV2 pg. 310). As Charles notes, verse 69:23, seems to be an interpolation within an interpolation (C pg. 140). Charles also observes that the first interpolator may have omitted text from the original *Parables* which picks up again at 69:26. Black proposes: "They could be an expansion of the poem on the oath to take account of later ideas about the spirits of nature" (BL pg. 249).

[1394] Many translate "mist" in place of storm cloud.

[1395] Charles has: "And all these believe" in place of "These all make confession."

[1396] For 69:24 (Isaac has 69:25; OTP1 pg. 49) Isaac has: "All these believe and give thanks in the presence of the Lord of the Spirits; they glorify with all their might, and please him in all this thanksgiving; they shall thank, glorify, exalt the Lord of the Spirits forever and ever!"

The Parable Ends

The Son of Man on his Throne of Glory in Judgement

26 They had great joy, and they praised and glorified and exalted,	62:7; 1Pet 1:20
because the name of the Son of Man had been revealed to them!	46:3; 48:2-3; Lk 1:31; Rev 3:12; 19:12
27 And he sat on the throne of his glory,[1397] and the whole	41:9; 45:3; Heb 1:3; Mt 19:28; 25:31; 26:64
judgement was given to the Son of Man,[1398] and he will	Jn 5:22, 27, 30; 9:39; 12:48; Dan 7:13-14
eliminate and destroy from the face of the earth those who	Mt 13:40-42; 25:31-46; Acts 10:42; 17:31
have led the world astray.	
28 They will be bound in chains, and in their assembling-place,	Jude 6; Rev 20:1-3; 2Bar 56:13
of destruction shall they be imprisoned, and all their works,	Isa 24:21-22
will vanish from the face of the earth.	10:12, 20-21; 38:1-2; 53:2
29 From then on there shall be nothing corruptible;	1Pet 1:4; 1Cor 15:42; Rom 8:19-21
for that Son of Man has appeared,	Rev 3:21; 14:14; 22:1; Jn 17:5; Mk 14:62
and has seated himself on the throne of his glory,	51:3; 61:8; 62:5; Mt 25:31; Heb 12:2
All evil shall pass away and depart from his presence.	Rev 19:15; 22:3; 2Bar 73:1
For the word of the Son of Man will prevail in the presence	Jn 1:1; 12:48; Mt 24:35
of the Lord of Spirits.[1399]	49
This is the third Parable of Enoch.	

Enoch Raised Aloft to the Son of Man and the Lord of Spirits

70 1 And after this, while he was living, his name was lifted up	Phil 2:9; Acts 1:9, TJob 53:8
into the presence of that Son of Man[1400] and into the presence	46:3; Sir 44:16; ApZeph 9:4
of the Lord of Spirits from among those who	Wis 4:10, 14; Jub 4:23

[1397] **"The throne of his glory" used here, and in 69:29, is a rare phrase. It is not from Christian sources and is recognized by the vast majority of scholars as the basis for the phrase in (Mt 19:28 and 25:31). This establishes that the Book of Parables was composed prior to the Gospel of Matthew and was known by him!**

[1398] **The son of man in Daniel 7:13 is revealed after judgement has been rendered (Dan 7:10). In the Parables, the Son of Man is revealed before being placed in a position of judgement: thus, matching the claims of the Son of Man/Christ in the New Testament. See (Jn 5:22, 27; 8:16, 26; 12:48; Acts 10:42; 17:31; Jas 4:12; 1Pet 4:5; and Rev 20:12-13). This is evidence that the Son of Man is modeled after the *Book of Parables* as well as Daniel.**

[1399] Olson renders: "for the word of that Son of Man will be powerful in the presence of the Lord of Spirits."

[1400] Like in 1En 48:2, the Son of Man is preexistent. Jesus also claimed this preexistence. "Your father Abraham rejoiced that he would see my day. He saw it and was glad." So the Jews said to him, "You are not yet fifty years old, and have you seen Abraham?" Jesus said to them, "Truly, truly, I say to you, before Abraham was, I am" (John 8:56-58). In this passage in John, Jesus can only be referencing (Jubilees 16:17-27) where Abraham rejoiced to know that the Messiah would come from his seed. This establishes that Jesus knew the Book of Jubilees, and considered it authoritative

dwell on the earth.[1401] [1402] 87:3
2 He was raised aloft on a chariot of the wind, and his name[1403] 12:1; 14:8; 39:3, 8; 52:1; Sir 4:13
vanished among them. 2Kgs 2:11; Gen 5:23, 24; Heb 11:5

A Possible Interpolation; Enoch Ascends

3 [From that day I was no longer counted among them;
and he placed me between two winds, between the north[1404] Heb 11:5
and the west, where the angels took the cords to measure 61:1-5; Ezek 40:2-3; Zech 2:1-2

[1401] Nickelsburg views 70:1-2 as the original conclusion to the Book of Parables (NV2 pg. 315). Nickelsburg says regarding 70:1-2: "I suggest that something like 70:1-2 constituted the original conclusion to the Book of Parables." And he continues "however, the fact that the author of 70:1-2 knows better than to attribute to the voice of Enoch an account that he is not in a position to transmit on earth leads me to ascribe the first-person material in 70:3-4 and chap. 71 to a later redactor or redactors" (R pg. 43 Nickelsburg). Concerning chapters 70-71, Heiser states: "These two chapters are considered summary additions placed at the end of the Book of Parables by either the writer or an editorial hand" (H2 pg.229). This view that the text originates with an editor is supported by the very abrupt change from third person in 70:1-2 to first person in 70:3. The shocking statement in (71:14-17) that Enoch the patriarch is the Son of Man, would argue that Heiser and Nickelsburg are correct that these two chapters after 70:2 are not original to the text. Interpolations were often made at the end of texts. This interpolation is more like 2 Enoch although it even goes beyond what is found there! The text used here, follows the majority reading for 70:1-2. This reading draws a clear distinction between Enoch and the Son of Man. Contending for the other view; Olson has identified Ethiopic manuscripts which he maintains bolster the short reading for 70:1 and argue for (70:3-71:17) being original to the text. Using them, 70:1 can be translated: "And it happened after this, while he was living, that the name of that Son of Man was raised into the presence of the Lord of Spirits" (Olson, Daniel C., "Enoch and the Son of Man in the Epilogue of the Parables," JSP 18 1998: 27-38). Using this minority translation for 70:1-2, Olson in his version translates: "Afterwards it came to pass that the immortal name of that Son of Man was exalted in the presence of the Lord of Spirits above all those who live on the earth. He was raised aloft on a chariot of wind, and his name became a household word." Olson's reading would equate the Son of Man with Enoch. The textual evidence for either reading is at a stalemate with texts on both sides of similar age and authority (NV2 pg. 317). **The majority reading is favored in the text before us, due to the abrupt change of tense, and its consistency with the remainder of the body of the Parables.**

[1402] **That the majority reading of 70:1-2 was part of the original *Book of Parables* may be shown by its probable usage in (Wis 4:10, 14); which is universally acknowledged to be speaking of Enoch as a prototype of righteousness. "(10) Being found well-pleasing to God, he was loved. While living among sinners he was transported. (14) for his soul was pleasing to the Lord. Therefore, he was hurried out of the midst of wickedness." If true, this would be the earliest extrabiblical (or Biblical for that matter) reference to the *Parables,* since the *Wisdom of Solomon* is dated by Winston to just after the resurrection of Christ during the reign of Gaius Caligula (AD 37-41).** Winston is certain it was composed in Egypt. (Winston, David, 1979. *The Wisdom of Solomon*, pgs. 21-25) Philo's *On Abraham* 3 (17) also mentions Enoch being transported. Philo lived ca. 15 BC to AD 50.

[1403] "His name" this is the person of Enoch. Olson translates this line as "his name became a household word" To support his translation: "Olson also refers to a fragmentary seventh-/eighth-century Sahidic Coptic Enoch Apocryphon, composed perhaps by a fifth-century Egyptian Christian, which he (Olson) thinks may have been inspired by 1 Enoch 70-71. That text reads: [God will bestow] upon you a [name more] famous than (that of) any man. You will be taken to heaven in your body, and you will be placed in the midst [of the] store-house [." (NV2 pg. 318).

[1404] Isaac has northeast. This is the place of the garden of righteousness in 77:3. "**The tradition that the garden became the habitat of the ascended Enoch is an old one attested already in Jub 4:23, a text from the first half of the second century B.C.E" (NV2 pg. 322).**

for me the place for the chosen and righteous.[1405] Jn 14:2-3; Rev 11:1; 21:15
4 There I saw the first fathers, and the righteous who from 32:3, 6; 60:8; 61:12
everlasting dwell in that place.[1406] [1407] Lk 16:22

Excursus: Options in interpreting 71:14.

1 Enoch 71:14 is easily the most controversial verse in 1 Enoch. It seems to be equating Enoch with the son of man. There are four options of dealing with this verse.

It is original to the text, and is identifying Enoch as the divine, pre-existent, mystical double of the "Son of Man"
This has become an increasingly popular view among scholars. It finds support in some of the oldest Ethiopic manuscripts.[1407a] Key to this interpretation is the controversy about the reading of 70:1-2. Stuckenbruck prefers the following reading. "Afterwards it happened that the living name of the Son of Man was exalted in the presence of the Lord of Spirits above all those who live on dry land." (P pg. 318). He sees this as lending support to 71:14 being genuinely original to the text. Olsen finds Jacob/Israel mysticism here in 1En 71:14, and 90:37-38. However he admits: "still, there has been no clue in the 'Parables' before chapters 70-71 that Enoch has actually been seeing himself in these messianic tableaux, and it may be that he is here granted a vision of a time when he will mysteriously merge with a distinct heavenly 'double,' an *antitype* preexistent with God, of whom the earthly Enoch, seventh from Adam, is a preeminent type."[1408] He finds a parallel with Jacob in the *Prayer of Joseph* A 7-8 (ca. AD 1st-2nd c.) which is a mystical interpretation of Jacob's wrestling match in Genesis 32. It comes very close to equating Jacob with the second power in heaven, but Jacob stops short of that point; describing himself as "the archangel of the power of the Lord and the chief captain among the sons of God" and "the first minister before the face of God"[1409] Jubilees also presents a high view of Enoch. "And in his life on earth he (Noah) excelled the children of men save Enoch because of the righteousness, wherein he was perfect. For Enoch's office was ordained for a testimony to the generations of the world, so that he should recount all the deeds of generation unto generation, until the day of judgement" (Jub 10:17). Another example of a heavenly double has survived as a part of the drama *Exagoge* (2nd-3rd century BC), a writing attributed to Ezekiel the Tragedian, which depicts Mose's experience at Sinai as his celestial enthronement. *Exagoge* 67–90 is preserved in

---

[1405] Here occurs an abrupt shift from third person to a "first person autobiographical narrative that continues through chap. 71 to vv.14b and 15b, the points at which the angel addresses Enoch in the second person" (NV2 pg. 315). This change is necessary for the description of the heavenly realm that follows.
[1406] For 70:4 Isaac has, "And there I saw the first (human) ancestors and the righteous ones of old, dwelling in that place" "The perspective of 70:4 (the garden is populated with 'the first fathers and the righteous') seems more appropriate to the time of the author than that of Enoch. The patriarch had only six generations of forebears including Adam, and according to the chronology of the Masoretic Text, all but Adam were still alive at the time of Enoch's removal, and the righteous were not a substantial quantity, to judge from the biblical record" (NV2 pg. 322). **This teaches that the righteous dead go to Paradise/Abrahams bosom (Lk 16:22-23) rather than a waiting space like Sheol or Hades.**
[1407] K translates: "who from *the beginning of* the world dwelt in that place."
[1407a] These are Eth. II manuscripts: EMML 6974, EMML 1768; EMML 2436, EMML 7584, EMML 2080 corrected, Abb 55 and Eth. I manuscripts: Remnant Trust, Gunde Gundi 151 and Parma 1296.
[1408] OL pg. 134.
[1409] *Prayer of Joseph* Frag A 7-9 OTP2 pg. 713 and Frag. C pg. 714.

fragmentary form in Eusebius of Caesarea's *Praeparatio evangelica.* (For others see Ladder of Jacob 2:7-19 (AD 1st century) and Bereshit Rabbah 68:12 (AD 300-500)).

Others find indications of Enoch's "son of man" status in the balance of 1 Enoch. Enoch is called the son of man in 61:10. "And he said to me: "Son of man, you here wish to know what is hidden." However, this can be taken in the human sense. Olson argues that a connection exists between 1En 14:8, 18-23 and Dan 7:9-10, 13 thus providing a link to the Danielic Son of Man but Daniel is more likely influenced by the Book of Watchers and the Book of Giants (4Q530 2.2.16-20) rather than vice versa. See also 1En 39:9. Stukenbruck makes a case that the scribe recording the transgressions of the 70 shepherds (commissioned in 89:61) may have been viewed by early readers as a heavenly Enoch; thus, leading to his later Son of Man status in 71:14.

Black postulated:

> It is by no means inconceivable that the tradition of Enoch as the Son of Man, preserved in the Parables, was also know to Jesus of Nazareth, and similarly interpreted and applied by him to his own role in his mission as prophet of the coming kingdom—not in terms of an Enoch *redivivus* Son of man-Messiah, but as an Enoch-like apocalyptic teacher and prophet, adopting and adapting the classic Enoch tradition to the Son of Man's futuristic role as eschatological Judge, but to his earthly ministry as Servant of the Lord.[1409a]

If 71:14 was original or was added prior to the Chrisitan era, it may be the reason the Parables were not more widely cited among Christians, as Jesus, not Enoch was for them the Son of Man. It could also explain its possible absence at Qumran. Charlesworth[1409b] sees John 3:13-15 as a possible "polemic against the claims associated with Enoch in the concluding chapters of the Parables of Enoch." "No one has ascended into heaven except he who descended from heaven, the Son of Man. And as Moses lifted up the serpent in the wilderness, so must the Son of Man be lifted up, that whoever believes in him may have eternal life." (John 3:13-15). Charlesworth states: "The link between John 3 and the Enoch traditions found in the Parables of Enoch is forged more strongly when one perceives that Enoch had claimed 'the Lord of the Spirits' had given him 'the lot of eternal life' (1En 37:4)." This link, however, could also be Jesus responding due to an interpolation of 70:3-71:17 into the text, although there is no manuscript evidence that the Parables of Enoch ever existed without chapters 70:3-71:17.

The text is corrupt

R. H. Charles proposed a textual corruption. He postulated a missing section between 1En 70:13 and 70:14 "wherein the Son of Man was described as accompanying the Head of Days, and Enoch asked one of the angels (as in 46:3) concerning the Son of Man as to who he was." Charles later changed his mind in his 1912 edition (pg. 142). "This chapter seems to belong to the Parables, though in the first edition I thought otherwise." Of this option, Nickelsburg writes: "Charles's tour de force, however, has no foundation in the MSS. and has been universally rejected by scholars."[1410] However this does not rule out all possible modes of textual corruption which

---

[1409a] "Charlesworth J. H. ed. 1992. The Messianism of the Parables of Enoch: Their Date and Contribution to Christological Origins. *The Messiah: Developments in Earliest Judaism and Christianity*. Fortress Press. Pg. 167.
[1409b] P pg. 175-176
[1410] NV2 pg. 328.

many have occurred prior to incorporation into the Ethiopic text. That Enoch and the Son of Man are again separated in 71:15 argues for textual corruption. He (The Son of Man) summons forth peace for you (Enoch). Charlesworth admits:[1410a] "The readings of the manuscripts often differ, disclosing a fluid text tradition, and it is not wise to over-interpret texts that may have been intentionally complex and seemingly disoriented." He continues in the footnote: "One wonders if the original text was changed through transmission." "One should not be focused only on the late medieval manuscripts but perceptive of what might have been in a putative original or *Untertext*."

It means "son of man" in the mortal sense
"Son of man" is used numerous times in Ezekiel and in the Noahic interpolation of 1En 60:10. It is possible to read the text of 1En 71:14 as "You are a son of man (born for righteousness)." This is the view of Ethiopic commentators.[1411] Isaac, a native speaker, takes this interpretation. The word "man" (*bəʾəsi*; ብእሲ) in the formulation "son of man" used in 71:14 and also the first occurrence of Son of Man in 69:29 is different from all other formulations of Son of Man in the Parables. Elsewhere in the text of the Parables, the word "man" in "Son of Man" is either *sabʾe*, (ሰብእ) 'people,' (46:2, 3, 4; 48:2; 60:10; 62:5) or *ʾəmäḥəyawə*, (እመሕያው) 'son of the mother of the living,' (62:7, 9, 14; 63:11; 69:26, 27, 29[2nd]; 70:1; 71:17).[1412] It should be noted that the Son of Man in 71:17 does use the common Ethiopic word *ʾəmäḥəyawə*. This makes 71:14 even more of an oddity due to its proximity with 71:17. 1En 71:14 is also odd; in that it is the only place in the parables where the Son of Man is referred to as being born. However (71:16-17) is clearly speaking of the Christ so it is difficult to see it's use in 71:14 in the mortal sense. Black discounts these differences in terms and attributes them to "the work of two different, probably Ethiopic. translators."[1412a] If this is true, then the whole significance of 71:14 is brought into question. What really matters is what the semitic language said, and unfortunately, we do not have an Aramaic/Hebrew manuscript of the Parables of Enoch. Stuckenbruck maintains that "not too much should be argued on the basis of the difference in terminology" (P pg. 315).

70:3-71:17 is a mid to late 1st century addition to the text.
Scholars that favor an addition include Nickelsburg, Knibb, Kvanvig, Uhlig, Collins, and Chiala. These scholars regard "the Parables of Enoch as a document that grew in several stages, respectively: the second century BCE (Maccabean period), the second half of the first century BCE (soon after the Parthian and Medes invasion of Palestine), and the first century CE (during which chs. 70-71 were added" (P pg. 315 n3). This view finds support for several reasons. Nickelsburg points out that the description of the heavenly realm in the rest of the Parables (39:3 – 39:14; 40:2-10) is presented in a matter-of-fact manner. "Chapter 71 is an altogether different story." "This recasting of material from 1 Enoch 14 (and Daniel 7) presents a graphic, vivid view of the heavenly world that the author(s) of the body of the Parables avoided even though they had the prototype in front of them. That the author(s) of the Parables responded to the traditional material in this understated manner makes it, in my view, unlikely that it was they who re-

[1410a] P pg. 200.
[1411] OL pg. 134.
[1412] See discussion NV2 pg. 328-332.
[1412a] BL pg. 207

presented in chap. 71 the terrifying reality previously described in chap. 14."[1413] In addition, unlike the rest of the *Parables*, the kings and the mighty are not mentioned in (70:3-71:17).

If (70:1-71:17) is a continuity, the parts do not logically fit together. Nickelsburg observes:

> First, if 70:1-2 describes Enoch's final departure from earth in the third person, how, after he is gone, does the same author suppose that the recipients of this book got a first-person narrative of his post-final ascension adventures? This is more likely a function of a second hand (possibly inserting a fragment of tradition) than the work of a single author.[1414]

If (70:3-71:17) is an addition, then this explains the strange language of 71:14. An early (1st century) kabbalistic redactor may have been attempting to bend the text to conform with the idea found in proto-gnostic (2 Enoch J 22:6-10), where Enoch says: "And I looked at myself, and I had become like one of his glorious ones, and there was no observable difference." The later Merkabah mystic text, (3 Enoch 3-16:1), has Enoch becoming Metatron,[1415] the highest of the archangels (cf. Targum Jonathan on Gen5:24; Clementine Homilies 18:13). However, even both 2 and 3 Enoch fall short of equating the Danielic Son of Man with Enoch; although (2En J 64:5) casts Enoch as "the one who carried away the sin of mankind." The balance of the Parables has endured numerous major interpolations, so an interpolation would certainly not be unusual here, especially given its position at the end of the Parables. It should be remembered that the Parables were translated from Aramaic to Greek then into Ethiopic; so much could have been "lost in the translation" (P pg. 357). Since this verse can be accounted for in many ways, it is no reason to reject the *Parables* and the remainder of 1 Enoch as "heresy."

Enoch Ascends into Heaven

71 1 After that my spirit was translated, and it ascended into the 12:1; 39:3-40:9; Sir 44:16; 49:14
heavens:[1416] and I saw the holy angelic sons.[1417] 69:4-5; Rom 8:14, 19; Gal 3:26; Lk 20:36
They were treading on flames of fire; 106:5; Ezek 28:14, 16
their garments were white, as were their tunics, Dan 7:9; 14:18-20; Mk 9:3
and the light of their faces (shone) like snow. Lk 9:29; Acts 6:15; Rev 15:6

[1413] NV2 pg. 331.

[1414] NV2 pg. 331. Changes in person are found in other ancient texts where unity is not in question (examples TJob 46:1; 4Ezra 6:28; Tobit 3:7; 1QapGen 21:23-30).

[1415] Metatron is named on a number of incantation bowls from Babylonia and in a 4th century Palestinian text Re'uyot Yehezqe'l (P Alexander, OTP1 pg. 229).

[1416] 71:1-4 borrows very heavily from chapters 14-18 of the *Book of the Watchers*. However, terms typical to the *Parables* are also used in the account, such as "secrets" or "hidden things," as are the titles typical of the *Parables* such as "Lord of Spirits" and "Son of Man." "In both the *Book of the Watchers* and the *Parables*, Enoch has ascended to heaven, has stood in the presence of the deity, and has toured the cosmos in the company of interpreting angels. For this reason, the section is best understood as an appendix to the *Book of Parables* that reflects primarily the *Book of the Watchers*" (NV2 pg. 323).

[1417] K, I and N have "sons of the holy angels." This title occurs elsewhere in 1 Enoch only in (69:4, 5 and 106:5). It may be the equivalent of the biblical term *benê-'elohîm*, "sons of God" in Genesis 6:2. Knibb notes this is probably a false translation of "the holy sons of God."

2 I saw two rivers of fire,	14:19; Dan 7:10
and the light of that fire radiated like hyacinth,[1418]	Ezek 28:13
and I fell on my face before the Lord of Spirits.	
3 Then the angel Michael, one of the archangels,	Jude 9; 1Thes 4:16; Dan 10:21
seized me by my right hand, and lifted me up	
and he brought me out to all the secrets	
and led me forth into all the secrets of mercy,[1419]	Lk 8:10
and he showed me all the secrets of righteousness.	49:2
4 He also showed me all the secrets of the ends of the heavens,	
and all the treasuries of the stars, and all the luminaries	
and where they emerge before the faces of the holy ones.	

Enoch Ascends to the Heavenly Palace

5 Then he translated my spirit—even me, Enoch—to the	1Kgs 8:27
heaven of heavens.[1420] There I saw in the midst of that	2Chr 2:6; 6:18; 2Cor 12:2
light, a house as it were, built of crystal stones,	14:9-12
and among those crystal stones were tongues of living fire.[1421]	Acts 2:3; 1Q29 1.3; 2.3
6 My spirit saw a circle that encompassed that house with fire;[1422]	
from its four sides ran rivers full of living fire,	Gen 2:10; Zech 2:5; Dan 7:10
and they surrounded the house.	
7 All around it were Seraphin, Cherubim, and Ophannin:[1423]	20:7; 61:10,12; Ezek 1:16-18; 10:2
these are they who sleep not[1424]	14:23; 39:13; 40:2
but keep watch over the throne of his glory.	2En 21:1
8 I saw angels who could not be counted,	40:1; 47:3; 60:1; 4Q530 2.2.16-19
thousands upon thousands, and myriads upon myriads,	1:9; 14:22; 60:1; Dan 7:10; Rev 5:11
encircling that house.	Heb 12:22
Michael, Raphael, Gabriel, and Phanuel, and the holy angels,	9:1; 40:9-10
who are above the heavens, all going in and out of that house.[1425]	Rev 15:5-6
9 Then Michael, Raphael, Gabriel, and Phanuel, and many holy	
angels without number, came forth from that house.	
10 With them was the Antecedent of Time. His head was white	46:1
and pure as wool, and his garments indescribable.	14:20; Dan 7:9; Rev 1:14

1418 Ethiopic *yākent* is elsewhere used to translate Greek *sapphiron* (Hebrew: *sappir*), so scholars consider "hyacinth" here to speak of sapphire" (H2 pg. 235) (cf. Ex 24:9-11; Isa 54:11; Ezek 1:26: 10:1).

1419 The doublet of "secrets of mercy" with "secrets of righteousness" brings to mind the future heavenly courtroom in the judgement.

1420 K has "highest heaven" in place of "heaven of heavens." This is the dwelling place of God (cf. I Kgs 8:27).

1421 Tongues of fire are mentioned in 14:9, 10, and 15, from which much of Chapter 71 is based. They also figure in the Dead Sea Scrolls, (see 1Q29 1.3; 2.3 (W pg. 145)); and at Pentecost in (Acts 2:3).

1422 For this line K has: "And my spirit saw a circle of fire surrounded that house."

1423 Ophannin are a special type of spiritual being linked to the Hebrew word ophan which is used in Ezekiel's vision of the glory of God in (Ezek 1:16-21). The "wheels", ophan, are described as living and having eyes in (Ezekiel 1:18-21).

1424 "These are they who sleep not" (cf. 1En 39:12-13; 40:2; 41:7; 61:12).

1425 **In 14:21 by contrast, no angel can enter the house. The house described here must correspond with the outer house described in 14:8-14.**

11 I fell on my face, and my whole body became relaxed, — 14:24; 60:3; Dan 10:8
and my spirit was transformed. I cried out with a loud voice, — 39:14; AscenIs 7:25
with a spirit of power, praising, glorifying and exalting. — 61:11; Isa 11:2
12 These blessings which came forth out of my mouth were — Heb 11:5; Gen 5:22-24[LXX]; Sir 44:16
well pleasing[1426] before that Antecedent of Time. — 61:6-12; Ps 19:14; Wis 4:10-15

Enoch is Identified as the Son of Man

13 Then the Antecedent of Time[1427] approached with Michael, — 2En 22:6-10; 67:2
Gabriel, Raphael and Phanuel, and thousands and ten — 1:9; 40:1; 60:1; Gen 32:30
thousands of angels without number.[1428] — Deut 33:2; Jude 14
14 That angel[1429] came to me and greeted me with his voice — PrJos

---

[1426] "Well pleasing" matches the reading in the LXX of (Gen 5:22, 24). Where "walked with God" is translated as "well pleasing." εὐηρέστησε δὲ Ἐνὼχ τῷ θεῷ = "and Enoch was well pleasing unto God," **The use of this phrase which can only be referring to Enoch early in the messianic passage of Wis 4:10-5:8 links Enoch with the Messiah of Isaiah 52-53 and incorporates elements of 1 Enoch 62:1-63:2. Was Enoch viewed by the author of the Wisdom of Solomon as a Christophany or a type of Christ?**

[1427] (1En 71:13-17) is astounding for two reasons. First in (71:13) "the Head of Days approaches Enoch with the four archangels and the thousands of angels without number" (NV2 pg. 327). This is without precedent outside Ezek 1. Secondly, and even more shocking, is the identification of Enoch as the Son of Man. Nickelsburg finds it unlikely that the usage of "Son of Man" refers to Enoch the patriarch as a human as it does to Ezekiel in the Book of Ezekiel. This major deviation from the remaining text of the *Parables* indicates that it is not original to the text of the *Parables*. **Unlike the remainder of the body of the *Parables,* the kings and mighty are not mentioned in 70-71. The strange switch from third person to first person in 70:3 is also suspicious. In addition, the end of Chapter 69 is the end of the third Parable and should thus end the *Book of the Parables*. This would indicate that chapter 70-71 were later additions.** Nickelsburg, after presenting even more evidence, sums up with the following statement "**If these sections, and especially chap. 71, are additions to the three parables, there are no grounds for asserting that the "author(s)" and the first transmitters of the Parables believed that the Righteous One/Chosen One, Anointed One/Son of Man was or would be the ancient patriarch Enoch**" (NV2 pg. 332). Such an identification would be highly offensive to both Jews and Christians. It is difficult to imagine it being original to the text. However, it is unmistakably found in the Ethiopic texts. It must be remembered that *The Book of Parables* relies only on Ethiopic and late medieval copies (R pg. 452) since no Aramaic text has been published. With no Aramaic text, it cannot be determined when chapters 70-71 were added to the book. Christopher Mearns argues that the *Testament of Abraham* (recension B chapter 11) is a reaction to the identification of Enoch as the Son of Man (Mearns, Christopher L., 2009. *Dating the Similitudes of Enoch in New Testament Studies* 25, Feb 5, 2009, pgs. 363-364). If this is true, it would indicate that chapters 70-71 were in the text as early as AD 75-100 when it is thought the Testament of Abraham was written (OTP1 pg. 875). Collins summarizes the issue: **"But as we have noted already, chaps. 70-71 are not a unit at all. Chap. 71 constitutes a second, or third, epilogue, and in my view, is most readily explained as a secondary addition. Even if the identification of Enoch with the Son of Man is accepted in chap. 71, the first epilogue in chap. 70 should not be harmonized with it. If the majority reading of 70:1 is accepted, as I think it should be, then the distinction it makes between Enoch and the Son of Man cannot be explained away"** (R pg. 224, Collins).

[1428] "The language here is that of an installation formula, as for example, in Ps. 2:7, and this fits well with a commissioning scene. The identification of Enoch as the Son of Man can be read as a first step toward the angelification of the seer in 2 Enoch 22 and of his identification with Metatron in 3 Enoch" (NV2 pg. 328).

[1429] It is not clear which angel this is. Some manuscripts say, "that one" in place of "that angel." Olson observes: "Most likely "that one" is Phanuel, the angel whose name derives from Gen 32:30-31, the wrestler with Jacob who bestowed upon him his new name while refusing to disclose his own. We recall that the closest literary parallel to Enoch in the PE is Jacob in the *Prayer of Joseph*." *Eerdmans Commentary on the Bible: First Enoch*

and said to me: "You are the son of man[1430] who is born for 46:3; Gen 5:22-24; Jub 10:17 OdesSol 3:7
righteousness, and righteousness abides upon you,[1431] 39:9; TAb B 11; 2En 22:10; 64:5
and the righteousness of the Antecedent of Time Isa 11:5
will not forsake you."
15 He also said to me:
"He summons forth peace for you in the name of the age that is to Heb 2:5; 6:5; Mt 12:32 4Q440 3.16; OdesSol 9:6
come;[1432] for from there has proceeded peace since the creation of the age. Mk 10:30; Eph 1:21
Therefore, it shall be yours forever, and forever and ever. 69:17
16 All shall walk in your ways, since righteousness never forsakes you. 46:3; Lev 26:12; Eph 2:22
With you will be their dwelling-places, and with you their inheritance, 39:4, 7; Jn 14:2-3; Rev 21:3
and from you they shall not be separated forever and forever and ever. 105:2; Rom 8:38-39
17 And so there shall be length of days with the Son of Man,
and the righteous shall have peace and an upright way Jn 14:27
in the Name of the Lord of Spirits forever and ever."] 108:13

[1430] Isaac notes: "This expression, 'son of man,' should be distinguished from the 'Son of Man.' 'Man' in the 'Son of Man' (elsewhere in the *Parables*,) is a translation of either *sabʾe*, 'people,' or *ʾegʷula-ʾemma heyyāw*, 'son of the mother of the living,' i.e. 'human being'; in the present case, however, we have *beʾesi*, 'man,' 'a masculine person.'" **This text follows Isaac and the interpretation of the Abyssinian Church in using "son of man." Ethiopian commentators and a few modern scholars interpret "son of man" here as meaning a mere mortal as it does throughout Ezekiel and possibly in 1En 60:10** (see the analysis above). Nickelsburg has: "You (are) that Son of Man." Knibb, Black and Olson have: "You are the Son of Man." Verse 15 seems to be an angel speaking on behalf of the Antecedent of Time. The person described in 16-17 is clearly the Messiah. The editor suspects corruption in the text and/or that 70:3-71:17 is an interpolation.

[1431] In the Testament of Abraham B chap. 11, Abel is the one to judge, and Enoch is reduced to a "scribe of righteousness". In the Prayer of Joseph C (AD 1st to 2nd century), as referenced by Origen, Jacob is identified as having been the archangel Israel prior to his life on Earth and having forgotten, is reminded of that fact by the archangel Uriel (OTP2 713-714).

[1432] **"Age that is to come" Charles asserts that this is the earliest use of this phrase** (cf. Mt 12:32; Mk 10:30; Lk 18:30; 20:35; Eph 1:21; Heb 2:5; 6:5). "The age to come" is after the second coming of the Messiah which will be in judgement.

The Book of Heavenly Luminaries

Background of *The Book of Heavenly Luminaries*

Original language: Aramaic, translated to Greek, but with no surviving Greek text. It was translated from Greek to Ethiopic (Ge' ez).[1433]

Author and provenance: Jew, Persia

Date: Persian period 550-330 BC, or earlier. This compilation and abridgment of astronomical, cosmological, and calendrical lore and law…has its roots in the Persian period and is probably the oldest of the Enoch traditions.[1434] This date is supported for the following reasons. 1. "It seems quite likely that the writer of the Book of the Watchers knows the Enochic astronomical work and uses its revelatory framework (Uriel to Enoch) and especially the contents of chap. 76."[1435] The Book of Heavenly Luminaries thus predates the Book of the Watchers. 2. "The original form is an example of Jewish literature from the eastern Diaspora, where the author learned the astronomy contained in it."[1436] "The background for much of the Enochic is almost certainly the primitive or traditional system attested in works such as MUL.APIN and Emuma Anu Enlil XIV."[1437] These sources (MUL.APIN and Emuma Anu Enlil), are so old they are translated from cuneiform fragments and texts. "Sources of the Emuma Anu Enlil date to 1950–1595 BCE with the MUL.APIN being edited between 1000 and 687 B.C.E." "Two clear-cut types of Babylonian astronomy can be distinguished: one a highly developed mathematical astronomy which flourished in the last three centuries before our era; the other, a rather primitive and crude astronomy which we find in texts of which the archetypes, though there is no direct evidence, possibly go back as far as Old-Babylonian times (i.e., about 1600 B.C.)."[1438]

Important notes: In the Abyssinian Church,[1439] as with the rest of 1 Enoch, it is regarded as part of the Old Testament. That the Book of Heavenly Luminaries was part of the Book of Enoch is demonstrated by a quote from Anatolius (ca. AD 269) preserved in *Historia ecclesiastica* by Eusebius 7.32 which reads "That the first month among the Hebrews straddles the equinox is shown also in the book of Enoch" (Cf. 1En 72:6, 9). Important similarities and differences exist between the Book of Heavenly Luminaries and 4Q208, 4Q209 and 4Q211 which are called Astronomical Enoch. A fragment of Q208 was dated to between 186-48 BCE (depending on the calibration method) by Mass Spectrometry.[1440] The text of The Book of Heavenly Luminaries has likely been reworked and was originally longer.[1441] Approximately 30% of the text is

---

[1433] NV2 pg. 564, 569.
[1434] N1 pg. 7-8. Olson considers the Book of Watchers to be older than the Book of Luminaries due to its apparent assumed knowledge of the speaker (Enoch), and the angelic guide (Uriel) from the Book of Watchers in 72:1. *Eeerdman's commentary on the Bible: First Enoch* (Introduction).
[1435] NV2 pg. 393.
[1436] NV2 pg. 383.
[1437] NV2 pg.383. E pg. 186.
[1438] Otto Neugebauer, *Studies in Ancient Astronomy* VIII.
[1439] Aka the Ethiopian Orthodox Tewahedo Church.
[1440] NV2 pg. 339.
[1441] NV2 pg. 444.

covered in the Dead Sea Scrolls.[1442] Evidence from Qumran indicates the Astronomical Book was once independent of the other Enochic booklets.[1443] "One should emphasize that there is no case where the Astronomical Book has been found in a manuscript (in the Qumran literature) together with another Enoch book."[1444] "In short, there may have been the notion of a collection of books of Enoch, but we have evidence only of the transmission of separate booklets."[1445] Some scholars have raised the possibility that the same calendar found in The Book of Heavenly Luminaries was used before the exile.[1446] "The 'Astronomy Book' may therefore preserve not only the official calendar of pre-exilic Israel but even ancient polemics against Gentile calendars."[1447] The book concerns astronomy, but not astrology, as there are no references to the zodiac or the planets. Since astrology is viewed as given by fallen watchers (1En 8:3), it makes sense it would not be promoted in the balance of 1 Enoch.

The *Book of Heavenly Luminaries* (Chapters 72-82)

The Law of the Sun

72 1 Book on the Motion of the Luminaries of Heaven: how each one of PsSol 18:10-12
them stands in relation to: their kinds, their period of rule, their seasons, 2:1; 82:7; 93:14; Gen 8:22
their names,[1448] their starting points and their months, as revealed to me Jub 2:9; 4:17-19; 6:4; Ps 147:4
by their leader Uriel,[1449] the holy angel who accompanied me.[1450] 20:2; 33:4; 80:1; Jer 31:35-36
He showed to me all their regulations[1451] as they are for all the years 80:6; Ps 89:1-5, 36-37; 148:5-6

[1442] N1 pg. 11.

[1443] NV2 pg. 532.

[1444] R pg. 103 Tigchelaar, *Remarks on Transmission and Traditions in the Parables of Enoch.*

[1445] R pg. 103 Tigchelaar, *Remarks on Transmission and Traditions in the Parables of Enoch.*

[1446] J. Milgrom, "Priestly ('P') Source, The Anchor Bible Dictionary 5. 458-459.

[1447] OL pg. 14. Eshel (E pg. 108) argues that a lunar calendar was used until priestly temple leadership switched to a solar calendar in the 3rd century BC before Antiochus IV later imposed a lunar calendar on the temple. (Dan 7:25)

[1448] The concept that the stars have names is also found in (69:21; Isa 40:26 and Ps 147:4). (See also 1En 82:9-20). To claim knowledge of the names and numbers of the stars is to claim special revelation from God since they cannot otherwise be known.

[1449] Uriel ("God is my light/fire") is very important as a guide in the *Book of Luminaries.* He is of the highest category of angels being second in the list of the four great angels (9:1) (Sariel=Uriel). He is the first of the seven holy angels mentioned in (20:2) where he is over the world and Tartarus. He accompanies Enoch in his travels in (21:4-10). Uriel was also Enoch's guide to the stars in (33:3-4). Uriel is named again in (74:2; 75:4; 78:10; 79:6, 80:1 and 82:7). Uriel is also mentioned in 4Ezra (4:1; 5:20; and 10:28). In (2 Enoch 23:3) an angel named Vrevoil shows Enoch the cosmos.

[1450] The author assumes that readers already know Enoch is the speaker, indicating as Olson proposes, that the *Book of Heavenly Luminaries* may be a continuation of and antedate the *Book of the Watchers.*

[1451] The cosmos obeys the laws of God. The comparison of the orderly cosmos with rebel angels and humans does not occur in the *Book of Heavenly Luminaries* but it does in the *Book of Watchers* (2:2-5:4). Genesis 8:22 is brought to mind here. "While the earth remains, seedtime and harvest, cold and heat, summer and winter, day and night, shall not cease." (See also Jub 6:4). These laws are to be in effect until the new creation. A change in their behavior is therefore a signal of the lawless one and the end of the age (1En 80:6; Dan 7:25). "By the time Jubilees 4:17-18 was written in the mid-second century, Enoch was known as an author who wrote about astronomical topics" (NV2 pg. 410).

of the world to eternity; until the creation[1452] will be made anew to 45:4-5; 91:16; Isa 65:17; 66:22 Ps 102:25-27; 2Bar 32:6
last forever.[1453] 2Pet 3:13; Rev 21:1; 4Ezra 7:75
2 This is the first law of the luminaries: the light (called) the sun
has its emergence through the gates of heaven in the east and it sets
among the gates of heaven in the west.
3 I saw six gates[1454] from which the sun rises, and six gates where Jub 4:17-18
the sun sets; the moon also rises and sets in these gates, as well as
the leaders of the stars together with those which they lead. 75:1; 80:1, 6; 82:10-14; Isa 40:26
Six gates are in the east and six in the west, and all of them are arranged
in sequence. And there are many windows to the right and to the left [1455] 75:7
of these gates.
4 First emerges the great light called the sun. Its roundness is as 41:5-7; Gen 1:16
the roundness of heaven and it is entirely filled with fire 73:2; 78:3-4
that illuminates and heats.
5 The chariot[1456] on which it ascends,[1457] is blown along by the wind 18:4; 73:2; 75:3-4,8; 2 Kgs 23:11

[1452] **This is an early statement that there will be a new creation and that the present world is only temporary.** It may only be predated by (Isa 65:17 and 66:22); or if one accepts a date for a third Isaiah in the fifth century BC it may be contemporary or even predate the Isaiah texts.

[1453] The concept of a new creation is common in second temple literature and the New Testament (cf. Jub 1:29; 4:26; 2Bar 32:1-6; 57:2; 4Ezra 7:75; Ps-Philo 3:10; 2Cor 5:17; Gal 6:15; 2Pet 3:13 and Rev 21:1). It is also found in Isaiah (65:17 and 66:22).

[1454] "In numerous Akkadian and Sumerian texts, the Moon, Sun, Venus, and the stars are said to pass through heavenly gates. As these astronomical bodies rise or appear in the sky, they are said to enter the heavens through gates. Conversely, as they set or disappear, they leave the heavens through gates" (Horowitz, *Gates to the Visible Heavens*," pg. 266). "These gates were conceived as being located on the eastern and western ends of the heavens" (NV2 pg. 420). Please see the examples below.

Gilgamesh IX.42-45,
"Go on, Gilgamesh, fear not!
The Mashu mountains I give to you freely (!),
the mountains, the ranges, you may traverse ...
In safety may your feet carry you.
The gate of the mountain ..."
To the rising of the sun ...
To the setting of the sun ...
To the setting of the sun ...
They caused to go out..."

Enuma Elish V.8-10
He fixed the heavenly stations of Enlil and Ea with it.
Gates he opened on both sides,
And put strong bolts at the left and the right.

(See also *Hymn to the Sun-God Shamash* 13-15)

[1455] Knibb has: "south and north" in place of "right and left."

[1456] "Chariots" "This echoes the imagery found in some cuneiform texts that Shamash rides upon a chariot" (NV2 pg. 421). "In Mesopotamian sources, Shamash travels through the underworld at night although there are varied ideas about the sun's nocturnal whereabouts and activities" (NV2 pg. 421, citing Heimpel, "Sun at night," 127-151).

[1457] 2 Enoch (AD first century) also has an astronomical section. Similarities include gates of the sun (2En 13-14) and moon (2En 16), the sun and moon traveling on a chariot (2En A 12).

When the sun descends from the sky, it returns by way of the north[1458] in 41:5; 77:3; 78:5; Eccl 1:5-6
order to travel again toward the east; and it is guided in such a way that
it enters in the proper gate and it shines again in the face of the sky.
6 In this way the sun emerges in the first month[1459] through the large *HE* 7.32.6-13; 4Q321
gate[1460]—the fourth of those six eastern gates.
7 In this fourth gate, from which the sun emerges in the first month,
there are twelve window-openings from which flames pour
whenever they are opened, in their proper season. 75:4, 7
8 When the sun rises in the sky it emerges through that fourth gate
for thirty mornings and the sun sets faithfully through this fourth Ps 104:19
gate in the west.
9 During this period, the day becomes longer over the (preceding) Gen 1:14-18
day, and the night becomes shorter than the (preceding)
night, for 30 days.
10 On that (thirtieth) day, the day is one ninth, or two units longer
than the night, the day being exactly ten parts and the night
exactly eight parts.
11 The sun rises from the fourth gate and sets through the fourth
(gate). Next it moves to the fifth gate in the east, for 30 mornings,
and it rises from it and it sets in the fifth gate.
12 Then the daytime increases two parts, so the day consists of
eleven parts and the night decreases to seven parts.
13 It returns again to the east and enters the sixth gate and it rises
and sets in the sixth gate for thirty-one[1461] days,[1462] in accordance
with that which this gate signifies.[1463]
14 During this time period, the daytime increases over the nighttime
until the daytime is double the night, such that the day is twelve parts
and the night grows shorter and is six parts.
15 Then the sun sets out to shorten the day[1464] and to lengthen the night.

[1458] Isaac has: "northeast." The idea is that the sun travels back to its place in the east through the north where it cannot be seen at night. The same cosmology is evident in (Eccl 1:5-6). A ritual for seeing the sun on its return to the east via the north is found in (*Sepher Ha-Razim* 4) which is based on (1En 72:5). (Cf. TJob 37:8)

[1459] **The first month is marked by the spring equinox. This is the beginning of the calendar year. Eusebius quotes *The Canons of Anatolius on the Easter Festival*, "That the first month among the Hebrews straddles the equinox is shown also in the book of Enoch"** (*HE* 7.32). **This quote is hugely significant, in that Anatolius (ca. AD 269) who Eusebius s quoting, considered a *Luminaries* type text to be part of The Book of Enoch as named by Origen** (Cels. 5:54). **Unfortunately, it is very doubtful that this original book of luminaries has come down to us in an intact form.** The fourth gate is the position of both spring and fall equinoxes. "Since the year begins at an equinox and during the first month the length of the period of light in the day increases, the year is understood to begin at the spring equinox" (NV2 pg. 424). This is the first Hebrew month Abib (Ex 12:1-2; 13:4; Deut 16:1); after the Babylonian captivity it was called Nisan (Neh 2:1). It corresponds to April.

[1460] "Large" likely means "important" or "notable" (NV2 pg. 423).

[1461] Several manuscripts read 30.

[1462] The sixth portal is the summer solstice. At the most northernly gate (6) the sun remains an extra day (31).

[1463] "Signifies" This sign has nothing to do with the zodiac which does not exist in Enoch's astronomy (BL pg. 395). In fact, Charles believes the cosmology here is designed to dispense with the signs of the zodiac (C pg. 152-153). The sign is the summer solstice itself, where the day length becomes double that of the night (72:14). See also (75:3).

[1464] The days begin to shorten now that the solstice is over.

When the sun returns to the east it enters the sixth gate and it rises
from it and sets for thirty mornings.
16 When the thirty mornings are completed, the day has decreased
exactly one part and the day is eleven parts and the night is seven.
17 Then the sun exits through this sixth gate in the west and goes
toward the east to rise in the fifth gate for thirty mornings and it sets
likewise in the western fifth gate.
18 By the thirtieth day, the day is two parts fewer, with the daytime
being ten parts and the night being eight parts.
19 The sun rises through the fifth gate and it sets in the fifth gate
in the west. Then it rises through the fourth gate for thirty-one
mornings in the east, in accordance with that which this gate signifies.[1465]
20 By the thirty-first day, the day equals the night and they are the
same: the night is nine parts and the day is nine parts.[1466]
21 The sun emerges from this (fourth) gate and it sets in the west.
Then it returns to the east, and rises through the third gate for thirty
mornings, and it sets in the west in the third gate.[1467]
22 During this time period, the night increases over the daytime;[1468]
each night longer than the last, and each day shorter than the last,
until by the thirtieth day: the nighttime is exactly ten parts and the
daytime eight parts.
23 The sun rises from this third gate and it sets in the west in the
third gate. The sun returns toward the east and emerges through the
second gate in the east for thirty mornings and it sets also in the
second gate of the western sky.
24 By the thirtieth day, the night is eleven parts and the day seven parts.
25 During this time period, the sun rises through this second gate and
sets in the west through the second gate. (Then) it returns eastward
to the first gate for thirty-one mornings and it sets in the first gate
in the western sky.
26 By the thirty-first day, the nighttime has increased to become twice
the daytime; the night is exactly 12 parts and the day is 6 parts.[1469]
27 The sun has thus completed the chief points of all its sections.[1470]
It then goes through these same appearances a second time, and
each gate for thirty mornings, and it sets opposite to them in the west.
28 During this time period, the night has decreased by a ninth part,

---

[1465] This sign is the equal day lengths of the autumn equinox.

[1466] The sun has now arrived at the autumnal equinox month in the northern hemisphere where it will spend 31 days. "Only in gates 2 and 5 does the sun always spend thirty days" (NV2 pg. 425).

[1467] The sun rise location now begins it journey to the south as autumn fades into winter.

[1468] This is a correct observation, that at this point, the night becomes longer than the day, as autumn progresses toward the winter solstice.

[1469] The sun has now reached the position of the winter solstice in the northern hemisphere. The day is divided into 18 parts of 80 minutes each rather than 24 parts of 60 minutes. The ratio of 12 to 6 may have derived from traditions in northern Asia. This ration would be found at 49 degrees latitude which equates with northern Asia (C pg. 153).

[1470] The sun has passed through each of the 6 gates at least once as it begins its journey north toward the vernal equinox. Similarities are seen with the layout of the temple in (Ezek 43:1-12 and 46:1-12).

that is by one part; and the night consists of eleven parts and the
day of seven parts.
29 The sun returns and enters[1471] the second gate in the east. It returns
to those chief points of its (route) for thirty days, rising and setting.
30 During this time period the night decreases in length with the night
becoming ten parts and the day eight parts.
31 Throughout these days the sun rises from the second gate and sets
in the west. It returns to the east and it rises in the third gate for
thirty-one mornings and sets on the western side of the sky.
32 During this time period, the nighttime decreases until it is nine parts,
with a daytime of nine parts. The night equals the day,[1472]
and the year is exactly 364 days.[1473] 4Q252 1.2.2-5; 4Q394 3-7 1.2-3
33 The length of the day and the night, and the shortness of day and
night, vary during the circuit of the sun.
34 For this reason, its course becomes longer day after day or
shorter night after night.
35 This is the law for the circuit of the sun
and its returnings, whenever it comes back and goes out.[1474]
This great luminary is called "the sun," for the duration of the years Ps 72:5, 17; 89:36-37; 4Q440 1.1
of the universe.
36 This one that rises is the great luminary, and it is named according Gen 1:16
to its appearance as the Lord has commanded. Sir 43:2-5
37 In this way it rises, and similarly it sets, and it does not grow dim 41:5-7; 73:3
nor rest,[1475] but travels day and night. Its light is seven times brighter 78:3-4; Isa 30:26
than the moon but the size of the two are equal.[1476]

Excursus: Similar content between the Book of the Luminaries and the Dead Sea Scrolls.

Book of Luminaries	Corresponding texts in the Dead Sea Scrolls
73:4-8; 74:3-10; 78:6-8; 10-16	4Q208; 4Q209 Frgs. 1-22, 26, 29-41; 4Q210 1.3.3-9
76:3-14	4Q209 Frgs. 23.1-2; 4Q210 1.2.1-10
77:1-4	4Q209 Frgs. 23:3-10; 4Q210 1.2.14-20

[1471] The verb tenses for this verse in the manuscripts, switch to perfect tense (i.e. the sun returned and entered). I have elected, as with most translators to keep the same verb tense as the rest of the text.
[1472] The sun has now returned to the vernal equinox.
[1473] Since 364 is an exact multiple of seven, the calendar has exactly 52 weeks, so that every date falls on the same day of the week every year. The year begins on Wednesday, since God created the luminaries on the fourth day (Gen. 1:14-19). (VF pg. 257). 4Q252 2.3-5 (W pg353) has Noah in the ark for 364 days "an exact year."
[1474] "Returns sixty times" is an additional phrase some Ethiopic manuscripts place in the middle of this verse. This may be a general statement that the sun spends two periods or about 60 days in each portal per year. Olson thinks it may be the remnant of a lost comment (OL pg. 150).
[1475] "The sun does not lessen or diminish, nor does it rest. Rather, it is always moving. This assertion contrasts with the idea in some cuneiform texts that the sun rests at night" (NV2 pg. 428).
[1476] This may be an observation from a total solar eclipse, where the moon totally covers the disk of the sun. Or just a general observation that they appear to be about the same size.

79:1	4Q209 Frg. 26.6
82:9-13	4Q209 Frg. 28
82:15-20	4Q211

"There is no doubt that something drastic happened between the Aramaic and the Ethiopic form of the Enochic astronomical work. In the absence of the Greek intermediate translation, we do not know the shape(s) of the text at that point, but the Ethiopic copies manifest an abbreviated version at several points."[1477] The Dead Sea Scrolls establish that *The Book of Luminaries* originally contained much more material than the text we have before us from Ethiopic.

Phases of the Moon

73 1 After this law, I saw another law about the smaller luminary, 4Q317; Gen 1:16
whose name is "the Moon."[1478] Sir 43:6-8
2 Its roundness is as the roundness of the sky, and the wind drives 18:4; 72:4-5
the chariot on which it rides. Light is given to it in measured portions.[1479] 75:3-4, 8
3 Each month its place of rising and setting vary, but its daylengths
are the same as those of the sun.[1480] When its light is full
it amounts to one seventh of the light of the sun. 72:37; 78:3-4; 91:16; Isa 30:26
4 In this way it rises with its beginning toward the east; it emerges 4Q208-209
on the thirtieth day and on that day it is visible. It becomes for you[1481]
the beginning of the month on the thirtieth day; with the sun
in the gate from which the sun rises. 4Q503
5 The halfmoon is of seven parts, and its whole disc is empty with
no light, except for a seventh part, one fourteenth part of its light.[1482] [1483]
6 When it has taken on a seventh part of half its light; then its
illuminated section is a half seventh part.

[1477] NV2 pg. 357.
[1478] Among the Dead Sea Scrolls, (4Q317 (W pg. 385-386) deals with the moon and its phases.
[1479] The moon phases are considered measured portions as they happen by exact degrees.
[1480] "Daylengths are the same as those of the sun" i.e. about 30 days each. Just as the sun defines 30-day months so do the phases of the moon. Unlike the sun's orderly movements, the moon's places of rising and setting vary greatly within each month. Sirach 43:6-8 seems to prefer the Lunar Calendar.
[1481] The phrasing "becomes for you [pl.]" is unique in the book. Elsewhere Enoch's oldest son, Methuselah, is the recipient of the information in the book (76:14; 82:1; cf. 79:1). It may be simply an idiomatic expression" (NV2 pg. 432).
[1482] VanderKam notes: "The writer appears to be describing the illuminated portions of the moon's surface (that is, the half of the moon facing the earth) on the first two days of a lunar month. **As the Aramaic copies show, he was severely abbreviating a lengthier table which supplied such information for a much longer time, possibly even an entire year"** (N pg. 100) (See 4Q209 7.2 (W pg. 300-301).
[1483] "Consequently, the first part of the verse expresses the distance the moon is from the sun, a distance or elongation that allows the new moon crescent to be seen" (NV2 pg. 433). Concerning the second part of 73:5 Vanderkam comments "…on the first day of a lunar month, a half of a seventh, that is, one-fourteenth of the moon's surface, is illuminated" (NV2 pg. 433).

7 It sets with the sun, and when the sun rises, the moon rises with it,
and it receives one half part of its light. During that night, at the
beginning of the moon's day, (which is the first day of its month), Haer. 2.28.2
the moon sets with the sun and it is dark that night in six seventh parts 78:6
and a half.
8 It rises and comes out on this day with exactly the seventh part
(of its total light). It emerges and recedes from the rising of the sun[1484]
and it is illuminated in the rest of its remaining days in its other
thirteen parts.[1485] [1486]

74 1 I saw another lunar circuit and law for it.[1487] According to that 4Q208; Ps 104:19
law it carries out the cycle of the months.
2 All this Uriel, the holy angel who is leader of them all,[1488] showed
me. I wrote down their positions as he showed them to me, and I
wrote down their months just as they were, and the phases of their
illumination, until full moon on the fifteenth day.[1489] [1490] 78:7
3 In one-seventh parts, it completes all its light in the east and 78.8
in the west.[1491]
4 In certain months it changes the location of its settings
(with the sun), but in certain months it goes its own individual way.[1492]
5 During two months it sets with the sun in these two middle gates;
that is, in the third and fourth gate.
6 It emerges for seven days, and it turns, and moves back to the gate
from which the sun rises, and it completes all its light. Then it recedes
from the sun, and enters for eight days the sixth gate from which the
sun rises.[1493]
7 When the sun emerges from the fourth gate, (the moon) comes out

---

[1484] Isaac has: "Then it comes out and recedes toward the east (away from) where the sun rises,"

[1485] "Thirteen parts" so has Charles. This is the clearest statement to convey the meaning. For the last sentence in 73:8 Olson has: "It recedes from the rising of the sun and in its remaining days becomes bright in its other six and other seven parts."

[1486] This text on the moon is abruptly ended here after day 2 of 14. Chapter 74 is viewed as a "disorganized chapter which obviously does not belong to the original composition" (BL pg. 397). Portions of this missing text may be found in (4Q208, 4Q209 and 4Q317 W pgs. 296-303 and 385-386).

[1487] Knibb has: "another journey and another law," Isaac has: "another system of rotation with its own regulation."

[1488] Uriel is the leader of all the heavenly bodies.

[1489] The waning and waxing of the moon each take 15 days.

[1490] DSS fragment (4Q209 25) may correspond with (74:1-2 or 78:9)? (N pg. 101).

[1491] Vanderkam notes numerous textual corruptions in verse three (NV2 pg. 440-441). This text follows his translation.

[1492] "Its own individual way" In other words not in the same gate with the sun. See 74:5-9.

[1493] "At the end of the verse (6) there is a mistake in the text because of an omission of some of the data. The text now says that the sun emerges from gate 6, which does not fit the pattern. Probably an earlier form of the text gave a fuller listing of the gates until the moon's return to gate 3, about which it would be appropriate to say that it was the one from which the sun rose" (NV2 pg. 447). Olson reconstructs 74:6 by adding the text in italics. "*When the sun rises through the 3rd gate,* it [the moon] goes forth for seven days, *to the 1st gate*, where it turns about, and it returns again in *seven days* to the gate where the sun rises [i.e., the 3rd]; and [there] its light is made full. Then it recedes from the sun, coming in eight days to the 6th gate, *turning about, and returning in seven days to the gate* through which the sun rises."

during seven days until it rises from the fifth[1494] (gate), and it returns
again, during seven days to the fourth gate, and it completes its light.
It recedes (from the sun), and it enters the first gate during eight days.
8 It again returns in seven days, to the fourth gate from which
the sun rises.
9 In this way I saw their positions, as the moon rises and the sun sets
during those days.

Comparison of the 354 and 364-day Calendar

10 When five years are added up, the total comes to thirty (extra)
days for the sun. All the days that result for one of those five years,
when complete, are 364 days.[1495] Jub 6:32-38
11 The extra amount for the sun and stars comes to six days;
for five years, six (extra) days, come to thirty days,[1496] and the moon
falls behind the sun and stars by thirty days.
12 The sun and the stars bring in every year with precision, all *Apol. A 4*
according to their eternal positions. They come neither early, nor late
by one day, by which they would change the year: each is exactly 1QS 1.13-15
364 days.[1497] 11QPs^a-Psalter 6
13 In three years there are 1092 days, in five years there are 1820 days,
with the result that in eight years there are 2912 days.[1498]
14 But for the lunar system by itself, the days in three years come
to 1,062; in five years it is fifty days fewer.
15 In five years there are 1770 days with the result that in eight years
the moon has 2832 days.
16 For in eight years, eighty days are lacking; the moon lags 79:5
by a total of 80 days by then.

[1494] Olson emends fifth to sixth.

[1495] **In Jubilees 6:32-38 the reader is urged not to use a lunar based calendar but rely on a solar based calendar of 364 days per year.** It is quite evident that these verses (10-17) are a later addition (BL pg. 399).

[1496] If using a 364-day year, one would expect this to be 50 days instead of 30 when comparing 354-to-364-day calendars. This verse seems to be comparing 354-day to 360-day years which VanderKam sees as a throwback to Mesopotamian astronomy. "Enochic astronomy shares much with a traditional form of Mesopotamian astronomy in which the year consisted of twelve thirty-day months or 360 days" (NV2 pg. 449). The passage mixes 364, and 360-day year, numbers. The passage seems to be comparing lunar 354-day years to solar 364-day years to arrive at the 10-day difference. The Greek lunar calendar was introduced by Menelaus and Antiochus IV (cf. Dan 7:25).

[1497] **Having the correct calendar is essential to knowing when to observe the festivals.** This is made plain in (1QS 1.14b-15a (W pg. 117) "They are neither to advance their holy times nor to postpone any of their prescribed festivals." "**Since the custodians of sacral calendars were priests, the 'Astronomy Book' supplies valuable evidence that *Enoch* traditions may have been passed down by a priestly group in rivalry with other priestly groups. That they were not originally a fringe sect is indicated by a singular fact: not a single dated event in the Old Testament falls on a Sabbath if we use the Enochic system (except for the Purim festival spoken of in Ester 9:13-22), suggesting that priestly editors of the Old Testament used the same 364-day solar method of reckoning. There are nearly a hundred such dates, so the statistic is significant**" (OL pg. 14 see text and note 24). **As in Jubilees 6:32-38, this text upholds the sun and stars as accurate dividers of time. The conclusion is that the solar calendar is superior to the lunar calendar.** For solar festival dates see (VF pg. 256-260).

[1498] The reason for the calculation in 74:13-16 is not clear, and the text is problematic for scholars. For an extensive discussion see (NV2 pg. 453-456).

17 Then the year is correctly completed in accord with their eternal positions, and the positions of the sun; they rise from the gate from which it rises and sets for 30 days.

Excursus: The 364-day calendar was superior.

By the second century BC, if not before, serious disputes arose among Jews concerning the lunar vs. solar calendar. Using the wrong calendar would lead to incorrect dates for festivals and sabbaths. Jubilees 6:23-38, the Temple Scroll and CD 3.14-15 all strongly advocated for the solar calendar for those reasons. Celebrating the festivals and sabbaths revealed by God's word on the wrong days would be a serious violation of God's revealed order putting humans out of sync with the parallel angelic order. This is attested in Jub 6:35. "…the divisions of times are ordained on the heavenly tablets, lest they forget the covenantal festivals and walk in the festivals of the nations, after their error and after their ignorance." The solar calendar is thought to be the traditional priestly calendar of the first and early second temple, used by both the Zadokite priests and Enochian Jews. The Hellenistic lunar calendar was introduced by Menelaus and Antiochus IV during the Maccabean crisis as referenced in Daniel 7:25.

Rabbinic Judaism continues to use the Hellenistic lunar calendar. "The lunar calendar, which Judaism follows to this day, requires a large number of human decisions. People must look at the stars and the Moon and report on their observations, and someone must be empowered to decide on the new month and the application of leap years." "By contrast, the 364-day calendar was perfect. Because this number can be divided into four and seven, special occasions always fall on the same day. This avoids the need to decide, for example, what happens when a particular occasion falls on the Sabbath, as often happens in the lunar calendar."[1499] This calendar was unchanging, and it appears to have embodied the beliefs of the members of an Enochic Jewish sect regarding perfection and holiness. This is one of many reasons the Enochic Jews/Essenes disassociated themselves from the temple dominated by the Pharisees. This could explain why Jesus may have celebrated the Passover at a different time than the Pharisees (cf. John 18:28; 19:14; Mt 26:17-19). Central to the calendar are the 4 days that correct it, one each quarter. The days occur on the two equinoxes and the two solstices. The deciphering of DSS scroll 4Q324d in 2017 revealed that these days were called (Tekufah).[1500] How the 364 day calendar was corrected to 365 ¼ days is not known; it may be that leap weeks were then added as needed.[1501]

Olson discounts "the theory that the Astronomy Book (of 1 Enoch) originated among diaspora Jews exposed to Babylonian astronomy" observing that "the 364-day calendar, has no true Babylonian parallel. All things considered; it is entirely possible that the Astronomy Book represents the official calendar of preexilic Israel." *Eerdmans Commentary on the Bible: First Enoch* (Kindle location 1461). Evidence of usage of the 364-day calendar in the time of David is found in 11QPs[a]-Psalter vs 5-6 where the author speaks of David "And he wrote three thousand

---

[1499] Eshbal Ratzon & Jonathan Ben-Dov. 2017. *A Newly Reconstructed Calendrical Scroll from Qumran in Cryptic Script.* Journal of Biblical Literature 136 (4): 905-936.

[1500] Ibid.

[1501] Johnson, Ken, 2020. *The Ancient Dead Sea Scroll Calendar: AND THE PROPHECIES IT REVEALS.* Ken Johnson has done work in fleshing out how this calendar may have functioned (https://dsscalendar.org). See also Calendars in the Dead Sea Scrolls (The literature of the Dead Sea Scrolls) James C.C. VanderKam

six hundred psalms; and songs to sing before the altar over the whole-burnt perpetual offering for every day, for all the days of the year: three hundred and sixty-four."

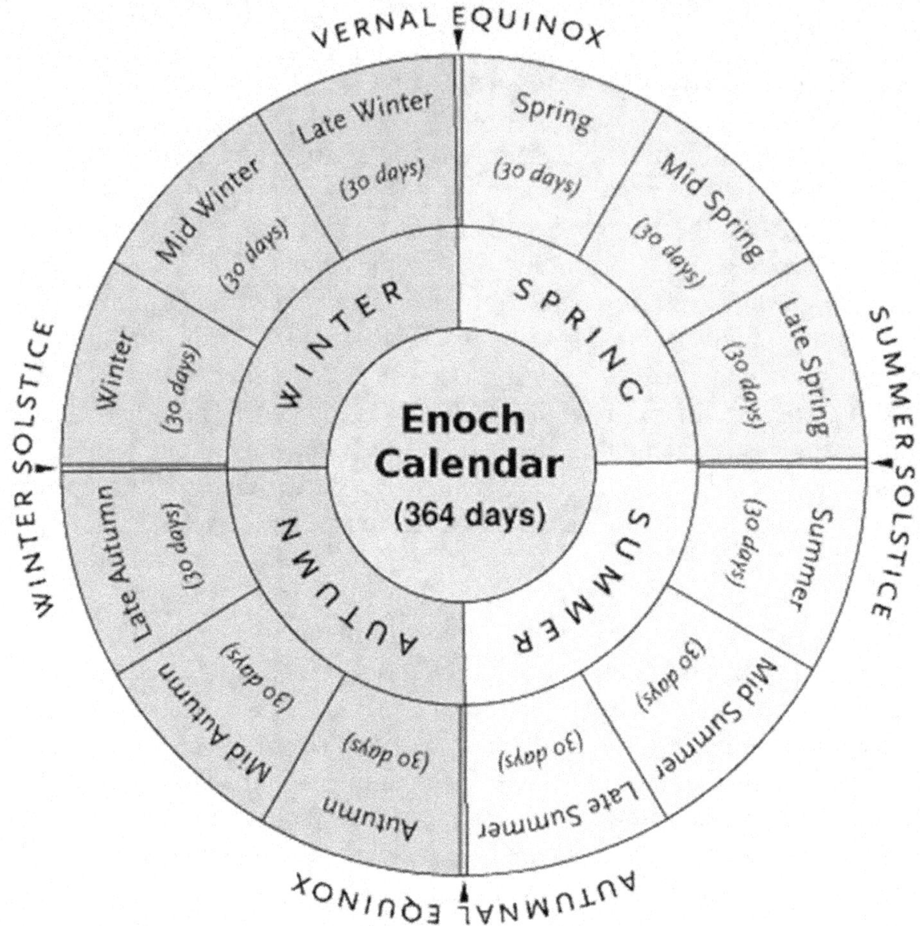

Source John Pratt, https://www.johnpratt.com. Used by permission.

Note: The four additional days, one each, are added at the times of the equinoxes and solstices.

The Leaders Over the Four Seasons

75 1 The leaders, at the head of (each) thousand (stars), who are 80:6; 82:4-20; 1Cor 15:41
appointed over the entire creation, and over all stars have to do with
the four additional days.[1502] They are inseparable from their positions, Jer 31:35
corresponding to the calculation of the year. They serve on these four

[1502] A similar thought is attributed to Papias writing around AD 130: "But Papias says, word for word: 'Some of them'—obviously meaning those angels that once were holy—'he assigned to rule over the orderly arrangement of the earth, and commissioned them to rule well.'" (Andrew of Caesarea, *On the Apocalypse*, chap. 34, sermon 12) These may be some of the same authorities and powers that Paul and Peter refer to (1Cor 15:24: Eph 1:21; 3:10; 6:12; Col 1:16; 2:10, 15 and 1Pet 3:22).

days which are not counted in the calculation of the year.[1503]
2 People err regarding them, (these four days),[1504] for these luminaries Jub 6:32-38
meticulously render service in the positions of the cosmos: 72:3
one in the first gate, one in the third gate, one in the fourth gate, 74:5; 82:10-11
and one in the sixth heavenly gate, so that the accuracy of the year is
achieved in the 364 positions of the cosmos.[1505]
3 For Uriel, the angel whom the Lord of eternal glory has forever 22:14; 1Cor 2:8; Jas 2:1
set over all the heavenly luminaries in the sky and in the cosmos,[1506] Jub 2:2
showed me the signs, the seasons, the year, and the days, so that they may 80:1
rule the firmament, appear above the earth, and be leaders of days and Ps 89:36-37; 136:8-9; 148:3
nights—the sun, the moon, the stars, and all the serving entities[1507] Deut 4:19
which make their revolution in all the heavenly chariots. 72:5; 73:2

The Twelve Gates of Heaven

4 In the same way, Uriel showed me twelve openings along the circuit
of the sun's chariot in the sky, from which the rays of the sun break forth, 72:7
and from which its warmth diffuses over the earth, whenever they are Ps 19:6
opened at their appointed seasons.
5 †(There are openings) for the winds, and for the wind (that brings) dew, 76:4, 6, 8
when the openings of heaven are opened, at the appointed times.†[1508]
6 I saw twelve open gates in the sky at the boundaries of the earth,[1509] 72:3
from which come out sun and moon and stars, and all the works of the
sky in the east and in the west.
7 There are many window openings to the right and to the left[1510] 72:3,7
of these. Each window at its time emits heat, like the gates from

---

[1503] Olson comments: **"astronomical knowledge is a matter not only of empirical observation but also of divine revelation. The cultic calendar belonged to those who knew about the angelic leaders and the exact handling of the four extra days. Ignorance of such things causes people to fall into error"** (OL pg. 154). The lunar calendar of the Jews did not have these four extra days. The Egyptian calendar had five days at the end of the year.

[1504] Other men who advocate a 360 rather than 364-day calendar cannot compete with the revelation from Uriel to Enoch. Appealing to Uriel leads credibility to the 364-day calendar. **"Coming down to the second century BCE, we find clear evidence of sharp disputes breaking out between Jewish advocates of the solar and lunar calendars. The Enochic calendar is the one championed in the Book of Jubilees, which attaches great religious portent to it, and by the Qumran community at the Dead Sea, where both Jubilees and Enoch were popular. Nevertheless, the 'Astronomy Book' itself seems to predate these lunar/solar debates since it describes the lunar calendar without a hint of disdain (78:15-16; 79:3-5), criticizing instead those who fail to correctly add the four days to the 360-day solar calendar (74:10-11; 75:1-2; 82:4-6)"** (OL pg. 14).

[1505] Gate one, winter solstice, gate three, autumnal equinox, gate four, vernal equinox, and gate six, summer solstice.

[1506] "Possibly the meaning of 'in the sky and in the world' is that the luminaries move through the sky but are seen in or have influence on the world" (NV2 pg. 460).

[1507] "Serving entities" The author does not refer to them as angels or other beings although he easily could have. Black speculates that these may be servants who are responsible for the return of the celestial bodies from their settings in the west to the eastern gates via the north (cf. 1En 72:5; 78:5)" (BL pg. 402).

[1508] Vanderkam omits verse five, stating: "The entire v. 5 appears to be the result of textual errors and for this reason has been omitted from the translation." Charles also brackets the entire verse. Dillman, Charles and VanderKam speculate it may be a gloss from chapter 76 or consist of ditto graphs from 75:4 and 75:6.

[1509] "A new element is explicit in v. 6: the gates are located on the boundaries of the earth" (NV2 pg. 465).

[1510] Knibb has: "to the north and south" rather than to the "left and right."

which the stars rise, as they are ordered, and in which they set 33:3; 36:2-3
according to their number.
8 I also saw chariots in the heavens racing through the cosmos,
above the openings,[1511] where the stars that do not set, revolve.
9 One of these circuits is larger than any of the others, and it makes
its way around the entire cosmos.[1512]

The Twelve Gates for the Winds

76 1 At the ends of the earth I saw twelve gates,[1513] opening in all
directions, from which the winds emerge and blow over the earth. Ps 135:7
2 Three of them are open at the front[1514] of the sky, (i.e. in the east), Rev 21:12-13
and three in the west, and three at the right side of the sky, and three
on the left side.
3 The first three are toward the east, three toward the north, the three 1Chr 26:14-16
after these on the left are toward the south, and three on the west. 34-36
4 From four of them come winds of healing and rejuvenation,[1515] Rev 7:1; 2Chr 7:14
but, through eight of them come winds [causing) calamities.
When they are sent, they bring devastation over the entire earth and its Job 37:9-13
waters, and everything in them which grow and sprout and creep Ex 20:11; Gen 1:20-25
both in the waters and on the land.[1516] [1517] [1518]

The Three Eastern Winds

5 The first wind that comes out from these gates is called "easterly," 18:2-5
emerging from the first gate in the direction of east, the one inclined
toward the south; come devastation, drought, heat, and ruin.
6 Through the second gate, the central one, (the wind) comes out
straight; and from it emerge rain and fruitfulness, prosperity and dew. 75:5?
Through the third gate, in the direction toward north, emerge cold

---

[1511] Some manuscripts say above and below.

[1512] For 75:9 Isaac has: "One (circuit) is larger than the rest of them all, and it circles the entire cosmos at the extreme ends of the earth." Vanderkam has: "One is larger than all of them and it is the one that encircles the whole world." This would be a star that circles the north star but is always visible. i.e., it never dips below the horizon.

[1513] These are different portals than those for the sun, moon and stars. These are found over the four directions, not just the east and west. It is not mentioned that they are ever closed.

[1514] "Front" or "face." **The ancient Hebrews considered the east as the front, so north was to the left and south was to the right. These gates are laid out like those in the walls of the New Jerusalem (Rev 21:12-13).**

[1515] These four winds bring to mind Rev 7:1. "After this I saw four angels standing at the four corners of the earth, holding back the four winds of the earth, that no wind might blow on earth or sea or against any tree."

[1516] "The 1:2 ratio of favorable to unfavorable winds is then documented for each direction, with the middle of the three gates in each case sending forth positive winds and other phenomena (vv.5-13)" (NV2 pg. 392).

[1517] "Winds and weather along with divisions of the earth are topics that are at home in cuneiform astronomical works" (NV2 pg. 471). "MUL.APIN mentions the winds in a number of passages and associates weather conditions with stars and winds." (NV2 pg. 471). "The winds figure in a number of the astrological assertions in MUL.APIN. For example, "if a man is made a ruler, and the East wind blows: his days will be short (II *iv* 11). The winds also play a role in the omens in the series *Enuma Anu Enlil*" (NV2 pg. 471).

[1518] This text attempts to incorporate the Aramaic with the Ethiopic text.

and drought.

The Three Southern Winds

7 Following these, the winds toward the south come out from three
gates. Beginning with the first gate, that is inclined toward east, there
comes forth the southern wind; the siroccos.[1519] Lk 12:55; Ps 11:6; Job 1:19
8 From the central gate, next to it there emerge a fragrant aroma,
dew, rain, prosperity and vitality.
9 Through the third gate, that is toward west, there emerge dew, Ex 10:13
rain, locusts,[1520] and devastation. Rev 9:3; Ps 105:32-34; Joel 2:20

The Three Northern Winds

10 Then the winds that are toward the north, and through the seventh Prov 25:23; Sir 43:17
gate which inclines eastward; there emerge from it dew, rain, locusts, Joel 1:2-7; 2:1-11
and devastation.[1521] [1522]
11 From the central gate in a straight direction there emerge vitality,
rain, dew, and prosperity. Then through the third gate on the north
inclining toward the west, there emerge mist, hoar-frost, snow, rain,
dew, and locusts.

The Three Western Winds

12 Following these are the winds in the direction toward the west.
From the first gate which inclines northward emerge dew, hoar-frost, Job 38:22-23
cold, snow, and frost.
13 Through the central gate there emerge dew, rain, prosperity and Lk 12:54
blessing. From the next gate in the direction toward the south there
emerge drought, destruction, deadly heat, and devastation.[1523]

1519 "Siroccos" Manuscript B: "the wind of death;" manuscript C: "the wind of heat." A sirocco is a Mediterranean wind that comes from the Sahara and can reach hurricane speeds in North Africa and Southern Europe, especially during the summer season.

1520 Isaac has: "young locusts" here and in (76:10, 11).

1521 Fragments of verses 76:4 to 76:10 have been found in the Dead Sea Scrolls (4Q210 Frag. 1 Col. 2 (W pg. 302)).

1522 For 76:10 Isaac has: "After these, there goes (the group) of the northerly winds whose name is the Sea. There proceed from the seventh gate, which is in the direction of the east, toward the south, dew, rain, young locusts, and desolation." VanderKam has: "Following these winds that are toward the north, whose name is "sea," and which emerge from the seventh gate that is toward the southeast—there emerge from it dew, rain, locust, destruction." "The verse in Ethiopic poses several problems. First, calling the north by the name *Sea* is unexpected in a Jewish work that many assume was written in Judea, and the commentators have repeatedly noted this. As Dillman put it, someone writing in Palestine would not call the north by this name; only an Egyptian or Abyssinian would do so" (NV2 pg. 477-478). In agreement with Charles and Olson, this text omits "whose is sea" which according to Knibb is considered a gloss.

1523 The last word of 76:13 and first part of 76:14 are found in (4Q209 23.1-2 and 4Q210 1.2.14 (W pg. 302)). This text is modified to conform with the Aramaic. For 13c-14 VanderKam has: "burning, and devastation. The twelve gates of the four quarters of the sky are completed. All their laws and all their punishment and their prosperity—I

14 The (description of) the twelve gates in the four quarters[1524]
of the sky are completed. I have shown you their fullness and 85:2; 91:1-2; 106:1, 4, 8; 107:3
explanation, my son Methuselah.[1525] 81:5; 82:1; 83:1; Gen 5:21

The Four Quarters, Seven Mountains and Seven Rivers

77 1 The first quarter[1526] [1527] is called "east" (*qedim*),[1528] because it is
the very "first" (*qudmay*);[1529] and the second is called "south" (*derom*)
because the Great One "dwells" (*dar*) there.[1530] 1:3-4; 25:3
And there the Blessed One will dwell from eternity.[1531] Rom 9:5; 2Cor 11:31
2 The great quarter[1532] they call "west" (*maarav*), because it is there 17:4
all the stars of heaven go, "hundreds setting" (*mein aravin*), and
hundreds entering, and all of them are stars. For this reason, it is
called "the west."
3 The north (is called) "north" (*tsippun?*), because in it all the vessels 72:5; 78:5
of heaven, "hide" (*tsepan*), gather, and make their circuits there, 17:3
traveling to the east side of the sky. The fourth quarter which is called
north is divided into three parts. One of them is the dwelling of the
sons of men, and one of them is for the oceans, gorges, forests, rivers,
mist, and darkness. The other part is for the deserts and
for the garden of righteousness.[1533] [1534] 32:3-6; 60:23; 61:12

---

have shown to you everything, my son Methuselah." Olson has: "deadly heat" in place of "burning." He notes that "the Dead Sea Scroll fragments appear to have the word "death" at this point."

[1524] The Ethiopic mss read *gates*, but the Aram has *quarters*" (See 14a in NV2 pg. 470 and note "e" in N pg. 105). (4Q210 1 ii 14) confirms that the four quarters are talking about directions similar to biblical usage (NV2 pg. 479).

[1525] Fragments of verses (76:14 to 77:4), in an expanded form, have been found in the Dead Sea Scrolls (4Q209 Frag. 23 and 4Q210 Frag. 1 Col. 2 (W pg. 302-303). An effort has been made to incorporate them into the present text.

[1526] This word means a "direction, a quarter, a region," (NV2 pg. 484).

[1527] Vanderkam notes that "geography is a frequent element in texts embodying the traditional form of Mesopotamian astronomy. The Akkadian phrase *kibrāt erbetti* refers to the four world regions located in the four cardinal directions" (NV2 pg. 483-484).

[1528] The Aramaic is included in italics to supply an indication of the word play involved.

[1529] Since the sun rises in the east, it was considered the first, or front of heaven.

[1530] This is recognized as referring to Mount Sinai.

[1531] "The first section of the chapter (77) is another of the places where the Aramaic fragments from Qumran have preserved a part of the original text (4Q209 23.3-10; 4 Q210 1.2 [14]-20). **The marked differences that separate the two versions at a number of places further document the thesis that the Book of the Luminaries is an abbreviated form of a longer astronomical book of Enoch"** (NV2 pg. 484).

[1532] Olson has "Great Quarter" based on a pun in the text. He speculates that "it is the great quarter because it must make room for the entire host of heaven when they set" (OL pg. 162).

[1533] It may be that the image here is that the dwelling of man is separated from the garden of righteousness by the area of water and darkness as envisioned by the ancients.

[1534] Concerning 77:3 Vanderkam notes when comparing the Aramaic (DSS) to the Ethiopic, "The Ethiopic manuscript tradition has either lost a section of text through scribal means or is a simple summary of the longer text now attested in 4Q209-210" (NV2 pg. 491). Olson provides a translation of the partial Aramaic text from the DSS which he considers a very early gloss by a learned scribe. He translates 77:3 as; "They call the north, 'North,' because there all the heavenly bodies 'conceal' themselves, gather together, turn about, and proceed to the east of

["East" (*madnah*) because from there the vessels of the sky rise
(*denah*). It is also called "east" (*mizrah*) because from there
hundreds rise upon the earth and shine (*zerah*).][1535]
4 I saw seven lofty mountains which are higher than all mountains 17:2; 18:6; 24:2; 32:1; Rev 17:9
on the earth; snow descends upon them; and the days, seasons, 82:7, 9
and years pass by.[1536]
5 I saw seven rivers on the earth, larger than all other rivers; one of them, 89:2
coming from the west, pours its waters into the Great Sea.[1537] 17:5; Num 34:6
6 Two come from the north to the sea, emptying their waters
into the Erythrean Sea in the east. 32:2
7 The remaining four emerge from the northern side toward their sea, Gen 2:10-14
two into the Erythrean Sea, and two discharge into the Great Sea,[1538]
[but some say into the wilderness.][1539] [1540] [1541] [1542]
8 I saw seven large islands in the sea and on the land; Jub 8:29; 9:13

---

the heavens. (They also call the east, 'East' [*mdnh*], because the heavenly bodies 'arise' [*dnhyn*] from there, and also 'East' [*mzrh*], because it is from there that they 'arise' [*zrhyn*].) And I saw the earth divided into three sections: one of them for the habitation of the sons of men, one of them for all the seas and rivers, and one of them for the deserts, and for the Darkness (?), and for the Paradise of Righteousness" (OL pg. 163). Like Olson, the language of this text attempts to mesh the Aramaic of the Dead Sea Scrolls with the Ethiopic text.

[1535] The bracketed section appears to be a gloss from a learned scribe found in the matching portion of the DSS. I have included it here, since it informs us of one of the functions of the east.

[1536] Perhaps the author "intends to say only that they always have snow on them, day after day, season after season, year after year" (NV2 pg. 495). Seven mountains are mentioned in other parts of 1 Enoch (18:6, 24:2, and 32:1?). Unlike the other passages, the author here says nothing about their direction, positions or alignment. The seven mountains imagery in 1 Enoch may aid in understanding the imagery of the seven mountains in (Rev 17:9).

[1537] The "Great Sea" is certainly the Mediterranean (Num 34:6). The river coming from the west is taken to be the Nile. There may be a corruption in the text with it coming from the west, or the author may have believed the Nile came from the southwest or the geography may be mystical. However, from the perspective of Israel, the Nile is to the west. The entire Indian Ocean including the Persian Gulf and the Red Sea were considered the Erythraean Sea.

[1538] "In the present context, with two rivers flowing from the north into this sea, commentators have identified the sea as the Persian Gulf and the two rivers as the Tigris and Euphrates" (NV2 pg. 496).

[1539] The bracketed text is likely a gloss.

[1540] These could match the four rivers of paradise (Gen 2:10-14). If a northern Eden is proposed, the two rivers the Tigris and Euphrates, are easily identified and they flow into the Erythrean Sea (Persian Gulf). The other two, the Pishon and Gihon, would be more mysterious to the author of the Book of Heavenly Luminaries and the interpolator, to the extent that their places of discharge are mysterious. The Great Sea under this scenario would be the Black Sea which is joined with the Mediterranean. The most likely rivers would be the Yesilirmak and the Kizilimak or possibly the Coruh. Two other candidates that discharge into the Mediterranean are the Ceyhan and Seyhan. Water in second temple literature is always seen as flowing from the dwelling of God, paradise, not to it from another place. In addition, God's dwelling is always on a mountain. A location for Eden near or under the flat topography of the Persian Gulf would be unlikely, if not ridiculous. The highlands of central eastern Anatolia, for many reasons, are a much more likely location for an earthly biblical Eden.

[1541] Commentators weigh in on 77:7: "The wording of the Ethiopic text is problematic" (NV2 pg. 496). Something seems missing in the text. The identification of the rivers is difficult. The end of the verse [and some say: into the desert]. May be a gloss (textual note) into the document. Even more surprising is the fact that in the Ethiopic copies the word for "wilderness" is as all commentators have noted, a transliteration of the Aramaic" (NV2 pg. 497). Olson speculates that the remaining four rivers are possibly the Indus and Ganges, followed by the Oxus and Jaxartes rivers but cautions against "asking for precise geography from a chapter like this one, which straddles the boundary between the real and the surreal" (OL pg. 162).

[1542] "Fragments 3 and 1 of the fourth-century Oxyrhynchus Papyrus 2069, published by Hunt in 1927, have been identified by Milik as containing bits of (1 Enoch 77:7-78:1; 78:8; 85:10-86:2; 87:1-3)" (N1 pg. 13).

two on the land[1543] and five in the Erythraean Sea.[1544] [1545]

The Sun and Moon: The Waxing and Waning of the Moon.

78 1 The names for the sun[1546] are as follows: the first Arjârês,[1547] 82:15, 18
and the second Tômâs.[1548]
2 The moon has four names: the first name is Asônjâ,[1549] the
second Eblâ, the third Benâsê, and the fourth Erâe.
3 These are the two great luminaries. Their roundness[1550] is Gen 1:14-19; Ps 136:7
as the roundness of the sky, and the size of the two of them 72:4; 73:2
is the same.[1551] [1552]
4 In the disc of the sun is combined seven parts of light beyond Isa 30:26
what the moon has. According to specific measure, light is placed 72:37; 73:3
(onto the moon), until the seventh part of the sun has been transmitted.
5 They set, passing through the gates in the west, and they return 72:5
via the north, to the eastern gates, and emerge through the gates of the
east upon the face of the sky.
6 When the moon rises, one half of one seventh part of its light shines 73:4-74:2
in the heavens, so as to be visible upon the earth. The portions of light 4Q210 1.3.3-9
become increasingly full each day until the fourteenth day, and its light 4Q503
is then fully complete.
7 Its light increases in fifteen steps, becoming increasingly full each

---

1543 "Two (islands) on the land" are likely islands surrounded by rivers.

1544 Manuscripts vary in the number of islands, and some have Great Sea. Knibb notes "(MSS) M "two on the land and five in the Erythraean Sea"; (MSS) GQTUD' "seven and two in the Erythraean Sea".

1545 For 77:7c-8 Isaac has: ". . . some say to the seventh desert. I (also) saw big islands in the sea and the land—seventy-two in the Erythraean sea." VanderKam has: ". . . but some say into the wilderness. I saw seven large islands in the sea and on the land—five on the land and two in the Erythrean Sea." "Islands on the land" is a puzzling statement. It could mean islands in rivers, islands near land, or a textual corruption. Some have drawn parallels with Jub 8:29, see also Jub 9:9-13. The Genesis Apocryphon xvi.11 is also a possible connection. The oldest manuscripts read "Erythrean Sea." Some scribes had "Great Sea" here which appears to be a later modification (NV2 pg. 498). Milik saw a potential reference to the mythical island beyond the circular ocean found in ancient Babylonian maps (M pg. 16; see his map on pg. 18).

1546 The Ethiopic word here is probably derived from *šemeš* the most common term for the sun in the Old Testament.

1547 **Arjares**: "means my light is the sun."

1548 **Tomas**: Knibb has: "Tomases." This word probably derives from hamāh, meaning heat, which is found in (Isa 24:23). This interpretation assumes a corruption in the text (OL pg. 162). Charles observes that the two names of the sun given here, correspond to the two seasons of the year in Palestine: Arjares being winter and Tomas being summer (C pg. 166-167). Nickelsburg thinks they are simply less commonly used names for the sun. (NV2 pgs. 503-504)

1549 I and N have Asenya, Alba, Banase and Era. **Asonja** may = "small man," **Elba** may = "the pale one" (Isa 30:26), **Banase** may = "full moon" (Prov 7:20 *hak kê se*) or "new moon" (Ps 81:3 *bak kê seh*) or *ben hasî* "son of the half" meaning halfmoon; **Erae**= yārēah "to shoot, dart" the most common name for the moon. These are examples of Hebrew names derived from the bible showing up in an otherwise Aramaic text.

1550 Some translate "roundness" as "circumference."

1551 Some manuscripts add "of their roundness is like the roundness of the sky" (N pg. 107).

1552 Even though the sun's diameter is 400 times that of the moon, from the perspective of earth, due to the Moon being 400 times closer, they appear to be the same size. This is especially apparent during a total solar eclipse when for a few minutes the corona of sun is the only part visible.

day until the fifteenth day, when its light is fully complete according
to the sign[1553] of the year. The course of the phases of the moon is by
parts that are halves of sevenths.[1554]
8 When it is waning, it decreases on the first day to fourteen parts of 4Q317
its light:[1555] on the next day it decreases to thirteen parts. On the third it
decreases to twelve parts and on the fourth it decreases to eleven parts,
and on the fifth it decreases to ten parts and on the sixth it decreases to
nine parts, and on the seventh it decreases to eight parts, and on the
eighth it decreases to seven parts, and on the ninth it decreases to six
parts, and on the tenth it decreases to five parts. On the eleventh it
decreases to four parts, and on the twelfth it decreases to three parts,
and on the thirteenth, it decreases to two (parts), and on the fourteenth
it decreases to half of one-seventh of its total light, and on the
fifteenth the entire remainder disappears wholly.[1556 1557] 74:3
9 During specific months, the moon (is visible) for twenty-nine days 78:15-17; 79:3-5
at times, and once for twenty-eight days.
10 Then Uriel showed me another law;[1558] (regarding) when light is
projected onto the moon, and from which side it is projected OdesSol 16:17
from the sun.[1559]
11 The entire time in which (the illumination of) the moon progresses,
it adds its light when facing the sun, until the fourteenth day when its
light is full. When the (lunar disc) is completely aflame, (then) its light
in the sky is complete.[1560]
12 On the first day it is called the "new moon," because on that day
light appears on it (for the first time).
13 (The light) becomes full, exactly on the day when as the sun sets in
the west, the moon rises from the east at nightfall. The moon shines all
night, until the sun rises opposite it, and the moon is then visible opposite
the sun.
14 From the side where the light comes to the moon, there again it
wanes until all its light is gone. A lunar day passes, and the moon's disc
remains empty without light.

1553 Black postulates "sign" should be "month" (BL pg. 409).

1554 The author shows a special attachment to the number seven, saying halves of sevenths rather than 14ths.

1555 Part of 78:8 was found in in the Greek text; Oxyrhynchus Papyri XVII 2069 frg. 3^{r}.

1556 Fragments of (78:6-8) were found in the Dead Sea Scrolls (4Q210 1.3 (W pg. 303).

1557 The waning moon always lasts 15 days but the waxing moon can take 14 or 15 days.

1558 "Another law" *te'zāz* ("commandment, decree, edict, law;" (cf. 72:2; 73:1; 74:1) (NV2 pg. 510).

1559 "The writer recognizes that the lunar illumination comes entirely from the sun (cf. 78:4), and that the surface of the moon visible from the earth receives light when it is located in places where the sun can shine on it." (NV2 pg. 510). See also 78:14.

1560 "The two linear sequences of 14 days increasing and 14 days decreasing illumination vary between the extrema 0 and 1, which remain valid for one day each—a pattern well known from linear schemes in Babylonian, Greek, and medieval astronomy" (Neugebauer, *Ethiopic Astronomy and Computus*, pg. 196).

The Lunar Year

15 It fashions three months of thirty days in its times; when it effects its
decrease it fashions three months of twenty-nine days each, in which it
makes its recession, in the first time and in the first gate, in 177 days.
16 In the time of its waxing, it becomes visible for three months of thirty
days each, and it becomes visible in three (other) months, for twenty-nine
days each[1561]

(79) 3 finishing at the sixth gate, because in the sixth gate its light
waxes to full.[1562] After that is the beginning of its diminishment
(79) 4 which is accomplished in the first gate in its proper season,
after the second 177 days are completed, or if reckoned with weeks,
25 (weeks) and two days.[1563]
(79) 5 In this way, it falls behind the sun and the order of the stars by 74:12-16
exactly five days in the course of one season, (i.e. half a lunar year)
during which time the horizon you see before you is traversed.[1564]

(78) 17 On some nights, its appearance resembles a mirror when the
light shines on it. On certain nights, this appearance resembles the 4QEnastr^{b} 26
image of a man. And during the day, sometimes it is indistinguishable
from the sky, for it has nothing in it except its light.[1565]

The Seasons and the Stars

79 1 Now my son,[1566] I have shown you everything, and the law of all 76:14; PrEv 9.17.8-9
the stars in the sky is completed.[1567] Wis 7:17-19
2 He (Uriel) showed me every one of their calculations for each day, 4QEnastr^{b} 25
each period of exercising dominion, each year, and the procession of 82:10; Ps 19:1-6

[1561] The Ethiopic text is severely disordered here, as proven by the DSS (4QEnastr^{b} 26) which reflects the order of rearrangement in this text, bringing in verses from Chapter 79. The reordering unfortunately creates confusion as it becomes difficult to find chapters and verses. However, altering the numbering would be even more confusing. The reordering makes sense of an otherwise disjointed text.

[1562] The moon's light has reached its full illumination.

[1563] "There are 177 days in six lunar months but 182 in six solar months in the Enochic calendar; the former number is explicit here and the second is implied by the difference of five days that is noted. As a result, the text is talking about this five-day deficit in six lunar months and calls it a "decrease, diminution" (NV2 pg. 518). Adding the 5 days to the 177 gives 182 days or one half of the 364-day solar calendar year.

[1564] **"The Aramaic evidence reveals that the lunar information now in 1 Enoch 79:3-5 actually preceded 79:1 at an earlier stage in the development of the text"** (NV2 pg. 516). As in this text, Olson places it between 78:16 and 78:17.

[1565] Olson follows Black's decipherment of the obscure DSS evidence (4QEnastr^{b} 26.4-6), supplemented with the Ethiopic text to arrive at the text used here for 78:17.

[1566] Enoch is transmitting the knowledge about the luminaries he received from Uriel to Methuselah. Pseudo-Eupolemus credited Enoch with discovering "astrology" from the angels (cf. PrEv 19.17.8-9; OTP2 pg. 881).

[1567] If the text is rearranged, as many scholars think, with 79:3-5 moved before 79:1, then 79:2, 3 and 6 give the impression of a conclusion to a more comprehensive work about the heavenly lights. "However, there is no textual evidence that 79:1-2 formed the end of an Enoch astronomical work" (NV2 pg. 516).

every one according to the command, every month, and every week.[1568] Gen 1:14-19

(82) 7 The account is accurate, and the computation exact, as recorded, 43:2
because Uriel (whom the Lord of the whole created world gave
instructions, on my behalf concerning the hosts of heaven) has
breathed over me,[1569] and revealed to me the luminaries, the months, 33:4; 72:1; 80:1
the festivals,[1570] the years and the days.[1571] 93:14; Jub 2:9: Sir 43:6-7
(82) 8 He has authority in heaven over night and day, in order to make Gen 1:3-4, 14-18
the light shine on mankind—sun, moon, stars and all the powers of
heaven which revolve in their circuits.
(82) 9 This is the law of stars, which set in their (proper) places, 2:1-2
according to their seasons, their festivals, their months and for *Apol. A 4*
their signs. [1572]
(82) 10 And these are the names of their leaders, who keep watch over
their seasonal entrances, who guide them in their places and their order, 72:3; 1Pet 3:22
in their seasons, in their months, according to their rule for all 2Bar 59:11
their jurisdictions.[1573]
(82) 11 First to enter, are the four leaders who separate the four parts of
the year; after them (enter) the twelve leaders of the orders who separate
the months; and the 360 heads over thousands (of stars) are the ones 75:1
who separate the days. Taking charge of the four additional days, are the
leaders who separate the four seasons of the year. 80:1,6
(82) 12 The chiefs of thousands are added in between one leader and
another, each bringing up the rear of the station, but nevertheless,
it is their leaders who make a division.[1574]

[1568] For 79:2 VanderKam has: "He showed me all their law for each day, each time in a jurisdiction, every year, its emergence, the command, every month, and every week." The use of week here is a week of days, not of years, as understood in the Book of Jubilees.

[1569] In place of "breathed on me" Knibb has "he inspired me."

[1570] **The use of "festivals," Knibb has "feasts," indicates that the Mosaic law has already been given, and the calendar is needed to determine festival days.** The terms used here luminaries, months, festivals, years and days, differ from 75:3, but use terms similar to Jubilees 2:9: days, sabbaths, months, festivals and years. **However, Jubilees has certain Jewish festivals such as Tabernacles (Jub 16:26-31) preceding the time of Moses, and Levi being a priest in the time of Jacob (Jub 32:1-11)!**

[1571] For 82:7 VanderKam has: "The account about it is true and its calculation is precisely recorded because the luminaries and the months, the festivals, the years, and the days he showed me, and Uriel, to whom the Lord of the entire creation gave orders for me regarding the host of heaven, breathed on me."

[1572] **The text is not talking about signs of the zodiac, since the rest of the Book of Heavenly Luminaries does not refer to the signs of the zodiac and neither does the MUL.APIN, the cuneiform compendium that shows a number of parallels with Enoch's astronomy** (NV2 pg. 558).

[1573] "Naturally, there are fixed places on the horizon through which the stars pass, just as there are for the sun and moon" (NV2 pg. 557).

[1574] 82:12 is puzzling. "The four leaders responsible for the four parts of the year are meant, and the one added presumably is one of these who effects one part of the fourfold division" (NV2 pg. 561). Charles humorously opines: "I don't understand this verse."

(82) 13 These are the names of the leaders[1575] [1576] who separate the four fixed parts of the year: Mîlkî'êl,[1577] Hel'emmêlêk, Mêl'êjal, and Nârêl.[1578]
(82) 14 The names of those whom they lead are: Adnâr'êl, Îjâsûsa'êl, and 'Ēlômê'êl. These three follow the leaders of the orders; that is, one of these follows each of the three leaders of the orders, who in turn follow those leaders of stations who separate the four seasons of the year.[1579]

Spring

(82) 15 At the beginning of the year Melkejâl[1580] rises first and
rules—the one called the southern sun; all the days that fall within 78:1
the period that he rules are 91 days.[1581] [1582]
(82) 16 These are the signs of the days that are to be seen on earth in the
days of his rule: sweat, heat, and calms.[1583] All the trees bear fruit and 3:1-5:1
leaves appear; a harvest of wheat, roses,[1584] and all the flowers which
bloom in the fields; but the trees of winter become withered. 3:1
(82) 17 These are the names of the leaders who are the subordinates: Berka'êl,[1585] Zêlebs'êl, and another one who is added, a chief of thousands, named Hîlûjâsph:[1586] and completed are the days of rulership with this one.[1587]

1575 **"It is worth highlighting that neither here nor in any other passage in the Book of the Luminaries are these leaders called angels. They are more likely luminaries with names"** (NV2 pg. 562).

1576 Origen (AD 185-254) referred to this section (82:13-20) in his *Homily on Numbers* 28:2. "'For he who made the multitude of the stars,' says the prophet, 'gives them all names.' Regarding these names the books called (of) Enoch contain many secret and mysterious things; but since these books do not appear to have authority among Hebrews" (NV2 pg. 349). This indicates he had a copy of the Book of Luminaries.

1577 Mîlkî'êl, "King, of God" is also found in (Gen 46:17; Num 26:45 and 1Chr 7:31). **This is a semitic name which thus argues for a semitic origin for the Book of Heavenly Luminaries.**

1578 Hel'emmêlêk, "God is King;" Mêl'êjal, "Fullness of God;" Nârêl, probably "Lamp of God."

1579 This section is incomplete since only two of the four 91-day periods are mentioned 82:15 and 82:18. The three entities named in 82:14 may have originally belonged to the description of one of the two seasons missing from the end of the Book of the Luminaries (They would have been after 82:20).

1580 Olson has Melkiel here.

1581 In the cuneiform texts, "Saturn (*ninib*) is the representative of the summer and has the name "south sun" (UT-URU-LU0" (NV2 pg. 564). However, Mîlkî'êl in 82:13 is the first mentioned and thus should be associated with spring, the first season in Enochic astronomy, rather than summer. The signs of his rule in 82:16 seem more spring-like April-June, than summer, July-September, who's signs are in 82:19.

1582 This is the spring equinox to summer solstice. The calendar described here has four equal 91-day periods from equinoxes to solstices. It is a very efficient calendar, superior to the Jewish 360-day calendar. For instance, the Passover meal in this calendar always comes on a Tuesday evening.

1583 I has: "dryness" in place of "calms"; N has "care." Some manuscripts have "sorrow." Care seems like a good fit for the season, since farmers are very busy, and the outcome is uncertain in late spring/early summer.

1584 Roses are not mentioned in the OT but are mentioned in other period sources (Sir 24:14; Wis 2:8; 1En 106:2).

1585 Berka'êl is also used in (Job 32:2, 6). It is a compound of the divine name and the word for blessing.

1586 Hîlûjâsph and Asfâ'êl (82:20) are reversals of each other, both of which mean "God increases."

1587 The three named in this verse (82:17) are each in charge of a month.

Summer

(82) 18 The next leader after him is Hêl'emmêlêk, who is named the bright sun; and the total of the days of his light are 91 days.[1588] 78:1; Rev 7:2
(82) 19 These are the signs of these days on earth: scorching heat, drought, trees bring their fruit to ripeness and maturity; the sheep mate and become pregnant; and people gather all the fruit of the earth, and everything which is in the fields, and the vats of wine. This takes place in the days of his rulership.
(82) 20 Here are the names of the leaders of the orders subordinate to them,[1589] and the chiefs of thousands: Gîdâ'îjal, Kê'êlhê'êl,[1590] and the name of one who is added to them as a head of thousands called, Asfâ'êl: and the days of the dominion of this one are completed.[1591] 4Q440 1.1, 4

(79) 6 This is the appearance and diagram of all the luminaries shown to me by the great angel Uriel, who is their leader.

(80) 1 At that time the angel Uriel addressed me, and said: See, I have shown you everything Enoch, and I have revealed everything to you so that you may see this sun and this moon, and those who guide the stars in the sky, as well as all who turn them—their tasks, their seasons, and their processions.[1592] [1593] 72:1; 82:7; 72:3; 75:1; 80:6; 82:10-11; 72:5; 73:2; 75:3

[1588] This is the summer solstice to fall equinox.

[1589] The plural "them" is textually based. One would expect it to be a singular him. It could be a textual error or it could be that "each 'leader of the orders' has two supervisors, the permanent monthly overseer and the main seasonal leader" (OL pg. 276).

[1590] Nickelsburg has Kê'êl and Hê'êl but suggests: "Again, one could suggest Semitic originals for the names" "The second and third names closely resemble each other and could be a doublet" (NV2 pg. 565). Olson combines the two names into Ke'elhe'el.

[1591] A fragment of a text similar to what one would expect of the extension of Chapter 82 was found in the Dead Sea Scrolls. It describes Autumn. "[(After 82:20) . . . the clouds that make dew] and rain to fall upon the earth, and see [. . .] herbs of the earth and tree. And [the sun] falls and enters [. . .] and winter comes, and the foliage of all the trees [withers and falls, except for four]teen trees for which such is not natural [. . .] their leaves re]m[ain . . .] (4Q211 1.2-6; W pg. 303) (cf. 1En 3:1). Vanderkam speculates this text preserves part of the lost ending of the Book of Luminaries (N pg. 115).

[1592] VanderKam has: "their work, their times, and their emergencies." Olson has: "their tasks, their seasons and their processions."

[1593] Many scholars see (1En 80:2-82:3) as an apocalyptic intrusion and thus not part of the original text.

Enoch Reads the Heavenly Tablets

81 1 Then he said to me:[1594] [1595]
"Enoch, look, at these tablets of heaven,[1596] read what is written on Dan 7:10; 12:1; Hab 2:2-3
them, and understand each and every item." Rev 20:12
2 So I looked at everything on the tablets of heaven, and I read 93:2; 103:2; 106:19; Jub 4:19
everything that was written and understood everything. I read the book, 89:71, 77; 104:1; 108:7; Ps 69:28
of all the deeds of mankind and of all the children of flesh on the earth, 1QS 3.13-18; 1QH$_a$ 9.7-29
unto the remotest generations of the world.[1597] [1598] TLev 14:1; 4Q504 6.12-14
3 Immediately I blessed the Great Lord, the King of Glory forever, 22:14
as he has fashioned all the works of the world.[1599] Jn 1:3
I praised the Lord because of his patience, and I wept on the earth
because of the sons of Adam.[1600] 90:41-42
4 Afterwards I spoke: "Blessed is everyone who dies righteous and 49:3; 102:4-5; 103:3; Mt 5:6 Rev 14:13
good,[1601] against whom a record of iniquity[1602] will neither be written, Dan 12:1; Rev 20:12; Rom 4:7-8
nor be found on the day of judgement."[1603] [1604] Rom 8:1; 14:12; 2Cor 5:10

Enoch Returns and Teaches Methuselah

5 Then the seven[1605] holy ones brought me and placed me on the 20; 87:2; 90:21-22

[1594] Nickelsburg makes a convincing case that 81:1-4 is the seventh stage in Enoch's journey that began in chapter 21, the one that supplies the missing Remiel unit. Remiel (Jeremiel) is also mentioned in (4Ezra 4:36; 2Bar 55:3; and ApZeph 6:15). See (NV2 pg. 532-534) for more information on this subject. Also "81:1-82:4 has significant literary relations with framework material in the Epistle of Enoch: 'The narrative in (81:1-82:4a) is continued not in chaps. (83-90) but in (91:1-10. 18-19 +93:11-94:5 +104:10-105:2)" (NV2 pg. 533). Nickelsburg believes 1 Enoch 81:1-82:4 appears to be a narrative bridge between the Book of the Watchers and chapters 91-105 (N1 pg. 337). Vanderkam, however, rejects the idea of 1En 81:1-4 being the seventh vision of the Book of the Watchers. Stating that "Nickelsburg's theory . . . does not adequately explain the elements that separate this passage from the sections in the Book of the Watchers" (NV2 pg. 538).

[1595] "Modern commentators have generally conceded that this passage (81:1-82:4$_{a-c}$) has been imported from another context" (N1 pg. 334). Olson disagrees, arguing that chapter 81 is original but disordered (OL pg. 273). This text follows Olson's order.

[1596] For 81:1b, Baty has: "Look on the book which heaven has dropped down" Isaac has: "look at the tablet(s) of heaven"

[1597] K and BL have: "eternity" in place of "the world."

[1598] This verse expresses the foreknowledge of God. The belief that tablets record the future of mankind, goes back to Mesopotamia (cf. Ps 139:16). Enoch sees the entire plan for earth, and praises God.

[1599] In place of "works of the world" VanderKam has: "deeds of eternity."

[1600] This text follows the Tana manuscript. Others read: "and blessed him because of the sons of Adam" or "and blessed him because of the sons of the world." For 81:3d VanderKam has: "but I wept for all the sons of Adam." Isaac has: "and I wept on account of the children of the people upon the earth." For support for "wept" see (90:41).

[1601] VanderKam has: "pious" in place of "good." Isaac has: "righteous and upright."

[1602] VanderKam has: "book of wickedness" (cf. 89:63; 97:6-7; 98:7-8; 104:7).

[1603] For 81:4c, Isaac has: "against whom no record of oppression has been written" **"For the righteous, there is a reassuring purpose in the tablets: their contents guarantee that there will be no condemnation for them, no day of judgement; rather, they will be blessed"** (NV2 pg. 537).

[1604] For 81:4d, Baty has: "and with whom a crime is not found."

[1605] Some later manuscripts say three, Knibb follows this reading. This may come from 87:2-3 and/or 90:31. The older Ethiopic manuscripts which read seven are preferred by most.

ground in front of the door of my house. They said to me: "Make — 1QH$_a$ 12.30-32; 15.39-40
everything known to your son Methuselah, and make all your children — Rom 3:10, 23; Isa 64:6; Ps 143:2
see that no flesh is righteous in the sight of the Lord, for he — Job 4:17; 9:2; Ps 14:1, 3
created them.[1606] — 1Kgs 8:46; 2Chr 6:36
6 We will leave you with your children for one year, until once — Prov 20:9; Eccl 7:20
again[1607]you have given them your last charges;[1608] so that you may teach — Jub 4:17-19; 4Q227 2
your children;[1609] and write it down for them, and testify to all your — 85:1-2; 91:1-3; 92:1; 93:2; 108:1
children. In the second year you shall be taken from their midst.[1610] [1611] — Jub 4:23; Gen 5:24
7 Be strong of heart!
For the good will proclaim righteousness to the good.[1612]
The righteous will rejoice with the righteous and congratulate — Rev 22:11
each other.[1613]
8 But sinners shall die with sinners, and the apostate will drown[1614]
with the apostate.

[1606] **That no one is righteous in God's sight is a basic Old Testament, Jewish and Christian doctrine. This necessitated the atoning work of Christ; see cross references.**

[1607] It may be that Enoch gave a charge to his children prior to dwelling with the celestial beings (i.e. walking with God) for the approximately 300 years.

[1608] Knibb has: "until you have regained your strength." VanderKam has: "until (you receive) another order." Nickelsburg has also proposed "until you give your commands twice" Following those readings the idea may be that Enoch is to remain with his family until he receives further instructions. More likely this is speaking of a patriarch giving the last instructions of a father to his children as in (Gen 49:1-33; 2Kgs 20:1; Isa 38:1 and the Testaments of the Twelve Patriarchs).

[1609] VanderKam has: "sons" in place of children, Isaac has: "and write it down for them and give all of them a warning" That Enoch has more children than Methuselah would indicate that his "stay with the angels was interrupted from time to time" (NV2 pg. 542). The mid-1st to mid-2nd century AD (Pseudo-Philo 1:15-17) reads. "And Enoch lived 165 years and begat Mattisalam. And Enoch lived after he begat Matusalam 200 years, and begat 5 sons and 3 daughters. But Enock pleased God at that time and was not found, for God translated him. Now the names of his sons are: Anaz, Zeum, Achaun, Pheledi, Elith; and of the daughters, Theiz, Lefith, Leath."

[1610] VanderKam divides Enoch's life into four parts. "At 65 years: he became the father of Methuselah when he was 65. For 300 years: he was with the angels. He was apparently brought back to human society. At 365: he was again with the angels and not returned to human society." **The present passage, then, is set near the end of the three-hundred-year period when he was with the angels**" (NV2 pg. 540). The 300 years is further established in Jub 4:21 where unlike the rest of Jubilees the Jubilee appears to be 50 years rather than 49. "And he was moreover with the angels of God these six jubilees of years, and they showed him everything which is on earth and in the heavens, the rule of the sun, and he wrote down everything." That Enoch was with the angels six full jubilees is also attested in (4Q227 2). Enoch is actually living with the holy ones in (1QapGen 2.19-23) (cf. 1En 106:7).

[1611] **The Book of Jubilees presents the following chronology of Enoch's life. "Between his sixtieth and sixty-fourth years, he was married (Jub. 4:20). In his sixty-fifth year, Edni bore him a son, Methuselah. During the next 294 years (six jubilees), he was touring the universe in the company of the angels. At some point during that period, he was sent to preach against the rebel watchers. He then returned to human company and wrote his testimony for humanity, presumably being taken by God at the end of the three hundred years mentioned in Gen 5:22" (N1 pg. 74). However, since he had other children (81:6) he must have returned home on occasion.**

[1612] VanderKam substitutes "pious" for good in both places on this line.

[1613] Isaac suggests "and congratulate each other" could also be translated "and present each other with gifts." Olson translates: "and they will exchange salutations among themselves." VanderKam has: "and they will greet each other." **The main idea is that the righteous will dwell eternally with the righteous and sinners with other sinners.** Did this text influence (Rev 22:11)? "Let the evildoer still do evil, and the filthy still be filthy, and the righteous still do right, and the holy still be holy?"

[1614] The term "go down" used by some other texts, means "submerged, sunk, drowned" (NV2 pg. 544). This of course brings flood imagery into the text.

9 Those who do what is right will also die because of the deeds 8:4; Isa 57:1-2; Rev 6:9
of men and will be gathered in because of the deeds of the wicked."[1615] Wis 4:10-11, 13-14
10 At that time, they finished speaking with me,[1616] and I came to my
people, blessing the Lord of the Ages.[1617] Ps 89:11

82 1 Now, my son Methuselah, I am telling you all these things and am *Defem* 1.3
writing (them) down for you. I have revealed to you everything, 37:2-3; 80:1
and given you the books[1618] about all these things. My son, preserve PrEv 9.17.9
the writings from the hand of your father, so that you may deliver them 104:11-13
to the generations of the world.[1619] [1620] 92:1
2 I have given wisdom to you and to your children, 91:10
and to your children yet to be, that they may transmit this wisdom which Ps 78:5-7; Joel 1:3
is beyond their thought[1621] to their children,[1622] and to generations *Defem* 1.3; Isa 55:8-9; Phil 4:7
of generations[1623] and to all those who are discerning. Eph 3:19
3 They will not sleep but understand, but they will listen
with their ears that they may master this wisdom. Sir 24:19-21; Ps 119:103
It will be better for those that partake of it than fine food.[1624] 69:24; Ps 19:8-11; 2En 48:7

Leaders Who Divide the Years/Calendar

4 Blessed are all the righteous ones! Blessed are all who walk in 99:10; Ps 1:1
the path of righteousness and do not err, like the sinners, in counting
all the days in which the sun traverses the sky. It enters in and comes
out through the gates for thirty days, along with the chiefs of thousands
(of the order of the stars), together with the additional four that Jub 6:23
separate the four seasons of the year, who lead them and with which

---

[1615] For 81:9 Isaac has: "But those who do right shall not die on account of the (evil) deeds of the people; it will gather on account of the deeds of the evil ones." VanderKam more correctly, has: "Those who do what is right will die because of the actions of people and will be gathered up because of the deeds of the wicked." It may mean the righteous along with the wicked will die in the flood caused by the wicked provoking the judgement of God. Alternately it could mean that the godless "persecute the righteous, even killing them" (NV2 pg. 544). In (Wis 4:11) Enoch; "was caught away, lest evil should change his understanding or guile deceive his soul."

[1616] Enoch's extended time with the watcher Elohim comes to a close.

[1617] Manuscripts vary here. VanderKam has: "world" in place of ages. Isaac has: "universe." Black has: "eternity."

[1618] Both uses of books in this verse are translated in the singular by Isaac. These are the books he was instructed to write in 81:6.

[1619] Knibb has: "eternity" in place of "the world."

[1620] **At this stage it appears Enoch has now reached the end of his time on earth, having fulfilled the angels charge to teach, record and testify to his children (81:6). Unlike in 1:2 where the writing is for a remote generation this writing is for all generations.**

[1621] VanderKam translates this literally as "above their thought" (NV2 pg. 547). **This likely means they would not have come up with this wisdom on their own if it had not been revealed to them.** Olson translates a minority text for the last sentence of 82:2: "All who are wise will sing praises, and wisdom will rest with their thoughts."

[1622] **Tertullian refers to this passage in (*de cultu feminarum*; *On the Apparel of Women* 1.3) "Enoch had given no other charge to Methuselah than that he should hand on the knowledge of them [Enoch's preachings] to his posterity." In the passage Tertullian is arguing for the authenticity of the book of Enoch which, in his opinion, was preserved by Noah, Methuselah's grandson, at the time of the flood"** (NV2 pg. 547).

[1623] Most β manuscripts. read "generations until eternity" (NV2 pg. 546).

[1624] **The hearers of this wisdom will prefer hearing it to sleep and fine food.**

they make their entry on the four days.[1625]
5 People err concerning them by not counting them in the complete 75:1-3; 80:7
reckoning of the year. Such people are mistaken and do not understand
them precisely.[1626]
6 For they belong to the reckoning of the year and are truly recorded[1627]
forever: one in the first gate, one in the third, one in the fourth and one
in the sixth (gate); so, the year is completed in 364 days.

Prophecy of Cosmic Disturbances

(80) 2 In the days of the sinners, winters will be cut short,[1628] [1629] 102:5; Mt 24:22; Mk 13:20
their seed will be late to their lands and fertile fields. EBar 4:3; *DivInst* 7.16
Everything on the earth will be turned back,

[1625] "75:1-3 and 82:4-8 – show very close parallels." "No Aramaic for either section has survived; as a result, it is not possible to check whether both sections were part of the Astronomical Book" (NV2 pg. 551).

[1626] Isaac has: "On this account there are people that err; they count them (the four?) in the computation of the year; for the people make error and do not recognize them accurately; for they belong to the reckoning of the year." For 82:5 Knibb has: "Because of them men go wrong, and they do not reckon them in the reckoning of the whole *course of the* world: for men go wrong in respect of them, and do not know them exactly. For they belong in the reckoning of the year." The sinners are those who fail to include the extra 4 days in their count, "whereas the righteous add them to the other 360 days." "Enoch may have in mind the book or one of the books he is leaving to Methuselah" (NV2 pg. 552).

[1627] "The word used for recorded (*lek 'un*; see also 103:2; 108:7) is related to a verb meaning "inscribe, impress, imprint, mark, set down in writing, compose" (NV2 pg. 552).

[1628] "Winter" literally: "rainy season." VanderKam has: "the rainy seasons will grow shorter" Isaac has: "and the winter(s) are cut short" The standard rendering is: "the years will be cut short." "The word "years" translates *keramāt*, which is not the normal term for a calendar year in the Book of the Luminaries, where *'āmat* performs that function" (NV2 pg. 523). Meanings for the singular form, *keramt,* include "rainy season, rains . . . winter, year" The text seems to be focusing more on lack of rainfall and the agricultural effects than cosmological effects in this section.

[1629] **The Epistle of Barnabas (4:3) (AD 70-AD 135) saw this passage as referring to a future time of cosmic upheaval related to the second advent of Christ. It reads: "The last stumbling block is at hand, concerning which the scriptures speak, as Enoch says. For the Master has cut short the times and the days for this reason, so that his beloved might make haste and come into his inheritance" (EBar 4:3). This is further evidence that the *Book of Heavenly Luminaries* was part of <u>*The*</u> *Book of Enoch,* not just writings attributed to Enoch and was likely among the texts Christ and the disciples would have considered scripture.** Jesus also referred to the days being cut short. "And if those days had not been cut short, no human being would be saved. But for the sake of the elect those days will be cut short" (Mt 24:22). The passage concerning cosmic disturbances following it (Mt 24:29-31) strengthens the connection. "Immediately after the tribulation of those days the sun will be darkened, and the moon will not give its light, and the stars will fall from heaven, and the powers of the heavens will be shaken. Then will appear in heaven the sign of the Son of Man, and then all the tribes of the earth will mourn, and they will see the Son of Man coming on the clouds of heaven with power and great glory. And he will send out his angels with a loud trumpet call, and they will gather his elect from the four winds, from one end of heaven to the other." (Mt 24:29-31) Other Old Testament passages describe celestial disturbances in the latter days (cf. Isa 13:10; 51:6; 60:19; and Joel 2:10, 31). **Olson sees this passage as satire. "The universe is not collapsing; it only seems that way to fools who follow wrong calendars and lag behind the true reckoning of the seasons. They do their planting too late, resulting in disastrous food shortages"** (OL pg. 176). **At the beginning of the passage, it could be taken as satire, but as the text develops, it is clearly talking about a future period which does not seem to be related to the great flood. The Epistle of Barnabas (4:3) did not see it as satire but as referring to a future time of cosmic upheaval related to the second advent of Christ.** (Cf. *DivInst* 7.16; 4Q385 4.3-6).

and will not appear at their times,[1630] Acts 1:7
the rain will be held back, Jer 3:3; 5:24-25; Amos 4:7
Rev 11:6; SibOr 3:540
and the sky will stand still,[1631] Lev 26:3-4; Ezek 34:26
(80) (5b) and famine will reach the extremities of the great chariot[1632] *DivInst* 7.16
in the west.[1633]
(80) 3 At those times the fruit of the earth will be late, and will not grow, Deut 11:14; 28:12; Hag 1:10
in their season, and the fruit of the trees Mt 21:18; Mk 11:12-14
will be withheld in their season. Jude 12; Jer 8:13
(80) 4 The moon will alter its order Isa 13:10; 34:4; 51:6; 60:19-20
and will not appear at its proper times. Mt 24:29; Lk 21:25; Joel 2:10,31
(80) (5a) At that time it will appear in the sky, Mk 13:24-25; 4Ezra 5:4
Rev 8:12
(80) (5c) and will shine very much more brightly than its 72:5; 2Kgs 23:11; Amos 8:9
normal light.[1634] Rev 6:13; 16:8; Isa 24:23
(80) 6 Many leaders of the stars will stray from the command, and 82:10-11; Lk 21:11,25; Rev 8:12
will alter their orbits and tasks, not appearing at the 72:3; 75:1; Dan 8:10; Jude 13
seasons commanded them.[1635] 18:13-16; 21:1-6; 102:2
(80) 7 The entire law of the stars will be concealed from the Ezek 32:7-8; Joel 2:10; 3:15

[1630] K has: "proper time."

[1631] (1En 80:2-8), which states that the laws of nature will change, appears to conflict with (72:1), which indicates they will stay the same. However, this can also be seen as a change in cosmological laws at the end of days. This is the only passage in the Book of the Heavenly Luminaires where a celestial object is said to alter its course. Charles sees (80:2-8) as an addition to the text (C pg. 147). However, if it is an addition, it would have been early to have been picked up in the Epistle of Barnabas. But it is telling that none of chapter 80 has been found among the DSS. Olson makes the case that chapters 80-81 are original to the text (OL pgs. 273-276).

[1632] "2 Kings 23:11 says that King Josiah burned the chariots of the sun—a feature that is understood to be an influence from Assyrian religion" (NV2 pg. 528). Olson has observed that "great chariot" was an ancient name for Ursa Major" (Olson, *Enoch*, 176 n). Ursa Major "is named 'wagon' in ancient sources such as MUL.APIN (see II I 68: 'If you are to observe the direction of the winds: the Wagon lies across where the North wind rises'" (NV2 pg. 528, quoting Hunger and Pingree, MUL.Apin, 87 with the comments on p. 131). The MUL.APIN influenced the *Iliad*, which in 18.487 (part of the description of Achilles shield) says that the Bear is called the "wain" which is a large heavy wagon used for farm use.

[1633] 80:5 is textually problematic. 80:5b is out of place in 80:5, fitting better in this location. Unfortunately, Aramaic does not include a passage for guidance. "The textual evidence is frustrating. None of the Ethiopic copies supports a change in or relocation of words in v. 5, and there is no Aramaic evidence for Chap. 80" (NV2 pg. 527).

[1634] For 80:5, I has: "In those days it will appear in the sky and it shall arrive in the evening in the extreme ends of the great lunar path, in the west. And it shall shine (more brightly), exceeding the normal degree of light." N has "At that time it will appear in the sky and will arrive at . . . at the edge of the great chariot in the west and will shine very much more (brightly) than its normal light." (Cf. Rev 16:8).

[1635] Pseudo-Hippolytus (AD 4th century) in *On the End of the World* (26) predicts cosmic disturbances associated with the Antichrist in the end times. "Under the eye of the spectators he will remove mountains from their places, he will walk on the sea with dry feet, he will bring down fire from heaven, he will turn the day into darkness and the night into day, he will turn the sun about wheresoever he pleases; and, in short, in (the) presence of those who behold him, he will show all the elements of earth and sea to be subject to him in the power of his specious manifestation." 4Ezra 5:4 likewise predicts "the sun shall suddenly shine forth at night and the moon during the day." This idea is found in the Bible in places like (Isa 13:10; 24:23; 60:19; Joel 2:10, 30-31; Mt 24:29; Lk 21:25; Rev 6:12-14; and Rev 8:12). It is also found elsewhere in 1 Enoch, see (102:2).

sinners,[1636] and the thoughts of those who dwell on earth will fall 75:2
into error concerning them. 82:4-6; Hos 13:4 LXX
They will turn from all their ways, fall into error, 19:1; Acts 7:42
and take them to be gods.[1637] [1638] Deut 4:19; 17:3; 11Q19.55.18
(80) 8 Evil will be multiplied upon them, and punishment[1639]
will come upon them so as to destroy them all."[1640] 1:7; Isa 13:9-11; Gen 6:17

[1636] Olson notes the Ethiopic text could be translated: "The whole order of stars will be *assigned by lot* over the sinners." Thus, alluding to (Deut 4:19-20).

[1637] VanderKam has: "They will turn back from all their ways."

[1638] Because the sinners don't understand the order of the stars, they develop inaccurate calendars and are led astray into worshiping the host of heaven. For 80:7 Isaac has: "All the orders of the stars shall harden (in disposition) against the sinners and the conscience of those that dwell upon the earth. Then they (the sinners) shall err and take them (the stars) to be gods." "Astral idolatry would be an obvious violation of the Scriptures, which warn against worship of the stars and would also oppose the clear teaching of the Book of the Luminaries, which subordinates even Uriel, ruler of all luminaries, to God" (NV2 pg. 529) (See Deut 4:19 and 17:3). The Temple Scroll (11Q19 55.15-21 (W pg. 623) provides for the stoning of individuals who worship the sun, moon, or any of the host of heaven. Other texts concerning star worship include: (2 Kgs 17:16; 21:3-5; 23:4-5; Jer 8:2; 19:13; Hos 13:4 LXX; Amos 5:26; Zeph 1:5; Acts 7:42-43).

[1639] **Lactantius in Divine Institutes 7.16 seems to be combining 1En 80:2-8 with concepts from the Book of Revelation to arrive at his eschatology. Note Lactantius finds no room for a pretribulational rapture when he could have easily included it. Quite the opposite, as he writes, "Of the worshippers of God also, two parts will perish; and the third part, which shall have been proved, will remain."** (Cf. DivInst 7.16-20). Isaac has "plagues" in place of "punishment."

[1640] Scholars speculate that *The Book of Heavenly Luminaries* was separated when *The Book of the Dream Visions* was added. In this case 91:1-10 and 92:3-5 may have originally been placed after 80:8 in the Book of Luminaries.

The Book of the Dream Visions

Background of The *Book of the Dream-Visions*

Original language: The original language was Aramaic, although the author may have drawn on some Hebrew sources.[1641] It was translated into Greek and the Greek into Ethiopic (Ge' ez). Interestingly the Ethiopic sometimes preserves the original Aramaic text better than the Greek version. "The Greek MSS that we possess are not the same Greek MSS used by the Ethiopic translators and doubtless contain errors from which the *Vorlage* of the Ethiopic translation was free" (T pg. 131). Knibb argued that the Ethiopic text may have been corrected against some Semitic language text such as Aramaic or Syriac. (T pg. 131).

Author and provenance: Jewish, Judea. "It can be safely assumed that the Animal Apocalypse (Chapters. 85-90) was written in Judea. The author's acquaintance with the events of the Maccabean revolt and the fact that he, or one of his associates, could update the apocalypse as events unfolded indicates that he was relatively close to the action" (T pg. 101).

Date: 165 BC. "In its present form, the latter vision dates to the time of Judas Maccabeus (ca. 165 B.C.E.), although a prior form *may* date to the end of the third century or beginning of the second century."[1642] The Animal Apocalypse 85:2-90:42 can be dated precisely to between 165 and 160 BC since the horned sheep of 90:9-12 is almost certainly Judas Maccabeus, leader of the Jewish revolt. "Enoch 90:12 plainly alludes to Juda's initial military successes against the Seleucids (166-165), but since there is no reference to his death in the spring of 160, Judas must have been alive when the 'Animal Apocalypse' was originally written."[1643]

Important notes: "There is no difficulty about the critical structure of this section. It is the most complete and self-consistent of all the sections, and has suffered least from the hand of the interpolator."[1644] Fragments of this section have been found in the Dead Sea Scrolls. Approximately 26 % of the text is covered in the Dead Sea Scrolls.[1645] However no parts of 83-84 have been found in the DSS. (1En 89:10-53) shares important parallels with (Acts 7:2-53). They are both summary histories of Israel. The Righteous One (Christ) of (Acts 7:52) and the sheep who was saved and brought to heaven share a number of common features. In addition, the placement of the killing of the prophets after the building of the temple in these histories are only found in (1 Enoch 89:50-52); and (Acts 7:50-52) while not in other contemporaneous writings.[1646] This indicates Stephen's (or Luke's) view of Israels history was influenced by the Animal Apocalypse (chapters 85-90).

[1641] N1 pg. 9.
[1642] N1 pg. 8.
[1643] OL pg. 15.
[1644] C pg. 179.
[1645] N1 pg. 11.
[1646] Oegema, R pg. 251 and 258.

The *Book of the Dream-Visions* (Chapters 83-90)

The First Dream Vision

Enoch's Vision of the Deluge

83 1 Now I will show you, my son Methuselah, all my visions which I Gen 5:21; Defem 1.3
have seen, recounting them before you.
2 Two visions I saw before I took a wife,[1647] and the one was quite unlike 85:3; Jub 4:20
the other; the first was when I was learning to write.[1648] The second, Jub 4:17
also was before I took your mother as wife. First, I saw a terrible vision,
and I made supplication to the Lord concerning it.
3 I had laid down in the house of my grandfather Mahalalel, and in a Gen 5:15-16
vision, I saw the heavens flung down,[1649] wrested loose and collapsing
onto the earth![1650]
4 And when it fell to the earth, I saw how the earth was swallowed Ex 15:12
up in a deep abyss, and mountains crashed down on mountains, and hills Isa 24:19-20
sank down upon hills! Lofty trees were ripped up by their roots,[1651] Ps 29:9-10
and hurled down, sinking also into the abyss!
5 At this, a word fell into my mouth, and I took it up crying: 13:8; 90:42
"The earth has been destroyed!"
6 My grandfather Mahalalel roused me as I lay near him, and said:
"Why do you cry out so, my son, and why do you wail like this?" 65:5
7 So, I recounted to him the entire vision which I had seen, and he
said to me: "My son you have seen a terrible thing. You have dreamed
a gravely powerful vision as to the secrets of the sins of the whole earth. 100:7
It must sink into the abyss and be destroyed with a great destruction.

[1647] According to (Jub 4:20) the wife of Enoch name was Ednî. She is named Edna in (1En 85:3), which is the Aramaic equivalent of Eden "paradise."

[1648] Isaac has: "when I (was beginning to) learn books" Writing arose in the fourth millennium BC or possibly somewhat earlier. (Collins, Steven, and Holden, Joseph M. 2019. *The Harvest Handbook of Bible Lands,* pgs. 21; 67-69) So this matches the time frame of Biblical Enoch.

[1649] **This is interesting imagery. Does it suggest a cosmic impact as precipitating the flood?**

[1650] "The eighth-century (B.C.E.) Aramaic Balam inscription from Deir 'Alla in the Jordan Valley raises some interesting questions with respect to the present text" In a similar fashion to this text; "The inscription preserves fragments of a first-person singular narrative in which Balaam receives a night vision, arises in the morning, weeping, and recounts the vision to his people. In the vision, Balaam has learned from the gods about a coming cosmic disaster, and the inscription has been made at the command of the gods in order to preserve the content of the vision" (N1 pg. 348). Some place the inscription as early as the 9th century BC. It is written in a very interesting Aramaic/Hebrew/Canaanite mix, to the extent that scholars cannot agree on the language. The inscription was found in 1967 attached to a fallen wall, at a site identified by many scholars as either Biblical Sukkot or Penuel (Gerrit van der Kooij, "Deir 'Alla, Tell," *The New Encyclopedia of Archaeological Excavations in the Holy Land* 1:338-342). These fragments are part of an inscription that had been written in red and black ink on plaster affixed to a wall that had collapsed during an earthquake, possibly the one mentioned in Amos 1:1 as having occurred during the reign of King Uzziah of Judah in the early eighth century BC (Aḥituv, Shmuel, *Echoes from the Past: Hebrew and Cognate Inscriptions from the Biblical Period* (Translated by Anson F. Rainey; Jerusalem: Carta, 2008) pg. 433).

[1651] I has: "uprooted." N has: "Tall trees were cut from their roots" This is a vivid description of a powerful flood. It is assumed by most scholars that he is talking about the flood but water is not mentioned in the text.

8 Now, my son, get up and make petition to the Lord of Glory, for you 22:14; 1Cor 2:8; Jas 2:1
are a man of faith;[1652] that a remnant may remain[1653] on the earth, 84:2-6
and that he may not obliterate the whole earth.
9 My son, from heaven all this will come upon the earth, and immense
destruction will take place upon the earth." 91:7
10 Then I arose, and prayed and made supplication and request, and
wrote down my prayer for the generations of the world, and I will show
everything to you, my son Methuselah. PrEv 9.17.1-9; *Defem* 1.3
11 So, when I had gone out below,[1654] I looked at the sky; at the sun 2:1-2; 41:5
rising in the east, the moon setting in the west, the waning of the stars Gen 8:20-22
and the whole earth—everything as he made it from in the beginning.[1655] 69:20-21
Then I blessed the Lord of judgement and magnified him, because he
had made the sun to go forth from the windows of the east, so that it
ascends and rises on the face of the heavens, and it sets out and
proceeds along the path which has been shown to it.[1656] [1657] 36:3

Enoch Beseeches the Lord to Leave a Remnant of Man

84 1 I lifted up my hands in righteousness and blessed the Great Holy 1:3; Ps 28:2; 63:4; 88:9; 134:2 Ezra 9:5; 1Kgs 8:22, 54
One, and spoke with the breath of my mouth, and with the tongue of flesh, 14:2; Neh 8:6; 1Tim 2:8
which God has created for the children of the flesh, that they Sir 51:22
should speak with it. He gave them breath and tongue and mouth that Jas 3:6-10
they should speak with it.
2 "Blessed are you, O Lord, King![1658] 9:4; 63:2-3
Great and mighty in your majesty,
Lord of the whole creation of heaven, 82:7
King of kings and God of the whole world![1659]
Your power, your kingship, and your majesty abide for ever and ever, Dan 2:44; 4:3; 7:27
and to all generations your dominion. 1Esdr 4:40; 1Tim 1:17; 6:16
All the heavens are your throne forever, Acts 7:49
and the whole earth your footstool for ever and ever. Isa 66:1-2; Mt 5:35
3 For you have made and rule all things, and nothing is too difficult Gen 18:14; Jer 32:17,27; Lk 1:37

[1652] B has: "(for thou art faithful)", I has: "for you are a man of faith." N has: "since you are faithful," This prayer may be the one in (1En 84:2-6).

[1653] **"Remnant may remain" A pun, in Hebrew Noah is *nûah* = "allowed to remain." Noah and his family will be the surviving remnant (cf. Gen 7:23).**

[1654] "Enoch 'went out' (*wad' a*) into the atrium to gaze aloft at the heavens with thanksgiving that all was as it always had been, with no signs of the heavens collapsing" (BL pg. 255).

[1655] A minority Ethiopic text renders the first part of 83:11 as: "And if I had gone out below and seen the heavens (etc.) and all the earth, then I would have known all things in it." (OL pg. 184)

[1656] **Enoch sees in the order of the movements of the cosmos, an answer from God to his prayer to preserve a remnant. That the movement of the heavens continue as before, assures him that God is still in control.**

[1657] I has: "starting to go the way that it was shown."

[1658] This is the petition Enoch mentions in (83:8-10). It begins in the way Jewish prayers begin even today (Tob 3:11, 1QH[a] 7.21; 8.26; 13.22; 18.16, 19.30, 32, 35, 22.34).

[1659] Nickelsburg has: "God of all eternity."

for you;[1660] 4Q203 9.4; Mt 19:26
wisdom does not escape you, and it does not turn away from 5:8; 48:1; 91:10; Prov 8:27-30
your throne or from your presence. Wis 9:4, 9; Sir 1:1
You know and see and hear all things,[1661] 63:3; 1QH$_a$ 9:27-31
and there is nothing hidden from you; you expose all things.[1662] Heb 4:13; Isa 24:21
4 And now the angels of your heavens are doing wrong, and against,[1663] 6:1; 9:8; 106:14; Job 4:18
the flesh of mankind abides your wrath until the great day 55:3; 60:25; 62:12; Rev 20:13
of judgement.[1664] Jn 3:36; Sir 5:6
5 So now, O God and Lord and Great King, I make supplication and 9:4; 91:13
request that you might fulfill my prayer, to leave me a remnant upon
earth, and not obliterate all human flesh. And make the earth without 67:2; Gen 7:23
inhabitant, so that there would be an eternal destruction.
6 Now, my Lord, remove from the earth the flesh[1665] which aroused
your wrath, but the righteous and true flesh establish as a seed-bearing 10:16; 93:2, 5, 10; Lk 13:19
plant forever. Hide not your face from the prayer of your 62:8; Ps 102:2
servant, O Lord!

The Second Dream Vision

The Animal Apocalypse

Adam to the Children of Seth

85 1 After this I saw a second dream, and I will show the whole dream 83:2, 10; Jub 4:19
to you, my son.[1666]
2 Enoch lifted up (his voice) and spoke to his son Methuselah, 91:1-3; Defem 1.3
"To you I speak, my son. Listen to my words! Prov 5:1
Open your ears to the dream vision of your father!
3 Before I married your mother Edna,[1667] I saw in a vision while 83:2; Jub 4:20, 27
lying on my bed and behold a bull emerged from the earth, Gen 2:7; Dan 4:10

[1660] God is omnipotent. A very similar phrase is in the *Book of Giants* (4Q203 9.4 (W pg. 295) or EnGiants[a] 9,10 (M pg. 317)).
[1661] God is omniscient.
[1662] Some manuscripts add "for you see all things" which is certainly a doublet of the previous line. This text follows Olson, who using the Tana text adds here: "you expose all things."
[1663] The Old Testament, New Testament and second temple literature does not view angels as infallible.
[1664] This the judgement of the flood.
[1665] The flesh to be removed by the flood is not just human, but also that of giants.
[1666] **It is significant that this second dream vision is referenced in (Jubilees 4:19). This indicates that The Book of Dream Visions was written prior to Jubilees (161-140 BC, OTP2 pg. 44) and was considered authoritative. Speaking of Enoch, it says: "While he slept he saw in a vision what has happened and what will occur—how things will happen for humanity during their history until the day of judgement. He saw everything and understood. He wrote a testimony for himself and placed it upon the earth against all humanity and for their history." (Jub 4:19, VanderKam translation)**
[1667] Edna is named Ednî the daughter of Dânêl or Daniel, Enoch's uncle, in (Jub 4:20). In (Jub 4:27), Methuselah's wife is named Ednâ, the daughter of Ezrael. Edna means "the Paradise" (M pg. 42).

and that bull was white.[1668] After it a young heifer[1669] came forth and Jub 3:5; Gen 2:21-23
along with her came forth two bull-calves, one of them black[1670] and Gen 4:1-2
the other red.[1671] [1672]
4 The black bull-calf struck down the red one and chased him across Gen 4:8-16
the land,[1673] and from then on, I could not see that red bull-calf.
5 But the black bull-calf grew up and a young heifer[1674] came to it. Jub 4:1, 9
I saw that many cattle issued from it, resembling it and they were Gen 4:17-22
following after it.
6 That first cow, went from the presence of that first bull in order ApMos 2:1-4:1
to seek the red bull calf, but did not find it, and she lamented bitterly Jub 4:7
over it, and searched for it.[1675] ApMos 3:3
7 I watched until that first bull came to her, and calmed her,
and from that time onward she cried no more.
8 After that she bore another white bull,[1676] and after him she bore Gen 4:25-5:4; *Vita* 49:1
many black bulls and cows.[1677] Jub 4:10
9 I saw in my sleep that white bull, that it likewise grew up, and
became a great white bull, and from him issued many white bulls Gen 5:6-8; Jub 4:8; 11-14
which resembled him.[1678]
10 These also began to sire many white bulls, which in turn resembled Gen 5:9-32; Jub 4:13-33
them, one following the other.

[1668] Isaac has: "snow white," this is Adam. White, is indicative of his purity and innocence. He comes forth from the earth as Adam does in (Gen 2:7). White identifies Adam's line in the Animal Apocalypse through Seth (85:8-9), Shem (89:9), Abraham (89:10), Isaac (89:11), and Jacob as a white ram (89:12) (N1 pg. 371).

[1669] Eve is depicted as a heifer here, since she had not yet borne children.

[1670] Cain is black, indicating his murderous character. "The image might possibly reflect the haggadic notion later attested in Jewish, Christian, and gnostic literature that Cain was begotten by Satan" (H1 pg. 371).

[1671] Abel is red indicating his spilled blood or perhaps his bloody sacrifice (N1 pg. 371).

[1672] **It is interesting that no mention is made here of Eve's temptation with the tree of knowledge. This indicates that the fall of the watchers (1En 86) was more important in the authors mind than the temptation of Eve. Eve's temptation is mentioned in the Parables (1En 69:6).**

[1673] "Chased him across the land;" This solid reading of the text, could mean that the vengeance for Abel's blood always follows Cain (See Gen 4:10, 14). Alternately the verbs could be transposed to chased and then killed. The image of Cain pursuing Abel is also mentioned in a much later (AD 200-300) gnostic text which says, "And carnal Cain pursued Abel his brother" (*The Hypostasis of the Archons* 90:21). A parallel and later (1st century BC to AD 1st century) account is found in the (*Apocalypse of Moses*, 2:1-4:1) but it does not mention a pursuit. (Jub 4:3-6) implies, as does (Genesis 4:12-16), that Cain was pursued.

[1674] **According to (Jubilees 4:1, 9); Cain married his sister Âwân or Avan, who was born after Abel but before Seth. She was the mother of the "other Enoch" from the line of Cain (Gen 4:17-18).**

[1675] Eve cannot find Abel and is distraught. According to (Jubilees 4:7) Eve mourned for Abel for 28 years!

[1676] This is Seth.

[1677] The rest of Adam and Eve's progeny are described as black (sinful) distinguishing them from the white, righteous line of Seth. **According to the ancient fictional work, (*The Life of Adam and Eve*, *Vita* 49:1 (OTP2 pg. 292)) (100 BC-AD 100), Seth had 30 brothers and 30 sisters.**

[1678] The sons of Seth are represented as white bulls. According to (Jubilees 4:8, 11) Seth married Azûrâ, his younger sister. "Seth came to be virtually deified in certain schools of Gnosticism" (OL pg. 188). Is this passage a hint of the Sethite theory? This is doubtful since in (1En 86), the ones who breed with the cattle, are obviously celestial beings rather than human.

The Fall of the Watchers, and the Violence of the Giants

86 1 Again, while looking upwards as I slept, I saw the heaven above,	88:1; Rev 9:1; 12:9; 4Q180 1.7-8
and behold a particular star fell from heaven,[1679] down into the midst	Lk 10:18; Isa 14:12; Ezek 28:17
of those large cattle and it fed and grazed among them.[1680]	Jub 4:15; *AdvHaer* 1.4
2 Then I saw the large and black cattle, and behold, the large and	
black cattle, began to make changes in their pastures, their stables	8:1; PseudClemHom 8:11-15
and their calves,[1681] and they began to moan one after the other.[1682]	8:2
3 Once again looking up to heaven in my vision, behold, I saw many	Jude 6; ADAM 32
stars descend and cast themselves down from heaven beside that	6:1-8 Gen 6:4; AThm 32
first star, and like it, they became bulls[1683] [1684]amongst those cattle,	TReu 5:6; Jub 4:22
and they were pasturing with them in their midst.[1685]	
4 As I watched, behold they all let out their organs, like horses,	90:21; Ezek 23:20; Jer 5:7-8
and began to mount the heifers among the cattle;	7:1-2; Gen 6:2-4; 4Q181 2.1-2
and they all conceived and bore elephants, camels and donkeys.[1686]	87:4; 89:6; Jub 5:1-3; 7:22

[1679] "A particular star fell from heaven," a fallen Watcher, Azâzêl, see 88:1, 6:7, 8:1 and 10:8 (See N1 pg. 195 for a discussion). **Azazel thus led the rebellion.** In antiquity, stars were usually, but not always, viewed both by Jews and pagans as celestial beings. However sometimes they are righteous humans. (Dan 8:10; 12:3; and probably Rev. 12:4) Fall in Aramaic, *nĕphal*, is the base word for *nephilim*. Is Jesus referencing language from this verse in Lk 10:18? For other references to fallen stars see (Isa 14:12; Rev 8:10-11; 9:1-6; 12:4, 9; TSol 20:14-17; and ApEl 4:11).

[1680] Fragments of (1En 86:1-3) have been preserved in the DSS (4Q207 1.1-5 (W pg. 285) or (4QEn^{f} 1).

[1681] "Make changes in their pastures, their stables and their calves" **The women gave up their homes, husbands and children due to their passion for the fallen watchers.** (1En 7:1-2).

[1682] Nickelsburg has: "and they began to moan, one after the other." Probably indicating sexual passion. Olson translates: "and they began to attack one another." Charles has: "began to live with each other." Black has "and they began to butt one another."

[1683] **These bulls are fallen watchers. Due to these bulls being dark skinned, supposedly like the Cainites who were descendants of Ham, some believe this supports the idea that Cainites intermarried with the Sethites producing giants. This was a view first floated by Julius Africanus (AD 160-240) and accepted by Augustine (AD 354-430) where they interpreted "sons of God" in Gen 6:1-4 as Sethites, and "daughters of men" as daughters of the Cainites. It is a view still taught by many in seminaries and churches today. There are several issues with this view. 1. 86:3 states that the fallen stars became bulls amongst those cattle" so this clearly states the origin of the black cattle being from the fallen stars. 2. This view is not supported by the context of the balance of 1 Enoch. (Chapters 6-10). 3. It is also difficult to envision how relations between two sets of humans would produce non-human beings, i.e. giants and monsters. 4. The watcher view was the only view espoused until the beginning of the third century, and as such, the Sethite view would have been unknown to all before that, including the Jews, Essenes, the Apostles of Christ and the early Christians!**

[1684] **The Testament of Reuben agrees with this text about the stars being transformed. Speaking of the watchers: "Then they were transformed into human males, and while the women were cohabiting with their husbands they appeared to them. Since the women's minds were filled with lust for these apparitions, they gave birth to giants"** (TReu 5:6).

[1685] The rebellion spreads, as other Watchers descend.

[1686] **This is a vision of the fall of angels in animal form. The aggressive salaciousness of stallions is well known. Note the progeny, elephants, camels, and donkeys are not uniform but are of three types. This matches the interpretation of (1En 7:2) being three types of watcher progeny rather than a reference to height. See also 10:9, and 88:2. "The particular species may be used as symbols because of the similarities between two sets of Aramaic words: *pîlîn* ("elephants") = *nĕpîlîn; gamĕlîn* ("camels") = *gibbōrin* ("giants"); 'ărodîn ("wild asses") = "elioud"** (Milik, *Enoch*, 240; and Tiller, *Commentary*, 240). **This description of the three classes in the Animal Apocalypse was written between 165-160 BC by an author who was very familiar with the Book of Watchers and squarely within the Enochic tradition. That he uses three types of progenies from the fallen angels in the**

5 All the cattle feared them and were terrified of them, and they began Jer 8:16-17; Gen 6:11-12
to bite with their teeth, and to devour and gore with their horns. 89:11,43; Jub 5:2
6 Furthermore, they began to eat those cattle,[1687] and behold all the 7:3-5
children of the earth[1688] began to tremble and shake in their presence
and were fleeing from them.

Excursus: Augustine's reasons for rejecting the Book of Enoch, and a response.

Augustine was a pillar in the church of the 5th century and was influential in the rejection of The Book of Enoch. Below are Augustine's comments on the Book of Enoch. To be fair to his position, I am including the entire passage. His views are fairly representative of church leaders at the time.

In the third book of this work we made a passing reference to this question, but did not decide whether angels, inasmuch as they are spirits, could have bodily intercourse with women.[1688a] For it is written, Who makes His angels spirits, that is, He makes those who are by nature spirits His angels by appointing them to the duty of bearing His messages. For the Greek word ἄγγελος, which in Latin appears as angelus, means a messenger. But whether the Psalmist speaks of their bodies when he adds, and His ministers a flaming fire, or means that God's ministers ought to blaze with love as with a spiritual fire, is doubtful. However, the same trustworthy Scripture testifies that angels have appeared to men in such bodies as could not only be seen, but also touched. There is, too, a very general rumor, which many have verified by their own experience, or which trustworthy persons who have heard the experience of others corroborate, that sylvans and fauns, who are commonly called incubi, had often made wicked assaults upon women, and satisfied their lust upon them; and that certain devils, called Duses by the Gauls, are constantly attempting and effecting this impurity is so generally affirmed, that it were impudent to deny it. From these assertions, indeed, I dare not determine whether there be some spirits embodied in an aerial substance (for this element, even when agitated by a fan, is sensibly felt by the body), and who are capable of lust and of mingling sensibly with women; but certainly I could by no means believe that God's holy angels could at that time have so fallen, nor can I think that it is of them the Apostle Peter said, For if God spared not the angels that sinned, but cast them down to hell, and delivered them into chains of darkness, to be reserved unto judgment. (2 Peter 2:4) I think he rather speaks of these who first apostatized from God, along with their chief the devil, who enviously deceived the first man under the form of a serpent. But the same holy Scripture affords the most ample testimony that even godly men have been called angels; for of John it is written:

---

same place of the story establishes that this was the original understanding of (1En 7:2). Neither the Animal Apocalypse, nor the DSS fragments support the idea of three different generations as found in the version by George Syncellus, although that interpretation has merit. Interestingly "Anakim", עֲנָק, the name of a giant tribe means "neck" or "long neck" Does this match the camels? (Cf. Bereshit Rabbah 26.6 numerous necklaces).

[1687] **These are the giants eating humans (cf. 1En 7:2-6)! This is attested elsewhere in ancient literature; (examples: Polphemus in the Odyssey; Jub 7:22; HE 1.2; Num 13:32?); and cannibal giants are abundant in native American folklore (David, Gary A., *Giants, Kachinas, and Cannibals*). This is especially concerning given the Lord's statement: "Just as it was in the days of Noah, so will it be in the days of the Son of Man" (Lk 17:26).**

[1688] Here is a lapse from the animal imagery.

[1688a] Cf. Cassian (AD ca. 360-435) *Conferences of the Desert Fathers* 8:20-21 who uses similar reasoning.

Behold, I send my messenger (angel) before Your face, who shall prepare Your way. (Mark 1:2) And the prophet Malachi, by a peculiar grace specially communicated to him, was called an angel. (Malachi 2:7)
But some are moved by the fact that we have read that the fruit of the connection between those who are called angels of God and the women they loved were not men like our own breed, but giants; just as if there were not born even in our own time (as I have mentioned above) men of much greater size than the ordinary stature. Was there not at Rome a few years ago, when the destruction of the city now accomplished by the Goths was drawing near, a woman, with her father and mother, who by her gigantic size over-topped all others? Surprising crowds from all quarters came to see her, and that which struck them most was the circumstance that neither of her parents were quite up to the tallest ordinary stature. Giants therefore might well be born, even before the sons of God, who are also called angels of God, formed a connection with the daughters of men, or of those living according to men, that is to say, before the sons of Seth formed a connection with the daughters of Cain. For thus speaks even the canonical Scripture itself in the book in which we read of this; its words are: And it came to pass, when men began to multiply on the face of the earth, and daughters were born unto them, that the sons of God saw the daughters of men that they were fair [good]; and they took them wives of all which they chose. And the Lord God said, My Spirit shall not always strive with man, for that he also is flesh: yet his days shall be a hundred and twenty years. There were giants in the earth in those days; and also after that, when the sons of God came in unto the daughters of men, and they bare children to them, the same became the giants, men of renown. These words of the divine book sufficiently indicate that already there were giants in the earth in those days, in which the sons of God took wives of the children of men, when they loved them because they were good, that is, fair. For it is the custom of this Scripture to call those who are beautiful in appearance good. But after this connection had been formed, then too were giants born. For the words are: There were giants in the earth in those days, *and also after that*, when the sons of God came in unto the daughters of men. Therefore, there were giants both before, in those days, and also after that. And the words, they bare children to them, show plainly enough that before the sons of God fell in this fashion they begot children to God, not to themselves — that is to say, not moved by the lust of sexual intercourse, but discharging the duty of propagation, intending to produce not a family to gratify their own pride, but citizens to people the city of God; and to these they as God's angels would bear the message, that they should place their hope in God, like him who was born of Seth, the son of resurrection, and who hoped to call on the name of the Lord God, in which hope they and their offspring would be co-heirs of eternal blessings, and brethren in the family of which God is the Father.

But that those angels were not angels in the sense of not being men, as some suppose, Scripture itself decides, which unambiguously declares that they were men. For when it had first been stated that the angels of God saw the daughters of men that they were fair, and they took them wives of all which they chose, it was immediately added, And the Lord God said, My Spirit shall not always strive with these men, for that they also are flesh. For by the Spirit of God they had been made angels of God, and sons of God; but declining towards lower things, they are called men, a name of nature, not of grace; and they are called flesh, as deserters of the Spirit, and by their desertion deserted [by Him]. The Septuagint indeed calls them both angels of God and sons of God, though all the copies do not show this, some having only the name sons of God. And Aquila, whom the Jews prefer to the other interpreters, has translated neither angels of God nor sons of God, but sons of gods. But both are correct. For they were both sons of God, and thus brothers of their own fathers, who were children of the same God; and they were sons of gods, because begotten by gods, together with whom they themselves also were gods, according to that expression of the psalm: I have said, You are gods, and all of you are children of the Most High. For the Septuagint translators are justly believed to have received the Spirit of prophecy; so that, if they made any alterations under His authority, and did not adhere to a strict translation, we could not doubt that this was divinely dictated. However, the Hebrew word may be said to be ambiguous, and to be susceptible of either translation, sons of God, or sons of gods.

Let us omit, then, the fables of those scriptures which are called apocryphal, because their obscure origin was unknown to the fathers from whom the authority of the true Scriptures has been transmitted to us by a most certain and well-ascertained succession. For though there is some truth in these apocryphal writings, yet they contain so many false statements, that they have no canonical authority. We cannot deny that Enoch, the seventh from Adam, left some divine writings, for this is asserted by the Apostle Jude in his canonical epistle.[1688b] But it is not without reason that these writings have no place in that canon of Scripture which was preserved in the temple of the Hebrew people by the diligence of successive priests; for their antiquity brought them under suspicion, and it was impossible to ascertain whether these were his genuine writings, and they were not brought forward as genuine by the persons who were found to have carefully preserved the canonical books by a successive transmission. So that the writings which are produced under his name, and which contain these fables about the giants, saying that their fathers were not men, are properly judged by prudent men to be not genuine; just as many writings are produced by heretics under the names both of other prophets, and more recently, under the names of the apostles, all of which, after careful examination, have been set apart from canonical authority under the title of Apocrypha. There is therefore no doubt that, according to the Hebrew and Christian canonical Scriptures, there were many giants before the deluge, and that these were citizens of the earthly society of men, and that the sons of God, who were according to the flesh the sons of Seth, sunk into this community when they forsook righteousness. Nor need we wonder that giants should be born even from these. For all of their children were not giants; but there were more then than in the remaining periods since the deluge. And it pleased the Creator to produce them, that it might thus be demonstrated that neither beauty, nor yet size and strength, are of much moment to the wise man, whose blessedness lies in spiritual and immortal blessings, in far better and more enduring gifts, in the good things that are the peculiar property of the good, and are not shared by good and bad alike. It is this which another prophet confirms when he says, "These were the giants, famous from the beginning, that were of so great stature, and so expert in war." Those did not the Lord choose, neither gave He the way of knowledge unto them; but they were destroyed because they had no wisdom, and perished through their own foolishness. Augustine, *City of God*, Book 15, Ch 23 (AD 420)

The following is a summarization of Augustine's points with a response.

1. While allowing that humans can be attacked sexually by spiritual forces. He "could by no means believe that God's holy angels could at that time have so fallen," as to mingle sensibly with women.

[1688b] Jerome is similar. Cf. Jerome's Commentaries on Galatians, Titus, and Philemon under Titus 1.12

Augustine is making an assumption that although evil beings have been known to attack women; God's holy angels could not have so fallen. This is an assumption based on nothing but his own thoughts, which are counter to the immense body of literature that reveals just the opposite. If angels have free will, then they can exercise it by sinning. Augustine's line of reasoning originated with Rabbinic Judaism not the Essenes, Second Temple literature or early church fathers (DialTrypho 79).

2. 2 Peter 2:4 is speaking of an original rebellion by angels who apostatized from God with the devil rather than a later fall like the 200 in the book of the Watchers.

   The Book of Watchers was very popular in the Judaism of Christ's day; as evidenced by the numerous copies found at Qumran. The specific language in 2 Peter 2:4 and Jude 6 obviously matches the backstory of the Book of the Watchers. It seems extremely disingenuous to deny what the Lord's brother and one of his prime disciples obviously believed. He is twisting the clear meaning of those scriptures.

3. The angels that fell were actually men because godly men are called messengers (angels) in Mark 1:2 and Malachi 2:7. This then sets up his argument for his promulgation of the Sethite theory.

   In the majority of copies, the Septuagint says "sons of God" in Gen 6:2, and virtually every English translation follows that lead. These were clearly heavenly beings. The Sethite theory maintains that the descendants of the Godly line of Seth were seduced by the daughters of Cain. When they mated, they produced the Nephilim. It is obvious that Genesis 6:1-4 is relying on a separate tradition well known to the readership of the time. It is not by accident that the translators of the LXX used "sons of God" since they knew the tradition of The Book of Watchers. Although the godly line of Seth was appreciated,[1689] *the Sethite theory of Genesis 6:1-2 did not appear in the literature until the third century when it was first tentatively proposed by Julius Africanus in AD 221. The Sethite theory would have thus been unknown and strange to Christ and His followers. Augustine is here making up and promulgating a new tradition that hinders an accurate understanding of scripture. Unfortunately, the Sethite theory is still taught today, even though the backstory of the watchers going back in history to ancient Mesopotamia is well documented and takes precedence.*

4. People occasionally grow to great stature today, so the Bible is simply referring to them when it speaks of giants.

   It seems odd to conjecture that two groups of humans, Sethites and the daughters of Cain, would produce offspring of great stature any more than occurs regularly. Again, given the known backstory, this new Sethite tradition is manufactured and imposed by authority figures on the church. Common sense would argue that crossing humans with humans would not produce giants and monsters.

[1689] *Ant* 1.3.1 §§72-73

5. These words of the divine book sufficiently indicate that already there were giants in the earth in those days, in which the sons of God took wives of the children of men, when they loved them because they were good, that is, fair.

   "In those days" means before the flood, and "also afterward," clearly means after the flood. That Augustine resorts to a paragraph of tortured exegesis to justify his position is concerning; especially in light of known tradition. One wonders what his real motive was. Obviously, in his time, the church was commendably and vigorously working to stamp out paganism. Having a tradition of celestial beings mating with humans and producing giants, as in Greek mythology, undermined their efforts.

6. The Book of Enoch has no place in the canon, because it was "not preserved in the temple of the Hebrew people by the diligence of successive priests; for their antiquity brought them under suspicion, and it was impossible to ascertain whether these were his genuine writings, and they were not brought forward as genuine by the persons who were found to have carefully preserved the canonical books by a successive transmission."

   Augustine is correct in questioning a biblical Enoch authorship, as he probably doubted that a manuscript could have been successfully preserved for such a great period of time. He does not seem to have knowledge of 1 Enoch beyond the Book of the Watchers. Many scholars doubt Augustine had a copy of any of the Books in 1 Enoch.[1690] *As a youth He was known to not have liked Greek although he could read it well.*[1691] *He was thus ignorant of the extensive New Testament parallels in the Parables, Dream Visions, Admonitions of Enoch and An Eschatological Exhortation (Ch. 108). He also seems to not have grasped the Essene's relationship with the Book of Enoch and early Christianity. He seems unaware that the rabbinic Judaism of his day bore no resemblance to the Judaism that birthed Christianity and that Aquila's translation was translated with an agenda in mind (see pgs.23). He was likewise ignorant of Christ calling the Book of Watchers scripture (cf. Mt 22:29-30 and 1Enoch 15:7). His out of hand decision to reject 1 Enoch was thus not an informed one, and has done serious damage to the Church ever since.*

Excursus: Did Jesus consider 1 Enoch to be scripture?

All three Synoptic Gospels contain an account of a dispute between Jesus and a group of Sadducees about the resurrection (Matthew 22:23-33; Mark 12:18-27; Luke 20:27-40). In this account, the Sadducees raise a scenario similar to that in the Book of Tobit (cf. Tobit 3:8) of a woman having seven husbands who each die. They then ask whose wife she will be in the resurrection? In response, Jesus refers to an evidently noncanonical scripture to justify why resurrected saints in heaven will not be married. "But Jesus answered them, 'You are wrong, because you know neither the Scriptures nor the power of God. For in the resurrection, they neither marry nor are given in marriage, but are like the angels in heaven.'" (Mt 22:29-30)." In Mark he also refers to the authority of scripture in his response. Jesus said to them; "Is this not the reason you are wrong, because you know neither the Scriptures nor the power of God? For

---

[1690] N1 pg. 14, 95.
[1691] Augustine, *Confessions* 1.13-14.

when they rise from the dead, they neither marry nor are given in marriage, but are like angels in heaven." In Luke, Jesus is recorded as giving the reason marriage is not necessary in Heaven. "And Jesus said to them, 'The sons of this age marry and are given in marriage, but those who are considered worthy to attain to that age and to the resurrection from the dead neither marry nor are given in marriage, for they cannot die anymore, because they are equal to angels and are sons of God, being sons of the resurrection.'" The reason given, is that since they are no longer subject to death, there is no reason to have progeny to replace those who have died, as in this world.

No scripture has been located in the Old Testament, or any other period literature, that matches His thought. However, (1En 15:4-7) does match. "You were holy ones, spirits, that live forever, yet you defiled yourselves upon the women, and have begotten (children) by the blood of flesh. Like the children of men, you have lusted after flesh and blood, just as they do who die and perish. It was for this reason I gave them wives that they might cast seed into them and thus, beget children by them, that nothing should ever fail them upon the earth. But as for you, you formerly were spirits that live forever, immortal for all generations of the world. For this reason, I did not appoint wives for you; because for celestial spirits, heaven is their dwelling." This matches the reasoning by Jesus in Luke. God did not provide wives for celestial beings, because they are immortal, and have no need to replenish their numbers since they do not die.

Jasko concludes "1 Enoch 15 is the best fit out of the extant Early Jewish literature."[1692] Olson speaking of (Lk 20:34-36) in reference to 1En 15:5-7 concurs: "This passage is surely the background against which Jesus's words should be understood."[1693] (OL pg. 46).

This establishes that Jesus considered the Book of Watchers, which was known to circulate separately at the time, as scripture. Given its abundance at Qumran, the way 1 Enoch was used and revered by early Christians, and its obvious use in 2 Peter, and Jude, this should not be a surprise.

What about the rest of 1 Enoch?

The theology of 1 Enoch forms the basis for the New Testament. While no other part of 1 Enoch is specifically called scripture in the New Testament; the books of Watchers, Parables, Dream Visions, the Admonitions, and Chapter 108 were heavily used in the New Testament, and are referenced and sometimes called scripture by Church fathers. The evidence would indicate that these were also considered scripture by Christ.

Are there other non-canonical books Jesus may have considered scripture?

That some non-canonical books were considered scripture by Christ, opens the possibility for more. Jubilees would be an immediate candidate, based on a comparison between John 8:56 and Jubilees 16:16-27. "Your father Abraham rejoiced that he would see my day. He saw it and was glad" (Jn 8:56).

[1692] Jasko, A. 2012. *Did Jesus Know 1 Enoch 15?*
[1693] OL pg. 56

> Lebsack writes: "Reading this for the first time, you probably overlooked this detail without giving it much attention. Upon closer examination, you then ask yourself, where in the standard "Old Testament" do we see where Abraham saw Jesus's day and rejoiced? Based on the context, Jesus was talking about something Moses wrote. Nowhere in the Pentateuch, nor anywhere in the standard "Old Testament" for that matter, do we see this detail Jesus said about Abraham. This detail however, is in the Book of Jubilees, which is a self-proclaimed work of Moses himself. In Jubilees 16, we see Abraham rejoicing several times about this festival. (20) "Then he [Abraham] built an altar there for Yahweh who had rescued him, and who was making him rejoice..." (25) "So he [Abraham] celebrated this festival for seven days, rejoicing with all his heart and all his soul..." (27) "And Abraham gave a blessing and rejoiced. So he named this festival the Festival of Yahweh, for it was a joy acceptable to the Most High God" (29) "For this reason it has been ordained on the heavenly tablets regarding Israel, that they should celebrate the Festival of Booths joyfully for seven days during the seventh month which is acceptable before Yahweh." The clues all point towards the chapter 16 passage from Jubilees describing Abraham's experience with the Festival of Booths/Tabernacles. It was during this very same festival that Jesus said this about Abraham rejoicing during it. Coincidence? It seems highly unlikely. When you read John 7-8 with the mindset that Jesus was referring to Jubilees, all the strange things he does and says suddenly seem to make perfect sense. (Lebsack, Phillip. *Did Jesus Fulfill and Reference Prophecy about Himself from the Book of Jubilees?*)

A large number of copies of Jubilees were known to be at Qumran (13-16 copies in 5 caves; VF pg. 197). In addition, Jubilees was embraced as an important text among early Christians who called it little Genesis, or Lesser Genesis (Leptogenesis).

Why are these books not in the cannon if Jesus considered them scripture?

By the fourth century, when the Old Testament canon was being finalized, it had been long forgotten that Jesus and Christianity obviously did not arise from the Pharisees, which became Rabbinic Judaism; but grew from the main Essene branch of Judaism. Josephus affirms that the Essenes had a different set of scriptures than the Pharisees. "They also take great pains in studying the writings of the ancients, and choose out of them what is most for the advantage of their soul and body" (War 2.8.6 §§136); "and will equally preserve the books belonging to their sect, and the names of the angels" (*War* 2.8.7 §§142). In the late fourth century (AD 390-405), when Jerome lodged in Bethlehem, meeting with Rabbinic Jews to translate their Hebrew scriptures into Latin, the Rabbinic Jews, inspired by Rabbi Akiba Ben Joseph, had long since stopped valuing (if they ever did) 1 Enoch and Jubilees.

Judgement of the Fallen Watchers and the Giants

87 1 Again I saw how they began to gore each other and devour one 7:6; 8:4; 9:2
another, and the earth began to cry out. Gen 4:10; Job 31:38
2 I raised my eyes once again to heaven, and in my vision behold I saw

descending from heaven beings who were like white men:[1694] 9:1; 46:1; 90:21-22; Dan 7:9
and four[1695] came forth from that place, and three others[1696] with them. 9:1; 20:1-8; 81:5
3 Those three who emerged last grasped me by my hand 12:1; 90:31; Jub 4:23-24
and took me up, away from the children of the earth, and lifted me onto 70:1-3; Gen 5:22, 24
a lofty place, and showed me a tower high above the earth,[1697]
and all the hills were lower.[1698]
4 Then they said to me: "Remain here until you witness everything
that happens to those elephants, camels, and donkeys and to the stars 86:4; 88:2; 89:6
and to the cattle—all of them."[1699]

Giants Kill Each Other and Fallen Watchers are Bound

88 1 Then I saw one of those four[1700] who had emerged first, and he Rev 20:1-3; Lk 10:18
seized that first star[1701] that had fallen from heaven and bound 10:4-5; 90:21; 2Pet 2:4; Jude 13
it by its hands and feet and cast it into an abyss: now that abyss was 18:10-16; 21:1-10; 90:24; Jub 5:6
narrow and deep, and desolate[1702] and dark.[1703] 92:5; Mt 8:12; 22:13
2 Another one[1704] drew a sword, and gave it to those elephants, camels, 10:9; 14:6; 87:4; 89:6
and donkeys. These proceeded to smite one another and the whole earth Gen 6:11; Jub 5:7, 9; 7:22
trembled because of them.[1705]
3 As I watched further in the vision, behold, one of those four[1706] who

---

1694 "Like white men" These are the seven archangels. Isaac has: "snow-white person." **The oldest Jewish text we have of spiritual beings in white garments is 1En 14:20 (the Great Glory), then Daniel 7:9 (the Ancient of Days) followed by this text. That makes this text the earliest instance of angelic beings depicted in white.** A celestial being in white next appears in (2Mac 11:8). Noah at birth is white (1En 106:2, 10). The temple priests and Essenes (*War* 2.8.3 §§123) were known for wearing white (cf. Eccl 9:8). The imagery of white garments explodes in the New Testament both with celestial beings (Mt 17:2; 28:3; Mk 9:3; 14:51-52; 16:5; Jn 20:12; Acts 1:10; Rev 1:14; 4:4; 19:14?) and saints (Rev 3:4-5, 18; 6:11; 7:9, 13, 14).

1695 Black postulates these four are: Michael, Sariel (also named Uriel) Raphael and Gabriel (BL pg. 260).

1696 Black postulates the three are: Raguel, Saraqael and Remiel (BL pg. 260). For seven archangels see (1En 20:1-8 and Rev 8:2).

1697 Charles views this as the heavenly temple, i.e., paradise. Wherever it is; it supplies a vantage point for Enoch who is later joined by Elijah (89:52) to view the unfolding events on earth. This is similar to the Christian rapture, where the saints are removed to paradise, to escape the wrath of God.

1698 God's dwelling is higher than all the hills where cultic activities occur; these will be covered in the flood (Gen 7:19, 20; 8:5).

1699 This verse again names the three types of watcher progeny. (See note 1686).

1700 This is Raphael, see 10:4.

1701 This is Azâzêl 10:4. Shemjazah (1En 10:11) is not mentioned.

1702 Some other manuscripts have "and enclosed" or "and worm infested" in place of "and desolate." Isaac has "empty" and suggests renderings based on other texts as; "serious" or "difficult."

1703 A very fragmentary part of chapter 88 was found among the Dead Sea Scrolls (4Q206 4.1 (W pg. 286) or 4QEn[e] 4 i (M pg. 238)).

1704 Gabriel, see 10:9.

1705 **The three types of "giants," *nĕpîlîn; gibbōrin and e*lioud, destroy one another in internecine war. This is also recounted in (Jub 7:22). "And they begat sons the Nâphîdîm, and they were all unlike, and they devoured one another; and the Giants slew the Nâphîl, and the Nâphîl slew the Eljô, and the Eljô mankind, and one man another."**

1706 Michael, see (1En 10:11).

had emerged, came down from the sky[1707] and he gathered up and took Mt 24:29; Rev 6:13; Jer 5:7-8
away the many stars whose, privy members were like those of horses, 86:3-4; Ezek 23:20; Jub 5:6
and bound them all hand and foot and he hurled them into a chasm 10:11-13; 2Pet 2:4; Jude 6
of the earth.[1708] Josh 10:11

Noah and the Flood

89 1 Then one of those four[1709] went to one of the white bulls, and he Gen 6:5-9:19; Jub 5:19-32
instructed him in a mystery,[1710] trembling as he was.[1711] Though born 10:1-3; Jub 5:21
a bull, he became a man.[1712] He built himself a great ship and lived 67:1-3; Gen 6:14-16
on it: along with three other bulls[1713] who also dwelt with him on Gen 7:1, 7, 13
that vessel. The ship was closed up[1714] and provided them cover. Gen 7:16; Jub 5:23
2 Once again, I raised my eyes to heaven and saw a lofty roof,[1715] 14:11
with seven cascading streams on it, and these streams poured 77:5; *Ant* 1.3.5; Jub 5:24
large quantities of water into an enclosed area.[1716]
3 I looked again, and behold chambers were opened up on the earth's Gen 7:11-12
surface, within that great enclosure,[1717] and the water began to
boil up and rise above the ground. I was looking at that enclosure till
the entire ground was covered with water.

[1707] Texts differ here. This text, as does Olson and Baty, follows EMML 2080 and one Eth2 manuscript which says "came down from heaven". Nickelsburg has: "one of those four who had come forth hurled stones from heaven and gathered and took all the great stars." Charles and Isaac also follow this reading. If it is hurled rocks; it may be an allusion to (Josh 10:11) where "the LORD threw down large stones from heaven." Hurling of rocks from heaven is found in Greek mythology (Hesiod, *Theogony* 675, 713-735 (730-700 BC). It is also interesting that the punishment for an ox who gores a person to death is stoning (Ex 21:28-29). Knibb is unique, having: "one of those four who had come out cast from heaven and gathered and took all the large stars."

[1708] This chasm is identified by R. H Charles and others as Beth Chaduda which is 3 miles southeast of Jerusalem (C pg. 189). (Cf. Martin, Ernest L. ed. Sielaff, David, 1981 (2010). *The Lake of Fire: Where Is it Located?*).

[1709] This is Uriel, see 10:1.

[1710] **In the Epic of Gilgamesh, concerning the flood; "Utanapishtim spoke to Gilgamesh, saying: "I will reveal to you, Gilgamesh, a thing that is hidden, a secret of the gods I will tell you!" (*The Epic of Gilgamesh* tablet 11). The Epic has other similarities to the flood account such as doves, sacrifices and of course, the flood.**

[1711] "Trembling as he was" is omitted in Aramaic texts. Charles translates it as "without his being terrified." Some manuscripts read "while he trembled" and others "without him trembling." **Noah may have been frightened of the angel Uriel, of the coming flood (*Ant* 1.3.7 §§96), or of the giants. *Jewish Antiquities,* (*Ant* 1:3:1 §§74) would support the tradition that he was afraid of the giants.**

[1712] Noah is here changed into a man. It is hard to imagine a bull building an ark. The wives and animals are not mentioned. This may be a step in the angelification of Noah since all the men in the animal apocalypse are angels.

[1713] The three sons of Noah, Shem, Ham & Japheth.

[1714] As in (Gen 7:16), God covers them in the ark.

[1715] The Aramaic (DSS account) is similar to the account in Genesis without the imagery of the cosmos as a grand building. Scholars, in this case, believe the Ethiopic text goes back to a better source than the DSS. Olson theorizes that the expansions in the Ethiopic text may go back to the original author making a second edition of the text (OL pg. 192). This text includes the fuller Ethiopic version. For a comparison see (OL pg. 193; T pg.258).

[1716] "Enclosed area" "The key word is the Eth. Noun *'asad*, which can designate an enclosed area such as a courtyard, and translate, for example, the Gk. … which can denote a building or village" (N1 pg. 375). Baty translates it as village. Was this the bowl of the Black Sea when it flooded from the Mediterranean through the Bosporus according to the Black Sea deluge hypothesis? Or was it another confined area near the Persian Gulf?

[1717] Is the enclosure a basin? This language could allow for a regional flood (cf. Jub 4:24). But flood accounts from oral traditions found throughout the earth would argue for a worldwide flood.

4 Water, darkness and thick cloud increased upon it.[1718] I watched the SibOr 1.217-218
height of the water, until it eventually poured over the enclosure, Gen 7:17-18; Jub 5:26
and it rose over the earth.
5 All the cattle of that enclosure were huddled together until I saw
them sinking and being engulfed and perishing in the water. Gen 7:21-23
6 Yet the vessel floated on the water, while all the cattle, elephants, 86:4; 87:4; 88:2; *Haer.* 4.36.4
camels, and donkeys[1719] sank to the bottom together with every 3Mac 2:4; SibOr 2:232
animal,[1720] so that I could no longer see them. They had no ability TNaph. 3:4b-5
to escape, (but) perished and sank into the depths.[1721]
7 Again, I watched in the vision until those cascading streams from
that high roof ceased, and the springs of the (underground) chambers Gen 8:2; 4Q206 4.2
closed up. Other deeps were at the same time opened up.[1722] Jub 5:29; 6:26; PrMan 3
8 Then the water drained down into these, until the earth appeared and 2Pet 2:5
the vessel settled down on the earth. The darkness withdrew and the Gen 8:4; Jub 5:28; *Ant* 1.3.5-6
light returned.

[1718] Olson observes: "Genesis says nothing about darkness at the Flood and light returning afterwards (89:8), but this was a stock feature in the Mesopotamian Flood traditions" (OL pg. 192). (See *Atrahasis* III, iii; *Gilgamesh* XI, ii, iii; Dally, *Myths from Mesopotamia* Pg. 31-32, 112-113; *Ziusudra* lines 202-208; SibOr 1:217-241; and Best, Robert M. 1999. *Noah's Ark and the Ziursudra Epic* pg. 257).

[1719] "Elephants and camels and donkeys" (three types of fallen angel progeny). This is the only place in all of 1 Enoch where giants are killed by the flood. In 1 Enoch 10:9 and 88:2 they kill each other through war. In Jubilees, they also kill one another (Jub 5:7-9; 7:22). According to (3 Baruch 4:10 (OTP1 pg. 666-667)) (1st-3rd century AD) either 409,000 (Gk) or 104,000 (Slav) giants were killed in the flood. (Cf. *Haer.* 4.36.4)

[1720] These are humans drowned in the flood.

[1721] Obviously, giants were on earth after the flood, as Moses, Joshua and David were fighting them, and North American native tradition is replete with descriptions (David, Gary A., *Giants, Kachinas, and Cannibals*). **Josephus, referencing Nicolaus of Damascus, says some people escaped the flood. "There is a great mountain in Armenia, over Minyas, called Baris, upon which it is reported that many who fled at the time of the Deluge were saved; and that one who was carried in an ark came on shore upon the top of it; and that the remains of the timber were a great while preserved" (*Ant* 1.3.6 §§ 95). Josephus, a Pharisee, elsewhere, had no problem with the fact that people other than Noah and his family survived the flood "which was the reason why there was no greater number preserved, since there was no place to fly to" (*Ant* 1.3.5 §§ 89). Pseudo-Eupolemus (prior to 1st century BC) goes even further: "Eupolemus, in his work 'On the Jews,' states that the Assyrian city of Babylon was first founded by those who escaped the Flood. They were giants, and they built the tower well known in history. When the tower was destroyed by God's power, these giants were scattered over the whole earth" (Praeparatio Evangelica 9.17.2-3 (OTP2 pg. 880)). He names a giant who escaped the flood as Belos (Praeparatio Evangelica 9.17.8-9; 9.18.2 (OTP2 pg. 881-882)). Belos is otherwise known in early traditions (OTP2 pg. 877). However, portions of the DSS seem to indicate that all the giants perished (4Q370 1.5-6) and of course (Gen 7:20-23) is quite explicit on this fact. The LXX of (Gen 10:1-9) indicates that Nimrod, the grandson of Ham and son of Cush, was the first of the post flood giants. "Now Chous (Cush) became the father of Nebrod (Nimrod). He was the first on earth to be a Giant. He was a giant hunter before the Lord God; therefore they will say, 'Like Nebrod a giant hunter before the Lord'" (Gen 10:8-9 LXX). This would indicate that a celestial being union with mankind occurred again. This would have occurred within a generation of the flood; thus, explaining how the giants reappeared on earth. This is repeated in the LXX of 1 Chronicles 1:10. In both passages it is very interesting that Nimrod is not mentioned with Cush's other sons but is set apart. Could there have been an illicit union between Cush and a fallen celestial being, or between Cush's wife and a celestial being? Tom Horn, with Michael Heiser's review, translated Gen 10:8 as: "And Nimrod began to change genetically becoming an (gibbor) the offspring of watchers on earth" (Horn, Thomas, 2012. *Apollyon Rising*).**

[1722] Fragments of 89:1-9, 10-16, 23-37, and 31-37 were found in the Dead Sea Scrolls (4Q206 4; 4Q204 4; (W pg. 286-287) or (4QEn[d] 2 i; 4QEn[d] 2 ii; 4QEn[d] 2 iii (M pg. 222-225) and (4Q En[e] 4 i; 4QEn[e] 4 ii; 4QEn[e] 4 iii (M 238-243)).

Shem to the Twelve Patriarchs

9 But the white bull which had become a man, came out of the vessel, Gen 8:18; Jub 6:1
and the three bulls with him. One of those three bulls was white[1723] Gen 9:18
like that first bull. and one of them was red as blood. and one black. 106:15-16
Then the white bull departed from them.[1724] Gen 9:29; Jub 10:15
10 They began to beget wild beasts and birds, so that there arose Gen 10:1-11:25
from them every variety of species: lions, tigers,[1725] wolves, dogs, hyenas, Lev 11:1-17
wild-boars, foxes, rock-badgers, pigs, swifts, falcons, ibises, eagles, 90:2
and ravens; and among them was born a white bull.[1726] [1727] Gen 11:27; Jub 11:14-17
11 And they began to bite one another. That white bull which was born Jub 11:2; 14:24; 16:12-13
amongst them begat a wild donkey[1728] and a white bull[1729] with it, and Gen 16:12, 15; 21:2
the wild donkeys multiplied. Gen 25:12-18
12 But the bull-calf which was sired by him begat a black wild boar[1730] Gen 25:22-26
and a white ram;[1731] of the flock; and the wild boar begat many other Gen 36
wild boars,[1732] and the ram begat twelve sheep.[1733] Gen 35:22-26

[1723] According to Nickelsburg, the red bull is Ham, symbolizing the curse of Canaan (Gen 9:25), and the bloody fate of the Canaanites who would be exterminated. The black bull is Japheth, black symbolizing the darkness of the north and the white bull is Shem (N pg. 376). However, Olson and Black have Japheth as red and Ham as black (OL pg. 192; BL pg. 264). White, worn by the Essenes (*War* 2.8.3 §§123), symbolized the purity of heavenly beings.

[1724] This references the passing of Noah.

[1725] Isaac has: "leopards" instead of "tigers"; "snakes" in place of "dogs"; "squirrels" in place of "rock-badgers"; "eagles" in place of "vultures"; and "striped crows" in place of "eagles."

[1726] White bull=Abraham, Lions=Chaldeans, tigers (leopards)= Syrians or Arameans, wolves=Egyptians, dogs=Philistines, hyenas=Moabites (OL pg. 192 asserts they are Arameans or Assyrians), wild boars=Edomites, Amalekites, foxes=Ammonites (Neh 4:3), rock badgers=?, pigs=?, swifts=unclean animals, birds (Lev 11:5, 7, 14) vultures= Macedonians. Ibises, eagles, ravens=unclean birds of prey (Lev 11:13-14), possibly Greeks, (N1 pg. 358). Even though the flood was to cleanse the earth, man soon fell into corruption again.

[1727] **It is thought that Stephen used (1 Enoch 89:10-53) as a framework for his summary speech of the history of biblical Israel in (Acts 7:2-53). "As for the relation between Acts 7:2-53 and 1En 89, Luke has used, according to Joachim Jeska,** (J. Jeska, *Die Geschichte Israels in der Sicht des Lukas: Apg 7,2b-53 im Kontext antic-jüdischer Sumnarien der Geschichte Israels,* FRANT 195) **the Greek version of 1En 89:10-53 as a model for his 'summary of the history of Israel' by adopting its structure and sequence of events and especially by placing the killing of the prophets after the building of the temple, which is found only in 1En 89:50-52 and Acts 7:50-52, but not in any other contemporaneous writings"** (R pg. 250, Oegema, *The Coming of the Righteous One in Acts and 1 Enoch*).

[1728] This is Ishmael, (see Gen 16:12); Ishmael and Isaac are listed in birth order. Ishmael is the progenitor of the Arabs and Midianites, the wild asses or donkeys of (1En 89:13,16).

[1729] This white bull is Isaac.

[1730] Esau, here depicted as a black boar, (an unclean animal) "reflects the bitter rivalry between Israel and Edom" (N1 pg. 377).

[1731] Jacob, a white ram, is a clear break with the line of white bulls. This may indicate that lives will now be shorter, and sheep are a common metaphor for Israel, which begins with Jacob (Pss 23:1-4; 74:1; 78:71-72; 79:13; 80:1; 95:7; Isa 53:6; Jer 50:6; Ezek 34; Zech 13:7).

[1732] These are the sons of Esau, the Edomites. They are symbolized by the black wild boars the animal most abhorrent to Israel. This is an indication of the depth of hatred felt for Edom especially when this text was written (BL pg. 264).

[1733] These are the twelve patriarchs.

Joseph to the Crossing of the Red Sea

13 When those twelve sheep had grown up, they gave up one of their own[1734] to the asses,[1735] and those asses in turn gave up that sheep to the wolves, so that sheep grew up among the wolves!

Ant 2.3; Gen 16:12; 37:17-36; 39-41; Jub 39:2

14 Then the ram led forth all the eleven sheep to dwell with it and to pasture with it among the wolves:[1736] and they multiplied and became many flocks of sheep.

Mt 10:16; Acts 7:2-53; Ex 1:7; Jub 45:1; 46:13; Gen 42-50; Ps 79:13

15 Then the wolves[1737] began to fear them,[1738] and they oppressed them, going so far as to destroy their little ones, and they cast their young into a river of deep water.[1739] Those sheep began to cry aloud on account of their little ones, and to complain to their Lord.[1740]

Ex 1:9-10; Jub 46:11-16; Ex 1:16-22; Jub 47:2

16 A sheep[1741] which had been saved from the wolves fled and came to the wild donkeys;[1742] I watched the sheep groaning and crying, beseeching their Lord[1743] with all their might, till the Lord of the sheep descended from a lofty abode[1744] at the call of the sheep, and he drew near and watched over them.

Ex 2; *Ant* 2.11

17 He summoned that sheep which had fled from the wolves, and spoke with it concerning the wolves, that it should warn them not to touch the sheep.[1745]

Ex 3:1-5:23; *Ant* 2.12

18 Then that sheep went to the wolves at the command of the Lord, and another sheep[1746] met it and went with it. Together the two went and entered into the assembly of those wolves.[1747] They spoke with them, and warned them not to touch the sheep from then on.

Ant 2.13; Ex 4:27; 5

19 After this, I saw the wolves, how they all the more harshly oppressed the sheep, with all their power; and the sheep cried aloud.[1748]

Mt 7:15; 10:16; Ezek 22:27; Did 16:3; Acts 20:29; Ex 5:4-23

20 Then their Lord came to the sheep and began to smite[1749] those wolves: and the wolves began to lament. Yet the sheep became quiet and thereafter ceased to cry out.

Ex 6-12; Jub 48:5-49:5; *Ant* 2.14

[1734] Joseph.

[1735] Asses=Ishmaelites (Gen 16:12; 37:28).

[1736] The sons of Israel move to Egypt.

[1737] Wolves=Egyptians.

[1738] Some manuscripts read: "to make them afraid."

[1739] Nile river.

[1740] The Ethiopic is again fuller than the Aramaic in (1En 89:15-16). The Aramaic omits: "to fear them" and "beseeching their Lord with all their might."

[1741] Moses

[1742] Ishmaelites/Midianites, Gen 16:12.

[1743] God

[1744] Mount Sinai.

[1745] Touch the sheep in order to harm them.

[1746] Aaron

[1747] Pharoah's court.

[1748] **Sheep and wolf imagery is used in the amazingly beautiful early Christian *Didache* (AD 50-135). "For in the last days the false prophets and corrupters will abound, and the sheep will be turned into wolves, and love will be turned into hate" (Did 16:3).**

[1749] Plagues of Egypt.

21 I looked at the sheep until they went out from the wolves; but the Ex 12:31-39; *Ant* 2.15
eyes of the wolves were blinded,[1750] and those wolves went forth in Jub 48:12, 17; Ex 14:4-9
pursuit of the sheep with all their forces!
22 Nevertheless the Lord of the sheep went with them, leading them, Jn 10:4-6, 14, 27; Ex 13:21-22
and all his sheep[1751] followed him; and his face was full of Ps 4:6; 77:20; 80:1-3; Num 6:25
glory—magnificent and terrible to behold. Ps 31:16; 67:1; 80:3; 119:135
23 But the wolves began to pursue those sheep till they encountered them Ex 14:5-9
by a body of water.[1752] Ex 13:18
24 That swamp of water was divided, and the water stood on this side and
on that, before their faces, and their Lord led them, placing himself Ex 14:19-31
between them and the wolves. Jub 48:13
25 The wolves still could not see the sheep as they proceeded into the
midst of the pool of water, but the wolves followed the sheep, and the
wolves ran after them into that swamp of water.
26 Then when they saw the Lord of the sheep, they turned back to flee Ex 14:24-25
before his face, but the swamp of water gathered itself together and *Ant* 2.16
suddenly it returned to its natural state. Then the water swelled Jub 48:13-14
and rose till it overwhelmed those wolves.
27 As I watched, all the wolves who pursued that flock perished.
They sank and they drowned, and the waters covered them over. Ex 14:28; 15:4-5, 10

Sinai to the Death of Moses

28 The flock of sheep passed on from that water, and went into a Ex 15:22-16:36
wilderness,[1753] where there was no water or grass; and they began to open 1:2; 90:6, 9, 10, 35
their eyes and see. I saw the Lord of the sheep pasturing them and giving *Ant* 3:1
them water and grass,[1754] and that sheep[1755] was continuing onward and Ps 23:1-2; 77:20; Ex 17:1-7
leading them.
29 Then that sheep ascended to the summit of a particular lofty crag,[1756] Ex 19:1-11, 17
and the Lord of the sheep delivered it[1757] to the flock while they all Ex 24:12; 31:18
stood at a distance.[1758]

[1750]This may refer to the darkness that was over the land (Ex 10:21-23). But more likely it reflects the blind rage of Pharoah (Ex 14:4-5). According to (Jubilees 48:12) Pharoah was inspired to pursue Israel by the "the prince of Mastema."

[1751] Children of Israel.

[1752] Olson has: "body of water," Black has: "sea of reeds," Nickelsburg has: "swamp of water." Knibb has: "stretch of water" Isaac has: "pool of water." Whichever terms are chosen, it does not appear to be a major part of the sea. The Ethiopic term for sea, baḥərä (ባሕረ) is not found in the passage. The word here is 'ayga māy (አይገ ማይ) "a marsh of waters, a watery marsh."

[1753] The wilderness of Shur and Sinai (Ex 15:22-26).

[1754] Manna

[1755] Moses

[1756] Sinai

[1757] It is unclear what "it" means. Some think it is Moses, and some the ten commandments (in which case 89:29 along with 93:6 would be the only two mentions of the Mosaic covenant in all of 1 Enoch). The Law was not of great importance to Enochian Jews.

[1758] "While they all stood at a distance" is a "precarious" reconstruction of the text by Milik pg. 243 (BL pg. 266). Olson keeps it while Nickelsburg, Knibb and Isaac omit it.

30 After that, I saw the Lord of the sheep who stood before them,
and his appearance was powerful, majestic and fearful, and all those Ex 19:11-19
sheep saw him and were terrified in his presence. Ex 20:18-19
31 They were all fearful of him and trembling. They cried out to the Deut 5:23-27
sheep which led them[1759] and to the other sheep[1760] which was with them,
saying: "We cannot stand before our Lord, or even look at him."
32 So that sheep which led them, ascended a second time to the summit Ex 32:1-7
of the crag. Meanwhile, the eyes of the sheep began to be blinded,[1761] 90:7, 26; Mt 15:14; Lk 6:39
and they strayed from the way which he had shown them, Ex 32:1-6
but that sheep[1762] did not know about these things.
33 Then the Lord of the sheep was filled with great wrath against the Ex 32:7-19
flock and that sheep discovered it, and descended from the summit of the
crag, and returned to the flock, and found the greatest part of them
blinded in their eyes and fallen away.
34 When they saw that sheep, they were afraid and wished to return to
their folds.
35 But that sheep took other sheep[1763] with it, and fell upon that flock;
and slaughtered every one that had gone astray. So, the sheep feared Ex 32:26-29
his presence. Thus, that sheep brought back those sheep that had fallen Jub 23:20
away, and they returned to their folds. [And when the straying flock
had returned to their folds] that [sheep] labored to reproach and
to slay and to trouble (everyone) who swore by [...........][1764] Ex 32:4, 20; 24; 32:27-35
36 I watched in the vision until that sheep was transformed,[1765] and Ex 34:29-35
became a man, and built a tabernacle[1766] for the Lord of the sheep, and he *Ant* 3.6; Ex 35-40
made all the sheep to stand at that tabernacle.[1767] Ex 33:8; Num 1-2
37 Then I watched until the sheep,[1768] which had met that sheep,[1769] Num 20:22-29; 32:11
which led the sheep fell asleep.[1770] I saw till all the full-grown sheep Deut 1:34-38; 2:14-3:17; 10:6
died, and young ones arose in their place, and they came to a pasture,[1771]

[1759] Moses

[1760] Aaron

[1761] Isaac has "dim-sighted." For blindness as a contemporary motif (cf. 4Q245 1.16; CD A 1.9). Later use by Jesus applied to the Pharisees, see (Mt 15:14; Lk 6:39).

[1762] Moses

[1763] The Levites carried out the death penalty on 3000 idol worshiping Israelites (Ex 32:25-29).

[1764] The DSS fragments show that verse 35 was longer in the Aramaic, but only a few words survive. The bracketed text is Tiller's reconstruction of the fuller Aramaic text of this verse from the DSS (cf. T 290-291, 295; M pg. 205; BL pg. 266). Tiller admits that the restoration is problematic and dismisses Milik's reconstruction as "of course, wrong". Cook reconstructs the text as "[. . .] all the ones who had strayed, and they began to [. . .] [. . .] that sheep brought back all the flock that had strayed to th[eir] folds. [. . ..] not [to] reveal or confront or oppress he swore [. . .] (W pg. 287). Tiller notes "Given the fragmentary state of the text, it is impossible to say whether the longer Aramaic text or the shorter Ethiopic text is original" (T pg. 295).

[1765] This transformation may refer to Ex 34:29-35 where Moses' faces shines as a result of his speaking with God..

[1766] Tabernacle is literally "house". Tiller proposes "dwelling, compartment" and postulates "this house represents either the tabernacle or the desert camp." (T pg. 296).

[1767] The 12 tribes camped around the Tabernacle (Num 1-2).

[1768] Aaron

[1769] Moses

[1770] This is the death of Aaron.

[1771] Pasture = the encampment before crossing the Jordan.

and approached a stream of water.[1772]
38 Then that sheep, their leader, which had become a man, withdrew
from them and fell asleep.[1773] All the sheep searched for him, and Jude 9; Deut 32:48-50; 34:5-8
made quite a loud outcry over him. *Ant* 4.8.48 §§320-326

Crossing of the Jordan to Solomon Building the Temple

39 I watched until they ceased crying for that sheep, and crossed that Josh 1:1-2; 3:14
stream of water. There arose two other sheep[1774] as leaders in the place Num 20:22-28; Deut 1:36-38
of those who had fallen asleep, and they led them. Deut 34:9
40 I looked till the sheep came to a very pleasant place; a beautiful Ex 3:8; Josh 18:1-9; 21:43-45
and glorious land.[1775] I saw that the sheep were satisfied, and the 26:1; Dan 8:9; 11:16, 41; Ex 20:6
tabernacle was in their midst in the pleasant land. 90:20; Ps 106:24; 1Chr 21:29
41 At times their eyes were open, and at other times were dim-sighted.[1776] Judg 2:18-19
Eventually another sheep[1777] arose and led them and brought 1Sam 3; 7:3-17
them all back, and their eyes were opened.
42 Then the dogs, and the foxes, and the wild boars, began to devour
the flock till the Lord of the sheep raised up a certain ram[1778] 1Sam 9-10
from among the sheep, which lead them.[1779]
43 This ram[1780] began to butt and pursue with his horns. Hurling 1Sam 11-15; 17
itself, against the foxes[1781] and after them, against the wild boars.[1782]
It destroyed many wild boars, and after them, it began to attack the *Ant* 6.5-7
dogs.[1783] [1784]
44 That sheep whose eyes were open,[1785] observed that ram of the flock,
until it forsook its path, and even began to strike the flock and 1Sam 15; 22:16-19

[1772] The Jordan River. They were actually camped around and on the Tel of ancient Sodom as they viewed Jericho in preparation for crossing the Jordan (Presentation by Steven Collins lead excavator of Tel el-Hamman).

[1773] This is the death of Moses on Mount Nebo.

[1774] This is Joshua and Caleb (Deut 1:34-38) and/or more likely Joshua and Eleazar (Num 20:22-28; *Ant* 4.8.48 §§324, 326) (T pg. 300).

[1775] "Glorious land" is used also in (Dan 8:9; 11:16, 41), once again showing the close association between these two apocalyptic books. Glorious land=land of Canaan/Israel.

[1776] This is a one phrase summary of the Book of Judges.

[1777] Samuel

[1778] Ram=King Saul; dogs=Philistines; foxes=Ammonites; wild boars=Edomites.

[1779] "A Greek text of (1 Enoch 89:42-49) was written into the margins of an eleventh-century tachygraphic manuscript discovered by Mai in the Vatican Library and published by him in 1844" (N1 pg. 13). It was deciphered in 1855. Tachygraphy is the abbreviated (shorthand) form of Greek and Latin used in the Middle Ages. The manuscript is Vatican MS 1809 (G^{vat}).

[1780] King Saul.

[1781] Ammonites, with Moab (Neh 4:3).

[1782] Amalekites/Edom, (Gen 36:9-12, 16; 1En 89:12).

[1783] Dogs=Philistines, (1Sam 17:43).

[1784] At this point in the Greek text, an additional line is found. Olson proposes that it read "And after them it began to attack those dogs" (OL pg. 198). It has been included here. This text is a combination of Ethiopic and Greek readings seeking the most accurate text.

[1785] This is Samuel. "Eyes were open" i.e.. had prophetic insight.

trample it down! So, it left the true path.[1786] *Ant* 6.7.4; 1Sam 28:3-25
45 Then the Lord of the sheep sent the sheep[1787] [1788] to another sheep,[1789]
and raised it to become a ram, and to lead the sheep instead of that ram[1790] 1Sam 16:1-13
which had deserted its way.
46 It went to it, and spoke to it alone, and raised up that ram, and made it *Ant* 6.8.1
the ruler and leader of the flock. But while this was going on,
those dogs[1791] continued to oppress the sheep.
47 The former ram pursued the second ram, and that second ram arose 1Sam 18-31; *Ant* 6.11
and fled before it. Then I looked at the first ram until those dogs 1Sam 31; *Ant* 6.14.7
pulled it down.[1792]
48a But the second ram arose and began leading the sheep. 2Sam 2:1-11; 5:1-5; 1Chr 11:1-3 Ps 78:70-72

49 Those sheep grew and multiplied; but all the dogs, and foxes, and 2Sam 5:17-25; 1Chr 14:8-17
wild boars[1793] feared, and fled from it. And the ram charged against 2Sam 8:2-14; 10:1-12:31; 21:22
all the wild beasts and killed them, and those wild beasts were once more *Ant* 7.4-5
powerless among the sheep, and robbed them no more of anything.[1794] 1Chr 18-20
48b That ram sired many sheep and fell asleep; and a young sheep[1795] 1Kgs 1-2
became a ram in its place: a prince[1796] and leader of the flock. 1Chr 29:22-25
50 Then that house[1797] became great and spacious—built for those sheep. TLev 10:5; 1Kgs 3:1
A tower lofty and great[1798] was erected upon that house for the Lord of 1Kgs 5-8; *Ant* 8.3; 2Sam 5:11
the sheep. That house was not high, but the tower was elevated *Ant* 8.4.4; 2Chr 2-4
and lofty.[1799] The Lord of the sheep stood on that tower and they 2Chr 7:1-3; Ezek 44:16
spread a full table before him.[1800] Ex 25:30; 1Kgs 8:10-13, 62-64

1786 For 89:44, Nickelsburg, following the Greek text has: "And the sheep whose eyes were open saw the ram among the sheep until it forsook its path and began to walk where there was no path."
1787 Samuel
1788 Both instances of the term sheep (Samuel and David) in 69:45 are literally "lamb."
1789 King David
1790 King Saul
1791 Philistines, see Goliaths taunt in (1Sam 17:43). "Am I a dog, that you come at me with sticks."
1792 This is Saul's death in battle, at the hands of the Philistines (1Sam 31).
1793 The Greek text omits "wild boars."
1794 That verse 49 belongs between 48a and 48b is confirmed by the Greek text.
1795 King Solomon
1796 "Prince" is appropriate here since God is the King of Israel.
1797 Jerusalem. **That this verse is likely the one alluded to in (TLev 10:5) shows that *The Book of the Dream Visions* was known and respected prior to the writing of the Testament of the Twelve Patriarchs in 137-107 BC** (OTP1 pg. 778, 792) (BL pg. 269). It also proves once again that 1 Enoch was not written by a biblical Enoch who would have had no knowledge of Jerusalem or a temple.
1798 The first Temple.
1799 Solomon's temple, standing tall on the Temple Mount, dominated the skyline of ancient Jerusalem.
1800 Contrast this full table with the polluted and impure table of (89:73) at the beginning of the second temple period. Olson notes: "The fact that they spread before him a full table is very important for Enochic theology, which apparently believed that the old Temple with its sacrifices and priesthood were legitimate but that the current Temple (built after the Exile) and its priesthood were defiled and unacceptable" (OL pg. 198).

From Solomon's Time to the Dispersion of Ten Tribes by Assyria

51 Still, I saw those sheep, that again they strayed and followed diverse 2Chr 10:16; 11:14-16; 12:1 2Chr 24:17-21
paths, abandoning their own house.[1801] The Lord of the sheep[1802] called 1Kgs 12:16-33; Lk 13:35
some from amongst the sheep[1803] and sent them to the sheep, but the Mt 23:31-37; Lk 11:49
sheep began to slay them![1804] Acts 7:51-52; 1Kgs 18:4, 13
52 One of them[1805] escaped safely and was not killed. It sprang away Rom 11:2-3
and cried out over the sheep. They wanted to slay it; but the Lord of the 1Kgs 18; 19:2-3; Mk 9:13
sheep rescued it from the hands of the sheep, and brought it up and 2Kgs 2:11; Mal 4:5
made it to dwell with me.[1806] 93:8; Mt 17:3,12
53 Then he sent many other sheep to that flock to testify against them 2Chr 36:15-16
and lament over them.[1807]
54 Eventually I saw when they abandoned the house of the Lord of the 2Kgs 16; 21:1-18; Jn 2:16
sheep and his tower, they went astray entirely, and their eyes were Mt 21:13; 23:38; Mk 11:17
blinded.[1808] I saw then that the Lord of the sheep worked much slaughter 1Kgs 15:16-22; Isa 53:6
on them in their pastures, because those sheep had invited that
slaughter[1809] and betrayed[1810] his place. 2Kgs 12:17-18; 16:5-20
55 He abandoned them into the hands of the lions, tigers,[1811] wolves, Jer 4:7; 5:6; 50:17; Lev 26:22 1Kgs 14:25-26; 2Chr 24:20
and hyenas, and into the hand of the foxes, and to all the wild beasts, 2 Kgs 23:26-29; 24:1-4
and those wild beasts proceeded to tear those sheep in pieces.[1812] Lk 10:3; Acts 20:29
56 I saw too that he abandoned that house of theirs and their tower, Barn. 16:5; Lk 13:35

[1801] This event is when Israel split from Judah by establishing an idolatrous worship center in Dan (1 Kings 12:25-33). Jesus refers to the temple as "your house" in (Mt 23:38; Lk 13:35) similar to the manner here. This is further evidence of Jesus having an Essene type worldview where they viewed themselves as outside the temple cult (*Ant* 18.1.5 §§19). His cleansing of the Temple (Jn 2:13-17, Mt 21:12) also indicated He viewed its worship as impure.

[1802] **That Jesus claimed to be Lord of the sheep and the Wisdom of God is evident from a close comparison between (1En 89:51; Lk 11:49; and Mt 23:34). The preincarnate Christ in (Mt. 23:34) is the one who sent the prophets, wise men, and scribes. In (Lk 11:49) it is the Wisdom of God (also see 1En 48:1-4) who sent them. Then finally the Son, is himself sent and rejected, leading to the destruction of the vineyard/Jerusalem (Mt 21:33-41).**

[1803] These are apostles, prophets, wise men and scribes sent to Israel and Judah. (Mt 23:34; Lk 11:49)

[1804] **In agreement with this passage, both Jesus (Mt 5:12; 21:35; 23:31-37) and Stephen (Acts 7:51-53) point out the inconvenient fact that the leadership of the Jewish nation, even during the first temple period, persecuted and killed the messengers God sent. This reference is specifically to the massacre of the prophets by Ahab and Jezebel in (1 Kings 18:13).**

[1805] **This is Elijah. Elijah joined Enoch in paradise making them the only ones who went to heaven without tasting death.**

[1806] **This is an interesting association of Enoch and Elijah given that many believe these two righteous men who never tasted death will be the two witnesses in Rev. 11:3** (See also Mt 17:11; Mal 4:5; *Haer.* 4.16.2).

[1807] This may be a reference to Jeremiah.

[1808] Isaac has: "their eyes became blindfolded."

[1809] Black proposes that "those sheep invited that slaughter" be translated "those sheep had invited that murderer," in reference to the appeal by Ahaz to Tiglath-pileser king of Assyria (2Kgs. 16:7) (BL pg. 270).

[1810] Isaac has: "vindicated" in place of "betrayed." This phrase is taken two ways by textual experts. One is, as here, that the Jews betrayed the Lord's temple by abandoning it and calling on heathen nations for help. The other is that the Lord vindicated or made right their desecration of the Temple by letting it be destroyed.

[1811] Nickelsburg and Isaac have: "leopards" in place of the more commonly translated "tigers."

[1812] Lions=Chaldeans, leopards=Arameans, wolves=Egyptians, hyenas=Moabites or Aram, foxes=Ammonites and/or Moabites.

and threw them all into the hands of the lions, so that they might tear Ezek 34:5-8; Isa 56:9; Jer 39:1
them in pieces and devour them—into the hands of all 2Kgs 23:27; Lam 2:7
the wild beasts.[1813] [1814] CD 1.2-4; Jerm 12:7-9
57 Then I began to cry out with all my might, and I appealed to the
Lord of the sheep, pointing out to him how the sheep were being
devoured by all the wild beasts.
58 But he remained silent,[1815] though he saw it, and he was perfectly Deut 28:63; Jub 15:33-34
happy[1816] to see them devoured, swallowed up, and carried off. 89:71,77; 94:10; 97:2; Ps 74:1
He left them in the hands of all the wild beasts for food. Isa 56:9-11; Ezek 34:5

Israel is Placed in the Care of the Seventy Shepherds

59 Then he summoned seventy shepherds,[1817] and left those sheep to 90:22-25; *Cels* 5.52; Ps 82:1-8

[1813] **Some scholars believe 1En 89:56 and verse 66 may be the passage combined, paraphrased and called scripture in (Barnabas 16:5) written (AD 70-135).** However, he applies it to the destruction of the second temple, when this is speaking of the destruction of the 1st temple and dispersion. It reads: "Again, it was revealed that the city and the temple and the people of Israel were destined to be handed over. For the scripture says: "And it will happen in the last days that the Lord will hand over the sheep of the pasture and the sheepfold and their watchtower to destruction. And it happened just as the Lord said" (Barn 16:5). **Milik and I see the Barnabas reference to be sourced more likely from (1En 90:26-28)** (M pg. 46). (1En 90:26-28) is referring to the final judgement and the destruction of the second temple; and so, would be more appropriate to the point the author of Barnabas was trying to make, as he would have been well aware of the distinctions between the two passages.

[1814] **The most likely fate of the Ark of the Covenant was that it was destroyed when the Temple was plundered by the Babylonians (cf. Lam 2:1 "he has not remembered his footstool in the day of his anger") The footstool of God is the Ark of the Covenant. Also see (Lam 2:7): "The Lord has scorned his altar, disowned his sanctuary; he has delivered into the hand of the enemy the wall of her palaces: they raised a clamor in the house of the lord as on the day of festival." From this it is clear that the Babylonians took full access to the temple. 1 Esdras stops just short of saying the ark itself was taken. "And they took all the holy vessels of the Lord, both great and small, with the vessels of the ark of God, and the king's treasures, and carried them away into Babylon."** (1Esdr 1:54 KJV) (See also 1 Esdras 1:51 LXX; 2Chr 36:19; Dan 1:2; 5:2-3, 23). 4 **Ezra (AD 70-120) says the ark was plundered; presumably after the Babylonian destruction of the Temple but it may be referencing the second Temple. "For you see that our sanctuary has been laid waste, our altar thrown down, our temple destroyed: our harp has been laid low, our song has been silenced, and our rejoicing has been ended; the light of our lampstand has been put out, <u>the ark of our covenant has been plundered</u>, our holy things have been polluted"** (4 Ezra 10:21-22 (OTP1 pg. 546). **Jeremiah, speaking before the Babylonian destruction, foresees a time when the Ark of the Covenant of the LORD "shall not come to mind or be remembered or missed; it shall not be made again"** (Jer 3:15).

[1815] Charles has: "remained unmoved;" in place of "remained silent." Isaac has: "he remained quiet and happy."

[1816] Nickelsburg has: "rejoiced" This was predicted long before in (Deut 28:63); "And as the LORD took delight in doing you good and multiplying you, so the LORD will take delight in bringing ruin upon you and destroying you. And you shall be plucked off the land that you are entering to take possession of it."

[1817] **Israel is here given to seventy shepherds (spiritual beings) (cf. Zech 10:3; TLev 16:1). "Whether these 70 angels are parolees from the 200 Watchers, or a different caste is not clear, but they enable the author to offer a new interpretation of Israel's sad post-exilic history. Disastrous international military and political events are really steered by human surrogates of these 70 shepherds (89:59-90:19) rather than by God directly. The author thus acquits God of all blame for excessive Jewish sufferings during this epoch"** (Olson pg. 15). Seventy nations that descend from the sons of Noah and are dispersed at the tower of Babel are named in Gen 10 (cf. Jub 15:31-32). As a symbol of reclaiming the nations for God, Jesus sent out 70 or 72 disciples (Lk 10:1). That the earth was divided among the "gods" is mentioned by Plato in *Critias* 109B-109C (360 BC): "I have before remarked in speaking of the allotments of the gods, that they distributed the whole earth into portions differing in extent, and made for themselves temples and instituted sacrifices." Paul's ministry to the gentiles involved "conquering,"

them, that they might pasture them. He spoke to the shepherds and their Ezek 34:1-31; Deut 32:8
assistants: "Every one of you from now on shall pasture the sheep, Sir 17:17; Jub 15:31
and everything that I command you, do.
60 I am handing them over to you exactly numbered, and I will tell
you which of them are to be destroyed. These you are to destroy." 63:9; Rom 1:24-28
And he handed those sheep over to them.[1818] Jer 15:3; 25:17-38
61 Next, he summoned another one[1819] and told him this: "Observe and 90:14, 22
mark everything that the shepherds do against these sheep; Lev 26:21-22; Isa 40:2
for they will destroy far more of them than I have commanded. Jer 12:7-10; 23:1-6; Zech 1:15
62 Every excess and destruction that is done by the shepherds, 89:68,70; Ezek 9:2-4, 11
write down, noting how many they destroy at my command, and how
many they destroy on their own volition. Make a record against each
individual shepherd regarding the destruction he causes.
63 By exact number, read out before me how many they destroy,
and how many they hand over to destruction, so that I may have this 89:70-71, 76
as a testimony against them. That I may know every deed of the 90:17, 20
shepherds, so that I may evaluate them and see what they do; whether 97:6; Jub 15:32
they abide by my command which I have commanded them or not.[1820]
64 Yet do not let them know it, and do not reveal it to them, or admonish
them. Merely record against each individual all the destruction of the Zech 11:4-9; 15-17
shepherds, one by one, in his own time, and bring it all up to me." Ezek 34:1-10
65 Then I watched while those shepherds pastured, <each> in their Zech 10:3
appointed time.[1821] They began to kill and destroy more than they had Isa 40:2; 56:9-11
been commanded, and they abandoned those sheep Ps 82:1-8; Jer 50:6

---

through the gospel of Christ, these 70 nations back into God's kingdom. Paul's strong desire to reach Spain (Tarshish/Tartessos, Gen 10:4; Rom 15:23-24) which is the most remote of the 70 nations may spring from the concept of these 70 nations. Ancient attestation that Paul did visit Spain is found in (*1 Clement* 5:5-7 (AD 70's); *The Muratorian Canon* 34-39 (AD 170); Cyril of Jerusalem (AD 315-386) *Catecheses, Lecture 17.26*; Chrysostom (AD 347-407) *Second Timothy, Homily 10 verse 20*; and Jerome (AD 342-460) *Amos, cap.* 5 which reads: "St. Paul having been in Spain, went from one ocean to another"). These 70 spiritual being shepherds; are judged in (1En 90:22-25). It is not clear if these are 70 different beings at the same time or in succession. Nickelsburg sees these as 70 periods of time. He bases this on (Jer 25:11-12; 29:10; Dan 9:2, 24) (N1 pg. 391-392). That they are periods of time is more evident in (90:1-27). Origen responds to Celsus, regarding this reference to the "sixty or seventy" in (*Cels* 5.52).

[1818] **The loyalty of the seventy shepherds is here tested by God. Will they destroy Israel, in order to enhance their domains, or obey God's limits on their treatment of His people.**

[1819] This "one" is most likely Michael; the prince of Israel (see Dan 10:21 and 1En 90:22). Black postulates that instead of "he summoned another one" the text may have read: "And he called a watcher, one of the seven white ones." Stuckenbruck proposes that this scribe may have been identified by early readers as Enoch himself (P pg. 326-327). He proposes this as a partial explanation for the Son of Man wording in 71:14.

[1820] The shepherds of the nations treated the dispersed Jews in different ways. The 70 celestial beings in charge of those nations have records strictly kept against them individually to memorialize their obedience to God's instructions. **God does not just test humans, but also high heavenly beings. That "gods" are accountable to God for their actions in regard to man, is evident in Psalm 82.**

[1821] Here it becomes apparent that these seventy appointed beings serve for defined periods of time as shepherds of Israel. "The first period of the angelic shepherds, which runs from 671/661-587/577 B.C.E. is initiated by Manasseh's apostacy and concludes after Nebuchadnezzar's destruction of Jerusalem and the exile to Babylon" (N1 pg. 393). Lions = Chaldeans lead by Nebuchadnezzar.

into the hands of the lions.[1822]

Excursus: The seventy shepherds of the nations.

Israel was given to the seventy shepherds (heavenly beings) of the nations and dispersed among them. (Zech 10:3; 11:4-9, 15-17; Jer 23:1-6; 25:34-36 and Ezek 34) have similar imagery but the shepherds appear to be human rather than heavenly beings. God here gives his special portion over to the "gods" they so desired in their false worship of the gods of the nations. That 70 beings rule the nations, is drawn from (Genesis 10 and Deut 32:8-9). "When the Most High gave to the nations their inheritance, when he divided mankind, he fixed the borders of the peoples according to the number of the sons of God. But the LORD's portion is his people," (Deut 32:8-9; See Deut[J] and LXX) This concept is seen in Sirach also: "He divided the nations of the whole earth. For every nation he appointed a ruler, but Israel is the Lord's portion" (Sir 17:17). It is also found in (Jub 15:31-32). This deepens and expands the imagery of Christ as the good shepherd[1823] who rescues the sheep from the negligent and wicked shepherds as was predicted (Ezek 34:11-24; Jer 23:5-6). Christ is the good shepherd, who will lead His elect out of the midst of the pagan nations ruled by the "gods of the nations."

The Destruction of the First Temple and Babylonian Exile

66 The lions and the tigers ate, and swallowed, the greater part of those Ps 80:13; 2Kgs 24:10-16
sheep, and the wild boars devoured along with them;[1824] and they Barn 16:5; 1Esdr 4:45; Ps 137:7 Obad 10-14
burned that tower and demolished that house.[1825] 93:8; 2Kgs 25:1-20; Jer 52:12-14
67 I grieved[1826] exceedingly on account of the tower, and because the 2Chr 36:19-22; 1Esdr 1:55
house of the sheep had been demolished. From then on, I was unable to 85:4; 2Bar 32:2-4
see whether those sheep were going into that house.
68 The shepherds and their servants delivered those sheep to all the 89:59; Jer 12:9-11
wild beasts, to be devoured. Each one of them received in his time a
definite number: and for each of them, that "other one" recorded in a 89:61-62
book how many of the sheep each one of them destroyed.

[1822] This imagery mirrors (Ezek 34:7-10). "Therefore, you shepherds, hear the word of the LORD: As I live, declares the Lord GOD, surely because my sheep have become a prey, and my sheep have become food for all the wild beasts, since there was no shepherd, and because my shepherds have not searched for my sheep, but the shepherds have fed themselves, and have not fed my sheep, therefore, you shepherds, hear the word of the LORD: Thus says the Lord GOD, Behold, I am against the shepherds, and I will require my sheep at their hand and put a stop to their feeding the sheep. No longer shall the shepherds feed themselves. I will rescue my sheep from their mouths, that they may not be food for them."

[1823] (Jn 10:11, 14).

[1824] Wild boars=Edom. This verse indicates that the Edomites were involved with the Chaldeans in the burning of the first Temple. This involvement is not found in the historical books of Kings and Chronicles but is found in (1 Esdras 4:45): "Thou also hast vowed to build up the temple, which the Edomites burned when Judea was made desolate by the Chaldees." Also (Ps 137:7) "Remember, O LORD, against the Edomites the day of Jerusalem, how they said, 'Lay it bare, lay it bare, down to its foundations!'" Animosity toward the Edomites is evident in other biblical texts. (Ezek 25:12-14; 35:1-15; Obad 10-14)

[1825] This is the Babylonian destruction of Solomon's Temple, with the city and walls of Jerusalem in 586 BC.

[1826] "Grieved" "Ethiopic *hazana* can be used of grief and sorrow or of anger and vexation" (BL pg. 272).

69 Every one of them killed and destroyed many more than was 89:60; Isa 40:2; Zech 1:15
decreed,[1827] and I began to weep and lament because of those sheep. Jer 13:17; Lk 19:41-42; Rev 5:4
70 In my vision I saw that one who wrote, how he made a record of Jer 25:12-14
each one that was destroyed by those shepherds, day after day. He carried 89:63; Ezek 34:1-10
the entire book up to the Lord of the sheep, laying it down and displaying
the record of everything they had done—all that each one of them had 99:3
taken away, and all that they had given over to destruction.
71 The book was read before the Lord of the sheep, and he took the 81:1-2; 89:77; 90:20; Jn 10:1-17
book from his hand, read it, sealed it, and put it away;[1828] 9:11; Dan 12:4; Rev 5-6

The Rebuilding of Jerusalem and Impure Temple worship

72 and from it I saw that the shepherds had been pasturing for twelve
hours.[1829] Behold three[1830] of those sheep returned, entered, Ezra 1-6; Neh 1-4
and began to build up all that had fallen down of that house. The wild 1Esdr 5:47-7:15
boars[1831] tried to hinder them, but they could not. Ezra 3-6; Neh 2:19; 4:1-5; 6:1-14
73 They began again to build as before, and they raised up that tower,[1832]
and it was named the high tower; and they began again to place a table CD 4:17-5:19
before the tower, but all the bread on it was polluted and not pure.[1833] 89:50; Mal 1:7, 12; TMos 4:8

[1827] **The belief that Israel received punishment more than they were due, is also found in (Isa 40:2) "that she has received from the LORD's hand double for all her sins." Also, (Zech 1:15) "And I am exceedingly angry with the nations that are at ease; for while I was angry but a little, they furthered the disaster."**

[1828] **The apparent inaction belies the plan to send Jesus the good shepherd (Jn 10:1-17); who will change everything by His first coming, and then in the final judgement when the book is finally opened (1En 90:20).** That a book of judgment exists, that is sealed, can also be found in (Dan 12:4 and Rev 5-6).

[1829] "The second period of the shepherds' activity runs from 587/577 to 426/416 B.C.E" (N1 pg. 394). Olson has a different starting date. He divides the four periods of angel rule into 12, 23, 23, and 12 hours. He begins period one at the "first regnal year of Nebuchadnezzar (650-604 BCE: cf. Jer 25:1). He ends that period at the beginning of the rebuilding of the temple after the exile. "If each hour represents seven years, the numbers come out right (12X7= 84 years: 604-520 BCE)" (OL pg. 202).

[1830] All manuscripts have three here, but manuscript 2080 has a correction over the sign for 2 which some scholars take as the original reading (NV2 pg. 389). In addition, the numbers two and three are often confused in Ethiopic. If it does indeed read three, the identity of these three is uncertain. Nickelsburg postulates they were Zerubbabel, and Jeshua (Ezra 5:2; 1Esdr 6:1-2) who were involved in rebuilding the temple. The third person is likely Sheshbazzar (Ezra 1:8-11; 5:14-16; 1Esdr 2:15; 6:18-20), who lead the return and who is said to have laid the foundations of the temple (Ezra 5:14-16; 1Esdr 6:18-20; cf. 1Esdr 2:12-15) (N1 pg. 394). For the possibility of the two being Ezra and Nehemiah see (Sir 49:11-13 and 2Mac 2:13).

[1831] The wild boars are elsewhere identified as Edomites. The author may know of an oral tradition involving the Edomites trying to prevent the rebuilding of the temple, but it is not found in the Bible or other ancient texts. (1Esdr 2:16-18), implicates the Samaritans as those seeking to prevent the rebuilding of the temple. (Neh 2:9-10 and 4:1-5) indicate an alliance lead by Sanballat the Horonite and Tobiah the Ammonite, that opposed the rebuilding of the wall. Israel and Judah, at the time, were part of what was known as the "province Beyond the River" (Neh 2:9; Ezra 6:6). (Ezra 4:7, 17; and 6:6) names those who were in opposition to the building of the temple, but none are identified specifically as Edomites. But a hint of Edomite involvement may be found in 1Esdr 4:50, where Darius commands the Edomites to give over the Jewish villages which they held.

[1832] This is the building of the second temple.

[1833] **"Employing language possibly taken from Mal 1:7 and 12, the author asserts that from its inception the cult of the Second Temple did not follow correct laws of ritual purity" (N1 pg. 395). See also the Dead Sea Scrolls (CD 4.17-5.20, and CD 6.11-20 (W pg. 55-57)) for a similar view from the authors of the Damascus**

74 Besides all these things, the eyes of the sheep had become so blind 89:32, 41, 53
that they could not see, and similarly even their shepherds, and they
were handing over their sheepfolds to severe destruction, and the flock
was trampled underfoot and devoured.
75 Yet the Lord of the sheep remained unmoved while they were 89:58; Ezek 34:12
scattered over the fields, mingling with the beasts,[1834] and they Ps 44:11; 1Pet 2:25
(the shepherds) could not rescue them from of the hands of the beasts.
76 The one who was recording the book brought it up, displayed it,
and read it aloud in the mansions of the Lord of the sheep. And he 89:16
implored and petitioned him on behalf of the sheep as he showed him 99:3
all the deeds of the shepherds, and he gave testimony before him 90:17
against all the shepherds.[1835]
77 And he took the actual book and laid it down beside Him and 9:11; 81:1-2; 89:70-71, 90:20
departed.[1836] Rev 20:12

From Alexander the Great into the Second Century

90 1 I continued watching until thirty-five[1837] shepherds had pastured 89:59
in this manner, and they all completed their respective times like
the first ones. Then others received them into their hands to tend
them in their respective times, each shepherd in his own period.
2 After this, I saw in my vision all the birds of heaven coming; 1Mac 1:1-9; Isa 34:11 LXX
eagles, falcons, ibises,[1838] and ravens, but the eagles[1839] led all *Ant* 12.1.1; Dan 8:8; 11:4
the other birds. They began to devour those sheep, and to dig out their TJud 21:8
eyes and eat their flesh.[1840] 1Mac 1:10-64

Document. This is evidence for a dissident tradition in turn of the era Judaism; that Jesus was sympathetic to, if not a part of (Mt 21:12-13; 23; Mk 11:15-16, 27-28; 12:38-40; 13:1-2; Lk 11:37-12:3; 19:45-47; 20:46-47; Jn 2:13-17). On priestly corruption (cf. 2Bar 10:18; 68:6; Ezek 22:26; *Ant* 18.2.2 §§33-35; Jer 5:31; 6:13; Lam 4:13).

[1834] **This refers to intermarriage with other nations (Ezra 9-10). Foreigners were prohibited from serving in the temple. In a related way, if Nephilim seed was still mixed with mankind, it would have been imperative that the pure line of humans be preserved. God is still silent and unmoved as he was before the exile.**

[1835] Olson reckons the second period (which is 23 hours) as being from the beginning of the second temple's construction to "359 BCE when Phillip II of Macedon came to the throne." "The hours remain seven years each (23 X 7 = 161 years: 520-359 BCE)" (OL pg. 202).

[1836] **The book is laid aside, waiting to be opened on the day of judgement** (1En 90:20, Rev 20:12).

[1837] All manuscripts are corrupt and say thirty-seven, but it should obviously be 35 (12+23). Note the total is 58 in 90:5 which would assume this is thirty-five. Most translators emend this to thirty-five as is done here.

[1838] Ibises ሆባይ (*hobay*) = Egyptians. (See Ant 2.10.2 §§ 246-247; PrEv 9.27.4ff) The serpent eating ibis was purportedly a symbol of the god Thoth, and the ibis cult itself was still thriving in the Greco-Roman period—excavations at Saqqara indicate upward of four million ibises mummified in the necropolis, and the Ptolemaic-era archive of Hor includes a reference to food for 60,000 ibises. (Smelik, K. A. D. 1979. *The Cult of the Ibis in the Graeco-Roman Period. With Special Attention to the Data from the Papyri*. in Studies in Hellenistic Religions pg. 303-325. See also Dungan E., 2023. *Ibises and Egypt in the Animal Apocalypse: A new identification*. Journal for the Study of the Pseudepigrapha 33.1, pgs. 3-18)

[1839] Eagles= "Ptolemies, whose coins regularly display an eagle on their reverse side" (N1 pg. 396).

[1840] "In the third period, which runs from 426/416 to 265/255 B.C.E., the historical events of note are the arrival of the Macedonians and the results of their oppressive activity" (N1 pg. 395). Olson sees these 23 periods as spanning from Alexander the Great to the takeover of Palestine by the Seleucid dynasty. Thus 23 X 7=161 years from 359-198 BC (OL pg. 204).

3 The sheep cried out because their flesh was being devoured by the birds. And as for me, I cried and protested in my sleep because of that shepherd[1841] who tended the sheep. Ps 79:1-3
4 I continued watching until those sheep were devoured by the dogs[1842] and eagles and ibises, and they left on them not a bit of flesh or skin or or sinew till only their bones stood there bare; then their bones too fell to the earth and the sheep became few. 103:9, 15; Sir 50:26 Mic 3:2-3 Ezek 37:1-14
5 I watched until twenty-three shepherds had undertaken the pasturing and had completed in their respective times fifty-eight periods.

Maccabean Revolt to the Kingdom of the Messiah

6 But behold, the white sheep gave birth to lambs![1843] And these began to open their eyes to see, and to cry to the sheep.[1844] Jub 23:26; CD 1:7-11 93:10; Dan 11:33-35; 12:3, 10
7 But even though they cried out to them, the sheep did not listen to their words, but were exceedingly deaf, and their eyes were extremely and severely blinded. Isa 53:6
8 Then in the vision, I saw that the ravens swooped down on those lambs and seized one of them.[1845] They dashed the sheep in pieces and ate them. 1Mac 1 2Mac 4:34-37
9 I looked until those lambs grew horns,[1846] but the ravens[1847] crushed their horns; and I saw until there sprouted a great horn on one of the sheep, and this opened their eyes![1848] Dan 7:8; 8:3-9 1Mac 2:1-3:9; Ezek 29:21

[1841] "That shepherd" is an especially brutal ruler who reigns under an angel shepherd who should have been protecting Israel. Dillman speculates that the identity of this shepherd is either Antigonius or Ptoemaeus (Black pg. 274-275).

[1842] Dogs=Philistines. Evidence that the Philistines were still an identifiable threat to Israel at this late time can be found in (Sir 50:26). Also 1 Maccabees, written around 100 BC, mentions "the land of the Philistines" in (1 Mac 3:24, 41; 4:22; and 5:66, 68). (1 Mac 10:83-85) mentions Jonathan Maccabeus (died 143/142 BC) as burning the temple of Dagon in Azotus, indicating a strong Philistine identity at that time. "The curse of the Philistines recorded in (Jub 24:28-33) attests to the animosity still felt for the Philistines in this period" (T pg. 347).

[1843] "This reform minded younger generation has often been identified with the Hasidim (1Mac 2:42-44; 7:13-17; 2 Mac 14:6), an originally pacifistic group which later endorsed armed revolt against the Seleucids" (OL pg. 204) (See also T pg. 104-105, 109-115). They may also be the parent group of the Yahad (E pg. 274). The sheep that did not listen would be the Jewish leadership. Their appeal would be to avoid apostacy by resisting the brutal persecution by Antiochus IV (it was even enforced by the high priest) which imposed Hellenistic practices on the Jews.

[1844] Nickelsburg comments concerning 1En 90:6-19. "This section recounts events in what the author expects to be the last years of human history before the eschaton. According to my chronology, these years, characterized by the activity of the final twelve shepherds, would be 265/255 to 181/171 B.C.E. But the present form of this section recounts, at least in part, events from the wars of Judas Maccabeus (166-161 B.C.E.), which appear to have been added to an earlier form of the Vision before Judas's death in 160" (N1 pg. 396). Olson sees the span of this period being from the "Seleucid takeover of Palestine to the onset of the last judgement." He here uses three and a half years for each period rather than seven. He thus calculates "(12 X 3 ½ =42 years, ca. 198-156)" (OL pg. 204).

[1845] "One of those lambs" This is believed by some to be the high priest, Onias III, murdered in 171 BC (2Mac 4:34-35) (E pg. 299). Others think it is referring to the martyrdom of the 90-year-old Eleazar who wished to serve as an example to those younger (2 Mac 6:18-31).

[1846] "The reference is unmistakably to the rise of the Maccabees" (BL pg.276).

[1847] Ravens=Syrians.

[1848] "Great horn on one of those sheep," This is Judas Maccabeus, hero of the Jewish war of independence (167-160 BC). He is not mentioned at all in the Book of Daniel and the Maccabees are only a little help (Dan 11:34). For ram or sheep in verses 90:10, 11 and 14, Baty has "dabela" which is a mountain goat with a large single horn.

10 They had vision, and their eyes were opened! That sheep cried out
to the flock, and the rams saw it and they all rallied to it. 2Mac 8:1; 1Mac 2:42-43
11 In spite of this, all those eagles, and falcons, and ravens, and ibises,
still kept tearing the sheep in pieces and swooping down upon them to Barn. 10:4
devour them. The sheep kept silent, but the rams protested and cried out.
12 Then the ravens battled and contended with that sheep. They sought
to lay low its horn, but they did not prevail over it.[1849] 1Mac 3:10-4:27
13 I watched them until the shepherds, the eagles,[1850] the falcons, and the
ibises came; and they called upon the ravens to smash the horn of that
ram,[1851] and they did battle and made war with it. But it fought back 1Mac 7:41, 42; 2Mac 12:22
against them, and cried out that its help might come.[1852] 1Mac 4:30-33; 2Mac 11:6-12
14 I continued watching till that man[1853] who had been recording the 89:61; DeSpec 27
names of the shepherds and bringing (them) before the presence of the
Lord of the sheep, came to the aid of the ram, revealing everything to it. *Ant* 13.10.3 §§282-283
He had come down for the help of that ram.
15 As I continued to watch, the Lord of the sheep came upon them in 89:16, 20; 2Mac 11:6-12; 12:22
wrath![1854] All who saw him fled, and they all fell into darkness before *Ant* 12.7.3-5; Ps 68:1
his face.[1855] 1Mac 5:40-44?; 2Mac 12:20-23?
16 All the eagles, falcons, ravens, and ibises assembled, and brought
with them all the wild sheep.[1856] So they all came together and
helped each other to smash to bits the horn of that ram.[1857]
17 Then I saw that man who wrote the book at the command of the Lord, 89:71, 76; Rev 20:12
until he opened the book of the destruction which those twelve last Ezek 34:1-10; Dan 7:10
shepherds had wrought, and he showed before the Lord of the sheep 89:63
that they had destroyed much more than their predecessors.[1858] Jn 21:15-17

[1849] This verse is proof that this text was written during the Jewish war of independence (167-160 BC) but before the death of Judas Maccabeus at the Battle of Elasa fought in April 160 BC; since his death is not recorded here (cf. 1Mac 9:1-21; *Ant* 12.11.1-2 §§ 420-434).

[1850] Eagles=Macedonians

[1851] Horn of that ram=Judas Maccabeus

[1852] Tiller (T pg. 63-78) presents the case that (90:16-18) was original to the text based on the authors prophecy of how events would play out. Tiller also postulates that (90:13-15) was added by a later scribe recounting the actual battles with the intervention of God and angels.

[1853] This is an angelic scribe, assumed to be the archangel Michael, the protector of Israel.

[1854] This appears to be referencing the battle of Beth-zur (early 164 BC) described in (2Mac 11:6-12, and *Ant* 12.7.3-5 §§.298-315) where the Lord sent an angel to save Israel or the battle at Carnaim (mid 163 BC) where God himself intervened (2Mac 12:20-23). For a discussion see (T pg. 74-76; 360).

[1855] Some Ethiopic manuscripts read "(his) shadow" in place of "darkness."

[1856] Most manuscripts read "wild sheep" but Nickelsburg emends to "wild beasts" since "wild sheep" does not appear otherwise in 1 Enoch. Some read "wild asses." If "Sheep of the field" or "wild sheep" is the correct reading, they symbolize the apostate Hellenized Jews who opposed Judas Maccabeus.

[1857] For verse 90:16 Isaac has: "All the eagles, vultures, ravens, and kites gathered, with all the sheep of the field lining up with them; and having thus come together in unity, all of them cooperated in order to smash the horn of the ram."

[1858] The last twelve spiritual beings/watchers/angels who reign over Israel are considered worse than those previous.

Messiah Returns in Judgement

18 As I continued to watch, the Lord of the sheep[1859] came to them!   1Pet 5:4; Rev 12:5; Bar 2:34
He took in his hand the staff of his wrath,[1860] and he struck the earth,   Num 16:31-33; 20:11 4Ezra 13:32-38
and the earth split open! All the beasts, and all the birds of heaven, fell   1:7; 56:8; Isa 11:4; Zech 14:4
away from among those sheep, and they sank into the (cleft) earth,   89:27; 99:2; Joel 3:2, 12
and it closed over them.   Ezek 30:24-25
19 While I continued to look on, a great sword was presented to those   91:12; Rev 6:4; 19:14-15; DivInst 7.19
sheep, and the sheep proceeded against all the beasts of the field to slay   38:5; 2Mac 15:15-16; Ps 149:6-9
them, and all the beasts and the birds of heaven fled before their face.   Zech 12:3-9; Mt 19:28; 25:31
20 Then, as I watched, a throne was erected in the pleasant land,   89:40; Ps 106:24; Dan 11:16, 41
and the Lord of the sheep sat upon it, and he received all of the   47:3; 81:1-2; 89:71; Zech 7:14
sealed books.[1861]   Dan 7:10; 12:4; Rev 5-6; 22:10
And they were opened before the Lord of the sheep.[1862] [1863] [1864]   Jub 30:22; Rev 5:9; 6:1; 20:12
21 The Lord summoned those men, the first seven white ones,[1865] and   20; 81:5; 87:2; Tob 12:15
commanded them to bring those stars before him, beginning with the first   10:4, 12; Rev 8:2
star which led the way,[1866] all the stars whose private parts were like   19:1; 86:1-4; 88:3; Ezek 23:20
those of horses, and they brought them all before him.   Jer 5:7-8
22 Then speaking to that man who had been writing before him—who
was one of those seven white ones—he said to him: "Seize those seventy   89:59; *Cels* 5.52; Jer 25:34-38
shepherds[1867] to whom I delivered the sheep, and who took and killed
more than I commanded them."   89:61
23 And behold I saw them all bound, and they all stood before him.   88:1, 3
24 Judgement was exacted first over the stars, and they were judged   53-56; Job 25:5
and found guilty. Off they went to the place of condemnation,   Rev 20:10
and they were hurled into an abyss, full of blazing fire,   10:6, 13; 18:11; Mt 25:41
and fiery pillars.[1868]   21:7-10; 89:59
25 And those seventy shepherds[1869] were judged, and found to be sinners,   Jer 49:19; 50:44; *Cels* 5.52

[1859] **Jesus Christ was called the good shepherd, great shepherd or chief shepherd (Jn 10:11, 14; Heb 13:20-21; 1Pet 5:4). He asks Peter to care for His sheep in (Jn 21:15-17). The imagery of the good shepherd as opposed to these 70 evil shepherds would not have been lost on the audience listening to Jesus.**

[1860] This is both a shepherd's staff and a royal scepter for the Lord of the sheep see 1En 90:20. That the earth splits open, reminds the reader of Korah's rebellion in (Num 16:31-33).

[1861] According to the Testament of Abraham (ca. AD 100) these are quite substantial books. "On the table lay a book whose thickness was six cubits, while its breath was ten cubits" (TAb A 12:7). (Cf. 4Q530 2.2.18)

[1862] **The opening of these books indicates that judgement is about to begin. Judgement has been long postponed as God laid the books aside (1En 89:71, 77). As in Revelation (5:9; 6:1), opening the seals indicates the beginning of judgement.** Cf. 2 Bar 24:1.

[1863] Here begins an interesting section expressing the author's (a patriotic Jew in 163-164 BC) messianic expectations.

[1864] This brings to mind other judgment scenes in scripture (Mt 25:31-46; Rev 20:11-15 and in 1En 53-56, 62).

[1865] The seven archangels (cf. Tob 12:15; Rev 4:5; 8:2, 6).

[1866] Azâzêl, (1En 10:8).

[1867] Some interpret these 70 shepherds as the 70 members of the Sanhedrin (Num 11:16; 2Chron 19:8; 1Mac 12:6).

[1868] Charles notes: "This final place of punishment is not to be confounded with the preliminary place of punishment in (18:12-16; 19:1-2; 21:1-6). It is that which is mentioned in (10:6; 18:11; 21:7-10; 54:6)" (C pg. 213).

[1869] Some interpret the seventy as watchers who were appointed over the nations (1En 89:59).

TLev 16:1
and they were cast into that fiery abyss. Mt 10:28; 25:41
26 I saw at that time that a similar abyss, full of fire, was opened in the 26:1; 27:1-3; 54:1
middle of the earth,[1870] and they brought those blinded sheep,[1871] and they 90:16; Zech 14:3-5; 2Bar 44:15
were all judged and found guilty and cast into this fiery abyss, and they Mt 18:8-9; 5:22,29,30 Rev 20:15
burned; now this abyss was on the south side of that house.[1872] Mt 10:28; 23:29-36
27 I watched as those sheep were burning; even their bones 48:9; Lam 1:13; Isa 66:24
were burning.[1873]

Destruction of Old Temple, Building of New, and Regathering of Israel

28 I stood up to watch as the old house was folded-up![1874] All the Barn. 16:5
columns were removed and all the beams and ornaments of the house Mt 23:38
were wrapped up along with it. It was taken out and put in a certain place
in the south of the land.[1875] [1876] 1Mac 4:41-48
29 I watched until the Lord of the sheep brought out a new house,[1877] Rev 3:12; 21:2; 10-12; Jub 1:17

[1870] The middle of the earth is Jerusalem (1En 26:1).

[1871] Jews who were blinded to the truth, i.e., apostates. Possibly those who sided with the Greeks in (1En 90:16). (1En 89:32) describes the golden calf worshiping Israelites as blinded.

[1872] **The final judgement will be in Jerusalem, this is the valley of Hinnom, Gehenna. The text reads literally: "this abyss was to the right of that house."** The text assumes that the reader is facing east.

[1873] Charles suggests this verse originally may have read: "I saw those sheep burning, yea their very selves." or, "I saw the sheep themselves burning."

[1874] "Folded-up," Most manuscripts read "he submerged" likely due to a spelling error. One manuscript (Tana) reads "they transformed it." **"The language of 'folding up,' used to describe the demolition of the old Jerusalem, may be meant to imply that it was as temporary as the Tabernacle, something to be used only until the permanent structure could be erected"** (OL pg. 208). In 1Mac 4:43 "the defiled stones of the temple were permanently moved to an unclean place" (T pg. 375-376)

[1875] The old Jerusalem is to be removed. Most of the city was in fact destroyed by the Romans in/after AD 70, but the new Jerusalem will be built by God (90:29; Rev 21:2, 10-14). This prophecy looks forward to a future fulfillment. The temple, even before the destruction of the second temple, was viewed as residing in the bodies of believers (Jn 2:19; 1Cor 3:16-17, 6:19-20; Eph 2:18-22; Rev 21:22; 4Q174 3.1-6; 1QS 8.4-10). There is therefore no need for a third temple. However, an expectation of a new temple can be derived from Old Testament prophecy (Ezek. 40-48; Isa 54:11-12; 60; Hag 2:7-9; Zech 2:6-13).

[1876] **This verse is paraphrased in The Epistle of Barnabas (probably AD 70-79; but certainly AD 70-135) and is called scripture. The author of Barnabas obviously considered it fulfilled prophecy. "Again, it was revealed that the city and the temple and the people of Israel were destined to be handed over. For the scripture says: "And it will happen in the last days that the Lord will hand over the sheep of the pasture and the sheepfold and their watchtower to destruction. And it happened just as the Lord said" (Barn 16:5). Viewed spiritually and without a strict chronology, 90:19-42 is a remarkable partially fulfilled prophecy concerning the Messiah who transforms those who follow Him (37-38), final judgement (20-27), the destruction of Jerusalem (28), resurrection of the elect, destroyed then assembled (33), Christ's resurrection (37-38), sanctification (33), salvation of the gentiles (beasts, birds, 30, 33), redemption (32), exaltation (30, 37-38), and the New Jerusalem (29, 33-36).**

[1877] This house (Jerusalem) has no tower (temple). In Ezek 40-48 and the Temple Scroll (11Q19 29.7-10; 36; 40-42 (W pgs. 606-612) God builds a much larger physical temple. **The New Jerusalem in 1 Enoch 90:29-36 does not contain a tower (temple). The only parallel to this is in Rev 21:22. "And I saw no temple in the city, for its temple is the Lord God the Almighty and the Lamb."** Also "And he carried me away in the spirit to a great, high mountain, and showed me the holy city Jerusalem coming down out of heaven from God" (Rev 21:10). **The idea of a new Jerusalem coming down from heaven was a familiar one in later Jewish Apocalypses** (cf. 4 Ezra 7:26; 13:36; 2Bar 32:2-4; Rev 21:2, 10) (C pg. 214). **But it appears the idea of a New Jerusalem originates in this text as possibly an amplification of (Isa 65:18).**

greater and loftier than that first, and raised it up on the site of the former	Heb 11:10; 12:22; 13:14 1Cor 5:1; 2Bar 32:4
which had been folded up. All its columns were new, and its beams	2Bar 4:2-7; Hag 2:7-9; Isa 54:11
were new, and its ornaments were new, and larger than those of the first,	Ezek 40-48; Tob 14:5; 5Q15
the old one which he had taken away. And all the sheep	TDan 5:12; Rev 21:22; Isa 60
were within it.[1878] [1879] [1880]	4Ezra 7:26; 13:36; Mic 4:1
30 I saw all the sheep that remained.[1881] And all the beasts of the earth,	Mic 4:6-7; 4Ezra 6:25-26; 12:34
and all the birds of heaven, were falling down and bowing down before	10:21; Dan 7:14, 27
those sheep,[1882] making petition to them and obeying them	Zech 2:11; 8:23; 14:16 1QM 12.14; 1QM 19.6-7; Rev 21:24; 2Bar 72:2-6
in every respect.[1883]	Isa 2:2-3; 11:10; 14:2; Zech 8:23 Isa 66:12,19-21; Mic 4:2
31 After that, those three who were clothed in white (the ones who had	Rev 3:4-5; 11:3-12
brought me up earlier) seized me by my hand, and also the hand of that	87:2-3; 4Ezra 6:26
ram[1884] was holding on to me, and they set me down in the midst of	89:52; Rev 11:3-4
those sheep who were free of condemnation.[1885]	Rom 8:1
32 All of those sheep were white, and their wool was abundant and	Isa 1:26; 4:3; 60:21; 1Cor 6:11

[1878] Some manuscripts very plausibly read: "And the Lord of the sheep was in the midst of it" (cf. Isa 8:18; Ezek 43:9; Joel 3:17; Zeph 3:17). Justin Martyr appears to be referencing this passage in *Dialogue with Trypho* 80.

[1879] **Ethiopian Christianity interprets the new house as referring spiritually to the church** (N1 pg. 105).

[1880] Did Herod see himself as fulfilling this prophecy when he enlarged the 2nd temple?

[1881] Isaac has "survived." Many Christians survived the siege of Jerusalem. Eusebius asserts that they were warned by an oracle to flee to Perea and settle in Pella (*HE* 3.5).

[1882] In place of "bowing down" both I and N have "worshiping."

[1883] **This idea is found in Revelation**: "By its light will the nations walk, and the kings of the earth will bring their glory into it," (Rev 21:24).

[1884] "Verse 31 presents two problems. The first is the identity of the ram. Is it Judas Maccabeus or is it Elijah, who had ascended to paradise to bring Enoch down. That the ram is Elijah seems most likely, since there is no indication that Judas has ascended to paradise to bring Enoch down. In that case we have here an early attestation of a tradition that joins Enoch and Elijah as eschatological agents" (N1 pg. 405). **This would argue that the two witnesses of Rev 11:3-13 are Enoch and Elijah. Olson observes: "The two anonymous "witnesses" in Revelation 11 are often identified as Moses and Elijah, but preference for such an interpretation is relatively recent. From the 2nd c. CE. until nearly modern times, the 'two witnesses' were almost exclusively identified as Enoch and Elijah"** (OL pg. 210). An example is (4Ezra 6:25-26) which can only be referencing Enoch and Elijah. "And it will be that whoever remans after all these things that I have told you of, he will be saved, and will see my salvation, and the end of my world. And they will see the men that have been taken up, who have not tasted death from their birth; and the heart of the inhabitants will be changed and turned into another meaning." Tertullian (AD 200) was of the same opinion: **"Enoch no doubt was translated, and so was Elijah; nor did they experience death: it was postponed, (and only postponed,) most certainly: they are reserved for the suffering of death, that by their blood they may extinguish Antichrist"** (*De anima* 50). Hippolytus (early 3rd century) also agrees: "By one week, therefore, he meant the last week which is to be at the end of the whole world of which week the two prophets Enoch and Elias will take up the half. For they will preach 1,260 days clothed in sackcloth, proclaiming repentance to the people and to all the nations" (*On Christ and Antichrist* 43). **"The Eastern Orthodox Church still teaches emphatically that Enoch and Elijah will return before Christ's coming"** (OL pg. 213).

[1885] An example of the majority reading for this last line is provided by Knibb, similar to some others. "and put me down in the middle of those sheep before the judgement was held." This present text follows a minority reading which reflects an emendation by Black, accepted also by Olson. Since the verse begins with a time indicator "after that" it would be extremely awkward to now go back in time to before the sheep were burned (1En 90:27). In addition, all the sheep in the following verse are pure so they would not be subject to condemnation. "Black's emendation involves deleting a single word from the text" (OL pg. 213). **This is the concept of grace, since all humans have already been identified as sinners in 1Enoch 81:5 (The Book of the Heavenly Luminaries).**

pure.[1886] Deut 30:3-8; Rev 7:13-14
33 All that had been destroyed[1887] and dispersed, and[1888] the beasts 51:1; Ezek 34:11-16; Dan 12:2
of the field, and all the birds of heaven, assembled in that house. 10:21; TLev 10:5; Isa 62:3-5
Zech 2:11; 8:7; Is 65:19
2Bar 78:7
TBenj 9:2; Ps 87; Hos 14:7
And the Lord of the sheep rejoiced[1889] with great joy because they had all Mic 4:2, 6-7; Zeph 3:17
Tob 14:6-7; PssSol 17:26
Jer 31:10-11; DialTrypho 139
become good and had returned to his house.[1890] Jn 14:2; Ezek 37:24-28
Isa 49:5-6
34 I continued watching till they laid down that sword,[1891] which had Ezek 34:25-31; Rev 19:14-15
been given to the sheep, and they brought it back into his house, and Mic 4:3, 8; 2Bar 78:7
sealed it up in the presence of the Lord. All the sheep enclosed[1892] Isa 49:19-20; 60:18; 2Mac 2:18
themselves within that house, but it did not contain them all.[1893] Zech 2:4; 10:10; Ezek 36:37-38
35 The eyes of them all were opened, and they saw clearly;[1894] 1Cor 13:12
there was not one among them that did not see.
36 I observed that the house had become large, and spacious, and it was 89:50; 91:13; Jn 14:2
very much full.

Messiah!

37 Then I saw that a white bull was born,[1895] with large horns, and all 85:3; 1Cor 15:45; Rom 5:14

[1886] **These are the saints cleansed by the blood of Christ.**

[1887] **The use of the term "destroyed" indicates that these sheep died and are now resurrected.**

[1888] Nickelsburg emends this "and" to "by" which is not supported by any text. All others have "and," which places all the beasts and birds (gentiles) within the temple. He reasons that "and" makes no sense with the rest of the verse as the beasts and birds could not return to the house, since they were not there to begin with. Nickelsburg also suggests "among" as a possible emendation. I have chosen to remain with "and" based on other passages like (1En 10:21) that include the Gentiles in the New Jerusalem, and the fact that "by" has no textual support. **This passage prophecies a massive conversion of the gentiles, which can only, at this point in history, have only been fulfilled by Christianity.**

[1889] "Rejoiced" (cf. Isa 62:3-5, 65:19; Zeph 3:17).

[1890] This house is the new Jerusalem. Revelation 21:22 is quite clear that there will be no temple in the New Jerusalem. "And I saw no temple in the city, for its temple is the Lord God the Almighty and the lamb." The New Jerusalem, is the Father's house, spoken of by Christ. "In my father's house are many rooms. If it were not so, would I have told you that I go to prepare a place for you? And if I go and prepare a place for you, I will come again and will take you to myself, that where I am you may be also" (Jn 14:2-3). **This verse is referenced in (TLev 10:5). "For the house which the Lord shall choose shall be called Jerusalem, as the book of Enoch the Righteous maintains."**

[1891] **God's ordained warfare, the time of the sword, is concluded (cf. 2Mac 15:15-16). This time of the sword is reflected in Revelation. "And the armies of heaven, arrayed in fine linen, white and pure, were following him on white horses. From his mouth comes a sharp sword with which to strike down the nations, and he will rule them with a rod of iron. He will tread the winepress of the fury of the wrath of God the Almighty" (Rev 19:14-15).**

[1892] In place of "enclosed themselves within" Ethiopic manuscript G has "were invited into."

[1893] Tiller suggests until it did not contain them all (T pg. 382).

[1894] Isaac has: "they saw the beautiful things" in place of "they saw clearly."

[1895] **It is significant that the messiah (white bull) is to be born rather than just appear from heaven. This indicates He is at least partially human. The parallel with the white bull in (1En 85:3) raises the imagery that this is a second Adam (cf. 1Cor 15:45; Rom 5:12-14).** Other passages from the Testament of the Twelve Patriarchs that describe the messiah include TLev 18; and TJud 24.

the beasts of the field and all the birds of the air feared him and made 10:21; Dan 7:13-14; Rev 12:5
petition to him continually. 48:4-5; 1Jn 3:2
38 As I watched, all their species were transformed,[1896] and they all 91:14; John 1:29; Ps 92:10
became white bulls! The first among them became an aurochs,[1897] Deut. 33:17; Rev 5:6; Zech 12:8
1QS 4:22-23
(the aurochs was a great beast and had great black horns on its head); 1Cor 15:21-22
and the Lord of the sheep rejoiced over them and over all the cattle. Ps 80:1
39 And as for me I fell asleep among them; and I awoke.
And I witnessed everything. 81:2-3
40 This then is the vision which I saw while I slept, and I awoke, and
blessed the Lord of righteousness and gave him praise. 22:14; 106:3
41 After that, I wept bitterly, and my tears did not cease until I had no Lk 19:41-42; 2Bar 32:5
more endurance left. They flowed down because of what I had seen,
for everything shall come to pass and be fulfilled. All the deeds of men, TLev 14:1
each in their order, were shown to me.[1898] [1899] TJud 18:1
42 On that night I remembered the first dream,[1900] and I wept because 81:3; Rev 5:4
of it. I was deeply troubled because I had seen that vision."[1901]

Excursus: When a lamb isn't a lamb.

The word this text translates as "Aurochs" in 1En 90:38 has vexed translators for centuries. Everyone agrees that the same word Charles translated as "Lamb" in 1En 90:38 symbolizes

---

[1896] **This is the new birth for Christians. All the elect, Jew and Gentile, will be transformed into the image of Christ (Rom 5:12-21; 1Cor 15:45-50; Phil 3:21; and 1QS 4.20-23).**

[1897] N admits that the text reads "word" in place of aurochs but translates it as ‹leader› in both places. OL and B translate "word" in place of aurochs. C has lamb. I has a noncommittal "something". K correctly postulates that 'word' (*nagar*) is derived ultimately from a transliteration of the Aramaic word for "wild ox" which is what he uses. Both uses of aurochs in this verse in Ethiopic are *nagar*. In Ethiopic it means 'thing, word, deed'. But it is an animal; as is everything else in the animal apocalypse. **In this passage the sheep and all the animals are restored to what their ancestors were; white bulls, and the Messiah is the largest, most glorious and most powerful of them all. Scholars agree this figure is the Messiah. His death is not evident here, but is implied, as the first bull returns as a great and powerful aurochs** (see Michell's reconstruction in the text box below. Mitchell's reconstruction is used in this text (Mitchell, David C. 2021. *Messiah Ben Joseph*, pg. 68). Mitchell makes a convincing case for this animal being an aurochs in (*Messiah Ben Joseph* 2021, pg. 63-68). The resurrection of Christ was prophesied also in (Ps 16:10, Isa 53:10-12, and Hos 6:2). **Putting Messiah to death resulted in Him returning in a vastly more powerful form.**

[1898] Enoch weeps over the apostacy, sin, and judgement he has seen in his vision. This vision may be referenced in the Testament of Levi (TLev 14:1). "And now, my children, I know from the writings of Enoch that in the end-time you will act impiously against the Lord, setting your hands to every evil deed; because of you, your brothers will be humiliated and among all the nations you shall become the occasion for scorn" (OTP1 pg. 793). But see (91:5-9).

[1899] Black notes that: "A free paraphrase of this verse occurs in a Greek Manichean writing (the writer introduces it as an actual quotation from the 'Apocalypse of Enoch')" (BL pg. 280). This was found in a copy of the Greek Cologne Mani Codex, 1 (AD 450) which is thought to have originally been composed in the mid third century AD. The text was discovered in 1969 at an indeterminate spot in the area of Asyūṭ (ancient Lycopolis) in upper Egypt. This unsurprisingly establishes the fact that the Manicheans had appropriated a least the Animal Apocalypse and certainly more of the Book of 1 Enoch in support of their heresy. Augustine was a Manichean in his early life. **The appropriation of 1 Enoch by heretical groups was a factor in the rejection of Enochic texts from Christian literature.**

[1900] The first dream was the cataclysm of the flood (1En 83-84).

[1901] Even though the vision ends very well, from Biblical Enoch's time to the end, much suffering must be endured.

Messiah. Not everyone agrees that it is a lamb. Baty and Olson call it a "word," Nickelsburg agrees, calling it a word. Isaac is least committal and calls it "something." Why then did Knibb translate it as wild-ox? The Ethiopian word is nagar, (thing, word, deed). However, everything in the Animal Apocalypse is; well; an animal. Scholars have been trying to guess the animal. The Ethiopic text was translated from Greek. The Greek word for "word" is *rema.* So the Ethiopic translator translated it as "word". However, the Aramaic word that the Greek was translated from, appears to have been carried over directly into the Greek text. *Rema* in Aramaic is the word for aurochs. Aurochs were ancestors of modern cattle; from modern cattle size, up to a larger size (3000 lbs. or 1361 kg.). They were very fearsome in antiquity, with large black horns. They are now extinct (since 1627) with the last one surviving in central Poland. They were native to Europe, the Levant, North Africa and the Indian subcontinent.

Figure 1: A bronze statue of an Aurochs in Rakvere, Estonia. "These are a little below the elephant in size, and of the appearance, color, and shape of a bull," "Their strength and speed are extraordinary; they spare neither man nor wild beast which they have espied." Julius Caesar in Commentarii de bello Gallico

Why would this animal be used? (Deut. 33:17) provides a clue. As Moses blesses the tribe of Joseph he says, "A firstborn bull—he has majesty, and his horns are the horns of a wild ox; with them he shall gore the peoples, all of them, to the ends of the earth: they are the ten thousands of Ephraim, and they are the thousands of Manasseh." Speaking of this passage, David C. Mitchell says of (1 Enoch 90:37-38); "The passage can now be interpreted as follows. The Messiah is born. His representation as an ox shows his lineage from Joseph, Ephraim and Joshua. His whiteness shows that he is a faultless *tsadik* (cf. Isa. 1.18; Ps 51:7); his large horns represent his majesty and power; the homage of the beasts and birds represents his acclamation among the nations. Nonetheless, this unblemished creature is destined to die, for he is a firstborn bull. Why is he a firstborn? He is called the 'first' among all those transformed and since his birth brings about the transformation of all other creatures into his own likeness, he is evidently the first of a new species."[1902]

Joseph's life is a powerful type of the life of Christ. He was despised out of jealousy, thrown in a pit (killed) by the sons of Israel. He was sold by those close to him for silver. He was separated from his father, taken away to Egypt, resisted temptation, falsely accused, arrested, "resurrected"

[1902] Mitchell, Daniel C. 2021. *Messiah Ben Joseph*, 2021 pg. 68.

from jail and placed at the right hand of power. He was found alive (second coming) and reunited with his brethren. He then showed compassion and forgave his brothers. Messiah ben Joseph is the suffering Messiah that Mitchell establishes was expected by the Jews.
The wild ox, aurochs, is a symbol of Joseph. Mitchell therefore translates this passage as follows; "37 And I saw that a white bull was born, with large horns, and all the beasts of the field and all the birds of the air feared him and made petition to him all the time. 38 And I saw till all their generations were transformed, and they all became white bulls; and the first among them became an aurochs (the aurochs was a great beast and had great black horns on its head); and the Lord of the sheep rejoiced over them and over all the oxen."[1903]

[1903] Ibid. These white bulls are the equivalent of the wise "*maskilim*" of Daniel 12:3 who will shine "like the stars forever and ever" as both books are contemporaneous with each other and the persecution by Antiochus Epiphanes.

The Admonitions of Enoch

Background of *The Admonitions of Enoch*, aka *Apocalypse of Enoch* or *The Epistle of Enoch* 91-105

Original language: Aramaic, translated into Greek and then into Ethiopic (Ge' ez).
Author and provenance: An educated, "wise", Jew in Judea (98:9; 99:10; 104:12-13) "This elite status notwithstanding, he is a powerful and impassioned protagonist for the poor and oppressed."[1904]
Date: 170-130s BC. "Thus, the Epistle of Enoch (1En 91-105) includes an apocalyptic discourse known as the Apocalypse of Weeks (93:1-10; 91:11-17) that was probably written around 170 B.C.E."[1905] "Dead Sea Scroll fragments indicate a latest possible date for the 'Admonitions' not much past 100 BCE."[1906]
Important notes: Numerous fragments of the *Admonitions of Enoch* were found in the Dead Sea Scrolls. Approximately 18% of the text is covered in the Dead Sea Scrolls. The preserved leaves of the 4th century Greek Chester Beatty-Michigan Papyrus contain the text of 1 Enoch 97:6-107:3. An estimate of the original size of that codex suggests that it contained the whole of the Epistle of Enoch plus the story of Noah's birth (chaps. 91 or 92-107).[1907] "Language and phraseology in the Epistle have been drawn from the earlier books of 1 Enoch. From this one may draw two conclusions. The author of the Epistle knew the earlier parts of the corpus. Second, his allusions presume that his audience knew (about) the accounts of Enoch's visions."[1908] (1En 91:1-10; and 92:3-5) are believed to have been a conclusion to *The Book of Heavenly Luminaries* or less likely *The Book of Dream Visions* that were artificially separated when *The Book of Dream Visions* was inserted in its present location. Speaking of the Greek text, Nickelsburg notes "The text of chapters 97-104 contains more than three dozen haplographies,[1909] often sizable ones" (Nickelsburg, "Enoch 97-104," pg. 153). Chapters 94-104:12 were not attested in Aramaic at Qumran but a Greek copy of 103:3-8 was found. 1En 105 does not appear in the Chester-Beatty/Michigan manuscript of the Epistle, which simply proceeds from 1En 104 into 1En 106. However, (4QEn^c 5 I (M pg. 206-209)) includes the joined text of (104:13-106:2). This indicates that the Admonitions of Enoch included chapter 105, and that the Birth of Noah was joined together with it in antiquity. Portions of chapter 93:3-8 were found in 1939, in a Coptic text ("Antinoë Fragment," TM 109718 / LDAB 109718) consisting of one third of a single leaf, dating from the sixth or seventh century.[1910] Boccaccini sees a major interpolation of section 94:6-104:6. He calls the much shorter mid-second century BCE remainder of the Epistle of Enoch the "Proto-Epistle of Enoch."[1910a] He views this "Proto Epistle" as pre-sectarian ie. before the Qumran Essenes split from the main Essenes and postulated that (94:6-104:6) was added by the main body. However, fragments of 1En 103:3-8

[1904] N1 pg. 428.
[1905] R. pg. 369, Piovanelli.
[1906] OL pg. 17.
[1907] N1 pg. 13, and 21.
[1908] N1 pg. 423.
[1909] A haplography is a scribal error where a letter or group of letters that should be written twice is written once.
[1910] N1 pg. 15, M pg. 81.
1910a Boccaccini, G. 1998. *Beyond the Essene Hypothesis* 104-113. Nickelsburg excludes 92, 94:6-104:9 (E 213).

may have been identified in cave 7. The fragmentary 4Q247 may be a pesher "commentary" on the apocalypse of weeks.

The Admonitions of Enoch (chapters 91-105)

Enoch Addresses his Children

91 1 "Now, my son Methuselah, call to me all your brothers;[1911] 82:1; 83:1
gather together to me all the children of your mother.
For a voice calls me and the spirit is poured out upon me, 14:24; Joel 2:28-29; Acts 2:4
so that I may reveal to you everything 49:1; 51:3; Zech 12:10
that will happen to you until eternity."[1912] Gen 49:1-2
2 At this, Methuselah went and summoned all his brothers to him
and assembled his relatives.
3 Then (Enoch) addressed all the children of righteousness, and said: 1QS 3.20
Hear, O sons of Enoch, all the words of your father,
and listen sincerely to the voice of my mouth; 85:2
for I testify to you and speak to you, my beloved ones.
4 Love uprightness and walk in it.[1913] 94:1
But do not draw near to uprightness with a double heart. 94:3; Jas 1:8; 4:8; $1QH_a$ 12.13-16
Do not even associate with those of a double heart.[1914] 97:4; 104:6; Ps 12:2; Sir 1:28
But walk in righteousness, my children;
and it will guide you along good paths, Prov 4:6-10; Wis 8
and righteousness will be your friend. Sir 7:18-31; 51:13-22

The Judgement of the Deluge

5 For I know that the state of wrong-doing will become increasingly prevalent on the earth,
and a great scourge will be executed on the earth.[1915]
Indeed, all iniquity will come to an end;
but it will be cut off from its roots, 91:11; Deut 29:18-19
and its whole structure will vanish.[1916] 83:4; 90:28
6 But iniquity will again rise to a climax on the earth, Mt 24:12, 37; Lk 17:26

[1911] According to (2 Enoch J 1:10 and 57:2), Methuselah's brothers were Regim, Riman, Gaidad, Ukhan and Khermion.

[1912] The Admonitions of Enoch is in the form of a testament, where a dying patriarch gives admonitions and instructions to those who remain. Enoch did not die, so his testament is pre-departure. A testament is a common form of Jewish literature in the second temple period. Good examples are the *Testaments of the Twelve Patriarchs* and (Gen 49:1-27).

[1913] N and OL have: "Love the truth and walk in it;" This line is placed in either verse 3 or 4 by various translators.

[1914] Isaac has "hypocrites" in place of double minded.

[1915] This scourge or chastisement would be the deluge.

[1916] For the last two lines of 91:5; Isaac has: "all (forms of) oppression will be carried out; and everything shall be uprooted; and every arrow shall fly fast."

and all the works of iniquity and violence and wickedness 2Thes 2:7-12
will dominate for a second time.[1917] 106:19; TLev 14:1; TJud 18:1

The Latter Time of Iniquity and Judgement

7 When sin, iniquity, blasphemy, and injustice of every kind, increase, 2Thes 2:3; 2Tim 3:1-5
along with perversity, apostasy, wickedness and uncleanness, TBenj 9:1; Mt 24:12
a great chastisement will come from heaven upon all these things.[1918] 83:9; Rom 1:18
The Holy Lord will come forth with wrath and punishment, 1:3-4; TMos 10:3
to execute judgement on the earth. Mt 25:12-46; Rev 19:11-20:15
8 In those days' violence[1919] shall be cut off from its roots,[1920] Prov 2:22
as well as the roots of iniquity, together with deceit, 10:14-16
and they will be destroyed from under heaven.
9 All the idols of the nations[1921] will be abandoned TMos 10:7; SibOr 3:606
and the strongholds[1922] will be burned with fire. 2Pet 3:7
They will be eliminated from the entire earth.[1923] [1924] Jer 10:11; Rev 21:8
They will be cast into the judgement of fire, LAE 49:3
and they shall perish in fierce, everlasting judgement. 1Thes 4:13-18

Excursus: Why is the verse numbering of the Admonitions of Enoch so out of order?

"At some point in the transmission of the 'Admonitions of Enoch.' A major displacement of text occurred. Probably a page with (1En 92:3-5; 93:1-10) on the front and (91:11-92:2) on the back was accidentally flipped over" (OL pg. 218). These verses are nearly intact in the DSS, proving conclusively that the sequence in the Ethiopic is wrong. "Verses 10-17 are textually problematic. Vv 11-17 have been displaced from their original location after 93:10 (where they are restored to their proper location in the Nickelsburg translation). Verse 10 appears to have been created to provide a transition when vv 11-17 were moved here." (N pg. 137). Scholars are by no means united in the proper order of the text. Olson orders the text as (91:1-10; 92:3-5; 93:1-10; 91:11-19; 92:1-2; 93:11-14; 94). Nickelsburg as (91:1-10; 91:18-19; 92:1-5; 93:1-10; 91:11-17; 93:11-14; 94). This text reflects Olson's order which is a minority view (See N1 pg. 414-415; and Olson, Daniel C., *Recovering the Original Sequence of 1 Enoch 91-93,* Journal for the Study of

---

[1917] This passage serves as a basis for the "days of Noah" statements by Christ (Mt 24:37; Lk 17:26), as it predicts a second time when the deeds of the antediluvian age will be replicated. This line, and the next one also, appear to be the ones referenced in TLev 14:1 and TJud 18:1; TSim 5:4?; and TBenj 9:1 which would favor the readings of (91:6-7) in this text, but compare (106:19). Charles has: "And transgression shall prevail in a twofold degree." Isaac is similar. Others are as above. (Isa 13:3) can also be read as forecasting a return of the giants to earth in the end times.

[1918] This passage is telling us about an end time (second coming) period of apostacy. While the language does not match; the concept is very similar to Paul's statements in (2Tim 3:1-5).

[1919] OL and K have: "wrongdoing" in place of "violence." Isaac uses: "injustice."

[1920] Instead of "roots" Isaac has: fountain.

[1921] C and I have "heathen" in place of "nations."

[1922] Or towers, (fortified tower) Charles has temples. Black proposes this may have originally read: "the images and effigies of the heathen will be burned with fire."

[1923] This seems to be teaching "the absolute rejection of the heathen," as Charles (C pg. 227) puts it. This would be the idea that no unbelievers will remain on earth after the judgement.

[1924] (1En 91:8b-9) is similar to the only Aramaic verse in otherwise Hebrew Jeremiah (Jer 10:11).

the Pseudepigrapha 11(1993) 69-94; and OL pg. 260). Charles and Beer ordered the text prior to the discovery of the Aramaic DSS and the previously numbered verse orders were proven inaccurate by the Aramaic.

The Resurrection of the Righteous!

10 Then the righteous shall arise from sleep,[1925] 38:2; 92:3; Dan 12:2; Isa 26:19
and wisdom shall arise and be given unto them.[1926 1927] 5:8; 91:10

(92) 3 The righteous shall arise from sleep—arise[1928] 1Cor 15:20-21?
and walk in the paths of righteousness, Eph 5:14
and all their ways of conduct will be in goodness and everlasting mercy.
(92) 4 He will be merciful to the righteous, giving them eternal truth. 1:8; Isa 53:12
He will give them power,
and they will live in goodness and righteousness
and they shall walk in eternal light. 1Jn 1:4-9; 4Q541 9.1.3-5
(92) 5 Sin will be destroyed in darkness forever, 10:5,16, 20; 88:1
and after that day it will never be seen again. 91:17; Rev 21:27

[1925] That the "righteous one" (translated "righteous" here) used in the Ethiopic is in a collective singular, indicates that the righteous as a group, are resurrected all at once, as in the rapture! **If this reading is correct, that makes this the earliest known reference to the rapture! This reading is made more likely, due to the common terminology of falling asleep in 1 Thessalonians 4:13-18; thus, potentially providing a link to this passage. Also, since this passage is occurring in an end time context; which in non-preterist historic Christianity, would be long after the resurrection of Jesus Christ; this is certainly referring to a general resurrection/rapture of the saints at the end of time. This rapture appears to be very near the time of the final judgement (see 1En 91:7-9).** Other, earlier passages, with a similar promise of a general resurrection of the righteous and unrighteous include (Dan 12:2 and Isa 26:19). This text follows the majority reading.

[1926] Dead Sea Scroll fragment (4QEn^g 1 ii) contains (1En. 91:10, 91:18-19 and 92:1-2). (4Q212 Frag 1.Col. 2-5) contains major sections of chapters 91-93. These Aramaic texts have been considered in the development of this text.

[1927] Nickelsburg has 91:10 followed by 91:18 and moves 91:11-17 to between 93:10 and 93:11.

[1928] **It should be noted that due to textual uncertainties, this passage can also be read as a prophecy of the resurrection of the Messiah. The Messiah reading is conceded as a possibility by Olson (OL pg. 218) and followed by Isaac.** "Righteous One" is used of the Messiah/Christ in scripture; (Isa 53:11; Acts 3:14; 7:52; 22:14; and elsewhere in 1En 38:2 and 53:6). That "Righteous One," is a collective singular, may have given rise to the idea in (Col 2:12) "having been buried with him in baptism, in which you were also raised with him through faith in the powerful working of God, who raised him from the dead." Isaac's messianic reading is as follows: "The Righteous One shall awaken from his sleep; he shall arise and walk in the ways of righteousness; and all the way of his conduct shall be in goodness and generosity forever. He will be generous to the Righteous One, and give him eternal uprightness; he will give authority, and judge in kindness and righteousness; and they shall walk in eternal light" (1En 92:3-4). With this interpretation, this passage is then a remarkable prophecy of His resurrection, given the phrase "arise from sleep." That this personage is given authority (92:4 in Issac's reading) perfectly applies, since Christ states numerous times, that he is given authority (Mt 9:6; 28:18; Jn 5:27; 17:2). That this person is given authority to execute judgement (92:4) typically can only apply to the Messiah/Christ (Acts 10:42; 17:31; 2Tim 4:1, 8) although there are exceptions (Wis 3:8; 1Cor 6:2-3). It is unfortunate, that given the extreme importance of this text, the identity of the "righteous" or "Righteous One" is not conclusive. Either reading is quite remarkable in its own way.

The Apocalypse of Weeks

(93) 1 After this, Enoch took up his discourse,[1929] saying:[1930]
(93) 2 "Concerning the sons of uprightness, and the chosen ones — 1:1-3; Eph 1:3-5
of eternity,[1931] and concerning those who have grown up from
the sprout of truth and righteousness, these things will I recount — 10:16; Isa 53:2-3
and make known to you, my sons. I, Enoch, have been shown
everything in a heavenly vision, and from — LAE 29:2-10
the words of the watchers and holy ones I came to know everything,
and from the tablets of heaven, I read and understood everything."[1932] — 47:3; 81:1-2; Jub 5:13
(93) 3 Then Enoch again took up his discourse and said: — 37:1; 60:8; Jude 14
"I was born the seventh in the FIRST WEEK; — Gen 5:24
and until my time, judgement was held back.[1933] [1934] [1935] — 60:5; 1Pet 3:19-20
(93) 4 After me, there will arise a SECOND WEEK in which — Gen 6:11-13
deceit and violence will spring up;[1936] — 6:6; 86:5-6; 106:13; Deut 29:18
and in it will be the first end, but in it a man[1937] will be saved. — 10:2; Jub 5:5; 2Pet 2:5
After that has ended, iniquity will increase, — 15:8-16:1; Jub 10:1-9; 1Tim 1:9
but an orderly arrangement will be made for sinners.[1938] — Jub 6:8; 7:20, 26-29; 11:2
(93) 5 Thereafter, in the THIRD WEEK, at its close,
a man[1939] will be chosen as a plant of righteous judgement; — 10:3, 16; Mt 7:15-20; Lk 3:8-9
and after him will come forth a plant of uprightness[1940] — Jub 1:16; 16:26; 21:24; 36:6
forever and ever.

[1929] "Discourse," is literally "parable."

[1930] **(1En 93:1) is considered by many scholars to be the true beginning of the fifth section of 1 Enoch. They are "divided about whether this 'Apocalypse of Weeks" should be dated ca. 170 BCE, or possibly even earlier"** (OL pg. 218). **Some think the Apocalypse of weeks was an older text incorporated into the *Admonitions of Enoch*.** The Apocalypse of Weeks is related to the later 2Bar 56-77 in form and genre (E pg.209).

[1931] Nickelsburg has: "chosen of eternity" as here. I, C, K, and O have "world" in place of eternity.

[1932] **Enoch has three sources for his knowledge: heavenly visions, the words of the watchers and holy ones, and the heavenly tablets.**

[1933] **"The fragment of a two-columned sixth/seventh-century Coptic MS., discovered in 1939, preserves the text of a small part of the Apocalypse of Weeks, 93:3b-4a + 5ab (recto) and 6c-7a + 8cd (verso)"** (N1 pg. 15).

[1934] Olson, as in this text, very plausibly translates the last line of 93:3 as: "and until my time judgement was held back" (cf. 1En 60:5; 1Pet 3:20). Nickelsburg has: "and until my time righteousness endured." **God's righteous judgement was withheld in patience before the flood.**

[1935] The ten weeks here in the apocalypse of weeks has "interesting similarities to the '70 weeks' prophecy in Daniel 9, since each of the ten 'weeks' in this apocalypse seems to represent seven generations" (OL pg. 218).

[1936] Fragments of verses 93:1-4 are found in the Dead Sea Scrolls (4Q212 Frag. 1 Col. 3 or 4QEn^{g} 1iii).

[1937] This is Noah. The first end was the deluge.

[1938] Olson translates the last line of 93:4 as: "but an orderly arrangement will be made for sinners." N has: "and a law will be made for sinners." OL suggests this verse is referring to the Tower of Babel with the law made for sinners being the division of the earth in Gen 10-11. That is the view in the Ethiopic church for this verse (OL pg. 220). It could also refer to the Noahic covenant (Gen 8:21-22; 9:11-17). Black cites (Jubilees 6:8; and 7:20) where God and Noah make laws for his sons. **Another plausible option, not mentioned by other scholars, is reflected in Jubilees 10:1-9, where the deception caused by demons unleased by the death of the giants, is mitigated when 90% of the demons are imprisoned by God at the request of Noah.**

[1939] This is Abraham.

[1940] **"Plant of righteousness" Israel is the plant of righteousness from which will come a Holy Seed** (Jub 1:16; 16:26; 21:24; 36:6; Isa 60:21; 61:3; 1QS 8.5; 11.8; 1QH 14:8; 16:7; 4Q418 81.13; and CD A 1.7-8 (W pg. 52)).

(93) 6 After that, at the completion of the FOURTH WEEK,
visions of the holy ones and of the righteousness ones will be seen,[1941] Ex 24:9-11; Deut 33:2
and a law for generations upon generations, and a Tabernacle
will be made for them.[1942]
(93) 7 Thereafter, there shall arise the FIFTH WEEK, and at its 1QS 8:5-8
conclusion, the Temple of the glorious kingdom[1943] 91:13; Barn. 16:6, 8; 2Sam 7:16
will be built for ever.[1944] [1945]
(93) 8 After this, in the SIXTH WEEK, all who are living in it will Rom 1:21; Eph 4:18; 4Q245 1.16
become blind, and the hearts of all of them will forget wisdom;[1946] TReu 3:8; TLev 14:4; TGad 6:2
and in that week a man will ascend.[1947] At its conclusion, the Temple 89:52; 2Kgs 2:11
of the kingdom will be burned with fire,[1948] 89:66; 4Ezra 5:28
and in it the whole race of the chosen root[1949] will be scattered.[1950] 89:68; 2Kgs 25:9-11; CD A 1.3-9
(93) 9 Thereafter, in the SEVENTH WEEK, a perverse generation will Dan 9:1-2, 21-27; Mt 17:17 Deut 32:20; Lk 9:41; 1QS 4.19
arise, and many will be its misdeeds 89:73-75; 99:2; 1Mac 1:10-15
and all its doings will be apostate.[1951] TLev 14:1; TJud 18:1

[1941] Holy and righteous=heavenly beings involved in the plagues of Egypt and/or the giving of the law. The law was given to Moses in the presence of heavenly beings. (**Ex 24:9-11**; Deut 33:2; Acts 7:53; Gal 3:19; Heb 2:2; *Ant* 15.5.5 §§136).

[1942] Nickelsburg translates this line as: "and a covenant for all generations and a tabernacle will be made in it." The covenant is the Mosaic Covenant/Torah and the enclosure is the Tabernacle (Ex 27:9). Olson translates "and an enclosure, will be made for them" Charles and Olson, view the enclosure not as a Tabernacle but as all of Palestine (C pg. 230 and OL pg. 220). But Ethiopian commentators see it as the fence of the Tabernacle (OTP1 pg. 74) and a Coptic fragment of this text supports the tabernacle view (M pg. 82). Yet another, but very unlikely, option is supplied by (Mishna Abot 1:1), which mentions a fence (presumably rabbinic rules) being around the Torah.

[1943] This is the first temple.

[1944] It is odd that the author says that the temple is built forever when in the next verse it is burned with fire. "Perhaps the author is thinking of the temple as an institution" (N1 pg. 447). **More likely he is thinking of the Temple of the Holy Spirit within the elect, which was a concept known even during the time when the Dead Sea Scrolls were written (1QS 8.5-10 (W pg. 129); 4Q174 3.1-10 (W pg. 256-257); John 2:18-21; 1Cor 3:16-17; 6:19). The author of the Epistle of Barnabas takes this view in Barnabas 16 after referencing this verse;** "'But it will be built in the name of the Lord.' So, pay attention, in order that the Lord's temple may be built gloriously. How? Learn! By receiving the forgiveness of sins and setting our hope on the Name, we became new, created again from the beginning. Consequently, God truly dwells in our dwelling place-that is, in us" (Barn 16:8).

[1945] **The Epistle of Barnabas (probably AD 70-79, but certainly AD 70-135) roughly quotes this verse or possibly 91:13**: "But let us inquire whether there is in fact a temple of God. There is—where he himself says he is building and completing it! For it is written: "And it will come to pass that when the week comes to an end, God's temple will be built gloriously in the name of the Lord" (Barn 16:6).

[1946] **This is the apostacy and idolatry associated with Israel and Judah prior to the exile. (Blind cf. CD A 1.9).**

[1947] **Elijah ascended to Heaven without facing death.**

[1948] **This was during the Babylonian invasion of 586 BC.**

[1949] **The "race of the chosen root" are the people from whom the descendant of David, the Messiah will come** (cf. Isa 11:1; 10; 53:2; Rom 15:12; Rev 5:5; 22:16; 4Ezra 5:28; TJob 1.5). Some MS read "the powerful root."

[1950] The Babylonian exile.

[1951] **The author does not even mention the building of the second temple, probably because it was regarded as so corrupt and apostate as to be an abomination (cf. 1En 99:2; and 104:10). For the abuses in the period see (Neh 5:1-13; 13:10-30). This section appears to be the text referenced in (TLev 14:1) "And now, my children, I know from the writings of Enoch that in the end-time you will act impiously against the Lord, setting your hands to every evil deed; because of you, your brothers will be humiliated and among all the nations you shall become the occasion for scorn" and (TJud 18:1) "For in the books of Enoch the Righteous I have read the evil things you will do in the last days." This may also be like the apostacy (apostasia) Paul talks about in (2Thes 2:3; and 1Tim 4:1).** I has: "criminal" and N has: "perverse" in place of "apostate."

(93) 10 And as that week reaches its close, the elect shall be chosen,[1952] Eph 1:3-5; Mt 22:14; Col 3:12 4Q245 1:18
to serve as witnesses of truth, Isa 43:10, 12; 1QS 8.6
from the eternal plant of righteousness, 10:16; 93:5; 104:12-13
to whom shall be given seven-fold wisdom and knowledge.[1953] [1954] [1955]

(91) 11 And they will uproot the foundations of violence, and the 91:5
structure of deceit which is on it and so execute judgement.[1956] [1957] 107:1
(91) 12 After this there shall arise an EIGHTH WEEK of righteousness, 2Mac 15:15-16; 1Mac 3:3, 12
in which a sword will be given to all the righteous, to exact a righteous 38:5; 90:19, 34; Rev 12:11 DivInst 7.19
judgement from all the wicked, who shall be delivered into their 95:3; 96:1; 98:12; 1QM 1:8-15

[1952] Additional cross references on the chosen are (Jn 6:70; Jn 15:16; 1Thes 1:4; Jas 2:5; 1Pet 2:4, 9; 5:13 and Rev 17:14). It is a very worthwhile study. **You definitely want to be one of the chosen!**

[1953] **This history/prophecy now arrives at the authors own day and his sect who received this knowledge. This elect group receiving sevenfold instruction are a special corps d'èlite, chosen from the midst of Israel (eternal plant of righteousness). "The elect are chosen, first of all, to be the recipients of wisdom and knowledge. In the context of the Epistle, this means a particular understanding of the divine law, other esoteric information about the cosmos, and the eschatological message of the coming judgement" (N1 pg. 448). Their identity has been proposed as the Hasidim of the Maccabean period (BL pg. 291), the Yahad who are so frequently mentioned in the DSS, or as Essenes or splinter groups thereof. Given the similarities between Enochic literature and the New Testament, one or more of these groups likely served as the incubator of early Christianity.**

[1954] Fragments of verse 93:10 are found in the Dead Sea Scrolls (4Q212 Frag. 1 Col. 4 (W pg. 288) or 4QEn^g 1 iv (M pg. 265-269).

[1955] Nickelsburg and Olson correctly insert 91:11-17 here. There is also a section missing here; "attested in Aramaic in a somewhat fuller, albeit fragmentary form, which indicates at least one line before v 11a" (N pg. 142 and N1 pg. 451). No Ge'ez manuscript to 1 Enoch 91-93 follows this original Aramaic sequence but all respect the out-of-order sequence as received thus demonstrating the fidelity of the Ethiopic scribes. Interestingly a 17th century Ethiopian commentary on the Apocalypse of Weeks (in Biblioteca Apostolica Vaticana Comb.S.8 (f.7r-9r) and the running commentary on the Mäṣḥafä Məśṭirä Sämay Wämedr follows the Aramaic sequence of weeks 1 to 10.

[1956] **With the discovery of the DSS, Aramaic 91:11 was found to be quite different from the Ethiopic. As always, unless the Aramaic is for some reason suspect, this text follows the Aramaic. Olson raises the possibility that the Ethiopic arose from a second version that was edited after the successful Maccabean uprising (OL pg. 220). Charles using only the Ethiopic has "[And after that the roots of unrighteousness shall be cut off, and the sinners shall be destroyed by the sword… shall be cut off from the blasphemers in every place, and those who plan violence and those who commit blasphemy shall perish by the sword.]**

[1957] **Week 7 ending in 91:11, brings us to the author's time during the persecution of Antiochus IV (E pg. 187). Weeks 8-10 (91:12-17) are prophecy, but also based on the struggle for freedom under the Maccabees. The weeks are of undetermined and variable periods. Attempts to systematize these weeks have been less than successful. A common interpretation is to make each week 700 years long. Week 8 (91:12-13) appears to be a climactic war won by the righteous who then acquire houses and build a house for God. This view likely helped inspire the two Jewish revolts against Rome. No wonder the Jews gave up on apocalyptic thought! (1En 91:13) is the period many Christians view as the millennium. Week nine (19:14) involves a judgment, that purges the earth of iniquity. This matches the chronology of Revelation 20 where the great white throne judgement follows the millennium. Week ten (91:15-16) describes a cleansing judgement of heaven followed by the creation of a new heaven. This is also the same as Revelation 20-21 where the new heaven follows the great white throne judgement. Following this is a period of eternal bliss described in 91:17 with Olson's addition (see footnote).** The Apocalypse of weeks forms a strong chiastic structure. Weeks one and ten: first and last judgement of the watchers; two and nine: first and last judgements on humanity; three and eight: the eternal establishment of the righteous and their roles as instruments of judgement; four and seven respectively to dual revelations—Mosaic and Enochic, and weeks five and six to the first temple, built and the destroyed (Barker, M 1987. *The Older Testament* London: SPCK pg. 59).

hands.[1958] [1959] 1Cor 6:2-3; 1QM 12.10-17
(91) 13 And with its completion they will acquire riches in Tob 14:5-7; Isa 65:21
righteousness,[1960] and there shall be built the royal temple 93:7; LAE 29:8-9; Zech 6:13
of the Great One, in glorious splendor, for all generations forever.[1961] [1962] 90:29; Barn 16:6; Ezek 40-48
(91) 14 After this, the NINTH WEEK will come; in which a
righteous and true judgement will be revealed to all the children PssSol 2:17; 8:8; Isa 42:1
of the entire earth. All the workers of evil shall entirely pass away from 10:20-21; Rev 20:11-15; 21:8
the whole earth,[1963] they will be cast into the eternal pit, 2Pet 3:7;
and all humankind shall look to the way of truth eternal.[1964] [1965] 50:2; 90:33; Isa 56:6-8; 66:18-24
(91) 15 After this, in the TENTH WEEK, in the seventh part,[1966]
(will be) an eternal judgement, and this fixed time of the Great Judgment 10:12; 1QM 1.8-15; 17:5-7, 15

[1958] **This week corresponds to the second coming of Christ in (Rev 19:11-21) followed by the extended time of peace and prosperity similar to the 1000-year reign of Christ in Rev 20:4. That this chronology precedes the much later Book of Revelation by roughly 250 years is astounding! One cannot properly understand end times eschatology without considering 1 Enoch. Christian eschatology has its roots in the Jewish sect(s) who embraced the end time beliefs of 1 Enoch and other second temple literature. Jesus Christ and many of His early followers were obviously a part of this group. The potential exists for a much better understanding of Christ's eschatology thru the study of 1 Enoch in conjunction with the Bible, the DSS, other second temple literature, and the anti-Nicene church fathers.**

[1959] ***The War Scroll*** **describes a battle of not just humans against humans, but also involving celestial beings on both sides (1QM 1.8-15; 17:5-7, 15; 18:1-3). The Thanksgiving Scroll also views the final war as being among celestial beings. "For God thunders with the roar of His strength and His holy dwelling roars forth in His glorious truth. Then the heavenly hosts shall raise their voice and the everlasting foundations shall melt and quake. The war of the heroes of heaven shall spread over the world and shall not return until an annihilation that has been determined from eternity is completed. Nothing like this has ever occurred" (1QH$_a$ 11.35-37 (W pg. 183). Likewise, the Testament of Levi describes the second heaven as populated by "the armies arrayed for the day of judgement to work vengeance on the spirits of error and of Beliar" (TLev 3:3 (OTP1 pg. 789)).**

[1960] **(1En 91:13, along with Isa 65:21 and Tob 14:5-7) may have been in his disciple's minds during Christ's teaching about the righteous acquiring houses. "And he said to them, 'Truly, I say to you, there is no one who has left house or wife or brothers or parents or children, for the sake of the kingdom of God, who will not receive many times more in this time, and in the age to come eternal life'" (Lk 18:29-30). This word for riches used in (91:13) is derived from Greek oikia (οἰκία) (meaning a house, household, dwelling, goods, property, means). This is the same word used in (Mt 19:29; Mk 10:29-30; and Lk 18:29-30).** For the idea of riches being acquired as spoils in an eschatological war; see also the *War Scroll* in the DSS (1QM 12.10-17; 19.4-6).

[1961] Fragments of verses 91:12-19 were found in the DSS (4Q212 Frag. 1 Col. 4 (W pg. 288-289) or 4QEn^g 1ii M pg. 260-263).

[1962] For the last lines of 91:13, Nickelsburg has: "and the temple of the kingdom of the Great One will be built in the greatness of its glory for all the generations of eternity." Hopes for the building of a New Jerusalem/eschatological temple were expressed in (Isa 56:6-8; 60; 65:17-25; Tob 13:9-18; Rev 21-22; 4Q554 and *The Temple Scroll).*

[1963] Other texts related to the workers of iniquity vanishing from earth are (Ps 6:8; Mt 7:23; 1En 10:20-22 and Rev 21:8).

[1964] Milik translates: "all [men shall see] the right eternal way" (M pg. 267). **Again, as in (1En 50:2-5; and 90:30, 33, 35) a conversion of the gentiles is prophesied.**

[1965] **The worldwide judgement of wickedness during week 9 follows a time of peace and prosperity (as in the millennium of Rev 20:2-3) that occurred in week eight. "The judgement (of weeks 8-10) proceeds in stages: (1) a judgement is given for Israel (or the elect of Israel) against her foes, external and internal; (2) this is followed by a universal judgment of mankind; and (3) the last stage, is the judgement of the angels and the condemnation of the watchers or fallen angels (91:15)"** (BL pg. 294).

[1966] "Seventh part," "The author is following the traditional schema of the 'Seventy Weeks' (of years) (7x70=490) or ten Jubilees (10x49=490)" (M pg. 254). **"The 'seventh part' of the 'Tenth Jubilee' is therefore, the final 'week (of years)'"** (BL pg. 294) (cf. Jub 1:29; Dan 9:24-27, TLev 16:1).

shall be executed with vengeance on the watchers.[1967] [1968] 100:4; Rev 12:7-9; 20:10
(91) 16 At that time, the first heaven[1969] shall pass away, 45:4; 72:1; Rev. 20:11; 21:1, 23
and a new heaven shall appear, and all the powers of heaven will rise, 2Pet 3:13; Ps 102:25-26 4Q440 1
shining for all eternity with seven-fold brightness.[1970] [1971] Isa 30:26; 65:17; 60:19-20; 66:22
(91) 17 After this there shall be many weeks without number—forever.
They will practice goodness and uprightness,
and from then on sin will never again be mentioned."[1972] [1973] 5:8-9; Isa 65:17; Rev 21:27
(91) 18 So now, I am speaking to you, my children, and revealing
to you the paths of righteousness, and the paths of iniquity; Deut 30:15-19; 4Q212 1.2
and I have shown them to you again, Jer 21:8
so that you may know what will come to pass.
(91) 19 Now listen, my children! Choose the paths of righteousness Prov 2:8-15
and walk in them. Refuse the paths of violence and do not walk in them. 91:1-4; 94:1-4
For all who walk in the paths of iniquity
shall be utterly destroyed.[1974] [1975] [1976] 5:5; 91:14; 2Thes 1:9; Rev 9:11

[1967] This text follows the DSS Aramaic. Ethiopian manuscripts vary greatly here, and may contain scribal additions. With variations, they in general read: "which will be executed among the watchers, and the great eternal heaven which will spring from among the angels." Knibb notes that "spring" in that manuscript, is a simple corruption of "take vengeance." This verse would correspond with the judgement of the devil and his angels in (Rev 20:7-10).

[1968] For the end of 91:15; Nickelsburg has: "and it will be executed on the watchers of the eternal heaven, ‹and a fixed time of the great judgement will be rendered among the holy ones›." Olson translates it as: "in which vengeance will be executed among the angels." This seems to indicate the watchers are again going to be active on earth or possibly they are wrested from prison at this time for judgement.

[1969] **As in Revelation 21:1, a new heaven and earth are created, beginning an endless and sinless eternity. In literature of the period only this text and Revelation 21:1 use the term "first heaven."**

[1970] **The luminaries of heaven are to be renewed in the end times, (1En 72:1; Jub 1:29; Isa 65:17; 66:22; Rev 21:1 and Rev 22:5). This judgement of the watchers and the wicked, cleanses heaven and earth of rebellion. Now that heaven and earth are cleansed of the unrighteous celestials and humans, the remaining obedient stars are free to shine with sevenfold brightness.** (Cf 4Q440 1.5)

[1971] Fragments of verses (91:10+91:18-19+92:1-2) are found in (4QEn^g 1 ii (M pg. 260-263)).

[1972] **In contrast to the sin of the righteous no longer being mentioned (91:17); the sin of the unrighteous will be remembered by the righteous (99:16).** Black has: "And sin shall be no more seen forever."

[1973] In the DSS, 91:17 has an addition from which only phrases can be deciphered. Olson reconstructs the phrases based on work by (Milik pg. 260 and Black pgs. 87, 294-295). His reconstruction reads as follows

. . .
. . . and will proceed. . .
. . . and they will pra[ise] him . . .(?)
. . . ear[th] will have rest . . .
. . . all generations forever . . .

This reconstruction reveals important information about the Book of Weeks (93:1-10 and 91:11-17) view of the final state. Earth will have rest forever (see 48:10a and 106:17b).

[1974] Very fragmented portions of (91:16-19 and 92:1-2) were found in the Dead Sea Scrolls (4Q212 Frag. 1 Col. 2 (W pg. 287), or 4QEn^g 1 ii (M pg. 260-263)). This establishes that if 91:18-19 and 92:1-2 were ever separate, they were joined by the end of the 2nd century, the date established for the fragment (E pg. 214). The Aramaic is a longer text than the Ethiopic. It is reflected in this text.

[1975] **"Utterly destroyed" This term is much more than simply the extinguishing of life; this apocalyptic term means absolute perdition, total destruction in Gehenna"** (BL pg. 282) (cf. Mt 5:29-30; 2 Thes 1:9; 1Tim 6:9; Heb 10:39; 2Pet 2:3; 3:7).

[1976] **Charles states: "This is one of the earliest non-canonical references to the "two ways"** (cf. Deut 30:15-20; Ps 1:6; Jer 21:8; 2En 30:14-15; TAsh 1:2-9; 4Q473; Did 1-2; 5).

Enoch's Epistle to the Righteous

92 1 The writings of Enoch the scribe, which he wrote and entrusted — *Defem* 1.3
to his son Methuselah. Enoch, the wisest of men, the one chosen — 71:14
from the children of the whole earth;[1977] — Gen 18:25; Ps 94:2
to all his sons and for all future generations, — CD 1.12
to all dwellers on earth who will observe uprightness and peace.[1978] — 94:4

God's Ways are Above Our Ways

2 Do not be grieved in your spirit on account of the times, — Jn 14:1, 27; 1Pet 3:14; Acts 1:7
for the Great Holy One has appointed times for all things.[1979] — 1QS 4.18-19; 4Q180 1.1
[... who is ab]le to know what is in the mind of [the Lord].[1980]
(93) 11 For who among all the sons of men is able to hear the words — Deut 4:33; 5:26; Ps 92:5;
of the Holy One and not be terrified?[1981] Or who can think his thoughts? — 14:24-15:1; Job 5:9; 9:10; 38:33
Who is the man who can behold all the works of heaven?[1982] — Isa 55:8-9; Jer 31:37; Eccl 11:5
(93) 12 Who can see a soul or spirit and be able to return to — Wis 7:17-18; 9:16
tell about it?[1983] Or who can ascend and discern their farthest limits, — 4Ezra 4:5-11
and understand them, or do as they do?[1984] — Prov 30:3-4
(93) 13 Or who is there among all the sons of men who can comprehend — Job 38:4-7, 18
the length and breadth of the whole earth? — Hab 3:6
Or who has been shown its entire extent and its shape?
(93) 14 And is there any man who can discern the length of the heavens — Jer 31:37; Isa 40:12; Job 11:8, 9
and what is their height, or upon what they are founded, or how great is — 33:4; 72:1; 82:7-8
the number of the stars?[1985] — Ps 147:4

Enoch's Advice to his Children and to the Righteous: Two Ways

---

[1977] The Ethiopic reads: "Enoch, the wisest of men, praised by all the sons of men and a judge of the whole earth." "While the primary meaning of this Ethiopic word is 'judge,' it can also translate words for 'ruler,' 'leader' and 'guide'" (N1 pg. 431). Aramaic reads as above.
[1978] The wording of the first two lines of 92:1 is uncertain.
[1979] **God is Lord of all time, and everything is totally in His control.** A similar concept is found in (1QS 4.18-19 (W pg. 121); 4Q180 1.1-4 (W pg. 269); and Acts 1:7).
[1980] This last line is found in the DSS but not the Ethiopic. The bracketed words are conjectured (W pg. 289).
[1981] The expected answer to all the questions in (93:11-14) would be "no human." However, Enoch is the exception, since by special revelation he would have extensive knowledge of these things. This section is known among commentators as the "nature poem."
[1982] At the end of 93:11 in the DSS, is a short phrase not found in the Ethiopic, which translates: "The splendor of..." and something about "resting." Olson plausibly conjectures: "or the resting places for the luminaries?" as a continuation of 93:11 (OL pg. 224).
[1983] The original text is uncertain for the beginning of verse (93:12) (N1 pg. 451).
[1984] In place of "or do as they do?" Nickelsburg has: "or make (something) like them?"
[1985] Ethiopic adds: "and where all the luminaries rest?" to the end of this line, but it is not in the Aramaic of the DSS (M pg. 270) (W pg. 289). Olson, theorizing it may have been misplaced, places it just after (93:11) (see note).

94 1 Now I say unto you my children, love righteousness and walk in it!
For the paths of righteousness are worthy of acceptance.[1986] 1Tim 1:15; 4:9; Mt 21:32
But the paths of iniquity shall quickly[1987] be destroyed and vanish. 107:1; Mt 24:43-44; Rev 3:3
2 The paths of wrongdoing and death will be revealed to men of note Lk 12:39-40; Ps 1:6; Deut 30:15
in their generation,[1988] and they will hold themselves far from them, Prov 4:14-15; 14:12; 16:25
and will not follow them. 91:4, 19; 97:4; 104:6; Jn 10:4-5
3 Now I say unto you, O righteous:
do not walk in the paths of evil, nor the ways of death! Ps 1:1; Prov 16:25; Jer 21:8
Stay away from them, lest you be destroyed! Prov 1:15-16; 2:13
4 But seek and choose for yourselves righteousness and an elect life.[1989] Deut 30:19; Mt 6:33
Walk in the paths of peace, Prov 3:17; Mt 5:9
that you may live and prosper. Lk 1:79
5 Hold fast my words in the meditations of your hearts, Prov 4:4
and do not erase them from your hearts! Josh 1:8; Tob 4:19
For I know that sinners will tempt men to debase wisdom,[1990] 104:10
and no place will be found for it, 42:1-3
and so there will be no decline in temptations.[1991]

Woes Against the Violent and Rich

6 Woe to those who build unrighteousness and violence,[1992] 91:5
and lay deceit as a foundation;
for quickly they will be thrown down,[1993] Mk 13:32; 1Thes 5:2; 2Pet 3:10
and they will not have peace. 5:4; 99:13; Isa 48:22; 57:21
7 Woe[1994] to those who build their houses through sin; 97:8; Jer 22:13

[1986] Fragments of verses (93:11-94:1) are found in the Dead Sea Scrolls (4Q212 Frag. 1 Col. 5 (W pg. 289) or 4QEn^g 1 v (M pg. 269-272)).

[1987] Isaac has: "soon" in place of "quickly" (cf. 95:6; 96:1, 6; 98:16; 99:9).

[1988] These "men of note" may be a reference to the future (future to Enoch) leaders of Israel; Moses, Aaron and the prophets (BL pg. 295). Alternatively, it may correspond to the chosen at the end of the seventh week, to whom wisdom is revealed in the midst of a perverse generation (93:9-10).

[1989] Nickelsburg, while using the term "elect life," postulates that a textual corruption may be involved, which if corrected, would result in a translation as "a good," or "a pious" life (N1 Pg. 458). Human free will is emphasized in the Admonitions of Enoch. Here humans can choose an elect life, by following the path of righteousness. **Predestination is not found anywhere in all of 1 Enoch.**

[1990] These dangers to wisdom are likely from Hellenism, and the sinners are Hellenizers and Sadducees (BL pg. 296).

[1991] Isaac has an interesting rendering of the last sentence of 94:5. "For I do know that sinners will council the people to perform evil craft; and every place will welcome it, and every advice (of the sinners) may not diminish. Nickelsburg has: "and none of the temptation will diminish."

[1992] Olson has: "iniquity and wrongdoing."

[1993] Isaac, extending the building imagery, has: "They shall soon be demolished" N has: "for quickly they will be overthrown."

[1994] **The Admonitions of Enoch have thirty-two "woes" (94:6-10: 95:4-7; 96:4-8; 97:7-10; 98:9-99:2; 99:11-16; 100:7-9; 103:5-8). Olson notes: "Arranging woes in strings like this is common to the Old Testament (Isa 5:8-22), the Apocrypha (Sir 2:12-14), and the New Testament (Matt 23:13-32 [=Luke 11:42-52] and Luke 6:24-26). Some of the New Testament examples, especially those in Luke 6, resemble these Enoch woes more than any of the Old Testament specimens" (OL pg. 238). Olson further observes: "The correspondences between**

for from all their foundations shall they be overthrown, Mt 7:26-27
and by the sword they will fall.
Also, those who accumulate gold and silver will perish 63:10; 97:8
by sudden judgement.[1995] 95:6; Prov 11:28; Ps 52:7
8 Woe to you rich, for you have trusted in your riches,[1996] 46:7; 96:4; Jas 5:1-6; Lk 6:24
but from your riches you will be parted, 97:8-10; 100:6; Lk 16:25
because you have not remembered the Most High in the days of Deut 8:17-18; Sir 41:1; Mk 10:23
your riches.
9 You have committed blasphemy and iniquity; 45:2
and have been prepared for the day of bloodshed, 99:6, 15; 100:1-3; Rev 14:14-20
and the day of darkness,[1997] and for the day of the great judgement. 98:10; Zeph 1:15; ApPet 20-33
Eccl 11:8; Joel 2:2;
Amos 5:18, 20

10 Thus, I speak and declare unto you: Deut 28:63; Job 15:23
He who created you, will also overthrow you,
and for your fall there will be no compassion; 98:12; Lk 94:10; 2Pet 3:9
4Ezra 7:131
your Creator will rejoice at your destruction.[1998] 89:58; 97:2; Ps 2:4; 37:13
11 And your righteous ones in those days shall be a reproach
to the sinners and the godless.[1999]

95 1 Oh that mine eyes were a fountain[2000] of waters Jer 9:1; 2Bar 35:2-3
that I might weep over you, Lk 19:41-42
and pour out my tears as a cloud of waters, Lam 3:48; Ps 119:136
and so find some relief from the grief of my heart!
2 Who appointed you to practice hatred and evil? Sir 15:20
The judgement will find you, sinners!
3 Do not be afraid of the sinners, O righteous; 96:1, 3; 97:1; Josh 8:1
for the Lord will again deliver them into your hands, 38:5; 91:12; Deut 3:2; 31:3-6
that you may execute judgement upon them according to your desires.[2001] Num 21:34

Luke and the 'Admonitions' include (1) thematic concerns, (2) parabolic imagery, and (3) Greek vocabulary (based on our sole surviving Greek copy of Enoch 97:6-107:3)."

[1995] Baty has: "gold and silver gotten by injustice." All others read similarly to this text. Knibb is typical: "and those who acquire gold and silver will quickly be destroyed in the judgement." Charles views this line as an interpolation (C pg. 235).

[1996] References to the rich trusting in wealth include: (1En 46:7; 63:10; 96:4; 97:8-10; Deut 8:17-18; Ps 49:6; 52:7; Prov 11:28; Jer 9:23; Mk 10:23; Lk 6:24-25; 12:21; and Jas 5:1-6). **(James 5:1-6) has notable parallels to this passage.**

[1997] For "Day of Darkness" compare: (Job 15:23; Eccl 11:8; Joel 2:1-2; Amos 5:18-20; Zeph 1:15 and Rev 16:10).

[1998] **God does rejoice at the destruction of the wicked, but He prefers repentance to destruction** (Ezek 18:23; 33:11; Lk 15:10; 2Pet 3:9).

[1999] 1En 94:11 seems out of place, but it is actually a continuation of 94:5. This is a literary device where a thought is interrupted, in this case by a warning to avoid evil, and then continued later in the text. It is used extensively in the parables (eight times) but only once here in the *Admonitions*.

[2000] Nickelsburg, as here, has "fountain" in place of "cloud" as found in some Ethiopic texts. He bases this on Jer 9:1, and the presumption of an Aramaic corruption.

[2001] "The present passage, in particular, is modeled on biblical exhortations set in the context of holy warfare." God "will deliver these enemies 'into the hands' of his people so that they can destroy them as they did in the past (Num 21:34; Deut 3:2; Josh 8:1-2; cf. Deut 7:18)" (N1 pg. 464).

4 Woe to you who bind with curses that cannot be reversed;[2002] 6:4-6; 8:3
healing will be far from you because of your sins.
5 Woe to you who repay your neighbor with evil; Prov 17:13; 24:29; 1Pet 3:9
for you shall be repaid according to your deeds. 100:7; Rom 2:6; 12:17
6 Woe to you, lying witnesses, Ex 23:1; Prov 19:5
and to all who weigh out injustice; Prov 22:8
for suddenly you shall perish.[2003] 16:1; 94:1, 7; 2Pet 3:10
7 Woe to you, sinners, because you persecute the righteous! Mt 5:10; Isa 3:11
For you yourselves will be delivered up and persecuted because of
iniquity, and its[2004] yoke will lie heavily upon you.

Excursus: Is Jesus referring to 1 Enoch 96:2 in Mt 24:9-30 and Lk 17:27-37?

	1 Enoch 96:2-3	**Mt 24:9-30 and Lk 17:27-37**
In an end times passage	X	X
Speaking of deliverance of the saints from the wrath of God	X	X
Saints have suffered	X	X
Saints taken alive	X	X
Sinners left behind	X	X
The lawless mourn	X	X
Mentions vultures	X	X

Rescue from the Sinners' Day of Tribulation (Rapture)

96 1 Be hopeful,[2005] O righteous; for the sinners will soon perish before Isa 41:12; Rev 3:3; Ps 73:19
you, and you shall have authority over them as you desire. 38:5; 91:12; 95:3; 98:12; 102:4
2 On the day of tribulation[2006] for the sinners, Deut 32:11; Rev 3:10
your young ones will mount up and rise like eagles, 100:5; Ex 19:4; Isa 40:31

[2002] Nickelsburg has: "Woe to you who utter anathemas that you cannot loose" Some manuscripts read "cannot be loosed" and others "can be loosed." Ancient magicians of the black arts would add hexes to supposedly make spells unbreakable.
[2003] Isaac has: "For you shall perish soon."
[2004] Some manuscripts read "their yoke."
[2005] Nickelsburg suggests that "be of good courage" or "fear not" may be replacements for "Be hopeful" (N1 pg. 465).
[2006] The "day of tribulation" or "day of the Lord" is a common way to refer to a time of personal or collective calamity. For other uses of the concept compare: (Isa 13:6, 9; Jer 46:10; Ezek 30:3; Joel 1:15; 2:1, 11, 31; Obad 15; Amos 5:18-20; Hab 3:16; Zeph 1:15; Mal 4:5; Acts 2:20, 1Cor 5:5; 1Thes 5:2; 2Thes 2:2; and 2Pet 3:10).

and higher than the vultures will be your dwelling place.[2007] [2008] Lk 17:37; Mt 24:28; Rev 12:14 1Thes 4:17

You will ascend[2009] and enter the crevices of the earth, Isa 2:10, 19, 21; Ex 33:21-23
and the clefts of the everlasting rock, like rock-badgers, Jer 16:16; 49:16; Isa 26:4, 20-21
before the lawless ones; who will moan and weep like sirens[2010] Isa 13:21LXX; Jer 50:39
because of you.[2011] [2012]
3 But as for you, fear not,[2013] you who have suffered;
for healing will be yours. 10:7; 95:4; Ps 73:26; 1QS 4:6-8
A bright light will shine on you, 38:2-4; 92:4; Mt 17:5; Acts 9:3-4 Jn 1:4

and a voice of rest you shall hear from heaven. Jub 23:31

Woes against the Rich Persecutors

4 Woe unto you sinners, for your riches make you appear to be Jas 5:1-6; Ps 73:3-10
righteous,[2014] 103:5-15; Lk 16:19-31
but your hearts convict you of being sinners, and this fact[2015]
will be a witness against you—a testament to your evil deeds! Jam 5:3

[2007] This text can be taken metaphorically of the righteous in the time of the Maccabees, or eschatologically of the future. **During the tribulation of the sinners, the elect will be hidden in places safe from the wrath of God (cf. Isa 26:20-21). All three animal examples (eagles, vultures and rock badgers) are secure in high places from the events and chaos below. (Mt 24:28 and Lk 17:37) also mention vultures or eagles and are quite enigmatic without the background of the text before us. Jesus Christ seems to use this passage in an eschatological manner, when he was speaking of the rescue/rapture of the end time saints in these two biblical passages, and the (vultures) gathering to Him (the corpse) (cf. Rev 12:14). 1 Enoch 96:2 adds the highly relevant fact that the lawless ones will be trying to destroy the righteous and will be upset that they have escaped from them and will soon return with vengeance. The lawless one is a term the Apostle Paul uses for the Antichrist (2Thes 2:8-9). This verse is a prime example of the usefulness of 1 Enoch in the study of Christian eschatology.**

[2008] All but Isaac have: "nest" in place of "dwelling place."

[2009] Nickelsburg has: "you will climb up" in place of "you will ascend"

[2010] The righteous elect have escaped persecution and death, having been whisked away to safety from the lawless ones. The lawless ones then lament, because they will very soon face imminent judgement from the combined forces of loyal celestial beings, and saints lead by the Chosen One. Sirens, in Greek mythology, would lure men to their destruction or accompany them in death. They were known for their lamentations. Translators use various terms for "sirens" which is used by (N, C, B, and I); BL uses "desert owls" OL and K use "satyrs." **However, sirens, in contrast to satyrs, were known for their wailing, and voices, so it seems the more appropriate term in context here. In either case, this is evidence of a Hellenizing influence, arguing once again that 1 Enoch was not written prior to widespread Greek influence in the Levant.** Sirens are famously present in the *Odyssey*, written in the 7th to 8th century BC. The LXX understands "sirens", when used in the Old Testament, to be demons of various types (cf. Isa 13:21 LXX; 34:11, 14; and Jer 50:39). Also see Rev 18:2 and Bar 4:35. That demons inhabit former human dwellings and cemeteries, is a staple belief of those who investigate such things.

[2011] Nickelsburg has: "And they will sigh because of you and weep like sirens" but he acknowledges that two manuscripts "omit *like,* making *sirens* the subject of the verb." Olson offers: "and into the clefts of the everlasting rock, like rock badgers, before the lawless ones, who will moan and weep like satyrs because of you." They may also be weeping because they know judgement is about to fall on them (Mt: 24:30).

[2012] Charles considered 96:2 as an interpolation. Most other scholars consider it to be original. **Interpolation or not, it was known to Christ, given (Mt. 24:28 and Lk 17:37).**

[2013] "Fear not" other uses include: (Isa 41:10, 13, 14; 43:1, 5; 54:4; Bar 4:5, 21, 27, 30).

[2014] **Humans mistakenly tend to think that material possessions indicate favor from God.** This is refuted by the story of Job and the rich man and Lazarus (Lk 16:19-31).

[2015] N has: "word" in place of "fact." The fact of them being rich is a witness against them as in James 5:3.

5 Woe to you who devour the very finest of the wheat, — Deut 32:14; Ps 81:16; 147:14
and quaff wine from large bowls,[2016] — Amos 6:6
but trample underfoot the poor with your might. — Jas 2:6; 5:4; Amos 5:11; Isa 3:14-15

6 Woe to you who have abundant water to drink whenever — Ps 73:12; Prov 5:15-18
you wish,[2017] [2018] for retribution will come suddenly,[2019] — 94:1; 1Thes 5:2-3; Ps 73:18-20
and you will be exhausted and wither away; — 48:1; Jn 7:37-38,
because you have forsaken the fountain of life.[2020] — Jn 4:10-14; Ps 36:9; Jer 2:13 Jer 17:13

7 Woe to you who commit iniquity, deceit, and blasphemy; — 1:9; 91:8; 94:6, 9; ApPet 20-33
it will serve as a testament of evil against you.
8 Woe to you, the powerful, who with might oppress the righteous; — Ps 73:8; Mal 3:5
for the day of your destruction is coming. — Lk 1:46-55
In those days, many good days will come for the
righteous—in the day of your judgement!

Excursus: Luke's writings and the Admonitions of Enoch.

The writings of Luke and the *Admonitions of Enoch* have long been known to display common themes and remarkable parallels.[2021] The links are so significant that it prompted Aalen to speculate concerning the origin of the Greek translation of 1 Enoch: "Was Luke personally acquainted with the man who translated 1 Enoch? Or was he perhaps himself that man? Nickelsburg assessed and refined Aalen's theory and found no proof of direct literary dependance. Aalen's speculation was disproven when very fragmented Greek copies, on papyrus, of 103:3-8, 12 dated to ca. 100 BC were at length identified in the Dead Sea Scrolls (7Q4.1; 7Q8; 7Q12 & 7Q14) (Flint, E pg. 224f. VF 313-319, but Nickelsburg disputes E pg. 237-39). In addition, 7Q4.2 appears to contain text from 98:11 or 105:1; 7Q11 from 100:12, and 7Q13 from 103:15 (VF 319). If the *Admonitions of Enoch* were in Greek well prior to the time of Christ it would stand to reason that the other existent portions of 1 Enoch were translated into Greek by the same time.

[2016] N has: "‹and quaff wine from the mixing bowl›," in his translation, but has: "and drink ‹wine from the krater›," (N1 pg. 467) in his commentary. A krater is an ancient Greek vessel used for diluting wine with water (i.e. mixing bowl). The rich indulge in rich food and abundant wine, while depriving and cheating the poor.
[2017] The sinners drink from every fountain but the true fountain (1En 48:1, John 7:37-38) This is a reference to the rich practicing idolatry in all its forms rather than seeking the true God. This fountain of life is to sustain the righteous through not only this life, but the next (22:9; Rev 21:6, and 22:1).
[2018] **Olson postulates that the *Admonitions of Enoch* were written during a drought where the rich had more access to water than others.** He points to (97:9-10; 98:2 and 100:11-13) as further evidence (OL pg. 230). Even in modern times, much of the world lacks access to clean drinking water.
[2019] Nickelsburg has: "for quickly you will be repaid, and cease and dry up," The wicked will not suffer a slow leak of water (the source of life in a desert) but a sudden catastrophic loss.
[2020] The Messiah is the inexhaustible fountain of righteousness (1En 48:1). In (John 4:7-15 and 7:37-38) Jesus Christ claims the fulfillment of this verse as the source of living water, which was an unmistakable claim to be the divine Messiah. This verse predicts that the Messiah will be rejected by the unrighteous as precisely happened. The wicked drink from every earthly fountain but not the spiritual fountain God provides.
[2021] (Aalen, S. "St. Luke's Gospel and the Last Chapters of 1 Enoch," *New Testament Studies* 13 (1966) 1-13); and (Nickelsburg, George W. E., "Riches, the Rich, and God's judgement in 1 Enoch 92-105 and the Gospel of Luke," *New Testament Studies* 25 (1979) 328).

Nickelsburg "cautiously suggests that the influence (of 1 Enoch on Luke) may go back to Jesus himself rather than Luke's redaction since similar themes are found in other strata of the Gospels."[2022] This would indicate that Jesus knew Greek and the Book of Enoch very well and Luke's apparent dependence on the admonitions is actually a reflection of Christ's knowledge! It is also evidence of the accuracy with which Luke transmitted the words of Christ![2023]

The texts below contain similarities in Greek vocabulary or expressions.

Admonitions of Enoch	**Luke**
102:10	10:29; 16:15; (cf. 18:9, 14; 20:20)

These verses above contain an extremely rare active use of "justify" dikaioō with a reflexive pronoun.[2024] In all Greek literature, this usage occurs only in these three passages!

104:8	12:5; (cf. 6:47)
98:3, 16; 99:9	13:3, 5
100:5	16:9
98:7; 99:10; 100:4; 101:1,6	1:32, 35, 76; 6:35 cf. Acts 7:48
103:4	20:38
104:1	10:20

The passages below contain similarities of conception, form, or structure.

97:8-10	12:15-21
98:9, 97:9, 103:3, 5; 104:5	16:19-31
94	6:24
96:4-5, 8	1:46-55

[2022] OL pg. 287-288.

[2023] **That Luke was written very early after the ministry of the Lord is evidenced by Paul's quotes of it in his epistles (Luke 10:7 in 1Tim 5:17-18; and Luke 22:19-20 in 1Cor 11:23-26). Matthew and Mark were also used by Paul (Mk 8:31; Mt 12:40 and 17:22-23 in 1Cor 15:3-4), (Mt 19:8-9; Mk 10:11-12 in 1Cor 7:10-11). In addition, (Mt 24:8-44) has numerous (13) distinctive parallels with (1Thes 4:14-5:8). If, as scholars believe, a Q gospel preexisted them all; then the time of the composition of the Gospel accounts was within a decade or two after the resurrection (AD 33). (1Cor was written in AD 53-55 and 1Tim ca. AD 65).**

[2024] OL pg. 246.

97 1 Take courage, O righteous! For the sinners will become an	
object of contempt and perish on the day of iniquity.[2025]	45:2; Jer 8:12
2 Be it known unto you, (sinners), that the Most High has your	
destruction in mind, and that the angels of heaven will rejoice	89:58; 94;10; Sir 16:9; Jer 51:48
over[2026] your destruction.[2027]	Rev 19:1-3; Lk 15:10
3 What will you do, O sinners?	4Ezra 16:17
And where will you flee on that day of judgement,[2028]	102:1-2; Lk 3:7; Rev 6:16-17
when you hear the sound of the prayer of the righteous?	99:3
4 You will not be like them; for this word will be	104:6
a testimony against you:	Mt 9:11, 11:18-19; Lk 5:30; 15:2
"You have been companions of sinners."[2029]	91:4; 94:3; Ps 1:1; 26:4-5; 50:18
5 In those days, the prayers of the righteous shall reach to the Lord;	8:4; 9:3; 47:2; 97:3; Rev 6:10
but for you, the days of your judgement shall come.	99:3; 104:3; Jn 5:28-29 Rom 2:16
6 The complete account of your lawless deeds will be read out	47:3; 81:4; 90:17, 20; Mt 12:36
in the presence of the Great Holy One,	1:3; 89:63, 71, 76; Rev 20:12-15
and your faces will be covered with shame.	46:6; 62:10; 63:11; 92:2 Isa 41:11-13; 44:9-11; 50:7
Then he will reject every deed which is grounded on unrighteousness.[2030]	Ezek 16:63; Eccl 12:14
7 Woe to you, sinners, whether out at sea or on dry land;	104:8; Ps 95:5; 139:9; Jonah 1:9
records of evil are kept against you.[2031]	100:10, 11; Deut 30:19
8 Woe to you who acquire gold and silver unjustly and say:	94:7-8; Jas 5:1-6
"We have become exceedingly rich, and acquired possessions;	Hos 12:8
and we have obtained everything we have desired.	Rev 3:17
9 Now let us do whatever we wish, for we have hoarded silver in	Judg 17:6
our treasure storehouses, and many are the goods in our houses."[2032] [2033]	Lk 12:16-21
10 But they are poured out like water!	98:2; Hos 5:10; Job 3:24
You are deceived, for your wealth will not abide.	94:8; Sir 11:18-19; Jas 5:1-3

[2025] BL has: "day of violence." **"The day of judgement is to be one of violent destruction of the wicked"** (BL pg. 299).

[2026] Nickelsburg, assuming corruption in the Aramaic, has: "make disclosure concerning" in place of "rejoice over."

[2027] Jesus turned this around and said the angels also rejoice over those who repent (Lk 15:10)!

[2028] **John the Baptist uses similar language in (Lk 3:7): "You brood of vipers! Who warned you to flee from the wrath to come?"** (Cf. Mt 3:7-8)

[2029] Olson translates 97:4 as: "And you! Who face this accusation: 'You have been the associates of the sinners': You will share their fate." **Jesus associated with sinners in order to save them. Were the Pharisees referencing this verse when accusing Jesus in (Mt 9:11; Lk 5:30 and 19:7)?** "And when the Pharisees saw this, they said to his disciples, 'Why does your teacher eat with tax collectors and sinners?'" (Mt 9:11) (Cf. Lk 15:2)

[2030] Isaac has: "built upon oppression" in place of "grounded on unrighteousness." For this line (N1, pg. 467), has; "then he will remove all the deeds that partook in lawlessness." "Verse 6c seems to refer to the final removal of sin from the earth (cf. 10:16, 20, 22, 91:14) (N1 pg. 473).

[2031] **"At sea or on the dry land" means everywhere. The idea is that no evil escapes the notice of God. All sinners will all be judged and all have sinned. That is why Christ's atonement for sin is such a precious gift.**

[2032] **Jesus most likely had this passage in mind in (Luke 12:13-21) as this is the most similar text. But the rich man's solution is to tear down his granaries and build bigger ones.** Other potential passages that draw from the same idea are (Sir 11:18-19; James 4:13-5:11; and Eccl 6:1-2).

[2033] Isaac has: "we have filled our treasuries (with money) like water. And many are the laborers in our houses." Nickelsburg has: "for silver we have gathered up in our treasuries, and many goods in our houses; and as water they are poured out."

But it will quickly take flight from you; Prov 23:4-5; Eccl 6:2
for you have acquired it all unjustly,
and you will be given over to a great curse. 5:5-7; 98:4; Prov 3:33

An Oath to the Wise

98 1 And now I swear unto you, to both the wise and the foolish,[2034] 99:6; 103:1; 104:1
that you will see many evils.[2035] Sir 34:11
2 For men will put on more beautiful adornments[2036 2037] Mt 11:8; Zeph 1:8
than women, and bright colors more than girls, 8:1; Lk 16:19-24
In royalty and in grandeur and in power,[2038]
(They will have to eat gold and silver for food 108:8-9; Ezek 7:19; Ex 32:20
and pour these for water within their houses![2039]
3 Because they are utterly lacking in knowledge and wisdom.)
Thus, they will perish, together with all their possessions Jas 5:1-6; Mt 6:19-20; Lk 13:3, 5
and all their splendor and glory;[2040] Phil 3:19; 1Tim 6:9
and in disgrace and misery, and great slaughter, 22:13; 99:11; Mt 13:42, 50
their spirits[2041] shall be cast into the fiery furnace. 100:9; 108:3; Rev 20:13-15
ApPet 20-33

Two Oaths Against the Sinners

4 I swear to you, sinners: that it was not ordained <for a man>
to be a slave, nor was <a decree> given for a woman to be Good Person 12.79; *Hypoth.11.4*
a handmaid: but it happened because of oppression.[2042]

2034 This text follows the reading of most Ethiopic manuscripts. But Greek and some Ethiopic manuscripts read "I swear to you wise, and not to the foolish." The foolish are addressed in (1En 98-102:3) and the wise in (1En 102:4-104).

2035 "Evils" is from the Greek text. Nickelsburg, Isaac and Knibb have "things." Another possible reading is: "many lawless deeds you will see upon the earth." (N1 pg. 469)

2036 Isaac has: "jewelry" in place of "adornments".

2037 **The rich and powerful indulge and adorn themselves with fine clothes. Compare to Matt. 11:8 "What did you go out to see? A man dressed in soft clothing? Behold those who wear soft clothing are in kings' houses." "Although the use of simile suggests that the author does not have in mind the critique of transvestitism in (Deut 22:5), his sarcasm regarding the impropriety is unmistakable"** (N1 pg. 475). Prohibitions on men and women mixing clothes may be found in: (Deut 22:5, 4Q271 3.1.3-4 (W pg. 67); 4Q159 2-4.6-7 (W pg. 232)) (cf. ApPet 31) and *Idol.* 16.

2038 These people were at the highest levels of society. They are probably the Seleucids.

2039 This reading follows Olson, who assumes a sarcastic tone in the text. Nickelsburg, following the Greek text, has: "And silver and gold will be among them as food, and in their houses, these will be poured out like water." BL has: "But silver and gold and purple and priceless things are destined to pass away. And your household goods will be poured away like water." K has: "and silver and gold and purple and honour and food will be poured out like water."

2040 **The dress and fate of the men in 98:2-3 matches very closely that of the rich man in (Lk 16:19-24).**

2041 **"The wicked are cast into Gehenna, apparently as incorporeal spirits: cf. 103:8; 108:3"** (BL pg. 301).

2042 **In a time of universal slavery, this text condemns slavery, saying it is not part of God's original plan, but is a creation of man. The Essenes were known to be opposed to slavery, (*Ant* 18.1.5 §§21; Good Person 12.79). Had 1 Enoch been valued, rather than disused, this prohibition on slavery may have found its way into the western Church. Can you imagine the human misery that would have been avoided if this statement on slavery had been promulgated and followed?** Biblical and other texts on slavery include (Ex 21:2-11; Lev 25:39-

Thus, lawlessness was not sent upon the earth; Sir 15:11-13
but men created it by themselves,[2043] [2044] 69:11; Jas 1:13-14
and those who do it will come to a great curse.[2045]
5 Likewise, neither is a woman created barren, Hos 9:14; Gen 20:18; 29:31
but because of the works of her hands, she is disgraced with childlessness.[2046] Sir 16:3
6 I swear to you, sinners, by the Great Holy One,
that all your wicked deeds are revealed in heaven, 97:6; 100:10; 104:7-8; Ps 73:11 97:7; Mk 4:22; Lk 8:17; 12:2-3
and none of your unrighteous acts will be covered up and hidden. Mt 10:26; 1Cor 4:5
7 Do not imagine in your spirits, or say in your hearts, Sir 16:17; 17:15, 19; Job 22:13
that they are not known or seen in heaven, 100:10; 1Tim 5:24-25; Ps 10:11 Ps 59:7; 94:7; Isa 29:15 Ezek 8:12
nor are they written down before the Most High. 81:1-2; 97:6; 104:7-8
8 From now on know! All your iniquities are written down Ps 64:5; 69:28
day by day until the day of your judgement![2047] 81:4; 104:7; 108:3; Rev 20:12

Woes Against the Wicked

9 Woe to you, fools, for you will perish because of your folly. Lk 12:20
You pay no heed to the wise; and good things will not come your way,
but evils will surround you.[2048]
10 Know this! You have been prepared for a day of destruction! 94:9; Rom 9:22
Do not hope to be saved,[2049] O sinners; you will depart and die,
knowing that you have been prepared for a day of great judgement;[2050] 45:2; 94:9; Ps 49:7-9; 2Pet 3:7
a day of anguish and great humiliation for your spirits.

46; Deut 15:12-18; and 4Q159 2-4.1-3 (W pg. 232)). Olson translates 98:4 differently. "I swear to you sinners: Just as a mountain has never, and will never, become a slave, nor a hill the handmaid of a woman, so also sin …"

[2043] **God did not create sin, man did.** Compare (James 1:13). The *Admonitions of Enoch* place the blame for sin on humans (98:4-5) and do not mention the fallen angel tradition.

[2044] (1En 98:4-6) has many parallels with (Sir 15-17).

[2045] The text of this verse (89:4) exactly follows Nickelsburg's translation, which "attempts to reach the original through a comparison of all texts" (N1 pg. 470). **He includes the Greek Chester Beatty—Michigan Papyrus (AD 4th century) in his analysis, which contains most of (1En 97:6-104:13) and the story of Noah's birth (1En 106-107). These manuscripts were not available to Charles, as they did not come to light until 1931.** Knibb is representative of the alternate reading: "I swear to you, you sinners, that as a mountain has not, and will not, become a slave, nor a hill a woman's maid, so sin was not sent on the earth, but man of himself created it, and those who commit it will be subject to a great curse."

[2046] In ancient times barrenness was attributed to demons or curses or as here, sin.

[2047] "The idea of heavenly books has a long history in the ancient Near East, and can be traced back to the texts of ancient Sumer, where one reads about tablets of life and tablets of human destiny." "In 1 Enoch, heavenly books have three kinds of contents. They record: human deeds, notably those of the sinners who oppress the righteous; the names of the righteous; and the rewards of the righteous" (N1 pg. 478). For an excellent summary of Heavenly Books see (N1 478-480).

[2048] The phrase at the end of 98:9 comes from the Greek text which adds: "but evils will surround you."

[2049] The sinners hoped to escape the judgement and enjoy eternal life.

[2050] The better Ethiopic manuscripts and possibly the damaged Greek manuscript reads as here. Knibb is representative of the alternative reading supported by most Ethiopic manuscripts: "rather you will go and die, for you know no ransom, for you are ready for the day of the great judgement" (cf. Ps 49:7-9).

11 Woe to you, stiff-necked and hard of heart who work   5:4; 16:3; Acts 7:51; 1QS 4:11
wickedness and eat blood![2051]   7:5; Lev 17:10; Deut 12:23
From where do you have good things to eat and drink and be satisfied?[2052]   100:8; Jub 7:27-33
Surely it is from all the good things which the Lord the Most High has   Jas 1:17; Eccl 2:24-25
placed in abundance on the earth! You will have no peace.   5:4
12 Woe to you who love the deeds of iniquity;[2053]   Prov 17:19; TLev 4:1
why do you cherish an expectation of good coming to you?
Know that you shall be delivered into the hands of the righteous, and they   38:5; Lk 21:24; Ps 149:6-7
will cut off your necks—put you to death without sparing you.[2054] [2055]   91:12; 95:3, 7; 103:12
13 Woe to you who rejoice in the suffering of the righteous;   104:2; Ps 79:2-3; Jer 22:19
for no grave will be dug for you.[2056]   Jub 23:23; 1Mac 7:17; Jer 8:1-2
14 Woe to you who nullify[2057] the words of the righteous;   Mk 7:13; Mt 15:6
for you shall have no hope of salvation.[2058]   98:10
15 Woe to you who write lying words, and words of error;   69:9-10; Jer 23:9-40; Mk 13:6
they write these down in order to lead many astray with their lies.[2059]   104:10; 4Q169 3-4.2.8; Mt 24:11
16 You yourselves have gone astray!   1QpHab 10.9-12
And you will not have peace, but suddenly die.   5:4; 16:1; 94:1,6; 95:6; 96:1, 6
2Pet 2:1; Mk 13:32; Job 34:20

[2051] **The prohibition on consuming blood was a fundamental law in Judaism, and in this verse, it appears to be directed at Jews who have fallen under the influence of Hellenizers (cf. Gen 9:3-6; Jub 6:7- 14; 7:27-33, 21:6; Lev 3:17; 7:26; 17:10-14; Deut 12:16, 23-25). It is one of the few observances of the law that James and the other leaders in Jerusalem required of Gentile Christian believers (Acts 15:20, 29; 21:25). This prohibition preceded Moses (Jub 6:10; 12-13; and Gen 9:4). The practice of eating blood appears to have originated with the giants; (1En 7:5) and the prohibition is a law forever (Jub 6:13-14). It is not mentioned in Genesis that the prohibition on eating blood is forever, but it can be assumed since it precedes the Mosaic law. These texts appear to be the basis of the prohibition on eating blood for Christians in (Acts 15:20 and 21:25). Christ's statements in (John 6:51-59) would indeed have been shocking to a first century Jew!**

[2052] **"Not content with enjoying the best of everything that God gives, these sinners eat blood and break the divine law;** (cf. Jub 7:28-32; 21:6; Acts 15:29)" (C pg. 243).

[2053] For a striking picture of those who love unrighteousness see (TLev 4:1); "For even when stones are split, when the sun is extinguished, the waters are dried up, fire is cowed down, all creation is distraught, invisible spirits are vanishing, and hell is snatching spoils by the sufferance of the Most High, men—unbelieving still—will persist in their wrongdoing."

[2054] "Cut off your necks" is missing in Greek. The punishment fits the crime of being stiff-necked (98:11).

[2055] This is the Jewish concept of the time of the sword (Ps 149:6-7). **It sounds barbaric to many but remember the suffering the Jews of the Maccabean period endured. (See 2 Maccabees 7; and *Ant* 12.5.4 §§248-256 for a sample). Few today would not call for vengeance after such atrocities. The Christian is to leave vengeance to God (Rom 12:16-21). However, self-defense (Ex 22:2-3; Lk 22:35-38) is allowed, and justice (Prov 29:4; Lk 11:42) is commended.**

[2056] The height of dishonor at the time, as today, in most cultures, is to not be buried (Tobit 1:17-20; 2:3-10; 4:3-4; 14:10-12; Ps 79:2-3; Isa 14:19; Jer 8:2; 14:16; 22:19; Jub 23:23; 1 Mac 7:17).

[2057] **"Nullify" This is exactly the same word Jesus uses in (Mt 15:6 and Mk 7:13), and in a similar context. "Then you no longer permit him to do anything for his father or mother, thus making void the word of God by your tradition that you have handed down. And many such things you do" (Mk 7:13). Olson notes that this exact idiom, ἀκυροῦντες or ἠκυρώσατε τὸν λόγον (making void the word), has not been found anywhere else but those two verses and (1En 98:14)** (OL pg. 236).

[2058] An alternate Ethiopic reading is "no hope of life."

[2059] Nickelsburg reads "with their lies <when they hear them.>"

Excursus: Remarkable prophecies from the Book of Enoch that have been fulfilled

Prophecy	Book	Reference
The light of God will shine on the elect Jn 1:4, 9; 1Jn 1:7	(Book of Watchers)	1En 1:8
Peace between God and the elect Jn 14:27; Rom 5:1	(Book of Watchers)	1En 1:8
Seventy generations from Enoch until Christ* Lk 3:23-37; 10:17-20	(Book of Watchers)	1En 10:12
A sinner (Judas?) will deny the name (Christ)* Mt 26:24; Mk 14:21 (But see Zech 11:12-13)	(Book of Parables)	1En 38:2
The Messiah will be rejected Mt 21:42; Mk 8:31; Lk 9:22 (cf. Mt 8:20)	(Book of Parables) (Admonitions of Enoch)	1En 42:1-2 1En 96:6?
The Messiah will return to heaven Lk 24:51; Jn 20:17; Acts 1:9	(Book of Parables)	1En 42:1-2
Blood of the Messiah to be a propitiation for sin* Eph 1:7; 1Pet 1:17-19; 1Jn 1:7	(Book of Parables)	1En 47:1, 4
The Messiah will reveal wisdom Mt 12:42; 13:54; Mk 6:2; Lk 2:40; 11:49	(Book of Parables)	1En 48:1; 51:3
The Messiah will be resurrected Mt 28:6-7; Mk 16:6; Lk 24:5-7; Jn 20:9	(Book of Dream Visions) (Admonitions of Enoch)	1En 90:37-38 1En 92:3?
The elect will be resurrected Mt 27:52-53; Jn 5:28-29; 11:43-44 *Mk 5:39-43; Lk 7:12-16; HE* 4.3	(Book of Watchers) (Book of Parables) (Book of Dream Visions) (Admonitions of Enoch)	1En 20:8 1En 51:1 1En 62:15 1En 90:33 1En 91:10 1En 92:3?
Events on the day of Pentecost* Acts 1:8; 2:2-4, 11, 14-41	(Book of Parables)	1En 61:6-7?
The Gentiles will be converted Acts 10:45; 11:1, 18; Act 15:12	(Book of Watchers) (Book of Parables) (Book of Dream Visions) (Admonitions of Enoch)	1En 10:21 1En 48:4 1En 90:30-38 1En 91:14
Messiah will transform His followers	(Book of Dream Visions)	1En 90:37-38

Acts 1:8; 4:13; Rom 12:2; 2Cor 3:18

Saints will be protected from the judgement that will fall on Jerusalem* *HE* 3.5	(Admonitions of Enoch)	1En 100:5
Enemies of God gathered in one place (Jerusalem) for destruction* *HE* 3.5; *War* 4.2.1 §§89; 6.9.4 §§428-429	(Admonitions of Enoch)	1En 100:4
Internecine war among defenders of Jerusalem *War* 4.6.1-2 §§354-376	(Admonitions of Enoch)	1En 100:1-2
Suffering during the Jewish revolts *War* 5.10.3 §§429-438; 6.3.4 §§201-213	(Admonitions of Enoch)	1En 99:4-7
Blood river at Jerusalem and Bar Kokhba revolt *War* 6.8.5 §§406; *Midrash Rabbah Lamentations* 2.2.6.6	(Admonitions of Enoch)	1En 100:2e
Jerusalem will be utterly destroyed *War* 7.1.1 §§1-4	(Book of Dream visions)	1En 90:28
Sinners hiding below ground will be sought out* *War* 3.7.36-3.8.1 §§336, 337, 340-344 *War* 6.8.4 §§392; *War* 6.9.4 §§429-434	(Admonitions of Enoch)	1En 100:4
The destruction of the Jewish nation an example to the entire world	(Admonitions of Enoch)	1En 100:6

*Prophecies first appearing in 1 Enoch

99 1 Woe to you who traffic in delusions,
and who for false deeds receive honor and glory.[2060] [2061] 4Q166 2.3-7
You will surely perish; you will have no salvation for good. 99:10
2 Woe to those who alter the words of truth, 104:9-10
and pervert the everlasting covenant,[2062] 93:6; 94:5; Isa 24:5; Mt 23:1-39
and yet consider themselves to be without sin!
They will be swallowed up in the earth.[2063] 90:18; Num 16:32; Jude 11
3 In those days, be ready, O righteous, Tob 12:12
to offer up your petitions as a reminder; 9:3; 96:4,7; Rev 5:8; Mal 3:16
laying them as a testimony before the angels,[2064] 89:70, 76; 97:5; 103:4; 104:1
so that they may bring the sins of the wicked before Acts 10:4; Rev 6:10; 8:2-4
the Most High as a reminder.[2065] Zech 1:12

Judgement on the Wicked at the Time of the End

4 At that time, the nations will be thrown into confusion, Mk 13:7-8
and the families of the peoples will be unsettled,[2066] Mt 24:7; SibOr 3:635f

---

2060 Isaac has: "Who glorify and honor false words."

2061 Chapter 99 has a constant confusion of the second and third person in the manuscripts. It is not known if this is attributable to the author or a misreading of Aramaic suffixes on the part of a scribe (BL pg. 303).

2062 **Nickelsburg has: "eternal covenant." "In the Hebrew Bible "eternal covenant" …refers variously to the Noachic covenant (Gen 9:16); the Abrahamic covenant (Gen 17:7; Ps 105:10); the sabbath (Ex 31:16-17; Lev 24:8); the Davidic covenant (2Sam 23:5; Isa 55:3); the covenant with Phineas (Num 25:13; cf. 1Mac 2:54); and in one instance the Mosaic covenant (Isa 24:5)" (N1 pg. 489). In this case it appears to be referring to divine law, the law of the Most High, see (TGad 3:1; and TAsh 5:4). This is evidence that the author's sect had a dispute with another group of Jews over the scriptures (words of truth) and God's relationship with them.**

2063 This text follows the Greek "swallowed up in the earth" (cf. 90:18; Num 16:1-3, 31-35; Jude 11) as opposed to the Ethiopic "trampled underfoot." These are people who consider themselves to be righteous, but the author considers them to be sinners. The picture of them being swallowed up by the earth, as happens to the Sons of Korah in (Num 16:32), may indicate that they are corrupting the priesthood, which by that time had become a political office.

2064 For angelic intercession on behalf of humans see the note at (1En 40:6).

2065 **This reminds one of a legal proceeding, where the prayers are saved as evidence to be used against the wicked.** The title "Most High" is found in all major sections of 1 Enoch (9:3; 10:1; 46:7; 60:1 ,22; 62:7; 77:1;(Great One) 94:8; 97:2; 98:7, 11; 99:3, 10; 101:6, 9).

2066 **This horrific text (99:4-6) was likely in the mind of Christ when he said in (Mt 24:15-22) "So when you see the abomination of desolation spoken of by the prophet Daniel, standing in the holy place (let the reader understand), then let those who are in Judea flee to the mountains. Let the one who is on the housetop not go down to take what is in his house, and let the one who is in the field not turn back to take his cloak. And alas for women who are pregnant and for those who are nursing infants in those days! Pray that your flight may not be in winter or on a Sabbath. For then there will be great tribulation, such as has not been from the beginning of the world until now, no, and never will be. And if those days had not been cut short, no human being would be saved. But for the sake of the elect those days will be cut short." (Cf. Mk 13:7-8; 14-23; Lk 17:29-33; Deut 28:52-57). The *Admonitions* and DSS (1QH^a 11.36-37 (W pg. 183); 4Q402 3-4.7-10 (W pg. 466); 4Q177 12-13.1.9-16 (W pg. 264)) present a somewhat more prolonged end time conflict. A strong case can be made that this prophecy was fulfilled during the first Jewish revolt (AD 68-70) (*War* 5.10.3-5.11.1 §§429-451; 6.3.4 §§201-213) and or the Jewish Bar Kokhba revolt, (AD 132-136). Those who were prudent enough to depart Jerusalem when the temple was violated by the zealots, before the siege began, had a chance at life just**

on the day of destruction of iniquity. 4Ezra 13:37
5 At that time, women bearing children will induce miscarriages, Mt 24:15-22; Lk 21:23-24
and pluck out and abandon their infant babes. 4Ezra 6:21; Lk 23:21
Those who are with child will abort; and nursing mothers will cast Deut 28:53-57; Isa 49:15
away their children. They will not go back to their infants, or to Mt 24:19; Mk 13:17; SibOr 8:84
their sucklings; nor will they show pity toward their loved ones.[2067] 69:12; *War* 5.10.3; 6:3.4
6 Again, I swear to you, O sinners, that wickedness is prepared 94:9; 98:1; 100:1-3
for the day of unceasing bloodshed.[2068] 38:5; Rev 14:19-20
7 You who worship stones, and carve images of gold, and silver, 46:7; 91:9; 104:9; Dan 5:4, 23
Isa 2:20; Ps 97:7; Lev 17:7
wood, stone and clay,[2069] and that serve phantoms, demons, 19:1; 46:7; *Idol.* 4;15; 4Q242 1.7
abominations, evil spirits, and all falsehood, not according to Jub 1:11; 11:4; 22:18; Rev 9:20
knowledge;[2070] no help will you find from them.[2071] Wis 12:24; 13:10-16; 14:12, 27
8 They will be led astray by the folly of their hearts. Rom 1:21-23; Isa 44:9-20
Their eyes will be blinded by the fear in their hearts Zeph 1:17; Jer 17:9
and the visions of their dreams will lead them away. Sir 34:1-8; Deut 13:1-3

---

as Jesus predicted (*War* 4.3.6 §§ 147-150). The accounts of the first revolt siege and fall of Jerusalem by Josephus are fodder for nightmares, and the carnage in the siege and fall of Betar in the Bar Kokhba revolt was even worse! Jesus unequivocally and accurately applies this to people who would be trapped in Jerusalem during the siege in AD 70. "But when you see Jerusalem surrounded by armies, then know that its desolation has come near. Then let those who are in Judea flee to the mountains, and let those who are inside the city depart, and let not those who are out in the country enter it, for these are days of vengeance, to fulfill all that is written. Alas for women who are pregnant and for those who are nursing infants in those days! For there will be great distress upon the earth and wrath against this people. They will fall by the edge of the sword and be led captive among all nations, and Jerusalem will be trampled underfoot by the Gentiles, until the times of the Gentiles are fulfilled" (Lk 21:20-24).

[2067]Nickelsburg, assuming a corruption in the Greek text, for the first sentence has: "At that very time, those who are giving birth will bring forth and they will sell and abandon their young infant." For 99:5 Isaac has: "In those days, they (the women) shall become pregnant, but they (the sinners) shall come out and abort their infants and cast them out from their midst; they shall (also) abandon their other children, casting their infants out while they are still suckling. They shall neither return to them (their babes) nor have compassion upon their beloved ones." **Although exposure of children, leading to death, and abortion, were commonplace in antiquity, both were condemned in early Jewish writings (200 BC to AD 200). Examples include: (Pseudo-Phocylides, *Sentences* 184-85; and Josephus, *Against Apion* 2.25). Abortion and infanticide were also condemned by Christians. Christian examples (1st to 2nd century) include: (*Sibylline Oracles* 2:281-85; *Didache* 2:2; *Epistle of Barnabas* 19:5; *Apocalypse of Peter* 25; Athenagoras, *A Plea for the Christians* 35; Tertullian, *Apology* 9 and *On the Soul* 27; Minucius Felix, *Octavius* 30; Hippolytus, *Refutation of all Heresies* 9:7; Cyprian, *Epistle* 48).**

[2068] **Tertullian's quote of 99:6-7 is slightly different. "I swear unto you, O sinners, that a just perdition is prepared against the day of blood. Ye that serve stones, and that make images of gold, and silver and wood and stone, and earthenware, and that serve phantoms, and devils, and spirits of ill name, and all false things not according to knowledge, ye shall find no help from them" (*Idol.* 4). The day of unceasing bloodshed is also known as the "time of the sword." (See note on 38:5).**

[2069] A similar list of idol materials may be found in the (*Prayer of Nabonidus 1:7-8*, or 4Q242 1-3.7-8 (W pg. 342); Dan 5:4; Wis 13:10; Rev 9:20 and Tertullian, *Of Idolatry* 4, see also *Of Idolatry* 15).

[2070] **"Behind the present passage lies a long tradition, as old as Deuteronomy (and to be taken up by the apostle Paul), which does not simply write off idols as dead and impotent (cf. Epistle of Jeremiah, Bel and the Dragon, etc.), but identifies the gods represented by the idols as supernatural beings of demonic character" (N1 pg. 495). The belief that idol worship was in actuality the worship of demons, was and is widespread among both Jews and Christians.** For a small sampling of references to idolatry being the worship of demons see (Ps 106:36-39; TJob 3:3-4; Origen Against Celsus 7.35; *Idol.* 15; *DialTrypho* 41 and Rev 9:20).

[2071] Verses 99:6-7 were attributed to Enoch and quoted verbatim by Tertullian in about AD 198; (Tertullian, *Of Idolatry* 4).

9 Through these things they will become godless and fearful;	1QpHab 12.10-13.4
for they have done all their works in a lie,	
and they have worshipped a stone.	91:9; 94:1
In one instant they will altogether perish.[2072]	Jub 22:22; TMos 10:7; Lk 13:3,5
10 Then blessed will be all who heed the words of the wise,	
and learn them, in order to follow the commandments of the Most High;	82:4
and walk in the paths of his righteousness,	Ps 1:1
and not apostatize with apostates; for they will be saved.	98:14; 99:1

Woes Against Rich Oppressors

11 Woe to you who spread evil to your neighbors;	108:3; $1QH_a$ 10.31; Ps 9:16
for you shall be slain in Sheol.[2073] [2074]	22:13; 98:3; Ps 30:3; Isa 14:15
12 Woe to you who lay the foundations of sin and deceit	103:7; Prov 11:1; Hos 12:7
and cause bitterness on the earth;[2075]	Amos 8:5; Ps 101:5
for because of it they will be brought to an end.[2076]	
13 Woe to those who build their houses by the hard labor of others,	94:7; 97:8-9; 98:4; Jas 5:1-6
and whose every building is constructed with stones and bricks of sin.[2077]	Sir 21:8; Jer 22:13; Hab 2:11-12
Woe to you, you shall have no peace.	5:4
14 Woe to those who reject the foundations and the timeless heritage	CD A 1:15-17
of their fathers and pursue after a spirit of error.[2078] [2079]	1Mac 2:19-20; 1Kgs 22:21-23
You shall have no rest.	63:1, 5, 6
15 Woe to you who practice lawlessness and assist wrongdoing,[2080]	
murdering their neighbors, all the way up to	103:15
the day of the great judgement.	45:2; 94:9; 98:10
16 For then he shall cast down your glory, and lay affliction on	
your hearts.[2081] He shall arouse his fierce anger to destroy all of you	38:5; Ps 78:38

[2072] This text of (99:9) follows the Ethiopic as per Olson. Nickelsburg following the Greek manuscript renders: "You and the false works that you have made and constructed of stone, you will be destroyed together."

[2073] The idea is spreading a net for others, as in hunting; again, repaying good with evil.

[2074] Verses 99:11-12 are missing from the Greek text. Olson notes: "if verse 11 is authentic, the 'Admonitions' here virtually identifies Sheol and Hell with each other. Enoch 103:7-8 also seems to blur the distinctions between the two, but not enough to show any advance over Enoch 22:11, 13, where Sheol is a place of torment as well as a waiting cell" (OL pg. 240). In the New Testament, Sheol/Hades and Hell/Gehenna/Lake of Fire are separate. (Lk 16:23; Rev 20:13-15).

[2075] For this second line of 99:12 some manuscripts read "And those who know the earth" which Olson speculates may mean "And those whose knowledge is worldly" (OL pg. 240).

[2076] For 99:12, Olson following a minority of Ethiopic manuscripts has: "Woe to you who make false and deceitful measuring balances, and who cause bitterness on the earth, for because of this, an end will be made of them" (cf. Prov 11:1; Hos 12:7; Amos 8:5).

[2077] This appears to be speaking of the very wealthy using forced labor to construct their palaces (cf. 98:4).

[2078] **"The idea of inherited tradition is a remarkable slip in this pseudepigraphic document, which attributes truth to Enoch's heavenly revelations rather than to tradition inherited from the forebears" (N1 pg. 498). Obviously 1 Enoch was not written by the Enoch of old as at that point there was no "timeless heritage" from his forefathers. This timeless heritage is seen by some as referring to the Mosaic Torah** (E pg. 218).

[2079] For this line Nickelsburg has: "and a spirit of error pursues you." For spirits of error see (1 John 4:6; 1En 15:9-16:1; and TReu 2:1-3:9).

[2080] "Assist wrongdoing," these are the Jews who collaborated with their gentile oppressors.

[2081] Black has: "put evil into your hearts."

with the sword. Rev 19:15
But all the holy[2082] and righteous will remember your sins. 27:2-3; 97:5-6; 99:3

Internecine Slaughter of Sinners

100 1 At that time, and in the same place,[2083] fathers will be slain 4Ezra 13:35-39; Hag 2:22
with their sons, and brothers will fall in death with one another. 56:7; Jer 13:14; Zech 14:13
100 (2e) from dawn until the sun sets, they will be killed together,[2084] GbRev 57
1c until their blood flows like a stream. 99:5-6; Joel 3:2, 13; Rev 14:20
2 For a man will not in mercy restrain his hand from killing his son, Ezek 38:21; Mic 7:6; SibOr 8:84
nor from his beloved one.[2085] The sinner will not withhold Mt 10:21, 34-36; Lk 12:53
his hand from the honored one, nor from his brother.[2086] Lk 21:16; Mk 13:12; Ps 79:3
3 A horse will wade up to its breast through the blood of the sinners,[2087] Ps 58:10; Isa 34:2-7 4Ezra 15:35; SibOr 5:373
and the chariot will sink to its axles. Ezek 32:5-6; Rev 14:14-20

[2082] The Greek text omits "the holy."

[2083] **This same place where judgement will occur is not identified but is viewed by most as Mount Zion. The Valley of Jehoshaphat named in (Joel 3:2, 13-17) is the Kidron Valley next to Jerusalem. This is also evident in (4Ezra 13:35-39) (cf. Ezek 39:4; Zech 12:2-3, 9; 14:12; Rev 14:20). In (Rev 16:16) Armageddon, Ἁρμαγεδών, Harmagedón, (mount of assembly) is a mountain (Mt. Zion), not a valley, and this bloodshed is outside the city (Rev 14:20).** (See Heiser, Michael S., 2015. *The Unseen Realm*, pg. 370-373). For a different and deeper analysis see (Hamp, Douglas, 2022, *An Etymology of Armageddon: Mountain of Megiddo or Sheaves in the Valley of Judgement*) who arrives at "the heap of the valley of the Judgement" which he also places in Jerusalem. **The place of the taunt in (Isa 14:13) is on the mount of assembly in the far north which is Mount Hermon. This matches the identification of Bashan as a mountain in opposition to God's dwelling in (Ps 68:15-17).**

[2084] 100:2e is repositioned here to create a series of distiches (N pg. 152). This text follows the Greek; Ethiopic reads "they will kill each other."

[2085] This text follows the Greek, Ethiopic reads "nor from his son's sons," in place of "nor from his beloved one."

[2086] **This appears to be a prophecy of internecine war during the siege of Jerusalem in AD 70 (War 4.6.1-2 §§354-376).** Charles, evidently dismissing the possibility of predictive prophecy, disagrees. "It is very probable that we have here a reference to the murder of Antigonus by his brother Aristobulus 1. Josephus (*Ant* 13.11.1,2,3 §§302-314) tells us that Aristobulus specially loved Antigonus, but moved by calumnies put him to death, and afterward died of remorse for his deed" (C pg. 248). **But his interpretation does not make sense, given that the fathers and sons are plural and the blood flowed like a stream.** As in (99:4-5), all human love and order will break down, even extending to familial relationships.

[2087] **Actual battles in the past that closely meet this description are found in an account of the Battle of Gephyrun in (2Mac 12:16); and the final scene of the fall of Jerusalem in (*War* 6.8.5 §§406). "Sennacherib, king of Assyria, boasted in the early 7th c. BCE: "My prancing steed, harnessed for my riding, plunged into the streams of their blood as (into) a river" (D. D. Luckenbill, Ancient Records of Assyria and Babylonia 2.127). A Jewish account of Hadrian's unspeakably brutal conquest of Betar (this city was Bar Kokhba's last stronghold in his war against Rome) in AD 134-135 uses similar language. "They slew the inhabitants until the horses waded in blood up to the nostrils, and the blood rolled along stones (with the size of 284 liters) and flowed into the sea, staining it for a distance of six kilometers. (In case you think that Betar is close to the sea: was it not in fact sixty kilometers distant from it?)" (*Midrash Rabbah Lamentations* 2.2.6.6). (Rev 14:20) also describes such an apocalyptic scene.**

Sinners Gathered for Judgement, Righteous Protected

4 The angels shall descend into (their) hiding-places on that day,[2088]   102:3; Rev 6:15-17
and those who aided iniquity will be gathered into one place;[2089]   TAb A 12:1-2; Mt 13:41,49
and the Most High will arise on that day,[2090]   1:3-4; 91:7, 15
to exact a great judgement on all the sinners.[2091] [2092] [2093] [2094]   2Thes 1:5-10
5 He will set a guard of the holy angels, over all the righteous   Mt 18:10; Prov 7:2; Acts 12:6-11
and holy;[2095] they will guard them as the apple of the eye,[2096]   4Ezra 7:85, 95; Deut 32:10
until every evil and every sin is brought to an end.[2097]   102:4-5; 103:3-4; Ps 17:8
From that time, the pious[2098] will sleep a sweet sleep,[2099]   Dan 12:2; Jn 11:11
and there will no longer be anyone to terrify them.   1Cor 15:6, 18, 20; 1Thes 4:13-15
6 Then the wise among men will perceive the truth,   99:10
and the sons of earth will understand all the words of this epistle,   102:3
and they will recognize that their wealth cannot save them   Jas 5:1-6; Zeph 1:18; 1Tim 6:17
when iniquity collapses.   83:7

[2088] **This could also be a prophecy of the Roman siege, as Jewish defenders made use of places of hiding to no avail. (Cf. *War* 3.7.36-3.8.1 §§336, 337, 340-344; *War* 6.8.4 §§392; *War* 6.9.4 §§429-434).**
In the future angels will likewise gather sinners, even when they are hidden (cf. Mt 13:38-41; and Rev 6:15-17). *The Testament of Abraham* A (TAb 12:1-11) has a ghastly scene of two angels with whips driving myriads of souls to the place of judgement.

[2089] **"One place" Jerusalem. The Jews gathered in Jerusalem to escape the Romans. (*War* 4.2.1 §§89)**

[2090] Greek and some Ethiopic manuscripts add "of judgement" here.

[2091] "The sinners" is a possible scribal addition found in the Ethiopic but not the Greek.

[2092] Texts where God arises include: (TMos 10:3; Num 10:35; Ps 7:6; 35:23; 44:23; and Isa 51:9).

[2093] Translating from the Greek, Milik has this verse referring to the fallen watchers. "On that day the angels will be hurled down, descending into the hidden places-those who helped support wrongdoing, and they will be gathered together" (M pg. 52). But Olson sees a reading similar to the text above as more likely (OL pg. 242).

[2094] **Given the context of the surrounding prophecies about the 1st Jewish revolt, this passage could mean that all the enemies of God were gathered into Jerusalem, "one place," where the Romans, as God's agent, exacted a great judgment on the sinners.**

[2095] Guardian angels watch over the righteous and holy (See Ps 91:11; Mt 18:10; and 1Cor 11:10). Charles notes "This verse has always been interpreted of the righteous on earth, but wrongly. The righteous here spoken of are not the living, but are righteous souls in the place of the departed" (C pg. 249). However, in context of the first Jewish revolt this would be the Christians protected in Pella (see note 2097).

[2096] "Apple of the eye", something precious and irreplaceable (N1 pg. 501). (Cf. Deut 32:10, Ps 17:8, Prov 7:2, and Zec 2:8).

[2097] **The Christians in Jerusalem, obeying a prophecy, fled to Pella and escaped the punishment that fell on the Jews who had so abused them and their Lord. "Meanwhile, before the war began, members of the Jerusalem church were ordered by an oracle given by revelation to those worthy of it to leave the city and settle in a city of Perea called Pella. Here they migrated from Jerusalem, as if, once holy men had deserted the royal capital of the Jews and the whole land of Judea, the judgement of God might finally fall on them for their crimes against Christ and his apostles, utterly blotting out all that wicked generation." HE 3.5**

[2098] Ethiopic has: "the righteous" in place of "the pious."

[2099] Sweet sleep. Some interpret this as meaning that the righteous of Jerusalem will not be molested again in life. The Jewish Christians returned to Jerusalem and rebuilt what had been destroyed. This included a Jewish/Christian synagogue in the site of the upper room which had presumably been destroyed (Kramer, Joel. 2020.Where God came down. pg.134-143). The long sleep of death (Jer 51:39, 57; Dan 12:2; Mt 27:52; Jn 11:11; and 1Thes 4:13). This should not be used as a proof text for the doctrine of soul sleep. For references of the state of the dead before the judgement, both righteous and sinners, consider the following (1En 22; 4Ezra 4:35-37; 7:75-101; 2Bar 21:23-25; 30:1-5; and Rev 6:9-10).

Woes Against Sinners

7 Woe to you, sinners, when you afflict the righteous, Wis 5:1
on the day of severe anguish,[2100] and burn them in fire;[2101] Rev 20:12; 2 Mac 7:3-5
for you will be recompensed according to your deeds! 95:5; 2Thes 1:6-9; Isa 3:11
8 Woe to you, stubborn of heart, 5:4; 16:3; 98:11; Mic 2:1-3 Rom 2:5
who lie awake in order to devise evil. Ps 36:4; Isa 29:20
Fear will lay hold on you, and there will be no one to help you! 103:10; Sir 51:7; Deut 28:29,31
9 Woe to all you sinners, because of the words of your mouth, 1:9; Jude 15
and on account of the deeds of your hands;
for you have strayed from works of holiness; Rev 20:15; 2Bar 44:15
in the heat of a blazing fire, you will burn! 98:3, 6-8; 103:7-8; Heb 10:27

Creation to Testify Against the Unrighteous

10 And now, know that from the angels he will inquire in heaven
into your deeds, and from the sun and the moon and the stars, 104:8; Deut 4:26; 3Bar 8:5
concerning your sins, because on the earth NJoA 3.3; ApPaul 4-7;ApMos 36
you passed judgement on the righteous.
11 Furthermore, he will summon to testify against you every cloud and 97:7; Mt 5:44-45; Hab 2:10-12
mist and dew and rain; for all of these have been withheld from you 80:2-6; Deut 11:17
so as not to descend upon you. Zech 14:16-18
They will pay you no mind because of your sins.
12 Therefore, offer gifts to the rain, that it be not withheld from Jer 3:3; 5:24-25
falling on you! And pay gold to the dew, to the clouds, and to the
mist that they may descend.[2102] 53:1
13 For if the snow and the hoar-frost and its cold Sir 39:28-31
do hurl themselves upon you, and the winds and their chill and 76:5-13; Ps 147:17
all their scourges, then you will not be able to withstand the cold Job 38:22-23
and their torments![2103]

[2100] "Severe anguish" in context, is a time of trouble when the sinners afflict the righteous. On times of trouble for the righteous, see (2Kgs 19:3; Job 5:6-7; Ps 50:15; 77:2; 86:7; Prov 24:10; Jn 16:33 and Acts 14:22).
[2101] "Burn them in fire" This may be referencing the horrible torture Antiochus Epiphanies inflicted on Jews in (167-165 BC) who would not renounce their faith (2 Mac 7:3-5).
[2102] In this sarcastic verse, the heavens cannot be bribed to bring forth dew and rain. In ancient times, Baal was seen as the one who provided fertility and rain. (1En 101:2) makes it plain that it is God, and not Baal that controls the rain. This is evidence that this passage was written during a drought.
[2103] The elements will descend on them, but it will not be for blessing; but rather to punish them.

Men Should Fear the Most High

101 1 So contemplate, the deeds of the Most High, O sons of men,[2104] 2:1-2
and fear to do evil in his presence.
2 If he closes the windows of heaven, and withholds the rain and the dew 89:2; 100:11; Gen 7:11 Isa 24:18 Jer 3:3; 5:24-25; 1Kgs 17:1
from descending on the earth because of you, what then will you do? Deut 28:23-24; 2Chr 7:13
3 Or if he sends his anger against you because of all your deeds, 1:9; 5:4
will you not be the ones who plead with him? 27:2
So why do you speak with your lips[2105] grandiose and harsh words
against his majesty? You will have no peace!

Parable of the Sea Captains

4 Observe the sea-captains who sail upon the sea.
Their ships are tossed about by the waves and are Jas 1:6
shaken by the storms.[2106] Distressed, Jonah 1:4-5; Sir 43:24; Wis 14:1
5 and beaten by the storm, they all fear, and throw all their goods 100:6; Acts 27:14-20
and possessions into the sea, for they are anxious in heart that the sea Ps 107:23-32
will swallow them up and they will perish in it.
6 Are not the entire sea and all its waters and all its turbulence[2107] Job 26:10; 38:8-11; PrMan 3
the work of the Most High? Has he not determined its limit, 69:18; Ps 65:7; 89:9; 104:5-9
and bound it together and confined it by the sand? Prov 8:29; Jer 5:21-24
7 At his rebuke it becomes afraid and dries up, and the fish die Ps 104:24-29; 105:29; 106:9 Nah 1:4
and everything in it! But you, sinners on the land, do not fear him! Isa 50:2; Rev 8:8-9
8 Did he not create heaven and earth and everything that is in them? PrMan 2; Ps 146:6
And who gave knowledge and wisdom[2108] to all who move on the
land and[2109] that are in the sea?[2110]
9 Do not the sea-captains fear the sea?
But sinners do not fear the Most High!

[2104] "This chapter is addressed not to the righteous (i.e. the sons of heaven), but to (wicked) humanity" (N1 Pg. 504). The point of this chapter is that man is helpless in the face of God's power. Creation fears and obeys God; sinners should repent and do likewise.

[2105] "With your lips," is omitted in Ethiopic.

[2106] Olson observes concerning 101:4-102:1: **"One of the literary Gems of the *Book of Enoch*, this brilliantly executed parable seems simple and straightforward, but in only a few verses it combines a host of Enochic images, including the Flood, the obedience of Nature, the uselessness of worldly goods in a crisis, God's power to bind and control chaos, the stubborn arrogance of the wicked, the connection between knowledge of the natural and spiritual realms, and the parallels between the first judgement and the last"** (OL pg. 244). Charles notes: **"They who go down to the sea in ships are filled with fear at the might of the sea: how much more should not men fear God by whom the sea has been made and of whom it is sore afraid?"** (C pg. 252).

[2107] Greek omits "and all its turbulence."

[2108] Greek omits "and wisdom."

[2109] Greek omits "on the land and."

[2110] By including earth and sea, all creation is included under God's control. This includes both chaos monsters, Leviathan and Behemoth.

End Time Terror!

102 1 In those days, when he hurls against you the flood[2111] Isa 66:24; Lk 12:49; 2Pet 3:7
of blazing fire,[2112]where will you flee to escape? 97:3; Wis 18:14-16
When he launches his voice,[2113] with a mighty sound against you, Rev 19:13-15; 22:12; Wis 18:15
will you not be shaken and afraid? 1:4-6; Ex 19:16, 19
2 The heavens and all the luminaries will shake and tremble in terror![2114] 23:4; Isa 13:10; 24:23; 34:4
All the earth will shake and tremble and be thrown into confusion! 1QH$_a$ 11:35-37; Mk 13:24
3 All the angels will carry out their commands, 100:4; Mt 13:39
and the sons of earth will tremble and shake,[2115] 14:20
seeking to hide themselves from the presence of the Great Glory! 1:5; 9:3; 2Pet 1:17; Rev 6:15-17 Isa 2:19; 26:20-21

As for you, sinners, accursed shall you be forever,
and you shall have no peace. 5:4

The Destiny of the Righteous: A Debate

4 Take courage, you souls of the righteous dead, 96:1; Rev 14:13
and be hopeful you pious who have died.[2116] 81:4; Isa 57:1-2
5 Do not grieve because your souls have gone down to Sheol in sorrow, 22
and during your lives your body of flesh did not fare
as your goodness deserved; because the days that you lived 108:11; 1Pet 4:6
were the days of sinners and the accursed of the earth.
6 Whenever you die, the sinners will say about you:[2117] Wis 2:1-4:9
"As we die, so the righteous die. Eccl 3:19
What have they gained from their deeds? 1Cor 15:32; Ps 73:1-19
7 See? Like us, they die in grief and darkness. Mic 7:7-9
What advantage do they have over us? Eccl 2:14-24; 3:20
We are exactly the same from this point. Eccl 6:6; 9:3
8 What will they receive, or what will they look upon, for eternity?[2118] 1Cor 15:35-49

[2111] **Black temptingly suggests "flood" may be better read as "tempest or perhaps whirlwind"** (Bl pg. 310).
[2112] **This will be Jesus Christ hurling this blazing fire. "I came to cast fire on the earth, and would that it were already kindled!** (Lk 12:49).
[2113] Charles translates: "launches forth his Word" in place of "launches his voice." Isaac has: "When he flings his word against you" (cf. Wis 18:15). Jesus Christ is called the Word of God; (Jn 1:1; Heb 11:3; 1Pet 1:23; 2Pet 3:5; 1Jn 2:14; Rev 1:2; 6:9, and 19:13) and will appear to judge the world; (2Tim 4:1; and 1Pet 4:5). Others (humans) will participate in the judgement (1Cor 6:2 and Rev 20:4).
[2114] **Even the heavenly beings will be terrified at the appearance of the Word of God. The fallen beings will seek hiding places, to no avail.** Other references to end time cosmic disturbances include: (91:5; Isa 13:10; 24:23; 34:4; Ezek 32:7-10; Joel 2:10-11; Mt 24:29; Mk 13:24-27; Rev 6:12-14; 8:12; 12:4; TMos 10:5).
[2115] This text follows the Ethiopic text. The Greek reverses the order of the second and third lines of 102:3.
[2116] (1En 39:4-5 and 104:6) have the righteous saints dwelling with the righteous heavenly beings. And 100:5 has the righteous dead being guarded by the holy angels.
[2117] **Scholars see striking parallels between (Wis 2:1-4:9 and 1En 102:6-103:15; 108:8-9, 13) (N1 pg. 78; BL pg. 310). Since *The Wisdom of Solomon* was written later, it would be dependent on The Admonitions of Enoch or a common tradition.**
[2118] For 102:8, N has: "Henceforth let them arise and be saved, and they shall forever see ‹the light›. But, look, they have died, and henceforth (and) forever they will not see the light."

But look! They too have died,
and from now on they will never again see the light.[2119] Job 10:20-21; Ps 49:19
9 Therefore, it is good for us to feast and drink, to plunder and sin, Lk 12:19; 17:27-30; Eccl 5:18
to strip men naked and amass possessions and see good days.[2120] 63:10; Isa 22:13; Mic 7:2
Ps 34:12

10 Consider then those who have made themselves righteous,[2121] 103:4-9; Lk 10:29; 16:15
and how they ended up; for no unrighteousness was found in them Ps 73
until their death.[2122] [2123]
11 But they perished and became as though they had never existed; Obad 16; Sir 44:8-10; Wis 2:2
and their souls descended into Sheol in pain." Job 10:19; 18:17; Jub 22:22

The Debate Settled in Favor of the Righteous

103 1 Now I swear to you, the righteous, by the glory of the Great One, 98:1; 99:6; 104:1
and by his magnificent sovereignty. By his majesty, I swear to you[2124]
2 that I understand the following mystery.[2125] 104:10, 12; 1Pet 1:12

[2119] **This is an untrue assertion by the sinners who deny the resurrection. Early Christians spent great effort in defending the resurrection and the judgment of the wicked** (Acts 4:2; 4:33; 17:18; 23:6-8; 24:21; and 1Cor 15:12-42).

[2120] This text is confusing as to who is speaking. In the text above, the argument of the unrighteous is carried through 102:11 with the rebuttal by the righteous beginning in 103:1. This makes sense with the strong oath to the righteous in 103:1. Olson, pursuing an alternate reading with a rebuttal beginning in 102:9, translates 102:9 as: I speak to you, O you sinners. You are well satisfied to feast and to drink—and to rob, and to sin, and to strip men naked, and amass possessions, and see good days." Nickelsburg translates (102:10-11) as: "Look, then, those who consider themselves righteous—of what sort their destruction has been—no righteousness was found in them until they died. And they perished and became as those who are not, and their souls descended with pain into Sheol."

[2121] "Those who have made themselves righteous" could be read "those who justify themselves."

[2122] The righteous (those who have made themselves righteous) appear to end up just like the unrighteous. This is the same thought as in Ps 73.

[2123] For 102:10 Nickelsburg has: "Look, then, those who consider themselves righteous—of what sort their destruction has been—no righteousness was found in them until they died." **Olson notes concerning the Greek text of this verse where he translates "made themselves righteous," "this active use of 'justify' (dikaioō) with a reflexive pronoun is found in Luke 10:29 and 16:15 but nowhere else in all Greek literature." These uses by Luke, which likely came from interviews of early Christians/apostles, may indicate that they not only knew the *Admonitions of Enoch* but had memorized it or had a Greek text in front of them. Or as Aalen, who sees direct literary dependence, asks: "Was Luke personally acquainted with the man who translated 1 Enoch? Or was he perhaps himself that man?" (Aalen, S., *St. Luke's Gospel and the Last Chapters of 1 Enoch*, *New Testament Studies* 13 (1966) 1-3). These two events in Luke are not found in other gospels. Nickelsburg "Cautiously suggests that the influence may go back to Jesus himself rather than Luke's redaction since similar themes are found in other strata of the Gospels" (OL pg. 288). This would indicate that Jesus knew Greek and the Book of Enoch very well.**

[2124] **1En 103:1 is a very strong and bold oath, especially from an observant Jew. The author is totally convinced of its truth and source. He is swearing on the authority of God and his throne. It is hard to imagine composition of a stronger oath.**

[2125] "A mystery is a divine secret, often of God's plan or purpose, revealed to those to whom God chooses to reveal it" (N1 pg. 522). Other mentions of a divine secret include: (Dan 2:28-30; 47; 1En 9:6; 10:7; 16:3; 1QpHab 7.5 (W pg. 84); Mt 13:11; Rom 11:25; Eph 1:8-9; 1Pet 1:12; Rev 17:7). The Yahad, mentioned so often in the DSS, were known for secret teachings (1QS 7.17-18; 8.11-12; 1QS 9.18 (W pgs. 128-129, 131); 1QH^a 26.14-16 (W pg. 204)). The Yahad formed a movement called the Way, which was involved in "preparing the way in the desert" (Isa 40:3) whose purpose was obviously preparing the way for the Messiah (Mt 3:1-3). (1QS 9.18-20 (W pg. 131)). **This**

For I have read the tablets of heaven; 81:1-2; 93:2; 108:3, 7
and I have seen the writing of what must be, and I know 106:19
the things that are written in them and inscribed concerning you.[2126] Mal 3:16
3 Good things, joy and honor, have been made ready and written down, Rev 21-22
for the spirits of the righteous dead. 81:4
Many good things shall be given to you in recompense for your labors, 2Cor 4:16-18; Rev 14:13
and your portion will be far better than the lot of the living! 2Mac 7:9, 14
4 The spirits of the pious who have died, will live and rejoice and be glad. 20:8; Rev 20:4-6; Jn 5:29
Their spirits shall not perish, nor their memory, from Wis 3:1-6; 5:15-16; Jub 23:31 Mt 26:13
before the face of the Great One through all the generations of the ages. 1:3; Ps 9:7; Isa 51:7; Mk 12:27
Therefore, do not fear their abuse.[2127] Mt 10:26-28; Lk 12:4-5
5 Woe to you, deceased sinners, when you die with your ill-gotten wealth.
Then those who are like you will say about you: Lk 16:9; 19-31
"Happy are the sinners! They have seen all their days, Ps 73:1-20
6 and now they have died with goods and wealth.
They have not seen affliction or slaughter during their lives.
They have died in splendor, Job 21:23
and judgement has not been executed on them during their lives."[2128] Job 7:9; Lk 16:25
7 Know this! That down to Sheol they will lead your souls;[2129] 22; 102:5, 11; Jub 7:29; 22:22
and there they will be in great distress[2130] 63:10; Rev 20:14-15; Mt 13:50
8 —in darkness, in snares, and in a blazing fire. 54:3; 100:9; Isa 66:24; 2Pet 2:4
Into great judgement your souls will come, 102:7; Jude 6; Jdt 16:17
and this great judgement shall be for all generations of eternity. 2Thes 1:5-10
Woe to you, for you shall have no peace! 5:4

A Lament of the Righteous

9 You who were righteous and holy in your lifetimes?
Do not say:[2131] "In the days of our misery we toiled laboriously and
experienced every trouble, and have met with much evil.

"Way" was the early name for Christians. It was the very early Christian group Paul persecuted: "But Saul, still breathing threats and murder against the disciples of the Lord, went to the high priest and asked him for letters to the synagogues at Damascus, so that if he found any belonging to the **Way**, men or women, he might bring them bound to Jerusalem" (Acts 9:1-2). "I persecuted this **Way** to the death, binding and delivering to prison both men and women" (Acts 22:4). (Cf. Acts 24:22).

[2126] **A very fragmented Greek copy, on papyrus, of 103:3-8 was at length identified in the Dead Sea Scrolls (7Q4.1; 7Q8; 7Q12). It is notable, in that it shows 1 Enoch was translated into Greek much earlier (150-50 BC) than previously thought** (Nebe, Muro, Puech, *Fragments of the Book of Enoch from Qumran Cave 7*) (E 230).

[2127] **What a promise 103:3-4 is for the elect! This is a clear statement of a resurrection to Paradise for those who have died in righteousness.** References to the resurrection of the righteous include: (1QH[a] 19.14-17; 20.5; 4Q 521; Lk 20:35-36; Jn 5:29; Acts 24:15; Rom 6:5; 1Cor 15:12-24, 42; Phil 3:10-11; and Rev 20:4-6).

[2128] (Lk 16:19-31) amplifies this concept in the parable of Christ about the rich man and Lazarus. "**Died in splendor" wicked King Herod's funeral was ostentatious in the extreme.** (War 1.33.9 §§670-673)

[2129] **The idea is that heavenly beings will compel the sinners to enter Sheol. "Sheol is here identified with Gehenna as the place for final punishment"** (BL pg. 314).

[2130] The author of (Ps 73) also wrestles with the prosperity of the wicked, but then considers their end.

[2131] Black argues that this should read: "Did you not say"

We have been exhausted, and have become few and our spirits small.[2132] Deut 28:62; Ps 107:39
10 We perished, and there was no one to help us with words or deeds. Deut 28:29
We were powerless and found nothing.[2133] We were ground down and
crushed,[2134] and had no expectation of survival from one day to the next. Deut 28:65-67
11 We hoped to become the head and have become the tail. Deut 28:13, 33, 44; Isa 9:14
We have toiled and labored, but were not masters of the fruits of our Deut 28:30-51
labor; instead, we have become food for sinners, Deut 28:31; Ps 14:4
and lawless men have laid their yoke heavily upon us.[2135] Mic 3:3; Deut 28:48; Lk 11:46
12 Our enemies have been our masters, and to those that goaded us
and penned us in,[2136] and to our enemies we have bowed our necks, 98:12
but they have shown us no pity.
13 We sought to depart from them that we might escape and be at rest, Deut 28:65; Job 3:13
but we found no place to flee and be safe from them. Ps 55:6-8
14 We complained to the rulers[2137] in our distress,
and we cried out against those who struck us down and devoured us,
but they did not receive our petitions
and they refused to listen to our voice.
15 They did not help us, finding no fault with those who oppressed[2138]
and devoured us. Rather they supported them against us,
and lent firm support to those who killed us and made us few.
They concealed their wrong-doing,[2139] and did not remove from us
the yoke of those who devoured us, scattered us and murdered us.
But they concealed our slaughter, and they have no recollection
of how they had lifted up their hands against us."

Encouragement to the Righteous; Warning to the Wicked

104 1 I swear unto you, that in heaven the angels remember Mt 18:10; Neh 5:19; Mal 3:16
you for good[2140] before the glory of the Great One, 14:2; 103:4; Dan 12:1

[2132] Black, without telling us why, has: "and lost heart" in place of "and our spirits small"

[2133] Greek has lost a substantial portion of this sentence. This text is a literal translation of the Ethiopic. Black, combines an Ethiopic text with Greek to arrive at: "We are *slain* and no protector of any kind have we found."

[2134] "Crushed", Nickelsburg states that this word may apply to a military defeat but it's Hebrew equivalent also denotes emotional collapse. He continues: "In either case it denotes violent and total annihilation" (N1 pg.526).

[2135] **The main point of this text is that the righteous are suffering the well-known curses of Deut 28:13-68, when it should be the sinners who suffer them!**

[2136] Black, assuming a mis-rendering of the Aramaic, conjectures: "and beheaded us" in place of "and penned us in." This would fit well with "bowed our necks" (BL pg. 315).

[2137] "Are these the rulers of the Seleucids?" (Bl pg. 315).

[2138] "There are substantial differences between G^b (Greek) and the underlying Greek version of Ethiopic in this verse (103:15) (BL pg. 316).

[2139] This may mean that lower authorities hid the oppression from those above them.

[2140] **"Remember you for good" "This expression is the precise equivalent of the cliché found frequently in later synagogue inscriptions…The present text appears to know this inscriptional convention, and it asserts that through the record compiled by the angels in heaven, the righteous and their deeds are remembered by God"** (N1 pg. 529).

and your names are written before the glory of the Great One.[2141] [2142]	Rev 20:12 ,15; Lk 10:20
2 Be of good courage, for formerly you were worn out by evils and	Mt 5:10; 13:43; 4Ezra 7:97, 125
afflictions, but now you shall shine and appear like the lights of heaven,	Dan 12:3; TMos 10:9;
and the portals of heaven[2143] will be opened unto you!	Deut 28:12; 2Bar 51:10
3 Your cry will be heard, and the judgement for which you cry will also	9:3; 103:14; Isa 35:4; Rev 6:9-11
appear to you; for inquiry will be required from the rulers	97:3, 5; 99:3, 16; Lk 18:7-8
concerning your affliction, and from all those who have helped them,	103:14-15
who oppressed you and plundered you.[2144]	
4 Be of good courage, and do not abandon your hope;	Heb 10:35; Mt 22:30
for you will have great joy like the angels of heaven.[2145]	Job 38:7; Lk 15:10; Mk 12:25
5 What obligation will you have? You will not have to hide on the day	Rev 6:16; 20:6; Isa 2:10
of the great judgement, and you will not be found out to be like sinners,	19:1; 84:4; 94:9; 98:10; 99:15
and the everlasting judgement will be (far) from you	91:15; 2Pet 3:9-10; 2Thes 1:8-9
for all generations forever.	
6 Fear not, O righteous, when you see the sinners growing strong and	Ps 1:1; 37:1-9; Jer 12:1
prospering: do not be companions with them,	91:4; 94:3; Barn. 4:2
but stay far from all their wickedness;	97:4; Mt 22:30; Lk 20:36
for you will be companions of the host of heaven.[2146]	69:11; Heb 12:22; Lk 2:13 2Bar 51:5,10,12; Rev 19:14 Wis 5:5; DivInst 7.26
7 For if you sinners, say: "None of our sins will be investigated and	Mt 10:26; Dan 7:10; Mal 3:16
written down" —every one of your sins will be recorded day by day!	81:4; Rev 20:12; Mt 12:36
8 Now I declare unto you that light and darkness, day and night,	Lk 8:17; 12:2-3; Ezek 9:2-11

[2141] The last phrase "and . . . One" is not found in the Greek text.

[2142] **This is the Book of Life. You really need to have your name in this book!** Some other mentions include (Jub 36:10; ApZeph 3:6-9; 9:2; Dan 12:1; Lk 10:20; Phil 4:3; Heb 12:23; Rev 3:5; 13:8; 20:11-12; and 21:27).

[2143] Greek has: "the windows of heaven" but if one wants to take this as portals between realms, the language will allow it.

[2144] (1En 104:3) is corrupt in both the Greek and Ethiopic but has fortunately been reconstructed in various ways by scholars. For 104:3 Olson has: "Your cry *will* be heard, and the judgement for which you cry will also appear. Insofar as it will be helpful to you, there will be an investigation by the angels concerning your afflictions, even concerning all those who joined with those who oppressed and devoured you."

[2145] (1En 104:4) is missing in the Greek, likely due to an accidental omission; but it was probably original.

[2146] **Wow! What a thought. That the resurrected righteous (as in 39:5) will be companions of heavenly beings; was also understood by the authors of the Thanksgiving Hymns ($1QH_a$ 19.13-17 (W pg. 196))** "For Your glory's sake You have cleansed man from transgression, so that he can purify himself for You from all filthy abominations and the guilt of unfaithfulness, so as to be joined wi[th] the children of Your truth, in the lot with Your holy ones, that bodies, covered with worms of the dead, might rise up from the dust to an et[ernal] council; from a perverse spirit to Your understanding. That he might take his position before You with the eternal hosts and spirits [of truth], to be renewed with all that shall be and to rejoice together with those who know." Also "I will dwell safely in a ho[ly] dwelling, [in] quietness and in ease [with the eternal spirits] in the tents of glory and salvation ($1QH_a$ 20.4-6 (W pgs. 197-198). "Corresponding to the compassion of God, according to His goodness, and the wonder of His glory, He brings some of the sons of the world near, to be reckoned with Him in [the council] [of the g]ods as a holy congregation, destined for eternal life and in the lot with His holy ones" (4Q181 1.3-4 (W pg. 270)) (cf. 1QS 11.7-9 (W pg. 134) $1QS_a$ 2.8-10 (W pg. 140) $1QH_a$ 11.23 (W pg. 182). 2 Baruch (AD 110-120) carries this idea further, even recognizing time travel, and it seems other dimensions! **"For they shall see that world which is now invisible to them, and they will see a time which is now hidden to them. And time will no longer make them older. For they will live in the heights of that world and they will be like the angels and be equal to the stars. And they will be changed into any shape which they wished, from beauty to loveliness, and from light to the splendor of glory** (2 Baruch 51:8-10 (OTP1 pg. 638)). "**And the excellence of the righteous will then be greater than the angels"** (2Bar 51:12 (OTP1 pg. 638)).

observe all your sins. 97:7; 100:10-11

Conclusion to the Admonitions

9 Do not go astray in your hearts, or lie, or alter the words of truth, TAsh 5:4
or declare the words of the Holy One are false. Do not give praise to 46:7; 94:5; 98:14; 99:2
your idols. For it is not to righteousness that all your lies and 99:7-9,14
all your error lead, but to enormous sin.
10 And now I know this mystery, that sinners will tamper with and 103:2; Prov 30:5-6
distort the words of truth, and pervert many. They will speak evil 94:5; 98:15; 99:2; Rev 22:18-19
words,[2147] and lie,[2148] and invent great fabrications,
and write "scriptures"[2149] in their own names.[2150]
11 If only they would write truthfully all my words in their languages,[2151]
and neither omit nor alter these words but write down accurately Rev 22:18-19
all that I testify to them.[2152] Jub 4:19, TZeb 3:4
12 And again, I know a second mystery. My books[2153] will be given 4Ezra 14:45-47; 1QapGen 19.24
to the righteous and holy and wise, to become a cause of joy in the truth, Dan 12:4, 9, 10
and for abundant wisdom.

2147 Greek omits: "speak evil words."

2148 **A prediction that people will fall into sin is common in the Testament of the Twelve Patriarchs. In four of these passages the writings of Enoch are referenced** (TSim 5:4; TLev 14:1; TDan 5:5-6; TBenj 9:1).

2149 Isaac, Milik (M pg.50) and Olson have "scriptures" here. Isaac relying on Ethiopic texts plausibly has: "my scriptures." Others have "books." **A reading of "scriptures" should be considered, as the author is likely not concerned about alterations of books of a non-scriptural nature, and the Ethiopic supports it.** Isaac is fully within bounds here, as the Ethiopic word he translates as scriptures in 103:10 is ወመጸሐፍተ, wämäṣaḥəfətä. The root word "masahaft" according to (Leslau's - *Comparative Dictionary of Ge'ez* (1987) pgs. 552 and 735) is the word for "sacred books, scriptures." In addition, the Greek has "scriptures in their names" in 1En 104:10. Following Isaac, the Ethiopic, Greek, and usage in context, this text is using scriptures in verse 10 but it could also apply in 12 and 13 in place of books. **This is important because it establishes that the author considers his own writing as scripture, likely along with the other Enochic texts existing at the time.**

2150 Ethiopic reads "own words" rather than "own names." Isaac has: "and write out my scriptures on the basis of their own words." This certainly carries the meaning of condemning those that are writing in their own authority or the mere human, rather than divine, origins of their writings. Speaking of 104:10, Nickelsburg opines: "Thus the text appears to have spoken about people who wrote writings in their own names. This could mean people who attached their own names to their literary compositions. But the idiom can also mean 'with their own authority.'" (N1 pg. 633-534). This gives us insight into why scribes composed their works in the names of famous patriarchs in place of using their own names. It would be interesting to know what "scriptures" the author is referring to. Nickelsburg speculates it may be works that rewrite the Torah such as Jubilees and the DSS Temple Scroll (N1 pg. 534). But this makes little sense, given that Jubilees is so full of Enochic references as to be considered Enochic in itself, and the Temple Scroll was found in cave 4, in association with most of the Enochic texts. This is evidence they were gathered from the same location. Milik seems closer to the mark when he suggests: "We must suppose him to be referring to the historical and apologetical works, in prose and in verse, of Demetrius, of Philon the Ancient, of Eupolemus, Artapan, Aristeas, Cleodemus-Malkâ, of pseudo-Hecataeus, Ezekiel the Tragic, and so on. Against this Graeco-Jewish religious literature he sets his own pseudepigraphal work" (M pg. 50).

2151 Nickelsburg considers *all my words in their languages*, to be an evident dittograph (scribal duplication) copied from the previous line (N pg. 162). Charles speculates that the languages referred to are Aramaic and Greek (C pg. 262).

2152 This thought is similar to (Rev 22:18-19).

2153 Isaac has: "scriptures" in place of "books." This is speaking of Enoch's Book (N1 pg. 534). The prophet's wish is fulfilled. *The Book of Admonitions*, despite 1400 years of being lost to the west, it is now "given to the righteous and holy and wise, to become a cause of joy in the truth and for abundant wisdom."

13 Indeed, to them, the books[2154] will be given,[2155] and they will believe in them, and all the righteous will rejoice and be glad to learn from them all the paths of truth.[2156]

105 1 In those days, the Lord, appointed them (the righteous) over the
sons of earth to testify with regard to them, according to their wisdom, 91:14
saying: "Instruct them, for you are their guides and rewards upon Pss 2:8-9
all the earth.[2157] [2158]
2 [For I and my son[2159] will be united with them forever in the paths 45:4; Prov 30:4; Jn 14:23;1Jn 5:5 71:16-17; 4Ezra 7:28, 29; 14:9
of truth, during their lives; and you will have peace.][2160] Rev 21:3; Jn 14:27
Rejoice, O children of uprightness." [Amen.][2161]

2154 Isaac again has: "scriptures" in place of "books."
2155 Greek omits, "Indeed, . . . given,
2156 Chapter 105 is omitted in Greek, but material corresponding to verse 1 and possibly the end of verse 2 is attested in Aramaic fragments (N pg. 162; OL pg. 252).
2157 Black suggests that based on a misunderstanding of an Aramaic term, this last line should be translated "you are their teachers and leaders over all the earth" (BL pg. 318).
2158 "A thin strip of 4QEn^c 5 i contains (parts of) seven words from 104:13 and 105:1-2, as well as a little of 106 and thus indicates that the chapter was part of the Aramaic" (N1 pg. 531). (4QEn^c 5 i (M pg. 206-209)) includes (104:13-106:2) thus indicating that **the Admonitions of Enoch and the Birth of Noah were joined together in antiquity.**
2159 It is disputed if "I and my son" refers to God and the Messiah, or Enoch and Methuselah. The former makes more sense in the context of being "united with them forever in the paths of truth." Especially if it is a Christian interpolation as some suspect.
2160 The first sentence of 105:2 was thought by Milik to be a Christian gloss (scribal note) since it was not found in the DSS fragments (M pgs. 54, 208). Most other scholars agree. The Aramaic is here incorporated into chapter 105 and the suspected gloss is included with brackets. The end of texts were prime locations for glosses and interpolations since they could be easily added there. Black speculates there may have been a line here referring "to Enoch himself and his son Methuselah" (BL pg. 319).
2161 Amen is not found in the Aramaic text (M pg. 208). **It is obvious that this is the end of a section of Enoch since it contains an admonition not to change the words, and a closing charge. It is clear that 106-107; "The story of Noah's birth was appended to the Enochic corpus to provide a conclusion that described the initiation of the events that would lead to judgement and the salvation that lay beyond it"** (N1 pg. 539). **The end of 1En 105:2 and the beginning of 106:1 were found on one of the DSS with only a space and a half between them thus establishing that the birth of Noah was appended to the Admonitions at an early date.**

The Birth of Noah

Background of *The Birth of Noah*

Original language: Aramaic, translated into Greek, then Ethiopic (Ge' ez). "This 'Book of Noah' was summarized in Aramaic, undoubtedly its original language, by the compiler of 1QGenesis Apocryphon."[2162] The text is attested in Ethiopic, and Greek, with fragments of Aramaic and Latin.

Author and provenance: Jewish, Palestine

Date: 150-33 BCE. This text "appears to be an ad hoc composition that makes use of a number of older traditions-including some from the Enochic corpus itself." [2163] "In its present form, then, it must be dated after the incorporation of the Epistle into the corpus in the first half of the second century B.C.E. . . . and before the copying of 4QEn^c in the last third of the first century B.C.E."[2164] "The account of Noah's birth (chaps. 106-107) was composed before the middle of the first century B.C.E. Subsequently, an editor added it to the Enochic collection in order to refer to the birth of a hero who was construed as the prototype of the righteous who would survive the great judgement and renew humanity in the new age."[2165] "The Dead Sea Scroll fragments show that these chapters were attached to the end of the 'Admonitions' by at least the end of the first century BCE."[2166] "That these chapters are an appendix—but a very early one—is proven by the DSS, which have a blank space-and-a-half between the end of 105:2 and the beginning of 106:1."[2167]

Important notes: 1QapGen 2.1-5.27 is a similar account found in the Dead Sea Scrolls. It may also have links with other Noachic material in chapters 65-67 and 83-84. The Birth of Noah was found in the Chester Beatty-Michigan Papyrus which dates to the third century AD. "A ninth-century Latin MS (MS Royal 5.E.XIII) includes an extract from the story of Noah's birth (106:1-18)."[2168] 1 Enoch 106 is attested in Latin in an eighth-century manuscript, which bears a press-mark from the fourteenth or fifteenth century that seems to point to its inclusion in an English monastic library.

The Birth of Noah; an Appendix (Chapter 106-107)

106 1 After a time I took a wife[2169] for Methuselah my son, and she Jub 4:27
bore a son. She called his name Lamech, saying: "Righteousness has

[2162] M pg. 55.
[2163] N1 pg. 542.
[2164] N1 pg. 542.
[2165] N1 pg. 26.
[2166] OL pg. 18.
[2167] OL pg. 252.
[2168] N1 pg. 14. M pg. 57, M pg. 80.
[2169] Methuselah married Edna, the daughter of Ezrael, the daughter of his father's brother (a cousin) (Jub 4:27).

been 'brought low' until this day."[2170]
And when he had come to age, Methuselah took for him a wife[2171]
and she conceived from him[2172] and bore a son.
2 And when the boy was born,[2173] his body was whiter than snow and 87:2; 90:21-22; Dan 7:9 Rev 1:14; 4Q534 1.1.1-2?
redder than a rose, his hair all white, and like white wool and curly.[2174] 46:1; Dan 10:6; ApPet 6-10
Glorious <was his face>;[2175] and when he opened his eyes, 1Q19 3
the house shone like the sun.[2176] Ex 34:29-30; Mt 17:1-2; Isa 60:1
3 And when he was taken up from the hands of the midwife,[2177] V*ita* 21:3
he opened his mouth and praised the Lord of righteousness.[2178] 22:14; 90:40; 4Ezra 6:21
4 His father Lamech was afraid of him and fled,[2179]
and came to his father Methuselah and said to him:
5 "A strange child has been born to me; he is not like any human,
but resembles the children of the angels of heaven! His form is different 69:4-5; 71:1
and he is not at all like us.
His eyes are like the rays of the sun, and his face is glorious.[2180] Acts 6:15
6 It seems to me that he has not sprung from me, but from an angel,[2181] 1QapGen 2:1

[2170] There is word play involved here. "Lamech" (*lmk*) and "brought low indeed" (*lw mk*) or "truly brought low" (*lm mk*) (OL pg. 252).

[2171] Lamech married a woman whose name was Bitenosh, the daughter of Barakiel, the daughter of his father's brother (a cousin) (Jub 4:28; 1QapGen 2.3 (W pg. 91).

[2172] Greek omits: "and she conceived from him."

[2173] Greek omits: "And when the boy was born."

[2174] Isaac has: "the hair of his head as white as wool and his demdema beautiful:" As for demdema, he notes: "This Eth. word has no equivalent in English. It refers to long and curly hair combed up straight that one calls *gofārē* in several modern Ethiopian languages, or "afro" in colloquial English." Charles observes that Noah's long beautiful locks are not mentioned in the Latin text and that it would be highly unusual for a newborn to have long hair. He therefore suspects corruption in the text (C pg. 264). Knibb sees "the tresses . . . glorious" as a gloss an omits it. Our text follows the Greek closely.

[2175] "<was his face>" is added to match 106:5.

[2176] He was shining is a result of being in the presence of God (Ex 34:29; Isa 60:1; Dan 10:6, 12:3; 1En 14:20-21; 71:1, 104:1-2; and Mt 17:1-2). In this vision of Noah, at his birth, he is born directly from the presence of God. This is a type of Jesus Christ descending to earth without sin, directly from the presence of God (Jn 3:13).

[2177] The Life of Adam and Eve (*Vita* 21:3) has an even more miraculous birth for Cain. "And she bore a son, and he was lustrous. And at once the infant rose, ran, and brought in his hands a reed and gave it to his mother. And his name was called Cain." Miraculous events around birth find parallels in scripture. Adam, Isaac, Jacob, Moses, John the Baptist and Jesus Christ all had unusual events surrounding their birth.

[2178] Nickelsburg has: "Lord ‹of eternity›" in place of "Lord of righteousness" in order to match the Latin text of 106:11.

[2179] You can't blame Lamech for being frightened! This is quite a hilarious scene.

[2180] **In the Dead Sea Scrolls, (1 QapGen 2:1-18 (W pg. 91-92)), a parallel account is found, where Lamech confronts his wife Bitenosh (compare Jubilees 4:28) about Noah's paternity, out of fear that Noah was conceived by a Watcher or Nephilim. She eloquently denies it, convincing Lamech by swearing an oath that he indeed was the father. The rest of the account (1 QapGen 2:19-5:27) is similar to that found here. "This version appears to be dependent on 1 Enoch 106-107 rather than on a common source, and in any event, the Apocryphon's version of Enoch's oracle was longer than in 1 Enoch 106-107"** (N1 pg. 76). **The supernatural conception of Noah is denied, but the supernatural conception of Jesus Christ is confirmed!** (Mt 1:20).

[2181] **Humans mating with spiritual beings would have been a very real concern in those preflood days. A parallel passage, (1QapGen 2:1(W pg. 91)) says, "then I decided that the conception was at the hands of Watchers, that the seed had been planted by Holy Ones or Nephil[im]." One of the reasons for patriarchs marrying within known family lines was to exclude fallen watcher bloodlines.**

and I fear him, lest some great wonder happen in his days on the earth.
7 I beg you, father, and beseech you; go to Enoch our father, 12:1; 65:1-2
and hear from him the truth; for his dwelling-place
is among the angels."[2182] [2183] 70:1-4; Jub 4:23
8 When Methuselah heard the words of his son, he came to me,[2184] 1QapGen 2.23
at the ends of the earth, where he had heard that I then was, 65:2; Jub 4:23; Ps 61:2
and he spoke to me: "My father, hear my voice and come to me."
I heard his voice, and went to him, and said: "Behold, here I am, my child.
Why have you come to me?"
9 He answered and said: "Because of an emergency I have come to you,
and because of a dreadful sight I have approached you here.[2185]
10 Hear me, my father, for a firstborn son has been born to my son 1Q19 3
Lamech, whose type and appearance is not like the form of a human.
His color is whiter than snow and redder than the flower of[2186] Mk 9:3; Rev 19:14
the rose, and the hair of his head is whiter than the whitest wool. Rev 1:14; ApPet 6-10
His eyes are like the rays of the sun; 1QapGen 5:2-23
and he opened his eyes and made the whole house bright.[2187] [2188]
11 When he was taken up from between the hands of the midwife,
he opened his mouth and blessed the Lord of eternity![2189]
12 His father, Lamech, my son, was afraid, and fled to me,
and he does not believe that he is his son,
but thinks that he is from the angels of heaven.
And so, I have come to you, because from the angels

[2182] A conflict exists between this text and the chronology of both the Masoretic and Septuagint texts of (Gen 5:21-29). In Genesis, Enoch had already been taken by God (Gen 5:24) before the birth of Noah (Gen 5:29). (Jub 4:16-28), agrees that Enoch had been taken prior to the birth of Noah. This can be resolved if the view is taken that in this vision Methuselah is visiting Enoch in paradise, see (Jub 4:23); or Enoch is visiting Methuselah on earth after his translation.

[2183] The parallel account of (106:4-8 in 1QapGen 2.19-25 (W pg. 92)) reads: "Thereupon I, Lamech, ran to Methuselah my father, and [told] him everything, [so that he would go ask Enoch,] his father, and come to understand the whole matter with certainty. For he, Enoch, is beloved and a friend [of God, and with the Holy Ones] has his lot been cast. They reveal everything to him. When Methusel[ah] heard [of these matters,] he set out for his father Enoch, in order to learn from him the truth of the whole affair [...] his will. Then he went the length of the land of Parvaim, and there he found Enoch [his father with the Holy Ones.] He [sa]id to Enoch, his father, "O, my father, my lord, I [have come] to you [...Hear] what I say to you. Do not be angry with me that I have come here [...]". (1QapGen) "can be dated paleographically to around the turn of the era, and by Accelerator Mass Spectroscopy between 73 B.C.E. and 14 C.E. Thus, the terminus ante quem for chaps. 106-7 appears to be a bit before the turn of the century" (NV2 pg. 279). Parvaim (*Oriental regions*), found in the above parallel account is the name of an unknown place or country whence the gold was procured for the decoration of Solomon's temple. (2Chr 3:6) It may be derived from the Sanscrit *purva*, "eastern," and is a general term for the east. Some have speculated that it is in northeastern Arabia.

[2184] Some Ethiopic manuscripts read "to us." Presumably meaning Enoch and the angels. Enoch did not die so he has not come back from the dead.

[2185] Greek omits: "and because of a dreadful sight I have approached you here."

[2186] Greek omits: "the flower of"

[2187] Greek omits: "and he opened his eyes and made the whole house bright"

[2188] Fragments of 106:2 or 10 are found in the DSS (1Q19 Frag. 3 (W pg. 289)).

[2189] Latin has: "Lord of eternity" "dominum viventem in secula" literally "Lord living forever" as in 1En 5:1. Ethiopic has "Lord of heaven" here.

you have the exact facts and the truth."[2190]

Enoch Answers Concerns about Noah and Prophecies the Deluge

13 Then I, Enoch, answered and said: "The Lord will restore — 4Q204 5.2 or 4QEnc 5 ii
his commandment upon the earth,[2191] just as I have seen and made — Isa 43:19
known to you, my son. That in the days of my father Jared,[2192] — 6:6; 37:1; Gen 5:18-20; 1QapGen 3.3; Num 16:30

they transgressed the word of the Lord
and violated the covenant of heaven.[2193] — 6-8; 86:1-4
14 And behold, they went on sinning and transgressed the custom. — Jub 5:1-4; 2Bar 51:5, 10
They changed[2194] in order to mate with women — 15:4-7; Jude 6
and commit sin with them. — Gen 6:1-4
They married some of them, and they went on begetting children.[2195]
17a They have borne on the earth giants,[2196] and these are not like spirits, — Rom 1:3-4; 8:4-16
but of flesh. — Gal 4:29
15 And there will be great wrath upon the earth and a deluge,
and there will be great destruction for one year. — Gen 7:11; 8:13-14
16 But this child which has been born to you will be left on the earth, — Gen 7:23
and his three sons will be saved with him, — 1Pet 3:20
when all people on the earth die,
17b and the earth will rest and be cleansed — Gen 6:11-13; 2Pet 1:4
of the great corruption that is on it.[2197] — 48:10; 91:17; 1QapGen 11.13-14
18 Now tell Lamech concerning the one who has been born:
'He is truly your son; and call this child who is born unto you 'Noah,'
for he will be your 'remnant,' for whom you will find 'rest.'[2198] — Jub 6:1-7; Sir 44:17; Gen 5:29
He and his sons will be saved from the corruption on the earth, and

---

2190 And . . . truth" follows Nickelsburg's rendering.
2191 Olson has: "In truth, the Lord will restore a new order on the earth"
2192 "Jared" see (1En 6:6; 37:1).
2193 (1QapGen 5:2-22 (W pg. 92-93)) has a different and expanded account of Enoch's response to Methuselah. DSS fragments contain portions of (106:13- 107:2) in (4Q204 5.2 or 4QEn^c 5 ii). This angelic covenant would have preexisted the Noahic covenant.
2194 "Changed" This word is attested in the DSS (4Q204 5.2.18 (W pg. 289)). **That the 200 angels altered their form in order to sin with women, is taught in the writings of the church fathers and other period writers:** (Pseudo-Clementine 12-13; Cyprian; *The Dress of Virgins* 14; *Octavius* 26; Philo, *Questions and Answers on Genesis* (*Quastiones et solutiones in Genesin*) 1.92; and Sulpicius Severus, *Historia sacra* (Sacred History) I.2)
2195 In both the Greek and DSS; 106:17a is inserted here after 106:14 and before 106:15. 106:17b is correct in its position.
2196 In Ethiopic this is literally "those who are tall."
2197 The flood cleansed the earth like baptism, as a picture of salvation, cleanses the Christian of sin (1Pet 3:20-21). Peter likely had this passage in mind.
2198 For 106:18ab, Nickelsburg has: "And now tell Lamech, 'He is your child in truth, and ‹this child will be righteous and› blameless, ‹And "Noah"› call his name, for he will be your remnant, from whom you will find rest.'" The name "Noah" may translate to "remnant who is left" (cf. Sir 44:17). **In the Masoretic text of Gen 5:29 the root of Noah's name means "console" (see 107:3). Whereas in the LXX, it translates to "rest." This indicates that the LXX (early to mid-3rd century BC) stands behind this text; so, it was written after the composition of the LXX. Noah is seen as a forerunner of the Christ (savior and cleanser of the world). Genesis (5:29) indicates that Lamech knew from the time of Noah's birth that he was special.**

from all the sins and injustice, which will be carried out
on the earth in his days.
19 Later on, there will come still greater wickedness than that which
was committed in their days on the earth.[2199]

For I know the mysteries of the Lord, which the holy ones have revealed
and shown me, and I have read them in the heavenly tablets.

Gen 6:5
1:5; 39:1; 91:6-7; Mt 24:12, 37
2Thes 2:7-12; TSim 5:4
TLev 14:1; TDan 5:5-6;
TBenj 9:1
47:3; 81:1-2; 93:2; 103:2

107 1 And I saw it written in them that generation after generation
will do evil in this way,[2200] and wrong will continue,
until there arise generations of righteousness.[2201]
Evil and wickedness shall end, and violence will cease
from the earth, and good things will come to them upon the earth.[2202]
2 Now go, my child, run and tell Lamech, your son, that this boy
who has been born, is truly and without deception his son."[2203]
3 When Methuselah had heard the words of his father Enoch—for
he had disclosed to him everything which is secret—he returned.[2204]
And the name of the child was called "Noah;" he who gladdens[2205]
the earth after all the destruction.[2206] [2207]

TLev 14:1
91:10-92:5; 2Tim 3:1-5
Rev 21:22-27
Rev 21:4, 8; Mt 7:25-33
1QapGen 5:2-23
1QapGen 5:24-27
Gen 5:29; Jub 7:1-6
10:16-19

[2199] **Jesus appears to be referencing the idea in this verse of a return of extreme wickedness in the end times. "And because lawlessness will be increased, the love of many will grow cold" (Mt 24:12). The apostle Paul echoed this theme of increased end time wickedness (2Thes 2:7-12) (cf. 1En 91:6-7).**

[2200] Greek reads: "that one generation [will be] wor[se] than another" Cook also differently translates the Aramaic: "each generation will be more evil than the last" (W pg. 290).

[2201] Cook has: "truth" in place of "righteousness." (W pg. 290).

[2202] This can only be Messiah's kingdom.

[2203] "That the child is Lamech's, is now emphasized in a positive and negative formulation… The double formulation has an exact parallel in the Demotic Magical Papyrus 5:15, 20" (N1 pg. 549) (See also 5.21 of the DMP). The Demotic Magical Papyrus, used for divination and magic is thought to have been composed early in the 2nd century AD.

[2204] Black translates "for he had disclosed to him the whole mystery."

[2205] Noah gladdens the earth after its destruction, as seen in (Jub 7:3-6) where "he celebrated with joy the day of this feast" after reestablishing agriculture on the earth. In the Masoretic text of (Gen 5:29), the root of Noah's name means "console."

[2206] Knibb, following the Greek has: "for he will comfort the earth after all the destruction."

[2207] Greek appends to the end of the text: "Epistle of Enoch"

An Eschatological Exhortation

Background of an Eschatological Exhortation, or simply Chapter 108.

Original language: Aramaic, translated into Greek and then Ethiopic.[2208] It is preserved only in Ethiopic (Ge' ez).

Author and provenance: Jewish, Judea.

Date: Chapter 108 was written after *The Book of the Parables* (20 to 4 BC) and before 1 Peter (62-63 CE). It thus dates from the very dawn of Christianity. "Since none of these parallels to the earlier chapters indicate the use of independent, more primitive tradition, it seems likely that chap. 108 was composed as the conclusion to a form of the corpus that included at least chaps. 1-71, 81:1-82:4 and 85-105."[2209] This independently attests to the existence of the Parables in the time of Christ even though they were not found among the DSS. "The similarities between 1 Enoch 108 and 1 Peter are remarkable and could indicate that something like the text of 1 Enoch 108 was part of "Peter's" theological repertoire."[2210] This is the last text added to the Book of 1 Enoch. "Chapter 108, a second appendix is not represented in any Aramaic or Greek fragments and is of an unknown date, but it contains no distinctly Christian ideas and is certainly in the Enochic tradition."[2211] "On the other hand, the origin of En. 108 is enigmatic, and the reason for its late addition (it is missing in the Chester Beatty-Michigan papyrus) to the Christian Enochic corpus is obscure."[2212]

Important notes: This short appendix to *The Book of Enoch* is critically important. That chapter 108 is dependent on 1 Enoch 18-21 is universally acknowledged.[2213] Parallels with the *Charter of a Jewish Sectarian Association/ Community Rule* (1QS 3.13-4:12) have been noted by the editor.[2214] Similarities between 108 and early New Testament (esp. 1 Peter) writings are numerous. Chapter 108 therefore provides a transition from the rest of the *Book of Enoch* to the New Testament. "While the evidence for a particular group known as the *Anawim* is tenuous, there are many lines of convergence between 1 Enoch 108 (and perhaps also the Epistle), some of the Qumranic materials, and the kinds of spirituality propounded in the Magnificat, parts of the Sermon on the Mount, and the Epistle of James. Further comparative study of these texts may

---

2208 N1 pg. 15; BL pg. 323.
2209 N1 Pg. 553.
2210 N1 pg. 560.
2211 OL pg. 18.
2212 M pg. 57.
2213 See Charles, Book of Enoch, p. 269.
2214 Does the association between (1QS 3.13-4.14), 1Enoch 108:3) and the New Testament indicate an association between the early Christian movement, the Yahad, and their parent Essene movement? The Yahad is a Jewish group whose charter is contained in (1QS, 4Q255-264a and 5Q11). Yahad =unity. For example, compare (1QS 4:13) Hell's outer darkness" to Christ's statements concerning outer darkness in (Mt 8:12; 22:13 and 25:30). Also compare the "generation of light" (1En 108:11) with "Sons of light" in (1QS 3.13, 24, 25) and "sons of light" in (Lk 16:8; Jn 12:36) and "children of light" in (Eph 5:8 and 1Thes 5:5). That the Yahad also called themselves the Way (1QS 9.18) as in (Acts 9:2; 19:9, 23) increases the possibility of an association. DSS pertaining to the Yahad, the Qumran sectarian texts, at a bare minimum include texts 7, 8, 9, 10, 12, 30, 101; 105; 125 and 128 in W.

reveal new insights into a common religious mentality that proliferated itself in a variety of groups and sects in early Judaism and primitive Christianity."[2215] The *Anawim* are the poor, meek, afflicted, and oppressed. This would be those who glory in God despite their poverty. (108:7-10) "A similar worldview is attested in the *Testament of Job*[2216] and among Christian texts, in Hebrews, James, and 1 Peter. Key parts of the preaching attributed to Jesus in Matt 5:3-12; 6:19-21, 23-34 | | Luke 6:20-23: 12:33-34; 12:22-32 also attest this kind of apocalypticized wisdom."[2217]

"The writer (of Chapter 108) is Essene in tone. Observe the honor paid to asceticism, the scorn of gold and silver in vv. 8-10, the blessed immortality of the spirit, but apparently not of the body, as well as the dualism of light and darkness so prominent in vv. 11-14"[2218] That this text was used in 1 Peter and James would argue that James and likely the inner circle of Jesus (Peter, James and John) were Essenes or a related group. Other evidence exists in a close comparison of the gospels and the descriptions of the Essenes in the writings of Josephus,[2219] Pliny,[2220] and Philo[2221] for a discerning reader. This is evidence that the earliest roots of Christianity are in the Essene tradition.

An Eschatological Exhortation (Chapter 108)

108 1 Another book which Enoch wrote for his son 37:2
Methuselah,[2222]who will come after him and maintain 1:2; 14:1; 92:1
the covenant[2223] in the last days. 99:2
2 You who have observed it, are waiting expectantly
in these days, until evildoers are brought to an end 1Pet 3:12; Dan 9:24
and the power of the sinners is finished.[2224]
3 Keep on waiting until sin passes away, for their names 10:20-22

[2215] N1 pg. 554.
[2216] The *Testament of Job* (100 BCE-100 CE) is a pre-Christian text which may have originated with the Therapeutae, Essenes or a similar group.
[2217] N1 pg. 553.
[2218] C pg. 269.
[2219] *War* 2.8.1-13 §§2.117-161; *Ant* 18.1.5 §§ 1.18-22.
[2220] Pliny, *Natural History* 5.73.
[2221] Philo of Alexander, *Good Person; (Quod Omnis Probus Liber Sit)* XII. §§75-85.
[2222] **This phrase indicates that *The Eschatological Exhortation* came after at least part of the rest of Enoch was composed. Chapter 108 has parallels from the rest of 1 Enoch, including the parables (in verses 7-10), in "situation and worldview" and "important motifs and imagery" (N1 pg. 553). Since none of these parallels to the earlier chapters indicate the use of independent, more primitive tradition..., it seems likely that chap. 108 was composed as the conclusion to a form of the corpus that included at least chaps. 1-71, 81:1-82:4, and 85-105" (N1 pg. 553). If, as appears proven beyond reasonable doubt, material was pulled from chapter 108 for Matthew, 1 Peter, James and Hebrews then this indicates that the vast majority of the corpus was completed prior to the composition of these books. Since the book of James is thought to have been written in AD 40-45, (ESV pg. 2389), this is further evidence that the entire corpus predates the ministry of Christ.**
[2223] "Maintain the covenant" so Olson, others have "keep the law." If this was written by a biblical Enoch, there was no mosaic law in his time, nor a Noahic covenant for that matter (cf. use of "covenant" in 99:2).
[2224] **108:2-13 has numerous word and idea similarities with Matthew; esp. the Sermon on the Mount (Mt 5:3-11; 6:19-21, 23-34) James, 1 Peter, and Revelation**. See cross references for some of them.

shall be blotted out[2225] of the Book of Life[2226] and out of the books of the holy ones,[2227] and their seed[2228] shall be destroyed forever. Their spirits shall be slaughtered,[2229] and they will cry out and groan in a desolate[2230] void,[2231] and in fire shall they burn; for there is no earth there.[2232]

47:3; 103:2; Ps 69:28; Rev 3:5; 13:8; 20:15; Dan 12:1
22:13; 1Pet 1:23; Gen 3:15; Ex 32:32; OdesSol 22:5
10:13; 22:12; 98:3; 99:11; Mt 10:28; Gen 1.2 LXX
Mt 8:12; 13:41-43; 22:13; 24:51; 25:30; ApPet 20-33
18:10-16; 21:1-10; Rev 20:14-15; 1QS 4.13-14

The Final Abode of the Wicked

4 I saw there something like a cloud, that could not be discerned, for because of its depth I was unable to observe (it). I saw flames of fire blazing brilliantly, and things like brightly shining mountains that revolved and shook from side to side.[2233]
5 I questioned one of the holy angels who was with me saying: "What is this brightness, for it is not heaven but only the flames of a blazing fire and the voices of crying and weeping, and groaning, and severe pain."
6 And he said to me: "This place which you see—here are cast the spirits of sinners and blasphemers,[2234] and of those who work wickedness and of those who alter everything which the Lord has established by the mouths of the prophets; things which must be accomplished.[2235]

18:13-15; 21:3
Jer 4:24
27:2
Isa 33:14
Lk 13:27-29
1:9; 91:7; ApPet 21, 27
104:10-11
99:2; Lk 1:70; Acts 3:18-21
103:2; 1Pet 1:10-12; Ezek 21:7; Lk 24:44

2225 Nickelsburg has: "erased" in place of "blotted out."

2226 **The wicked will have their names blotted out of the Book of Life. This passage sheds light on (Rev 3:5) which appears to be dependent on this passage.** "The one who conquers will be clothed thus in white garments, and I will never blot his name out of the book of life." Other references to names being blotted out include (Ex 32:32-33; Ps 9:5; 69:28; Rev 3:5).

2227 One Ethiopic manuscript has: "book of the Holy One." Manuscripts differ.

2228 Nickelsburg has: "spirits" in place of "seed."

2229 "Spirits slaughtered" see (1En 22:13 and 98:3; 99:11). These spirits are not annihilated because they "cry out and groan."

2230 **"Desolate" Charles links this word to the Greek word in the LXX used in Gen 1:2 for formless which in Hebrew is תֹהוּ (tohu) which is defined as formlessness, confusion, unreality, emptiness. This type environment is commonly described in accounts of near-death experiences. "Another woman in childbirth felt herself floating on water, but at a certain point, 'It was no longer a peaceful feeling; it had become pure hell. I had become a light out in the heavens, and I was screaming, but no sound was going forth. It was worse than any nightmare. I was spinning around, and I realized that this was eternity; this was what forever was going to be.... I felt the aloneness, the emptiness of space, the vastness of the universe, except for me, a mere ball of light, screaming.'"** (Bush, Nancy Evans, and Greyson, Bruce, *Distressing Near-Death Experiences: The Basics,* The Journal of the Missouri State Medical Association. 111(6): 486–491).

2231 Knibb has: "chaotic desert place," Nickelsburg has "desolate, unseen place," Isaac has: "invisible wilderness" Black has: "a place deserted and void."

2232 **The description of hell in 108:3 is very similar to descriptions by Christ in (Mt 8:11-12; 13:42; and Mk 9:43-48).**

2233 **The imagery of the desolate void, flames, and revolving mountains shows the authors familiarity with the Book of Watchers (18:10-16; 21:1-10).**

2234 **The sinners are here imprisoned in the place prepared for the devil and his angels as in (Mt 25:41).**

2235 Isaac has: "...through the mouth of the prophets, all of which have to be fulfilled." **Jesus Christ may have this text in mind in (Lk 24:44) "Then he said to them, "These are my words that I spoke to you while I was still**

7 For there are books and records about them in heaven above, so that the angels may read them and know what destiny awaits the sinners,[2236] and the spirits of those who have gone astray; have defiled their bodies, have revenged themselves against God, and have
outdone evil men."[2237] [2238]

47:3; 81:1-2; 103:1-4; AscenIs 7:27
1Pet 1:10-12; Rev 5:1; 20:12-15; Mk 13:32
7:1; 19:1; SibOr 2:216

The Blessed Fate of the Persecuted Righteous

8 Those who love God, and have not loved gold and silver
nor any of the good things which are in the world:
but gave over their bodies to torture.[2239]
9 Who, since they came into being, craved not
after earthly food,[2240] but regarded themselves as a breath
that passes away and lived accordingly.[2241] The Lord
tested them much, but their spirits have been found pure
so that they might bless his Name.
10 I have recounted all their blessings in the books.
He has assigned them their reward, for they have been
found to have loved heaven more than their life that is
in the world.[2242] [2243] Although they were trampled
underfoot by evil men, and experienced abuse and

97:8-10; 98:2; Jas 5:3; 1Pet 1:8, 18; Acts 3:6
Good Person XII (76); Mt 6:19-21, 24; 1Jn 2:15
48:7; 102:5; *War* 2.8.3, 5, 10
96:5-7; Jn 6:27
Wis 2:2-5; 5:9-14; Mt 4:4; Job 7:7-8; Eccl 1:2
Jas 1:2-4, 9-10; 4:14; 1Pet 1:24; Dan 12:10
Wis 3:5-6; 1Pet 1:7; Dan 11:35; Mt 5:11-12; ApPet 3
1Pet 3:9; Ps 11:5; 103:1-4; Prov 17:3
Lk 10:20
Mk 10:30
48:7; Mt 19:29; Jn 12:25; 15:19; Rev 12:11; 1Jn 2:15
Ps 34; Heb 11:10-16
Mt 5:10-12

---

with you, that everything written about me in the Law of Moses and the Prophets and the Psalms must be fulfilled" and also Peter in (Acts 3:18) "But what God foretold by the mouth of all the prophets, that his Christ would suffer, he thus fulfilled." This is the only express mention of prophets in 1 Enoch.

[2236] **Angels seem very interested in the affairs of humans. But they do not have access to all the information. "But concerning that day and hour no one knows, not even the angels of heaven, nor the Son, but the Father only"** (Mt 24:36).

[2237] This text of 108:7 follows the minority reading of Ethiopic manuscript, Tana, as translated by Olson. "The variants all involve small spelling changes in the Ethiopic script, so they must have originated in the Ethiopic phase of textual transmission. The majority reading introduces a streak of ascetic self-mortification not typical of Jewish literature and not found elsewhere in *Enoch* but common in Christian literature throughout its early centuries, Ethiopian Christianity included. Of the two readings, therefore, Tana seems more likely to reflect the Jewish original and the other MSS later revisions at the hands of Christian scribes" (OL pg. 256). Isaac follows a similar reading as Olson. As with Olson and Isaac, this text references the judgement of fallen celestial beings. Other manuscripts following the majority reading are quite different, typified by Nickelsburg's translation: "For there are books and records about them in heaven above, so that the angels may read them and know what will happen to the sinners and the spirits of the humble, and those who afflicted their bodies, and were recompensed by God: and those who were abused by evil men:"

[2238] Nickelsburg says concerning 108:7-10: **"By contrast with the sections that precede and follow it, this lengthy poetic description of the righteous and their attitude, actions, and plight is shot through with terminology that occurs rarely in the rest of 1 Enoch"** (N1 pg. 556).

[2239] **This description is very much like the description of the Essenes in (Josephus, *War* 2.8.3, 5, 10; and Philo of Alexander, *Good Person; (Quod Omnis Probus Liber Sit)* XII. §§76).**

[2240] (Cf. Jn 6:27) "'Do not work for the food that perishes, but for the food that endures to eternal life, which the Son of Man will give to you. For on him God the Father has set his seal.'" Also (Jn 4:34) "Jesus said to them, 'My food is to do the will of him who sent me and to accomplish his work.'"

[2241] "And lived accordingly" is literally "and kept this." Nickelsburg has: "and to this they kept."

[2242] Many manuscripts read: "life which is forever."

[2243] **These are martyrs who loved Heaven (God) more than life (Rev 12:11).**

reviling, yet they endured and blessed me.
11 Now I will summon the spirits of the good who belong
to the generation of light,[2244] and I will transform those
who <have descended into> darkness,[2245] who in
their flesh were not rewarded with honor as their
faithfulness deserved.
12 Indeed, I will bring forth in shining light[2246] those who
have loved my Holy Name,[2247] and I will seat each one
on his throne of honor.[2248]
13 They shall be resplendent for ages that cannot be
numbered. For righteous is the judgement of God,
and to the faithful he will show faithfulness, because
they abide in the paths of truth.[2249]
14 They shall see those who were born in darkness cast
into darkness, while the righteous are resplendent.
15 And seeing them shine, sinners will cry aloud;
and they,[2250]for their part, will depart to where the days
and times are prescribed for them."[2251]

1Pet 3:16; 4:4, 16
22:3; 61:12; Mt 24:31; 1Jn 3:2
Lk 16:8; Jn 12:36; 1Thes 5:5; Eph 5:8; 1QS 3:13,24-25
102:5,7; 1Pet 2:9; Col 1:13

Mt 5:14-16
62:16; Dan 12:3; 2En 22:8-10; ApPet 17
Rev 3:21; 4:4; 11:16; 20:4; Mt 19:28; Ps 105:3
1Pet 5:4, 6; 2Tim 4:8; Eph 2:6
Mt 13:43; Wis 3:7-8
71:17
2Tim 2:13
1QS 3.13-4.26; Ps 119:75; Jn 17:17
55:4; 62:10; 63:11; Jn 8:12; Eph 5:8
39:7; Mt 8:12; 22:13; 25:30; 1Pet 2:9
48:9; 2Bar 51:4-6; Wis 5:1-8; Dan 12:3

2244 **"Generation of light or sons of light," see references to (Eph 5:8; 1Thes 5:5; and Col 1:12-13). In the War Scroll (1QM 1.3, 9, 11, 13, 14 (W pg. 148) "Sons of Light" is used extensively as a term for the Jews who will fight the Sons of Darkness in the final battle.**

2245 This reading follows Nickelsburg. See 102:7. **These would be the righteous dead who descended into the darkness of death but whom God has exulted. Charles and others have: "those who were born in darkness." Either way, it is a witness to a belief in the resurrection and transformation of the righteous dead.**

2246 **The shining lights are actually the spiritual bodies of the elect.**

2247 **Profaning the name of God is done by disobedience to His commandments, as well as using the name of God in an unworthy manner. (1QS 6.27-7.1)** Therefore, Christ's statement in Jn 14:15, that **"If you love me, you will keep my commandments" applies here. A person honors God's Holy Name by living a righteous life.**

2248 **Jesus Christ promised that his followers would sit on thrones** (Mt 19:28; and Lk 22:30). This was taken to heart by the mother of the sons of Zebedee when she requested that her sons be seated "one at your right hand and one at your left, in your kingdom" (Mt 20:20-23). Christ explained that: "to sit at my right hand and at my left is not mine to grant; but it is for those for whom it has been prepared by my Father." **This indicates that those who are to reign and their relative positions will be chosen by the Father. Paul also informed us that the saints will be enthroned. "(God) raised us up with him and seated us with him in the heavenly places in Christ Jesus, so that in the coming ages he might show the immeasurable riches of his grace in kindness toward us in Christ Jesus"** (Eph 2:6-7).

2249 Olson renders 108:13 as: "They will be resplendent for seasons without number, for God's judgement is truth, and to the faithful he will show faithfulness in the home of the ways of truth" (cf. Ps 119:75; Jn 17:17).

2250 To add to their agony, the wicked will be able to view the righteous in their shining paradise at least temporarily (1En 48:9; 62:12-13; Wis 5:1-8; 2Bar 51:4-6; Lk 16:23).

2251 Many of the Ethiopic manuscripts end this passage with phrases such as: "Here ends the Revelation of the Secrets of Enoch." (Tana) or "The Vision of the secrets of Enoch. Here is completed the account and vision and prophecy of Enoch, which will be fulfilled before him" (EMML 2080) (OL pg. 258).

SUBJECT INDEX

n means note #

B

E

F

G

H

I

J

K

L

M

N

O

P

Q

S

T

U

SCRIPTURE AND OTHER WRITINGS INDEX

n means note #

Old Testament

Lamentations

Ezekiel

New Testament

Apocrypha, Pseudepigrapha and Jewish works

Church Fathers and other Christian period writers

New Testament Apocrypha and Pseudepigrapha

Dead Sea Scrolls

Ancient Mesopotamian Egyptian and Greek texts

Pre-Classical and Classical Greek

www.ingramcontent.com/pod-product-compliance
Lightning Source LLC
Chambersburg PA
CBHW081652120626
46550CB00010B/2867

* 9 7 9 8 9 9 2 3 0 0 0 0 0 *